World-Systems Evolution and Global Futures

This series seeks to promote understanding of large-scale and long-term processes of social change, in particular the many facets and implications of globalization. It critically explores the factors that affect the historical formation and current evolution of social systems, on both the regional and global level. Processes and factors that are examined include economies, technologies, geopolitics, institutions, conflicts, demographic trends, climate change, global culture, social movements, global inequalities, etc. Building on world-systems analysis, the series addresses topics such as globalization from historical and comparative perspectives, trends in global inequalities, core-periphery relations and the rise and fall of hegemonic core states, transnational institutions, and the long-term energy transition. This ambitious interdisciplinary and international series presents cutting-edge research by social scientists who study whole human systems and is relevant for all readers interested in systems approaches to the emerging world society, especially historians, political scientists, economists, sociologists, geographers and anthropologists.

This book series is indexed in Scopus.

All titles in this series are peer-reviewed.

Alex M. Feldman · Yannis Stamos

Zero Sum Political Economy

History from Antiquity to the Present

Springer

Alex M. Feldman
Research, Humanities and Social Sciences
CIS-Endicott International University
Madrid, Spain

Yannis Stamos
Center for Hellenic Studies
Harvard University
Washington DC, WA, USA

ISSN 2522-0985 ISSN 2522-0993 (electronic)
World-Systems Evolution and Global Futures
ISBN 978-3-032-18325-5 ISBN 978-3-032-18326-2 (eBook)
https://doi.org/10.1007/978-3-032-18326-2

This Springer imprint is published by the registered company Springer Nature Switzerland AG
The registered company address is: Gewerbestrasse 11, 6330 Cham, Switzerland

"The struggle of man against power is the struggle of memory against forgetting."
(Kundera, 2023/1978, p. 4)

"Non tibi illud apparere si sumas potest"
(Fairclough, 1909, II.4.414 [Plautus])

"Man Proposeth, God disposeth.
Living well is the best revenge.
Poverty is no sinne.
Hee begins to die, that quits his desires.
Every one is a master and servant.
He that trusts in a lie, shall perish in truth."
(Herbert, 1640, proverb 524)

For Pilar
and especially for Alan,
in the hope that he'll grow up in a less
zero-sum world.

Acknowledgements This book benefited from conversations with and comments by Francisco López-Santos Kornberger and Valerio D'Angelo, two lifelong friends and scholarly sparring partners. We owe them both a sincere debt of gratitude for their insightful feedback. Any remaining errors are our own.

Competing Interests The authors have no competing interests to declare that are relevant to the content of this manuscript.

About This Book

This book offers an alternative narrative of the global history and current state of affairs of political economy, interpreting it as ultimately based on varied manifestations of zero-sum logic. The book develops around a single premise: that the whole history of sovereign political economy, from the earliest Near Eastern slave empires to the currently passing age of the Anthropocene, can be read in terms of predictable cycles of systematic violence against excluded faraway or domestic populations and future generations based on zero-sum logic. The major argument of the book is that zero-sum thinking comprises the very beating heart of almost all models of sovereign political economy. The book tells the story of time without lines, empire without fall, enterprise without growth—and the eternal recurrence of zero-sum thinking, which has characterized human history since long before the fashionable worship of eternal economic growth. It also, in the process, seeks to change how the West has viewed the East across the immense span of Afro-Eurasia, Oceania and the Americas.

This book charts the past and present affairs of human sovereign political economies, interpreting all their forms as based on zero-sum logic, from the earliest slave empires to the currently passing Anthropocene. All involve predictable cycles of structural violence against excluded faraway or domestic populations and future generations—regardless of the fashionable worship of eternal economic growth. If every system begins with its Alpha and ends with its Omega, then the entire history of political economy is an infinite ouroboros whose cerebrospinal fluid is zero-sum.

Contents

Part I The Ancien Regime: The World Until 1776

1 **Prologue: The Endless Finitude of the Household Regime** 3
References 12

2 **Law and Wealth** 15
The Original Pyramid Scheme 16
Livestock 19
Get All the Gold Part 1: Bullionism 20
Tribalism and the Blood Feud 22
Potlatch Societies 25
References 29

3 **Feudalism and Mercantilism** 33
Feudalism (Negligible Economic Growth) 37
Get All the Gold Part 2: Mercantilism 43
Mythologies of Feudalism and Mercantilism 48
The Myth that Roman Laws and Feudal Laws Were Different 49
The Myth That Feudalism Has Been Exclusive to Latin Christendom 50
The Myth That Feudalism and Mercantilism Are Mutually Exclusive Economic Systems 54
Dynasties and Mafias 57
Two Models of Ancient Imperial Expansion 62
References 64

Part II "You Know Why They Call it the 'American Dream'...?" (1776–1929)

4 The Birth of Liberal Economic Expansion 77
Sinomania and Physiocracy 79
Frontiers, Population Valves and the Economics of Hope 83
The Malthusian Challenge 87
The Myth of Linear Industrial Progress 90
Liberalism Confronts Slavery 94
References 99

5 The First Failure of Liberalism 105
The Standardizations of Gold and Liberalism 107
Pivot Points on the Last Frontiers 112
Myths of Eternal Economic Growth—Part 1 115
The Technocratic Myth of Liberal Imperialism 120
Social Darwinism Part 1: Eugenics 125
References 134

Part III "...Because You Have to be Asleep to Believe it." (1929–2008)

6 Nationalism, Socialism and Zero-Sum Thinking 145
Autarky: Corporatism and Blood and Soil 148
Whose Golden Age? 154
Stagflation and Zero-Sum Thinking 162
References 166

7 Neoliberalism 173
Neoliberalism Confronts Communism 176
The Technocratic Myth of Global Free Markets & Free Trade 183
Disaster Capitalism: from Creative Destruction to Shampoo Economics 195
References 205

Part IV Refeudalization: The World Since 2008

8 The NeoFailure of Neoliberalism 221
The Myth of Eternal Economic Growth—Part 2 224
Social Darwinism Part 2: Meritocracy 231
TINA Strikes Back 235
Neo-Feudalism: Highway to Serfdom 241
References 250

9 Unipolarity, Multipolarity and Zero-Sum Thinking 263
Pandora's Pandemic: Disaster Capitalism and COVID-19 265
Autarky Part 2: 21st-c. Neo-Mercantilism 269
Cold War II: the Anthropocene Between Thalassocracy and Tellurocracy 279
References 290

10 Epilogue: History Instructs 307
Convergence: Infinite Tyranny? 308
Zero-Sum Tribalism 308
Inevitability and Eternity 309
Awe and Absurdity 310
Divergence: Infinite Growth? 313
Progress and Regress 314
Credit and Debt 315
Abundance and Degrowth 318
References 326

Index 333

About the Authors

Dr. Alex M. Feldman is an economic historian and professor at CIS-Endicott International University of Madrid.

Dr. Yannis Stamos is an intellectual and cultural historian and a postdoctoral fellow at Harvard University.

Part I

The Ancien Regime: The World Until 1776

Prologue: The Endless Finitude of the Household Regime

1

Abstract

The book begins by recognizing the original meaning of the term "economy" as envisioning the management of sovereign wealth as a household, where resources would always be finite and must therefore be conserved accordingly. It lays out the central premises and arguments for the use of the term "zero-sum thinking," taking into account the origins of the terms in Anglo-American scholarship during the early decades of Cold War I (1950s–1970s). It stipulates that zero-sum thinking is just as foundational to liberal politico-economic thought as it is to the politico-economic thought of fascist and communist totalitarian regimes (autarky), as well as all the overtly theocratic regimes before them. It organizes the structure of the book into four parts—each part representing given cycles of history determined by various interacting ideologies of sovereign political economy. Each part contains two chapters and each chapter contains three to six subsections, the themes of which tend to repeat in familiar patterns over generations, centuries and millennia.

> Ἐν ἀρχῇ ἦν ὁ λόγος, καὶ ὁ λόγος ἦν πρὸς τὸν θεόν, καὶ θεὸς ἦν ὁ λόγος. (John 1:1 *SBLGNT*)

> The *aleph* is […] the beginning of sound in the throat that is heard by its opening [… and] cannot be explained by any other in the European languages. (Spinoza, 1925, pp. 287–288)

Resources have always been viewed by humans as scarce, if not as entirely limited. As sustenance, resources might even be downright definitive for human survival:

> When Adam and Eve ate the forbidden fruit of the tree of knowledge and asserted the right to choose for themselves, they were cast out of the world of abundance into scarcity; to "eat bread in the sweat of their faces." The moral theme is that knowledge and the exercise of

A. M. Feldman and Y. Stamos, *Zero Sum Political Economy*, World-Systems Evolution and Global Futures, https://doi.org/10.1007/978-3-032-18326-2_1

choice are burdens in a world of divinely imposed or natural scarcity. (Lowry, 2003, esp. p. 14)

The point to faith was originally as an alleviation of the scarcity of resources, which emerges from phrases like "salvation" and "God shall provide." Thus, divine appeasement to ensure access to scarce resources (food, water, land, gold, etc.) has always required sacrifice (whether human, animal or other). This was true in the foundations of both the Abrahamic and Vedic faiths.

In the Vedic tradition, the oldest part of the earliest of the *Vedas*, the *Samhita* of the *Rigveda*, contains the *Arayakas* (the *Forest/Wilderness* books), which detail (in the verses of the *Brahmanas* and *Aranyakas*) the proper reasons and prayers for divine sacrifice. For these earliest Vedic prayers of sacrifice, the purpose was primarily to ensure wealth amid scarcity and victory against enemies:

> O god Savitr, bind thou in the furthest distance with a hundred fetters him who hateth us and whom we hate, thence let him not free.
> Araru is smitten away from the earth, the place of sacrifice.
> ...
> Thou art the good luck of the sacrificer.
> We have reached the path which leadeth to bliss, without a foe.
> Whereby a man defeateth all his foes and winneth wealth. (Keith, 1914, pp. 9, 28)

The Vedic hymns of sacrifice expressly beseech divinity for wealth in return for sacrifice: "Pragâpati, no other than thou embraces all these created things. May that be ours which we desire when sacrificing to thee: may we be lords of wealth!" (Müller, 1885, p. 6). Similarly, the Zoroastrian *Zend-Avesta* explicitly equates divine sacrifice with salvation: "I offer my sacrifice and homage to thee, the Fire, as a good offering, and an offering with our hail of salvation, even as an offering of praise with benedictions, to thee, the Fire, O Ahura Mazda's son! Meet for sacrifice art thou, and worthy of our homage" (Darmestetter, 1885, p. 106).

The situation was no different further East: the sheer quantity of archaeological evidence of both human and animal sacrifice in ancient China demonstrates that it was as much a method of ensuring divine favor as maintaining control; so much so that according to the UCLA sinologist Plutschow (1995/1996), "the Chinese premodern state was built upon sacrifice." In the book of *Pa Yih* of the *Confucian Analects*, the logical connection of sacrifice, salvation and power is made quite clear: "Someone asked the meaning of the great sacrifice. The Master said, 'I do not know. He who knew its meaning would find it as easy to govern the kingdom as to look on this;' – pointing to his palm" (Legge, 1861, III.XI).

In the Abrahamic tradition, after Adam's and Eve's expulsion from the Garden of Eden and the births of Cain and Abel, the sacrifices of the brothers are described as relative: God's favor of Abel's sacrifice was relative to his disfavor of Cain's sacrifice. They each worked hard and sacrificed to please God, but they were graded on a curve; it was a game of favor and Abel won while Cain lost.

> In the course of time Cain brought some of the fruits of the soil as an offering to the Lord. And Abel also brought an offering – fat portions from some of the firstborn of his flock. The Lord looked with favor on Abel and his offering, but on Cain and his offering he did not look with favor. So Cain was very angry, and his face was downcast. (Genesis 1:3–5, *NIV*)

The point to sacrifice and hard work has always been to foster or merit future prosperity. Therefore, when couched in terms of wealth and prosperity, the ultimate and eternal scarcity of resources could equally bear unfortunate implications. For example, the cynical outlook on the scarcity of resources has also been "get it while the gettin's good," or even the Jack Sparrow version, "take what you can; give nothin' back." This alternative to the "God will provide" perspective on the scarcity of resources is truly disturbing when taking in the proverbial God's eye-view.[1] It also explains why, as the Tanakh originally made clear, the true ownership of wealth lay only with God: "'The silver is Mine, and the gold is Mine,' says the Lord of hosts." (Haggai 2:8). In contrast, the *Epic of Gilgamesh*, with its own account of the great flood, and unlike Noah, who only loaded aboard his ark his family and wild animals, demonstrates that before animals and family, the most important thing to preserve amid the deluge was gold and silver (Sandars, 1972).

The New Testament warned that, by viewing wealth as ownable by humans (private property), humans would harden their hearts to the poverty of others, that values are tantamount to beliefs: "For where your treasure is, there your heart will be also" (Luke 12:34). In contrast, the verse implies that by giving away wealth, the heart is humanized. Or rather that it conforms to the theological logic of God's realm, according to which God alone is infinite and the true owner of everything—a similar ideal is shared by Plato. Yet the New Testament also recognizes the ultimate truth of wealth and its ownership by humans, that the haves will always be have-mores and the have-nots will always be have-lesses: "to those who have everything, more will be given; from those who have nothing, everything will be taken" (Matthew 22:29). The recognition of human ownership of wealth is made further explicit in the famous verse "Truly I tell you, it is hard for someone who is rich to enter the kingdom of heaven. Again I tell you, it is easier for a camel to go through the eye of a needle than for someone who is rich to enter the kingdom of God" (Matthew 19:23–24), and similar verses appear in Mark 10:24–27, Luke 18:24–27 and in the Quran 7:40. The Quran also warns against the logic of wealth hoarding: "Satan threatens you with poverty and orders you to immorality, while Allah promises you forgiveness from Him and abundance. And Allah is All-Encompassing and All-Knowing" (Quran 2:268). In their

[1] The authors wish to thank Routledge since parts of this section are derived from Feldman, A. M. (2024). *Orthodox mercantilism: Political economy in the Byzantine Commonwealth* (pp. 2–7). Routledge.

compulsions toward divine submission as opposed to submission toward earthly wealth and power, these verses reveal the eternal human notion that wealth and power comprise a game of economic winners and losers, a mentality which must be avoided at all costs, yet which has always invited temptation. In other words, if the classic Golden Rule teaches our ideal of humanity, that we must treat others as we would like to be treated, the common flippant variation of the Golden Rule is more revealing of the reality of humanity: "He who has the gold makes the rules."

For most of human history, political, social and economic issues were all bundled together under the heading *Theology*, never separately domiciled until quite recently. If man is created in the image of God, then the study of God (theology) is tantamount to the study of man (anthropology). By implication, the rule of God (*Theocracy*) is the rule of man. Most governing systems throughout human history have been theocracies of one form or another, be they monarchies, oligarchies, or any of their variants. Even in the United States, the commonly described democracy has borne the caveat "Under God" in its pledge of allegiance since 1954 (Public Law 83–396, 68 Stat. 249, H.J.Res. 243). Regardless of the differences between Judaism, Christianity and Islam, across the various boughs, branches and offshoots of Western Civilization, they all spring from the same Abrahamic fountainhead. And the scripture associated with each one, the Tanakh, the New Testament and the Quran, were essentially early constitutions concerned with the *who, what, where, when, why* and *how* of ruling. The *word* (*logos*) of each of these scriptural revelations was meant to rule; in effect, the word was *with* God and God *was* the word. Therefore, the existential point to the Abrahamic faiths is the goal of the ruler. By extension, Judaism, Christianity and Islam were, above all, originally philosophies of rulership, of government. As such, they were each adopted by various governing structures and dynasties throughout history, or, as commonly called, regimes, and in each case, the regime has its own way of thinking about wealth and value.

By far the most common way of thinking about wealth and value goes back to the origins of the word "economy". In Greek, *oikonomia* (οἰκονομία) was the term for household management, and thus, we arrive at the central point: when thinking about how wealth is created and preserved throughout history, the regime is usually thought of as a household. That's why we still use the word economy to talk about a concept much bigger than the typical individual household: the common household, i.e. the regime. This is most clearly outlined in the *Oeconomicus* of Xenophon (Eide & Whitaker, 2016; Leshem, 2016; Lowry, 1988; Pomeroy, 1994; Williams, 2008), and even in the New Testament, which lays out that the ultimate circuit of bullion began and ended with Caesar ("Give to Caesar what is Caesar's, and to God what is God's" [Matthew 22:17]). The driving of the moneychangers from the Temple by Christ was not a reaction against the profanity of profit so much as a reaction against the mixture of the sacred with the profane (Sedlacek, 2011, pp. 139–141). The conceptualization of regime and, later, state economies as households would accompany economic history to this day, reinforcing ideas about scarce or limited resources (austerity, spending cuts as paths to economic recovery, etc.). This implies that the original purpose of an economy (the law of the household) ultimately seeks answers for the impossible question of potentially unlimited human endeavors, necessities and growth versus ultimately limited resources – the household's endless finitude. Furthermore, this explains why economics, as a discipline of the social sciences, has largely and only quite recently come to dominate the other social sciences, particularly history, theology and philosophy (Bulgakov & Evtuhov, 2000; Nelson, 2001, p. 38).

Ironically, the logic of hoarding and protectionism was cautioned against in holy scriptures (even if its implications may nevertheless have been indulged), yet it is clear in Classical texts. For example, in the works of Hesiod, perhaps the clearest and earliest statement of this logic of value emerges in the Greek myths of the *Theogony*, specifically about the inheritances of Zeus, Poseidon and Hades, the values of which (*timai*) they perceive as ultimately limited in scope.

> Their *timai* are "powers" to be used actively in each sphere, and the general context implies a "zero-sum" concept of *timê*, leading to competition and resentment – here, to Poseidon's fearful resentment of Zeus' attempt to restrain him, since he is after all *homotimos* with his brother god (*Iliad* 15.18). (Boedeker, 1983, p. 81)

Similarly, *theomachoi* such as Bellerophon, Sisyphus, Salmoneus fight a war against the gods in order to claim ultimately limited divine privileges for themselves, even if later heroes chose more diplomatic means of engaging with the gods (Graziosi, 2016). Hesiod's *Works and Days* focuses on the finitude of time and resources, compared to the infinitude of human necessity, endeavor and labor (Sedlacek, 2011, p. 96).

Returning to Xenophon, it is true enough that his *Oeconomicus* did not specifically advocate the protection or hoarding of wealth, but it does deal with landownership and the returns of investment therefrom: "(34) Now, nothing shows a larger increase (35) than a piece of land reclaimed from barren waste and bearing fruit a 100-fold." However, perhaps his true macroeconomic insight is demonstrated in his *Πόροι ἢ περὶ Προσόδων* (*De Vectigalibus/On Revenues/Ways and Means*), which is essentially a political economy for the Athenian regime. There, he specifically advocated the favor of thalassocratic merchants a—reasoning we would doubtlessly call protectionist (even mercantilist) were it written a millennium and a half later:

> It would also be an excellent plan to reserve front seats in the theatre for merchants and shipowners, and to offer them hospitality occasionally, when the high quality of their ships and merchandise entitles them to be considered benefactors of the state. With the prospect of these honours before them they would look on us as friends and hasten to visit us to win the honour as well as the profit. (Xenophon, 2008, III)

In one of the most prescient bits of logic, he explains the reason for the accumulation and hoarding of silver (and by extension other forms of bullion) in order to protect its ownership:

> No one when he has got sufficient furniture for his house dreams of making further purchases on this head, but of silver no one ever yet possessed so much that he was forced to cry "enough." On the contrary, if ever anybody does become possessed of an immoderate amount he finds as much pleasure in digging a hole in the ground and hoarding it as in the actual employment of it. And from a wider point of view: when a state is prosperous there is nothing which people so much desire as silver. (Xenophon, 2008, IV)

Understanding this is crucial in the development of stoicism (and the original form of cynicism named after Diogenes of Sinope), which essentially taught that less is more—an explicit rejection of the logic of hoarding. Therefore, many "ancient authors have little to say on marginal utility theory and the non-zero-sum games of trade," precisely because they understood that the simplicity of merchants' logic was beneath the rationalism of higher forms of logic and other human concerns. For classical Greek authors, simply making as much money as possible was obviously predicated on the logic of wealth acquisition and hoarding, since it was clear enough to them that the merchant's gain derived from another's loss. Thus, for Aristotle, proper inquiry of economic affairs could not be detached from ethics (Dierksmeier & Pirson, 2009, p. 418). Similar sentiments can be evinced for the next several centuries, especially from the works of Cicero, Cato and Terence onward, and were common among the ruling class of the Roman empire both long before and long after the top-down process of Christianization commenced in the reign of Constantine the Great (d. 330) (Hanchey, 2013).

After the Fourth Crusade, in which Latin Christian armies stormed and looted Constantinople in 1204, Roman (Byzantine) thinkers and statesmen like George Akropolites and Nikephoros Gregoras extensively discussed the economic problems of scarce resources, and they frequently advocated various policies of wealth hoarding and protectionism. George Gemistos Plethon even insisted on economic protectionism and hoarding wealth and land, having presented a comprehensive program of essentially mercantilist economic reforms to the despot of the Morea (the Peloponnese), Theodore II and the emperor Manuel II (Akropolites, 2007, pp. 230–235; Dölger, 1924, nos. 2945, 2956; Gregoras, 1829, pp. 41–44, 229; Labuk, 2016; Laiou & Morrisson, 2007, pp. 229–230; Peritore, 1977; Siniossoglou, 2011; Thiriet, 1958, nos. 342, 551, 575; Woodhouse, 1986).

At the personal level, the Byzantine author Alexios Makrembolites describes a hypothetical conversation in his 14th-c. *Dialogue Between the Rich and the Poor*, which is equally striking in its personal logic of hoarding and protectionism. In the interpretation of the Byzantinist Dionysios Stathakopoulos,

> there's an instance where the poor are saying to the rich, "Well, you know back in the day" – they mean the Komnenian period – "the rich were creating charities and hospitals and orphanages and none of us were hungry, and you could not hear the cries of the poor all around." Then the rich say, "Yes, but these were other times, we owned the whole world back then; now we have so little, and the little that we have, we're not going to share with you, because then our children will become like you." (Stathakopoulos & Feldman, 2020)

Whereas generations of statesmen implemented official policies of hoarding and protectionism as a matter of course, such economic behavior was little different from the decisions made by everyday folks. A rich merchant or a poor share-cropping peasant were both driven by the same cruel calculus of need for scarce resources—only the former had more access than the latter.

For most of recorded history, back at least to the law code of Hammurabi, if not in the Sumerian king list and the *Epic of Gilgamesh*, wealth was defined primarily by gold and land. One bought or produced the other, just as wealth begot power and vice versa. Distinctions between wealth and power (and gold and land) have always existed, but these were dwarfed by the distinctions between these and the opposite—the lack thereof. Most questions have been answered in relation to how gold and land have traditionally been claimed, preserved and defended. As Rousseau wrote in his *Discourse on Inequality* (1755), "The first person who, having enclosed a plot of land, took it into his head to say this is mine and found people simple enough to believe him, was the true founder of civil society" (Rousseau, 1992, p. 44).

This is ultimately about law, which, as generations of thinkers have discussed, protects the wealth of the wealthy and limits access to it for the rest—the oldest story of haves and have-nots. But it is not always about finding the right answers so much as asking different questions. For example, seldom has the question been asked: why the eternal struggle and/or scramble for these resources? In a word: finitude. Although it has rarely been demonstrated, humans have almost always assumed that there is a fixed amount of gold and land available in the world—the rare assumption which is usually confirmed. If we take gold and land as the traditional definition of wealth, then we are presented with an eternal paradox: how are we to distribute a finite supply of wealth given an ever-increasing supply of human need and endeavor? Otherwise, humans, like other animals, will return to the Law of the Jungle and fight over finite resources using the logic of "your gain is my loss." This paradox was only recently given a formal logical term: zero-sum thinking, a term largely linked to the emergence of a new strand of economic analysis in the post-war era.

Game theory, as this strand became known, gained its academic bona fides in the 1950s–1970s as the two Cold War superpowers engaged in round after round of nuclear brinkmanship. They were at odds for many reasons, but the central one was the supremacy of one ideology or the other. The proxy wars and other geopolitical games these superpowers played were predicated on the concept that only one party could win, meaning that the other side would lose. It was only after the fall of the Berlin Wall that game theory concepts became better known beyond Cold War politics, increasingly so in the realm of psychology. Among its various concepts, one of the most relevant has become the idea of the zero-sum game.

Aside from some behavioral economics papers, there are very few books explicitly employing zero-sum thinking as a framework for analyzing political economies, but all have a very different approach and discuss zero-sum logic as the trait of only a particular time, place or system. For example, at the outset of the neoliberal period in the 1980s, the MIT dean of political economy, Thurow (1980,

1985) advocated a much more active social democracy, recognizing that Eisenhower's famous exhortations were as true in the context of the 1930s–1950s as they would wind up being in the 1980s–2000s. Unfortunately, however, his words were twisted by those like Ayau (2007) who propagated neoliberal market fundamentalism and largely fell on deaf ears. More recently, zero-sum thinking has been discussed in relation to climate change and green transitions in the growing drumbeat of climate policy, specifically in the form of Alf Hornborg's ecological economy and the works of Carlo Jaeger and his collaborators (Hornborg, 2012; Jaeger et al., 2012). Simultaneously, the baton was taken up by the *Financial Times* journalist Rachman (2011), who has dealt extensively with the concept as applicable in what he saw as a new emerging post-2008 global economy. His analyses, however, fail to put zero-sum logic in a much longer historical context and display obvious Anglo-American geopolitical biases. Finally, in the past several years, a new batch of books about zero-sum strategies and economies such as by Kolenda (2021), McAtee (2021) and Raitt (2019) have envisioned new models where politics and economics are walked back from the brink of what the journalist Giridharadas (2019) calls a "Winners Take All Charade."

Yet, the idea of a zero-sum game, supported by zero-sum thinking, is the oldest, simplest, most basic form of thinking about political, social and economic relations throughout history and across the world. As Freud (1993) told Einstein in 1932, "The living being [...] defends its own existence by destroying foreign bodies." Either you have the finite resources or you don't, and by exchanging something of value for something else of less value, you have less. Everyone wants more without having to forfeit something. This is where the phrase "To have your cake and eat it too" comes from, as well as a major component of the ruling philosophy of most varieties of contemporary political conservatism, which advocate deriving as much benefit as possible without thinking about the negative downstream consequences—somewhat like "après moi, le déluge." Nevertheless, zero-sum logic is not confined to either the political-economic left or to the right, as various partisanship would suggest. Rather, it can be evinced in every corner of human public life from the remotest past to the present. Some have even wondered whether "zero-sum thinking and egalitarian sharing might be inherent to the design of the human brain" (Tupy, 2016). Recent examples include the relationship between political ideology and zero-sum thinking (Davidai & Ongis, 2019), the majoritarian fear of increased rights for minority communities (Drutman, 2019), and the idea that wealth and power are not only preserved but increased by hoarding wealth and preying on the weak—prevalent from the words of George R. R. Martin (placed in the mouth of Tyrion Lannister) to the logic of Collins (2021), Raikes (2019) and Mechanic (2021).

In the English-speaking world, it remains quite common, especially for neoliberal economists like Rubin (2003, 2018), to dismiss zero-sum thinking exclusively as a "peasant" or "folk" phenomenon, forgetting, if not outright ignoring, the ubiquity of zero-sum thinking among the peasants, "folks" *and* the ruling classes in English-speaking countries both before and after the advent of liberal economic expansion in the wake of Adam Smith's publication of the *Wealth of Nations* in

1776 (Foster, 1965). More recently, it has become common to address zero-sum thinking not as simply a feature of "peasant society" in faraway lands of poor, starving miserables, but rather as an omnipresent feature across economic thought (Johnson et al., 2018). In the narrow logic of the apologists of unfettered (neo-) liberal capitalism, solely Marxists have a zero-sum mindset, in which "the prosperity of others came at the expense of their own prospects" (Reed, 2018; many of Reed's arguments against socialism pertaining to its long-term effects can equally be made regarding liberalism). Instead, the ultimate goal of this book is to demonstrate that zero-sum thinking is the dominant logic of political economy throughout history. Historians refer to the prevalence of economic forces in the shaping of the trajectory of history as "historical materialism." If there is in fact a "*homo oeconomicus*" standing upright on his own two legs without leaning on the fashionable myth (Sedlacek, 2011, p. 108), it is likely that his guiding logic is zero sum.

This is also the reason that this book addresses zero-sum thinking at the heart of various philosophies of political economy. While it deals extensively with the world of Eurasia, due to the sheer length and breadth of its written historical record in many scripts and faiths, it also addresses the extensions of Old-World faiths into the New Worlds. In other words, the spread of various Christianities (and Islam into Australasia) into new lands as ruling faiths presupposed that rulers have always implicitly understood that there is a finite amount of land on earth over which to rule. This was just as true in the Islamic conquest of Constantinople (1453) as in the Catholic conquest of Granada (1492) and Tenochtitlan (1522), the Orthodox conquest of Kazan (1552) and the Anglican settlement of North America and Oceania. After all, it was the contact and competition between these rival ecumenical empires over seemingly finite land which drove their spread well into the nineteenth century. During the nineteenth century, as ecumenical empires gradually and violently transformed into nation-states, the same assumptions of zero-sum competition for land and gold remained well into the twentieth century. Even during the twentieth century, when these nation-states were subsumed by various ideological forces (communism, fascism, liberalism) which replaced the old ecumenical empires, the zero-sum logic remained in the brutal calculus of political economy. This book will explore how zero-sum thinking can be traced as a thread through the fabric of time.

Accordingly, the book is structured into four main chronological parts, each organized based on the zero-sum logic of the basic economic systems of the era. The first part deals with the ancient world and its predominant economic systems of feudalism and mercantilism (covered in this chapter and Chap. 2), both of which rested on the pillar of zero-sum logic and endured largely until the advent of the first true innovation: liberal economic growth in the late eighteenth century (exemplified by Adam Smith's *Wealth of Nations* published in 1776). But this had its limits, as will be discussed in the second part, covering the period from 1776 to 1929. Within part two, Chap. 3 covers much of the nineteenth century and the zero-sum logic embedded within Malthusianism and colonialism, while Chap. 4 mostly covers the early twentieth century up to the 1920s and the shortcomings of economic institutions built for eternal economic growth. Picking up after 1929, part three deals with the dominant economic paradigms of the era until 2008: Keynesianism's attempts to balance economic growth with equality in Chap. 5 and then in Chap. 6, the emergence of neoliberalism during the 1970s–1980s. Finally, part four addresses the world since 2008, describing the gradual processes of economic consolidation and ossification of wealth and power to unprecedented degrees. In it, Chap. 7 focuses on the (neo)failure of neoliberalism while Chap. 8 delves into the transition from unipolarity to multipolarity. Finally, the wider ramifications of zero-sum logic for historical understanding are discussed in the epilogue.

References

Akropolites, G. (2007). *The history* (R. Macrides, Trans.). Oxford University Press.

Ayau, M. E. (2007). *Not a zero-sum game: The paradox of exchange.* University Francisco Marroquín.

Bulgakov, S., & Evtuhov, C. (2000). *Philosophy of economy: The world as household* (Russian Literature and Thought). Yale University Press.

Boedeker, D. (1983). Hecate: A transfunctional goddess in the Theogony? *Transactions of the American Philological Association, 113*, 79–93. https://doi.org/10.2307/284004

Collins, C. (2021). *The wealth hoarders: How billionaires pay millions to hide trillions.* Polity Press.

Darmestetter, J. (Trans.). (1885). *Sacred books of the East.* Clarendon Press.

Davidai, S., & Ongis, M. (2019). The politics of zero-sum thinking: The relationship between political ideology and the belief that life is a zero-sum game. *Science Advances, 5*(12). https://www0.gsb.columbia.edu/mygsb/faculty/research/pubfiles/26169/eaay3761.full.pdf

Dierksmeier, C., & Pirson, M. (2009). Oikonomia versus chrematistike: Learning from Aristotle about the future orientation of business management. *Journal of Business Ethics, 88*(3), 417–430. http://www.jstor.org/stable/40295009

Dölger, F. (1924). *Regesten der Kaiserurkunden des Oströmischen Reiches: Regesten von 565–1025.* Verlag C. H. Beck.

Drutman, L. (2019). *American politics as a zero-sum game.* New America: Resilience. https://resilience.newamerica.org/american-politics-as-a-zero-sum-game/

Eide, S., & Whitaker, K. (2016). A philosopher and a gentleman: Xenophon's *Oeconomicus. Arion, 24*(2), 93–100. https://doi.org/10.2307/arion.24.2.0093

Fairclough, H. R. (Ed.). (1909). *The Trinummus of Plautus.* Macmillan.

Foster, G. M. (1965). Peasant society and the image of limited good. *American Anthropologist, 67*, 293–315. https://doi.org/10.1525/aa.1965.67.2.02a00010

Freud, S. (1993, March). *Why war? A letter from Freud to Einstein.* UNESCO Courier. https://en.unesco.org/courier/marzo-1993/why-war-letter-freud-einstein

Giridharadas, A. (2019). *Winners take all: The elite charade of changing the world.* Penguin.

Graziosi, B. (2016). Statues crumbled. Review of *Battling the Gods: Atheism in the Ancient World* by T. Whitmarsh. *London Review of Books, 38*(15).

Gregoras, N. (1829–1855). *Byzantina historia* (L. Schopen & I. Bekker, Eds.). Weber.

Hanchey, D. (2013). Cicero, exchange, and the Epicureans. *Phoenix, 67*(1–2), 119–134. https://doi.org/10.7834/phoenix.67.1-2.0119

Herbert, G. (1640). *Outlandish proverbs* (Proverb 524). T. P. for Humphrey Blunden.

Hornborg, A. (2012). *Global ecology and unequal exchange: Fetishism in a zero-sum world.* Taylor & Francis.

Jaeger, C., et al. (Eds.). (2012). *Reframing the problem of climate change: From zero sum game to win-win solutions.* Routledge.

Johnson, S., Zhang, J., & Keil, F. (2018). *Psychological underpinnings of zero-sum thinking*. https://doi.org/10.2139/ssrn.3117627

Keith, A. B. (Trans.). (1914). *The Veda of the Black Yajus School, entitled, Taittiriya Sanhita, Part 1: Kandas I–III*. Harvard University Press.

Kolenda, C. D. (2021). *Zero-sum victory: What we're getting wrong about war*. University Press of Kentucky.

Kundera, M. (2023/1978). *The book of laughter and forgetting*. HarperCollins.

Labuk, T. (2016). 'Nationalist' discourse and the political myth in the memoranda of Georgios Gemistos Plethon. *Miscellanea Byzantina, I*, 81–130.

Laiou, A. E., & Morrisson, C. (2007). *The Byzantine economy*. Cambridge University Press.

Legge, J. (Ed.). (1861). *The Chinese classics: With a Translation, Critical and Exegetical Notes, Prolegomena, and Copious Indexes: Vol. 1: Confucian analects, the great learning, and doctrine of the mean* (J. Legge, Trans.). Trübner & Co. https://www.google.com/books/edition/The_Chinese_Classics/XAdJSH6CkyUC

Leshem, D. (2016). Retrospectives: What did the ancient Greeks mean by oikonomia? *Journal of Economic Perspectives, 30*(1), 225–238. https://doi.org/10.1257/jep.30.1.225

Lowry, S. T. (1988). *The archaeology of economic ideas: The classical Greek tradition*. Duke University Press.

Lowry, S. T. (2003). Ancient and medieval economics. In W. J. Samuels, J. E. Biddle, & J. B. Davis (Eds.), *A companion to the history of economic thought* (pp. 9–27). Blackwell. https://doi.org/10.1002/9780470999059.ch2.

McAtee, S. (2021). *Zero-sum economics*. Splat Concepts.

Mechanic, M. (2021). *Jackpot: How the super-rich really live—And how their wealth harms us all*. Simon & Schuster.

Müller, F. M. (Trans.). (1885). *Sacred books of the East* (Vol. 6). Clarendon Press.

Nelson, R. H. (2001). *Economics as religion: From Samuelson to Chicago and beyond*. Pennsylvania State University Press;

Peritore, N. P. (1977). The political thought of Gemistos Plethon: A renaissance Byzantine reformer. *Polity, 10*(2), 168–191. https://doi.org/10.2307/3234257

Plutschow, H. (1995/1996). Archaic Chinese sacrificial practices in the light of generative anthropology. *Anthropoetics, I*(2). https://anthropoetics.ucla.edu/ap0102/china/

Pomeroy, S. B. (1994). *Xenophon, Oeconomicus: A social and historical commentary*. Clarendon Press.

Public Law 83–396, 68 Stat. 249, H.J.Res. 243, enacted June 14, 1954. https://www.govinfo.gov/app/details/STATUTE-68/STATUTE-68-Pg249-3

Rachman, G. (2011). *Zero-sum world: Politics, power and prosperity after the crash*. Atlantic; American version: *Zero-sum future: American power in an age of anxiety*. Simon & Schuster.

Raikes, J. (2019, June 17). Can power be anything but zero-sum? *Forbes*. https://www.forbes.com/sites/jeffraikes/2019/06/17/can-power-be-anything-but-zero-sum/

Raitt, G. (2019). *The metaphysics of market power: The zero-sum competition and market manipulation approach*. Hart Publishing.

Reed, L. W. (2018, April 5). The XYZs of socialism. *Foundation for Economic Education*. https://fee.org/resources/the-xyz-s-of-socialism/

Rousseau, J.-J. (1992). *Discourse on the origin of inequality* [D. A. Cress, Trans.] Hackett Publishing.

Rubin, P. H. (2003). Folk economics. *Southern Economic Journal, 70*(1), 157–171. https://www.jstor.org/stable/1061637

Rubin, P. H. (2018). Zero-sum thinking and economic policy. *Behavioral and Brain Sciences, 41*, e185. https://doi.org/10.1017/S0140525X18000511

Sandars, N. K. (Trans.). (1972). *The epic of Gilgamesh*. Penguin Group.

Sedlacek, T. (2011). *Economics of good and evil: The quest for economic meaning from Gilgamesh to Wall Street*. Oxford University Press.

Siniossoglou, N. (2011). *Radical Platonism in Byzantium*. Cambridge University Press.

Spinoza, B. (1925). Compendium grammatices linguae hebraeae. In *Opera* (Vol. 1). C. Winter.

Stathakopoulos, D., & Feldman, A. M. (2020). *Episode 5: The Gift*. Dumbarton Oaks Byzantine Podcast. https://www.doaks.org/research/byzantine/podcast/episode-5-the-gift

Thiriet, E. (1958). *Regestes des délibérations du Sénat de Venise concernant la Romanie*. La Haye-Mouton.

Thurow, L. (1980). *The zero-sum society: Distribution and the possibilities for economic change*. Basic Books.

Thurow, L. (1985). *The zero-sum solution: Building a world-class American economy*. Simon & Schuster.

Tupy, M. L. (2016, September 6). The loathing of commercial capitalism has ancient roots. *Foundation for Economic Education Online*. https://fee.org/articles/the-loathing-of-commercial-capitalism-has-ancient-roots/

Williams, B. R. (2008). An economist looks at Xenophon's *Oeconomicus*. *The Classical Outlook, 85*(3), 102–105.

Woodhouse, C. M. (1986). *George Gemistos Plethon: The last of the Hellenes*. Oxford University Press.

Xenophon. (2008). *On revenues* (H. G. Dakyns, Trans., Book III) [Ebook]. Project Gutenberg. https://www.gutenberg.org/ebooks/1179

Law and Wealth

2

Abstract

The second chapter lays out the most ancient aspects of sovereign political economy from the earliest writings in major scriptural traditions (Abrahamic, Vedic, Sinic, Hellenic, etc.). It incorporates the earliest socioeconomic conceptions of **the original pyramid scheme**. It covers the earliest, most foundational politico-economic modes of production and legal frameworks (from Hammurabi to Akhenaten to Moses to Graeco-Roman law). In doing so, it demonstrates that the earliest laws were meant not so much to curb violence as to protect property rights (including ownership of both humans and animals)—both forms of **livestock**, which was the original form of non-zero-sum wealth. Conversely, it also discusses the original finite resources—bullion and land. In terms of bullion, the predominant ancient form of politico-economic thought is typically called **bullionism (to accumulate as much as possible)**. In terms of land, the predominant ancient foundations of politico-economic thought were concerned with ideas about **tribalism and blood feuds**. Thus, in order to mitigate the violence caused by laws which have protected the wealth of the wealthy, the earliest politico-economic traditions, as Marcel Mauss explained in *The Gift*, required **potlatch societies** where mutual obligations were to be fostered by various forms of gift-giving patronage networks between haves and have-nots.

> Anyone who studies present and ancient affairs will easily see how in all cities and all peoples there still exist, and have always existed, the same desires and passions. Thus, it is an easy matter for him who carefully examines past events to foresee future events in a republic and to apply the remedies employed by the ancients, or, if old remedies cannot be found, to devise new ones based upon the similarity of the events. But since these matters are neglected or not understood by those who read, or, if understood, remain unknown to those who govern, the result is that the same problems always exist in every era. (Machiavelli, 1517/1950, Book 1, Chapter 39)

A. M. Feldman and Y. Stamos, *Zero Sum Political Economy*, World-Systems Evolution and Global Futures, https://doi.org/10.1007/978-3-032-18326-2_2

William Faulkner is far more straightforward: "The past is never dead. It's not even past." The past's patterns purify the perplexity of the present and formulate the fog of the future—for those willing to see (Faulkner, 1951, p. 73). Historians of various specialties love to debate various set-piece topics *ad aeternum.* For military historians it's the relative importance of strategy versus tactics, for cultural historians the meaning of the very term "culture," for political historians "great man history" versus the history of mass movements, for economic historians the relative importance of the ideas of Adam Smith or Karl Marx. But all historians, regardless of their specialty, are drawn to the recurring debates over periodization: what is the difference between the ancient, the medieval and the modern? Where are the lines? Who drew them, when and why? Who paid for them to be drawn? Which spurious intellectual entrepreneurs first benefitted from the concept of the tripartite division of history (ancient/medieval/modern)? What do these lines in time imply about the cultures we inhabit and what are the consequences for our minds and our societies?

As historians, we believe that these divisions are often arbitrary, fetishized and essentialized, frequently taking on lives of their own. There is little difference between the ancient world and the medieval world, save for the pervading authority of various forms of faith—Judaism, Christianity, Islam, Hinduism, Buddhism, Confucianism, etc. The holy scriptures of these faiths were effectively ancient constitutions, which could be transferred and implemented in new places under new dynasties. They guaranteed governance, law and order. These three items, commonly thought of as archetypical components of the "social contract," are equally suffused with meaning about the endless finitude of resources. Whether we discuss the laws of various faiths in context or one-by-one, we can see that their laws have always governed access to seemingly finite resources. The purpose of this chapter will be to examine this state of affairs not by region, era or faith, but topic: the ways in which religions have always functioned as social pyramids, the ways they've traditionally conceived of infinite resources (such as men and beasts) and the ways they've conceived of bullion, land, tribalism and charity; in short, the ancient social contract.

The Original Pyramid Scheme

Most of human history since the dawn of agriculture can be told as a story of "barbarous" outsiders invading previously "civilized" agrarian regions and cities dominated by landowning insiders in order to access their wealth, i.e. finite supplies of gold and land as well as potentially infinite resources of food and livestock (including humans/slaves). The gods that accompanied the finite conception of the agrarian grain supply also accompanied the finite conception of wealth in general (Cauvin, 2000). Across much of Eurasia, this was largely the case right up to the 15–16th centuries CE, after which time, the "civilized" insiders found themselves butting up against each other in various zero-sum struggles for arable land. The first "barbarian" to interlope into the "civilized", agrarian world could be argued as Enkidu in the Epic of Gilgamesh, although the title could easily go to Sargon of Akkad who invaded Sumer from the north and first consolidated power throughout Mesopotamia between the 24–23rd centuries BCE. Then came Hammurabi's Babylonians in the eighteenth century BCE, then Mursili's Hittites in the sixteenth century BCE, then Tukulti-Ninurta's Assyrians in the thirteenth century BCE. The Hyksos and later the Sea Peoples accomplished similar feats in Egypt during the late bronze and early iron ages. Still later, the Achaemenids of Persia and the Macedonians of Greece enlarged the known world yet further.

A similarly violent churn pattern of migration/invasion can be evinced in ancient China with the Xiongnu peoples in the third century BCE and then the "Five Barbarians" (Xiongnu, Jie, Di, Qiang, and Xianbei) peoples in the fourth century CE, up to the Mongols who established the Yuan dynasty in the thirteenth century CE and the Manchus who established the Qing dynasty in the seventeenth century CE. In the Indus valley civilization, analogous cycles occurred from the migration or invasion of the Indo-Aryan peoples in the fifteenth century BCE and then the Scythians/Sakas peoples in the second century BCE, followed by the Mughals in the sixteenth century CE and so on. Even in Mesoamerican folklore, the Aztec foundation myth can be seen largely as a migration story from the "barbarous" wilderness to the "civilized" agrarian world of Lake Texcoco, which the Aztecs later dominated with allied city-states by propagating and enforcing formal, natural laws (the law of the jungle; might makes right) (Offner, 2023). In each of these examples, likely beginning with Hammurabi in the Near East, a set of laws was laid down, and after every conquest, the laws were superseded or renewed by the new ruling dynasty and a new cycle of surplus, growth, competition, crisis and stabilization started (Slatyer, 2012). We typically tend to take the inequality that was promulgated by law for granted without much skepticism: "contemporary "big history" writers—such as Jared Diamond, Francis Fukuyama and Yuval Noah Harari", Graeber and Wengrow (2021b, November 4) note, "often talk about inequality as the natural result of living in larger groups with a surplus of resources."

The original purpose of law was to solidify the wealth and legitimacy of the ruling dynasty. This was just as true for the Code of Hammurabi ("eye-for-an-eye") as it was for Mosaic law and for later pagan Graeco-Roman laws such as the Constitution of the Athenians, the Law of the Twelve Tables and the Gortyn Code. The scholarly discussion about their similarities goes back to the nineteenth century (Assmann, 2010; Van De Mieroop, 2016, pp. 152–155; Wright, 2009). The curtailment of murder, rape, theft and abuse was merely a byproduct of the dynasty's jurisdiction. At the frontiers of the jurisdiction, where the agrarian met the nomadic and pastoral, or mountainous, these violent behaviors were always commonplace. Once adopted and systematized, laws created a top-down power structure: the ruler, his few priests, lords and warriors at the top, and the majority of the merchants, craftsmen, peasants and slaves at the bottom. For centuries, law codes changed little; usually, laws were simply reproduced by a new ruler upon his succession or conquest and later ascent to power. Even before it was codified into religious codes, laws preserved the wealth and legitimacy of the powerful, while creating social pyramids in the process; effectively, a caste system. Organized religion didn't bring law; law brought organized religion. This was as true *before* Solon created his famous Athenian Constitution as it was a *result* of it. The reason Solon unburdened the dependent farmers (*hektemoroi*) from their debt-bondage (*seisachtheia*) was because they were indebted—and thus compelled to sell themselves into slavery—due to the finitude of arable land in Attica protected by the Athenian rulers (the landowning dynasties). Regardless of the origins of the social pyramid, enslavement is still as old as debt, agriculture or possibly even war itself.

There is a case to be made that the inception of Judaism itself was the result of an attempt to avoid the ancient social pyramid. This concept was symbolically diffused within the books of Genesis and Exodus as the founding myth of the Jewish people as distinct from (albeit geographically connected to) the slave empires of Egypt and Mesopotamia while contrasting them with Israel and Judaea (Assmann, 2008, 2018). Abraham was originally a refugee from the Mesopotamian social pyramid and his descendants were refugees from the Egyptian social pyramid. Joseph and Moses were the primary social climbers in the Torah, the former most deliberately and the latter more fortuitously if not apprehensively. Yet, even escaping slavery in Egypt did not cause its abolition in Judaism or save Canaan from the same fate. Mosaic laws, implemented by the Davidic dynasty (and later the Hasmonean and Herodian dynasties), achieved similar results in Canaan, later known as Israel and Judaea. Comparable social pyramids were reproduced under the Assyrians and later the Achaemenid Persians. The original Jewish rebellion against slavery became largely metaphorical and rhetorical once the former slaves had found liberty; they enslaved the Canaanites as soon as they arrived.

All these early law codes, which preserved the wealth and legitimacy of the ruling dynasty and generated social pyramids, provided the foundations for "axial age" civilizations, which first provided the axis on which the gears of history turn through their philosophical and moral transformations. This concept was first coined by the German philosopher Karl Jaspers, but it has a much broader literature. Historians who focus on the axial age have also noticed that the phenomenon of early law codes creating social pyramids was not limited to the ancient Near East (Harari, 2011). Comparable phenomena were evident in early Vedic laws of India and Chinese legal traditions rooted in Confucian principles (Armstrong, 2006; Arnason et al., 2005; Bellah & Joas, 2012; Eisenstadt, 1986; Jaspers, 1953). Even Aztec laws accomplished similar social pyramids in the pre-Columbian Americas (Offner, 1983). Production of food, ore, timber, wool and all manner of other commodities from ceramics to tools and weapons was meant to flow upwards as tribute, while stability and order was guaranteed from the top. The anthropologist Eric Wolf (1982) and the historian John Haldon (1993) called this the "tributary mode of production."

This oppressive order posed as a necessity against the endless churn of migration, invasion and social mobility; basically what seemed to sedentary regimes to be chaos itself (Brown, 2010). However, the necessity for order also functioned itself as a curtailment not only of murder, rape, theft and abuse, but of much human endeavor which ultimately led to various forms of enslavement, whether outright or through some form of serfdom or other legal classification. In the words of British prime minister William Pitt the Younger (before the House of Commons, 18 November, 1783), "Necessity is the plea for every infringement of human freedom. It is the argument of the tyrant; it is the creed of slaves." John Milton (1667) made a similar observation in *Paradise Lost*: "So spake the fiend, and with necessity, The tyrant's plea, excus'd his devilish deeds" (Book IV, line 393).

Livestock

Necessity, as the saying goes, is also the Mother of Invention. If the Invention of the social pyramid may claim descent from Mother Necessity, the womb was a shared inheritance. Invention's brother, Replication, was just as much a son of Necessity as Cain and Abel were sons of Eve after her departure from Eden. Just as Cain, the farmer, confronted Abel, the herder, out of jealousy of divine favor, Invention, the social pyramid, confronted Replication out of jealousy of his divine favor. Replication is the human propensity to domesticate ad infinitum.

Not all of human history rests on zero-sum logic. In fact, since the beginning of recorded history, a very striking primary pillar of human economic thought rests on the exact opposite: potentially unlimited supply. This is neither gold nor land, but what they encapsulate. Whereas gold and land have always been seen as finite, land is especially valuable due to what it offers: food in the form of plants and animals, which is *not* finite. Land is also where (wo)men and beasts live, which have economic value all their own: they can be domesticated. Domesticated beasts provide labor as well as infinite commodities like meat, wool and milk (which may be hard to store and trade but much less so in the form of cheese). On the other half of the livestock ledger, domesticated humans supply all sorts of slave labor to the social pyramid, both productive and reproductive labor, including care work and forced sex work. Just as with domesticated livestock, the more docile the slave, the more valuable (Burja, 2021; Hare & Woods, 2020; Hribal, 2007; Stetka, 2020). As Stephanie Kelton argues, what governments have always truly been after is the labor of their own subjects or citizens, and the more easily coerced the better (Kelton, 2020, pp. 23–31). This is a fundamental rejection of what David Graeber called "the myth of barter," in which the liberal narrative goes that money was simply invented to replace the barter system. In fact, it was debt, and commonly debt *slavery* (the idea of chartalism) which shows that taxes have always been more commonly paid in *kind* (that is, through typically *slave labor*) than in cold, hard cash. Slavery and slave labor have typically been the rule, not the exception, throughout written history—and they've come with a predictably grim set of economic incentives, behaviors and expectations.

Slave revolts have also been common (and commonly feared) for millennia, even before Spartacus. Throughout history, slavers have implemented strategies to keep slaves docile, while slaves have developed methods to foment agitation and awareness of their condition. The slavers' primary strategy involves setting slaves against each other ("divide-and-rule"). The slaves' usual strategy, involving forms of protest and agitation, aims to prevent docility and division. While divide-and-rule seems more prevalent historically, the strategy of the enslaved is perhaps older, being a primary theme in the Book of Exodus. The divide-and-rule approach was brought to the New World by Old World slave empires. Although Old World and Mediterranean slavery originally functioned within pagan economic systems, and later became associated with monotheistic differences (Christians and Muslims enslaving each other), New World slavery primarily involved monotheistic peoples enslaving pagans (native Americans and Africans). Despite the common distinction drawn between Afro-Eurasian religiously-based slavery and American racially-based slavery, the potentially unlimited economic exploitation in both systems suggests there was, in fact, little fundamental difference (Eltis & Engerman, 2011; Eltis et al., 2017; Fynn-Paul, 2009; Wheat, 2010).

Get All the Gold Part 1: Bullionism

The real measure of wealth and power has always been valued in terms of inelastic, finite commodities. The two most basic are gold and land. Most wars have been waged over restricted access to limited supplies of either—one affords the other. Land, if especially well-endowed, contains mines; mines produce new value, and if the owner is incredibly lucky, gold. Ipso facto, whoever legally controls the land controls the gold and vice versa, resulting in the social pyramid. Hence, bullionism has been the earliest and simplest form of political economy: in short, one way or another, get all the gold. This remained the basic political economy of all dynastic power structures for millennia, from the very beginning of written records between myth and history. Cain and Abel have been cast as representatives of the earliest farmers competing with herders for ownership of seemingly finite land (Quinn, 2009). This competition resulted in murder, the earliest legal recourse of which was the blood feud and the tribalism which sustained it—detailed in the following subsection.

Nevertheless, the successors of Cain and Abel continued the competition for restricted access to seemingly finite gold and land; this is the story of history (typically what we now consider ancient and medieval history). Whether we now call them Sumerians, Egyptians, Babylonians, Macedonians, Mongols, Mauryans or Ming, and whether they engaged more in herding or farming, they ultimately competed among themselves and others for access to ownership of resources perceived as finite like gold and land. For most of recorded history, all sedentary, organized city-states, kingdoms, empires and dynasties had basically the same standardized political economy, which we now call bullionism—a useful word since it includes both gold and silver. In short, bullionism was, and remains, the political economy which attracts bullion—or money.

In a nutshell, once a regime (a ruler, a dynasty or a ruling class) had consolidated its rule (jurisdiction) over a region, it set about acquiring as much gold as possible, and once bullion had been brought within the jurisdiction, laws and policies were implemented to restrict the outflow of bullion and to make bullion easily accessible for the regime. Such laws can be seen for example in early Roman history in the *lex Minucia de triumviris mensariis* which was an amendment of sorts to the Laws of the Twelve Tables, passed in 216 BCE, to alleviate the problem of the growing numbers of Roman citizens in debt selling themselves into slavery (Niczyporuk, 2011). With the incoming gold and silver, the regime would pay soldiers to expand its frontiers and return the investment back to the regime in a circular system. The survival of the regime depended on the degree of success and efficiency of the circuit of the bullion it invested to return as tax. The loss of land or bullion would eventually result in the weakening of the regime. For example, during the mid-tenth century, the khans of Khazaria were weakened by the outflow of bullion without it returning; they couldn't pay enough soldiers sufficiently to resist the onslaught of the Rus' (Feldman, 2022).

Over time, laws were added which increased the effectiveness of the circuit, thereby protecting the economic viability of the regime. These laws aimed, for instance, at maintaining a positive trade balance, which would ensure more inflow of bullion than outflow. Legally boosting the likelihood of further inflows of bullion would then pay for more soldiers to further expand the jurisdiction of the regime. This is how many countries have come to hold the shapes they currently do.

And this wasn't simply a European, Christian, nor even still a specifically Abrahamic phenomenon. The same held true for most dynastic regimes the world over. The earliest Islamic thinkers in the wake of the death of the Prophet Muhammed advocated political-economic policies which resembled bullionism. Even by the 14th c. in North Africa, ibn Khaldun, perhaps the greatest Islamic thinker of the age, noted that the value of bullion for a regime was only as strong as its own circuitous supply from the taxes of its subjects (what is now called the Laffer curve) and the demand of its neighbors, and therefore a regime predictably interferes in the commercial sphere to protect its own interests (Hosseini, 2003; Ibn Khaldun, 1969, pp. 276–278; Oweiss, 1988; Weiss, 2009). The Hindu Vijaynagar regime in southern India during the 14–17th centuries also consciously interfered with commerce to protect its interests to maintain trade surpluses and prevent the outflow of bullion (Mahalingam, 1940). The famous Chinese "Debate about Salt and Iron" from over two thousand years ago crystallized the position many Chinese thinkers have taken to advocating a regime's strong regulation of commerce for its own fiscal benefit (Gale, 1931/1967; Gale et al., 1934; Wagner, 2001; Wan, 2012). The Mayan *Popol Vuh* expressed the ruler's need for precious metals even if only meant for his warriors as a symbol of his divine authority and sovereignty (Christenson, 2007, pp. 240–242, 294).

Ultimately, the drive, usually by some regime or another, to obtain and preserve access to as much gold and silver as possible is called bullionism. Bullion has been most commonly obtained in one of three ways: by mining, trading or raiding. Once it has become accessible, it is then fed into the circuit. The first option has always been the least risky and the most preferable. Consequently, most and usually the shallowest gold mines have been exhausted from a relatively early era, although there are still deep gold mines in operation, such as in South Africa. For much of history, whenever a regime could gain access to silver or gold mines, it has immediately monopolized control over them, such as for instance the Árpád dynasty's 11th-c. monopolization of control over the silver mines near today's town of Banská Štiavnica in Slovakia. Four centuries later, the Ottoman dynasty monopolized control over the fortified silver mines of Novo Brdo after defeating the Branković dynasty in 1441, and the resulting dearth of available bullion in both Latin and Orthodox Christendoms was felt as far away as England, where wages fell accordingly ("the Great Bullion Famine") (Dyer, 1989, p. 219; Engel, 2001; Pamuk, 2000). The second option is to conduct commerce for the purpose of importing as much bullion as possible and restricting its export as much as possible. This usually requires pursuing ethically questionable business practices combined with having convenient natural boundaries: mountains and rivers are common, but an island location perhaps makes this easiest—this was the English crown's preference for centuries. The third option is the riskiest: to go to war for booty. This has frequently been the primary cause of warfare throughout history, although it has usually been justified with other, more noble *casus belli*, like the love of a woman—or of God.

Nevertheless, the logic of bullionism has always been the same: more bullion for one regime means less for another, and consequently, more soldiers for the former and fewer soldiers for the latter, making it likely that the survival of the former regime would come at the expense of the latter in their efforts to expand or protect their respective jurisdictions. This is one of the commonest and oldest forms of zero-sum thinking about political economy.

Tribalism and the Blood Feud

Zero-sum competition for seemingly finite access to bullion and land, being the most frequent cause of violence, has perhaps the longest history of all. The causes of violence, being simple, are in turn exacerbated by one of the simplest features of human psychology: tribalism. It is commonly thought that tribalism is endemic to any form or instance of warfare, and may very well be an ineradicable aspect of the human condition. Whatever else tribalism may be labeled, "otherization," "us-versus-them," "groupthink," etc., it would be hardly controversial to suggest that tribalism, based on exclusion, takes many forms and has done so since time immemorial.

Before we proceed, some clarifications are in order regarding the use of the much-debated term of "tribalism". We use the term in a global context, not limited to Native American or African groups, but as a phenomenon observable across various societies and throughout history. Importantly, we do not frame "tribalism" as a primitive stage in a supposed linear progression of societal development, nor do we tie it to the discourses of civilization versus barbarism. Instead, we view it as a complex form of social organization and identity formation that can be seen in numerous contexts where group cohesion based on (perceived) shared traits or interests occurs. While the term first appears in the first chapter, it is not something we describe in the manuscript as restricted *only* to premodern societies. Our perspective aligns with a more nuanced understanding of "tribalism" as a universal human behavior that transcends geographical and cultural boundaries, rather than as a term mired in historical prejudices. It also converses with Realistic Group Conflict Theory, which emphasizes the relation of conflict with (perceived) zero-sum conditions (Fog, 2017). Our position is that such words should not be necessarily avoided because they were abused generations ago by eugenicists and social Darwinists to justify colonialism, racism, Jim Crow, apartheid and so forth. This specific term has a significant analytical utility as it encompasses multiple patterns of identity formation and otherization, in-group and out-group affects and practices.

Indications of internecine strife and warfare appear in the earliest archaeological records nearly everywhere. The earliest form of sovereignty was basically a militocracy, namely sovereignty by crude force; or as Charles Tilly (1975) famously wrote, "war made the state, and the state made war" (p. 42). Anthropologists and evolutionary biologists have concluded that the propensity for tribal warfare among clans and extended families of apes persisted throughout the evolution of anatomically contemporary humans (Diamond, 2006; Wrangham & Peterson, 1996). The earliest grave stelae in bronze-age Near East attest to brutal, seemingly interminable periods of warfare punctuated by short, feeble, unstable and perpetually disintegrating peace. The earliest written record of a battle, the famous battle of Kadesh between the ancient Egyptian and Hittite slave empires in the thirteenth century BCE (the late bronze age) over hegemony over the Levant, is hardly the first (Hasel, 1998). According to the interpretation of Homer in the *Epitome* of Apollodoros, the Mysians (possibly Hittites) also aided the Trojans against the Mycenaeans during the Trojan War (thirteenth century BCE)—somewhere between myth and history. In fact, the Trojan war itself has been interpreted as a conflict over finite control of the Dardanelles Straits, which the Hittite Tawagalawa Letter has been interpreted as mentioning. Later, according to Thucydides and Plutarch, the major war between the Trojan War of Homer (thirteenth century BCE) and the Persian Wars of Herodotus (sixth century BCE) was the Lelantine War fought between Eretria and Chalkis over the finite central, fertile plains of the Greek island of Euboea in the 8–7th century BCE (Apollodorus, 1921, Epitome 5.12; Bryce, 2005; Hoffner, 2009; Lambert, 1982; Sommer, 1975). Although the causes of every conflict since have been veiled by seemingly nobler justifications (love, religion, glory, even democracy), the base reasons have always come down to hegemony, control or some kind of access to land and/or bullion. In short, with vanishingly few exceptions, most wars are turf wars.

The reason for the emergence of various forms of monotheism was originally to transcend tribalism. Yet, even though religious allegiances were meant to surpass pagan tribalism via collective loyalties to common sets of laws and subjection to a common authority, they nevertheless resulted in rival religions and by extension, rival religious identities, to say nothing of the rival dynasties which manifested them. Ultimately, tribalism has also been shown to transcend both time and confessional doctrine (Jaffrelot, 2003; Keeley, 1996; Marx, 2005).

It may be helpful to think of visceral "tribalism" as an extension of network theory. Neurological studies have demonstrated that typical human brains are not adapted to socially keeping track of large populations of other humans, usually referred to as "Dunbar's number" (Dunbar, 1992). In a brief summary, having reached a connection limit for a sheer quantity of other people a given person can be acquainted with (about 150), many neurologists have formulated that the natural reaction for the brain is to resort to some amalgamation of stereotypes, hierarchical schematics, and other oversimplified structures in order to manage information about so many other people (Bernard et al., 1987; Dunbar, 2010; Fiske & Taylor, 2013, pp. 32–33; Killworth & Bernard, 1979; Killworth et al., 1984; McCarthy et al., 2000).

While this might suggest that "tribalism" and zero-sum thinking are ineradicable aspects of human neurology—if only for the sheer fact that the typical human brain cannot be familiar with so many other people and creates conceptions of "us versus them"—a closer examination reveals a more complex picture. The social psychologist Cory Clark and her colleagues have surmised that the human mind

> was forged by the crucible of coalitional conflict. For many thousands of years, human tribes have competed against each other. Coalitions that were more cooperative and cohesive not only survived but also appropriated land and resources from other coalitions and therefore reproduced more prolifically, thus passing their genes (and their loyalty traits) to later generations. (Clark et al., 2019)

Interestingly, while this description emphasizes inter-group conflict, it also demonstrates the crucial role of intra-group cooperation. The success of these coalitions wasn't solely determined by zero-sum competition with other groups, but significantly by their ability to foster non-zero-sum cooperation within the group. This suggests that, even in our evolutionary past, non-zero-sum strategies were key to human success and expansion. Therefore, while zero-sum thinking may be a strong tendency, particularly in inter-group contexts, it is not an inescapable aspect of human nature. Rather, our evolutionary history points to a capacity for both competitive and cooperative strategies, with the latter often providing a significant advantage.

This interpretation aligns with recent anthropological research which challenges the notion that these cognitive limitations rigidly determine social structures. Graeber and Wengrow (2021a) argue that human societies have historically demonstrated remarkable flexibility in social organization, often transcending the constraints suggested by Dunbar's number. They provide evidence of large-scale prehistoric societies that developed methods to maintain social cohesion beyond the proposed 150-person limit, such as seasonal variations in social structure or complex political systems including some based on mathematical principles. This suggests that while zero-sum thinking and tribalism may be cognitive tendencies, they are not immutable. As Graeber and Wengrow (2021a) note, early human societies were capable of "self-conscious social experimentation" (p. 326), which indicates a capacity to innovate beyond apparent cognitive limitations.

Nonetheless, inter-tribal conflict solidified the legality of the blood feud and the feudal contract meant to mitigate it. The concept of fief, codified in the *Libri Feodorum* (a 12th-century collection of legal customs from Northern Italy), connected the feud to the contract of property exchanged for service (serfs' labor). This text attempted to mitigate the eternality of the blood feud by establishing who, where, when and how fiefs could be apportioned, attained, maintained, bequeathed, disputed and forfeited. The legal concept of the fief itself—essentially heritable land ownership in exchange for fealty to another lord—was conditioned by the zero-sum logic of finite possessable land and bullion. But given the valuable livestock on that land, a lord's ownership of land came at the price of his obligations both to superiors and vassals. Thus, feudalism also concretized the idea of patronage and charity as well—*noblesse oblige*.

This was the real heritage of feudal law: to reduce feuds by applying separate legal classifications to different social classes, with heritability following. In French legal terminology, this was referred to as private law, or "privi-lege," resulting in "feudal privilege" (Ganshof, 1952, pp. 106–108). The goal of feudal privilege was to facilitate a stable social structure to minimize tribal feuding by appealing to a common set of laws (in the 9–11th centuries, Roman bishops/popes instituted legal doctrines which became called the *Peace and Truce of God*) (Cowdrey, 1970). Yet, the byproduct was a more durable, hardened social pyramid, where the chaos of social mobility decreased in seemingly zero-sum, fixed proportion to the order of upward-facing fealty and downward-facing charity and patronage (Bloch, 1961, pp. 125–126; Davis, 2008; Duby & Ariès, 1993, p. 27; Gluckman, 1955; Holland, 2009; Pocock, 1987).

Potlatch Societies

The firmly established social pyramid, enshrined by law, preserves the wealth of the wealthy and, to ensure the consent and goodwill of the powerless, engenders the need for charity and patronage—the original soft power. Once people shared the same religion, they couldn't enslave each other (although they could and did enslave members of other religions for centuries). So how would the social pyramid—essentially a caste system—be maintained with reduced slavery? Almsgiving.

The concern for human righteousness when giving and receiving alms is universal. The sacrifice of personal property through almsgiving forms a major part of every world religion and is literally written into every holy scripture, divine revelation or commentary thereupon. In Judaism, it's called *Tzedaka*; in Christianity, the Septuagint translation and New Testament used the word *Eleemosyne*; in Islam, *Zadak*; in Hinduism, Buddhism, Jainism and Sikhism, *Dāna*; in Confucianism, *Ren*. This was noticed by James G. Frazer, who discussed, among many other topics, the comparative necessity for sacrifice and almsgiving across all world religions, both Abrahamic and Vedic, in his *Golden Bough.*

The Tanakh extensively references almsgiving, which is often interchangeable with the term for righteousness, *tzedaka*, even in the Book of Genesis (18:19 *NIV*): "For I [the Lord] have chosen him [Avraham], so that he will direct his children and his household after him to keep the way of the Lord by doing what is right [tzedaka]." The Book of Isaiah (1:27 *NIV*) first teaches that "Zion will be redeemed by justice; and those in her who repent, by righteousness [tzedaka]" (Isaiah I:27 *NIV*). Later, Isaiah 54:14 (*NIV*) declares: "In righteousness [tzedaka], you [the Lord] will be established." One of the longest passages about tzedaka [righteousness], appears in the Book of Deuteronomy (15:7–11 NIV), which consciously acknowledges that law creates wealth disparity between the haves and the have-nots. Later in the Tanakh, the Book of Psalms (41:1 *NIV*) declares: "Blessed are those who have regard for the weak." Maimonides is hardly the first rabbi to discuss tzedakah, but as one of the most well-known rebbeim on the topic, he defined eight levels of charity based on a scale between vanity and genuine righteousness (Maimonides, 2003, Hilchot Mat'not Ani'im 10:7–14). Even those at the very bottom of the social pyramid are not exempt from the necessity to sacrifice something for tzedaka. According to the common interpretation of the Talmud, "Since it is not the quality of the sacrifice that counts but the effort made by the sacrificer, the meager offering of the poor man may be worth more than the rich man's large sacrifice" (Steinsaltz, 1976, p. 176). In effect, Halakhic law in Judaism underpinned a social system of hereditary castes, where certain priestly clans such as the Kohanim and Leviim occupied roles which required perpetual mutual obligations with those born into lower castes, not unlike the brahmins in Hinduism.

Similar concepts appear in the New Testament and the Quran regarding the differing capacities and roles in the giving and receiving of alms. A common verse in Luke 21:1–4 relates:

> He looked up and saw the rich putting their gifts into the treasury. And He saw a poor widow putting in two small copper coins. And He said, "Truly I say to you, this poor widow put in more than all of them; for they all out of their surplus put into the offering; but she out of her poverty put in all that she had to live on."

The Quran provides specific instruction for almsgiving in response to poverty and destitution:

> The alms are only for the poor and the needy, and those who collect them, and those whose hearts are to be reconciled, and to free the captives and the debtors, and for the cause of Allah, and (for) the wayfarers; a duty imposed by Allah. Allah is knower, Wise. (Qur'an 9:60).

Building on this, Islamic judicial thinkers have formulated certain criteria of wealth level for almsgiving, a kind of graduated charity system based on income (Qaraḍāwī, 1999). Having evolved from Islamic law (Sharia) into taxation based on income, the emergence of Islamic social structures used legal concepts of taxation like *kharaj*, *jizye*, and *iqta* which perpetuated various versions of potlatch societies.

The Vedas teach that Dāna brings benefits for the giver in the future:

> The Gods have not ordained hunger to be our death: even to the well-fed man comes death in varied shape,
>
> The riches of the liberal never waste away, while he who will not give finds none to comfort him,
>
> The man with food in store who, when the needy comes in miserable case begging for bread to eat,
>
> Hardens his heart against him, when of old finds not one to comfort him.
>
> Bounteous is he who gives unto the beggar who comes to him in want of food, and the feeble,
>
> Success attends him in the shout of battle. He makes a friend of him in future troubles,
>
> No friend is he who to his friend and comrade who comes imploring food, will offer nothing.
>
> Let the rich satisfy the poor implorer, and bend his eye upon a longer pathway,
>
> Riches come now to one, now to another, and like the wheels of cars are ever rolling,
>
> The foolish man wins food with fruitless labour: that food – I speak the truth – shall be his ruin,
>
> He feeds no trusty friend, no man to love him. All guilt is he who eats with no partaker.
>
> (Griffith, 1896, 10.117)

The potlatch society fostered by the Vedas facilitated the legal concepts in the Dharmasastra or Hindu Law. For centuries, the legal concepts contained in the Dharmasastras perpetuated the caste system in Hinduism, its own potlatch society which endured for centuries (Dumont, 1980, pp. 66–73, 193; Hiltebeitel, 2011; Olivelle, 2008, pp. 240–245).

The Book of Mencius in the Confucian canon is devoted to the proper way to give and receive and how patronage must be performed:

> Wan Chang said, "Why is it a Gentleman does not place himself under the protection of a feudal lord?"
>
> "He does not presume to do so," said Mencius. "According to the rites, only a feudal lord who has lost his estate places himself under the protection of another. It would be contrary to the rites for a Gentleman to place himself under the protection of a feudal lord."
>
> "But if the ruler gives him rice," said Wan Chang, "would he accept it?"
>
> "Yes."
>
> "On what principle does he accept it?"
>
> "A prince naturally gives charity to those who have come from abroad to settle."

> "Why is it that one accepts charity but refuses what is bestowed to one?"
>
> "One does not dare presume."
>
> "Why does one not dare presume?"
>
> "A gate-keeper or a watchman accepts his wages from the authorities because he has regular duties. For one who has no regular duties to accept what is bestowed on him is for him to show a lack of gravity."
>
> "If it is permissible to accept gifts from the ruler, I wonder if one could count on their continuance?"
>
> "[...] If, in spite of one's claim to like good and wise men, one is able neither to raise them to office nor to take care of them, can one be truly said to be like such men?"
>
> (Lau, 1970, pp. 150–156)

For Mencius, being the good and wise man that he was, the only proper way for a lord to patronize a good and wise man is to raise him to high office (Lai & Lee, 2002).

In all the religions and their injunctions on the proper method of giving and receiving charity, the most common concept is the idea of obligation, or reciprocity (in Greek, υποχρέωση). The mutual obligations involved in giving and receiving were meant to cement the social roles of each (except perhaps in the case of Maimonides, who advocated giving enough to permanently change the social relationship—for Mencius this came through high office), and to dispel the vanity that also typically accompanies charity.

One of the most outspoken proponents for the direct relationship between vanity and charity was Bernard de Mandeville in the 17–18th centuries, who is generally credited as one of the first to advocate greed as a benefit to the common good due to the self-conscious universal human need to launder reputation by giving to charity. To this day, psychologists remain intrigued by the propensity for western individualism to elicit acts of generosity, even if the underlying logic beneath it is rather more prosaic (Rhoads et al., 2021; Sedlacek, 2011, pp. 183–190). Emile Durkheim's nephew Marcel Mauss showed that by giving generously to charity, the wealthy became patrons to the powerless, ensuring the devotion and reverence of the powerless and the continued benefit of the powerful through their philanthropy, or what other sociologists have referred to as "noblesse oblige"; in other words, gift-giving structures, or, essentially, systems of almsgiving. Mauss called this a "Potlatch" society after the term used by the landowning native American communities of the Pacific Northwest. By giving just enough to maintain their wealth to continue giving, the powerful landowners of these communities could maintain their status and use it to continue their efforts to gain more wealth from their lands in order to give more away (Barnett, 1938; Clutesi, 1969; Graeber, 2001, pp. 188–208; Mauss, 2002; Rosman, 1972). Similar observations can be made about much of the world due to the seeming finitude of land. In effect, potlatch patronage has been the silent glue which held the fiefdom, or the landowner-based feudal social fabric together. Even in the 21st-c. US tax code, which gives reductions for giving to charities, it still is (26 U.S.C. § 501, 2024).

And although conservatives lament the erosion of older potlatch systems, there is always another class of nouveau riche to replace them with a newer version of the same structure.

This also explains why the base of the social pyramid—the caste system—has also been the most susceptible to authoritarianism. Trained to believe that they have the most to gain from the status quo and to harbor ethnic chauvinist beliefs by the ruling dynastic and feudal institutions which maintain their place through divide-and-rule strategies, the slaves, peasantries and working classes have always been the most numerous and ardent defenders of the status quo—because they depend on the patronage and beneficence of the powerful. In this way, potlatch philanthropy makes the weak dependent on the strong (the poor dependent on the rich) and preserves the social and economic hierarchies of patronage which preserve or ossify into private laws—the privileges of feudalism.

References

26 U.S.C. § 501 (2024).

Apollodorus. (1921). *The library* (J. G. Frazer, Trans.). Harvard University Press.

Armstrong, K. (2006). *The great transformation: The world at the time of Buddha, Socrates, Confucius, and Jeremiah*. Atlantic Books.

Arnason, J. P., Eisenstadt, S. N., & Wittrock, B. (Eds.). (2005). *Axial civilizations and world history*. Brill.

Assmann, J. (2008). *Of God and gods: Egypt, Israel, and the rise of monotheism*. University of Wisconsin Press.

Assmann, J. (2010). *The price of monotheism* (R. Savage, Trans.). Stanford University Press.

Assmann, J. (2018). *The invention of religion: Faith and covenant in the book of Exodus* (R. Savage, Trans.). Princeton University Press.

Barnett, H. G. (1938). The nature of the potlatch. *American Anthropologist, 40*(3), 349–358.

Bellah, R. N., & Joas, H. (Eds.). (2012). *The axial age and its consequences*. Harvard University Press.

Bernard, H. R., Shelley, G. A., & Killworth, P. (1987). How much of a network does the GSS and RSW dredge up? *Social Networks, 9*(1), 49–63.

Bloch, M. (1961). *Feudal society* (L. A. Manyon, Trans.). Routledge & Kegan Paul.

Brown, P. (2010). *Empires and barbarians*. Oxford University Press.

Bryce, T. (2005). *The Trojans and their neighbours*. Taylor & Francis.

Burja, S. (2021, May 17). Why civilization is older than we thought. *Palladium Magazine*. https://www.palladiummag.com/2021/05/17/why-civilization-is-older-than-we-thought

Cauvin, J. (2000). *The birth of the gods and the origins of agriculture*. Cambridge University Press.

Christenson, A. J. (2007). *Popol Vuh: Literal translation* [Ebook]. Mesoweb Publications. http://www.mesoweb.com/publications/Christenson/PV-Literal.pdf

Clark, C. J., Liu, B. S., Winegard, B. M., & Ditto, P. H. (2019). Tribalism is human nature. *Current Directions in Psychological Science, 28*(6), 587–592. https://doi.org/10.1177/0963721419862289

Clutesi, G. (1969). *Potlatch* (2nd ed.). The Morriss Printing Co.

Cowdrey, H. E. J. (1970). The peace and the truce of God in the eleventh century. *Past & Present, 46*, 42–67.

Davis, K. (2008). *Periodization & sovereignty: How ideas of feudalism & secularization govern the politics of time*. University of Pennsylvania Press.

Diamond, J. M. (2006). *The third chimpanzee*. HarperCollins.

Duby, G., & Ariès, P. (1993). *A history of private life: Revelations of the medieval world*. Belknap Press.
Dumont, L. (1980). *Homo hierarchicus: The caste system and its implications* (Revised ed.). University of Chicago Press.
Dunbar, R. I. M. (1992). Neocortex size as a constraint on group size in primates. *Journal of Human Evolution, 20*, 469–493.
Dunbar, R. I. M. (2010). *How many friends does one person need? Dunbar's number and other evolutionary quirks*. Faber & Faber.
Dyer, C. (1989). *Standards of living in the later Middle Ages: Social change in England c. 1200–1520*. Cambridge University Press.
Eisenstadt, S. N. (Ed.). (1986). *The origins and diversity of axial age civilizations*. SUNY Press.
Eltis, D., & Engerman, S. L. (Eds.). (2011). *The Cambridge world history of slavery* (Vol. 3). Cambridge University Press.
Eltis, D., Engerman, S. L., Drescher, S., & Richardson, D. (Eds.). (2017). *The Cambridge world history of slavery* (Vol. 4). Cambridge University Press.
Engel, P. (2001). *The realm of St. Stephen: A history of medieval Hungary, 895–1526*. I. B. Tauris.
Faulkner, W. (1951). *Requiem for a nun*. Random House.
Feldman, A. M. (2022). The decline and fall of Khazaria: Might or money? *Восток (Oriens). Bulletin of the Russian Academy of Sciences, Institute of Oriental Studies, 4*, 75–84. https://doi.org/10.31857/S086919080021412-0
Fiske, S. T., & Taylor, S. E. (2013). *Social cognition: From brains to culture*. Sage.
Fog, A. (2017). *Warlike and peaceful societies: The interaction of genes and culture*. Open Book Publishers. https://doi.org/10.11647/obp.0128
Fynn-Paul, J. (2009). Empire, monotheism, and slavery in the greater Mediterranean region from antiquity to the early modern era. *Past & Present, 205*(1), 3–40.
Gale, E. M. (Trans.). (1931/1967). *Discourses on salt and iron: A debate on state control of commerce and industry in ancient China* (Reprint). Ch'engwen.
Gale, E. M., Boodberg, P., & Liu, T. C. (1934). Discourses on salt and iron. *Journal of the North China Branch of the Royal Asiatic Society, 65*, 73–110.
Ganshof, F. L. (1952). *Feudalism* (P. Grieson, Trans.). Longmans, Green & Co.
Gluckman, M. (1955). The peace in the feud. *Past and Present, 8*(1), 1–14.
Graeber, D. (2001). *Toward an anthropological theory of value: The false coin of our own dreams*. Palgrave.
Graeber, D., & Wengrow, D. (2021a). *The dawn of everything: A new history of humanity*. Penguin.
Graeber, D., & Wengrow, D. (2021b, November 4). Ancient history shows how we can create a more equal world. *New York Times*. https://nyti.ms/3o2PLMB
Griffith, R. T. H. (1896). *The hymns of the Rigveda: Translated with a popular commentary* (2nd ed.). (Original work published 1889).
Haldon, J. F. (1993). *The state and the tributary mode of production*. Verso.
Harari, Y. N. (2011). *Sapiens: A brief history of humankind*. Penguin Random House.
Hare, B., & Woods, V. (2020). *Survival of the friendliest: Understanding our origins and rediscovering our common humanity*. Penguin Random House.
Hasel, M. G. (1998). *Domination and resistance: Egyptian military activity in the southern Levant, 1300–1185 B.C.* Brill.
Hiltebeitel, A. (2011). *Dharma: Its early history in law, religion, and narrative*. Oxford University Press.
Hoffner, H. A., Jr. (2009). *Letters from the Hittite kingdom*. Society of Biblical Literature.
Holland, T. (2009). *Millennium: The end of the world and the forging of Christendom*. Abacus.
Hosseini, H. S. (2003). Contributions of medieval Muslim scholars to the history of economics and their impact: A refutation of the Schumpeterian great gap. In J. Biddle, J. Davis, & W. J. Samuels (Eds.), *A companion to the history of economic thought* (pp. 28–45). Blackwell.
Hribal, J. (2007, September 22–23). What would Frederick Douglass and John Africa think of Michael Vick? *Counterpunch*. https://www.adaptt.org/documents/Vick.pdf

Ibn Khaldun. (1969). *The Muqaddimah: An introduction to history* (F. Rosenthal & N. J. Dawood, Trans.). Princeton University Press.
Jaffrelot, C. (2003). For a theory of nationalism. *Questions De Recherche, 10*, 1–51.
Jaspers, K. (1953). *The origin and goal of history* (M. Bullock, Trans.). Routledge & Kegan Paul.
Keeley, L. H. (1996). *War before civilization: The myth of the peaceful savage*. Oxford University Press.
Kelton, S. (2020). *The deficit myth*. PublicAffairs.
Killworth, P. D., & Bernard, H. R. (1979). A pseudomodel of the small world problem. *Social Forces, 58*(2), 477–505.
Killworth, P. D., McCarthy, C., & Bernard, H. R. (1984). Measuring patterns of acquaintanceship. *Current Anthropology, 25*(4), 381–397.
Lai, P.-C., & Lee, P. (2002). Traditions of giving in Confucianism. *Alliance Magazine*. https://www.alliancemagazine.org/analysis/traditions-of-giving-in-confucianism/
Lambert, S. D. (1982). A Thucydidean scholium on the 'Lelantine War.' *Journal of Hellenic Studies, 102*, 216–220. https://doi.org/10.2307/631143
Lau, D. C. (1970). *Mencius*. Penguin Books.
Machiavelli, N. (1950). *The discourses of Niccolò Machiavelli* (L. J. Walker, Trans.; Vol. 1). Yale University Press. (Original work written c. 1517).
Mahalingam, T. V. (1940). *Administration and social life under Vijayanagara*. University of Madras Press.
Maimonides. (2003). *Mishneh Torah* (J. J. Baker, Trans.). http://www.panix.com/~jjbaker/rmbmzdkh.html (Original work composed ca. 1170–1180).
Marx, A. W. (2005). *Faith in nation: Exclusionary origins of nationalism*. Oxford University Press.
Mauss, M. (2002). *The gift: The form and reason for exchange in archaic societies* (W. D. Halls, Trans.). Routledge.
McCarthy, C., Killworth, P. D., Bernard, H. R., Johnsen, E., & Shelley, G. (2000). Comparing two methods for estimating network size. *Human Organization, 60*(1), 28–39.
Milton, J. (1667). *Paradise lost: A poem in ten books*. Samuel Simmons.
Niczyporuk, P. (2011). Mensarii, bankers acting for public and private benefit. *Studies in Logic, Grammar and Rhetoric, 24*(37), 105–115.
Offner, A. (2023). Law before European contact: Mesoamerica. In J. Rosado & C. Goebel (Eds.), *A companion to Latin American legal history* (pp. 29–48). Brill Nijhoff. https://doi.org/10.1163/9789004436091_003
Offner, J. A. (1983). *Law and politics in Aztec Texcoco*. Cambridge University Press.
Olivelle, P. (2008). *Caste and purity in collected essays*. Firenze University Press.
Oweiss, I. M. (1988). Ibn Khaldun, the father of economics. In G. N. Atiyeh & I. M. Oweiss (Eds.), *Arab civilization: Challenges and responses: Studies in honor of Dr. Constantine Zurayk* (pp. 112–127). SUNY Press.
Pamuk, Ş. (2000). *A monetary history of the Ottoman Empire*. Cambridge University Press.
Pocock, J. G. A. (1987). *The ancient constitution and the feudal law: A study of English historical thought in the seventeenth century*. Cambridge University Press.
Qaraḍāwī, Y. (1999). *Fiqh az-zakat: A comparative study: The rules, regulations and philosophy of zakat in light of the Qur'an and Sunna* (M. Kahf, Trans.). Dar Al Taqwa.
Quinn, D. (2009). *Ishmael*. Random House.
Rhoads, S. A., Gunter, D., Ryan, R., & Marsh, A. (2021). Global variation in subjective well-being predicts seven forms of altruism. *PsyArXiv*. https://doi.org/10.31234/osf.io/k3y7u
Rosman, A. (1972). The potlatch: A structural analysis. *American Anthropologist, 74*(3), 658–671.
Sedlacek, T. (2011). *Economics of good and evil*. Oxford University Press.
Slatyer, W. (2012). *Life/death rhythms of ancient empires—Climatic cycles influence rule of dynasties*. Trafford.
Sommer, F. (1975). *Die Ahhijava-Urkunden: Mit 9 Tafeln*. Olms.
Steinsaltz, A. (1976). *The essential Talmud* (C. Galai, Trans.). Jason Aronson.
Stetka, B. (2020, October 31). *How humans domesticated themselves*. NPR Health.

Tilly, C. (1975). Reflections on the history of European state-making. In C. Tilly, G. Ardant, & L. W. Pye (Eds.), *The formation of national states in Western Europe* (pp. 3–83). Princeton University Press.

Van De Mieroop, M. (2016). *Philosophy before the Greeks: The pursuit of truth in ancient Babylonia*. Princeton University Press.

Wagner, D. B. (2001). *The state and the iron industry in Han China*. Nordic Institute of Asian Studies Publishing.

Wan, M. (2012). Discourses on salt and iron: A first century B.C. Chinese debate over the political economy of empire. *Journal of Chinese Political Science, 17*, 143–163. https://doi.org/10.1007/s11366-012-9190-6

Weiss, D. (2009). Ibn Khaldun on economic transformation. *International Journal of Middle East Studies, 27*(1), 29–37. https://doi.org/10.1017/S0020743800061560

Wheat, D. (2010). Mediterranean slavery, New World transformations: Galley slaves in the Spanish Caribbean, 1578–1635. *Slavery & Abolition, 31*(3), 327–344.

Wolf, E. R. (1982). *Europe and the people without history*. University of California Press.

Wrangham, R. W., & Peterson, D. (1996). *Demonic males: Apes and the origins of human violence*. Houghton Mifflin.

Wright, D. P. (2009). *Inventing God's law: How the covenant code of the Bible used and revised the laws of Hammurabi*. Oxford University Press.

Feudalism and Mercantilism

3

Abstract

The chapter lays out how the most ancient aspects of political economy gradually transformed across multiple scriptural and theological traditions (Abrahamic, Vedic, etc.). Across all these traditions, the original pyramid schemes, which were enlarged to mitigate tribalism and blood feuds, facilitated systems of land ownership which is now recognizable as **feudalism (which presupposed negligible economic growth**). This chapter also traces the process by which bullionism became synonymous with what we now call **mercantilism**. Both of these terms derived from various legal systems which sought to socioeconomically limit access to ownership of the original finite resources (land and bullion). However, much economic historiography over the past several generations has erected various **mythologies of feudalism and mercantilism**: the myth that Roman laws and feudal laws were different, the myth that feudalism has been exclusive to Latin Christendom, and the myth that feudalism and mercantilism have been mutually exclusive economic systems. By dispelling these myths, the reader can see that dynastic regimes across time and space have always come to power by breaking laws—that there has never been either structural or legal difference between **dynasties and mafias**. This zero-sum political economy, which enshrined the logic of "conquer or be conquered," has engendered **two models of ancient imperial expansion**—tellurocracy (land power) and thalassocracy (sea power), a state of affairs which combined both feudalism and mercantilism and continued up to the eighteenth century, until a new and increasingly successful form of political economy began to be pioneered: liberalism.

Very few ancient agrarian regimes didn't fit the bill outlined in the previous chapter. Regimes based on agrarianism were always heavily dependent on laws regulating and limiting accessibility of land ownership and subsequently potlatch

A. M. Feldman and Y. Stamos, *Zero Sum Political Economy*, World-Systems Evolution and Global Futures, https://doi.org/10.1007/978-3-032-18326-2_3

networks of philanthropy and charity to reduce social aggression and foster interdependence between castes. In one way or another, human ownership of finite commodities like gold or land resulted in tribal blood feuds, which necessitated laws to quell the violence. These laws, in turn, which solidified caste-based social pyramids, initiated potlatch societies. We may consider any number of cases of agrarian societies: the ancient human social structures in places as far flung as Iceland, Japan, Madagascar, Volga Bulgaria, Hungary or even the African Songhai.

We may consider the human inhabitation of Iceland, which was founded as a colony of refugees from zero-sum wars over land in ancient Scandinavia, and now often celebrated as a haven of economic equality, progressive taxation and a healthy middle class. For much of its history between the promulgation of early law codes beginning in the tenth century and facilitating the Goðorð system, until well after its late 13th-c. pledge of allegiance to the Norwegian crown, it resembled most other potlatch societies all the way back to the Book of Judges in the Tanakh: a smattering of chieftain dynasties acted as judges and controlled the finite amount of land on the island, which solidified into a social pyramid in order to reduce tribal feuding and thereby developed into a durable, quasi-potlatch feudal society. This did not lessen after allegiance to the Norwegian crown in 1282; it simply reinforced the pyramid (Jakobsson, 2009; Sigurðsson, 1999, p. 211).

The case of Japan is not dissimilar. Now a NATO partner state and theoretically a liberal democracy since its postwar constitution, most of Japanese history is essentially a story of various versions of a feudal potlatch society with intermittent wars for hegemony by a ruling class of chieftain dynasties (daimyos) squabbling over fiefs (han), the finite amount of land on the main island. The competition spread to the northern island of Hokkaido as well, being "intensified for the limited supply of arable land in northern Honshu, [where] the Ainu [people] were increasingly regarded in a more negative light by the Japanese" (Day, 2008, p. 86). Although various branches of an imperial dynasty had existed since time immemorial, rule over the entire main island was a bicameral affair: emperors had shoguns who wielded the real power; the shogun's dynasty was typically the most powerful of the daimyos; and therefore the periodic wars these daimyos fought against each other were as much for survival as for supremacy. Because all wealth and status was inherited due to Confucian laws, the Bakuhan caste system emerged as the basic Japanese social pyramid (ritsuryo): the four Confucian social categories below daimyo lords, i.e. warriors, peasants, craftsmen and merchants (Diamond, 2005; Duus, 1998; Ohnuki-Tierney, 1993; Totman, 1981; Visočnik, 2014).

As in Iceland and Japan, the history of Madagascar is pockmarked with the signs of zero-sum thinking. For centuries, various feuding chieftain dynasties acted as judges controlling portions of the finite amount of land on the island over which they constantly squabbled. These chieftainships, essentially fiefs but alternatively traditional kingdoms, gave rise to the various ethnic groups on the island, defined primarily by language and region based on their respective control by one dynasty or another. From the mid-sixteenth century, one dynasty, the combination of the Vazimba and Hova clans, produced the Imerina family which would gradually bring the other dynasties on the island under their authority and solidify a pyramidal caste system called *fanjakana arindra*, or "organized government", which involved enslavement as well. By the late eighteenth century, these dynasties were gradually brought under the control of Andrianampoinimerina, and his son, Radama, brought the entire island under his authority in the early nineteenth century with British support (the slave trade didn't hurt either) (Bloch, 1971; Campbell, 1981; Chapus & Dandouau, 1961, p. 47; Miller et al., 1989, p. 143; Raison-Jourde, 1983, p. 239).

But pyramidal potlatch societies are not confined to "primitive," small-scale island societies rather than being the norm for continental-based societies. Some indicative examples from Eurasia and Africa are Volga Bulgaria, Hungary and the Songhai. Located at the Volga-Kama confluence in western Eurasia, a dynasty emerged in the early tenth century due to the legendary conversion to Islam by the ruler, Almuš, which, as revealed by plenty of archaeological evidence, was the main catalyst for agrarian sedentarization and urbanization in the region. His descendants, the Islamic Almušid dynasty, spread their authority over surrounding areas, which later became known as Volga Bulgaria. Castles were built, and inside and around them cities, mosques and slave markets appeared, as well as in the surrounding areas of their respective jurisdictions. Silver coins traded up from Khwarezmia in Central Asia and Baghdad further south were at first used as currency to traffic in pagan slaves. Later they were double struck and soon they were melted down and restruck into expressly Volga Bulgarian coins imitating the silver coins of the Caliphate. The Islamic laws which meant to reduce tribal feuding by a common allegiance to Islam eventually limited access to a seemingly finite amount of land over which the Almušids could feasibly exercise jurisdiction, often by appointing supporters and relatives to rule nearby districts. The result was a feudal, slave-based potlatch society which endured remarkably well until the Mongol invasions of the mid-thirteenth century (Curta, 2013; Gagin, 2008, esp. p. 134; Goldina & Chernykh, 2005, esp. p. 42; Gubajdullin, 2002; Ivanova et al., 2013; Izmailov, 2009; Kazakov, 1992; Khalikov, 1991; Khuzin, 2015; Mako, 2011, esp. pp. 212–217; Sitdikov et al., 2015, esp. pp. 170–172; Zhivkov, 2015, p. 241, n. 75–76).

Much like the Almušids who created what would become Volga Bulgaria, the tenth century also saw the emergence of a ruling dynasty, the Árpáds, in the old Roman province of Pannonia, or the Carpathian Basin, which later became Hungary, or Magyarok. The first Árpád to successfully adopt Christianity, Stephen, according to legend was crowned in Esztergom on Christmas day in the year 1000. Although he fought many wars against steppe nomads and the hardline pagans in primitive settlements, Christianity eventually brought written law, later agrarian sedentarization, urbanization and top-down centralized (pyramidal) rule. Like the Almušids, Stephen's Árpád descendants spread their rule (or conquered) as far as possible, appointed minor family members as appanage rulers in provincial areas, monopolized whatever silver mining they could find (in today's Slovakia) and apportioned out fiefs to their supporters. Christianity laid the administrative groundwork of a feudal, potlatch society that only many centuries later created the nation of Hungary (Bartlett, 2007; Berend, 2001; Engel, 2001, pp. 40–44; Heather,

2008; Herold, 2016, esp. pp. 117–120; Klaniczay, 2004; Pálóczi-Horváth, 1989, pp. 32–33; Róna-Tas, 1999; Wolf, 2003, esp. p. 330).

Lastly, the Islamic Sonni dynasty, which ruled the Songhai realms of West Africa, came to power during the fifteenth century and imposed monotheism on the subject populations in a top-down manner not unlike the previous examples. Once their power had been consolidated, the Sonni rulers expanded their jurisdictions at the expense of neighboring dynasties, most notably the Keita family of Mali and the Mossi families to the south. By the time the Askia dynasty came to power in the Songhai capital of Gao in the late fifteenth century, a stable social pyramid had been erected due to the limitations to agrarian land ownership. As in the previous cases, tributary systems were implemented where rulers apportioned nearby provinces and towns, essentially fiefs, to relatives and supporters in exchange for loyalty. The only major difference between the Songhai and the previous cases is that, due to the prevalence of its goldfields, the Songhai domain is one of the few where salt was as much if not more valuable than gold. Consequently, gold was traded northward beyond the jurisdiction of the ruling dynasty in exchange for salt and other valuable commodities. Nevertheless, the feudal social structure is unmistakable (Abitbol, 1999; Cissoko, 1996; Dalgleish, 2005; Iliffe, 2007, pp. 72–78; Shaw, 1997, pp. 199–217; Willard, 1993, esp. 88–89).

There are few historical exceptions which, due to their common traits of limited land ownership and preference for other life ways, favored other modes of production. In certain other places, horticulture and extremely limited agriculture has been practiced, which has resulted in small population densities in comparison with the land associated with these populations, such as the Aborigines of Australia and New Guinea or the mountain dwellers of upland Southeast Asia, or Zomia (Diamond, 2005; Scott, 2009). In Zomia, it is notable that this was deliberate, since the mountain dwellers had fled and resisted the sedentary, feudal (and slave-based) empires and kingdoms of the neighboring lowlands of India, China and Indochina. Alternatively, the cases of preference for nomadic pastoralism to agrarianism on the grasslands of various continents are exceptions to agrarianism which prove the rule: the Mongol and Turkic peoples of the Eurasian steppe (Beckwith, 2009); the Sioux and Comanche peoples of the American plains; the Maasai peoples of the East African Serengeti. It should also be mentioned that mountain peoples and steppe peoples alike took slaves; nomadic, pastoral social pyramids were just as brutal (if not more) as sedentary, agrarian social pyramids. Nomads and mountain dwellers have been as likely to build pyramidal-shaped earthen tombs (called 'kurgans') as Egyptians and Mayans—which is not itself evidence of pyramidal social structures, but can be indirectly indicative. However, in all ancient societies, one feature of human economic endeavor proved seemingly permanent: the negligibility of economic growth.

Feudalism (Negligible Economic Growth)[1]

In agrarian societies, which have predominated throughout most of human history, there was usually very limited economic growth. Although land could produce potentially infinite goods, the land itself was ultimately finite and the limits of crop yields themselves would be enough to limit population growth. Among nomads and mountain dwellers, their small horticultural, aquacultural and pastoral (stockbreeding) economies were just as constrained; even though livestock could reproduce infinitely, the ultimate finitude of the land itself was no different from agrarian economies. Elsewhere, the fishing peoples who practiced aquaculture were not constrained by finite land, but were still constrained by the amount of fish that could be expected to be caught. In all of these lifeways, however, economic growth was rarely, if ever, sought as an end in itself. Growth happened sporadically in specific locations whenever new lands were conquered and booty and spoils were distributed among the victors. After the initial orgy of violence and greed in the wake of conquest, lands would be settled by the peasants and slaves of the victors, who would till the soil, breed their herds and return to the low-growth agrarian or pastoral economies. Certainly commerce and marketplaces existed between the buyers and sellers of various commodities, as well as rudimentary forms of credit and debt, but it was usually not enough to engender an organised pursuit of economic growth on the part of the rulers (Cohen, 1992; Niczyporuk, 2011).

No wonder then that 18th-c. French economists called themselves "physiocrats"—because to them it was *physically* manifest that all power and wealth in the end derived from the land. This is why laws were ultimately necessary not to prevent crime, but to preserve the social order and limit access to resolutely finite land ownership. Crime prevention was just a byproduct. Private laws (privileges), which applied to different members of different social strata, were heritable and meant to make the order durable. Lords got one set of laws, merchants another, and peasants another. The ultimately negligible economic growth rates of ancient agrarian and pastoral societies are not born out in ancient economic statistics; they did not exist. Instead, they are born out by the function of social pyramids which effectively fulfilled the same purpose as economic data: they provided the basic information about heritable social status and access to seemingly finite wealth, measured in gold and land (Piketty, 2014, pp. 428–258; Stein, 1999, pp. 61–67). Or, in the words of Susan Reynolds (2001), "even in a laissez-faire capitalist society, and however little the man in the street may like to recognize the fact, property is to some extent limited by social controls" (p. 54).

Most wealth—that is to say, value (primarily inelastic land and gold)—was seldom created; it was bequeathed, traded, stolen, confiscated, taxed and/or forfeited.

---

[1] This section is largely based on Feldman, A.Mesibov, *Orthodox Mercantilism: Political Economy in the Byzantine Commonwealth* (Abingdon: Routledge, 2024), 18–12. Elsewhere in Part 1, certain passages are also drawn from other parts of the same publication.

For those fortunate enough to be born into a landowning family, and doubly so for those whose landowning families owned mines on those lands, wealth could be created by being dug from the ground. But this was seldom enough to concretize an idea of economic growth for its own sake. Instead, and most of all, wealth was bequeathed and inherited. The same economic logic which kept wealth (which bought status) within the family was also the force behind the emergence of dynasties. Therefore, as long as wealth and status could only be primarily inherited, birth became the most important determining factor for wealth and status for most of history. This is not to say that this was a hard and fast economic law of history. The stories of the emergence of various dynasties and noble families or business dynasties are well known and have been typically well promoted. But these are the exceptions which prove the rule: dynasties of kings, sultans, emperors, magnates, barons, dukes and emirs emerged for various reasons, but their initial wealth and status usually came, in one way or another, at another's expense; and their children (usually the firstborn males) would inherit their wealth and status. As Thomas Piketty observed, there is little need to prove this occurrence. Its obviousness never needed to be stated in the annals of history. This is why Piketty referenced well-known, albeit fictional, works of 18–19th-c. literature by Henri de Balzac and Jane Austen to prove the point. Even though he called this state of affairs "patrimonial capitalism," it could easily apply a millennium before, to the 8–9th century (Arnason, 2003, pp. 195–322; Piketty, 2014, pp. 2–15, 240–242).

While earlier scholarship has clarified the interdependence of agrarian societies and some kind of sacred law code (Davis, 2008; Kehoe, 2007), very little scholarship has demonstrated the connection between ancient law codes and perpetually low-growth-rate agrarian economics. Simply put, by adopting a given form of monotheism (with its corresponding scriptural traditions, laws and so forth), a ruling dynasty preserved its wealth (measured in land, precious metals or other finite commodities) according to the law code it relied on for legitimacy. Because rulers assumed that social mobility was always negligible and that fundamentally wealth (inelastic gold or land) was finitely available in the world, wealth and resources were seen as scarce. So it should be no surprise that rulers typically thought of maintaining their wealth as a "zero-sum game;" in other words: your gain is my loss. In this light, the pagan attraction to monotheism becomes quite understandable: sacred scriptures provided sacred laws, which preserved the wealth and legitimacy of the ruling dynasty. This also explains why after espousing a form of monotheism, dynasties often jealously protected their lands from encroachments by rival faiths, as they would protect their coffers. Is it any wonder why warnings about Islamic expansion written by Byzantine emperors like John VI Kantakouzenos (who nevertheless maintained friendly relationships with Islamic rulers) were copied and translated into Slavonic in the Balkans and Eastern Europe centuries after Constantinople fell to the Ottomans?

Protecting one's finite resources was never exclusive to the ruling dynasty. For most of history, everyone has lived by the same laws of finitude, from the lowliest peasant up to the kings, emperors, sultans, caliphs, emirs, popes, patriarchs, czars, khans, sons of heaven or God's regents on earth. This is what created the feudal private laws (privileges) in the potlatch society discussed in Chapter 1 in the first place: vassals and suzerains.

Today we are less likely to use terms like "vassals" and "suzerains" than similar terms like "rentiers" and "landlords." The legal function of rent in a feudal society was simple—and little different from the social relations between 17–19th-c. American planters and sharecroppers (nor perhaps indeed today). One owned the finite land while the other paid them rent to live on it and work it. This was the essential purpose of privilege and gave rise to what Karl Marx called the "feudal mode of production," or what Eric Wolf and John Haldon called the "tributary mode of production." In the basic, ideal situation, the landlord, or landowner, increased their wealth by the labor of the rentier, then would protect their family and generously (and visibly) give to charity. Their children would inherit their respective statuses, obligations and debts, and the relations would continue. Of course, this was not always true, and rentiers, sharecroppers, serfs and peasants sought ways to reduce the rent by whatever means necessary, while the landowner would seek ways to increase it—usually by appealing to the king or emperor to change the laws. Judging by the many failed revolts of slaves, peasants, serfs and sharecroppers, using the same bare muscles and tools for their own ends as were normally used on their masters' behalf, the latter was usually more successful (Bryer, 2002; Haldon, 1993; Haley, 2011). Rent-seeking, on the part of the wealthy, whether through commerce or through land and title, was not meant to produce more overall wealth or growth; it was simply the individual's ends which justified the means.

At a higher level, the situation becomes a bit more fluid. The wealth and power of the landlords, when combined, meant that kings, sultans, emperors (and American presidents through Lincoln) were not always free to alleviate the crushing poverty of the peasants, serfs, slaves and sharecroppers. More often than not, in order to maintain their crowns rather than being deposed, imprisoned or worse, they were compelled to reduce taxes on the nobility and increase it on the poor. This became one of the major differences of feudal rent versus imperial rent. For centuries, kings and emperors wrestled with this dilemma—whether to allow the nobility to ruthlessly exploit their peasants, serfs and sharecroppers or to directly tax the poor instead of the nobility—and it went in both directions. The intractable wealth and power of established landowning dynasties emerges in different places at different times based on the relative strength and establishment of law; in other words, cycles of order and chaos.

In Western Eurasia, where our respective specialties lay, the concentrated wealth and power of entrenched landowning dynasties truly becomes apparent over the course of the 9–eleventh centuries. Even though self-sufficiency was the ideal, it was impossible due to the finitude of land. As one of the most famous economic historians of Byzantium has put it, "the image of the man reposing under his own olive and fig trees, a picture that goes back to the Old Testament, is a compelling one and recurs over time." While this ideal of autarky, or self-sufficiency, is regarded as a common literary ideal more than an economic reality, it is also necessary to point out that the reason why "in practice, this ideal was either unattainable or inadequate, and landlords did not in fact shun the market" is/was that "in economic thought, it was superseded, certainly in the course of the tenth century, if not earlier, by the less proper but equally powerful stress on profit" (Laiou, 2002). And profit from agricultural production was always limited by the finitude of land.

Numerous Christian kings and Roman (Byzantine) emperors, such as Basil II after centuries of the *"pronoia"* system, were so threatened by the revolts of powerful landowning dynasties called "*dynatoi*"(e.g. Bardas Phōkas, Bardas Sklēros, Geōrgios Maniakēs, Leōn Tornikios, etc.), that they enacted legislation to try to curb the wealth and power of the landed magnates and were inclined to support merchants and ship-owners with mercantilist policies at the zero-sum expense of feudal *dynatoi* (Ashburner, 1910; Brown, 2012; Heather, 2013; Jacoby, 2017; Kehoe, 2007; Macrides, 1986; McGeer, 2000; McKee, 2000; Moroney, 2009). It wasn't enough, however. From the late eleventh century through the fifteenth century, powerful landowning dynasties like the Komnenians and Palaiologans took over the throne and imposed their own legislation which solidified the power of the nobility and essentially outsourced the rights to tax the serfs, peasants and smallholders ("paroikoi", a legal status which was made hereditary in 1079) to monasteries and other noble dynasties—a practice which later became known as tax farming (Guillou, 1974, p. 400; Oikonomides, 2002, esp. pp. 1022–1024). Religious institutions such as Orthodox and Catholic monasteries alike, like landed magnate dynasties, would also use their landownership to buy up the nearby lands of smallholders and then profit from the labor of the peasants. This situation became so widespread in the Orthodox world that, by the mid–sixteenth century, Nil of Sora and Maximus the Greek teamed up to lead mass movements (called the "non-possessors," or *nestyazhateli*) of disenfranchised peasants against the organized power of landowning monasteries (Merianos, 2017; Preiser-Kapeller, 2015). Lenin and Trotsky weren't born from Mother Russia without older siblings.

One notable exception to this situation appeared under the Piast dynasty beginning in the 13–14th c. in what later became Poland. The last Piast king Casimir III successfully resisted the combined power of his nobility and clergy and inaugurated tax and land legislation which favored his constituencies of Jews and peasants. He became known as the Polish Justinian (although Justinian's laws were notoriously unfavorable to Jews), the only king of Poland to receive the epithets "the Great" and the "King of Peasants and Jews" (Berend et al., 2013; Knoll, 1972; Urbańczyk & Rosik, 2003, 2008). Consequently, the Jews residing in the Polish (and later, the Polish-Lithuanian) realm became so numerous that, by the partition of Poland in the late eighteenth century, Czarist laws were implemented to confine Jewish settlements to this "Pale of Settlement." Even the movie *Schindler's List* depicts the Nazis occupying Poland as referencing 600 years of Jewish life in Poland—due to the beneficial policies of Casimir III.

Such royal magnanimity was not the norm, however, and regardless of religion, practices of tax farming and the further constraints of the legal rights of peasants and serfs continued for centuries. For example, the Abbasid, Mamluk, Ottoman, Mughal and Qing dynasties all across Eurasia were notorious for their centuries of tax farming policies and resulting caste systems characterized by rent-seeking landed magnates lording over peasants and serfs (Butcher & Dick, 1993; Ermis, 2014; Haldon, 1993; Reda, 2018; Von Glahn, 1996). In China, Confucian laws perpetuated the *"fengjian"* caste system (Bloom, 1999; Byres & Mukhia, 1985, pp. 213–218; Wu, 1952; Zhufu, 1981). In the various Islamic caliphates, these quasi-feudal systems have been called "*iqta*". The major distinction between Latin Christian feudalism and the *iqta* caste system is that the possession of the *iqta* (by a *"muqti"*) was not always hereditary—not so dissimilar from the Roman/ Byzantine *"pronoia"* system. However, Byzantine and Islamic ruling dynasties were always under pressure from noble dynasties to allow these systems to become hereditary, and by the 13–14th centuries, they did, becoming comparable to the heritability of Latin Christian fiefdoms. The pressure stemmed from rent-seeking noble dynasties competing with each other for a seemingly finite slice of the pie to bequeath to their eldest children and thereby strengthen their dynastic wealth and power. Similar developments occurred in the Ottoman timar system of *agas* and *agaluks* (Cahen, 1953; Darling, 1996, p. 71; Duri, 1969; Inalcik, 1994; Küpeli, 2007; Lewis, 1979; Murphey, 1990; Özel, 1999).

Lachman Dev was born into the somewhat wealthy Sodhi caste in 1670 in Kashmir. Betraying his caste as a young man, he joined a Sikh force in a rebellion in 1709 against the reigning Islamic Mughal dynasty (who traced their sovereignty back to Genghis Khan). After defeating the Mughal-appointed governors in several battles, he rose in prominence as a rebel leader as his force confiscated the captured land and bullion of the previous Mughal-appointed governing dynasties. Like Maximus the Greek and Nil of Sora, he aimed to alter landownership laws in his new domains, redistributing large tracts of land to smallholder peasants and outlawing the local *zamindari* and *taluqdari* caste systems of inherited, rent-seeking, landowning aristocracy. As you can imagine, the zamindars and taluqdars which had previously benefited handsomely from the Mughal rule were unamused. Between their complaints of dispossession and his spreading jurisdiction in lands the Mughals themselves had previously held sovereignty over, the Mughals marched against Lachman Dev, now Banda Singh Bahadur, and his scrappy Sikh army in Autumn 1710. After five more years of skirmishes, stalemates, posturing and politicking, the set piece battle came in Spring 1715 at Gurdas Nangal, where after a monthslong siege, he, his family and his army were captured in a day which still lives in infamy: 7 December (Cicero was assassinated for comparable reasons on the same day). Paraded through the streets of Delhi in an iron cage surrounded by overlookers' jeers and his compatriots' heads on pikes, he and his followers were demanded to renounce Sikhism and accept Islam (and the Islamic caste system). Refusing, he and his family were put to death in such a gruesome manner that you can look it up if you want to know more (Saggo, 2001; Singh, 1935).

In Muscovy and, later, the Russian Czardom, the large-scale inheritance of Byzantine ecclesiastical legislation (like the *Ekloga* and the *Nomokanon*) beginning in the late thirteenth century, and respectively translated into the *Zakon Sudnyj Ljudem* and the *Kormchaja Kniga*, drastically solidified the wealth and power of landowners and monasteries at the expense of the peasants and serfs (Beneshevich, 1987; Bibikov, 2019; Bulanin, 2017; Mulcahy, 2001; Psarev, 2018; Tikhomirov,

1961; Vernadsky, 1937; Zakon Sudnyj Ljudem, 1977). Unsurprisingly, the non-possessors (*nestyazhateli*) were finally defeated at the Stoglavyj Council in 1551. This isn't just some outdated Marxist narrative either; it comes directly from the legal sources as well as birch bark letters regarding business transactions, accounts and debts which clarify the private laws (privileges) applied to different members of social strata (Cherepenin, 1969; Kovalev & Noonan, 2000; Meyendorff, 1996, pp. 179–180; Schaeken, 2012; Weickhardt, 2001, 2005). From the Sudebniks of 1497 and 1550, up to the Ulozhenie of 1649, which was enforced well into the 19th-c., the legal status of peasants and serfs was hereditary and increasingly constricted, just as the legal statuses of the landlords and merchants were hereditary and increasingly empowered through laws regulating legal rights, taxation and inheritance (Bushkovitch, 1980; Dewey, 1956; Feldbrugge, 2018; Kaiser, 1980; Kleimola, 1975; Vernadsky, 1937). By the early seventeenth century, the increasingly oppressive caste-based feudalization began to reach beyond the settled urban areas and into the steppe, triggering a series of rebellions by the nominally Orthodox cossacks against the land-hungry policies of the czars and their local governing representative dynasties (Avrich, 1976). The same feudalism enshrined in the ecclesiastical jurisprudence of Latin Christendom and Byzantium, from the thirteenth century, was engendered in Russia as well. In this light, it's not difficult to see why and how the idea emerged of Moscow as the "Third Rome" (Christian, 1995; Meyendorff, 2010; Momotov, 2003; Petrukhin, 2006; Reyerson et al., 2006; Schapov, 1969, 1978, 1993; Telitsyn, 2013).

Further west, the *encomienda* systems in the Two Spains (the Habsburg-ruled Americas) created the same feudal privileges and social structures of tax farming which replaced tribalism ("caciquismo") in smaller potlatch societies conquered by the conquistadores. The cruelty of the *encomienda* system and the abuses of the *conquistadores-encomenderos* toward their new slave-subjects became so notorious even in the sixteenth century that the Habsburg crown instituted the *New Laws of the Indies* in 1542. These inaugurated the *hacienda* system instead, essentially plantation-fiefdoms (*fincas*) which aimed to strengthen Catholicism by reducing the enslavement of the native Americans. To make up for the reduced local slavery, merchant-slavers brought in African slaves collected and sold from African tribal rulers to the New World, thereby generating the Atlantic triangular trade. Similar social structures existed in the *fazendas* (plantation-fiefdoms) of Portuguese America, later Brazil (Lockhart, 1969; Menéndez Pidal, 1966, pp. 102–143; Mörner, 1973; Vassberg, 1986, pp. 142–146; von Wobeser, 1983; Yeager, 1995). The brutality of these Old World systems brought to the New World became so notorious, that in contemporary Protestant kingdoms, which always sought to distance themselves from Catholicism, it became known as the "Black Legend" promulgated in works like Robert Ashley's *A Comparison of the English and Spanish Nation* (1589). Yet, the "Black Legend" comprised primarily a form of religious propaganda more than authoritative difference between Catholic and Protestant regimes. Slavery, feudalism and the triangular trade were just as prominent in English and Dutch colonial economies as they were further south.

By the 17–18th centuries, kings such as Louis XIV and others were able to reduce the power of the nobility, but in doing so, they simply increased their own. For example, one of the hallmarks of absolutist rule was the attempt to abolish feudal tax farming (the *'ferme générale'*), which didn't increase the tax burden on the nobility so much as result in absolutist taxation on the peasantry. In other words, this represented a zero-sum understanding of taxation within the social pyramid. Either the peasantry or the nobility would foot the tax bill; the burden's decrease for one constituency came at the expense of another.

Get All the Gold Part 2: Mercantilism[2]

The way mercantilism is typically explained makes most people fall asleep. Fortunately it's quite simple, but it's nothing to glaze your eyes at. The same zero-sum logic applied by a regime to taxation would equally apply to other revenue streams. Interested most of all in expanding their physical possessions, regimes instead looked to protect their domains and authority over them by limiting the outflow of gold and silver, which, in the hands of their enemies, could be otherwise dangerous—used to pay enemy soldiers (and more gold in enemies' hands would inevitably mean more enemy soldiers at the gates). This invariably meant that regimes and dynasties were always tempted by economic policies which would strengthen themselves and weaken their enemies, or as Richard Wiles (1974) summarizes, "the mercantilist are said to have viewed the world as being composed of a fixed quantum of sources and thus one nation's gain implied a loss to another" (p. 56). The temptations of coin debasement to increase short-term buying-power, protectionism, capital controls and the endemic pursuit of bullion (bullionism) have always been present in various regimes' policies throughout history. Put together, these policies are commonly called mercantilism, which is essentially a developed set of protectionist policies tacked onto bullionism. These policies are also indicative of mercantilist thought: to expand for the purpose of acquiring more bullion in order to fuel more expansion to survive or overpower rival regimes (Heckscher, 1994; Magnusson, 1993; McCormick, 2001; Minchinton, 1969; Wennerlind & Stern, 2013). In essence, a trade war has always been tantamount to a real war.

The first of these protectionist policies, coin debasement is basically ancient inflation. Regimes and dynasties were always tempted to debase their coins to ramp up short-term buying power for wars and other costly matters of state. In other words, a regime has a finite, inelastic amount of bullion. True, regimes, families and even individuals could and did indebt themselves borrowing on credit (typically in early speculative bubbles) (Polybius, 1979, IV.17), but this was usually limited to winning one war or another in order to repay the debt (before the

[2] This section is largely based on Feldman, A. Mesibov, *Orthodox Mercantilism: Political Economy in the Byzantine Commonwealth* (Abingdon: Routledge, 2024), 13–18. Elsewhere in Part 1, certain passages are also drawn from other parts of the same publication.

nineteenth century, debt was hardly ever a fiscal policy for its own sake) (Graeber, 2011). Debasement was frequently a less risky short-term solution than debt even if it had nefarious long-term consequences. By decreasing the amount of gold or silver in every coin minted and paid to the soldiers in order to pay for ever more soldiers, a regime could stretch a relatively inelastic commodity to the limit. Of course, it was risky and came at a price commensurate with the bullion itself. If the war was lost or the price of victory didn't recoup the costs, a period of chaos and uncertainty might ensue—soldiers revolting, civil wars, slave insurrections, invasions by neighbors, loss of finite land, downfalls of dynasties, floods, droughts, famines, and so on. In short, a general period of crisis, misery, destruction, poverty and death.

However, this hodgepodge of disasters didn't stop debasement from happening all the time. It did. Arguably ever since the Roman Third Century Crisis, debasement caused many crises in the Roman empires as well as in the Islamic caliphates right up to the fall of the deposition of the last Ottoman caliph in 1922. Up to the mid-eleventh century, for example, the Roman/Byzantine *nomisma* (or bezant, solidus), was so stable it's been called the "dollar of the middle ages," until it was debased during wars with Pechenegs and Seljuks and caused the implosions of a few ruling dynasties. The accession of a new dynasty in 1081, the Komnenians, saw the reformation of the currency, which was stabilized for another couple of centuries until another round of debasement following the Fourth Crusade in 1204 (Kaplanis, 2002; Morrisson, 2002, pp. 944–946). Also during the eleventh century, the first Christian Rus' princes—the descendants of Rjurik, Vladimir and Jaroslav—minted a few fistfuls of gold and silver coins until they ran out of bullion. Silver and gold mines not being abundant in the area, Byzantine and (largely) Islamic coins travelled northward presumably in exchange for slaves, furs and mercenaries—which were then melted down into mostly base-metal (with varyingly small amounts of silver) ingots called *grivny.* Due to their scarcity and the resulting zero-sum thinking, many were hoarded and silver almost completely disappeared from circulation in Eastern Europe for a few centuries and was largely replaced by debt and "fur money"—what is now known as the Rus' Coinless Period (Feldman, 2018; Gruszczynski et al., 2021; Guletskij & Doroshkevich, 2018; Huletski & Petrov, 2021; Kuleshov, 2020; Khudokormov & Drozdov, 2018; Noonan, 1987; Pavlova, 1994; Pritsak, 1998; Spasskij, 1962). These were early demonstrations of Gresham's law that bad money drives out good money.

After capturing the fortified Serbian silver mines in the 1440s, the Ottoman silver coin, the akce, was 85% silver; by the time lord Elgin infamously hacked off the marbles from the Parthenon, the same coin was less than half of 1% silver (Malanima, 2009, p. 198; Pamuk, 2000, pp. 112, 131). In the mid-sixteenth century, Henry VIII of England instituted such a monetary policy of debasement that it is now called the "Great Debasement"—and he was called "Old Coppernose" (Knafo, 2013, p. 78; Li, 2009; Mackie, 1963, p. 606; Owen, 2012). A century later, the widespread debasement of Spanish silver in the Viceroyalty of Peru caused such a scandal when it appeared in the Iberian Peninsula that Peninsular mints switched almost entirely to straightforwardly copper coins instead (Motomura, 1994). In each of these examples, the zero-sum logic which underpinned coin debasement is easily observable: a regime had a finite amount of bullion, and therefore would be tempted to stretch its short-term spending power by debasing the supply of bullion in each coin it minted.

Like coin debasement, policies of protectionism also indicate zero-sum logic, and have therefore been present for centuries. In Western Eurasia, arguably the first instance of protectionism is noticeable beginning in the Roman empire of the 4–6th centuries, when exporting iron, millstones, salt and bread beyond imperial jurisdiction (presumably to "barbarians" or Persians) was prohibited. Simultaneously, there were also tax exemptions for importing goods required by the imperial treasury, household and guardsmen (de Laet, 1949, p. 475). From the 6–9th centuries, the *Justinianic Code* incentivized agricultural goods for export, while objects intended for the needs of the court and the army continued to remain incentivized for import. Wine, olive oil, garon (a kind of ancient fish sauce similar to today's Worcestershire sauce), flax, wool, weapons and materials from which they were manufactured, and, most importantly, gold and silver wares, pearls, precious stones, as well as ingots of gold and silver bullion were included later through the 9th-c. *Basilika* Roman law code (Blume & Kearley, 2008, vol. 1, Dig. 39.4.11; Blume & Kearley, 2008, vol. 2, Cod. 4.41.1–2, Cod. 4.63.2; Troianos, 2007, 56.1.20). In efforts to fiscally weaken enemies such as the Sassanid dynasty of Persia, Justinian also granted imperial corporations (such as one led by John Tzibus) the right to maritime trade monopolies, much like it happened with the mercantilist India companies over a thousand years later (Dewing, 1921, II.15.1–26; Greatrex & Lieu, 2002; Galbraith, 1987, pp. 38–39; Martindale, 1992, p. 638; Sears, 1997). While imports were encouraged in order to prevent civil strife such as the 6th-c. Nika riots, trade was specifically discouraged with non-Christians. By the 8th c., the *Book of the Eparch* (*Eparchikon Biblion*) basically sought to ensure the lowest possible prices on as many goods as possible, even if it was also an instrument which limited access to seemingly finite profit. Constantinople being by far the largest Christian marketplace, Christian merchants with imports were essentially forced to obey such protectionist measures, not just for the protection of other Christian merchants but also Christian consumers (Banaji, 2001, pp. 217–218; Harris, 2003, pp. 5–6; Jacoby, 2017; Koder, 2013; Nicole, 1894, 5.3, 6.8, 9.3; Sorochan, 1995, esp. p. 124). This was a legal-moral system which sought to balance profit-seeking with social justice, albeit imperfectly.

Capital controls were another way that the Roman-Byzantine imperial regime sought to prevent the outflow of bullion from imperial jurisdiction and to "accumulate reserves of metal whenever it could" (Morrisson, 2002, p. 940; Preiser-Kapeller, 2016). From the sixth century on, emperors and chroniclers alike (Prokopios, Leo VI the Wise, George Gemistos Plethon, etc.) constantly remarked on their dependence on the amount of bullion they had access to, keeping large reserves of it within their jurisdiction (Altwater, 1961, pp. 95–97; Moravcsik & Jenkins, 1967, 13.12–13.28; Sewter, 1979, p. 368; Troianos, 2007, nos 52–62; Wortley, 2010, pp. 263–264). As in imperial China, Christian emperors always concentrated on preventing bullion and other limited goods of value from reaching those variously deemed as foreigners, enemies and/or barbarians (Atik, 2021; Hendy, 1985, pp. 224–226; Jacoby, 2000, 2013; Merianos & Gotsis, 2018; Preiser-Kapeller & Mitsiou, 2019). By the twelfth century, Roman/Byzantine authors remark about the "mass-production process that was affected by [those] who worked 'for whole months, even years, night and day to watch over and control the flux and reflux of the gold'." After 1204, the diffusion of imperial monetary policy had been adopted by local rulers in the Balkans and Anatolia, and Venetian bullionism and *ducats* largely replaced imperial monetary policy as the main "international media of exchange" (Grierson, 1982, pp. 269–275; Morrisson, 2002, pp. 915–966).

Together, coin debasement, protectionism, capital controls and bullionism comprise policies which indicate the zero-sum logic of mercantilism. And it was certainly not confined to the Roman/Byzantine empire—nominally Christian or otherwise; what was true for Constantinople and its emperors would have been true for any other city and its rulers. All their policies were predicated on the same set of seemingly permanent economic assumptions: first, the assumption of a perpetually negligible economic growth rate—typical in agrarian societies; second, the belief in a basically inelastic amount of wealth (ultimately measured in bullion and/or land) available for possession, and therefore, that acquiring such wealth would usually presuppose zero-sum thinking, necessitating capital controls, protectionism, customs duties and even sometimes coin debasement (Galbraith, 1987, pp. 40–41; Heckscher, 1994, pp. xii-14; Johnson et al., 2020, esp. pp. 3–5, 36).

Therefore, it was not just Constantinople which sought to maintain a positive trade balance—i.e., exporting high-quality crafts, finished wares and local specialties while effectively seeking to accumulate bullion reserves and other necessities and maintaining currency controls. Constantinople's trade balance was a simple, yet effective model and other cities and regimes increasingly inherited the model even before 1204—such as the Black Sea cities of Amastris and Cherson (today's Amasra and Sevastopol') (Carter, 2003, pp. 27–40; Feldman, 2013, pp. 96–100; Romanchuk, 2000, pp. 86–130; Sharp, 2011, pp. 53–117; Zavagno, 2009, pp. 129–151). An autonomous city council which frequently acted on behalf of commercial interests emerged in Thessaloniki in the 11–15th centuries, just as was common in other imperial cities like Venice, Genoa and Pisa—even in the Norman kingdom of Sicily (Kambouri-Vamvoukou & Katsoni, 2016; Necipoğlu, 2003; Penna, 2012). Similar developments occurred during the same period all over the Black, Mediterranean and Red Seas—in the later case, where the Mamluk regime maintained similar policies (Christ, 2017). Across the Black Sea, the Byzantine economic model was also later implemented in Kiev, Novgorod and subsequently, elsewhere in the Rus' lands, where bullion brought from Byzantium had "a mercantile and not merely a military role" (Feldman, 2018; Martin, 2006; Morrisson, 2002, p. 964; Shepard, 2009).

Protections for domestic merchants, relentlessly pursuing bullion, instituting capital controls and other forms of protectionism and so forth became widespread throughout both Latin and Orthodox Christendoms by the late thirteenth century, resulting in specifically merchant classes focused on Constantinopolitan commerce. It is no surprise that legal adjudication using Justinianic law and specialized maritime law (the *Rhodian Sea Laws*, inserted into the 9th-c. *Basilika*) is so well attested among the archetypal mercantilist cities and classes throughout Christendom (Ashburner, 1909; Cameron & Neil, 2003, p. 59; Galbraith, 1987, p. 45; Kadens, 2015, esp. p. 264; Kontogiannopoulou, 2015; Reinert & Fredona, 2017, esp. pp. 3–6). The major difference, however, was that for the Byzantines after 1204, the Western Christians, as well as Jews, could no longer always be considered "domestic" merchants. In fact, from the early thirteenth century and later, Justinianic law repurposed as Venetian law applied to retrospective Byzantine cities such as Candia, Crete, supported and resulted in urban, merchant classes engaged in pursuit of commercial profit which did not always benefit (and frequently undercut) the Roman/Byzantine emperors—further weakening Constantinople (McKee, 2000, pp. 168–178; Mell, 2014; Prinzing, 2015; Schiffman, 2005). By the time the Ottoman sultan Mehmed II al-Fatih conquered Constantinople on 29 May, 1453, the resultant inability of Latin Christian merchant ships to reach the Black Sea contributed to the zero-sum inaccessibility of bullion in Latin Christendom and the necessity to find a route to the spices, slaves and bullion considered to be available in the East Indies. Yes, the voyages of Da Gama, Columbus and Cabot were the direct results of the fall of Byzantium a generation before.

And, in the midst of what economic historians call the "Great Bullion Famine," if they were after new sources of cash bullion through spices, they could also get it through slavery. And where better to find slaves than from nearby Islamic and pagan lands?

It should come as little surprise, then, that Latin Christian dynasties in Iberia (Aviz—Portugal, Trastámara—Castille and León) replicated Orthodox Christian mercantilist laws and policies before and after conquering the New World. Ferdinand and Isabella had also inherited the imperial title of the Roman/Byzantine emperor from its last heir, Andreas Palaiologos (whose sister, Zoe/Sophia Palaiologina brought her own imperial Roman/Byzantine inheritance to her marriage to the grand prince Ivan III the Great of Russia, who codified the Sudebnik of 1497). Nevertheless, using their *encomiendas* and *haciendas* in the New World to mine as much bullion as possible (particularly in the Peruvian mines of Potosí, now Bolivia), the bullion of the New World was systematically shipped back to the Old World (which also explains the symbolic colors of Venezuela's national flag)—to pay for wars against heretics and infidels (Muslims, pagans, foreigners, etc.). The clearest method for paying for these wars was to ensure that gold and silver returned across the Atlantic without falling into the hands of English privateers or sinking to the bottom of the sea, entered the principal port of Cádiz, later Sevilla, and later still El Escorial outside Madrid, and seeped out as little as possible except insofar as to pay for ships, soldiers, mounts and ordnance. Thus, the same Christian laws which limited access to finite bullion in Constantinople could be repurposed and augmented for Madrid. After all, Castilian law *derived* from Canon law (Nogués-Marco, 2010, pp. 23–24). Shortly after the *New Laws for the West Indies* were announced, the Habsburg dynasty (under Charles V) also announced laws closer to home in order to limit the amount of bullion which could fall into the hands of foreigners—the same heretics and infidels:

> We have been informed that there is so much greed to take gold coins out of our kingdoms, that both foreigners and natives are involved in the business of collecting gold coins and paying for them more than their value, in order to take them out to other kingdoms, thus making profits, with no fear of the punishments that our laws provide; as the laws of our kingdom stipulate that no one can pay for coins more than their value. (Nogués-Marco, 2010, p. 25)

It was not for nothing that the Spanish armada, with papal blessing, sailed for Elizabeth's Protestant England only 17 years after defeating the Islamic Turks in Orthodox Greece at the Battle of Lepanto (1571). Less well-known is that Elizabeth sent an English armada against Spain the following year in 1589, which was largely defeated, but managed to establish the first English East India Company and privileged it with a commercial monopoly before she died in 1603. By the turn of the seventeenth century, with its addenda of capital controls and protectionism on top of bullionism, mercantilism had become the de facto political economy of the various Christian Protestant, Catholic and Orthodox dynasties in seemingly zero-sum competition with each other for finite land and bullion. Capital controls weren't just aspects of Christian mercantilism either: even the Sunni Ottomans recognized the importance of the mercantilist policy of preventing outflows of bullion from beyond their jurisdiction from the late eighteenth century (Ermiş, 2014, pp. 168–186).

Unfortunately, however, several misguided myths have grown up around feudalism and mercantilism, namely that the zero-sum logic at the heart of mercantilist and feudalist theories, policies and laws was confined to Latin Christendom and only during the 16–19th centuries. On the contrary, as the following section will demonstrate, feudalism and mercantilism have been (and arguably remain) universal across time and space.

Mythologies of Feudalism and Mercantilism[3]

Having adopted various confessions, including their scriptural traditions, laws, legitimacies and sovereignties, various lands ruled by various dynasties gradually emerged throughout the Old World whose courts fostered literature which reveals the zero-sum logic of their social orders—this is usually preserved in law codes,

[3] This section is largely based on Feldman, A. Mesibov, *Orthodox Mercantilism: Political Economy in the Byzantine Commonwealth* (Abingdon: Routledge, 2024), 177-187. Elsewhere in Part 1, certain passages are also drawn from other parts of the same publication.

but occasionally it appears elsewhere in theoretical discussions about tax, commerce, land-ownership, inheritance and the distribution of the spoils of war. Many of their most prominent merchants and landlords also supplied plenty of written material about optimizing the political economy, in other words, schemes for how the ruling dynasty can get rich quick—not unlike early 21st-c. bitcoin advertisements. Nevertheless, many myths and misleading assumptions surround the seemingly mystified trajectories of feudalism and mercantilism, not least because of cliches, stereotypes and plain old intellectual slovenliness shot through recent (and conceptually Eurocentric) economics textbooks. Three myths are the most pervasive, and arguably the most nefarious: **first**, that Roman law and feudal law were structurally different; **second**, that feudalism and mercantilism were primarily Christian phenomena; and **third**, that feudalism and mercantilism were/are different systems of political economy.

The Myth that Roman Laws and Feudal Laws Were Different

The original Justinianic Christian Roman law, the *Corpus Juris Civilis* (*Codex Justinianus* [Blume & Kearley, 2008]), was meant to centralize imperial power and implement Christian legal principles in a top-down fashion. It was augmented by subsequent law codes such as the *Ekloga* (Burgmann, 1983; Freshfield, 1926), *Basilika* (Troianos, 2007), *Procheiron* (Freshfield, 1928), *Eisagoge* (Signes Codoñer & Andrés Santos, 2007) and *Farmer's law* (Ashburner, 1910), which formed the core of 9–11th century Roman/Byzantine land legislation. These codes sought to protect smallholders and/or peasants ("paroikoi") and maintain the legal system (called "pronoia") of landownership in a durable way into the foreseeable future ("pronoia" literally means "forethought")—therefore, land-ownership legislation up to the 10–11th centuries sought to limit the heritability of legal status by provincial noble clans—"dynatoi" (meaning the "powerful," or "dynamic") (Macrides, 1986; McGeer, 2000, pp. 102–121; Troianos, 2011).

The same Roman legal norms and practices inherited from the *Corpus Juris Civilis* were maintained in Latin Canon law as well. However, western imperial administration was not always as durable for the long term as it was in contemporary Constantinople. By the mid-11th c., the primary distinctive legal-economic issue between Eastern and Western Christendom was the permission of inheritance of landed estates in the *Edictum de beneficiis regni Italici* implemented by the Western (Holy) Roman emperor Conrad II in 1037 in an attempt to placate his nobles and curry their support for his wars (king John's signing of the Magna Carta at Runnymeade in 1215 was little different). This became the core legal innovation in the *Libri Feodorum* by the time of their codification in the mid-thirteenth century (Dilcher, 2013; Landau, 2008; Reynolds, 2001, p. 44; Ryan, 1997; Weimar, 1990). Therefore, Roman/Byzantine law was only mainly distinguishable from feudal law by the issue of whether landlords could automatically bequeath their estates (fiefs) to their sons, thereby creating powerful noble dynasties which sought more wealth and power by buying up or conquering as much seemingly finite land as possible (rent-seeking)—often at the expense of neighbors, smallholders, peasants and serfs (Stein, 1999, pp. 18–21).

However, by the era of the reconquest of the Palaiologan dynasty (late 13th c.), when Roman/Byzantine lords were legally permitted to form dynasties (even though this had been tacitly acceptable since the ascendancy of the Komnenian dynasty in the late eleventh century) (Laiou, 2011), although issues of liturgy and sovereignty between Eastern and Western Christendom remained, there was neither functional nor structural distinction between feudal law and Roman law. In effect, by the late thirteenth century, Roman law *was* feudal law.

The Myth That Feudalism Has Been Exclusive to Latin Christendom

This is a common misconception due to the origin of the term "feudalism" in the Latin Christian context of the *Libri Feodorum*. Centuries of attorneys, judges, scholars and legal theorists have debated when, where and why this obscure group of 13th-c judicial books from Northern Italy became the basis of agrarian political economy which inspired worldwide revolutions against it centuries later. Many have certainly tried to deny its relevance outside Northern Italy (Davis, 2008). But the expansion and endurance of the social pyramid enshrined in the legal classifications and hereditariness of the *Libri Feodorum* can also be evinced in many ancient laws the world over. As we have already seen, similar laws in various languages and under various guises resulted in similar feudal privileges and pyramidal social relations were promulgated everywhere, from the Roman/Byzantine Orthodox world of Eastern Europe and Coptic East Africa, to the Islamic world, to the domains of Hinduism, Buddhism, Confucianism and the pre- and post-Columbian Americas as well.

Throughout the Orthodox Christian world of Eastern Europe, Roman/Byzantine laws were translated from Greek and Latin (*Corpus Juris Civilis*, *Nomokanon*, *Ekloga*, *Basilika*, *Procheiron*, *Eisagogue*) into Slavonic laws (*Kormchaja Kniga*, *Zakon Sudnyj Ljudem*, *Knigi Zakonnye*), alongside Armenian, Georgian, Ethiopian and Coptic laws. In each of these cases, these law codes were quite durable for a time (let's call it the 'pronoia' system)—until princes, nobles and monasteries, whose wealth and status had been made legally hereditary since the thirteenth century, had gained control over as much finite land as they could, which ushered in various forms of feudalism based on different degrees of heritable privileges and rights limiting ownership of finite land. This necessitated the regime's ownership of as much land as possible. Whereas heritability of landownership by provincial dynasties may have been a variegated factor of Orthodox jurisprudence over the centuries, in a nutshell, the zero-sum logic of finite land was always built into the law itself. The seeming finitude of land in these examples of Orthodox political economy was manifest everywhere from Ivan the Terrible's 16th-c. eastward expansion, to the Romanovs' 17–19th-c. southward and westward expansions, to

Eleftherios Venizelos' attempt to implement the *Megali Idea* in early-1920s Anatolia, to the land grabs based on ethno-religious identities in the wake of the collapse of Yugoslavia in the early 1990s. It is still apparent from Nagorno-Karabakh, to Ethiopian policies in Tigray, to Russian policies in North Ossetia and Eastern Ukraine.

Islamic Sharia laws transplanted the *"iqta"* system into newly Islamized lands under Islamic dynasties, where the major distinction between Latin Christian feudalism and the *iqta* system is that the possession of the *iqta* (by a *"muqti"*) originally was theoretically not hereditary (comparable to the Roman/Byzantine "pronoia" system), and like the pronoia system and the Latin Christian feudal system, was made hereditary by the 13–14th centuries—when muqtis could own and bequeath to their firstborn sons iqtas much like Latin or Orthodox lords could own and bequeath fiefs to theirs. Unsurprisingly, this increasingly led to hereditary aristocracies and serfdom. The Mamluks themselves were a military aristocracy built on slavery and enserfment, while the Ottoman "timar" system continued a variation of the "iqta" system into the 19–20th centuries 101 (Cahen, 1953; Christ, 2021; Darling, 1996; Duri, 1969; Ermiş, 2014; Inalcik, 1994; Küpeli, 2007; Lewis, 1979; Murphey, 1990; Özel, 1999; Reda, 2018). Similar landowning castes of *taluqdars* were perpetuated by the Mughal dynasty (and even the British Raj) from Delhi into the nineteenth century. The 11th-c. Persian *Siyasetname*, for example, a kind of Machiavellian guide for princes, advises them to think of their slaves and subjects as sheep and their vezirs as sheepdogs (not dissimilar from the Christian "flock"). And consequently, much as in Orthodox Christian political economy, the seeming finitude of land (and its distribution) was built into Islamic law, jurisprudence (*"fiqh"*) and political economy—even in the same source (Darke, 2012, chs. 4–5, 50; Lambton, 1953). By the late fourteenth century, when ibn Khaldun wrote his famous *Muqaddimah* in Qalᶜat ibn Salama (today's Algeria), the need for various dynasties to continuously conquer new lands to bring in new revenue in other means to sustain their ever-increasingly luxurious lifestyles is a vital element of his conception of the predictably grim cycles of political economy (Ibn Khaldun, 1969, pp. 124–160; Weiss, 1995, pp. 31–33). The resulting necessity to expand over land against non-Muslims, heretics or rival dynasties was manifest everywhere from the early Islamic conquests of the 7–9th centuries, to the Ottomans' 13–17th-c. northward and westward expansions, to Mustafa Kemal Ataturk's counterattack against king Constantine of Greece in early-1920s Anatolia and the Saudi dynasty's defeat of the Hashemite dynasty in 1920s Arabia. It is still apparent today from the expansionary attempts of the Islamic dynasties who control the Islamic State in Syria and Iraq, the Taliban in Afghanistan, Boko Haram in West Africa, the Azerbaijani militants of Nagorno-Karabakh and the Moro Conflict in the Philippines.

Hindu laws in the *Dharmasastra* and the Code of Manu achieved similar results as feudal laws—by making legal classifications based on hereditary castes. Human behavior was regulated through different crimes and punishments applied to different castes:

> If a Sudra hurls abusive words at a virtuous Arya, his tongue shall be cut out. If, while he is speaking, walking on the road, lying in bed, or occupying a seat, a Sudra pretends to be equal to Aryas, he should be flogged. If a Sudra kills a man, steals, or appropriates land, he should be executed and his property confiscated. If a Brahmin is guilty of these crimes, however, he should be blindfolded. Alternatively, those who transgress their specific duties should be kept in secret confinement until they relent. If they do not relent, they should be banished. A teacher, an officiating priest, a bath-graduate, and the king may save him from punishment, except in the case of a capital crime.
>
> If someone takes a piece of land on lease and it produces no harvest because he puts no effort into it, then, if he has the means, he should be made to pay the landowner what would have been his due. An indentured farmhand who quits working should be flogged; so also a herdsman, and his flock should be impounded.
>
> If someone takes charge of cattle and lets them die or become lost, he should pay restitution to the owners. (Olivelle, 1999, Āpastamba, 2.27:14–21, 2.28:1–4, 2.28:6)

Like the agrarian societies of the Latin and Orthodox Christendoms as well as Islam, Hindu laws, which presupposed an agrarian Hindu society, privileged landownership (*zamindar*), and as a result, created a quasi-feudal society. This was as true under the dynasties of the Mauryas and Guptas in the fourth century BCE–sixth century CE, as under the ruling dynasties of Mysore, Kerala, Tamil and Karnataka up to the 17–18th centuries (Chauhan, 2004; Habib, 1997; Sharma, 2005; Thakur, 1989). Because land (and therefore landownership) was always regarded as physically finite, it also created a concept of a finite Hindutva—a fixed "Hindu world"—which is incidentally the same ideology used by the BJP in today's India, and presides over land disputes based on Hinduism and other faiths from the Ayodhya district of Uttar Pradesh, to the Bengali Hindu homeland, to the Panun Kashmiri homeland.

Buddhist laws of zero-sum landownership achieved similar results further east under the *Maṇḍala* legal models for the antique imperial social structures of Indochina we now call the Khmer (*Devarāja*), the various branches of the ruling dynasties of Siam/Thailand (*sakdina*), and so on. The agrarian *shan* regimes of Burma, for example, were built on the essentially feudal principles of *Maṇḍala* and legitimated by Buddhism (Baker & Phongpaichit, 2017; Charney, 2006; Chutintaranond, 1990; Tambiah, 1976; Vickery, 1998; Wolters, 1999). The original Buddhist Theravada laws in the *Dhammasattha* (originally influenced by Vedic principles of the *Dharmasastra*), as in the ideal conception of law in the Vedic Dharmasastra and Islamic Sharia, were meant to maintain a long-term cosmic order—not dissimilar from the "pronoia" or "iqta" systems (Huxley, 1990, 1997; Lammerts, 2010; Lieberman, 2003; Lingat, 1952–1955). This was achieved in the same way as in the other faiths—through hereditary legal status within the pyramidal social structure. The Buddhist feudal legal principles present in the *shan* agrarian institutions of Burma were only deconstructed in 1959. And the zero-sum concept of land meant for Buddhist sovereignty has led to violence even today in the Myanmar government's policies toward the Islamic Rohingya. Perhaps the most striking assessment of feudalism in agrarian Buddhist legal and social principles lies in the continuing debate in Tibet about whether Tibetan Buddhism can be described as "feudal" before Tibet's annexation by the People's Republic of China in 1950. Whereas the Chinese argument centers on the annexation's legitimacy as a means of alleviating the Tibetan peasants' oppression under feudalism, the Dalai Lama's counterargument, aside from pointing out the hypocrisy and illegality of the annexation, proclaims that "necessary reforms were initiated"—presumably in reference to centuries-long social stratification, peasant oppression and noble/monastic privileges and ownership of finite land (Goldstein, 1971; Office of Tibet, 1996).

Little more needs to be said about the way in which the pyramidal social structure in agrarian societies further east necessitated expansion. Dominated by Confucian legal principles (which we've already discussed) Confucian laws in China, ruled by whichever dynasty, for centuries perpetuated the *'fengjian'* feudal system, which Mao Zedong rebelled against, and which is gradually (and quietly) being reimplemented under Xi Jinping (Bloom, 1999; Byres & Mukhia, 1985, pp. 213–218; Wu, 1952; Zhufu, 1981). Similar Confucian-based legal principles were enshrined for centuries in Korea and Japan under codes like the *Gyeongguk daejeon* and *Ritsuryo* respectively, which maintained similar feudal legal structures (Crewe, 1996; Deuchler, 1992; Haley, 1994; Mesheryakov, 2003). In each case, the ruling dynasties were always pressured to expand their rule to new lands in order to distribute spoils to supporters and family members who could not always benefit from the existing system. This is apparent from Chinese Tang and Qing westward expansion into the Tarim Basin in the seventh and seventeenth centuries, to Korean Joseon westward expansion into Manchuria in the seventeenth century, to Japanese Tokugawa and Shōwa westward expansion into Korea and Manchuria in the sixteenth and twentieth centuries.

Even in the pre-Columbian Americas, by the year 1486, the Aztec agrarian regime's chief concern was to "instill fear in the enemy and to show that the Aztecs were the masters of all the riches of the earth and controlled all the finest lands." Like the other examples above, their powerful families who served the Aztec sovereign were mostly concerned with "access to land (most likely controlled by nobles)" (Durán, 1994, p. 319; Nichols et al., 2017, p. 5). In all these cases, the political-legal model of agrarian social pyramids ensured that castes would be hereditary, thereby ensuring the long-term stability of the ruling dynasty and the loyalty of its noble families through access to finite landownership (Arnason & Hann, 2018; Butcher & Dick, 1993; Haldon, 1993; Ma & van Zanden, 2011).

The reason why local Mesoamerican tribes and communities preferred to ally with the newly-arrived conquistadores was because of their subjugation within the feudal pyramids that were already there. Of course, like all short-term thinking, these temporary alliances came with unfortunate long-term consequences—namely that their children and grandchildren would pay the price of subjugation for centuries into the social pyramids of the Old World empires. And much as in the zero-sum conception of the tax burden (either the peasantry or the nobility would pay more to sustain the pyramid), the circumstances of New World subjects changed in accordance with the circumstances of Old World subjects. Essentially, for Old World kingdoms and empires with overseas possessions in the New World such as England, Spain, France, Portugal and the Netherlands, the slow, gradual enfranchisement of their own peasantries came at the expense of the enslavement or enserfment of their conquered subjects in the New World—this has been termed the "discovery of feudalism" (Davis, 2008).

This also feeds into the myth (which we've received even from esteemed economics professors in the US—such as at the University of Amherst) that somehow, feudalism ended in western Europe at some relatively early date, i.e., the sixteenth century, but continued throughout the rest of Eurasia (and presumably Latin America)—feeding a narrative of a "divergence." The "Great Divergence," as it's become commonly known, has been presented as the reason for economic differences between the "West" (always English-speaking countries, often including Western Europe, sometimes parts of Central and Eastern Europe) and "the Rest." Usually the story goes like this: Western Europe (principally England) got rid of feudalism in the sixteenth century—under Elizabeth I—while it slowly became more oppressive in the East. The Eurocentrism and Orientalism inherent in this narrative are unmistakable, but the real damage is done in the self-delusion that generations of impoverished English-speakers, who have been told that their poverty is their own fault, can claim distinction from generations of impoverished speakers of other languages. The implications of that situation still resonate in the twenty-first century—Trump and Brexit are only the most obvious recent manifestations.

The Myth That Feudalism and Mercantilism Are Mutually Exclusive Economic Systems

This is the greatest misconception of all, that feudalism and mercantilism have been seen as two different, mutually exclusive economic systems. The typical idea is that by some stable, if debatable date, feudalism transitioned into mercantilism—and this is usually only discussed while describing the so-called "European middle ages." Based on the commonly accepted notion of the "industrial revolution," some business historians look back further and label other developments (such as "the techniques of modern business, not least of accounting and banking" that "created the world of pre-Industrial global capitalism") as revolutionary. They term it the "commercial revolution," which, according to this version of history, marked the medieval transition toward the Renaissance and early modernity. Such histories even misguide the reader that Venice was independent from Byzantium since the late-ninth century; it wasn't until at least 1054, if not 1204 (Reinert & Fredona, 2017, p. 3). Of course explanations such as this presuppose a Latin Christian (read Eurocentric) framework of time—can the "middle ages" or the "Renaissance" apply equally or suitably to Orthodox Christendom, Islam or the faith-based civilizations further east?

This goes along with the commonly reproduced myth that mercantilism "remained confined among the European nations, and not a single country from the Muslim East could adopt the system or contend them" (Bhandari, 2009; Islahi, 2008–2009). Nothing could be further from the truth; all human political economy was always beholden to the zero-sum logic of mercantilism. Basic mercantilist principles even appear in Aztec society, where, according to the *Codex Florentino*, private merchants ('Pochteca') were essentially appointed as Aztec imperial corporations to maintain commercial policies, ply trade routes and exchange items for the benefit of the ruling dynasty (Anderson & Dibble, 1959; Hirth, 2016; van Zantwijk, 1985, pp. 125–177). Islamic dynasties were just as beholden to the same zero-sum logic of political economy as Christian dynasties. However, capital controls and other protectionist measures were not equally or effectively enforced everywhere. It wasn't that mercantilist policies were exclusive to Christian regimes; Christian merchants were simply more successful at procuring inelastic bullion from Islamic regimes than Islamic merchants were at procuring bullion from Christian regimes. Basically, following the Islamic conquest of Constantinople in 1453, capital controls were more effectively enforced by Christian regimes, and therefore by the 17–18th centuries, Christian merchants and maritime powers like Venice and Genoa had more market power than Islamic merchants whose home regimes privileged wealth in land over bullion (Masters, 1988). By the time that Christian merchants began to trade further east, such as in China, the 17–18th-c. Chinese response to Christian mercantilism was not dissimilar from Islam, in that classical Chinese political economy privileged land over bullion for protectionist policies (Von Glahn, 1996). In both Islam and China, Christian merchants dealt with legal systems focused on regulating access to finite land but regulated access to bullion rather more loosely. Therefore, Christian merchants were essentially able to procure more bullion by comparison (Anievas & Nişancioğlu, 2015).

It's not surprising, then, that the expansion of Christian mercantilism and the success of Christian merchants in procuring bullion from outside of Christendom during the 16–18th centuries is seen as the golden age of mercantilism. From the writings of Christian merchants like Antonio Serra (who conveniently ignored the fact that the Christian Romans/Byzantines implemented mercantilist policies just like their pagan Roman forebears) to Jean-Baptiste Colbert, Thomas Mun and Philipp Wilhelm von Hornick, it's little surprise that this period is seen as defined by mercantilism in Europe and the Americas. But it was equally defined by feudalism insofar as the ultimate purpose of bullion was to purchase more immovable assets like status, power and land. Feudalism in Europe didn't end when mercantilism began—although it *was* conveniently described, or *'discovered'* as such during the 17–18th centuries. Rather, the end purpose of the merchant classes who manifested mercantilism, was always to buy into the finite share of land as rent-seekers in the feudal, agrarian societies of Latin and Orthodox Christendom (Davis, 2008; Day, 2008, p. 165; Ekelund & Robert, 1981).

This became most apparent after decades of papal relaxation of anti-usury laws, which were originally meant to regulate maritime loans (for mercantile bullion procurement), and which of course led to widespread dissatisfaction with the papal status quo by the early sixteenth century, mediated by zero-sum assumptions about the distribution of land and laws governing access to it. Protestantism wasn't theological as opposed to economic—the economic *was* the theological. The 16–17th-c. conflagrations of migrations, revolts and wars of religion in Latin Christendom were compounded by food shortages stemming from the worsening climate during the little ice age and of course zero-sum thinking about wealth (Diamond, 2005). One of the clearest illustrations of this can be seen in the figure of Jacob Fugger.

Jacob Fugger was born into a wealthy merchant dynasty in the free imperial city of Augsburg in 1459, pledged his life to money-making, and, in operating with his brothers, initially made money from the ground (near the same mines monopolized by the Árpád dynasty in Pannonia in the eleventh century)—mining ore to create new wealth in the forms of primarily copper and silver. Once converted into gold, it bought and promoted Habsburg emperors, bought off popes, engaged in rent-seeking, built social housing (but only for Catholics—a clearly potlatch initiative), indirectly inspired the first European speculation markets in Tulips, as well as peasant wars and revolts against papal corruption and oppression (such as in 1525, the year he died), lobbied against the Catholic Church's regulation of usury, financed the Portuguese spice trade, and so on. As a lifelong Catholic, that he stood staunchly against the new Protestant movement and was personally denounced by Martin Luther should come as no surprise. It's no hyperbole to suggest that his wealth and ruthlessness inspired the Reformation itself. Later Protestants would see themselves as protesting the same thing as Christ when he drove the money-changers from the Temple: the unholy mixture of the sacred with the profane, exactly as embodied in the Fuggers' mixture of financial and ecclesiastical power. His epitaph, likely personally dictated, read: "second to none in the acquisition of wealth... as he was comparable to none in life, so after death he is not to be numbered among the mortal" (Cameron, 2017; Chancellor, 1999, p. 15; Häberlein, 2006; Hümmerich, 1922; Steinmetz, 2015; von Pölnitz, 1999, p. 255). Is it any wonder that his reign of money inspired so much anger from fellow Catholics who had been told that both God and Mammon cannot be served at once?

Whether historians regard his dynasty's activities to be legal or illegal, mercantilist or feudalist, right or wrong, depends solely on subjective considerations (especially given the papal corruption under the Borgias and lack of enforcement of anti-usury laws). Similarly, some historians posit that the transition from feudalism to mercantilism occurred during the 12–15th centuries—others the 15–18th centuries. They base their logic on arbitrary notions of periodization ("medieval" versus "early modern") or predominant political economies in various regimes (e.g. Venice versus the Holy Roman Empire). But aside from the arbitrariness and eurocentrism, the problem is that the logic is ultimately circular: feudalism never entirely disappeared because it was not just about paying homage but it was about legal hereditary principles applied to different classes of rent-seeking people (feudal privileges)—just as mercantilism never truly disappeared because it was about legal principles for protecting the finite wealth of the regime—the ruling institutions. In reality these two legal systems are not mutually exclusive at all: they worked together to govern limited access to the original zero-sum, finite commodities—land (feudalism) and bullion (mercantilism) (Magnusson, 1994, xi–xxxv). Both rest on natural laws of finitude: one could even call their combined system of political economy *physionomy*. Fittingly, both feudalism and mercantilism rest on zero-sum thinking: one's loss is another's gain. Conquer or be conquered.

Dynasties and Mafias

Expansion is therefore always necessary; if one does not expand at another's expense, one will pay the requisite expense oneself—conquer or be conquered; eat or be eaten. Owing to the zero-sum thinking shot through most versions of political and behavioral economy, much of history has always been a dog-eat-dog affair with pretty veneers like "democracy," "progress" or "liberty" painted over it. Almost all expansion has been led by men who rape, pillage and plunder their way to unrivalled wealth, power and legitimacy, found dynasties and whose heirs use their inheritance of wealth, power and legitimacy to continue expansion or fail to do so either by disinterest or by defeat at the hands of another rival. Likewise, the successful ruling family expands, and eventually most historical political units are families which operate not unlike what we may now consider a mafia structure—by rewarding junior members of the clan or other supporters with key posts and/or appanage positions at the frontiers of the clan's power base, which, as it grows bigger, increasingly resembles a monarchy or imperial family. As prophesied by Jesus of Nazareth, "And from the days of John the Baptist until now the kingdom of heaven suffereth violence, and the violent take it by force" (Matthew 11:12 *KJV*).

But, the reader may object, surely a crime family and a ruling family are fundamentally different—the former breaks the law while the latter makes the law. A very famous and highly regarded Byzantine historian once made this objection at a formal academic conference over wine and cheese. It's true that a "mafia" as an archetype for a ruling dynasty may appear at first glance misleading on the basis that mafias are typically thought of as engaging in illegal profiteering activities. Yet consider that families may engage in illicit or violent activities until their wealth and/or power eclipses those of the ruling dynasty, for example in a coup, conquest, marriage or some such momentous elite event, and the new dynasty takes power, thereby mitigating the consequences of their previous activities. In this way, a family considered to be criminal can occasionally achieve power through alliance with a leading representative of the predominant religion, erasing their criminality and retrospectively rendering them legitimate. A prime example is Basil I the Macedonian, who rose from peasant to co-emperor of New Rome (Byzantium) in the 860s, brutally murdered the legitimate reigning emperor Michael III in 867, founded a dynasty through his least favorite son (Leo VI the Wise may have been the biological son of Michael, since his mother was evidently passed around), appointed other loyal friends and family members to key positions and then commissioned chronicles which cast Michael as a "drunkard." Nearly every dynasty in history was created by someone who came to power through alliance or violence, was loyally supported by blood relations, allies or both, received legitimacy through a judicial-religious structure, and who rewarded friends and family with spoils—not so essentially dissimilar from what we would consider a mafia operation (cf. Tilly, 1985).

Consider also the Davidic line in the Tanakh. According to the traditional story in the Book of Samuel, David was a lowly shepherd, who achieved power by killing Goliath in single combat, supplanting king Saul, receiving legitimacy from the elders of Israel in Hebron, murdering his own soldier Uriah the Hittite just to impregnate his wife Bathsheba, and then founding a dynasty and awarding his loyal family members and supporters with wealth and power. The Achaemenids of Persia emerged triumphant when Cyrus II successfully revolted against his master, the Median king Astyages, allowed the enslaved Jews in Babylon to return to Judaea (a potlatch initiative), and initially distributed family members and supporters across the empire as satraps, or local governors of provinces. The Ptolemies of Egypt and the Seleucids of Persia who both came to power after Alexander's conquests against the Achaemenids had similar policies. The Hasmonaeans who came to power after successfully resisting the Seleucids in the Maccabean Revolt apportioned power to junior dynasts as political favors. In Rome, after the death of Caesar and the ascendancy of Octavian Augustus and his successors, the Flavians, the Antonines and the Severans all built dynasties by violence and spoils, which endured with varying success. One of the most durable dynasties were the Constantinians due to their founder, Constantine the Great, who simultaneously vanquished his pagan enemies, consolidated his rule by distributing spoils to his supporters and family members and adopted Christianity.

Further to the East, the record is little different. The Sassanians of Persia came to power through the spoils of violence and then replicated the basic political system of the Achaemenids. In the wake of the early Islamic conquests of Muhammad and his successors in the 7–9th centuries, the Umayyads led by Mu'awiya conquered their enemies and awarded their supporters and family members with appanages of their empire, a level of corruption which led to the rise of the Kharijites and the first Islamic *fitna* (civil war within Islam). In the 850s, the Abbasids did the same against the Umayyads in the name of Islamic piety, and set out distributing spoils accordingly. The Carolingians, Ottonians, Piasts, Árpáds and Angevins achieved similar results in the name of Latin Christian piety (9–13th centuries) at the same times that the Doukids, Rurikids, Komnenians, Asenids and Palaiologans each came to power through various amounts of violence and alliance, used Orthodox Christianity for legitimization and then awarded their supporters and family members with pieces of the pie (finite land).

On and on it goes. In the mid-eleventh century, a petty lord who had inherited a province (which was incidentally an appanage awarded to his ancestor as a political favor by another dynasty), claimed power over a small island off the coast of far western Eurasia. After winning the ensuing battle by killing his rival in a particularly gruesome manner, he distributed the appanages of his new empire on the main island to his loyal friends and family, and founded a royal house which would eventually splinter into the Plantagenet and Blois dynasties. Even today, the legitimacy of the kings and queens of England depends on descent from a man with multiple names: originally he was William the Bastard, today he is commonly called William the Conqueror, but perhaps more appropriately, he could be called William the Mobster. Was the foundation of the Yuan dynasty of China much different? It depended on descent from Kublai Khan—Ghengis Khan's grandson—a family which purportedly murdered (by some historians' estimates) tens of millions of people across the dark, bloodsoaked badlands of 13th-c. Eurasia. After Kublai's conquests, he distributed the spoils and appanages similarly—as did his cousins in their conquests in the Ilkhanate of Persia and the Golden Horde of Russia. Up until the deposition of the last Mughal sultan (Bahadur Shah Zafar) in 1857, descent from Genghis Khan (through Tamerlane—himself perhaps one of history's worst killers) was the main determining factor of legitimacy in the largest agrarian empire in South Asia. The later Qing dynasty achieved similar results as Genghis Khan's progeny in the ancient lands of China again several centuries later (Kuzmin & Dmitriev, 2015). The Safavids, Qajarids and Pahlavids did the same again when each respectively murdered or overthrew the last monarch of the previous dynasty, distributed spoils to friends and family, and legitimized their actions through religious piety (of Shi'a Islam), thereby reconquering the ancient lands of Persia in later centuries. The early Ottomans' ability to operate almost as a corporate unit awarding towns and beyliks (lands under the jurisdiction of a *Bey*, or a local lord, namely, *principalities*) to family members and supporters in Anatolia and the Balkans at least until the early fifteenth century is well documented. The Japanese, whose organizational similarities with the Turks have a long and well-deserved history of comparison, saw a family called the Tokugawas emerge victorious and legitimate from a brutal generations' long civil war on the main island of Honshu during the 15–16th centuries by eliminating enemies and distributing spoils of the pie. Was the Joseon family—commonly considered the foundational dynasty of the unified Korean people—any different? The first Joseon ruler, Taejo, in a violent coup, overthrew the last ruler of the previous dynasty, the Goryeo (whose ascent itself is shrouded in bloody, 10th-century legends), declared a new dynasty (whose power would endure until 1910) and appointed family members and supporters to key positions.

And the saga continues. Why belabor the point with well-known stories of the ascents, operations and maneuverings of the Tudors, Romanovs, Habsburgs, Valois, Hohenzollerns or Bourbons in Orthodox, Latin and later Anglican Christendom? Despite his ascent from a minor noble family in Corsica, upon his coronation as the new "Emperor of France" after his extensive conquests in the 1790s and 1800s, Napoleon divorced his wife, married a Habsburg princess and installed his brother on the Spanish throne—directly attempting to repeat the French Bourbon victory over the Spanish Habsburgs a century before. Or consider the Saudi royal family, which came to power through a political alliance with the fundamentalist Wahhabist sect of Sunni Islam in the 1740s. Initially, the distribution of spoils was limited to supporters and family members. Yet, with the discovery of oil at an opportune time in the twentieth century (and after using petrodollars to buy tanks and airplanes to brutally destroy the Hashemite dynasty in control of Mecca and Medina during the 1920s—itself a zero-sum fight for control of the Arabian peninsula), along with an expedient wartime alliance with the winning side in WWII, the Saudi royal family by now numbers in the thousands. The Saudis have seemingly bought the loyalty of their entire subject population through appointments to comfortable functionary positions paid for by petrodollars—along with nearly the entirety of the PGTA. Lastly, Kim il-Sung used a communist-inflected political religion to overthrow the Japanese and American-backed post-WWII power structure in Korea, defeated the UN forces in North Korea in the early 1950s, not only declared himself "dear leader," but also rewarded his supporters with the spoils of his conquests, and founded a new dynasty which reigns into the 2020s. How else besides a zero-sum war for finite land on the Korean peninsula can the 1950–1953 Korean War be summarized?

Are the various American political dynasties very different? Even the Bushes recognize that four dynasties have largely oligopolized power in the US:

> The American electorate has a long-running, if tortured, romance with political dynasties in general. We love to grumble about them. Another Bush running for office? Another Clinton? Come on. But we also love to embrace them, up and down the political ladder. Just ask the Roosevelts or the Udalls or the Sununus or the scores of other clans for whom politics has become the family business. … Many Americans find the whole concept of political dynasties distasteful. Legacy politicians can carry a whiff of inherited power and entitlement that seems downright undemocratic. Way back in 2013, when the political world was waiting for Jeb Bush to become the third member of his family to run for president, his doting mother, Barbara, shared her reservations: "I think it's a great country, there are a lot of great families, and it's not just four families or whatever," she told the "Today" show. "There are other people out there that are very qualified, and we've had enough Bushes." (Cottle, 2023)

But remove one dynasty and get another. After working as a family corporation (whose patriarch went to jail), didn't the Kushners marry into the Trumps to solidify their status and power (Bernstein, 2020)? Is it any different for the Cheneys, Romneys, Pences, Longs, Quayles and McCains in the rest of the Republican party? And are the dynasties which dominate one party much different from the dynasties that dominate another? Haven't the Clintons, Obamas, Cuomos, Pelosies, Manchins and Bidens worked together closely and apportioned key positions, ambassadorships and infrastructure projects to their loyal supporters to ensure their continued domination of the Democratic party at least ever since the 1990s? After all, the Bidens' criminal scandals are just as publicly salacious as the Trumps'—and their progeny are just as aware of it (Rogers, 2023).

Many American political dynasties have formed political alliances with business dynasties like the Adelsons, Waltons, Cargill-MacMillans, Kochs, Lehmans or Morgenthaus in order to fund reelection campaigns and pass tax cuts for allied corporations (Meier, 2022). This has been going on since long before the Supreme Court's 2010 Citizens United decision, back to when the du Ponts, Bells, Edisons,

Carnegies, Morgans, Vanderbilts and Rockefellers formed and maintained their own corporate dynasties which funded political dynasties like the Lodges, Delano-Roosevelts, Tafts, Hoovers and Kennedys. Such fortunes were at times made, as in the case of the Delano family, from foreign drug addiction, at other times, from domestic drug addiction (the Sacklers). They were always maintained by exploitation, manipulation and abuse. For the Kennedys, the money came from insider financial and alcohol trading respectively before the 1929 Crash and 1933 repeal of Prohibition (Nasaw, 2012). As Joseph Stiglitz (2024) writes, "many of America's richest families acquired their wealth with more than a whiff of exploitation and bad behavior-abuse of market power (Rockefeller), pushing opioids (the Sacklers), or through the opium or slave trades" (p. 162). Even the Adams family functioned as a political dynasty, coming to power through tax evasion, insurrection and propagandism and then producing two presidents (John and John Quincy) and several other statesmen. Corporate or political, the ultimate purpose was always to prosaically perpetuate, in Abigail Disney's (2021) words, "blueprints for dynastic wealth," which explains why the lucky inheritors of the dynastic wealth and power can rarely see it for what it is: "if you are a fish, it is hard to describe water, much less to ask if water is necessary, ethical." America is no different from any other empire with a few wealthy, powerful families monopolizing or oligopolizing its inner workings (Hess, 2015; Jasanoff, 2023; Nyhan, 2014).

Zero-sum understandings of political dominance have always been the reverse side of the metaphorical coin from zero-sum understandings of market dominance. Even the darling of Canada's liberal class (and of many liberals the world over), Justin Trudeau, inherited his wealth, status and political connections and fashioned them into high office through a combination of effort, birth (luck), publicity and sheepish submission to corporate finance. Or in Greece, have the Papandreou, Karamanlis or Mitsotakis political dynasties truly operated by the same laws as everyone else? The same can be said about the Assad dynasty in Syria, the Marcos and Duterte families of the Philippines, the Fayez family of Jordan, or any other political dynasty in various Latin American countries sometimes, albeit perhaps unjustly, called "Banana Republics."

And the cycle repeats. In nearly every case, the award for being born into the right family or backing the winning side has been a chance at a seat at the table in the room where it happens—a piece of a seemingly finite pie. If wealth and power could not or would not need to be secured through violence, it could alternatively be secured through political alliances. As the old Habsburg dynastic advice goes: "Let others fight wars. You, happy Austria, marry." Whether gained by carrot or by stick, by hook or by crook, successful families which have become ruling dynasties through varying manipulative combinations of intimidation, violence, addiction, insider trading, alliance and spoils distribution have operated not entirely differently from what we would consider to be mafias. The questionability of their morally or legally suspect activities would or could always be dismissed upon successfully attaining wealth, power and legitimacy at the zero-sum expense of another. When successful, an attempt at usurping power creates its own legality. In order to make the law, first you have to break the law; at a certain point, might *does* make right. As Honoré de Balzac wrote in 1834, "The secret of great fortunes without apparent cause is a forgotten crime, because it was covered up properly." Or in the words of Ralph Waldo Emerson (1902), "Piracy and war gave place to trade, politics and letters; the war-lord to the law-lord; the privilege was kept, whilst the means of obtaining it were changed" (p. 168). Whether we view them as criminal mafias or legitimate ruling dynasties, the wars and/or rapacious enterprises they've engaged in or bankrolled since the dawn of recorded history have basically been turf wars over finite resources—whether they're Carolingians in the conquest business, Boeings in the bomb business or Hiltons in the hotel business. They, their family members and supporters, like their rivals, have always been after the most valuable commodity. A piece of the political pie has always been the goal—the bigger the better—*because* they've always seen the pie itself as finite.

Two Models of Ancient Imperial Expansion

Imperial expansion also functioned as the natural substitute for welfare states—there was no ancient form of a bureaucratized "welfare state" as may be recognized today. However, by endeavoring to conquer lands from neighboring dynasties, welfare could be ensured for supporters based on new lands and booty to distribute. In effect, small-scale feuds (and feudalism) between local dynasties and later faiths gradually became replaced by ever larger scale feuds (and feudalism). By the late eighteenth century, imperial dynasties and their faiths which vied for land and power with zero-sum logic competed across entire continents and oceans. This explains why the same ancient imperial war for control over seemingly finite land and bullion as late as the mid-eighteenth century is called many names on different continents: the French and Indian War in the Americas and the Seven Years War in Eurasia.

Though not mutually exclusive, usually various powers lean their ambitions for expansion—and therefore martial concentration—toward one theater of battle: either land or sea. Some, like the various imperial families of Rome/Byzantium, found ways to relatively evenly divide their limited resources toward a mutual disposition for both types of expansion over land and/or sea. Similar remarks could be made about American Manifest Destiny up to 1898 and Madrid's ecumenical empire across both land and sea—also up to 1898. Based on whether they have dominated and drawn their power from the land or the sea, empires have been called either tellurocratic or thalassocratic.

Tellurocracy refers mainly to contiguous, land-based agrarian empires, which have traditionally pursued geographical expansion. This is the most common kind of imperial expansion—especially in Eurasia. The relative consistency of Eurasian climates and geographical proximity typically facilitated the expansions of many of the biggest, most famous tellurocratic Eurasian empires (Huntington, 1907; Meyer, 2000; Preiser-Kapeller et al., 2020; Turchin, 2009). Characteristic examples include Sparta, Macedonia/Persia, China, the 13th-c. Mongol empire, Russia, the Mughals, Islamic Caliphates including the Ottomans and Safavids. More recent examples include Napoleonic France after the Louisiana Sale, and the short-lived Greater Germanic Reich established by the Nazis as well as the Soviet imperium under Stalin and afterwards.

Conversely, thalassocracies derive imperial power from maritime expansion. Early thalassocracies were also produced by a combination of geographical proximity and climatic consistency. Unsurprisingly, this has been less common throughout the heartland regions of Eurasia, but more common around the edges—near sea lanes. Most early thalassocracies from the late-Bronze-Age Sea Peoples to the Iron-Age Greek and Phoenician colonizations and the 11–16th-c. Venetian, Genoese and Aragonese dominations of various port colonies throughout the Mediterranean and Black Seas were locally confined. Similar observations may be made for the various 7–14th-c. kingdoms and sultanates of the Java Sea (Srijiaya-Majapahit) as well as the 8–15th-c. kingdoms and commercial (Hanse) leagues of the North and Baltic Seas (Kulke, 2016; Sulistiyono et al., 2018).

Even the 11–15th-c. Crusades were essentially overseas attempts at "proto-colonialism" by Christian sovereignty. This was then applied within Europe, particularly with the German expansion eastwards and the so-called Northern Crusades, which, as usual, combined religious conversion with land grabs. Carried out by Christian orders such as the Templars, this *Ostsiedlung* would prefigure (and inspire) later German ambitions of expansion toward Eastern Europe in search for "living space," in an effort to plunge the Iron Cross into the supposed heartlands of atheism and Judaism (i.e. the Soviet Union) (Mitterauer, 2010; Prawer, 1972). It was not for nothing that Hitler's 1941 invasion of the Soviet Union was codenamed "Operation Barbarossa" and characterized as a "crusade" (Harrisville, 2019; Stahel, 2018).

Beginning with the 15th-c. colonizations (and genocides followed by Jewish slave-settlement) of the Canaries and Azores (Albertino & Agostinho, 2011, p. 24), and then the voyages of Vasco da Gama and Columbus, the Iberian ecumenical empires of the families of the Trastámara-Habsburgs (Spain) and Aviz (Portugal) engaged in primarily maritime expansion. In fact, the obvious corruption of the three dynasties involved in the 1494 Treaty of Tordesillas to divide the world between them (blessed by the Borja papal dynasty) led the Valois king of France, Francis, to declare, "The sun shines for me as it does for others. I would very much like to see the clause of Adam's will by which I should be denied my share of the world" (Lacoursière, 2005, p. 28).

The very same 16–18th century thalassocratic expansion pioneered by the Holy Roman Spanish, Portuguese and French, also later fed into the Protestant Dutch and English crowns, which, having separated from the legal domination of Roman Catholicism and simultaneously gained and lost some of their American colonies, sought to shore up their political economies with a new plan for expansion. Rather than relying on the age-old plans for either thalassocratic or tellurocratic expansion based on the zero-sum finite amount of land available to be conquered and settled in the world, the new Protestant kingdoms began to pioneer a new possibility: potentially unlimited economic expansion based on the supposedly non-zero-sum infinite amount of wealth to be gained through production, consumption and commerce alone.

References

Abitbol, M. (1999). La fin de l'Empire songhay. In B. A. Ogot (Ed.), *Histoire générale de l'Afrique. V: L'Afrique du xvie au xviiie siècle* (pp. 341–368). UNESCO.

Albertino, F., & Agostinho, N. (2011). *Exorcising devils from the throne: São Tomé and Príncipe in the chaos of democratization.* Algora Publishing.

Anderson, A. J. O., & Dibble, C. (Eds. & Trans.). (1959). *The Florentine codex* (Book 9). University of Utah Press.

Anievas, A., & Nişancioğlu, K. (2015). *How the West came to rule: The geopolitical origins of capitalism.* Pluto Press.

Arnason, J. P. (2003). *Civilizations in dispute: Historical questions and theoretical traditions.* Brill.

Arnason, J. P., & Hann, C. (Eds.). (2018). *Anthropology and civilizational analysis: Eurasian explorations.* SUNY Press.

Ashburner, W. (Trans.). (1910). The farmer's law. *Journal of Hellenic Studies, 30*, 85–108.

Ashburner, W. (1909). *The Rhodian sea-law.* Clarendon Press.

Atik, K. (2021). A comparison of Komnenos era Byzantine and Song era Chinese diplomacy with nomad. *Journal of Turkish Research Institute, 70*, 343–358. https://doi.org/10.14222/Turkiyat4433

Atwater, R. (Trans.) (1961). *Procopius: Secret history.* University of Michigan Press.

Avrich, P. (1976). *Russian rebels, 1600–1800.* W.W. Norton & Co.

Baker, C., & Phongpaichit, P. (2017). *A history of Ayutthaya: Siam in the early modern world.* Cambridge UP.

Balzac, H. de. (1834). Le père Goriot. *Revue de Paris.* https://quoteinvestigator.com/2013/09/09/fortune-crime/

Banaji, J. (2001). *Agrarian change in late antiquity: Gold, labour, and aristocratic dominance.* Oxford University Press.

Bartlett, R. (2007). From paganism to Christianity in medieval Europe. In N. Berend (Ed.), *Christianization and the rise of Christian monarchy* (pp. 47–72). Cambridge University Press.

Beckwith, C. I. (2009). *Empires of the Silk Road: A history of Central Eurasia from the Bronze Age to the present.* Princeton University Press.

Beneshevich, V. N. (1987). *Древнеславянская кормчая XIV титулов без толкований.* Болгарская Академия Наук.

Berend, N. (2001). *At the gate of Christendom: Jews, Muslims and "Pagans" in medieval Hungary, c. 1000–1300.* Cambridge University Press.

Berend, N., Urbańczyk, P., & Wiszewski, P. (2013). *Central Europe in the High Middle Ages: Bohemia, Hungary and Poland c.900–c.1300.* Cambridge University Press.

Bernstein, A. (2020). *American oligarchs: The Kushners, the Trumps, and the marriage of money and power.* Norton.

Bhandari, S. (2009). Free trade, ottoman empire, and mercantilism. *International Trade eJournal.* https://doi.org/10.2139/ssrn.1624049

Bibikov, M. V. (2019). «Закон судный людем» и византийская эклога в свете средневековых правовых традиций. *Российская история*, 4, 82–91. https://doi.org/10.31857/S086956870005844-9

Bloch, M. (1971). The implications of marriage rules and descent: Categories for Merina social structures. *American Anthropologist, 73*(1), 164–178.

Bloom, I. (1999). The evolution of Confucian tradition in antiquity. In W. T. de Bary, W.-t. Chan, & R. J. Lufrano (Eds.), *Sources of Chinese tradition* (Vol. 2). Columbia University Press.

Blume, F. H., & Kearley, T. (Trans.). (2008). Annotated Justinian Code (Vols. 1–2). University of Wyoming Law Library. http://www.uwyo.edu/lawlib/blume-justinian/ajc-edition-2/books/ (Original work compiled 529–534 CE).

Brown, P. (2012). *Through the eye of a needle: Wealth, the fall of Rome, and the makings of Christianity in the West, 350–550 AD*. Princeton University Press.

Bryer, A. A. M. (2002). The means of agricultural production: Muscle and tools. In A. E. Laiou (Ed.), *The economic history of Byzantium* (Vol. 1, pp. 101–113). Dumbarton Oaks.

Bulanin, D. M. (2017). «Кормчая Книга» и «Книга Кормчий»: семантика названий двух древнерусских книг. *Русская Литература, 2*, 5–18.

Burgmann, L. (Ed.). (1983). *Ecloga: Das Gesetzbuch Leons III. und Konstantinos' V* (Forschungen zur byzantinischen Rechtsgeschichte, Bd. 10). Löwenklau-Gesellschaft. (Original work composed 726 CE).

Bushkovitch, P. (1980). *The merchants of Moscow, 1580–1650*. Cambridge University Press.

Butcher, J., & Dick, H. (1993). *The rise and fall of revenue farming: Business elites and the emergence of the modern state*. Martin's Press.

Byres, T., & Mukhia, H. (Eds.). (1985). *Feudalism and non-European societies*. Frank Cass.

Cahen, C. (1953). L'évolution de l'iqṭāᶜ du IXe au XIIIe siècle. *Annales: Economies, Sociétés, Civilisations, 8*, 25–52.

Cameron, A. (2017, October 24). The man who gave us the Reformation–and it wasn't Martin Luther. *The Conversation*. https://theconversation.com/the-man-who-gave-us-the-reformation-and-it-wasnt-martin-luther-85196

Cameron, R., & Neil, L. (2003). *A concise economic history of the world: From Paleolithic times to the present* (4th ed). Oxford University Press.

Campbell, G. (1981). Madagascar and the slave trade, 1810–1895. *The Journal of African History, 22*(2), 203–227.

Carter, J. C. (Ed.). (2003). *Crimean Chersonesos: Chora, city, museum, and environs*. UTA Institute of Classical Archaeology.

Chancellor, E. (1999). *Devil take the hindmost: A history of financial speculation*. Macmillan.

Chapus, G.-S., & Dandouau, A. (1961). *Manuel d'histoire de Madagascar*. Maisonneuve & Larose.

Charney, M. W. (2006). *Powerful learning: Buddhist literati and the throne in Burma's last dynasty, 1752–1885*. University of Michigan Press.

Chauhan, G. C. (2004). *Origin and growth of feudalism in early India: From the Mauryas to AD 650*. Munshiram Manoharlal Publishers.

Cherepenin, L. V. (1969). *Новгородские Берестяные Грамоты Как Исторический Источник*. Издательство «Наука».

Christ, G. (2021). Was there economic decline in Mamluk Egypt in the late Middle Ages? Demographic shock, industrial transformation, and a move towards a knowledge economy. *Vierteljahrschrift für Sozial- und Wirtschaftsgeschichte, 108*(2), 190–223. https://doi.org/10.25162/vswg-2021-0007

Christ, G. (2017). A king of the two seas? Mamluk maritime trade policy in the wake of the crisis of the 14th century. *Ulrich Haarmann Memorial Lecture 13*. EB-Verlag.

Christian, D. (1995). *A history of Russia, Central Asia and Mongolia, Volume II: Inner Eurasia from the Mongol Empire to today, 1260–2000*. Wiley.

Chutintaranond, S. (1990). Mandala, segmentary state and politics of centralization in medieval Ayudhya. *Journal of the Siam Society, 78*(1), 88–100. http://www.siamese-heritage.org/jsspdf/1981/JSS_078_1i_SunaitChutintaranond_MandalaSegmentaryStateInMedievalAyudhaya.pdf

Cissoko, S. M. (1996). *Tombouctou et l'Empire songhay: Épanouissement du Soudan nigérien aux XVe-XVIe siècles*. L'Harmattan.

Cohen, E. E. (1992). *Athenian economy and society: A banking perspective*. Princeton University Press.

Cottle, M. (2023, June 14). He's no Jack Kennedy. *New York Times*. https://www.nytimes.com/2023/06/14/opinion/rfk-jr-biden.html

Crewe, J. (1996). *Sources of Korean tradition*. Columbia University Press.

Curta, F. (2013). Markets in tenth century al-Andalus and Volga Bulghâria: Contrasting views of trade in Muslim Europe. *Al-Masaq, 25*(3), 315–321.

Dalgleish, D. (2005). Pre-colonial criminal justice in West Africa: Eurocentric thought versus Africentric evidence. *African Journal of Criminology and Justice Studies, 1*(1), 55–69.

Darke, H. (Trans.). (2012). *The book of government or rules for kings: The Siyar Al Muluk or Siyasat-nama of Nizam Al-Mulk*. Taylor & Francis.

Darling, L. (1996). *Revenue-raising and legitimacy: Tax collection and finance administration in the Ottoman Empire, 1560–1660*. Brill.

Davis, K. (2008). *Periodization & sovereignty: How ideas of feudalism & secularization govern the politics of time*. University of Pennsylvania Press.

Day, D. (2008). *Conquest: How societies overwhelm others*. Oxford University Press.

de Laet, S. (1949). *Portorium: Étude sur l'organisation douanière chez les Romaics, surtout à l'époque du Haut Empire*. De Tempel.

Deuchler, M. (1992). *The confucian transformation of Korea: A study of society and ideology*. Harvard University Asia Center.

Dewey, H. W. (1956). The 1497 Sudebnik—Muscovite Russia's first national law code. *American Slavic and East European Review, 15*(3), 325–338. https://doi.org/10.2307/3001097

Dewing, H. B. (Trans.). (1921). *Procopius: History of the Wars* (Books I–II). Harvard University Press.

Diamond, J. (2005). *Collapse: How societies choose to fail or succeed*. Penguin.

Dilcher, G. (2013). Das lombardische Lehnrecht der Libri Feudorum im europäischen Kontext. *Vorträge und Forschungen, 76*, 41–91. https://doi.org/10.11588/vuf.2013.0.33709

Disney, A. (2021). I was taught from a young age to protect my dynastic wealth. *The Atlantic*. https://www.theatlantic.com/ideas/archive/2021/06/abigail-disney-rich-protect-dynastic-wealth-propublica-tax/619212/

Durán, D. (1994). *History of the Indies of New Spain* (D. Heyden, Ed.). University of Oklahoma Press.

Duri, A. A. (1969). The origins of the iqṭāᶜ in Islam. *Al-Abḥāṯ, 22*, 3–22.

Duus, P. (1998). *Modern Japan*. Houghton Mifflin.

Ekelund, R. B., & Robert, D. (1981). *Mercantilism as a rent-seeking society: Economic regulation in historical perspective*. Texas A&M University Press.

Emerson, R. W. (1902). *English traits* (Original work published 1856). George Routledge and Sons.

Engel, P. (2001). *The realm of St. Stephen: A history of medieval Hungary, 895–1526*. I. B. Tauris.

Ermiş, F. (2014). *A history of Ottoman economic thought: Developments before the nineteenth century*. Routledge.

Feldbrugge, F. J. M. (2018). *A history of Russian law: From ancient times to the Council Code (Ulozhenie) of Tsar Aleksei Mikhailovich of 1649* (Vol. 66). Brill Nijhoff.

Feldman, A. M. (2013). The historiographical and archaeological evidence of autonomy and rebellion in Chersōn: A defense of the revisionist analysis of Vladimir's baptism (987–989). [MRes thesis, University of Birmingham] (pp. 6–100).

Feldman, A. M. (2018). Bullion, barter and borders in the Rus' coinless period. *Midlands Historical Review, 2*, 1–12. http://www.midlandshistoricalreview.com/wp-content/uploads/2018/07/Feldman-Bullion-Barter-and-Borders.pdf

Freshfield, E. H. (Trans.). (1926). *A manual of Roman law: The Ecloga*. Cambridge University Press. (Original work composed 726 CE).

Freshfield, E. H. (Trans.). (1928). *A manual of Eastern Roman law: The Procheiros Nomos*. Cambridge University Press. (Original work composed ca. 870–879 CE).

Gagin, I. A. (2008). Волжская Булгария: от посольства багдадского халифа до походов князя Святослава (X в.). *Вопросы Истории, 3*, 131–142.

Galbraith, J. K. (1987). *Economics in perspective: A critical history*. Houghton Mifflin.

Goldina, R. D., & Chernykh, E. M. (2005). Forest and steppe: A dialogue of cultures. *Acta Orientalia, 58*(1), 41–58.

Goldstein, M. C. (1971). Serfdom and mobility: An examination of the institution of human lease in traditional Tibetan society. *The Journal of Asian Studies, 30*(3), 521–534.
Graeber, D. (2011). *Debt: The first 5,000 years*. Melville House.
Greatrex, G., & Lieu, S. N. C. (2002). Justinian's second Persian war: The northern front (540–562). In G. Greatrex & S. N. C. Lieu (Eds.), *The Roman Eastern Frontier and the Persian Wars: Part II, AD 363–630* (pp. 115–117). Routledge.
Grierson, P. (1982). *Byzantine coins*. Methuen.
Gruszczynski, J., Jankowiak, M., & Shepard, J. (Eds.). (2021). *Viking-age trade: Silver, slaves and Gotland*. Routledge.
Gubajdullin, A. M. (2002). Фортификация городищ Волжской Булгарии.
Guillou, A. (1974). *La civilisation byzantine*. Arthaud.
Guletskij, D. V., & Doroshkevich, N. A. (2018). Меховые деньги древней Руси XI–XIII вв. Рифтур Принт.
Häberlein, M. (2006). *Die Fugger: Geschichte einer Augsburger Familie (1367–1650)*. Kohlhammer.
Habib, I. (1997, August 9). History and Interpretation. *Frontline*. Accessed 13 May, 2021. https://web.archive.org/web/20090422150140/http://www.hinduonnet.com/fline/fl1416/14160600.htm
Haldon, J. F. (1993). *The state and the tributary mode of production*. Verso.
Haley, J. O. (1994). *Authority without power: Law and the Japanese paradox*. Oxford UP.
Haley, J. O. (2011). The evolution of law: Political foundations of private law in medieval Europe and Japan. In D. Ma & J. L. van Zanden (Eds.), *Law and long-term economic change: A Eurasian perspective* (pp. 19–45). Stanford University Press.
Harris, J. (2003). *Byzantium and the Crusades*. Bloomsbury.
Harrisville, D. (2019). Unholy crusaders: The Wehrmacht and the reestablishment of soviet churches during operation Barbarossa. *Central European History, 52*(4), 620–649. https://doi.org/10.1017/S0008938919000876
Heather, P. (2013). *The restoration of Rome: Barbarian popes and imperial pretenders*. Macmillan.
Heather, P. J. (2008). Ethnicity, group identity, and social status in the migration period. In I. H. Garipzanov, P. J. Geary, & P. Urbańczyk (Eds.), *Franks, Northmen, and Slavs: Identities and state formation in early medieval Europe* (pp. 17–49). Brepols.
Heckscher, E. F. (1994). *Mercantilism*. Routledge.
Hendy, M. F. (1985). *Studies in the Byzantine monetary economy, c. 300–1450*. Cambridge University Press.
Herold, H. (2016). The natural environment, anthropogenic influences and supra-regional contacts at 9th–10th-century fortified elite settlements in central Europe. In N. Christie & H. Herold (Eds.), *Fortified settlements in early medieval Europe* (pp. 107–120). Oxbow.
Hess, S. (2015). *America's political dynasties: From Adams to Clinton*. Brookings Institution Press.
Hirth, K. G. (2016). *The Aztec economic world: Merchants and markets in ancient mesoamerica*. Cambridge UP.
Houben, H. (2002). *Roger II of Sicily: Ruler between East and West* (G. A. & D. Milburn, Trans.). Cambridge University Press.
Huletski, D., & Petrov, A. (2021). Finances and trade of ancient Rus', fur money in the context of theory and practices of fiat emissions in the 11th–12th centuries. *Rus', Lithuania, Horde: Journal of Numismatics and Sigillography, 9*, 57–60.
Hümmerich, F. (1922). *Die erste deutsche Handelsfahrt nach Indien, 1505/06: ein Unternehmen der Welser, Fugger und anderer Augsburger sowie Nürnberger Häuser*. R. Oldenbourg.
Huntington, E. (1907). *The pulse of Asia: A journey in Central Asia illustrating the geographic basis of history*. Houghton Mifflin.
Huxley, A. (1997). The importance of the Dhammathats in Burmese law and culture. *The Journal of Burma Studies, 1*, 1–17. https://doi.org/10.1353/jbs.1997.0008
Ibn Khaldun. (1969). *The Muqaddimah: An introduction to history* (F. Rosenthal & N. J. Dawood, Trans.). Princeton University Press.
Iliffe, J. (2007). *Africans: The history of a continent*. Cambridge University Press.

Inalcik, H. (1994). *An economic and social history of the Ottoman Empire, 1300–1914*. Cambridge University Press.
Islahi, A. A. (2008–2009). Mercantilism and the Muslim states: Lessons from the history. *Hamdard Islamicus, 32*(3), 23–43.
Ivanova, M. G., Zhurbin, I. V., & Kirillov, A. N. (2013). Fortifications at Idnakar settlement: The findings of interdisciplinary research. *Archaeology, Ethnology and Anthropology of Eurasia, 41*(2), 108–119.
Izmailov, I. L. (2009). Ислам в Волжской Булгарии. *Восток. Афро-Азиатские Общества: История и Современность, 2*, 5–12.
Jacoby, D. (2017). Byzantine maritime trade, 1025–1118. In B. Flusin & J.-C. Cheynet (Eds.), *U doron eimi tas graphas blepon noei - mélanges Jean-Claude Cheynet* (pp. 627–648). Association des Amis du Centre d'Histoire et Civilisation de Byzance.
Jacoby, D. (2000). The Byzantine outsider in trade (c.900–c.1350). In D. C. Smythe (Ed.), *Strangers to themselves: The Byzantine outsider* (pp. 129–147). Ashgate.
Jacoby, D. (2013). Between the imperial court and the Western maritime powers: The impact of naturalizations on the economy of late Byzantine Constantinople. In A. Ödekan, N. Necipoğlu, & E. Akyürek (Eds.), *The Byzantine court: Source of power and culture* (pp. 95–103). Koç University Press.
Jakobsson, S. (2009). The process of state-formation in medieval Iceland. *Viator, 40*(2), 151–170. https://doi.org/10.1484/J.VIATOR.1.100426
Jasanoff, M. (2023). The history of Nepo babies is the history of humanity: From ancient dynasties to modern fortunes, family has long defined our past, present, and future. *The New Yorker*. https://www.newyorker.com/magazine/2023/05/29/the-world-a-family-history-of-humanity-simon-sebagmontefiore-book-review
Johnson, S. G. B., Zhang, J., & Keil, F. (2020, April 30). Win–win denial: The psychological underpinnings of zero-sum thinking. *PsyArXiv*, 1–55. https://doi.org/10.31234/osf.io/efs5y
Kadens, E. (2015). The medieval law merchant: The tyranny of a construct. *Journal of Legal Analysis, 7*(2), 251–289. https://doi.org/10.1093/jla/lav004
Kaiser, D. H. (1980). *The growth of the law in medieval Russia*. Princeton University Press.
Kambouri-Vamvoukou, M., & Katsoni, P. (Eds.). (2016). Thessaloniki in the Age of Comnenoi and Angeloi. In B. Krsmanović et al. (Eds.), *Proceedings of the 23rd International Congress of Byzantine Studies, Belgrade, 22–27 August 2016: Round tables* (pp. 561–590).
Kaplanis, C. (2002). The debasement of the dollar of the Middle Ages. *The Journal of Economic History, 63*, 768–801.
Kazakov, E. P. (1992). Культура ранней Волжской Болгарии. Этапы этнокультурной истории.
Kehoe, D. P. (2007). *Law and the rural economy in the Roman Empire*. University of Michigan Press.
Khalikov, A. Kh. (1991). Ислам и урбанизм в Волжской Булгарии. In P. N. Starostin, A. Kh. Khalikov, & F. Š. Khuzin (Eds.), *Биляр - столица домонгольской Болгарии* (p. 48). Kazan'.
Khudokormov, A. G., & Drozdov, V. V. (2018). Деньги и денежное обращение в России в допетровский период. *Методология и история экономической мысли, 10*(4), 7–32. https://doi.org/10.38050/2078-3809-2018-10-4-7-32
Khuzin, F. Š. (2015). On the process of sedentarization of Volga Bulgars. *Journal of Sustainable Development, 8*(7), 68–74.
Klaniczay, G. (2004). The birth of a new Europe about 1000 CE: Conversion, transfer of institutional models, new dynamics. *Medieval Encounters, 10*(1–3), 99–129.
Kleimola, A. M. (1975). Justice in medieval Russia: Muscovite judgment charters (Pravye Gramoty) of the 15th and 16th centuries. *American Philosophical Society, 65*(6), 5–93.
Knafo, S. (2013). *The making of modern finance: Liberal governance and the gold standard*. Routledge.
Knoll, P. W. (1972). *The rise of the Polish monarchy: Piast Poland in East Central Europe, 1320–1370*. University of Chicago Press.
Koder, J. (2013). The authority of the Eparchos in the markets of Constantinople (according to the Book of the Eparch). In P. Armstrong (Ed.), *Authority in Byzantium* (pp. 83–110). Ashgate.

Kontogiannopoulou, A. (2015). Τοπικα Συμβουλια στις Βυζαντινες Πολεις. Παραδοση και Εξελιξη (13ος-15ος αι.). Ακαδημία Αθηνών.

Kovalev, R. K., & Noonan, T. S. (2000). What can archaeology tell us about how debts were documented and collected in Kievan Rus'? *Russian History, 27*(1–4), 119–154. https://doi.org/10.1163/187633100X00047

Kuleshov, V. S. (2020). О Новгородском денежном счете XI века, или краткая редакция Правды Русской как позднесредневековый фальсификат. *Novogardia, 1*, 336–347.

Kulke, H. (2016). Śrīvijaya revisited: Reflections on state formation of a Southeast Asian Thalassocracy. *Bulletin de l'École française d'Extrême-Orient, 102*, 45–95. https://doi.org/10.3406%2Fbefeo.2016.6231

Küpeli, I. (2007). Iqta als „islamischer Feudalismus"? [Iqta as "Islamic feudalism"?]. Grin.

Kuzmin, S. L., & Dmitriev, S. (2015). Conquest dynasties of China or foreign empires? The problem of relations between China, Yuan and Qing. *International Journal of Central Asian Studies, 19*, 59–92.

Lacoursière, J. (2005). *Canada Quebec 1534–2000*. Septentrion.

Laiou, A. E. (2002). Economic thought and ideology. In A. E. Laiou (Ed.), *The economic history of Byzantium* (Vol. 3, pp. 1123–1144). Dumbarton Oaks.

Laiou, A. (2011). Constantinople under the Palaeologus. In A. Laiou & C. Morrisson (Eds.), *The Byzantine World III—Greek Empire and its neighbors, xiii th–xv th century* (pp. 131–143). Presses Universitaires de France.

Lambton, A. K. S. (1953). *Landlord and Peasant in Persia*. Oxford UP.

Lammerts, D. C. (2010). *Buddhism and written law dhammasattha manuscripts and texts in premodern Burma*. PhD thesis, Cornell University.

Landau, P. (2008). Feudistik und Kanonistik. Ein neuer Quellenfund zum lombardischen Lehnrecht. *FS Elmar Wadle*, 525–536.

Lewis, B. (1979). Ottoman land tenure and taxation in Syria. *Studia Islamica, 50*, 109–124.

Li, L.-F. (2009). After the great debasement, 1544–51: Did Gresham's law apply? *Economic History Working Papers*, 126. London School of Economics. http://eprints.lse.ac.uk/27874/1/WP126.pdf

Lieberman, V. (2003). *Strange parallels: Southeast Asia in global context, c. 800-1830, Volume 1: Integration on the Mainland*. Cambridge UP.

Lingat, R. (1952–1955). *Les régimes matrimoniaux du sud-est de l'Asie: essai de droit comparé indochinois*. Éditions de Boccard.

Lockhart, J. (1969). Encomienda and hacienda: The evolution of the great estate in the Spanish Indies. *Hispanic American Historical Review, 59*, 411–429.

Mackie, J. D. (1963). *The earlier Tudors, 1485–1558*. Oxford University Press.

Macrides, R. (1986). Nomos and Kanon on paper and in court. In R. Morris (Ed.), *Church and people in Byzantium: SPBS 20th Spring Symposium of Byzantine Studies, Manchester* (pp. 61–85). Centre for Byzantine.

Magnusson, L. (1994). Eli Heckscher and mercantilism—An introduction. In E. Heckscher, *Mercantilism* (M. Shapiro, Trans.). Routledge.

Magnusson, L. (Ed.). (1993). *Mercantilist economics*. Kluwer Academic Publishers.

Mako, G. (2011). The Islamization of the Volga Bulghars: A question reconsidered. *Archivum Eurasiae Medii Aevi, 18*, 199–223.

Malanima, P. (2009). *Pre-modern European economy: One thousand years (10th–19th centuries)*. Brill.

Martin, J. (2006). Coins, commerce and the conceptualization of Kievan Rus'. In K. L. Reyerson, T. G. Stavrou, & J. D. Tracy (Eds.), *Pre-modern Russia and its world: Essays in honor of Thomas S. Noonan* (pp. 161–172). Harrassowitz Verlag.

Martindale, J. R. (1992). *The prosopography of the later Roman Empire* (Vol. 3, AD 527–641). Cambridge University Press.

Masters, B. (1988). *The origins of western economic dominance in the Middle East: Mercantilism and the Islamic economy in Aleppo, 1600–1750*. New York University Press.

Ma, D., & van Zanden, J. L. (2011). *Law and long-term economic change: A Eurasian perspective.* Stanford UP.
McCormick, M. (2001). *Origins of the European economy: Communications and commerce AD 300–900*. Cambridge University Press.
McGeer, E. (Ed.). (2000). *Land legislation of the Macedonian emperors.* Pontifical Institute of Mediaeval Studies.
McKee, S. (2000). *Uncommon dominion: Venetian Crete and the myth of ethnic purity.* University of Pennsylvania Press.
Meier, A. (2022). *Morgenthau: Power, privilege, and the rise of an American dynasty.* Random House.
Mell, J. L. (2014). Cultural meanings of money in medieval Ashkenaz: On gift, profit, and value in medieval Judaism and Christianity. *Jewish History, 28*(2), 125–158. https://doi.org/10.1007/s10835-014-9212-3
Menéndez Pidal, R. (1966). *The Spaniards in their history* (W. Starkie, Trans.). W. W. Norton. (Original work published 1947)
Merianos, G. (2017). More than a shepherd to his flock: Eustathios and the management of ecclesiastical property. In F. Pontani, V. Katsaros, & V. Sarris (Eds.), *Reading Eustathios of Thessalonike* (pp. 309–330). De Gruyter.
Merianos, G., & Gotsis, G. (2018). *Managing financial resources in late antiquity: Greek Fathers' views on hoarding and saving.* Palgrave Macmillan.
Mesheryakov, A. (2003). On the Quantity of written data produced by the Ritsuryō state. *Japan Review, 15*,187–199.
Meyendorff, J. (1996). *Rome, Constantinople, and Moscow: Historical and theological studies.* St Vladimir's Seminary Press.
Meyendorff, J. (2010). *Byzantium and the rise of Russia: A study of Byzantino-Russian relations in the fourteenth century.* Cambridge University Press.
Miller, D., Rowlands, M., & Tilly, C. (1989). *Domination and resistance.* Routledge.
Minchinton, W. E. (Ed.). (1969). *Mercantilism: System of expediency?* D.C. Heath & Co.
Mitterauer, M. (2010). The crusades and protocolonialism: The roots of European expansionism. In *Why Europe? The medieval origins of its special path* (pp. 194–231). University of Chicago Press. https://doi.org/10.7208/9780226532387-009.
Prawer, J. (1972). *The Crusaders' Kingdom: European Colonialism in the Middle Ages.* Praeger Publishers.
Meyer, W. B. (2000). "Climate and Migration." In A. Bell-Fialkoff (Ed.), *The role of migration in the history of the Eurasian Steppe: Sedentary civilization vs. "Barbarian" and Nomad.* Palgrave Macmillan.
Momotov, V. V. (2003). *Формирование Русского Средневекового Права в IX-XIV вв* [Monograph].
Moravcsik, G., & Jenkins, R. J. H. (Eds. & Trans.). (1967). *De Administrando Imperio of Constantine VII Porphyrogenitus* (2nd ed.). Dumbarton Oaks.
Mörner, M. (1973). The Spanish American hacienda: A survey of recent research and debate. *Hispanic American Historical Review, 53*(2), 183–216. https://doi.org/10.2307/2512251
Moroney, G. (2009). Slave society and economic development of the late Roman world. In *Slave societies and markets in the Roman Empire* (pp. 684–728). Brill.
Morrisson, C. (2002). Byzantine money: Its production and circulation. In A. E. Laiou (Ed.), *The economic history of Byzantium* (Vol. 3, pp. 909–966). Dumbarton Oaks.
Motomura, A. (1994). The best and worst of currencies: Seigniorage and currency policy in Spain, 1597–1650. *The Journal of Economic History, 54*(1), 104–127.
Mulcahy, R. G. (2001). *Canon law in medieval Russia: The Kormchaia kniga as a source of law* (Unpublished MPhil thesis). University of London.
Murphey, R. (1990). Ottoman census methods in the mid-sixteenth century: Three case histories. *Studia Islamica, 71*, 115–126.
Nasaw, D. (2012). *The patriarch: The remarkable life and turbulent times of Joseph P.* Penguin.

Necipoğlu, N. (2003). The aristocracy in late Byzantine Thessalonike: A case study of the city's archontes (late 14th and early 15th centuries). *Dumbarton Oaks Papers, 57*, 133–151.

Nichols, D. L., Berdan, F., & Smith, M. E. (2017). *Rethinking the Aztec economy (Amerind studies in anthropology)*. University of Arizona Press.

Nicole, J. (Trans.). (1894). *Le Livre du Préfet ou l'édit de l'empereur Léon le Sage sur les Corporations de Constantinople*. Georg & Cie, Libraires-Éditeurs.

Niczyporuk, P. (2011). Mensarii, bankers acting for public and private benefit. *Studies in Logic, Grammar and Rhetoric, 24*(37), 105–115.

Nogués-Marco, P. (2010). *Bullionism, specie-point mechanism and bullion flows in the early 18th century Europe* [Doctoral dissertation, Universitat de Barcelona]. http://diposit.ub.edu/dspace/bitstream/2445/35759/1/PNM_THESIS.pdf

Noonan, T. S. (1987). The monetary history of Kiev in the pre-Mongol period. *Harvard Ukrainian Studies, 11*(3–4), 384–443.

Nyhan, B. (2014). Another season of 'Dynasty' for voters. *The New York Times*. https://www.nytimes.com/2014/04/29/upshot/another-season-of-dynasty-for-voters.html

Office of Tibet. (1996, February 2). Traditional society and democratic framework for future Tibet. *Tibetan Government-in-Exile*. https://web.archive.org/web/20080410151700/http://www.tibet.com/WhitePaper/white4.html

Ohnuki-Tierney, E. (1993). *Rice as self: Japanese identities through time*. Princeton University Press.

Oikonomides, N. (2002). The role of the Byzantine state in the economy (J. Solman, Trans.). In A. E. Laiou (Ed.), *The economic history of Byzantium* (Vol. 3, pp. 973–1058). Dumbarton Oaks.

Olivelle, P. (1999). *Dharmasūtras: The law codes of Āpastamba, Gautama, Baudhāyana, and Vāsiṣṭha*. Oxford University Press.

Owen, J. (2012, December 19). Old Coppernose—Quantitative easing, the medieval way. *Royal Mint Blog*. http://blog.royalmint.com/old-coppernose-quantitative-easing-the-medieval-way/

Özel, O. (1999). Limits of the Almighty: Mehmed II's 'land reform' revised. *Journal of the Economic and Social History of the Orient, 42*(2), 226–246.

Pálóczi-Horváth, A. (1989). *Pechenegs, Cumans, Iasians: Steppe peoples in medieval Hungary*. Corvina.

Pamuk, Ş. (2000). *A monetary history of the Ottoman Empire*. Cambridge University Press.

Pavlova, E. (1994). The coinless period in the history of northeastern Rus': Historiography study. *Russian History, 21*(4), 375–392.

Penna, D. (2012). *The Byzantine imperial acts to Venice, Pisa and Genoa, 10th–12th centuries: A comparative legal study*. Eleven International Publishing.

Petrukhin, V. J. (2006). Феодализм перед судом русской историографии. *Одиссей: Человек в истории*, 1, 161–170.

Piketty, T. (2014). *Capital in the twenty-first century* (A. Goldhammer, Trans.). Belknap Press.

Polybius. (1979). *The rise of the Roman Empire* (I. Scott-Kilvert, Trans.). Penguin Classics.

Preiser-Kapeller, J. (2015). Piketty in Byzanz? Ungleichverteilungen von Vermögen und Einkommen im Mittelalter. *Das Andere Mittelalter*. https://www.dasanderemittelalter.net/news/piketty-in-byzanz-ungleichverteilungen-von-vermogen-und-einkommen-im-mittelalter/

Preiser-Kapeller, J. (2016). The frontiers of administration and the limits of income: Aspects of the "management of shortage" in the late Byzantine Patriarchate [Conference paper]. *23rd International Congress of Byzantine Studies*. https://www.academia.edu/23988250

Preiser-Kapeller, J., & Mitsiou, E. (2019). Mercantile and religious mobility between Byzantines, Latins and Muslims, 1200–1500: On the theory and practice of social networks. *Medieval Worlds, 9*, 187–217.

Preiser-Kapeller, J., Reinfandt, L., & Stouraitis, Y. (Eds.). (2020). *Migration histories of the Medieval Afroeurasian transition zone: Aspects of mobility between Africa, Asia and Europe, 300-1500 C.E. (Studies in global migration history 13)*. Brill.

Prinzing, G. (2015). In search of diasporas in the Byzantine "successor state" of Epirus (c. 1210–1267). In G. Christ et al. (Eds.), *Union in separation: Diasporic groups and identities in the Eastern Mediterranean (1100–1800)* (pp. 123–136). Viella.

Pritsak, O. (1998). *The origins of the old Rus' weights and monetary systems*. Harvard University Press.
Psarev, A. (2018). *Chasing Canon 15 of the First and Second Council in Constantinople* (861). (Unpublished PhD thesis). Queen's University Belfast.
Raison-Jourde, F. (1983). *Les souverains de Madagascar*. Karthala.
Reda, A. (2018). *Prophecy, piety, and profits: A conceptual and comparative history of Islamic economic thought*. Palgrave Macmillan.
Reinert, S. A., & Fredona, R. (2017). Merchants and the origins of capitalism. *Harvard Business School Working Paper*, 18-021. https://www.hbs.edu/ris/Publication%20Files/18-021_b3b67ba8-2fc9-4a9b-8955-670d5f491939.pdf
Reyerson, K. L., Stavrou, T. G., & Tracy, J. D. (Eds.). (2006). *Pre-modern Russia and its world: Essays in honor of Thomas S. Noonan*. Harrassowitz.
Reynolds, S. (2001). *Fiefs and vassals: The medieval evidence reinterpreted*. Clarendon Press.
Rogers, K. (2023, July 1). Hunter Biden's daughter and a tale of two families. *New York Times*. https://www.nytimes.com/2023/07/01/us/politics/hunter-biden-daughter-arkansas.html
Romanchuk, A. I. (2000). *Очерки истории и археологии византийского Херсона*. Изд-во Уральского университета.
Róna-Tas, A. (1999). *Hungarians and Europe in the early Middle Ages: An introduction to early Hungarian history* (M. Bodóczky & N. Bodóczky, Trans.). Central European University Press.
Ryan, M. (1997). 'Ius commune feudorum' in the thirteenth century. In A. Romano (Ed.), *Colendo iustitiam et iura condendo... Federico II Legislatore del Regno di Sicilia nell'Europa del Duecento. Per una storia comparata delle codificazioni europee* (pp. 51–65). Edizioni de Luca.
Sagoo, H. (2001). *Banda Singh Bahadur and Sikh sovereignty*. Deep & Deep Publications.
Schaeken, J. (2012). *Stemmen op berkenbast: berichten uit middeleeuws Rusland: dagelijks leven en communicatie*. Leiden University Press.
Schapov, J. N. (1969). Церковь и становление древнерусской государственности. *Вопросы Истории, 11*, 55–64.
Schapov, J. N. (1978). *Византийское и южнославянское правовое наследие на Руси в XI–XIII вв.* Наука.
Schapov, J. N. (1993). *State and church in early Russia, 10th–13th centuries* (V. Schneierson, Trans.). Aristide D. Caratzas.
Schiffman, D. A. (2005). The valuation of coins in medieval Jewish jurisprudence. *Journal of the History of Economic Thought, 27*(2), 141–160. https://doi.org/10.1080/09557570500114293
Scott, J. C. (2009). *The art of not being governed: An anarchist history of upland Southeast Asia*. Yale University Press.
Sears, S. D. (1997). *A monetary history of Iraq and Iran, ca. CE 500 to 750* (Unpublished doctoral dissertation). University of Chicago.
Sewter, E. R. A. (Trans.). (1979). *Fourteen Byzantine rulers: The Chronographia of Michael Psellus*. Penguin.
Sharma, S. R. (2005). *Indian feudalism* (3rd rev. ed.). Macmillan.
Sharp, R. (2011). *The outside image: A comparative study of external architectural display on Middle Byzantine structures on the Black Sea Littoral* (Unpublished doctoral dissertation). University of Birmingham.
Shaw, F. L. (1997). *A tropical dependency: An outline of the ancient history of the Western Sudan with an account of the modern settlement of northern Nigeria*. Black Classic Press.
Shepard, J. (2009). "Mists and portals": The Black Sea's north coast. In M. M. Mango (Ed.), *Byzantine trade, 4th–12th centuries* (pp. 421–441). Ashgate.
Signes Codoñer, J., & Andrés Santos, F. J. (Trans.). (2007). *La Introducción al derecho (Eisagoge) del patriarca Focio*. Consejo Superior de Investigaciones Científicas (Original work composed ca. 879–886 CE).
Sigurðsson, J. V. (1999). *Chieftains and power in the Icelandic commonwealth*. Odense University Press.
Singh, G. (1935). *Life of Banda Singh Bahadur*. Sikh History Research Department.

Sitdikov, A. G., Izmajlov, I. L., & Khayrutdinov, R. R. (2015). Weapons, fortification and military art of the Volga Bulgaria in the 10th–first third of the 13th centuries. *Journal of Sustainable Development, 8*(7), 167–177.

Sorochan, S. B. (1995). Случайность или система? Раннесредневековый византийский меркантилизм. *Древности-1995. Харьковский историко-археологический ежегодник*, 122–132.

Spasskij, I. (1962). *Русская Монетная Система*. Moscow: Издательство Государственного Эрмитажа.

Stahel, D. (Ed.). (2018). *Joining Hitler's crusade: European Nations and the invasion of the Soviet Union, 1941*. Cambridge University Press. https://doi.org/10.1017/9781108225281

Stein, P. (1999). *Roman law in European legal history*. Cambridge University Press.

Steinmetz, G. (2015). *The richest man who ever lived*. Simon & Schuster.

Stiglitz, J. E. (2024). *The road to freedom*. Penguin.

Sulistiyono, S. T., Masruroh, N. N., & Rochwulaningsih, Y. (2018). Contest for seascape: Local thalassocracies and Sino-Indian trade expansion in maritime Southeast Asia during the early premodern period. *Journal of Marine and Island Cultures, 7*(2), 74–93. https://doi.org/10.21463/jmic.2018.07.2.05

Tambiah, S. J. (1976). World conqueror and world renouncer: A study of Buddhism and polity in Thailand against a historical background. Cambridge UP.

Telitsyn, V. L. (2013). *Русское иго, или Нашествие ушкуйников на Золотую Орду*. Алгоритм.

Thakur, V. K. (1989). *Historiography of Indian feudalism towards a model of early medieval Indian economy, c. AD 600-1000*. Commonwealth Publishers.

Tikhomirov, M. N. (1961). *Закон Судный Людем*. Академия Наук СССР.

Tilly, C. (1985). War making and state making as organized crime. In P. Evans, D. Rueschmeyer, & T. Skocpol (Eds.), *Bringing the state back in* (pp. 169–191). Cambridge University Press.

Totman, C. (1981). *Japan before Perry: A short history* (10th ed.). University of California Press.

Troianos, S. N. (2011). *Οι πηγές του βυζαντινού δικαίου*. Sakkoula.

Troianos, S. N. (Trans.) (2007). *Οι Νεαρές Λέοντος ΣΤ΄ του Σοφού*. Irodotos (Original work compiled ca. 867–879 CE).

Turchin, P. (2009). A theory for the formation of large Agrarian empires. *Journal of Global History, 4*, 191–217.

Urbańczyk, P., & Rosik, S. (2003). The kingdom of Poland, with an appendix on Polabia and Pomerania between paganism and Christianity. In N. Berend (Ed.), *Christianization and the rise of Christian monarchy* (pp. 263–318). Cambridge University Press.

Urbańczyk, P., & Rosik, S. (2008). Slavic and Christian identities during the transition to Polish statehood. In I. H. Garipzanov, P. Geary, & P. Urbańczyk (Eds.), *Franks, Northmen, and Slavs: Identities and state formation in early medieval Europe* (pp. 243–272). Brepols.

van Zantwijk, R. (1985). *The Aztec arrangement: The social history of Pre-Spanish Mexico*. University of Oklahoma Press.

Vassberg, D. E. (1986). *Tierra y sociedad en Castilla: Señores, poderosos y campesinos en la España del siglo XVI*. Editorial Crítica.

Vernadsky, G. (1937). *Studies in the history of Moscovian private law of the 16th and the 17th centuries: Inheritance, the case of the childless wife*. Cedam.

Vickery, M. (1998). Society, economics, and politics in Pre-Angkor Cambodia: the 7th–8th Centuries. Centre for East Asian Cultural Studies for UNESCO.

Visočnik, N. (2014). Living on the edge: Buraku in Kyōto, Japan. *Anthropological Notebooks, 20*(2), 127–143.

von Pölnitz, G. (1999). *Die Fugger* (6th ed.). Mohr & Siebeck.

Von Glahn, R. (1996). Myth and reality of China's seventeenth-century monetary crisis. *The Journal of Economic History, 56*(2), 429–454.

von Wobeser, G. (1983). *La formación de la hacienda en la época colonial. El uso del agua y la tierra*. Instituto de Investigaciones Históricas, UNAM.

Weickhardt, G. G. (2001). The canon law of Rus', 1100–1551. *Russian History, 28*(1–4), 411–445. https://doi.org/10.1163/187633101X00235

Weimar, P. (1990). Die Handschriften des Liber Feudorum und seiner Glossen. *Rivista Internazionale di Diritto Comune, 1*, 31–98.

Weiss, D. (1995). Ibn Khaldun on economic transformation. *International Journal of Middle East Studies, 27*(1), 29–37. https://doi.org/10.1017/S0020743800061560.

Wennerlind, C., & Stern, P. J. (Eds.). (2013). *Mercantilism reimagined: Political economy in early modern Britain and its empire*. Oxford University Press.

Wiles, R. C. (1974). Mercantilism and the idea of progress. *Eighteenth-Century Studies, 8*(1), 56–74. https://doi.org/10.2307/2737891

Willard, A. (1993). Gold, Islam and camels: The transformative effects of trade and ideology. *Comparative Civilizations Review, 28*(28), 80–105.

Wolf, M. (2003). 10th–11th century settlements, earthen forts, and crafts. In Z. Visy & M. Nagy (Eds.), *Hungarian archaeology at the turn of the millennium* (pp. 326–332). Teleki Laszlo Alapitvany.

Wolters, O. W. (1999). *History, culture and region in Southeast Asian perspectives*. Cornell UP (Institute of Southeast Asian Studies, revised ed.).

Wortley, J. (Trans.). (2010). *John Skylitzes: A synopsis of Byzantine history, 811–1057*. Cambridge University Press.

Wu, T.-K. (1952). An interpretation of Chinese economic history. *Past & Present, 1*, 1–12. https://doi.org/10.1093/past/1.1.1

Yeager, T. J. (1995). Encomienda or slavery? The Spanish Crown's choice of labor organization in sixteenth-century Spanish America. *The Journal of Economic History, 55*(4), 842–859.

Zakon Sudnyj Ljudem (Court Law for the People). (1977). (H. W. Dewey & A. M. Kleimola, Trans.; Michigan Slavic Materials). University of Michigan Slavic Publications.

Zavagno, L. (2009). *Cities in transition: Urbanism in Byzantium between Late Antiquity and the Early Middle Ages, (500–900)*. Archaeopress.

Zhivkov, B. (2015). *Khazaria in the ninth and tenth centuries* (D. Manova, Trans.). Brill.

Zhufu, F. (1981). The economic history of China: Some special problems. *Modern China, 7*(1), 3–30. https://doi.org/10.1177/009770048100700101

Part II

"You Know Why They Call it the 'American Dream'...?" (1776–1929)

4 The Birth of Liberal Economic Expansion

Abstract

The fourth chapter explains how Eurasian regimes looked to the Qing dynasty's Chinese empire, engendering a period of so-called **sinomania and physiocracy**, which was little more than an enshrinement of feudalism and mercantilism as the paramount universal program of political economy. Caught between the zero-sum socioeconomic pyramids of both national and ecumenical slave regimes, their working classes were increasingly compelled to emigrate toward the New World in search of **frontiers, population valves and the economics of hope**. In response, **the Malthusian Challenge** of Old World economists proposed that only by increasing limits on access to ownership of finite resources like gold and land could working populations be adequately disciplined (i.e. clearances). The ensuing suffering was seemingly mitigated by the beginnings of the "Industrial Revolution." This ostensibly new historical phase brought unprecedented growth coupled with unprecedented immiseration for the working classes. Despite economic expansion far surpassing demographic expansion since industrialization, this often came at the zero-sum expense of working classes in the Eurasian empires. The expanding pie was still managed based on zero-sum principles and the **myth of linear industrial progress** framed the industrialization of production as a "revolution" while avoiding a real one. The unintended consequence of this was that the forces of **liberalism confronted slavery**, enshrining the former as victors in a zero-sum struggle against slavers.

A nation is born stoic and dies epicurean.—Will Durant

1776 was a busy year for Anglo-Americans. As the rosy-fingered dawn sunlight first percolated through the single-paned windows of the genteel redbrick

A. M. Feldman and Y. Stamos, *Zero Sum Political Economy*, World-Systems Evolution and Global Futures, https://doi.org/10.1007/978-3-032-18326-2_4

townhomes on the Philadelphian morning of July 3rd, the heady gentlemen-revolutionaries at the Continental Congress completing the draft of the separatist document in the nearby Palladian statehouse were overcome with both exhaustion and ecstasy. The Testament had been a long time coming in their eyes. Eleven years later, another Philadelphian convention would seek to overturn what Alexander Hamilton and Elbridge Gerry (of "Gerrymandering" infamy) deemed "an excess of democracy" (Holton, 2005). Loyalists be damned. The multi-paned propaganda first germinated by the singular Thomas Paine, published anonymously only seven brief months prior, on January 10th, had finally borne fruit.

Just over a month after the publication of Paine's pamphlet, on February 17th, the London publishers Strahan and Cadell printed the very first volume of Edward Gibbon's arch-famous tome, *The History of the Decline and Fall of the Roman Empire*. The first thousand copies sold out in a matter of months and a new batch of 1500 had to be produced by June 3rd, a month before the synod in Philadelphia. Ever since, Gibbon's works have been admired and reviled alike for their rationalist and secularist views of human history as a steady march of linear progress—commonly deemed "Whig history." Accordingly, the English-speaking conceptualization of history became standardized as a trajectory leading from the ruins of the Roman Empire to the glories of the British, and after 1956, the American one. Furthermore, the tripartite division of history into ancient, medieval and modern periods became commonly accepted in the West, a lingering byproduct of which is the separate academic discipline of the "Classics."

Nevertheless, almost a month after the publication of Gibbon's work, on 9 March 1776, this Whiggish, linear conception of time struck a new hour with Strahan and Cadell's publication of Adam Smith's *An Inquiry into the Nature and Causes of the Wealth of Nations*. In a single-paned window into his mind, Smith single-handedly reversed British imperial economic policy and forever altered the past, present and future of economic thought. Incidentally, a month later, Smith, working with Strahan and Cadell, published David Hume's 5-page treatise, *My Own Life*, which summarized some of the famous philosopher's many ideas, including his defense of rationalist linear time, free trade, inequality and, perhaps most intriguingly, that private property must be earned because of the inherent scarcity of resources.

It almost seems that in a single year, as in the declaration of Year One in the French Revolution (16 years later), the world was born anew, a solution to everything prior. The problem was that it wasn't.

There's a case to be made that Gibbon and Smith (and perhaps less-so Hume) were just as influential to America's founding principles as Franklin, Jefferson, Adams and Washington. There's little doubt about America's "Anglo-liberal-Protestant inheritance" (Douthat, 2021). Several convincing cases have been presented. Three points stand out.

First, Gibbon's Whiggish, linear, supposedly rationalist march of history from Roman ruins to English supremacy was never seriously challenged either in America or in Britain; nor was Adam Smith's thesis, which sought to chuck mercantilist economic thought into the dustbin of history (Smith, 1776, Book IV, chapter 8). The jury is still out on whether it ever even cleared the maw of the can.

Second, America's inheritance of the British empire was never seriously challenged in the aftermath of World War II, due to the same slovenly Whiggish intellectual assumptions which guided Gibbon. Similarly, America's inheritance of Britain's economic model, derived from the individualist intellectual assumptions guiding Smith, ensured that Britain was not the only "nation of shopkeepers," as any celebrant of American small business will attest. Perfidious Albion was the direct forerunner of the American Dream (de Tocqueville, 1835, Vol. II, Ch. XIX; Douglas, 2012).

Third, only progress and growth can forestall decadence and corruption; in the works of the classical liberal economists who followed Smith, notably Ricardo, this proved as evident for individual enterprise as it did for corporate, public and imperial enterprise (Beckstein, 2019; Pasinetti, 1981, pp. 91–93). Apologists for growth have consistently and successfully argued that only an ever-growing pie can preempt social aggression, societal collapse and the kind of zero-sum thought which engenders conclusions such as "your gain is my loss" (Foster, 1965; Johnson et al., 2018; Różycka-Tran et al., 2015; Rubin, 2003). Zero-sum thought, the classic hallmark of mercantilist economics, which Smith himself railed against, has also been on trial for crimes such as Britain's Malthusian response to the Irish Famine, the American government's broken promises to Native Americans' land rights, Canadian, Australian and South African outright sequestrations of land, the Armenian, Assyrian and Pontic Genocides, the Holodomor, the Holocaust and every genocide since.

Despite liberal attempts to prevent them, these Malthusian tragedies nevertheless occurred due to zero-sum thinking, as evident in between the lines of liberal authors as in the lines of their detractors. That's the story of this chapter.

Sinomania and Physiocracy

Western economic ideas have not always reigned supreme. Before liberalism caught on around the turn of the nineteenth century, there was a sweep of economic thinking within much of Christendom related to Western perception and admiration of China. Many manifestations of this admiration can be found in the artistic and intellectual products of the time. Perhaps the most famous is what came to be labeled as *Chinoiserie*, the 17–18th-c. European trend of Chinese-inspired design and decoration. But Western fascination with China also had a far-reaching impact on Enlightenment political and economic thought. Many early-Enlightenment thinkers saw imperial China as a more advanced civilization than the European and presented China as a model for the West before the Whiggish concept of 'historical progress' became vogue (discussed later).

This movement truly began with the return of a well-known French Jesuit missionary, Philippe Couplet, from China back to Christendom, who first translated the basic works of Confucianism into Latin. His first Parisian edition, entitled *Confucius Sinarum Philosophus* (1687), inaugurated a wave of admiration for Confucian economic thought in Latin Christendom. Soon afterward, a school of economic thought began to orbit around the Sun King, led by Francois Quesnay (labelled also the "Confucius of Europe"), who called themselves physiocrats. In his writings, Quesnay praised the Chinese reverence for traditional agrarianism (and therefore landownership) as the ultimate derivation of all wealth. The Confucianism which underpinned it all through the concept of "*wu-wei*," in his understanding, was based on the same seemingly "natural laws" he understood in Europe, which he developed into the concept of *laissez-faire*. Good governance was conceptualized as a grand agrarian bargain between the aristocracy and the monarchy to allow each to protect their interests at the zero-sum expense of the poor, landless and powerless (Dodds, 2018, pp. 47–70, esp. 54).

In another great irony of economic history, the economic idea which *isn't* typically associated with either the French or Chinese is the very one spawned in the former language and inspired by the latter. China was considered as a wealthy country in Europe, indeed one of the wealthiest in history, but as a static one, not on a course of ever-increasing development and wealth creation. This was attributed largely to its heavy restrictions on international trade and reliance on domestic agriculture—the *fengjian* feudal/tributary mode of production. However, while Enlightenment admirers of China, like Quesnay, emphasized its stability and age-old prosperity as being in keeping with "natural law," things changed as the Whiggish notion of "progress" started taking hold, coupled with a different conception of the natural order of things, namely that of *laissez-faire* economics (particularly in the sense of unimpeded commercial activity rather than the one that Quesnay had evinced in Chinese imperial policy on agriculture). The idea that merchants and planters were always locked in a zero-sum conflict of economic interests took hold (later this continued under the conflict between capital and labor for instance). As Mariana Mazzucato writes,

> The Physiocrats worried that some classes in society (the merchants and the landlords) were siphoning too much value out of the system, so that the true source of value creation - agriculture - would be hurt. This is why they called the merchants and the landlords, who they believed extracted more wealth than they created, *the sterile class*. (Mazzucato, 2020, p. 192, emphasis in the original)

Ultimately, Quesnay's Chinese-inspired physiocracy was little more than an attempt to erect a coherent, unified economic system out of feudalism. In other words, physiocracy is essentially an 18th-c. French aristocratic veneer painted over the defense of traditional feudal-landowner prestige. Consider Quesnay's logic in his seminal *Philosophie rurale* (1763):

> That one returns to the source of this payment, by following the course of the circulation of the bullion representative of the wealth in the different hands, through which it is passed, one will find that it comes uniquely from the land, which solely produces all the goods of our use. (de Mirabeau & Quesnay, 1763)

John Kenneth Galbraith was incorrect to suggest that this consideration was unique to the French landed nobility (Galbraith, 1987, p. 47). After all, the same logic is most glaringly exhibited 800 years earlier in the *prooimion* of the 10th-c. Byzantine agronomical compilation, the *Geōponika* (1895/2002): "Knowing that the polity consists of three elements – the army, the clergy, and agriculture – you have devoted no less care to the latter, which is best able to preserve human life" (p. 231).

That the greatest economic concern should be for agronomy (and by extension, land ownership) is no surprise in a world of apparently finite land, even in the late eighteenth century. Accordingly, late-18th-c. economic thinkers like the Spanish Gaspar Melchor de Jovellanos, reading early translations of Adam Smith's *Wealth of Nations*, wrote critiques of the French physiocratic feudal aristocracy, since, in reality, it was an economic charade of beneficent "natural law" built on zero-sum foundations (de Jovellanos, 1786, 1794). It's true that the derivation of wealth from land can always be improved through new crops (like the New World potato, tomato and tobacco brought to the Old World), better practices of farming and land redistribution (usually for the benefit of large landowners—called *"Binnenkolonisation"* in Prussia, *"Landesausbau"* elsewhere on the Continent, or alternatively, the "Clearances" in Britain) or better technology to dig and drain deeper mines. But ultimately, the same zero-sum assumptions about land would inevitably return.

It's on the same physiocratic assumptions that the various romantic approaches to mining in the 18–19th centuries were based. By the turn of the nineteenth century, most of the easily accessible ore had long been extracted from Old World mines and expensive new methods and technologies were required to extract more. This caused win–win obsessive romanticism and credit bubbles, just as silly and nefarious as tulipmania, railway mania or bitcoin mania. The clearest examples of this can be seen in the Americas, from the legends of El Dorado through the Gold Rushes of California and Alaska and 19–20th-c. "resource nationalism" to the present day. Besides the miner's own degree of accessibility to the wealth of the ore itself, the only major difference between old North and South American mining towns today is the degree to which they are romanticized as sites for tourism. Most North American mining towns have become repurposed for tourism. In South America, mining towns like Copiapo, Chile, are still in use for mining, but "lack the history of competing mining companies, and do not have locally established banks" (Rose, 1938; Wise & Wise, 2017). Anyone familiar with Winston Graham's *Poldark* novels (or the hit BBC series from 2015) will immediately recognize the romanticism of mining copper as the hero, Ross Poldark, makes his money honestly from the ground rather than dishonestly like the villain, George Warleggan, through usurious banking and other sinister, zero-sum schemes.

Alternatively, consider the romanticism of the less familiar Greek mines in the creation and bursting of the bubble that went down in history as *Lavreotika* (1869–1875). In the mid-1860s mining operations began in Lavrion, a place famous for its mines in antiquity and the role these played in Athenian hegemony. The widespread demand for stocks of the Lavrion mines led to an incipient, unofficial stock market in Greece; stocks were sold at cafes in the center of Athens—the

Athens stock exchange was officially established on Sofokleous Street only after Lavreotika, in 1876. But it also led to the first financial scandal in modern Greek history. Most importantly, the scandal constituted (and was considered by several contemporaries) a huge upward transfer of wealth. One of the wittiest writers and intellectuals of the time, Emmanouil Roidis (1836–1904), was among those who succumbed to the Lavrion stock mania. Even though the share-buying craze was promoted by perceptions of the situation as a win–win game, Roidis was quick to satirize the actual zero-sum underpinnings of Lavreotika when the bubble burst (Consiglio et al., 2012; Minoglou, 2002). "It is unfair, we think, for our local mining enterprises to be accused as completely sterile and unproductive, while, on the contrary, on the ruins of each and every one of them there has been erected a majestic Hall of fine marble." No one was spared from his biting remarks: big bankers and merchants for accumulating their wealth at the expense of everyone else, shareholders for being imbeciles, and himself for being one of them (as was Adam Smith when the South Sea Bubble burst) (Theotoumpis [Roidis], 1875).

Yet, wherever the mine was located, to a regime, all this mined ore either brought gold from abroad or was gold itself. Once above ground, it rejoined the age-old bullion circuit within the regime's jurisdiction or, more precisely, was paid as taxes to the regime and pittance wages to the miners while the remainder was pocketed by the new class of mining speculators, who, at the very least, had formed a symbiotic relationship with the regime and were allowed to use their wealth to invest in land and rent-seeking, just as had always been done. The major difference was that this new class of speculating and rent-seeking mine owners existed in the West, as opposed to the East.

Ultimately, the zero-sum assumptions that undergirded the eulogy of Chinese stasis were replaced with a critique of a stagnant political economy, incompatible with Whiggish progress, leveled from a free-market vantage point. In the writings of Adam Smith, the pendulum swung in the other direction, where China had to take Europe (Britain specifically) as its model. This became increasingly apparent as British merchants, supported by the British navy (in what might be called an early implementation of "state capitalism"), were able to extract increasingly favorable commercial treaties for themselves at the expense of the Qing regime, ultimately culminating in the Chinese loss of the mid-19th-c. Opium Wars and the beginning of China's "Century of Humiliation." Chinese money sucked from opium dens funded the early industries and railroads of Britain and the United States (Bradley, 2015; Rieber, 2014). The failure of ecumenical feudalism (physiocracy) occurred both in Europe and in China; it was just that citizen Capet paid the price at the foot of a guillotine over a century and a half before citizen Pu Yi died of natural causes in 1967, decades after being overthrown. They each "had the bad luck to be a historical leftover" (Behr, 1987, p. 256; The New York Times, 1967).

Frontiers, Population Valves and the Economics of Hope

Perhaps the most tragicomic episode in the sordid history of manias and bubbles of financial speculation about easily available riches at the frontiers of the ancient zero-sum social pyramid is the story of Sir Gregor MacGregor, the Catholic son of an affluent sea captain in the British East India Company. After a series of adventures in the New World fighting against the Spanish empire in Simón de Bolívar's revolutionary army, MacGregor turned up in London claiming to be the Cazique of Poyais ("cazique" comes from the Spanish word for a local tribal ruler, "cacique"), one of the supposedly newly established sovereign nations in Central America. After publishing a fictitious description of this Poyaisian El Dorado (under a pseudonym), he spent a couple of years convincing the upper and lower classes alike in London, Edinburgh and Glasgow that they could get rich (or richer) quick by investing in prospects for "globules of pure gold" and high agricultural yields in Poyais (Strangeways, 1822). Mind you, Lord Byron claimed the latter just the same in his periodic trips to London to raise investments for the Greek War of Independence around the same time. Poyais quickly became the "land of opportunity" on the London Stock Exchange. Poyaisian government bonds and land deeds were sold to gullible Londoners and particularly Scotsmen, to whom MacGregor appealed using their national pride (typical affinity fraud, which has worked just as well to convince poor men of any nation to fight and die in war). Hundreds of lower-class settlers and emigrants disembarked from two ships between 1822–1823 on the Black River Mosquito coast of present-day Honduras with little more than hopes, dreams and Poyaisian land deeds. Soon enough, hundreds died miserable deaths, succumbing to starvation, malaria and yellow fever after it became clear that it was all "the most audacious fraud in history." By the time the grim news from Honduras reached the British navy, which accordingly intercepted another several ships full of hundreds of defrauded settlers en route to Poyais, MacGregor was already in Paris playing the same game. He was imprisoned in Paris in December, 1825 and acquitted in May, 1826, later retiring comfortably in Caracas (Hasbrouck, 1927; London Quarterly Review, 1823; Sinclair, 2003/2004). The ideals of hope, profit, settling and zero-sum grifting at the American frontier have a history all their own.

The first War for Independence in the Americas was the original culmination of Scottish dreams of national sovereignty. The American Revolutionary War was the latest Protestant rich man's civil war for national sovereignty from an ecumenical empire, this time the Anglican one, in a succession back to the English Civil War (the 1860s American Civil War continued this hallowed tradition). After all, Jefferson's formula of the "pursuit of happiness" directly followed from Locke's "pursuit of property"—finite or otherwise. But Jefferson drew a major distinction between the brutally exploitative social pyramid of England and the English pursuit of property in America:

> England exhibits the most remarkable phaenomenon in the universe in the contrast between the profligacy of it's government and the probity of it's citizens. and accordingly it is now

> exhibiting an example of the truth of the maxim that virtue & interest are inseparable. it ends, as might have been expected, in the ruin of it's people. but this ruin will fall heaviest, as it ought to fall, on that hereditary aristocracy which has for generations been preparing the catastrophe. I hope we shall take warning from the example and crush in it's birth the aristocracy of our monied corporations which dare already to challenge our government to a trial of strength, and to bid defiance to the laws of their country. (Jefferson, 1816)

English lions being led by donkeys has plenty of precedence. Nevertheless, the new United States of America's seemingly infinite frontier served to catalyze an important subchapter in the history of zero-sum thinking.

Frontiers have always existed. Why did the American frontier, specifically, between Christian and pagan, Protestant and Catholic, and simultaneously between free and enslaved, engender such fantasies of unending possibilities, growth and abundance? Similar ideals were purported for the vast, seemingly empty lands in Australia and Canada. The lands were never empty but had been occupied since time immemorial by Aboriginal and indigenous peoples. Yet, the mentality of settler colonialism was, and remains, one of seeing native peoples as little more than animals. Nevertheless, it seemed that there was enough land for all the economically disenfranchised at the bottoms of the ancient social pyramids of the Old World to come and make a new start in these New Worlds, particularly in the United States (since Canada and Australia were preserved primarily for the excess population of Britain). This was also true throughout *all* the Americas (Elliott, 1998, pp. 20–26). Few thought about how to reform the social pyramids of the Old World. America would be the population valve for the Old World and the economic engine of hope for its immiserated hordes of lower castes. The idea that there was potentially unlimited wealth available ultimately manifested in land ownership was a foundational factor in the American idea. Or, in other words, steadily increasing population density, along with the economic consequences of feudal rent-seeking and the resultant necessary territorial expansion, have always been a major factor in Anglo-American history. As Noah Webster wrote in 1787:

> The power of entailing estates is more dangerous to liberty and republican government, than all the constitutions that can be written on paper, or even than a standing army. Let the people have property, and they will have power--a power that will for ever be exerted to prevent a restriction of the press, and abolition of trial by jury, or the abridgement of any other. (Webster, 1787/1968)

There was seemingly always enough room for all the poor and disenfranchised of the Old World to come to the New World to make it on their own—to buy cheap and abundant land and to settle and profit from renting it to others, or in the corporate buzzword of the time, "competency" (Vickers, 1990, pp. 3–29). This was made explicit by George Washington himself (1785): "Rather than quarrel abt territory, let the poor, the needy, & oppressed of the Earth; and those who want Land, resort to the fertile plains of our Western Country, to the second Land of promise, & there dwell in peace, fulfilling the first & great Commandment."

That didn't stop Washington himself from fighting for the English Crown and Ohio Company for investments in 80,000 hectares of land along the Ohio River during the French and Indian (or Seven Years) War. The American founding fathers were above all would-be feudal lords and land speculators who rebelled against the British because the crown sought to limit wars against native tribes caused by the wealthiest colonists stealing their land in the first place, as it did not wish to be used as their military instrument in their endeavor to buy, claim, settle and/or rent as much finite land as they could (Holton, 2021). This was why, as Aziz Rana (2011) notes, for these wealthy Anglo-American colonists, absolute freedom was an

> exclusivist ideal, accessible only to Anglo-Saxons and select Europeans, whose heritage, land practices and religion made them particularly suited to self-rule. Such exclusivism presupposed that settler security, as well as more grandiose dreams of utopian peace, required the subordination of internal and external enemies, who threatened Anglo social and political supremacy. Thus freedom and domination were bound together. (p. 97)

The French alternative model which didn't seek to gobble up as much finite land from the native tribes but focused on trade and Catholic proselytizing instead would have constituted a drastically different historical timeline, but it wasn't to be in the world Washington helped to build (Anderson, 2000; Taylor, 2001). "Washington and other land-hungry inhabitants of Virginia were keen to break out of the increasingly crowded English colonies along the eastern seaboard and seize the fertile Indian lands across the Appalachian Mountains for themselves" (Day, 2008, p. 116). At first, access to land in his newly established United States of America was exclusively available to "free white person[s] ... of good character," based on the Naturalization Act of 1790, which was itself based on the Plantation/Naturalization Act of 1740 (recall, plantation = fief), which was meant as "An Act for settling such foreign Protestants [...] in America" (Peters, 1845, p. 103). Indeed, American political economy has always been defined in terms of Whiteness, Protestantism and Individualism (even if Jews too were allowed to come to America in 1740, they have only been integrated because of a process of "whitening" and expansion of the Protestant ideal into that of "Judeo-Christianity" after WWII) (Achcar, 2024; Barkan, 1999; Brodkin, 1998; Henriques, 1907).

This was also the underpinning idea of "settler colonialism," in which natives (the noble savage) were always the "last of their kind"—as in James Fenimore Cooper's rendition of the French and Indian War in the year 1757, *The Last of the Mohicans* (1826). White Protestant immigrants and settlers were continually permitted to claim land, always at the expense of the native Americans (Cooper, 1826; Dunbar-Ortiz, 2014; Smith & Warrior, 1996). The early-19th-c. dissolution of the Iroquois Nation and the settlement of Upstate New York by land-hungry White Protestant New England settlers was a case in point (although far from the only one). Similarly, settler colonialism and Protestant economic liberalism went hand in hand. The Philadelphian Protestant Henry Charles Carey, who published Fenimore's *Last of the Mohicans*, was also one of the earliest Americans to promote

Smithian growth (liberal economic expansion) as the primary political economy for the new American Republic (Carey, 1837). Of course, the seemingly infinite land available for individual ownership was only part of the ledger: in fact there was a finite amount of land to sequester from the natives, and by the time the American frontier was officially closed around the turn of the twentieth century, the process of the rent-seeking feudalization (over-extraction, exploitation, etc.) of the American population accelerated in earnest—with Vanderbilt, Rockefeller, JP Morgan, and so forth.

The same Protestant zero-sum logic of land enclosures and clearances in the British Isles and on the Continent was brutally replicated in the fledgling United States after the War of 1812 with White Protestant settlers up to the Mississippi River. In fact, the Andrew Jackson administration's entire policy toward the native Americans rested on the same zero-sum logic of land ownership, as evident in his letter to the Creek nation on March 23, 1829:

> In my talk to you in the Creek nation, many years ago, I told you of this new country, where you might be preserved as a great nation, and where your white brothers would not disturb you. In that country, your father, the President, now promises to protect you, to feed you, and to shield you from all encroachment. Where you now live your white brothers have always claimed the land. The land beyond the Mississippi belongs to the President, and to none else; and he will give it to you for ever. (Jackson, 1829)

It is a historians' consensus (almost cliché) that Uncle Sam's broken promises of favorable land grants (now small, impoverished or casino-based reservations) to the native Americans go far back (Calloway, 2008). Events like these American enclosures occurred with surprising regularity throughout the 19–20th centuries across the planet:

> ... populations were forcibly removed en masse from settings where their production and labor were illegible and inappropriable and were relocated in colonies and plantations where they could be made to grow cash crops (tea, cotton, sugar, indigo, coffee) which might contribute to the profits of landowners and the fiscal power of the state. (Scott, 2009, pp. 10–11)

Yet, due to the seemingly infinite land available to settle, the entire idea of America always rested on infinite wealth and abundance, gradually reaching almost mythical status by the late nineteenth century. There need be no contradiction between the foundation of American principles in both 1619 and 1776; coming to the New World and actually eking out a living in it (if not prospering at the zero-sum expense of many others) was always a morally ambiguous affair (Willick, 2021). Of course now we know that the streets were never paved with gold. There was never enough gold for everyone in the first place. If there had been, in a system where value is predicated on scarcity, the gold itself would have been worthless anyway.

The Malthusian Challenge

As in the Old World, however, zero-sum logic dictated that the freedom available to the White man came at the expense of the Black man. Black Africans were still chattel slaves brought to the Americas by the thousands for their cheap labor which padded the agricultural and mining profits of the landowners and their shareholders in London, Stockholm, Copenhagen, Paris, Lisbon or Madrid—lest we forget their construction of the White House and other American monuments. The hope of freedom on the frontier was never available to Black Africans; their hope of escape lay chiefly in the other direction, as manifested in Hans Jonatan's story from enslavement to freedom.

Born to a Black slave woman in 1784 in the Danish West Indies, owned by Heinrich Ludvig Ernst von Schimmelmann, Hans came to Copenhagen with his owner in 1801. After escaping and joining the Danish navy in the First Battle of Copenhagen against the British, he received his freedom, only to be indicted by Heinrich's wife Henriette Catharina on the grounds that he was still her slave. He argued in court that Danish law prohibited slavery. Ultimately, her argument, that slavery was only prohibited in Denmark proper but permitted in the New World, won out given her Whiteness and assurance that she had planned to sell him back in St. Croix. He escaped a second time, this time to Iceland, where he married and lived out his days until 1827 as a free, albeit peasant farmer (Loftsdóttir & Pálsson, 2013; Pálsson, 2016). Denmark, like the other Protestant national empires, quietly continued to ignore that its freedom and prosperity was paid for at the expense of the Black slaves its citizens owned across the ocean, until by 1878, it could no longer.

> The wealth of the colonial era is [still] visible in the elegant Rococo and Baroque mansions of Copenhagen. The first tribute to the people who suffered to create that wealth appeared on April 2, [2018], when a statue was unveiled of a black woman [named Mary Thomas] who led a [..] rebellion against Danish rule on St. Croix [in 1878]. (Sorensen, 2018)

During a time before the widespread abolition of slavery, the prosperity or freedom of thousands of von Schimmelmanns in the Old World rested in the enslavement of millions of Hans Jonatans and Mary Thomases in the New World. There's good reason why the ancient expression "out of sight, out of mind" is so timeless. Early on in the nineteenth century, this was understood by the subsequent economists to come to grips with the downstream brutal realities of Adam Smith's liberal ideas about profit put into action. For example, by formally recognizing that "profits depend on high or low wages, wages on the price of necessaries, and the price of necessaries chiefly on the price of food, because all other requisites may be increased almost without limit," David Ricardo and other post-Smith abolitionist economists recognized the zero-sum logic that the maximization of the profit of the merchant or shareholder was contingent on the minimization of the cost of labor—and slave labor was by far the most profitable (Ricardo, 1817/2010, Chapters V,

XXVI). Or as Percy Bysshe Shelley wrote in 1821 (pertaining to the Matthew Effect, from the Parable of the Talents at Matthew 25:29):

> To him that hath, more shall be given; and from him that hath not, the little that he hath shall be taken away. The rich have become richer, and the poor have become poorer; and the vessel of the State is driven between the Scylla and Charybdis of anarchy and despotism. (Shelley, 1839/1840, pp. 42–43)

Therefore, even though post-Smith economists sung the songs of free trading and free markets leading to greater liberty and prosperity, they recognized that these came with costs which would best be paid by other people: millions of enslaved Blacks in the New World or millions of peasants in other lands altogether. The most prominent of these economists was Thomas Malthus, whose concept of rent was derided by Ricardo as "infirm," and who nevertheless theorized that there are finite resources (primarily grain), which humans, reproducing at a potentially infinite rate, will eventually outstrip and therefore fight over, with clear-cut victors and vanquished (Malthus, 1798). Such logic presupposes that most agrarian societies operated according to the ancient zero-sum social pyramid wherein the peasants or slaves at the base would reproduce at an unsustainable rate were it not for the ruling classes extracting the surplus production. Therefore, in Malthusian calculations, it is always necessary for the ruling classes to extract the maximum share of surplus production from the lower classes in order to ensure limitations of their ability to reproduce (Tisdell & Svizzero, 2020, pp. 202–227). Unsurprisingly, Karl Marx called him a "lackey of the bourgeois" (Neurath, 1994, p. 5), as his principles are the ruling-class version of zero-sum thinking, which could be easily used to attack or divide dissenters, lower classes and minorities.

Consider the case of Joseph Priestley, born into a comfortably affluent family of Protestant dissenters against royal Anglicanism (its own form of ecumenical sovereignty), who met a like-minded Scotsman in the figure of James Keir when he arrived in Birmingham in 1780 and promptly joined the Lunar society of wealthy early industrialists and philosophers with the likes of Matthew Boulton, James Watt and Erasmus Darwin. A lifelong intellectual, Priestley was invited to a fancy dinner party at the Royal Hotel in Birmingham by Keir to commemorate the second anniversary of the storming of the Bastille (14 July, 1791) as "Friends of Freedom." Fired into a fit of rage against this display of out-of-touch liberal intelligentsia, and egged on by local landowners who maintained the Anglican potlatch system, the lower classes rioted in Sparkhill, destroying Priestley's and several other Lunar Society member's homes, along with a Quaker meeting house, in the name of "King and Country," who were furious at this "inner elite of magnates." Priestley eventually took his family and inherited money to America in 1794, and finally settled in Pennsylvania, buying 300,000 acres of land to be leased or sold (with interest) in 400-acre plots (Martineau, 1997; Rose, 1960, esp. p. 70; Sheps, 1989). To this day, one of his most famous works is entitled *An Account of a Society for Encouraging the Industrious Poor*, an early exposition of the classic British division of the poor (divide-and-rule tactics) into "strivers and shirkers," as routinely chronicled in *The Guardian* (An Account of a Society1787; Jowit, 2013). This was an early expression of "producerism," a set of ideas that hold that society can be divided into classes of producers and consumers (makers and takers); accordingly, the former should always be advantaged at the zero-sum expense of the latter.

The earliest clearcut example of Malthusian limitations on access to food and land for the peasants of England after Wellington's victory at Waterloo can be seen in the infamous "Corn Laws" of 1817, which limited England's imports of grain in order to artificially keep prices high, benefiting the landed nobility who controlled access to grain in early oligopolies. The resulting rioting of starving peasants in Manchester's St. Peter's field was crushed by British cavalrymen, who killed 18 and injured hundreds. Later known as the Peterloo massacre, this was Britain's Malthusian warm-up to its response to the Irish Potato Blight, in which the British governor of Ireland, Sir Charles Trevelyan, forbade any relief for the starving Irish in order to thin the Catholic population and make more room for the Protestant settlers from England as well as discipline or at least proselytize Protestantism among the supposedly prolifically reproducing Catholics (Fahey, n.d.; Fogarty, 2014; Smith, 1962; The Great Irish Famine Online, n.d.).

Similar policies can be evinced in the distribution of finite land for 19th-c. treaties and then broken promises toward native populations by governments like the United States, Canada, Australia and South Africa, where outright sequestrations of land were more common for the benefit of White Protestant settlers. By extension, European colonies in 19th-c. Africa displayed similar policies as well as the American policy of redlining based on Blackness and Whiteness in the 1930s–60s. Are 21st-c. Israeli policies in East Jerusalem or Hebron so different? Every round of land reform (clearances, redistribution or both) is predicated on the zero-sum logic of finite land, which, in multiethnic societies, usually results in gains for members of one ethnic group at the expense of another (Albertus, 2021a, 2021b).

In every case, the previous status quo was both a cause and an effect of the violence and instability it would take to reform it—and land reform was at the center of the issue. Thomas Skidmore's 1829 treatise "The Rights of Man to Property! Being a Proposition to Make It Equal Among the Adults of the Present Generation" begins with a blunt statement of his position: "One thing must be obvious to the plainest understanding; that as long as property is unequal; or rather, as long as it is so enormously unequal, as we see it at present, that those who possess it, will live on the labor of others, and themselves perform none, or if any, a very disproportionate share, of that toil which attends them as a condition of their existence, and without the performance of which, they have no just right to preserve or retain that existence, even for a single hour." For Skidmore, Malthus' eternal underlying zero-sum conflict was truly about labor and ownership—he occupied an ideological midpoint between Malthus and Marx. Thus, it is not possible, Skidmore asserts, to "maintain a doctrine to the contrary of this position, without, at the same time, maintaining an absurdity no longer tolerated in enlightened countries;

that a part, and that a very great part, of the human race, are doomed, of right, to the slavery of toil, while others are born, only to enjoy." Skidmore was not a political theorist. He was, at the time of his writing, a machinist who had taken a prominent role in the newly formed New York Working Men's Party. He wrote its platform, which included a call for land redistribution to every man and unmarried woman over the age of 21, an end to commercial monopolies and an end to the hereditary transfer of wealth. His ideas germinated directly in the Anti-Rent War (also known as the Helderberg War), a tenants' revolt in upstate New York from 1839 to 1845—and commonly deemed the "end of feudalism" in New York State. It was the same reason why, at the time, Pierre-Joseph Proudhon proudly proclaimed that "Property is theft!" Such zero-sum analysis explains why even in the twenty-first century, economists like Paul Krugman and Daniel Susskind consider that "Malthus was right about the whole of human history up until his own era" (Krugman, 2008; Susskind, 2024, pp. 11–28, 241). The German phrase encapsulated the entire ethos of the working classes vs the bourgeoisie classes in 1848: "the freedom to read vs the freedom to feed."

Christian morality remained the major engine of resistance to both Malthusian law-of-the-jungle doctrines and movements toward land reform—especially among Christian thinkers in Europe and America. The resistance to the seeming repugnance of Malthus' ideas was mirrored in central Europe by resistance to those of Kant, Fichte and Hegel as well—devoid as they remain of moral guidance. The scale of the sacrifice of Christian morality at the altar of politico-economic utility (not to mention moral relativism) led the poet Heinrich Heine to prophesy the rise of Nazism in 1834 and the scholar Robert Heilbroner to profile the zero-sum thinking in the rise of Nazism in 1996 (Heilbroner, 1995, p. 8; Kossoff, 1983, p. 126).

Even if the zero-sum logic inherent in Malthus' reasoning was primarily economic, it also played a role in the chauvinism of ethnic cleansing and genocide, as in the case of the British government's response to the Catholic Irish during the Potato Blight, and even throughout the 20th c. Whether or not governments passively or ineffectually tried to avert these Malthusian miseries, plausibly denied their role in them or actively implemented them, they nevertheless occurred as a direct result of the ruling-class zero-sum thinking at the heart of Malthusianism. Regardless of whether Malthus can ultimately be vindicated or vilified, his zero-sum ideas are still with us today, and they manifest across the board, as their espousal in Michael Moore's documentary *Planet of the Humans* (2019) suggest (Harris, 2020; Mann, 2018; Ridley, 2015).

The Myth of Linear Industrial Progress

> For those who live inside a myth, it seems a self-evident fact. Human progress is a fact of this kind. If you accept it you have a place in the grand march of humanity. Humankind is, of course, not marching anywhere. (Gray, 2013, p. 12)

Malthus' are not the only ideas from this historically pivotal era which have had such an unusually long afterlife. If Malthusianism represents the intellectual embodiment of ruling-class zero-sum thinking, then Whiggism represents the exact opposite: eternal optimism and belief in a long, linear march of history progressing ever further toward liberty and prosperity. As Daniel Susskind summarizes, "Adam Smith, David Ricardo and John Stuart Mill ... took for granted in their work the prospect of an impending 'stationary state'," which, each in their own way, sought to escape through the political-economic concept of "progress." Hence, in the era of Malthus, the birth of the progressivism fetish was simultaneously the birth of the Law of Diminishing Returns (Susskind, 2024, pp. 30–37, 242–245).

To this day, the Latin word "Excelsior," which every New York schoolkid must learn means "ever upward," is emblazoned as the motto on the New York state coat of arms and flag (in use 1777, adopted 1778), and flanked by the goddesses Liberty and blindfolded Justice, crown underfoot, bearing the Phrygian cap, sword, scales and standing astride a shield showing the deified Hudson River (or Atlantic Ocean) before the mountains of New York state (typically Mount Beacon), with the rising sun above and an eagle on top of a hemisphere over all (Laws of New York, 2020). The religious heraldry is hard to miss.

Over the course of the seventeenth and eighteenth centuries, overtly religious symbols and ideas of historical development were largely replaced with the Enlightenment idea of progress in much of Western (primarily Protestant) Christendom. In a later instance of US civic symbolism, installed in mid-18th-c. Washington, the Senate is adorned with a pediment titled "Progress of Civilization" (Day, 2008, p. 143). Today, the Enlightenment narrative of historical progress still suffuses countless history books—especially those focusing on economic history, for example by the much-celebrated Niall Ferguson: "Though the line of financial history has a saw-tooth quality, its trajectory is unquestionably upwards" (Ferguson, 2008, p. 358). Yet despite its secular pretensions, the Enlightenment concept of progress had its own religious undertones and implications. It was not just economically or geographically deterministic but incorporated previously religious elements of utopianism or even apocalypticism (such as in the Catholic writings of Thomas Moore and the Protestant writings of John Milton), seeing history as moving in the direction of an inevitable endtime, which could resemble either heaven or hell. However, the Enlightenment ideals of particularly English thinkers gradually abandoned the hellish eschatology and embraced the heavenly. They moreover functioned as a general framework for understanding the world and the passing of time, just as religious systems had done before, but now, like Protestantism, they were detached from the ecumenical church and instead secularized.

As a result, the idea of progress influenced the way mechanization and industrialization was framed from the very beginning of what came to be termed as the "industrial revolution." Industrial development was seen as unequivocally positive (in the eyes of the entrepreneurial class/bourgeois, not the working classes/proletariat), contributing to or being part of the overall trajectory of history toward inevitable human progress (Susskind, 2024, pp. 47–53). Every major phase of transition to new technologies has subsequently claimed the title of a "revolution," as the idea of "the industrial revolution" was constructed from the Whig idealization of history as the ever upward and forward progress of history to greater aggregate human wealth, prosperity and freedom (Butterfield, 1931/1965; Mayr, 1990; Torr, 2000).

Simultaneously, the Whig version of history seeks to *learn from history so as not to repeat it*, but, like all highways to hell paved with good intentions, the right lessons haven't been learned so much as mixed up—due to the underlying simplicity of the Whig model of history itself. Given the historical parallels commonly drawn between various historical eras of plague and disease, one of the most striking examples of the Whiggish conception of history lies in the ever less nuanced interpretation of the mid-14th-c. Bubonic Plague and the socio-economic revolutions it supposedly portended.

From the early nineteenth century, English-language historiographies soon became rife with ideas about how serfdom was abolished in England in the sixteenth century shortly before Catholicism and how the "middle classes" were created from a very early period—usually as a consequence of the fourteenth-century Black Death. "The Black Death was the prehistory both of enclosure and of the Reformation" (James, 2011). Unfortunately these accounts elide the facts that English serfs and peasants fulfilled the same socio-economic roles, that the English peasant and proletariat classes remained for centuries later—arguably even until today and that the Black Death had similar effects across all of Latin Christendom (not just England).

Such interpretations of the mid-14th-c. Bubonic Plague is rather about the period of their composition than about the period they examine and occurs more commonly in thought-piece journalism than rigorous historical inquiry (North, 2021). Pandemics such as during the mid-fourteenth century didn't completely and permanently alter the social fabric: "by the time later epidemics hit, the elite had found ways to preserve their fortunes and even their health" (Wade, 2020). The ruling classes and the church still ruled and the peasants may have briefly had more leverage but the pyramidal social structure was still zero-sum, even if one generation of peasants had more leverage in the rural labor market. If the zero-sum underpinnings of the economies affected by the Plague were made clearer through the temporary payment increases of the peasantry due to labor shortage, another side-effect of the pandemic had much more lasting and markedly zero-sum repercussions: "Although the Black Death caused short-term losses for Europe's largest companies, in the long term, they concentrated their assets and gained a greater share of the market and influence with governments" (Bell et al., 2020, pp. 35–42; Russell & Parker, 2020).

In a way the early 19th-c. historical revisionism of the Black Death is still here with us today. The 19th-c. story went that the Black Death had made way for greater labor rights for English serfs and peasants, followed by the demise of feudalism under the great Protestant queen Elizabeth I, and then by the magnanimity of the British empire, which brought freedom, prosperity and civilization to all the darkened corners of the earth (in a highly melanin-conscious sense as Rudyard Kipling's "White Man's Burden" indicates). How far removed from the

19th-c. narrative is a contemporary take on the historical consequences of the Plague such as this? "As modern research is increasingly making clear, the roots of the industrial revolution of the eighteenth century lay in the industrious revolution of the post-plague world: as productivity rose, aspirations were cast upwards and levels of disposable wealth increased along with opportunities to spend it" (Frankopan, 2015). Yet such an interpretation begs another, more important question: if the Bubonic Plague wiped out millions all across Afro-Eurasia around the mid-fourteenth century, why did it have such a special effect on a tiny island in the far northwest of Europe, thereby explaining the industrial revolution nearly half a millennium later? The referenced research here doesn't even mention the 14th-c. Bubonic Plague. Although, it *does* discuss the beginnings of the industrial revolution (de Vries, 1994; van Zanden, 2002).

Undoubtedly, a fundamental change occurred in the method and mode of production in the early nineteenth century in England and the emerging United States of America (largely in the northern states such as Connecticut, Massachusetts and New York). A period of incredible economic transition shifted a largely agrarian society of peasants and landlords to an industrial society of proletarians, factory managers and owners. This is pretty well-known as the Whigs' much-heralded industrial revolution, but it did little for improving the miserable living conditions of the working poor of the mid-nineteenth century, which so inspired (and revolted) Friedrich Engels and his associates for decades afterward (Engels, 1844/1892).

But what exactly made it a revolution? Gottfried Wilhelm Leibniz defined a revolution as "overarching, ultimately irreversible movement" (Koselleck, 2006, p. 247). Yet, the "industrial revolution" did not fundamentally change political-economic relations between workers/peasants and the ruling classes. The only concrete way that liberal industrial growth "revolutionized" political relations was that vacancies were newly created at the ruling table for the merchants (Harcourt et al., 2017–2018). Otherwise, liberalism's real success during this era was only due to capital's willingness to pay its laborers more than in other nations, which allowed these national commonwealths to expand. Calling it a "revolution" looked like avoiding a political revolution by labelling the phenomenon an economic one (Susskind, 2024, pp. 182–185).

Elsewhere, liberal economic growth was obstructed by very real limits imposed by the beneficiaries of agrarian (feudal) production and the old monarchies and aristocracies of Europe. As Alexander I of Russia marched with his surviving conscripted peasants and mounted Cossacks, bows and arrows slung from their shoulders, into Paris in 1813 and forced Napoleon to abdicate the throne, suddenly, the Parisian population had become royalists. In the United States, as northern liberalism (along with abolitionism) increasingly threatened the "Southern way of life" throughout the 1830s–1850s, the scions and representatives of agrarian Southern landowning slavers resisted the encroachments of northern-originated industrial policies like tariffs and other measures which they worried jeopardized the source of their wealth. As the historian Charles Sellers observed, the root cause of increasingly ossified oligarchies in the United States was the finite amount of wealth which could be extracted from the land on either side of the Mason-Dixon line, and control of the economic markets was tantamount to control of the political markets: "Republican ambiguity was rooted in the constitution, which made American politics a zero-sum game by requiring an electoral majority to win the potent presidency" (Sellers, 1994, p. 38). Otherwise, had Southern planters adopted liberal industrialism *en masse*, there might not have been a Civil War in the first place. But it was not to be. The myth of industrialism as "revolutionary" is very clearly demonstrated by the outbreak of the American Civil War (Atkeson & Kehoe, 2007; Hillstrom & Hillstrom, 2005; Kornblith, 1998; Licht, 1995).

It's not that the mechanization of production was a myth by itself—this was largely true for both of the first two periods of industrialized production in the early and the late parts of the nineteenth century (Appleby, 2010; Chandler & Hikino, 1990; Hobsbawm, 1999; Hull, 1996; Kranzberg & Pursell, 1967; Landes, 2003; Mokyr & Strotz, 1999). However, the headiness of the era was unevenly distributed; it was the sole fiefdom of the industrialists. On the other half of the ledger, the millions of artisans (cobblers, butchers, coopers, smiths, potters, etc.) who had previously worked for themselves and local outfitters gradually became low-wage workers in warehouses, slaughterhouses and factories (Laurie, 1989). The zero-sum implications of mechanization were not lost on Eric Hobsbawm, who saw in Luddite machine-breaking a form of "collective bargaining by riot" (Hobsbawm, 1952, pp. 57–70). You'd think that as the efficiency of the consumption of resources (such as coal or other fossil fuels) increases, then demand would decrease, but you'd be wrong—as efficiency increases, paradoxically so too does demand. This was noted in the mid-nineteenth century by English economist William Stanley Jevons, and named after him—the "Jevons Paradox." In fact, like the myth of trickle-down economics which is believed, like a tide, to raise all boats, Jevons demonstrated a far greater truth of economic history: the greater the consumption, the greater the demand for consumption—and the fewer resources for ever fewer people to consume (Alcott, 2005; Bauer & Papp, 2009; York & McGee, 2016). So, instead, the *real* myth is that the mechanization of production would fulfill the Whiggish promise of ever greater historical progress, liberty and prosperity for all.

Liberalism Confronts Slavery

Before the workers could be enfranchised, the tens of millions of serfs and slaves across the world had never stopped yearning or fighting for freedom from their exploited position in the brutal social pyramids into which they were born. And just as ruling-class abolitionism became fashionable among would-be liberals like João Carlos Pereira Leite (the Brazilian feudal landlord of the "fazenda jacobina" in Mato Grosso), would-be Spartacuses like Vitório Sule found dissension even within their own ranks—including their very wives.

Such a wife to Vitório Sule was Sabina da Cruz during the Malê Slave Revolt of Bahia in Brazil in 1835. Overhearing her husband discussing plans for an Islamic slave revolt against their Christian owners, she reported the information to a confidant and freedwoman named Guilhermina. Guilhermina promptly informed the authorities further up the social pyramid about Vitório, the "straw boss" of the slave revolt. When they prematurely confronted the slaves later that night in Ladeira da Praça, Salvador, a fight ensued and Vitório was killed. The needless pain caused is compounded by the tragic irony of her actions. Imagine the hopelessness contained in her tears over her husband's broken body—which embodied a movement for her own emancipation (Reis, 1835/1995, pp. 74, 129, 184–185, 249). Contrary to what nineteenth-century British utilitarian ethicists (and economists) would have us believe, humans have never acted entirely according to their own best interests—in fact often quite the opposite.

Why else would tens of thousands of well-heeled liberal abolitionists (many of them Whigs) abandon their inherited economic interests when it was widely, if grudgingly understood that their own prosperity and privilege (directly or indirectly) derived from the enslavement of millions of others? Many were motivated by genuine faith in divine justice—a faith which *always* requires the toppling of the prosaic pyramid. Zero-sum logic was never exclusively relegated to the enslaved when everyone is confined within the same pyramid. Faith-based or otherwise, such liberal sentiments drove the cause of abolitionism for generations across the globe, from the Jacobin feudal landlords of Mato Grosso (who supported the Sabinada abolitionist revolt in 1837) to the financial supporters of British abolitionists like Frederick Douglas and William Wilberforce, to the well-fed supporters of Russian liberals like Nikolay Alexeyevich Milyutin, agitating against Russian serfdom.

The United States was not the only government attempting to liberalize its economy toward industrial expansion and finding out that it was impossible without wrestling with the age-old systems of slavery, serfdom and feudalism. In line with his ideals, Napoleon had previously abolished feudalism in France only to brutally try (and fail) to impose slavery in his possessions in the Caribbean, i.e. Haiti. His successors did impose debt imprisonment on the Haitians however, and by the time the Bourbons were restored, slavery still continued (Girard, 2005; Sévillia, 2003, p. 256). America was in fact unexceptional: the same residues of feudalism, serfdom and slavery remained in Brazil, Japan, as well as several other ecumenical empires such as those of dynasties like the Hanoverians, Ottomans, Habsburgs, Qing and Romanovs.

The liberalization reforms which included political, economic and social programs in Japan and the Ottoman empire were known as the Meiji and Tanzimat, which also accompanied the popularization of the Ottoman imperial political economy (Pamuk, 2009). The push toward Japanese liberalism was an especially striking case study since it stemmed from primarily one incident in 1853 when the US admiral Matthew Perry pulled into Tokyo harbor and fired a 21-gun salute. In Brazil, pressure toward the abolition of slavery began mounting in the 1830s with several failed slave revolts, resulting in its eventual abolition in 1850 with the passage of the Eusébio de Queirós Law—aimed more at prosaically preserving the status quo than subverting it (Graden, 1987, pp. 249–282). For everything to stay the same, everything had to change.

The other major empire which personally belonged to the Romanov family, Russia, began its wrestling match with economic liberalization and abolishing serfdom since the turn of the nineteenth century before Alexander I faced down the guns of Borodino and the cause was accelerated and animated by the Decembrist uprising against the accession of Nicholas I in 1825. It was already a priority at the outset of the Crimean War (1853–1856), and in the wake of defeat and humiliation it had already become a platitudinous piety of polite society when Alexander II fully committed so that by 1861, he was known as the Liberator. In fact, there were sweeps of rumors across the Russian empire throughout the 1850s that Czar Nicholas was offering emancipation for any serf who wished to join the army to fight in the War (especially against the British Light Brigade at Balaklava) (Bugler Martin Landfried, 1890). Ironically, so many Russian serfs requested to be conscripted that the army was overwhelmed by the sheer number of serfs seeking emancipation in this way, and was forced into crushing these uprisings of the very Russian serfs who so desperately sought to join them (Moon, 1992, pp. 691–704).

By comparison, the upending of China's fengjian Confucian feudal system, temporarily beset by the Taiping Rebellion and loss of the Opium Wars with Britain, wouldn't also arrive successfully until the early twentieth century (Chesneaux, 1973, pp. 23–24; Curwen, 1977; Kuhn, 1970; Lee & Campbell, 1998; Michael, 1966, pp. 4–16; Rhee, 2007; Spence, 1996; Wagner, 1982; Wu, 1952). No matter whether 10 or 20 million died in Taiping's arguably bloodiest civil war in human history, the land and labor legal reforms that followed were still endorsed by the leadership of the concurrent International Workingmen's Association. And they directly inspired Sun Yatsen's republican revolution a couple of generations later (Hayford, 2018, pp. 90–126; Wang, 2024; Youwen, 1973). In the meantime, the ecumenical Eurasian empires did not need to simultaneously wrestle with the vested interests of slave owners due to their divine-right and absolute monarchies. However, the price was still paid in blood just as it was in the aspirationally democratic United States.

Nevertheless, popular liberal abolitionism was steadily growing throughout the 1840s–70s across Eurasia and the Americas. With the apparent success of industrialization (and the profits from wage-driven manufacturing outweighing those of slave/serf-driven agriculture), the mid-19th-c. forces of liberalism were coming for the forces of enslavement the world over. The real reason the pagan or Christian Roman Empires (namely Byzantium and the Holy Roman Empire) never industrialized wasn't for lack of interest in or imagination of new technologies so much as for their zero-sum political-economic models, which relied on slavery, serfdom or peasantries and therefore didn't require industrialization. In the United States of America, which never ultimately resolved the internal contradictions within Whig history of ever-increasing liberty, freedom and justice, the continued reliance on slave labor seemingly ad infinitum was enough to break the party for good by the outset of the Civil War in 1860—being replaced by Abraham Lincoln's Republican party.

The American Civil War, fought by Marxist Prussian-American men like August Willich to destroy slavery, was equally a labor revolt against the concentrated capital of the southern landowning oligarchs of their day (Chan, 2017). Their combined market share was termed by 19th-c. thinkers as "slave power": "The 'slave power' thesis was the belief that a slaveholding oligarchy ran the United States for its own benefit. It had ruled the nation for decades, went the argument, and now intended to expand slavery across the continent and even further into the North" (Bouie, 2022). The slave oligarchy is not a recent conception limited to the 21st-c. pages of the NYT either. The first Republican platform in Pittsburgh (1856) denounced how the US constitution had been "resolved upon the dethronement of the principles of republicanism and the establishment in their stead of an oligarchy, bound together by a common interest in the ownership of slaves" (The New York Times, 1856). The slave oligarchs, utilizing the new technology of the cotton gin, had gobbled up as much finite land as possible in order to cement their status at the top of the American social pyramid. Even the *History Channel* acknowledges that by 1860, such dynasties comprised about 1% of the Confederacy's population, even if between 26–32% of the White confederate population owned slaves in various slave states (Pruitt, 2016; *Selected Statistics...*, n.d.). The only political market share left outside the landowning planters' dominions in the Democratic party belonged to the Know-Nothings' bigotry. How did the plantation owners manage to convince millions of poor White farmers, most with few if any slaves at all, to fight and die in a rich man's war to preserve an institution against their own interests? Banal bigotry of course—or as Lincoln articulated the false dichotomy between the Democrats and the Know-Nothings:

> As a nation we began by declaring that 'all men are created equal.' When the Know-Nothings get control, it will read 'all men are created equal, except Negroes and foreigners and Catholics.' When it comes to this, I shall prefer emigrating to some country where they make no pretense of loving liberty - to Russia, for instance, where despotism can be taken pure, and without the base alloy of hypocrisy. (Lincoln, 1855)

Aside from "states' rights," poor southern Whites were told it was about preserving the racial hierarchy of the zero-sum pyramid. No matter how poor a White man might be, he was still above the Black man; in other words, a pyramidal potlatch system of institutionalized racism maintained him and he would fight—and die if necessary—to preserve it. By opposing slavery, the labor leaders and unionist soldiers of the era fought to destroy the corrosive effect that slavery had on the price of labor of all workers (Richards, 2000). It was not for nothing that Abraham Lincoln passed the "Anti-Coolie Act" ("An Act to Prohibit the 'Coolie Trade' by American Citizens in American vessels") in February 1862, in order to prohibit American slave lords from importing cheap foreign indentured labor (Chinese or Indian "coolies") to replace or reinforce the racialized labor hierarchy. Paradoxically, it was only in destroying slavery (and the Whig party itself) that liberalism finally made some hesitating progress toward prosperity for all. In other words, liberalism was the phoenix which arose from the ashes of both Whiggism *and* slavery.

Similarly, no matter how many northern carpetbaggers ventured south in search of business opportunities to get rich at the zero-sum expense of the defeated Confederates, it didn't change the overall economic calculus of industrialization. Wage slaves ("coolies" of whatever race) or chattel slaves still occupied the same place in the zero-sum pyramid even if managing the uppitiness of the former was more profitable than the docility of the latter; the ingredients were tweaked and substitutions made, but the recipe wasn't significantly altered. Slave labor could be exploited either in the cotton fields or in the factory—but the latter guaranteed more returns of investment than the former, precisely because workers received a pittance in wages. Liberalism, with or without industrialization, has never been very different from feudalism or mercantilism except insofar that it promises economic expansion and rarely delivers it. But the system itself only differs based on various amounts of human exploitation. The poorly paid coolies and industrial workers were at risk of injury or death in a warehouse fire or machinery accident just as peasants, serfs and slaves were terrorized by the whip, the chain and the noose.

As liberal emancipatory and abolitionist movements triumphantly arose in cities across the world, rural serfs and slaves did not always behave as their beneficent, upper-class abolitionist compatriots expected, instead often turning to their priests and erstwhile masters for guidance in their newfound freedom (and responsibility for their own hunger), rather than the abstract ideals of the intelligentsia and their frequently (though not always) champagne-soaked sociological critiques of capital with thinkers like Lassalle essentially straddling the fence between the liberals and the socialists. (Lassalle, 1863) Lincoln himself was for much of his political career portrayed as a flip-flopper, fence-sitter and rail-splitter. Gradually and peacefully or immediately and violently, in one part of the world or many, slavery was replaced: in the countrysides, sharecropping substituted slavery (again, little different from old-fashioned lord-and-peasant rent-seeking feudalism); in the cities, wages became the new form of peasanthood, whose meek earners early socialists called the proletariat—a word dug from the pages of Livy. This was the real legacy of the failure of Reconstruction: the liberation from serfdom and slavery remained incomplete due to the prioritization of the income of their wealthy patrons and benefactors in a restructured zero-sum potlatch system. Or, as the sociologist W. E. B. du Bois (1935) called it, a "counter revolution of property" after the American Civil War.

Now the price of the labor of free men would be cast in opposition to the price of labor of the recently freed serfs and slaves. Not only that, the wages of the sharecroppers and proletarians came in direct opposition to the income of the landowners and factory owners—in their own zero-sum argument, their ability to create more jobs for more workers. For precisely this reason, as the job-creating class, they would always lobby governments to allow them to pay their workers less and less (which of course allowed them to take more and more—a continuation of the liberal myth of trickle-down economics). This was the true impact of liberalism's triumph over slavery. Based on the works of economists like Ricardo and Lassalle, we call this zero-sum state of affairs the "iron law of wages" (Baumol, 1983).

References

Achcar, G. (2024, March 21). The whitening of European Jews and the misuse of Holocaust memory. *Verso*. https://www.versobooks.com/blogs/news/the-whitening-of-european-jews-and-the-misuse-of-holocaust-memory

Albertus, M. (2021a, April 11). How authoritarians turn rural areas into their strongholds. *The Atlantic*. https://www.theatlantic.com/ideas/archive/2021/04/how-land-reform-underpins-authoritarian-regimes/618546

Albertus, M. (2021b). *Property without rights: Origins and consequences of the property rights gap*. Cambridge University Press.

Alcott, B. (2005). Jevons' paradox. *Ecological Economics, 54*(1), 9–21. https://doi.org/10.1016/j.ecolecon.2005.03.020

An Account of a Society for Encouraging the Industrious Poor. (1787). Pearson and Rollason.

Anderson, F. (2000). *Crucible of war: The Seven Years' War and the fate of empire in British North America, 1754–1766*. Knopf Doubleday Publishing Group.

Anonymous. (1823). The Poyais bubble. *London Quarterly Review, 28*, 158–161.

Appelbaum, D. M. (2013). Biblical nationalism and the sixteenth-century states. *National Identities, 15*(4), 317–332. https://doi.org/10.1080/14608944.2013.814624

Appleby, J. O. (2010). *The relentless revolution: A history of capitalism*. Norton.

Atkeson, A., & Kehoe, P. J. (2007). Modeling the transition to a new economy: Lessons from two technological revolutions. *American Economic Review, 97*(1), 64–88.

Barkan, E. R. (1999). *U.S. immigration and naturalization laws and issues: A documentary history*. Greenwood Press.

Baumol, W. J. (1983). Marx and the iron law of wages. *The American Economic Review, 73*(2), 303–308.

Bauer, D., & Papp, K. (2009). Book review perspectives: The Jevons Paradox and the myth of resource efficiency improvements. *Sustainability: Science, Practice, & Policy, 5*(1). https://doi.org/10.1080/15487733.2009.11908028

Beckstein, M. (2019). Political conservation, or how to prevent institutional decay. *Constellations, 26*(4), 623–637.

Behr, E. (1987). *The last emperor*. Futura.

Bell, A. R., Prescott, A., & Lacey, H. (2020). What can the Black Death tell us about the global economic consequences of a pandemic? In M. Billio & S. Varotto (Eds.), *A new world post COVID-19: Lessons for business, the finance industry and policy makers* (pp. 35–42). Edizioni Ca' Foscari. (Reprinted from *The Conversation*, 2020, March 4). https://theconversation.com/what-can-the-black-death-tell-us-about-the-global-economic-consequences-of-a-pandemic-132793

Bouie, J. (2022, May 27). It's not looking too good for government of the people, by the people and for the people. *The New York Times*. https://www.nytimes.com/2022/05/27/opinion/uvalde-senate-gun-control.html.

Bradley, J. (2015). *The China mirage: The hidden history of American disaster in Asia*. Little, Brown & Co.

Brodkin, K. (1998). *How Jews became white folks and what that says about race in America*. Rutgers University Press.

Butterfield, H. (1965). *The Whig interpretation of history*. W.W. Norton. (Original work published 1931)

Calloway, C. G. (2008). *First peoples-a documentary survey of American Indian history*. Bedford/St. Martin's.

Carey, H. C. (1837). *Principles of political economy*. Carey, Lea & Blanchard.
Chan, A. (2017, August 1). Karl Marx, communists and the civil war: Interview with Robin Blackburn. *HistoryNet*. Retrieved March 27, 2026. https://historynet.com/karl-marx-communists-civil-war-interview-robinblackburn/?f
Chandler, A. D., Jr., & Hikino, T. (1990). *Scale and scope: The dynamics of industrial capitalism*. Harvard University Press.
Chesneaux, J. (1973). *Peasant revolts in China, 1840–1949* (C. A. Curwen, Trans.). Norton.
Consiglio, J. A., Martínez Oliva, J. C., & Tortella Casares, G. (Eds.). (2012). *Banking and finance in the Mediterranean: A historical perspective*. Ashgate.
Cooper, J. F. (1826). *The last of the Mohicans: A narrative of 1757*. H.C. Carey & I. Lea.
Curwen, C. A. (1977). *Taiping rebel: The deposition of Li Hsiu-ch'eng*. Cambridge University Press.
Day, D. (2008). *Conquest: How societies overwhelm others*. Oxford University Press.
de Mirabeau, V. R. M., & Quesnay, F. (1763). Philosophie rurale ou Économie générale et particulière de l'agriculture, réduite à l'ordre immuable des lois physiques et morales qui assurent la prospérité des empires. *Libraires associés*. Accessed 18 May, 2021. http://archive.org/details/philosophierura00quesgoog
de Tocqueville, A. (1835). *Democracy in America* (H. Reeves, Trans.). Saunders & Otley.
Dodds, P. (2018). 'One vast empire': China, progress, and the Scottish enlightenment. *Global Intellectual History, 3*(1), 47–70. https://doi.org/10.1080/23801883.2017.1381927
Douthat, R. (2021, July 10). Why a patriotic education can be valuable. *The New York Times*. https://www.nytimes.com/2021/07/10/opinion/sunday/history-education-patriotic.html
du Bois, W. E. B. (1935). *Black reconstruction in America: 1860–1880*. Harcourt, Brace & Co.
de Vries, J. (1994). The Industrial Revolution and the Industrious Revolution. *Journal of Economic History, 54*(2), 249–270.
Douglas, M. (2012). Foreword: "No free gifts." In M. Mauss, *The gift: The form and reason for exchange in archaic societies* (W. D. Halls, Trans., pp. i–xxiii). Routledge.
Dunbar-Ortiz, R. (2014). *An indigenous peoples' history of the United States*. Beacon Press.
Elliott, J. H. (1998). *Do the Americas have a common history? An address by J. H. Elliott*. John Carter Brown Library.
Engels, F. (1892). *The condition of the working-class in England in 1844: Trans Florence Kelley Wischnewetzky*. George Allen & Unwin Ltd.
Fahey, B. (n.d.). Documentation. *Irish Hunger Martyrs*. http://www.irishhungermartyrs.org/the_evidence.html
Ferguson, N. (2008). *The ascent of money: A financial history of the world*. Penguin Press.
Fogarty, C. (2014). *Ireland 1845–1850: The perfect holocaust and who kept it "perfect."* Fogarty Publishing.
Foster, G. M. (1965). Peasant society and the image of limited good. *American Anthropologist, 67*, 293–315. https://doi.org/10.1525/aa.1965.67.2.02a00010
Frankopan, P. (2015). *The silk roads: A new history of the world*. Bloomsbury.
Galbraith, J. K. (1987). Economics in perspective: A critical history. Houghton Mifflin.
Girard, P. (2005). Liberte, Egalite, Esclavage: French revolutionary ideals and the failure of the Leclerc Expedition to Saint-Domingue. *French Colonial History, 6*(1), 55–77. https://doi.org/10.1353/fch.2005.0007
Graden, D. T. (1987). An act even of public security: Slave resistance, social tensions, and the end of the international slave trade to Brazil, 1835–1856. *The Hispanic American Historical Review, 76*(2x), 249–282. https://doi.org/10.2307/2517141
Gray, J. (2013). *The silence of animals: On progress and other modern myths*. Farrar, Straus & Giroux.
Harcourt, B. E. et al. (2017–2018). Modalities of Revolt, 1–13. *Uprising Seminar Series*. Columbia University. Accessed 21 May, 2021. http://blogs.law.columbia.edu/uprising1313/1-13/
Harris, J. (2020, May 2). Michael Moore's 'Planet of the Humans' offers dangerous solutions to the climate crisis. *Medium*. https://medium.com/climate-conscious/michael-moores-planet-of-the-humans-offers-dangerous-solutions-to-the-climate-crisis-c25d59c96270

Hasbrouck, A. (1927). Gregor McGregor and the colonization of Poyais, between 1820 and 1824. *The Hispanic American Historical Review, 7*(4), 438–459. https://doi.org/10.2307/2505996

Hayford, C. (2018). New Chinese military history, 1839–1951: What's the story? *Frontiers of History in China, 13*(1), 90–126. https://doi.org/10.3868/s020-007-018-0006-0

Heilbroner, R. (1995). *Visions of the future: The distant past, yesterday, today, and tomorrow.* Oxford University Press.

Henriques, H. S. Q. (1907). The political rights of English Jews. *The Jewish Quarterly Review, 19*(2), 298–341. https://www.jstor.org/stable/1451130

Hillstrom, K., & Hillstrom, L. (Eds.). (2005). *The Industrial Revolution in America: Iron and steel, railroads, steam shipping.* ABC-CLIO.

Hobsbawm, E. J. (1952). The machine breakers. *Past & Present, 1*(1), 57–70.

Hobsbawm, E. J. (1999). *Industry and empire: From 1750 to the present day* (2nd ed.). New Press.

Holton, W. (2005). An 'Excess of democracy': or a shortage?: The federalists' earliest adversaries. *Journal of the Early Republic, 25*(3), 339–382. http://www.jstor.org/stable/30043335

Holton, W. (2021). *Liberty is sweet: The hidden history of the American revolution.* Simon & Schuster.

Hull, J. O. (1996). From Rostow to Chandler to you: How revolutionary was the Second Industrial Revolution? *Journal of European Economic History, 25*(1), 191–208.

Jackson, A. (1829, March 23). Letter to the creek Indians. G. Peters, & J. T. Woolley (Eds.), *The American presidency project.* Accessed 18 May, 2021. https://www.presidency.ucsb.edu/node/342176

James, T. (2011, 17 February). Black death: The lasting impact. *BBC History.* Accessed 21 May, 2021. http://www.bbc.co.uk/history/british/middle_ages/black_impact_01.shtml

Jefferson, T. (1816, 12 November). Letter to George Logan. *Founders Online, National Archives.* Accessed 25 May, 2021. https://founders.archives.gov/documents/Jefferson/03-10-02-0390

Johnson, S., Zhang, J., & Keil, F. (2018). *Psychological underpinnings of zero-sum thinking* [Working paper]. https://doi.org/10.2139/ssrn.3117627

Jowit, J. (2013, January 8). Strivers v shirkers: The language of the welfare debate. *The Guardian.* https://www.theguardian.com/politics/2013/jan/08/strivers-shirkers-language-welfare

Kornblith, G. J. (1998). *The Industrial Revolution in America.* Houghton Mifflin.

Koselleck, R. (2006). *Begriffsgeschichten: Studien zur Semantik und Pragmatik der politischen und sozialen Sprache.* Suhrkamp Verlag.

Kossoff, P. (1983). *Valiant heart: A biography of Heinrich Heine.* Associated University Press.

Kranzberg, M., & Pursell, C. W., Jr. (Eds.). (1967). *Technology in Western civilization* (Vol. 1–2). Oxford University Press.

Krugman, P. (2008, March 25). Malthus was right! *The New York Times.* https://archive.nytimes.com/krugman.blogs.nytimes.com/2008/03/25/malthus-was-right/index.html

Kuhn, P. A. (1970). The Taiping Rebellion. In J. K. Fairbank (Ed.), *Cambridge history of China* (Vol. 10, pp. 264–317). Cambridge University Press.

Landes, D. S. (2003). *The unbound Prometheus: Technical change and industrial development in Western Europe from 1750 to the present* (2nd ed.). Cambridge University Press.

Lassalle, F. (1863). *Offenes Antwortschreiben an das Central-Comité zur Berufung eines Allgemeinen Deutschen Arbeiter-Congresses zu Leipzig.* https://mdz-nbn-resolving.de/details:bsb11753187

Laurie, B. (1989). *Artisans into workers: Labor in nineteenth-century America.* University of Illinois Press.

Lee, J., & Campbell, C. (1998). Headship succession and household division in three Chinese banner serf populations, 1789–1909. *Continuity and Change, 13*, 117–141.

Licht, W. (1995). *Industrializing America: The nineteenth century.* Johns Hopkins University Press.

Lincoln, A. (1855, 24 August). Letter to Joshua F. Speed. *Abraham Lincoln Online.* Accessed 27 March, 2026. https://www.abrahamlincolnonline.org/lincoln/speeches/speed.htm

Loftsdóttir, K., & Pálsson, G. (2013). Black on white: Danish colonialism, Iceland and the Caribbean. In J. Nordin & M. Naum (Eds.), *Scandinavian colonialism and the rise of modernity* (pp. 37–52). Springer. https://doi.org/10.1007/978-1-4614-6202-6_3

Malthus, T. (1798). *An essay on the principle of population*. J. Johnsom. Accessed 20 May, 2021. https://www.gutenberg.org/files/4239/4239-h/4239-h.htm#:~:text=The%20Project%20Gutenberg%20Etext%20of%20An%20Essay%20on,on%20the%20Principle%20of%20Population%20Author%3A%20Thomas%20.

Mann, C. C. (2018). *The wizard and the prophet: Two remarkable scientists and their dueling visions to shape tomorrow's world*. Knopf.

Martineau, D. (1997). Playing detective: The Priestley riots of 1791. *Birmingham Historian, 12–13*, 11–18.

Mayr, E. (1990). When is historiography Whiggish? *Journal of the History of Ideas, 51*(2), 301–309. https://doi.org/10.2307/2709517

Mazzucato, M. (2020). *Mission economy: A moonshot guide to changing capitalism*. Penguin.

Michael, F. (1966). *The Taiping Rebellion: History and documents*. University of Washington Press.

Minoglou, I. P. (2002). Ethnic minority groups in international banking: Greek diaspora bankers of Constantinople and Ottoman state finances, c. 1840–81. *Financial History Review, 9*(2), 125–146. https://doi.org/10.1017/S0968565002000112

Mokyr, J., & Strotz, R. H. (1999). The Second Industrial Revolution, 1870–1914. In V. Castronovo (Ed.), *Storia dell'economia mondiale* (pp. 219–245). Laterza.

Neurath, P. (1994). *From Malthus to the club of Rome and back: Problems of limits to growth, population control, and migrations*. M.E. Sharpe.

North, A. (2021, 1 April). What the history of pandemics can teach us about resilience. *The New York Times*. Accessed 21 May, 2021. https://nyti.ms/2ObO4yh

Pálsson, G. (2016). *The man who stole himself: The slave odyssey of Hans Jonathan*. University of Chicago Press.

Pamuk, S. (2009). *The Ottoman economy and its institutions*. Ashgate.

Pasinetti, L. L. (1981). *Structural change and economic growth: A theoretical essay on the wealth of nations*. Cambridge University Press.

Peters, R. (1845). *A century of Lawmaking for a new nation: U.S. congressional documents and debates, 1774–1875*. Charles C. Little & James Brown.

Pruitt, S. (2016, May 3). 5 myths about slavery. *History*. https://www.history.com/.amp/news/5-myths-about-slavery

Rana, A. (2011). *The two faces of American freedom*. Harvard University Press.

Reis, J. J. (1995). *Slave Rebellion in Brazil: The Muslim uprising of 1835 in Bahía*. Trans Arthur Brakel. Taylor & Francis.

Rhee, H. (2007). *Asian millenarianism: An interdisciplinary study of the Taiping and Tonghak rebellions in a global context*. Cambria Press.

Ricardo, D. (1817). *On the principles of political economy and taxation*. John Murray.

Richards, L. L. (2000). *The slave power: The free North and Southern Domination, 1780 to 1860*. Louisiana State University Press.

Ridley, M. (2015, December 14). The long shadow of Malthus. *Standpoint Magazine*. https://standpointmag.co.uk/text-january-february-2016-matt-ridley-long-shadow-of-malthus/

Rieber, A. J. (2014). *The struggle for the Eurasian borderlands: From the rise of early modern empires to the end of the First World War*. Cambridge University Press.

Rose, C. (1938). *Copper mining in South America* [Professional degree thesis]. University of Missouri. https://scholarsmine.mst.edu/professional_theses/156

Rose, R. B. (1960). The Priestley riots of 1791. *Past & Present, 18*, 68–88.

Różycka-Tran, J., Boski, P., & Wojciszke, B. (2015). Belief in a zero-sum game as a social axiom: A 37-nation study. *Journal of Cross-Cultural Psychology, 46*(4), 525–548.

Rubin, P. H. (2003). Folk economics. *Southern Economic Journal, 70*(1), 157–171.

Russell, E., & Parker, M. (2020, June 3). How pandemics past and present fuel the rise of large companies. *The Conversation*. https://theconversation.com/how-pandemics-past-and-present-fuel-the-rise-of-large-companies-137732

Scott, J. C. (2009). *The art of not being governed: An anarchist history of upland Southeast Asia*. Yale University Press.

Selected statistics on slavery in the United States. (n.d.). Weber State University Faculty. https://faculty.weber.edu/kmackay/selected_statistics_on_slavery_i.htm

Sellers, C. G. (1994). *The market revolution: Jacksonian America, 1815–1846.* Oxford UP.

Sévillia, J. (2003). *Historiquement correct. Pour en finir avec le passé unique.* Perrin.

Sheps, A. (1989). Public perception of Joseph Priestley, the Birmingham Dissenters, and the Church-and-King Riots of 1791. *Eighteenth-Century Life, 13*(2), 46–64.

Sinclair, D. (2004). *The land that never was: Sir Gregor MacGregor and the most audacious fraud in history.* Da Capo Press. (Original work published 2003)

Smith, A. (1776). *An inquiry into the nature and causes of the wealth of nations.* W. Strahan and T. Cadell.

Smith, A. D. (2003). *Chosen peoples: Sacred sources of national identity.* Oxford University Press.

Smith, C. W. (1962). *The great hunger: Ireland 1845–1849.* Harper & Row.

Smith, P. C., & Warrior, R. A. (1996). *Like a hurricane: The Indian movement from Alcatraz to Wounded Knee.* New Press.

Sorensen, M. S. (2018, 14 April). *Iceland's 1st black citizen? An ex-slave and war hero Denmark now disregards.* The New York Times.

Spence, J. D. (1996). *God's Chinese son: The Taiping Heavenly Kingdom of Hong Xiuquan.* Norton.

Susskind, D. (2024). *Growth: A history and a reckoning.* Belknap Press.

Taylor, A. (2001). *American colonies.* Viking.

The Great Irish Famine Online. (n.d.). Geography Department, University College Cork. https://dahg.maps.arcgis.com/apps/MapSeries/index.html

The New York Times. (1856, Feb. 22). The aggressions and usurpations of the slave power: Declaration of principles and purposes of the republican party. Address of the Republican Convention at Pittsburg. *The New York Times.* https://timesmachine.nytimes.com/timesmachine/1856/03/01/77048257.pdf?pdf_redirect=true&ip=0

The New York Times. (1967, October 19). Pu Yi, last emperor of China and a puppet for Japan, dies. https://timesmachine.nytimes.com/timesmachine/1967/10/19/83637619.pdf

Tisdell, C., & Svizzero, S. (2020). The ability in antiquity of some Agrarian societies to avoid the Malthusian trap and develop. *Forum for Social Economics, 49*(2), 202–227. https://doi.org/10.1080/07360932.2017.1356344

Torr, C. (2000). The Whig interpretation of history. *South African Journal of Economic and Management Sciences, 3*(1), 52–58. https://hdl.handle.net/10520/AJA10158812_263

van Zanden, J. L. (2002). The 'revolt of the early modernists' and the 'first modern economy': An assessment. *Economic History Review, 55*(4), 619–641.

Vickers, D. (1990). Competency and competition: Economic culture in early America. *William and Mary Quarterly, 47*, 3–29.

von Thott, H. (1735). *Allerunderdanigste uforgribelige tanker om kommerciens tilstand og opkomst.* J. C. Bie.

Wade, L. (2020, 14 May). From black death to fatal flu, past pandemics show why people on the margins suffer most. *Science.* Accessed 21 May, 2021. https://www.sciencemag.org/news/2020/05/black-death-fatal-flupast-pandemics-show-why-people-margins-suffer-most

Wagner, R. G. (1982). *Reenacting the heavenly vision: The role of religion in the Taiping Rebellion.* University of California Press.

Wang, S. (2024). Differences in perspectives on the Christian revolution of the Taiping Heavenly Kingdom in China. *HTS Theological Studies, 80*(3). https://doi.org/10.4102/hts.v80i3.10122

Webster, N. (1787, 10 Oct). *An examination into the leading principles of the federal constitution.* Pamphlets 58–61 The Founders' Constitution Vol. 1, Ch. 16, Doc. 17. The University of Chicago Press. http://presspubs.uchicago.edu/founders/documents/v1ch16s17.html

Willick, J. (2021, July 2). The 'Hustlers' who started America. *The Wall Street Journal.* https://www.wsj.com/opinion/the-hustlers-who-started-america-11625249906

Wise, J. M., & Wise, Y. K. (2017). *Comparison of South and North American historic mining towns.* South America to the World. https://www.southamericatotheworld.com/comparison-of-south-and-north-america-historic-mining-towns/

Wu, T. (1952). An interpretation of Chinese economic history. *Past & Present, 1*(1), 1–12. https://doi.org/10.1093/past/1.1.1

York, R., & McGee, J. (2016). Understanding the Jevons paradox. *Environmental Sociology, 2*(1), 77–87. https://doi.org/10.1080/23251042.2015.1106060

Youwen, J. (1973). *The Taiping revolutionary movement*. Yale University Press.

The First Failure of Liberalism

5

Abstract

This chapter explains how, following the victories of the forces of liberalism against slavers in the late nineteenth century, the political economy of **liberalism** and its concomitant monetary policy, the **gold** standard, both underwent a period of **standardization**. The success was so complete that it planted the seeds of its own demise. By the end of the nineteenth century, the thalassocratic national empires, espousing politico-economic ideologies of liberalism, had gobbled up all remaining lands on earth, putting an end to the population valves and placing **pivot points on the last frontiers**. These historical developments were accompanied by trickle-down **narratives of eternal economic growth** and defense of colonial policies through **technocratic myths of liberal imperialism** (White Man's Burden, Anglo-Saxonism, etc.). As the national empires increasingly collided with each other in their quests for more finite resources (gold, land, etc.), they sponsored pseudoscientific racial theories to justify their expansionist policies and racial social pyramids. Both became known as **social darwinism (eugenics)**, a staple of public discourse and ideology both before and after WWI—and were explicitly connected to the autarkic (neofeudalist/neomercantilist) political economies which arose alongside them.

If the seeds of liberalism's downfall were sown in its triumph over slavery, they were planted not by planters or slaves, but by the same liberals whose virtue-signaling abolitionism masked exploitative practices at home. As the old Manhattan proverb goes: the only unforgivable offense in polite society is genuine poverty. Once the social pyramid re-emerged in the familiar form of industrial capitalism, it returned to prioritizing short-term profit over long-term stability. Or as one analyst put it: "*Après moi, le déluge*! is the watchword of every capitalist and of every capitalist nation. Hence Capital is reckless of the health or length of

A. M. Feldman and Y. Stamos, *Zero Sum Political Economy*, World-Systems Evolution and Global Futures, https://doi.org/10.1007/978-3-032-18326-2_5

life of the labourer, unless under compulsion from society" (Marx, 1867, Vol. 1, III.X.V).

Every slave has a master, and every master, a slave—the same applies to workers and bosses across industries. History's banal patterns return with new costumes but familiar scripts. The "trashcan of history," a phrase attributed to Trotsky but coined by the Anglo-Irish Augustine Birrell (1885), begs the question: whose history is being discarded? (Safire, 1983). Birrell, like many liberal imperialists, mediated irreconcilable factions in Ireland, a microcosm of the larger imperial dilemmas in India, Palestine, and beyond—places where finite land and zero-sum thinking bred violence. Unlike the communists who overthrew old orders, liberal imperialists clung to fairytales of prosperity for all.

Late-19th-c. abundance (during the Belle Époque, Victorian era, Gilded Age) benefited only the ruling classes of industrial empires. Elsewhere, under older religious and cultural systems, lifecycles continued, untouched by the linear "economic miracles" at Eurasia's edges. While liberal economists praise the industrial revolution's virtuous cycles, they often ignore the colonial plunder and subjugation that made such growth possible (Arnason, 2018). Certain economic historians like Brad de Long promote fantasies about a "long twentieth century" beginning in 1870 with the "Industrial Revolution" which created virtuous cycles of growth and lifted millions from agrarian poverty in the industrializing nations (*Slouching Towards Utopia*). What his rhetorical sleight-of-hand hides, however, is that this capitalist miracle came at the zero-sum expense of millions more whose agrarian lands were conquered by these same nations as colonies from which to extract cheap labor (coolies), resources and rent.

On settler frontiers—like the United States, South Africa, and Australia—the myth of endless land fueled expansion and masked dispossession. As land, taken from indigenous (particularly non-Christian) peoples by imperialists and settler-colonists, ran out and capitalism matured into consolidation and financialization, new tensions emerged. Unionization movements faced zero-sum suppression not only through force but by pitting workers against each other along racial and national lines. This divide-and-rule tactic was used, for instance, during the 1877 U.S. railroad strike of the Workingman's Party, when White and Black workers united to halt the rail system and demand better pay, working conditions and an end to child labor. In response, elites used strikebreakers, police, and symbolic diversions like the St. Louis "Veiled Prophet" (resembling a klansman) fair to undermine solidarity by privileging White over Black workers. The fair, with its Black and Jewish caricatures, distractions of "industrial progress" and manufactured pageantry, offered one White worker an aspirational taste of elite indulgence, undermining demands for justice. It was only in 1972 that labor activist Gena Scott slid down a power cable and unmasked the "prophet" as Monsanto executive Tom Smith—her car was bombed (Spencer, 2000).

By the twentieth century, imperial competition for land and resources between political dynasties and underwritten by corporate and financial dynasties turned liberal "win–win" rhetoric into the beggar-thy-neighbor mercantilist calculus of zero-sum reality. Battleships became poker chips; colonies, currencies and chauvinism remained. When the cosmic contradictions reached a breaking point, liberalism's failures and broken promises helped fuel the world wars. This is the story of the chapter—and it begins with the gold standard.

The Standardizations of Gold and Liberalism

While the conflict between liberalism and slavery hinged on the price of labor to be paid by the employer, or *Capital* (and by extension, the oligopoly of land ownership), the next great conflict would center on the currency in which that price would be paid. Traditionally this was inelastic (finite) gold or silver bullion. Yet, since liberalism had seemingly defeated lord-and-serf feudalism, now it would purportedly come for its zero-sum brother, mercantilism.

The reason that liberalism (particularly when practiced by English-speakers) surpassed mercantilism (particularly when practiced elsewhere in Eurasia, especially within Habsburg domains) is typically explained because of liberalism's inherent superiority over mercantilism—the great misunderstanding (and conceit) of Smith's "invisible hand". In reality, liberalism surpassed mercantilism not because of some inherent superiority so much as the fact that the Habsburg, Bourbon and other imperial authorities did not regulate essentially mercantilist commerce as well as the Anglican authorities allowed free traders to exploit the bullion leaking from Habsburg and Bourbon domains. Napoleon and his successors actually exacerbated the continental problem that bullion leaked from their domains and pooled in places of free-trade like London, Amsterdam and New York, where for most of the nineteenth century, access to high finance was relatively limited.

In the United States, bullion was shipped to Fort Knox, where it undergirded the value of the paper money being printed. Plenty of cheap land on the frontier and bullion piling up in Fort Knox underwriting more and more paper money in circulation made the United States a magnet for more than just Irish famine refugees: for starving peasants and workers of imperial social pyramids across Eurasia. Yet, "for all the gold in Fort Knox," it didn't change the ancient, zero-sum logic of bullion itself (bullionism). Based only on a gold standard, there couldn't be enough accessible for everyone. The paradox went back to Ricardo:

> A currency is in its most perfect state when it consists wholly of paper money, but of paper money of an equal value with the gold which it professes to represent. The use of paper instead of gold substitutes the cheapest in place of the most expensive medium, and enables the country, without loss to any individual, to exchange all the gold which it before used for this purpose, for raw materials, utensils, and food, by the use of which both its wealth and its enjoyments are increased. (Ricardo, 1817, ch XXV)

Such reasoning is fine when there's a relatively limited amount of people using paper money theoretically backed by a gold standard, but is unsustainable at a larger scale. It gradually became apparent that the gold standard was a paradox:

ensuring economic growth predicated on a finite supply of bullion. This suited big-city London and Wall Street bankers who had direct access to the bullion itself, but not workers and main street citizens who would be left bartering nickels and dimes at best or driving themselves into debtors' prison at worst. The zero-sum inelasticity of bullion effectively separated the prospects of the bankers from the proletarians, inadvertently resulting in a zero-sum struggle between them. It was in the bankers' interests to gaslight the small people and deny the obviousness of the zero-sum implications of the gold standard while it was in the interests of workers and small businesses to prove the obvious. Thus, working-class politics began to appear as zero-sum to the banking class, who naturally denied the fundamentally zero-sum nature of the inelasticity of the gold standard.

By the late nineteenth century, Anglo-American monetary debates shifted to bimetallism: a gold *and silver* standard. The opening of the gold standard to include silver was the first step in a sequence which gradually came to separate fiat currency (in dollars) from the zero-sum logic of bullionism, thereby making money more accessible to businesses rather than the exclusive domain of regimes and bankers. The ancient art of bullionism could be practiced with greater access to credit and internally by companies and individuals who need not always be bankers, which further encouraged liberal economic expansion (Knafo, 2013). However, due to the zero-sum nature of bullion, the more accessible it became within nations like the United States and empires like Britain, the less accessible it became outside. This relegated poorer countries, empires and regions to even poorer, more dependent statuses, since available bullion, naturally attracted to pre-existing pools of bullion in Britain and the United States, was shipped to New York or London (Bloomfield, 1959, p. 16).

Since the British Empire enforced the gold standard across its international trade—rigidly binding bullion to policy—workers' immiseration and the anxiety over wealth flows became fertile ground for antisemitic conspiracy theories (Carter, 2021, June 19). These narratives blamed "international financiers," often coded as Jewish, for manipulating markets. Prominent thinkers like Jeffrey Hobson articulated these ideas, even as Anglo-American liberal elites overlooked them to reassure tellurocratic Eurasian regimes (Habsburg, Romanov, Qing, Ottoman, Qajar), claiming that liberal order would secure prosperity and stability (Hobson, 1902, pp. 112–114, 240–242). Nothing could be further from the truth, but this was yet another case of "Apres moi, le déluge." As long as the supply of bullion for monetary standards (gold *or* bi-metallic) could temporarily keep relative pace with the growing population in the American landscape and British empire, rapidly filling with White settlers or colonists (themselves dispossessing indigenous peoples), liberalism itself could retain its preeminence. However, its temporary success over slavery was also attracting ever more economists—a worrying sign (Boettke, 2019).

Along with the triumph of liberalism over slavery came the codification of liberalism. In effect, liberalism became classicized into "classical" and "neoclassical" forms, with proponents, practitioners and pundits agreeing in the basic formats while differing slightly at the edges on this or that bit of incremental tweakage. In most instances, the proper role of government became minimized to ensure maximum productivity with ideals like "laissez-faire" liberalism and interests only in protecting private property (ie., finite access to land ownership). Ferdinand Lassalle denigrated such intellectual packaging of governmental liberalism as little more than a "night-watchman state" (Long & Machan, 2008; von Mises, 1985, p. 37). For economists like Lassalle, such a minimalist philosophy of government invited, if not outright incentivized, the private consolidation of markets (banking, industry, agriculture, textiles, etc.) by a few behemoth oligopolies. Limited government was seen as problematic in Eurasia and Latin America long before the United States of America (the latter most succinctly in the works of Ruben Darío) (Jáuregui, 1998). But in Lassalle's time, business was booming and the long-term structural issues inherent in liberalism were being cloaked by the establishments of Germany and Italy as new, classically liberal nation-states. Why worry about future problems when things are going well?

Free-market competition peaked shortly after the mid-19th c. abolitions of serfdom and slavery, only to then start turning into a more aggressive type of internal and, soon, national-imperial competition that was simultaneously its very opposite—most rapidly in the United States, but also in Napoleon III's France and Victorian Britain. The 1870s were a time of nation-state building with the kingdoms of Germany, Italy, Serbia, Montenegro, Bulgaria, Romania and the newly independent—and deeply indebted—republics of Latin America. There was also a time of deep depression (the stagnation of the "Long Depression" in the United States or the *Gründerkrise* in Eurasia lasted into the 1890s) and emerging corporate oligopolies, cartels and trusts. The big-business "robber barons" and their dynasties in the United States were mirrored by the *zaibatsu*, *confindustria* and *Großunternehmen* in empires like Japan, Italy and Germany. The French and British empires called theirs the "chartered companies" and "le parti colonial." These organizations or agglomerations of firms could employ tactics conducive to oligopolization, e.g. fix prices to temporarily sell at a cost to drive competitors with lower capital reserves out of business.

If the inescapable economic truth is that both God and mammon cannot simultaneously be served (a zero-sum question nevertheless), it's clear where the loyalties of like-minded business titans have always lain. Around the turn of the century, such internally oligopolistic and externally imperialistic business practices became a frequent topic of examination—and critique—even by conservative economists. There was no real government regulation of business; the idea hadn't been pioneered yet. One striking example is the notion of "cut-throat" competition that eventually leads to oligopolies, discussed in the treatise *The Philosophy of Wealth* (1886) by leading American classical liberal economist John Bates Clark. He called his idea "marginal utility theory," which laid out the basic zero-sum structure of finite market-share: individuals and/or companies will compete in a given market until enough have been driven out of business or bought out by bigger competitors until only a few survivors remain, who eventually agree to trusts to control the finite pie. In other words, competitive markets have always bred anti-competitive monopolies, oligopolies and corrupt crony capitalism, resulting in legalized bribery (lobbying) of governmental representatives to maintain and expand their slice of the pie—at the expense of the workers, the consumers, the voters who elect the representatives (Clark, 1886, pp. 123–130; Schumpeter, 1942, pp. 82–85).

Reflecting the trajectory of Clark's changes of mind, from Christian socialism, inspired by his studies in Europe and familiarity with German economic thinkers, to staunch American libertarianism, it's easy to understand why Christian socialism could never catch on in the United States the way it did in a geographically confined and relatively more homogeneous nation like Bismarck's German Empire. Basically, the real reason why Clark became a libertarian was to counter the labor protesters in the wake of the Haymarket Riot of 1886 who argued that they were being exploited, manipulated and conned. No, Clark (1899) countered, else "every right-minded man should become a socialist" (p. 4), rather their earnings were commensurate with their production instead of their relative power in the social pyramid. He trusted that they had not read Smith and Ricardo who said the opposite. The tragedy was that although he was wrong about the former point, he was largely correct about the latter (Adler, 2010, January 4). So, while in 1886 he laid bare the zero-sum logic of competition and its negative ramifications both for small business and workers, he later went on to normalize and partly conceal this logic by fusing economic theory with social Darwinism. Calling his creation "economic Darwinism," he conceded that "Though the process was savage, the outlook which it afforded was not wholly evil. The survival of crude strength was, in the long run, desirable" (Clark, 1888, p. 2).

This major shift in Clark's economic thought reflects a broader shift in American economic thinking. Initially relying on ideas that migrated from Germany to the United States (along with US economists who had gone to Germany for studies), US economic thinking gradually moved in an autonomous, original direction in the late 19th-early 20th c. (which was more conditioned by homebrewed American big business interests than by the German engineering of social-democratic or statist ideals) (Backhaus, 2012). This political economy would be most clearly espoused by Alfred Marshall, whose work came to define the long liberal decadence in the first decades of the twentieth century (Marshall, 1890).

Like industrialization itself, the professionalization of economics as a distinct discipline became widespread and soon cohered into various schools of liberalism, where professorial chairs were handed down to favorites like rent-seeking fiefdoms. For example, Ludwig von Mises and his students in the Austrian school emphasized a subjective method he called "praxeology" to deduce abstract economic conclusions about human behavior (an early version of the "homo economicus" model with stereotypes and caricatures dressed in the costumes of hard-scientific data), while other Austrians like Carl Menger and his students developed their own ideas of "marginal utility" which was basically a version of the law of diminishing returns, but for commodities. In the early era of the Chicago school, Jacob Viner, a Jewish Québécois economist, even came to Chicago to argue that Adam Smith "did not foresee that England would soon need a new set of regulations to protect her laboring masses against new, and to them dangerous, methods of industrial organization and industrial technique." He also wrote a book on economic thought, venturing no further back than English foreign trade since the sixteenth century (Viner, 1927, esp. p. 231). Other Chicago economists like Frank Knight, Henry Calvert Simons and their students emphasized the importance of the return of investment based on risk and uncertainty and disparaged corporate trusts for reducing "perfect competition" as well as monetarism, which purported to keep the supply of money low in order to keep the supply of labor cheap and easily accessible for corporations and business owners. They imagined that the ideal of perfect competition could be maintained perpetually rather than being constantly thwarted by corporate mergers and trusts for their own monopolistic benefit. Different economists have always emphasized different methods and concepts of money-making and trickle-down economics, since their careers rose and fell by how their ivory tower superiors (university deans and chancellors appointed from on high) received their work, even if they all agreed on the basic form of liberal economic expansion: that the forces of supply and demand maintain a social pyramid based on financial incentivization which solidifies the ancient zero-sum social pyramid by promising (without always delivering) the high tides to raise all boats—little different from ancient promises of afterlives in paradise. Freud's "narcissism of small differences" didn't only apply to John Cleese's People's Front of Judaea.

As with all triumphal hubris, with the false triumph of liberalism came certain decadent misconceptions, chief among them that economic (and imperial) expansion was unlimited and could last forever (Heffer, 2017). The other major one was that the West had irrevocably *diverged* from the East—which is still wrongly taken as an article of faith to this day, a concept popularly termed "the Great Divergence," around which a cottage huckster industry of misguided historiography and Western chauvinism has grown (Feldman, 2024; Grinin & Korotayev, 2015). More on this later.

The idea that a Great Divergence has taken place has proven an enduring one. But the Great Divergence wasn't between Western *progress* and the backward East, so much as between the allure of short-term benefits for liberalism at the zero-sum expense of long-term stability for nations which prided themselves on their democratic bonafides. Economic expansion, like all expansion, has always been predicated on someone else's exploitation, manipulation, dispossession or poverty, even if the beneficiary is justified by grit and gumption—while the history is conveniently swept under the proverbial rug. The real man-behind-the-curtain has never been pulling utopian pyrogenic non-levers so much as dystopian workaholic all-nighters. Yet regardless of the political propaganda and win–win economic ideologies officially sanctioned by any and all the Eurasian or American empires, the zero-sum finitude of land available for colonization and possession on the planet was promptly becoming the geopolitical pivot point putting liberalism to pasture.

Pivot Points on the Last Frontiers

One of those points would pivot on the ancient region of Axum in East Africa, where, while the rest of the world agonized over slavery, a local aristocratic dynasty since the seventeenth century produced five sons and daughters sometime during the 1830s–50s. The politically-connected family had grown rich by tax-farming (or rent-seeking) gold lifted directly from one community and then showering another with the potlatch fruits of redistribution. The third of the brood, a girl named Taytu Betul, was married off to an officer in the army of the Ethiopian emperor Tewedros II at the age of ten. Three marriages later, she landed the emperor Menelik II himself in 1889, along with the ownership of thousands of slaves, becoming a veritable nineteenth-century Queen of Sheba. Involved with her new husband's establishment of Addis Ababa as the new imperial capital in response to Italian expansion from their nearby colony in Eritrea, she tore up their false treaty of friendship (Wuchale)—the Italian version legally labeled Ethiopia as an Italian protectorate. Several years later, she met the Italians as a commander in the Battle of Adwa in 1896, where they were completely routed and Ethiopia preserved its independence. The empress never managed to provide an heir, and that, combined with her nepotism and discriminatory prejudices in court, saw her eventually overthrown (Munro-Hay, 1991, p. 48; Prouty, 1986, pp. 27–30). It didn't change the fact that the empire of Italy still had designs on carving out the ancient lands of Ethiopia, the last African lands as yet unclaimed by European national empires, for itself.

By the 1885 Treaty of Berlin, the divvying up of Africa was emblematic of something bigger: the carving up of the entirety of the earth's habitable surface by its richest, most powerful dynasties and national empires. It was the latest development in a long process of maneuvering for control over finite land throughout the world, or what we now call colonialism. As in Ethiopia a couple decades hence, the intermittent efforts to retain power over their ancestral lands (by violence and/or diplomacy, by hook or by crook) by members of the previous ruling dynasties of Hawaii, Madagascar, Cambodia, Zululand and many other smaller or agrarian kingdoms the world over had little effect without industrial production of guns, bombs, ships and fortresses to protect their limited lands and resources from the encroachments of foreign empires (Cock & Nathan, 1996, p. 23; Edwards, 2007, pp. 15–20; Laborde, 1879, pp. 112–120). In this brave new Malthusian world (which in some respects was little different from the zero-sum Law of the Jungle), as the Japanese ruling class quickly recognized, there were two options: conquer or be conquered, colonize or be colonized, be a master or be a slave. There were seemingly finite resources available in the world (land, gold, and increasingly fossil fuel) to provide for one's people and only might could make right. Or as the dilemma was worded in *The Nation* in 1902:

> A problem is rolling up before which Japanese statesmen are appalled. At the present rate of increase, there will, before the middle of this century, be a hundred million people to

> provide for. It is this prospect that is leading Japanese statesmen to make such frantic efforts to secure opportunity for colonization. (The Nation, 1902, p. 187)

In the late 1890s, the last frontiers of North America, South Africa and Oceania became fully settled, claimed or bought (by predominantly White Protestant settlers)—the end result of manifest destiny on various continents (Ferns, 2015). Wealthy land speculators had long since claimed as much finite land of the western frontier as possible and had used the American military for their own purposes when the natives got in their way. For the United States, Hawaii and Alaska were the last remaining frontiers, which were also increasingly colonized by White Protestant settlers, different cultures and waves of whom formed what Colin Woodard has called "American nations." Whether in Oceania, South Africa or North America, all bore certain measures of the White Protestant cultural traits derived from liberalism, first noticed in 1893 by the University of Wisconsin history professor Frederick Jackson Turner (although the theme has been somewhat broadened since then) (Fischer, 1989; Turner, 1894; Woodard, 2011). This involved first the physical, then cultural, dispossession and genocide of indigenous peoples: after the last Indian Wars had yielded to massacres like Wounded Knee, the Killing Times and Coniston, native children were kidnapped, taken from their mothers to be raised by bureaucrats with White Protestant manners in public boarding schools in order to assimilate the indigenous peoples into the dominant White Protestant societies (Adams, 1995; Allam & Evershed, 2019, March 3; Barrington, 2008; Buti, 2004; Day, 2008; Milloy, 1999; van Krieken, 1999). With the closing of the frontier and the swallowing up of the last continentally contiguous (and outlying) lands in Oceania, South Africa and North America, the race was on to claim all remaining lands elsewhere on the globe.

For the United States, a country with a large standing army and a brand new blue-water navy underwritten by Theodore Roosevelt, the remaining option beyond resource extraction on a limited continent, where land, gold, oil and housing stock were quickly being bought up by rent-seeking speculators, was geographical (maritime) expansion at the expense of another, older empire. Enter the ancient Catholic ecumenical thalassocratic empire, Bourbon-ruled Spain, whose last remaining appanages lay in Cuba, Puerto Rico and the Philippines. The Spanish-American war of 1898 may have changed the linguistic and confessional ingredients of imperialism, but the same expansionist recipe had remained.

The United States was not the only one which swallowed up remaining land: the same held true for the Russians in Manchuria and East Asia, the British in South Africa (the First Boer War of the 1880s was now followed by the Second Boer War, fought to secure access to the Transvaal Gold Rush), the Japanese in Korea and many European colonial powers across Africa and Indochina, including the Italians, who initially failed in their genocidal intentions against the Ethiopians, and the Germans, who succeeded against the Herero (Day, 2008, pp. 179–180). The scramble for new colonies and lands was widespread not only in the late nineteenth century, but also well into the twentieth due to zero-sum logic of the finitude of habitable land to claim for possession, and then rent-seeking.

The scholarly result of such imperial expansionist designs came in the form of two texts which implicitly seemed to confirm this situation. The first was American admiral Alfred Thayer Mahan's *The Influence of Sea Power Upon History*, received with critical acclaim across the largely thalassocratic English-speaking world when it appeared in 1890. After the assassination of the US president William McKinley, who had defended the American annexation of previously Spanish Catholic Philippines by saying, "There was nothing left for us to do but to take them all, and to educate the Filipinos, and uplift and civilize and Christianize them" (Olcott, 1916, v. 2, p. 110), his vice-president Theodore Roosevelt himself wrote to Mahan: "I am greatly in error if it does not become a naval classic" (Mahan, 1890; Turk, 1987). Every English-speaking statesman was suddenly a "big ship man." Although it only deals with the 17th to 18th centuries, the main argument of the book is that naval power is a determinative factor in history, which ensures ruling dynasties' access to resources, finite or otherwise. For the next century, Anglo-American national budgets were decided by bets on dollars to dreadnoughts.

While the American admiral focused on the sea at the expense of the land, an English bookman advanced a new theory of landmass-based global geopolitics in a short, but highly influential article published in 1904: Halford Mackinder. Filling in the other half of the geographical geopolitical ledger ignored by Mahan, he divided the world into three major terrestrial spheres: the Eurasian heartland, the intermediate sphere and the outlying Islands (including the Americas). By the time he published what he termed the end of "the Columbian epoch" in the smoking ruins of the British imperial concentration camps of the Boer War, "the world, in its remoter borders, has hardly been revealed before we must chronicle its virtually complete political appropriation" (Mackinder, 1904). This acknowledgment of the finitude of habitable territory for imperial population valves was followed by further geographical expositions spotlighting the geopolitical importance of Eurasia, which Mackinder deemed the heartland of the world, and whoever controlled it would control the world (Huntington, 1907). For most of the rest of the twentieth century in the wake of the rise of nationalism and decline of imperialism, based on a combination of Mahan and Mackinder, the world may have been divided by various ideologies such as fascism, communism and liberalism, but it was divided by geography into the Old World, the Middle World and the New World (inner Eurasia, outer Eurasia and the New World), which explains why the definitive version was published using American public subsidies in 1942 (Mackinder, 1942). This logic moreover underpinned the German *Drang nach Osten* and the Nazi *Lebensraum* in the 1930s–1940s (see chapter 5 below). Even today, much discussion of geopolitics and geographical determinism in both Eurasia and the Americas is dominated by footnotes to Mackinder (de Blij, 2012; Dugin, 2012; Kaplan, 2018; Kitsikis, 2002; Maçães, 2018; Marshall, 2015; Simon, 2011).

With the closing of the last frontiers, particularly the American frontier, which prized the "rugged individualism" of the WASP frontiersman, and memorialized in minstrel shows and "Wild Bill," individualism was repurposed for an alternative world of liberal economic expansion rather than specifically geographical expansion. As the frontier inevitably became settled by WASPs, one of the most strident late-19th-c. American arch-liberals, Henry George, argued in his book *Progress and Poverty* against rent-seeking extraction and for a progressive land-value tax (which would replace income tax, tariffs VAT and all other taxes) to be redistributed as a "citizen's dividend" to offset the zero-sum expense borne by the urban poor and renting classes; his ideas essentially heralded some of the first pioneering models of Anglo-American land redistribution. According to his theory, landlords would eventually disappear, transportation would be socialized, land use would be made more efficient (through agricultural incentivization). George, whose economic philosophy quickly became termed "Georgism," observed that taxes on labor discouraged productivity (a potentially infinite supply) while taxes on land did *not* discourage land ownership (due to its finitude). Samuel Gompers, despite his comfort with big business ("The greatest crime an employer can perpetrate on his employees is to fail to operate at a profit"), was a committed Georgist (Heron, 1954). Land value taxes had, after all, been advocated by Adam Smith, John Stewart Mill, and as we will discuss later, John Maynard Keynes and Milton Friedman. Even today, smaller states like Denmark, Taiwan and Singapore use George's principles of clearly finite land to maintain progressive land taxes and encourage the efficient use of finite land.

Myths of Eternal Economic Growth—Part 1

The personal responsibility ideal of "pulling oneself up by one's bootstraps," which had been widely regarded as a preposterous idea in the nineteenth century, became embedded at the heart of the archetype of American individualism, much like independence and self-sufficiency was proposed for the standard Eurasian collective nation-state during the same period. The great popularizer of these myths in America was the rags-to-riches author, Horatio Alger. Born into respectable New England puritanical aristocracy, his father paid for his Harvard education and a grand tour of Europe, but was always in the creditors' crosshairs. Returning to New England at the outset of the American Civil War in 1861, his family connections landed him a series of positions as an editor, teacher and minister in the local aristocracy (the "Boston Brahmins") as a budding morality writer for temperance and abolitionism until a church pedophilia scandal in 1866 drove him to New York. There he spent his time writing moralistic tales about how poor street urchins could strike it rich. This new writing style was much more lucrative, landing him a publishing contract and a tutoring gig for the rich kids of an international banker named Seligman. His novels often involved a conscientious boy being taken in by a wealthy older gentleman and given a job at the expense of some other, seemingly undeserving boy. One's rise required another's fall—and the only realistic aspect of the bootstraps was to use the boot to step on the other boy's neck. By his death in 1899, Alger's writing consisted mostly of stale old hits of individual pluck and beneficent luck. Like the KKK, his work enjoyed a revival in the 1920s, but afterwards, public interest again plummeted. He made his money hawking these bootstrap ideals to others who believed them, bought his books and contributed to his routinely insecure riches—he estimated that he made $100 k between 1866 and 1896 (Nackenoff, 1994, 1997; Scharnhorst, 1980; Scharnhorst & Bales, 1981, 1985).

In the end, Alger's modest riches came from swindling others. Unregulated liberalism led directly to more versions of grift, abuse, corruption and exploitation, a different form of feudalism under a new guise: industrial oligarchy, or in the vocabulary of the time, monopolies, trusts and robber barons. Liberal policies *did* foster industrial economic growth, and simultaneously raging inequalities from freezing Russian imperial winters of bolshoi ballet, balls, and imperial industrialization around the turn of the twentieth century to the industrialist, imperialist and banking-friendly policies of Bismarck and Napoleon III and certainly throughout much of the British empire and America—at least for Whites in Anglo-American countries, and bourgeois classes and/or national majorities in Eurasia.

In the wake of the carving up of the finite surface of the earth and its rent-seeking exploitation as well as the standardization of national currencies to the price of finite gold (which suited international bankers in New York and London most of all), all matters of business and state became matters of finite market share and market saturation. It's little surprise that corporate consolidation of wealth and power came at the same time as imperial consolidation of control over land, gold and other finite resources like newly important petroleum. As corporate dynasties like the Vanderbilts, Rockefellers, Morgans, Carnegies, Bells, Rhodes', etc., grew as powerful as entire national empires, they increasingly relied on various myths to maintain their status. Chief among them is the Smithian myth that only trickle-down (potlatch) economics could produce growth and that socioeconomic success and failure were completely the result of individual decisions over a lifetime.

The first layer of this myth was that individual success could be available to all: it didn't require a massive scale of exploiting or manipulating others in a zero-sum socio-economic pyramid. All that was required was hard work and perhaps a dash of luck here or there. Failure or poverty, on the other hand, was simply a mark of an individual's moral or genetic defects.

The second layer of the myth of trickle-down economics was that the wealthy and successful were the only ones who knew best how to handle finite resources like land or money (pegged to the gold standard) because they were the benevolent creators of gainful employment for everyone else. Even if men like Cecil Rhodes, Andrew Carnegie or John Rockefeller didn't provide enough jobs for everyone, as great patrons of social welfare and the common good, the feudal ideals of *noblesse oblige* inherited and reconciled with the industrial era meant that they gave generously to warm-hearted philanthropic causes (Carnegie, 1901). Therefore, these captains of industry or empire should not be expected to obey the same laws or pay the same rate of taxes as everyone else.

The final layer of the myth was that these men were simply geniuses who created innovations which improved human life—rather than extracted finite value from preexisting, rent-seeking business models. The ultimate fact that such models seemed eternal meant that there could never be any alternative; economic liberalism must be the only way. Therefore, these genuflecting "captains of industry" must be glorified, without whom the countless impoverished wretches (previously preached to by Alger) would be penniless and shirtless, even if they could be made so anyway by the industrialists. Fortunately, the industrial titans instead made shows of clothing and feeding the masses through their potlatch benevolence.

The central core of the myth was the producerist idea that without such "captains of industry," society would be composed of takers rather than makers, the same simplistic division of society emblematic of every era when growth and profit are valued above solidarity and equity. In reality, the money and power of the "captains of industry" came at the zero-sum expense of the wretches whose labor they exploited for their aggrandizement, and whom they repaid with crumbs from their tables through pittances as wages and potlatch charitable causes. Rent-seeking returned as land and housing speculation. The social pyramid became the shape of a tall, thin, top-heavy skyscraper, first manifest in Manhattan's Flatiron Building. There wouldn't be enough work for the entire base of the pyramid, whose denizens would be consigned to fighting just to get onto the bottom rung of the zero-sum social pyramid in the first place. This was also the beginning of the "prosperity theology" derived from the Parable of the Talents (Matthew 25:14–30/ Luke 19:11–27—or simply, the "Matthew Effect").

The zero-sum logic used to manipulate is also used to justify the status quo—the social pyramid of haves and have-nots, which was later lampooned by Bertolt Brecht as the rich man's preferred scriptural method to gaslight the worker into his own exploitation (Bowler, 2013; Brecht, 1934; Herzog, 1994, pp. 150–168). He (primarily it was a White, Anglo-Saxon Protestant male) was told that by working hard enough and long enough ("hustling") he too could access the American dream. In reality, this form of dream *hoarding*, even in the nineteenth century, was a form of class warfare waged by the top down. As the economist Alfred Marshall wrote in 1890, "The children of the working classes go to the grave carrying underdeveloped abilities and faculties; which, if they could have borne fruit, would have added to the material wealth of the country" (bk. IV, ch. IV, sec. 5.2). The brutal reality of such dashed dreams, however, led only to painful hypertension, constant stress and anxiety, mental illness, overwork and exploitation either of the individual or foisted onto other individuals in a perpetual psychological pyramid scheme, and the resulting social malaise came to be known by a number of names, even if the Protestant work ethic at its foundation was one and the same. Sigmund Freud and other psychologists called it "neurasthenia"; in the British empire, it was called "brain fag"; one surgeon called it "Newyorkitis"; William James simply called it "Americanitis"; when it came home to roost in Eurasia, sociologists like Emile Durkheim, Marcel Mauss and Karl Marx called it "anomie" and "alienation" (Ayonrinde, 2020; Beard, 1869; Daugherty, 2015; Durkheim, 1933; Erwin, 2002, pp. 361–362; Girdner, 1901; Marx, 1964; Van Deusen, 1869). Exorbitant profits came at the expense of millions of those who believed the bootstraps mythology and willingly bought its "successories," such as the British motivational posters of Parker-Holladay Co., brought to the United States and Canada in the 1920s. The rich stay rich and the poor stay poor because neither can imagine any alternative model to their confinement within the same zero-sum social pyramid.

John Kenneth Galbraith aptly described one of the main causes for the repeating cycles of "speculative euphoria and programmed collapse" as "the specious association of money and intelligence". He rightly observed that in capitalism there prevails a belief that "the more money, the greater the intelligence that supports it". He went on to explain that.

> in a world where for many the acquisition of money is difficult and the resulting sums palpably insufficient, the possession of it in large amount seems a miracle. Accordingly, possession must be associated with some special genius. This view is then reinforced by the air of self-confidence and self-approval that is commonly assumed by the affluent. On no matter is the mental inferiority of the ordinary layman so rudely and abruptly stated: "I'm afraid that you simply don't understand financial matters." (Galbraith, 1994, pp. 13–14)

The fact that the cheap labor of millions of poor wretches has been required for the self-aggrandizement of the captains of industry was first noticed by economists like Alfred Marshall who congratulated industrialists for putting otherwise idle talent buriers to good use. Their labor itself, because for want of capital it was all the laborers had to offer the marketplace, was only later noticed as its own form of monopolization. This was called monopsony by the economist Joan Robinson, since few buyers (employers) would substantially control the potentially infinite (labor) market as the major purchasers of goods and services offered by many would-be sellers (that is, many laborers selling their potentially infinite labor to comparatively fewer buyers, or employers). Joan Robinson also observed that the same central problem of employers' low-rate wage-fixing had a deep impact on conventional laissez-faire liberalism: "One of the main effects (I will not say purposes) of orthodox traditional economics was … a plan for explaining to the privileged class that their position was morally right and was necessary for the welfare of society" (Polychroniou, 2021). Ever since Adam Smith, employers' low-rate wage-fixing was just considered "the natural state of things, which nobody ever hears of" (Smith, 1776, I.VIII).

When the wealth furnished by exploited workers was legally fashioned into dynastic inheritance over the course of generations, economists gradually detected the reappearance of legal privileges for prestigious families separate from the public sphere. By the first decade of the twentieth century, this was called refeudalization in Eurasia, or second serfdom, characterized by economists and sociologists like Thorstein Veblen by a continuation of the dynastic inheritance of zero-sum wealth into the industrial era from the feudal era (Giordano, 2003; Hudson, 2012, p. 5; Veblen, 1899).

Few saw the entropic (yet predictable) development of industrial relations as clear-eyedly and soberly as a transatlanticist Jewish labor leader. Born shortly after Horatio Alger into a poor family in London (when Engels was writing about them), the Gompers family chased the American dream into the cigar sweatshops of the Lower East Side. From a bench in a workshop owned by a German immigrant-socialist named David Hirsch, and under the tutelage of Karl Laurrell (the former secretary of the International Workingmen's Association), Samuel Gompers gradually built a labor movement to counterbalance the reigning American monopsony, racial division, inequality, strikebreaking and intimidation (Livesay, 1987). By the turn of the twentieth century, toggling his American Federation of Labor (AFL)'s support between the imperialist and/or isolationist distractions du jour, he stood firmly against two things: the rapacity of concentrated capital and the cheaper labor of other immigrants (particularly Chinese) (Babcock, 1974; Gompers, 1925; Greene, 1998; Grubbs, 1968; Mandel, 1963; Mandel, 1955; Mink, 1986; Reed, 1930; Saxton, 1971; Taft, 1957; Whittaker, 1969).

Samuel Gompers' Anglo-American chauvinism used producerism to agitate for better pay and working conditions on behalf of the producers rather than the extractors of finite resources using cheap, infinite labor: "Until some limitations are placed upon the absolutism of these absentee coal operators in West Virginia, the government of West Virginia will continue to be Russianized and the people can be naught but serfs" (Corbin, 2011, p. 28). Gompers recognized that the improvements in the domestic labor conditions of Americans (predominantly White ones) could only come at the zero-sum expense of cheaper labor coming from other countries (like himself) (Currarino, 2011). Accordingly, he supported calls to limit East Asian immigration to the US, first beginning in the 1870s, in his "American Manhood against Asiatic coolieism" (1908): "As a fitting close to this document we submit the remarks made by one of the greatest of American statesmen, Hon. James G. Blaine, February 14, 1879: 'Either the Anglo-Saxon race will possess the Pacific slope or the Mongolians will possess it'" (Gompers & Gutstadt, 1908, p. 22).

The zero-sum logic of race versus race, or capital and labor in the social pyramid was tantamount to the zero-sum logic of maker and taker; imperialism and landownership—perhaps best exemplified in the caricatures of George Frederick Keller in the San Francisco WASP.

By the early 1910s, continual geographical expansion had worked well for a time (the 1912–13 Balkan Wars are a clear example), until it could not be condoned by public opinion or international agreements (Bismarck's secret 1887 reinsurance treaty with the Romanovs, which precluded an Eastern front war, died when he was dismissed by Wilhelm II in 1890)—at which time, the need for some kind of geographical expansion to justify and perpetuate grotesque inequities ran up against the same need by rival powers. The fact that the great powers were all socioeconomically interconnected was used by Norman Angell in his 1909 book *The Great Illusion* to argue that such economic interdependence meant that the horrendous warfare of the Napoleonic era had permanently passed into the dustbin of history. His *Great Illusion* was itself an illusion: the royal dynasties that ordered their working classes to total war just five years later did so not *despite*, but *because* they were so interdependent. As Jean-Yves Le Naour observed in his own *Grande Illusion* in 1914 (arguably in response to Angell's *Illusion*), they were more afraid to forfeit the cause of expansion than whatever the cost in blood and treasure it would take to attain it—precisely because they held the zero-sum assumption that without expansion, they would be required to forfeit their finite resources for someone else's zero-sum gain. Hence, attempts at continuous expansion were one of the factors determining the beginning of World War I (Angell,

1909; Le Naour, 1914). Another Frenchman, Edmond Théry argued in his *La transformation Économique de la Russie*, published shortly before the outbreak of the war in 1914, that the economic future of the Romanov imperial czardom would be bright, wealthy and powerful—at the expense of the other powers (Théry, 1914).

WWI was also the result of market saturation in major European national empires, a ruling class effort to distract the exploited working classes with imperial glory, nationalism and racial chauvinism, which meant that eventually the working classes of the rival European nations would need to be pitted against each other in a zero-sum struggle for national/racial supremacy, if not survival (Boemeke et al., 1999). The differences between the experiences of the lions in their trenches from the donkeys who led them from their HQs bear their own witness; there is little reason to dwell on the quietude of any front—Western or Eastern, indigenous or imperial, labor or capital, have or have-not:

> It is the book's central argument that this was really the game all governments were playing: each feared its own people, each wanted them to be in a rage with foreigners instead of with their rulers. What Disraeli called 'a spirited foreign policy', and held up as the best way to turn discontent outwards, had come to be accepted by statesmen everywhere as their domestic cure-all, heedless of the fact that it was bringing a European war closer and closer. (Barraclough, 1982; Kiernan, 1983, January 10)

The Technocratic Myth of Liberal Imperialism

> In some decades, nothing happens; in some weeks, decades happen. —Vladimir Lenin

Euthemia was born ca. 1909 in a quaint village overlooking the southern Black Sea. A member of the Pontic Greek minority of the Pontus region in northeastern Anatolia, her early years were recalled in Greek, going to the Orthodox church and her family paying the special tax for non-Muslims, the *jizya*, to the Islamic Ottoman authorities. Then, in the midst of Istanbul's occupation in WWI, Russian encroachments in the western Caucasus, rising Turkish nationalism in Anatolia and the downfall of the Ottoman caliphate, the new Turkish authorities (the Committee for Union and Progress, better known as the Young Turks) ordered the removal of all Christian minorities in central and eastern Anatolia, including Pontic and Cappadocian Greeks, Armenians and Assyrians to guarantee living space for the Islamic majority. Like tens of thousands of other families, Euthemia's family was ordered on a death march into the Syrian desert. Hundreds of thousands died: raped and/or killed on the roadside by Ottoman guards (predominantly Kurdish Hamidiye cavalry regiments), left to thirst or starve, forced into slave labor squadrons or simply abandoned to the elements upon arrival in the desert. Separated from her dying family, Euthemia was taken in as a domestic servant by an Assyrian family who couldn't pronounce her name, and was renamed Sano. There she was married and emigrated to the United States. Decades later, her daughter Thea told her mother's story about the effect on the Christian minority of the decline and fall of the Ottoman empire (Halo, 2001; Hedges, 2000; Papageorgiou, 2014).

Similar stories of state-sanctioned pogroms against the roadkill of history unite these Christian minorities with the millions of Jewish and Islamic minorities as collateral damage in the declining and falling Russian empire on the other side of the Black Sea: these were some of the first systematic genocides of minority populations which occurred as a consequence of the finance-fueled implosions of the great tellurocratic Eurasian ecumenical empires as the speculating bankers and statesmen of New York and London looked the other way.

Every imperial conviction needed to maintain a legal fiction to justify its condition and disguise the imposition of the colonizer on the colonized. As the historian Caroline Elkins has put it:

> If Britain's civilizing mission was reformist in its claims, it was brutal nonetheless. Violence was not just the British Empire's midwife, it was endemic to the structures and systems of British rule. [...] British officials also obsessed over the rule of law, insisting this was the basis of good government. But in the empire, rule of law codified difference, curtailed freedoms, expropriated land and property and ensured a steady stream of labor for empire's mines and plantations, the profits from which helped fuel Britain's economy. By the 20th century, the empire was replete with legal exceptionalism in the form of martial law and states of emergency needed to maintain control. While lawful, these states of exception granted extraordinary powers of repression. When security forces needed more discretion, or when their actions constituted unsanctioned violence, British officials rendered their behavior legal by amending old regulations and creating new ones. This recurring phenomenon turned the exceptions into norms. (Elkins, 2022, June 4)

Many millions of people around the world were impoverished, dispossessed, enslaved, mutilated, or outright murdered by British legal exceptionalism. The "rule of law" was simply "rule *by* law" which could only be hidden as long as other empires did not encroach on their turf. By the time that the imperial German Hohenzollern dynasty successfully emulated the British Hanoverians' policies overseas at their zero-sum expense in the late nineteenth century, the imperial status quo's days were numbered. Following British industrialization, Germany also industrialized, since industrialization as a political-economic model diffused across Europe. Yet Germany could produce goods of the same quality for cheaper and would overtake Britain in the production of materials that were central to the "Second Industrial Revolution", such as steel and chemicals (Hobsbawm, 1987, 1994). And so Britain went to war with Germany in 1914 because of the unlearned historical lesson of the Thucydides Trap.

Thus, the 1920s began with a pandemic and a liberal economic crisis that crossed the borders which had just been set by WWI and ended with an even bigger liberal economic crisis which was as global as WWI, if not more. Between the depletion of their gold stocks, the resulting debasements of their currencies, and the growing resentment of their peasants and workers due to their increasing awakening to their own industrialized exploitation in their respective social pyramids, WWI (and their inability to finance it) broke the concentrated capital and sovereignty of the remaining agrarian (largely unindustrialized) tellurocratic

Eurasian ecumenical empires. By the early 20th c., the tipping point for these dynasties had arrived and down fell imperial lines which had never previously fallen. The Confucian Qing, Sunni Ottomans, Shi'a Qajarids, Catholic Habsburgs, Protestant Hohenzollerns and Orthodox Romanovs all fell shortly before or after WWI (the Buddhist Chakri, the Anglican Windsor and the Shinto Japanese dynasties managed to survive WWI). Most were replaced by various forms of republics (save for Persia, which got a new ruling dynasty, the Pahlavids). The final implosions of these ecumenical tellurocratic empires were often very violent—it wasn't always clear who or what constituted an Austrian, a Russian, a Turk, or a Chinaman, since the Romanovs, Habsburgs, Qing and Ottomans ruled over so many vast regions and the peoples which inhabited them—causing some of the first systematic genocides. This was the byproduct of Woodrow Wilson's call for democratic creation of nation-states from empires (national self-determination).

As Tacitus wrote in his *Annales, Miseram pacem vel bello bene mutari* ("A bad peace is even worse than war") (Alfred, & William, 1876, III, XLIV). The same words were used ubiquitously to describe the fallout of the Peace of Versaille. Aside from giving brutal permission for ethnic cleansing in the name of national self-determination, the Treaty of Versailles indebted and impoverished nations essentially indefinitely. As the Treaty consigned entire generations to debtor's prison, primarily in Germany, Keynes forewarned in his *The Economic Consequences of the Peace* of a global conflagration hitherto unimagined in the decades following 1919 (Garcia, 2017, July 26; Keynes, 1920). The first sign of Keynes' prescience came in the form of the Spanish Flu, which exacerbated the 1920–1921 Depression, causing a decline in workers' spending power from Flu deaths, from veterans returning to manufacturing, displacing what had previously been a tighter labor market and from European hyperinflation, which chased still more gold to the United States (Barro & Ursua, 2009, May 5; Metzer, 2000; Vernon, 1991). Of course, the decline in the spending power of everyday folks mattered little as long as one could keep the labor market loose, the unions at bay and the workers docile. Between the reduction of the size of government by the Wilson administration in the wake of Versailles and the Spanish Flu, Harding's tax wizardry of lowering rates while raising revenue, an unexpected monetary stimulus to revive consumer demand and the financialization of all remaining causes of economic instability, it was "the last governmentally unmediated business cycle downturn" (Grant, 2014; Kuehn, 2011). Still, for American bank vaults to swell with Eurasian gold, it would come at the zero-sum expense of Eurasian financial institutions perpetually reliant on the gold standard.

Even in 1924, Keynes made it clear to the American public that the central problem of the Gold standard was that a finite commodity could never keep pace with a growing global population. In other words, Keynes pointed out that the central zero-sum problem with the gold standard was that this "barbarous relic" ensured that enough wealth to eat would never be available to most (Keynes, 1924, March 30). This didn't stop some historians from claiming that WWI had nothing to do with zero-sum thinking. Niall Ferguson may well have a point that WWI and

WWII were truly one and the same war, but he misses the larger issue by painting an overly rosy picture of liberal globalization before WWI:

> ...some severe economic crises did not lead to wars. Certainly, it is now impossible to argue (though Marxists long tried to) that the First World War was the result of a crisis of capitalism; on the contrary, it abruptly terminated a period of extraordinary global economic integration with relatively high growth and low inflation. (Ferguson, 2006, xxxvii–xxxviii)

Yet the times which it spelled an end to also constituted the period of the highest increase in economic inequality, imperialism, colonialism and the accumulation of greater amounts of inherited wealth concentrated for ever fewer privileged heirs—in short, refeudalization for everyone else. That a period of such opulence and decadence for the few and increasing resentment and immiseration of the many led to war should come as little surprise: Martin Luther's denunciations of Jacob Fugger and ambivalence about the bloody 1525 Peasants' Revolt would easily represent the same historical forces at work. Ferguson certainly has a point that WWII was an extension of WWI, but by the same token, the Great Depression of the 1930s was an extension of the long depressions of the 1870s–1890s as symptoms of the failure of liberalism.

It didn't stop Keynes' detractors (at the time or today [Beaudreau, 2006]) from trying to discredit his ideas using the logic of the fear of missing out. But this is misleading since it assumes that only WWI was not begun for economic reasons due to some "crisis of capitalism." No, the crisis was zero-sum Malthusian thinking about land, food, bullion and colonial sovereignty: if all the land in the world was gobbled up by rival great powers, then a finite amount of opportunities for geographical expansion would surely ensue, and ensue it did. This was the "crisis of capitalism," which Ferguson tries to pin on the "Marxists" in a rhetorical sleight of hand. The strongest followers of Marx are those who endorse the idea of class warfare and wage it from the top down.

As a result, as the 1920s wore on, Keynes found himself vindicated by every major international event—the American immigration act of 1924, the increasingly adversarial Anglo-American relations (symbolized by the United States' "War Plan Red" in the event of war against Britain and Canada [Bell, 1997; Holt, 1988; Major, 1998]) and naval arms races (up to the Washington Treaty, 1926), the increasingly obsolete Kellogg-Briand Pact of Paris (1928), the Americans (led by Senator Henry Cabot Lodge) refraining from joining Woodrow Wilson's liberal initiative of the League of Nations, etc. Essentially, the failure of the League of Nations was equivalent to the failure of liberalism itself—the forces of communism and fascism were steadily becoming models too successful to resist.

The political extremism which resulted from the corporate consolidation, commodification and financialization of every aspect of life didn't go unnoticed. This was an environment that witnessed the first usage of the term "technocracy", shortly after WWI (Smyth, 1921). Like under the *ancien* Regime, the wealthy were able to transfer their holdings and incomes abroad (to Dutch and Swiss banks where they hedged against the Reichsmark) to avoid paying taxes at the zero-sum expense of the working poor. During the German hyperinflation of the 1920s, the Berliner Tageblatt reported:

> The Business taxes bring nearly no income because any kind of expense can be written off [...] including the cost of private cars for the company owner and directors. The respect for our taxes has fallen so low that many hundreds of thousands of well-off citizens haven't even paid their taxes for the year 1920. The entire tax system is a shaky house of cards. (Fergusson, 1975, pp. 89–96)

Corporate consolidation, speculative financialization, stock buy-backs and oligopolization in the corporate world of WWI's winning powers throughout the 1920s (including corporate kickbacks even to Calvin Coolidge) demonstrated over and over again that the ABCs of liberalism, which had been so promising in the mid-nineteenth century especially during its triumph over slavery, were rapidly devolving into little more than a popular parlor game of rackets and speculative decadence (Chancellor, 1999, pp. 207–210). Self-regulation by private markets operating under private laws had major impacts on the public:

> The original self-regulatory organization was the New York Stock Exchange, created in 1792. Prior to the New Deal, the Stock Exchange functioned as a private club, and its failure to enforce transparent and fair dealing had vast consequences for the public well-being when markets periodically crashed. (Kuttner & Stone, 2020, April 8)

As Paul M. Warburg, scion of the German-Jewish banking dynasty turned American monetary reformer opined in March, 1929:

> History, which has a painful way of repeating itself, has taught mankind that speculative overexpansion invariably ends in overcontraction and distress... If orgies of speculation are permitted to spread too far, however, the ultimate collapse is certain not only to affect the speculators themselves, but also to bring about a general depression involving the entire country. (Warburg, 1929)

The result might be termed the XYZs of liberalism: low economic growth due to oligopolistic cartelization and consolidation of corporate wealth and power during the gilded age lead to declining spending power of most citizens, then widespread stock market speculation, then declining birth rates—later called "secular stagnation" by the economist Alvin Hansen. This only became more apparent when the stock market crashed on Black Tuesday, 1929, and corporate greed and speculation at the top of the social pyramid shattered the grand potlatch illusion (that a trickling-down rising tide lifts all boats). After taking power in the fallout of the Hoover's order for MacArthur and Patton to destroy the Bonus Army encampment at Anacostia Flats, FDR's New Deal advisors, Adolf Berle and Gardiner Means argued uncontestedly that corporations would need to be reorganized to redistribute zero-sum power (and therefore wealth) downwards (Berle & Means, 1932, pp. 124, 278; Smith et al., 2019).

Initially, most American overseas imperialism before WWI was concerned with maintaining authority over Cuba, the Philippines, Hawaii, Alaska and Panama as landholdings in the global zero-sum competition for territory. But after WWI, the defining feature of the American foreign policy portfolio became more diversified: sugar, oil and fruit had become the cash crops du jour and Wall Street would be remiss to allow control over access to these profitable resources (which could draw in even more bullion) to fall to rival power players or to local populations. By extension, the US corporate interference in Latin American countries' political and economic affairs (Mexico, Honduras, Panama and Cuba), was meant to lure as much gold back to New York as possible—and made for the first "Banana Republics" as coined by O. Henry in 1904 and lamented by the proud Latin American arielist followers of Ruben Darío) (Jáuregui, 2008). The American general Smedley Butler was hired to conduct public foreign policy on behalf of private interests, and later confessed himself an economic hit man in the November 1935 issue of the socialist magazine *Common Sense* and his 1935 book (*War is a Racket*) (Butler, 1935; Schmidt, 1998, p. 231).

These revelations appeared shortly after Butler outed a fascist plot by Wall Street to overthrow FDR and install a dictator friendlier to them (The New York Times, 1934, November 21). As one historian observed in 1950: "In March, 1934, the New Deal was a year old. The economic collapse which had provoked it and the confused but determined activities of the New Deal had become, by then, profoundly disturbing to men whose gods were Adam Smith and Herbert Spencer" (Rudolph, 1950).

Social Darwinism Part 1: Eugenics

> "Cruel men believe in a cruel god
>
> and use their belief to excuse their cruelty."
>
> Bertrand Russell, *BBC London Calling*, 1947
>
> [=*The Faith of a Rationalist*].

Smith and Spencer together formed the pillars of a secular worldview that would prove insidiously religious in character. Among modern ideas, few would be so deleterious as those related to genetics, evolution and natural selection. Research on genetics and heredity like that conducted by early-19th-c. Austro-Hungarian monk Gregor Mendel, or by later scholars influenced by him like Charles Darwin, would take a dangerous turn with the work of those who prescriptively applied evolutionary concepts to human society Spencer, a leading figure among them. The long afterlives of these ideas demonstrate how scientific thought was captured to justify extreme social inequality and greed, but this could only happen because of how pervasive they were: the so-called "unity of nature" had been embraced as common sense and cosmic law (Gillham, 2013; Teicher, 2020). The way the ideas themselves evolved as they took on a life of their own would even come back to bite some of those who first championed them.

Robert Fitzroy was a lifelong friend of Charles Darwin and captain of the HMS Beagle who was deeply interested in ideas about the "unity of nature" to be used to predict future weather. Shortly after Darwin's publication of *The Origin of Species* in 1859, as a pioneer of the new science of weather forecasting, he could see the storm clouds ironically gathering around the very ideas that Darwin and he had so vociferously championed. Racked with guilt, regret and fear about how his and Darwin's ideas would be used, he slit his own throat in London in 1865 (Browne, 2002, p. 264; Desmond & Moore, 1991, p. 495; Nichols, 2003). A year later, in 1866, army surgeon Cesare Lombroso, fresh from the University of Pavia interested in "unity of nature" theories and working for the Savoyard Italian monarchy, was promoted to a lectureship position where he sought to explain the causes of brigandage and crime. His ideas quickly turned into racial theory as he promoted the idea of anthropological criminology, biological determinism and the racial inferiority of southern Italians who later left Italy and found success in the Americas. The triumph of his ideas was such that they were fully adopted by the fascists after the installation of Mussolini in Rome. Lombroso's own daughter and son-in-law fled fascism for Switzerland where they died in 1944 at the height of the Holocaust, partly inspired by her own father's "racial science" (Gibson, 2002; Gould, 1996; Wolfgang, 1961).

Lombroso was an illustrative example of Fitzroy's fears about the terrible ways in which Darwin's ideas could backfire. From the publication of his books on the evolution of animals and humans in the third quarter of the nineteenth century, Darwin's evolutionary ideas were almost immediately utilized to construct understandings of race, justify socioeconomic stratification (feudalism), and theorize national identity, which were later subsumed into a set of theories called "Social Darwinism." Social Darwinism thus took form in the late 19th c. as a distinct ideological trend that built on Malthusianism combined with an oversimplified interpretation of Darwin's concept of evolution through natural selection. Social Darwinism boiled Darwin's evolutionary ideas down to "survival of the fittest", a phrase coined by Herbert Spencer, the primary social Darwinist, instead of Darwin himself (Darwin, 1866; Stucke, 2008, p. 973).

The upper-class advocates of Social Darwinism sought to use this somewhat neopagan law-of-the-jungle concept of biological determinism to justify the widening gap between the top and the bottom of the eternal social pyramid and the increasingly draconian laws criminalizing poverty in the late nineteenth century. Spencer may be known for his rejection of nationalism and imperialism as governmental overreach and for his advocacy of laissez-faire ideas about individual freedom and personal responsibility, which could now be considered as "proto-libertarianism." However, earlier in life, he enthusiastically adopted Malthusian ideas about warfare and imperial expansion at the zero-sum expense of "inferior races" to be cleansed from the earth, which guided late-19th-c. White Men's Burdens (McKinnon, 2010; Lindqvist, 1996; Spencer, 1864, p. 444). In the third quarter of the nineteenth century, Spencer also pioneered the idea that there could be no real alternative to the classical liberal political economy (Spencer, 1851, pp. 42, 307). In this sense, Spencer was among the first intellectuals who used evolutionary ideas to justify war as a purifying force (and thus the zero-sum struggle of "strong" vs "weak"), a late-19th-c. strand of thought that escalated into the two world wars that stained the first half of the twentieth century.

By using Social Darwinism to engage in deliberate social engineering, a new science arose: race science, which soon became known as "Eugenics." It was in fact Darwin's cousin, Sir Francis Galton (born on the same site as Joseph Priestley's old Birmingham manse), who coined the term in his 1883 book *Inquiries into Human Faculty and its Development*. Galton, a great advocate of his own genius for inventing and popularizing neologisms, created the field of "historiometry," the study of human progress, which he later used to advocate zero-sum ethnic cleansing given the depletion of available land for imperial, national and racial occupation, writing: "There exists a sentiment, for the most part quite unreasonable, against the gradual extinction of an inferior race." Yet despite the intellectualized veneer of continuous evolution and liberal progress, as the biomedical historian, Marius Turda has demonstrated, Eugenics was more an heir of Malthus than anyone else, inaugurating a zero-sum struggle of the self-appointed superior and strong vs the inferior and weak, or in other words, 'us' vs. 'them' (Darwin, 1859; Spencer, 1873).

When the zero-sum implications of Social Darwinism, Malthusianism and Eugenics propounded by self-described liberal thinkers came in the late nineteenth century to the inhabitants of the great Eurasian ecumenical, feudalist and mercantilist empires like those of the Romanovs and the Qing, these ideologies ironically influenced thinkers who used their zero-sum foundations to directly challenge them. Their intellectual fingerprints can be found all over the land-reformist and/or Marxist works of Nikolay Chernyshevsky, Peter Kropotkin, Maxim Gorky, Vladimir Chertkov and Mikhail Bakunin (Figes, 1996; Kembaev, 2010; Kropotkin, 1906; Orekhanov, 2014; Paperno, 1988; Yedlin, 1999). Similarly, when Darwin's natural selection came to imperial China, it came through the filter of Spencer's ideas, resulting in land reformist models recommended by the intelligentsia to the Qing emperors. Due to the ownership of all the finite land in China by centuries of fengjian aristocrats, Galton even suggested that the Qing emperors should colonize Africa due to their racial superiority over the "Negros." In Japan, Spencer's ideas spurred on the Meiji Reformation and the eventual colonization of Korea (Galton, 1873, 5 June; Jin, 2019; Pyle, 1969; Schwartz, 1964; Selden, 2005, p. 202).

When Galton died in 1901, his longtime eugenics student, Karl Pearson, took up his banner and waved it impetuously above the prospect of zero-sum death matches between entire nations:

> History shows me one way, and one way only, in which a high state of civilization has been produced, namely, the struggle of race with race, and the survival of the physically and mentally fitter race. If you want to know whether the lower races of man can evolve a higher type, I fear the only course is to leave them to fight it out among themselves, and even then the struggle for existence between individual and individual, between tribe and tribe, may

> not be supported by that physical selection due to a particular climate on which probably so much of the Aryan's success depended. (Pearson, 1901, pp. 19–20)

The horrors of trench warfare hardly changed his zero-sum outlook on racial survival in a fully-populated world. Similarly, Pearson advocated his mentor's position on China conquering Africa from the racially inferior Blacks: "the Hindoo and still more the Chinaman might, to the great advantage of general world progress, replace the negro in many districts of Africa." Advocating biological determinism as a deciding factor in British immigration policy, a paper he co-authored with Margaret Moul concluded its first part in this way: "*The admission of aliens to a crowded country is only advisable when those aliens in physique or mentality are the superiors of the autochthonous race.* This has so far not been demonstrable in the case of the Polish and Russian Jews" (Pearson & Moul, 1925, p. 51; emphasis in the original).

The Social Darwinism of racial and national eugenics espoused by Spencer, Galton, Pearson and their intellectual heirs (who themselves inherited zero-sum assumptions from Malthus rather than Darwin) fostered imperial chauvinism, antisemitism and national competition for seemingly finite resources, as the intelligentsias of aspiring national empires espoused such ideas as an auxiliary tool in their respective states' efforts to compete with established (mostly Anglo-American and French) great powers. For instance, the German racial theorist Ernst Haeckel waved the same banner as Pearson shortly before the outbreak of WWI, maintaining that:

> The Caucasian, or Mediterranean man (Homo Mediterraneus), has from time immemorial been placed at the head of all the races of men, as the most highly developed and perfect.... This species alone (with the exception of the Mongolian) has had an actual history; it alone has attained to that degree of civilisation which seems to raise men above the rest of nature. (Haeckel, 1914, Vol. 2, p. 429)

The example of Japan, which was often included in broader categorizations like the "Mongolian man" mentioned above by Haekel, gave Westerners a lot of pause for thought from the late 19th c. onwards. The Japanese victories over their Asian neighbors (Hokkaido, Taiwan, mainland China, Korea) and a major European/Eurasian power (imperial Russia) led to a reconsideration of their alleged inferiority. However, this reconsideration was subsumed again into a Social Darwinist—and often Eurocentric—framework. On the one hand, Japanese nationalists regarded themselves as naturally superior to their neighbors and as justified to expand at their expense or treat them as inferior beings. On the other hand, Westerners increasingly perceived Japan as a special case within Asia that resembled Europe, as evinced by the labeling of Japan as the "Prussia of the East" and of the Japanese as "Honorary Aryans" or "*Herrenvolk* of the Orient". The term "Herrenvolk" indicated a "master race;" inferior races may be allowed to exist beneath it, but certainly not to economically surpass it. In other words, the term promoted a racialized social pyramid through the new "science" of eugenics and Darwinian ideas about natural selection. This also explains why Friedrich Engels connected social and economic Darwinism to Malthusianism in order to delegitimize both ideologies as distortions of older Hobbesian misconceptions about iron laws of human societies:

> The whole Darwinists teaching of the struggle for existence is simply a transference from society to living nature of Hobbes's doctrine of bellum omnium contra omnes and of the bourgeois-economic doctrine of competition together with Malthus's theory of population. When this conjurer's trick has been performed..., the same theories are transferred back again from organic nature into history and it is now claimed that their validity as eternal laws of human society has been proved. (Engels, 1875)

The *Herrenvolk* social pyramid was already the default setting throughout the British empire: in Australia, most aborigines were simply and unceremoniously eliminated in battle or hunted down like animals (Welch, 1988; Windschuttle, 2005). In the United States, after large tracts of land were claimed from the indigenous peoples, the population was replaced by the *Herrenvolk* social pyramid: Whites on top with their own ethnic categories and Blacks, Reds and Yellows on the bottom. Museums designed to categorize various races based on their objects (often stolen) and brought to the White man's country would support and justify the status quo (Kuper, 2023). The ancient ideas about slavery, segregation, racism and the domestication of humans as livestock (as discussed in chapter 1) were updated to reflect and perpetuate the same social pyramid; only now, they also included new methods, such as the new science of craniometry, which was becoming increasingly popular around the turn of the century (Das, 2017, October 25; Lewis et al., 2011; Orsucci, 1998). The confluence of class solidarity and ethnonational solidarity facilitated the creation of official, racially delineated social pyramids, which largely characterized the culture wars of the 1920s across the English-speaking world (Vickery, 1974).

By the early twentieth century, eugenics became the lodestar of US federal socioeconomic policy and the *Herrenvolk* social pyramid increasingly relied on lynchings to maintain itself. As the American labor unionist and civil rights activist Asa Philip Randolph put it in a 1919 column in *The Messenger*, it is "the economic arrangement in the South" that constitutes the "fundamental cause of race prejudice, which is the fuse that causes the magazine of capitalism to explode into race conflicts." He blasts "prejudice as the chief weapon in the South which enables the capitalists to exploit both races" and warns that in actuality "capitalism knows no color line" and that capitalists "will coin the blood, sweat and suffering of white women and white children or black women and black children into dollars and dividends" (Randolph, 1919). Such eugenicist and white supremacist (*Herrenvolk*) social architecture institutionally relied on the old "divide-and-rule" stratagem and effectively amounted to a "war against the weak" (Black, 2012). One historian writes: "In the nineteenth century, employers' ability to pay Black workers a fraction of white wages made whites see free Black people as threats to their livelihood. In the early twentieth century, new immigrants were added to this competitive dynamic, and the result was zero sum" (McGhee, 2021).

Rightly then, reformers and labor rights advocates like William Jennings Bryan who denounced the zero-sum gold standard also denounced social darwinism. (Paul, 2009).

If Darwin's contribution to discrimination was unintentional, the story is quite different for thinkers like Houston Steward Chamberlain, the son-in-law of the arch-antisemite of the 19th-c. German art scene Richard Wagner, or even Arthur de Gobineau and Vacher de Lapouge, who deliberately promoted theories of scientific racism and normalized the concept of an "Aryan master race" (de Lapouge, 1899; Dennis, 1995; Guski-Leinwand, 2016; Hecht, 2000). These ideological outgrowths of social darwinism became so widespread after the last quarter of the nineteenth century that even John Maynard Keynes flirted with eugenics and Malthusianism in the late 1920s (Kelly, 2020; Keynes, 2013, p. 86; Magness & Hernandez, 2017; Toye, 2000).

The same ideas were simultaneously reproduced for an American ideological marketplace, most helpfully right before American entries into each World War, and most notably by three men. First was the American liberal economist-turned-racial-theorist, William Z. Ripley, who later became known for his critiques of Wall Street speculative practices and corporate consolidations for the inequality and resulting American unrest they caused in the early decades of the twentieth century, but his 1899 publication, *The Races of Europe: A Sociological Study*, had managed to perpetuate the white supremacist and antisemitic racial theories of the day (The New York Times, 1926, September 26). This was followed by Madison Grant's *The Passing of the Great Race*, published shortly before America's entry into WWI in 1916, which changed Ripley's "Teutonic" man into "Nordic" man, the archetype of the Aryan master race. Carleton Coon delivered the *coup de grâce* of the American eugenics trilogy about two decades later, which essentially reprised and updated Ripley's racial pseudoscience for the American audience of the day in Coon's own *The Races of Europe: A Sociological Study* (1939), entitled after the treatise Ripley had published forty years prior and dedicated to him. The fact that Mohammed Limnibhy, coming from an "inferior" race of Riffian Berber Moroccans, worked as a close associate of the racial theorist Carleton Coon during the Spanish Bourbon dynasty's imperial Rif War against his neighbors in the '20s and later came to America to visit his old colleague, goes to show just how deeply embedded these racial ideas had become (Coon, 1931).

In the early decades of the twentieth century, the pseudoscientific obsession with genealogical and genetic inheritance masked the very real obsession with economic inheritance. The more people believed in bootstraps self-made-manhood, the more it acquired the aura of mystique and distracted from the fact of inherited wealth and power. Economic inequality during the Gilded Age was a growing conundrum which progressives like TR and Taft sought to ameliorate, but after WWI it worsened until, by the late 1920s, the highest levels of inherited inequality were registered leading many to call it a new feudalism (Gordon, 2008; Piketty, 2014, pp. 348–351; White, 2017, pp. 752–758). By the 1930s, Alvin Hansen referred to the widespread cynical macroeconomic outlook of the time as "secular stagnation," which he feared would amount to "a check to economic progress as investment opportunities were stunted by the closing of the frontier and the collapse of immigration" (W., 2014, August 16). Even the *History Channel*, an outlet which frequently contains more pawn shop reality shows than actual historical documentaries, concedes that "income inequality increased so much during the 1920s, that by 1928, the top one percent of families received 23.9 percent of all pretax income", a situation which according to the Pew Research Center has only been surpassed since 2013 (a clear connection to the neo-feudalism that we discuss in chapter 7) (Little, 2021, March 23; DeSilver, 2013, December 5).

The pseudoscientific racism of Social Darwinism and economic folk-wisdom like "pick yourself up by your bootstraps" were both ideologies meant to justify the greed which perpetuated the unequal status quo. A great irony was that the concept of the "bootstraps" success story began as a satire in the nineteenth century and was never taken seriously until it became normalized, even mobilized in the early twentieth century. Rather than addressing their own zero-sum greedy practices, racial and genetic explanations were deemed far more suitable to those preferring to protect (and expand) their share of the pie. This is why, in the early twentieth century, American judges like Oliver Wendell Holmes Jr could justify sentencing Carrie Buck, a woman characterized as "feeble-minded", to involuntary sterilization, stating that "three generations of imbeciles are enough" (Lombardo, 2022). It was also why the era's predominant liberal economic system ("industrialization") required certain populations to be systematically disenfranchised, so that other populations could be enfranchised at their zero-sum expense. In the United States, the failure of Reconstruction led to the "Jim Crow economy," as the ruling class sought to maintain its position by ensuring that poor whites would socioeconomically remain above Blacks (Mitchell, 2000). As Rev. Dr. Martin Luther King Jr. described the psychology and the hunger of poor whites in his 1965 speech in Montgomery, Alabama, "no matter how bad off he was, at least he was a white man, better than the black man. And he ate Jim Crow" (King Jr., 1965/1983). Eugenics advocates, both in the United States and the British empire, also used their theory to justify curtailing immigration by perpetuating the idea that nonwhites, foreigners or any of their self-professed undesirables were genetically inferior and their progeny would undermine the natural supremacy of white American or British racial stock (Dickerson, 2021, April 5; Serwer, 2019, April 15). In fact, the entire discourse surrounding Social Darwinism and eugenics, when applied to immigration policy in the late nineteenth and early twentieth century, was downright zero-sum, even in well-regarded news magazines like *The Atlantic*:

> The question to-day is not of preventing the wards of our almshouses, our insane asylums, and our jails from being stuffed to repletion by new arrivals from Europe; but of protecting the American rate of wages, the American standard of living, and the quality of American citizenship from degradation through the tumultuous access of vast throngs of ignorant and brutalized peasantry from the countries of eastern and southern Europe. (Walker, 1896)

Such eugenicist ideologies of immigration restriction were internalized by the businessmen who inherited their money, property, and business acumen from their business dynasties. They also inherited the predominant potlatch social contract from Carnegie's *Gospel of Wealth.* It was not for nothing that Joseph Conrad described the banality of the antihero Kurtz of his *Heart of Darkness* as a product of the society of his time: "All Europe contributed to the making of Kurtz." But by the late 1920s, as the American labor movement was just beginning to gain political and economic strength, the two movements were combined by reformists like Richard T. Ely, Washington Gladden, Josiah Strong, Walter Rauschenbusch, and Doris Day who used Christian principles to create the "social gospel." Nevertheless, it made little difference against the era's predominant Eugenics and Social Darwinism until socioeconomic policy reforms were largely implemented in the New Deal era (Aiken & McDonnell, 1970; Rader, 1966; Rauschenusch, 1917).

Yet it wasn't just in America but throughout the industrializing world that Social Darwinism and Eugenics existed to justify the greed and inequality of the refeudalizing post-WWI era (or even before that, the proletarianization of the nineteenth century) and coexisted with the social gospel. Christian socialism gained traction in the British empire in the form of the Church of England's Christian Social Union as a method of addressing refeudalization caused by the steady structural inheritance of massive economic inequality (Inglis, 2007; Jones, 1968). Greece produced its own leader of the cause of social gospel in the "Awakening Movement" led by Apostolos Makrakis, whose efforts led to his collision with the wealthy and powerful and his own incarceration (Karageorgoudis, 2005). All the major Greek Christian organizations hail from this originating movement. Even though Makrakis came to blows with the Greek church, the ensuing organizations formed a symbiotic relationship with both church and state, fostering socially regressive mentalities and authoritarianism, co-operating with dictatorships, and promoting anticommunist hysteria (Makrides, 2004; Moustakis, 1983). In France, a Catholic-inflected social gospel trend was influenced by the early-19th-c. thinker Henri Saint-Simon, becoming an entire movement, Saint Simonianism, one of whose most prominent followers was none other than Emile Durkheim (Carlisle, 1987; Durkheim, 1958). Saint Simonianism also came to Germany in the form of the German Youth Movement (*Jugendbewegung*, an update from the Young Germany movement of the 1840s) (Butler, 1968). One of the foremost manifestations of this new German social movement was the Christian Social Party of Germany, established in the 1870s, founded by Adolf Stoecker, who advocated Christian potlatch social policies (a *Herrenvolk* democracy) at the zero-sum expense of racial minorities—primarily Jews, who were vilified as corrupt financiers and usurers based on the forged *Protocols of the Elders of Zion* (1899) (Telman, 1995). Stoecker was also a professor of economics who represented the right wing of the so-called Socialists of the Chair (*Kathedersozialisten*). Much like neoliberalism after the crises of the 1970s, this conservative ideological current was first incubated in academia and gathered steam only after the crisis of 1873. Being an amalgamation of social reform, economic protectionism, paternalism, militarism and nationalism, it provided a promising alternative to laissez-faire capitalism. A paradigm change was underway in Germany that would define its political economy long after the 1870s (Fricke, 1970, pp. 245–255).

So, social darwinism and eugenics were promoted under the guise of science alongside social gospel, both as the spearhead of technocratic modernity and as the shield of anti-secular traditionalism. But it was moreover enshrined in law, as elites who control the state often tend to do with their zero-sum ideologies and practices. The most infamous legal framework of this sort was that of Nazi Germany. The 1935 Nuremberg Laws have been much publicized, but there was also a plethora of other less-known legal "innovations" that followed. Even less-known is that the Nazis did not in reality innovate as much as they copied US legislation, finding the treatment of Blacks by the US federal government a very welcome blueprint for the way they would deal with their "Jewish Question", with segregation and ghettos being a prime example (this was later noticed by Dr. W. E. B. du Bois in his "The Negro and the Warsaw Ghetto") (Du Bois, 1952; Whitman, 2018). In fact, some Nazis considered American Jim Crow laws "*too* racist" (Whitman, 2018, p. 5).

This didn't stop German (and later Nazi) eugenics advocates such as Hans F. K. Günther, like their industrializing brethren in the United States and the British empire, from basing their political programs on racial and national theories (Bergman, 1992). Likewise, Japanese eugenicists and criminologists based their agendas on blood types (Becker, 2006, p. 294). These pseudoscientific theories of social darwinism and eugenics also underwrote German and Japanese militarism and imperialism in their advocacy of expansion to mirror the Anglo-American model (Gow, 2004; Ito, 2019; Brendon, 2000, pp. 438–464, 633–660). For example, Hans Grimm's 1926 novel *Volk ohne Raum* (*A People without Space*) presented an idealized version of an expanded Germany, whose supposedly racially superior Aryans ought to take the lands of racially inferior peoples like the Slavs, just as the British and Americans had done elsewhere in the world. Another German eugenics proponent named Adolf Hitler used such ideas in his *Mein Kampf* (1925), and later, following his orders, the Nazi propaganda apparatus produced material like the 1940 films *Der ewige Jude* and *Jud Süss* to justify his policies of racial annihilation. He also compared the Slavs to animals and considered them unclean, lazy, and narrow-minded. His belief in their inferiority is succinctly expressed in a September 17th, 1941 comment of his: "The Slavs are a mass of bom slaves, who feel the need of a master." To Hitler, the inferiority of the Slavs necessitated a Germanic White's Man's Burden to civilize them (or at least put them to work) and expropriate their lands—not dissimilar from White Americans' "manifest destiny" beyond the Mississippi or British imperial policy beyond the Indus: "If the English were to be driven out of India, India would perish. Our role in Russia will be analogous to that of England in India. [...] The Russian space is our India. Like the English, we shall rule this empire with a handful of men" (Trevor-Roper, 1953, pp. 33–34).

These ideas about primordial, perhaps even biological national or racial taxonomies that circulated already in the late 19th c., and constituted a crude application of Darwin's theories to human societies interacted with ideological currents that had captured the imagination of intellectual elites, such as Nietzscheanism (critique of Christian ethic of charity and empathy for the weak coupled with lionization of the strong), producing an explosive mixture in the process.

> While the Spanish had been fortified by religion, the Germans and other more recent supplanters were fortified by fashionable notions of racial science, with evolutionary theories and ideas of social Darwinism causing people to see the world in terms of "the survival of the fittest." (Day, 2008, p. 90)

Both the genocidal and the economic implications of this mixture would be reinforced and manifest more openly in the 1930s and 1940s: forced sterilization programs, euthanasia of the physically and mentally ill, industrialized genocide. The arguments employed by early exponents of these ideas and the Nazis alike would often rely clearly on zero-sum thinking, e.g. emphasizing the cost of treating people with hereditary diseases, money "wasted" that could be spent otherwise. Even in the case of Carrie Buck, the woman sentenced to forced sterilization by the US Supreme Court, the petition of the Superintendent of the Virginia Colony in which she was held, argued that, were she to be sterilized, she could be released back into society, "and thereby relieve the Commonwealth of Virginia of the burden of the support of her custodial care" (Petition of A.S. Priddy, 1924).

Even if the emergence of Social Darwinism as a distinct theory with scientific pretensions and explicit applicability is largely a thing of the past, it remains with us today as the worldview that is the guiding principle of a few influential organizations and many "successful" personalities—even if, as we will see in chapter 7, it has adopted the veneer of meritocracy. But if there is some truth in the social darwinist narrative, it is that the fittest are not the best but the most ruthless. It's far from the greatest social arrangement when the most antisocial and manipulative personalities climb to the top of the zero-sum social pyramid. Rather than advancing the health of the social body, as it purports, social darwinism encourages the development and predomination of dysfunctional and destructive personality types at the expense of society—and ultimately the unraveling of the social fabric itself (Radkiewicz & K Skarżyńska, 2021; Sharpe, 2024).

References

Adams, D. (1995). *Education for extinction: American Indians and the boarding school experience, 1875–1928*. University Press of Kansas.

Adler, M. (2010, January 4). Bringing overpaid executives to heel. *Los Angeles Times*. http://www.columbia.edu/~ma820/bringing.overpaid.executives.to.heel.html

Alfred, J. C., & William, J. B. Tr., (1876). *Tacitus. Annales*. Macmillan.

Aiken, J., & McDonnell, J. (1970). Walter Rauschenbusch and labor reform: A social gospeller's approach. *Labor History, 11*(2), 131–150.

Allam, L., & Evershed, N. (2019, March 3). The killing times: The massacres of Aboriginal people Australia must confront. *The Guardian*. https://www.theguardian.com/australia-news/2019/mar/04/the-killing-times-the-massacres-of-aboriginal-people-australia-must-confront

Angell, N. (1909). *The great illusion: A study of the relation of military power to national advantage*. Heinemann.

Arnason, J. (2018). Mauss revisited: The birth of civilizational analysis from the spirit of anthropology. In J. Arnason & C. Hann (Eds.), *Anthropology and civilizational analysis: Eurasian explorations* (pp. 1–33). SUNY Press.

Ayonrinde, O. (2020). 'Brain fag': A syndrome associated with 'overstudy' and mental exhaustion in 19th century Britain. *International Review of Psychiatry, 32*(5–6), 520–535. https://doi.org/10.1080/09540261.2020.1775428

Backhaus, J. (Ed.). (2012). *Handbook of the history of economic thought: Insights on the founders of modern economics*. Springer.

Babcock, R. (1974). *Gompers in Canada: A study in American continentalism before the First World War*. University of Toronto Press.

Barro, R., & Ursua, J. (2009, May 5). Pandemics and depressions. *The Wall Street Journal*. https://www.wsj.com/articles/SB124147840167185071

Barrington, J. (2008). *Separate but equal?: Māori schools and the Crown, 1867–1969*. Victoria University Press.

Barraclough, G. (1982). *From Agadir to Armageddon: Anatomy of a crisis*. Holmes & Meier.

Beard, G. (1869). Neurasthenia, or nervous exhaustion. *The Boston Medical and Surgical Journal, 80*(13), 217–221. https://doi.org/10.1056/NEJM186904290801301

Beaudreau, B. (2006). *The economic consequences of Mr. Keynes: How the second industrial revolution passed Great Britain*. Universe.

Bell, C. (1997). Thinking the unthinkable: British and American naval strategies for an Anglo-American war, 1918–1931. *International History Review, 19*(4), 789–808.

Bergman, J. (1992). Eugenics and the development of Nazi race policy. *Perspectives on Science and Christian Faith, 44*, 109–124.

Berle, A., & Means, G. (1932). *The modern corporation and private property*. Macmillan.

Birrell, A. (1885). *Obiter dicta*. Elliot Stock.

Black, E. (2012). *War against the weak: Eugenics and America's campaign to create a master race*. Dialog Press.

Bloomfield, A. I. (1959). *Monetary policy under the international gold standard, 1880–1914*. Federal Reserve Bank of New York.

Boemeke, M., Chickering, R., & Förster, S. (Eds.). (1999). *Anticipating total war: The German and American experiences, 1871–1914*. German Historical Institute.

Boettke, P. (2019). What happens when the economic past is left to the kindness of its enemies? *The Independent Review, 24*(2), 279–287.

Bowler, K. (2013). *Blessed: A history of the American prosperity gospel*. Oxford University Press.

Brecht, B. (1934). *Threepenny novel*. Allert de Lange.

Brecht, B. (1956). *Threepenny novel* (A. B. Bowles, Trans.). Grove Press.

Brendon, P. (2000). *The dark valley: A panorama of the 1930s*. Knopf.

Browne, E. J. (2002). *Charles Darwin: The power of place* (Vol. 2). Princeton University Press.

Buti, A. (2004). The removal of indigenous children from their families—US and Australia compared. *University of Western Sydney Law Review, 8*, 125–152.

Butler, E. (1968). *The Saint-Simonian religion in Germany: A study of the Young German movement*. Fertig.

Butler, S. (1935). *War is a racket*. Round Table.

Carlisle, R. (1987). *The proffered crown: Saint-Simonianism and the doctrine of hope*. Johns Hopkins University Press.

Carnegie, A. (1901). *The gospel of wealth and other timely essays*. Century.

Carter, Z. (2021, June 19). The real problem with globalization. *The Atlantic*. https://www.theatlantic.com/politics/archive/2021/06/globalization-bretton-woods-keynes-history/619232/

Chancellor, E. (1999). *Devil take the hindmost: A history of financial speculation*. Farrar, Straus and Giroux.

Clark, J. B. (1886). *The philosophy of wealth: Economic principles newly formulated*. Macmillan.

Clark, J. B. (1888). The limits of competition. In J. B. Clark & F. H. Giddings (Eds.), *The modern distributive process* (p. 2). Ginn.

Clark, J. B. (1899). *The distribution of wealth: A theory of wages, interest and profits*. Macmillan.

Cock, J., & Nathan, L. (1996). *War and society in colonial Malawi*. Currey.
Corbin, D. (2011). *Gun thugs, rednecks, and radicals: A documentary history of the West Virginia mine wars*. PM Press.
Coon, C. (1931). *Tribes of the Rif*. Peabody Museum.
Currarino, R. (2011). *The labor question in America: Economic democracy in the Gilded Age*. University of Illinois Press.
Das, S. (2017, October 25). Racism, eugenics and the domestication of humans. *UCL Culture Online*. https://blogs.ucl.ac.uk/museums/2017/10/25/racism-eugenics-and-the-domestication-of-humans
Darwin, C. (1859). *On the origin of the species by means of natural selection*. Murray.
Darwin, C. (1866). Letter no. 5145 to A. Wallace. *Darwin Correspondence Project*. https://www.darwinproject.ac.uk/letter/?docId=letters/DCP-LETT-5145.xml
Daugherty, G. (2015, 25 March). The brief history of Americanitis. *Smithsonian*. Accessed 27 March 2026. https://www.smithsonianmag.com/history/brief-history-americanitis-180954739/
Day, D. (2008). *Conquest: How societies overwhelm others*. Oxford University Press.
De Blij, H. (2012). *Why geography matters: More than ever*. Oxford University Press.
De Lapouge, G. (1899). *L'Aryan, son rôle social*. Fontemoing.
Desmond, A., & Moore, J. (1991). *Darwin*. Joseph.
Dennis, R. (1995). Social Darwinism, scientific racism, and the metaphysics of race. *Journal of Negro Education, 64*(3), 243–252. https://doi.org/10.2307/2967206
DeSilver, D. (2013, December 5). U.S. income inequality, on rise for decades, is now highest since 1928. *Pew Research Center*. https://www.pewresearch.org/short-reads/2013/12/05/u-s-income-inequality-on-rise-for-decades-is-now-highest-since-1928/
Dickerson, C. (2021, April 5). America never wanted the tired, poor, huddled masses. *The Atlantic*. https://www.theatlantic.com/magazine/archive/2021/05/united-states-immigration-exclusion/618390/
Du Bois, W. E. B. (1952). The Negro and the Warsaw Ghetto. Orthodox Jewish Congregations of America. https://europe.unc.edu/wp-content/uploads/sites/314/2021/02/DuBois-The-Negro-and-the-Warsaw-Ghetto.pdf
Dugin, A. (2012). *The fourth political theory*. Eurasian Movement.
Durkheim, É. (1933). *The division of labor in society*. Free Press.
Durkheim, É. (1958). *Socialism and Saint-Simon* (A. Gouldner & C. Sattler, Eds. & Trans.). Antioch Press.
Edwards, P. (2007). *Cambodge: The cultivation of a nation, 1860–1945*. University of Hawai'i Press.
Elkins, C. (2022, June 4). The imperial fictions behind the Queen's Platinum Jubilee. *The New York Times*. https://www.nytimes.com/2022/06/04/opinion/the-imperial-fictions-behind-the-queens-platinum-jubilee.html
Engels, F. (1875, November 12–17). Engels' letter to Pyotr Lavrov in London. *Marx-Engels Correspondence*.
Erwin, E. (2002). *The Freud encyclopedia: Theory, therapy, and culture*. Routledge.
Feldman, A. M. (2024). *Orthodox mercantilism: Political economy in the Byzantine Commonwealth*. Routledge.
Ferguson, N. (2006). *The war of the world: Twentieth-century conflict and the descent of the West*. Penguin.
Fergusson, A. (1975). *Das Ende des Geldes. Hyperinflation und ihre Folgen für die Menschen am Beispiel der Weimarer Republik*. Finanzbuch.
Ferns, N. (2015). Manifest destiny crosses the Pacific: The utility of American expansion in Australia, 1850–1901. *Australasian Journal of American Studies, 34*(2), 28–43. http://www.jstor.org/stable/44779732
Figes, O. (1996). Maxim Gorky and the Russian revolution. *History Today, 46*(6), 16.
Fischer, D. H. (1989). *Albion's seed: Four British folkways in America*. Oxford University Press.
Fricke, D. (Hrsg.). (1970). *Die Bürgerlichen Parteien in Deutschland. Handbuch der Geschichte der bürgerlichen Parteien und anderer bürgerlicher Interessenorganisationen vom Vormärz bis*

zum Jahre 1945. Band 2: Fraktion Augsburger Hof – Zentrum. VEB Bibliographisches Institut Leipzig. S. 245–255.
Galbraith, J. K. (1994). *A short history of financial euphoria*. Penguin.
Galton, F. (1873, June 5). Africa for the Chinese: To the editor of The Times. *The Times*. https://galton.org/letters/africa-for-chinese/AfricaForTheChinese.htm
Garcia, C. (2017, July 26). When Keynes pondered Malthus. *Financial Times*. http://ftalphaville.ft.com/2017/07/26/2191314/the-lessons-of-keynes-pondering-malthus/
Gibson, M. (2002). *Born to crime: Cesare Lombroso and the origins of biological criminology*. Praeger.
Giordano, C. (2003). Interdependente Vielfalt: Die historischen Regionen Europas. In K. Kaser (Ed.), *Europa und die Grenzen im Kopf* (pp. 113–134). Wieser-Verlag.
Girdner, J. (1901). *Newyorkitis*. Stokes.
Gillham, N. (2013). The battle between the biometricians and the Mendelians: How Sir Francis Galton's work caused his disciples to reach conflicting conclusions about the hereditary mechanism. *Science & Education, 24*(1–2), 61–75. https://doi.org/10.1007/s11191-013-9642-1
Gompers, S. (1925). *Seventy years of life and labor*. Dutton.
Gompers, S., & Gutstadt, H. (1908). *Meat vs. rice: American manhood against Asiatic coolieism, which shall survive?*. Asiatic Exclusion League.
Gordon, R. J. (2016). *The rise and fall of American growth: The U.S. standard of living since the civil war*. Princeton University Press.
Gould, S. (1996). *The mismeasure of man*. Norton.
Gow, I. (2004). *Military intervention in pre-war Japanese politics: Admiral Kato Kanji and the Washington system*. RoutledgeCurzon.
Grant, J. (2014). *The forgotten depression, 1921—The crash that cured itself*. Simon & Schuster.
Greene, J. (1998). *Pure and simple politics: The American Federation of Labor and political activism, 1881–1917*. Cambridge University Press.
Grinin, L., & Korotayev, A. (2015). *Great divergence and great convergence: A global perspective*. Springer.
Grubbs, F., Jr. (1968). *The struggle for labor loyalty: Gompers, the A. F. of L., and the pacifists, 1917–1920*. Duke University Press.
Guski-Leinwand, S. (2016). 3. "Wissenschaftlicher Antisemitismus": Abriss zu seiner Begriffsgenese und zu seinen Ausprägungen im 20. Jahrhundert. In *Psychologie und Totalitarismus: Die Abwendung vom Humanitätsgedanken in der Psychologie und die Folgen (ca. 1895–1945)* (Lang). https://doi.org/10.3726/b10520/13
Halo, T. (2001). *Not even my name*. Picador.
Haeckel, E. (1914). *The history of creation (Vol. II* (6th ed.). Appleton.
Hecht, J. (2000). Vacher de Lapouge and the rise of Nazi science. *Journal of the History of Ideas, 61*(2), 285–304. https://doi.org/10.2307/3654024
Heffer, S. (2017). *The age of decadence: Britain 1880 to 1914*. Random House.
Hedges, C. (2000, September 17). A few words in Greek tell of a homeland lost. *The New York Times*. https://www.nytimes.com/2000/09/17/nyregion/a-few-words-in-greek-tell-of-a-homeland-lost.html
Heron, A. (1954). *Reasonable goals in industrial relations*. Stanford University Press.
Herzog, W., II. (1994). *Parables as subversive speech: Jesus as pedagogue of the oppressed*. John Knox Press.
Hobsbawm, E. (1987). *The age of empire: 1875–1914*. Weidenfeld & Nicolson.
Hobsbawm, E. (1994). *The age of extremes: The short twentieth century, 1914–1991*. Vintage.
Hobson, J. (1902). *Imperialism: A study*. Allen & Unwin.
Holt, T. (1988). Joint Plan Red. *MHQ: Quarterly Journal of Military History, 1*(1), 48–55.
Hudson, M. (2012). The road to debt deflation, debt peonage, and neofeudalism. *Economics Institute of Bard College Working Paper*, 708, 5. https://www.levyinstitute.org/pubs/wp_708.pdf
Huntington, E. (1907). *The pulse of Asia: A journey in Central Asia illustrating the geographic basis of history*. Houghton Mifflin.

Inglis, K. (2007). *Churches and the working classes in Victorian England (Original work published 1963)*. Routledge.
Ito, T. (2019). *Militarismus des Zivilen in Japan 1937–1940: Diskurse und ihre Auswirkungen auf politische Entscheidungsprozesse*. Iudicium.
Jáuregui, C. (1998). Calibán, ícono del 98. A propósito de un artículo de Rubén Darío. *Revista Iberoamericana, 64*(184–185), 441–449.
Jáuregui, C. (2008). *Canibalia: canibalismo, calibanismo, antropofagia cultural y consumo en América Latina*. Iberoamericana.
Jin, X. (2019). Translation and transmutation: The origin of species in China. *British Journal for the History of Science, 52*(1), 117–141. https://doi.org/10.1017/S0007087418000808
Jones, P. (1968). *Christian socialist revival, 1877–1914: Religion, class, and social conscience in late-Victorian England*. Princeton University Press.
Kaplan, R. (2018). *The return of Marco Polo's world: War, strategy, and American interests in the twenty-first century*. Random House.
Karageorgoudis, E. (2005). *Χριστιανισμός και πολιτική κατά τον Απόστολο Μακράκη [Christianity and politics according to Apostolos Makrakis]*. Vryennios.
Kelly, D. (2020). Malthusian moments in the work of John Maynard Keynes. *Historical Journal, 63*(1), 127–158. https://doi.org/10.1017/S0018246X19000104
Kembaev, Zh. (2010). Федералистские идеи М. А. Бакунина относительно объединения народов Европы и всего мира [M. A. Bakunin's federalist ideas regarding the union of the peoples of Europe and the whole world]. *Право и политика, 11*, 2016–2025
Keynes, J. M. (1920). *The economic consequences of the peace*. Macmillan.
Keynes, J. (1924, March 30). On the mysteries of American finance; The gold standard "a barbarous relic," and other opinions in his "Monetary Reform." *The New York Times*. https://www.nytimes.com/1924/03/30/archives/mr-keynes-on-the-mysteries-of-american-finance-the-gold-standard-a.html
Keynes, J. M. (2013). *The collected writings of John Maynard Keynes* (3rd ed.). Cambridge University Press.
Kiernan, V. (1983, January 10). Royal mysteries. *London Review of Books, 5*(1), 3–5. https://www.lrb.co.uk/the-paper/v05/n01/v.g.-kiernan/royal-mysteries
Kitsikis, D. (2002). Une vision géopolitique: La Région intermédiaire. *Relations Internationales, 109*, 15–28.
King Jr., M. L. (1965, March 25). Our God Is Marching On! (How Long, Not Long). In J. M. Washington (Ed.), *Speeches and writings of Martin Luther King Jr.* (Harper & Row, 1983).
Knafo, S. (2013). *The making of modern finance: Liberal governance and the gold standard*. Routledge.
Kropotkin, P. (1906). *Conquest of bread*. Putnam.
Kuehn, D. (2011). A critique of powell, woods, and murphy on the 1920–1921 depression. *Review of Austrian Economics, 24*(3), 273–291. https://doi.org/10.1007/s11138-010-0131-3
Kuper, A. (2023). *The museum of other people: From colonial acquisitions to cosmopolitan exhibitions*. Profile.
Kuttner, R., & Stone, K. (2020, April 8). The rise of neo-feudalism: The private capture of entire legal systems by corporate America goes far beyond neoliberalism. *The American Prospect*. https://prospect.org/economy/rise-of-neo-feudalism/
Laborde, J. (1879). *Relation de Madagascar sous le règne de Ranavalona I*. Firmin-Didot.
Le Naour, J.-Y. (1914). *La grande illusion*. Perrin.
Lewis, J., DeGusta, D., Meyer, M., Monge, J., Mann, A., & Holloway, R. (2011). The mismeasure of science: Stephen Jay Gould versus Samuel George Morton on skulls and bias. *PLOS Biology, 9*(6), Article e1001071. https://doi.org/10.1371/journal.pbio.1001071
Lindqvist, S. (1996). *Exterminate all the brutes*. New Press.
Little, B. (2021, March 23). Why the roaring twenties left many Americans poorer. *History Channel*. https://www.history.com/news/roaring-twenties-labor-great-depression
Livesay, H. (1987). *Samuel Gompers and organized labor in America*. Addison-Wesley.

Lombardo, P. (2022). *Three generations, no imbeciles: Eugenics, the Supreme Court, and Buck v. Bell*. Johns Hopkins University Press.

Long, D., & Machan, T. (Eds.). (2008). *Anarchism/minarchism: Is a government part of a free country?* Ashgate.

Maçães, B. (2018). *The dawn of Eurasia: On the trail of the new world order*. Yale University Press.

Mackinder, H. J. (1904). The geographical pivot of history. *The Geographical Journal, 23*(4), 421–437.

Mackinder, H. J. (1942). *Democratic ideals and reality: A study in the politics of reconstruction*. National Defense University Press.

Mahan, A. T. (1890). *The impact of sea power on history*. Little, Brown & Co.

Makrides, V. (2004). Orthodoxy in the service of anticommunism: The religious organization Zoe during the Greek civil war. In P. Carabott & T. Sfikas (Eds.), *The Greek civil war: Essays on a conflict of exceptionalism and silences* (pp. 159–174). Ashgate.

Major, J. (1998). War plan red: The American plan for war with Britain. *The Historian, 58*(1), 12–15.

Magness, P., & Hernandez, S. (2017). The economic eugenicism of John Maynard Keynes. *Journal of Markets and Morality, 20*(1), 79–100.

Mandel, B. (1963). *Samuel Gompers: A biography*. Penguin.

Mandel, B. (1955). Samuel Gompers and the Negro workers, 1886–1914. *Journal of Negro History, 40*(1), 34–60.

Marshall, A. (1890). *Principles of economics*. Macmillan.

Marshall, T. (2015). *Prisoners of geography: Ten maps that tell you everything you need to know about global politics*. Scribner.

Marx, K. (1964). *Economic and philosophic manuscripts of 1844*. International Publishers.

Marx, K. (1867). *Das Kapital* (Vol. I). Otto Meissner.

McGhee, H. (2021). *The sum of us: What racism costs everyone and how we can prosper together*. Penguin.

McKinnon, A. M. (2010). Energy and society: Herbert Spencer's 'energetic sociology' of social evolution and beyond. *Journal of Classical Sociology, 10*(4), 439–455. https://doi.org/10.1177/1468795X10385184

Meltzer, A. H. (2000). Lessons from the early history of the Federal Reserve. *Atlantic Economic Journal, 28*, 269–278. https://doi.org/10.1007/BF02298317

Milloy, J. (1999). *A national crime: The Canadian government and the residential school system 1879–1986*. University of Manitoba Press.

Mitchell, T. (2000). From reconstruction to deconstruction: Undermining black landownership, political independence, and community through partition sales of tenancies in common. *Northwestern University Law Review, 95*(2), 505–580.

Mink, G. (1986). *Old labor and new immigrants in American political development: Union, party, and state, 1875–1920*. Cornell University Press.

Moustakis, G. (1983). *Η γέννηση του Χριστιανοφασισμού στην Ελλάδα [The birth of Christian-fascism in Greece]*. Kaktos.

Munro-Hay, S. C. (1991). *Aksum: An African civilisation of late antiquity*. Edinburgh University Press.

Nackenoff, C. (1994). *The fictional republic*. Oxford University Press.

Nackenoff, C. (1997). The Horatio Alger myth. In P. Gerster & N. Cords (Eds.), *Myth America: A historical anthology II*. Brandywine Press.

Nichols, P. (2003). *Evolution's captain: The dark fate of the man who sailed Charles Darwin around the world*. HarperCollins.

Olcott, C. (1916). *The life of William McKinley* (Vol. II). Houghton Mifflin.

Orsucci, A. (1998). Ariani, indogermani, stirpi mediterranee: Aspetti del dibattito sulle razze europee (1870–1914). *Cromohs, 3*, 1–9.

Orekhanov, G. (2014). В. Г. Чертков в жизни Л. Н. Толстого [V.G. Chertkov in the life of L.N. Tolstoy]. ПСТГУ.

Papageorgiou, P. (2014, December 19). Συνέντευξη: Η Σάνο Χάλο, η "Γιαγιά των Ποντίων." *Armenian Weekly*. https://www.pontosnews.gr/309061/synentefxeis/synentefxi-i-sano-chalo-i-giagia-ton-p/
Paperno, I. (1988). *Chernyshevsky and the age of realism: A study in the semiotics of behavior*. Stanford University Press.
Paul, D. B. (2009). Darwin, social Darwinism & eugenics. In G. Radick & M. Hodge (Eds.), *The Cambridge companion to Darwin* (pp. 219–245). Cambridge University Press.
Pearson, K. (1901). *National life from the standpoint of science*. Black.
Pearson, K., & Moul, M. (1925). The problem of alien immigration into Great Britain, illustrated by an examination of Russian and Polish Jewish children. *Annals of Eugenics, 1*(2), 5–54. https://doi.org/10.1111/j.1469-1809.1925.tb02037
Piketty, T. (2014). *Capital in the twenty-first century* (A. Goldhammer, Trans.). Harvard University Press.
Polychroniou, C. (2021, October 13). Chomsky, Pollin and Lapavitsas: Are we witnessing the demise of neoliberalism? *Truthout*. https://truthout.org/articles/chomsky-pollin-and-lapavitsas-are-we-witnessing-the-demise-of-neoliberalism/
Prouty, C. (1986). *Empress Taytu and Menilek II: Ethiopia 1883–1910*. Red Sea Press.
Pyle, K. (1969). *The new generation in Meiji Japan*. Stanford University Press.
Radkiewicz, P., & Skarżyńska, K. (2021). Who are the 'Social Darwinists'? On dispositional determinants of perceiving the social world as competitive jungle. *PLoS ONE, 16*(8), Article e0254434. https://doi.org/10.1371/journal.pone.0254434
Rader, B. (1966). Richard T. Ely: Lay spokesman for the social gospel. *Journal of American History, 53*(1), 61–74. https://doi.org/10.2307/1893930
Randolph, A. (1919). Lynching: Capitalism its cause; socialism its cure. *The Messenger*, 9–12. https://www.marxists.org/history/usa/pubs/messenger/1919-03-mar-Messenger.pdf
Rauschenbusch, W. (1917). *A theology for the social gospel*. Macmillan.
Reed, L. (1930). *The labor philosophy of Samuel Gompers*. Columbia University Press.
Ricardo, D. (1817). *On the principles of political economy and taxation*. John Murray.
Rudolph, F. (1950). The American liberty league, 1934–1940. *American Historical Review 56*, 19–33.
Safire, W. (1983, October 16). On language; dust heaps of history. *The New York Times*. https://nyti.ms/29yvYCj
Saxton, A. (1971). *The indispensable enemy: Labor and the anti-Chinese movement in California*. University of California Press.
Scharnhorst, G. (1980). *Horatio Alger Jr*. Twayne Publishers.
Scharnhorst, G., & Bales, J. (1981). *Horatio Alger Jr.: An annotated bibliography of comment and criticism*. Scarecrow Press.
Scharnhorst, G., & Bales, J. (1985). *The lost life of Horatio Alger Jr*. Indiana University Press.
Schmidt, H. (1998). *Maverick Marine: General Smedley D. Butler and the contradictions of American military history*. University Press of Kentucky.
Schumpeter, J. (1942). *Capitalism, socialism and democracy*. Harper.
Schwartz, B. (1964). *In search of wealth and power*. Harvard University Press.
Selden, M. (2005). *Political economy of Chinese development*. Routledge.
Serwer, A. (2019, April 15). White nationalism's deep American roots. *The Atlantic*. https://www.theatlantic.com/magazine/archive/2019/04/adam-serwer-madison-grant-white-nationalism/583258/
Sharpe, M. (2024). After trickle down, kicking down: On Jordan Peterson, naturalizing inequality, and neofascist indirect apologetics. *Critical Sociology, 0*(0), 1–19. https://doi.org/10.1177/08969205241284282
Simon, T. (2011). *Eurasia's new frontiers: Young states, old societies, open futures*. Cornell University Press.
Smith, A. (1776). *An inquiry into the nature and causes of the wealth of nations* (Book I, Chapter VIII). Strahan & Cadell.

Smith, A., Tennent, K., & Russell, J. (2019). Berle and Means's The modern corporation and private property: The military roots of a stakeholder model of corporate governance. *Seattle University Law Review, 42*(2), 535–563.
Smyth, W. (1921). *Technocracy. First, second and third series. Social universals.* University of California Press.
Spencer, H. (1851). *Social statics.* Chapman.
Spencer, H. (1864). *Principles of biology.* Williams & Norgate.
Spencer, H. (1873). *The study of sociology.* King & Co.
Spencer, T. (2000). *The St. Louis Veiled Prophet Celebration: Power on Parade, 1877–1995.* University of Missouri Press.
Stucke, M. (2008). Better competition advocacy. *St. John's Law Review, 82*(3), 951–1036.
Taft, P. (1957). *The A.F. of L. in the time of Gompers.* Harper.
Teicher, A. (2020). *Social Mendelism: Genetics and the politics of race in Germany, 1900–1948.* Cambridge University Press. https://doi.org/10.1017/9781108583190
Telman, D. (1995). Adolf Stoecker: Anti-Semite with a Christian mission. *Jewish History, 9*, 93–112. https://doi.org/10.1007/BF01668991
The Nation. (1902). Vol. 74. New York Evening Post Co.
Théry, E. (1914). *La transformation économique de la Russie.* Économiste européen.
Toye, J. (2000). *Keynes on population.* Oxford University Press.
Trevor-Roper, H. (1953). *Hitler's table talk 1941–1944.* Weidenfeld & Nicolson.
Turda, M. (Ed.). (2013). *Crafting humans: From Genesis to eugenics and beyond.* VR Unipress.
Turner, F. J. (1894). The significance of the frontier in American history. *Annual Report of the American Historical Association* (pp. 199–227). Government Printing Office.
Turk, R. (1987). *The ambiguous relationship: Theodore Roosevelt and Alfred Thayer Mahan.* Greenwood Press.
van Deusen, E. (1869). Observations on a form of nervous prostration, (neurasthenia) culminating in insanity. *American Journal of Insanity, 25*(4), 445–461. https://doi.org/10.1176/ajp.25.4.445
van Krieken, R. (1999). The 'stolen generations' and cultural genocide: The forced removal of Australian indigenous children from their families and its implications for the sociology of childhood. *Childhood, 6*(3), 297–311. https://doi.org/10.1177/0907568299006003002
Veblen, T. (1899). *The theory of the leisure class: An economic study of institutions.* Macmillan.
Vernon, J. (1991). The 1920–21 deflation: The role of aggregate supply. *Economic Inquiry, 29*(3), 572–580. https://doi.org/10.1111/j.1465-7295.1991.tb00847.x
Vickery, K. (1974). 'Herrenvolk' democracy and egalitarianism in South Africa and the U.S. South. *Comparative Studies in Society and History, 16*(3), 309–328. http://www.jstor.org/stable/178268
Viner, J. (1927). Adam Smith and laissez faire. *Journal of Political Economy, 35*(2), 198–232. http://www.jstor.org/stable/1823421
von Mises, L. (1985). *Liberalism (Original work published 1927).* Fox & Wilkes.
Warburg, P. (1929, March 9). Vol. 128, No. 3324. *Commercial and Financial Chronicle.* https://fraser.stlouisfed.org/title/1339/item/517038
Welch, A. R. (1988). Aboriginal education as internal colonialism: The schooling of an indigenous minority in Australia. *Comparative Education, 24*(2). 203–215. http://www.jstor.org/stable/3099076.
White, R. (2017). *The republic for which it stands: The United States during reconstruction and the Gilded Age, 1865–1896.* Oxford University Press.
Whitman, J. (2018). *Hitler's American model: The United States and the making of Nazi race law.* Princeton University Press.
Whittaker, W. (1969). Samuel Gompers, anti-imperialist. *Pacific Historical Review, 38*(4), 429–445. https://doi.org/10.2307/3637623
Windschuttle, K. (2005). White Australia and Sixties-generation historians. Lecture presented at the NSW Higher School Certificate History Extension Conference, University of Sydney. http://www.kooriweb.org/foley/resources/history/wind60shistorians.html

Wolfgang, M. (1961). Pioneers in criminology: Cesare Lombroso (1835–1909). *Journal of Criminal Law, Criminology, and Police Science, 52*(4), 361–391. https://doi.org/10.2307/1141263
Woodard, C. (2011). *American nations: A history of the eleven rival regional cultures of North America.* Viking.
Yedlin, T. (1999). *Maxim Gorky: A political biography.* Praeger.

Part III

"...Because You Have to be Asleep to Believe it." (1929–2008)

Nationalism, Socialism and Zero-Sum Thinking

6

Abstract

This chapter deals roughly with the period from the 1920s to the 1970s. From the ruins of WWI to the disintegration of the Keynesian paradigm, zero-sum thinking has appeared in guises ranging from models of self-sufficiency to their very opposites. First, we see the zero-sum implications of two principal aspects of **autarky** (essentially neomercantilism): one had to do with the symbiosis of state and big business at the expense of workers and other national economies (corporatism); the other is what found its foremost example in the ideology of **blood and soil**, namely the quest for national self-sufficiency at the expense of ideologically determined foreigners both inside and outside national borders. Amid the havoc wrought by autarky, the Bretton Woods agreement concretized the US Dollar as the world's reserve currency and capitalism's so-called **golden age** (of the national majorities at the expense of the minorities) in the decades after WWII. These *Trente Glorieuses*, fostered by Keynesian social democracy, had their own zero-sum features hidden underneath trickle-down narratives of eternal economic growth. The Cold War cracks began to appear during the 1970s, as the two nuclear superpowers were unable to keep their promises to their working classes, engendering yet more cycles of **stagflation and zero-sum thinking** and the collapse of Keynesian social democracies.

> The whole problem with the world is that fools and fanatics are always so certain of themselves and wiser people so full of doubt. —B. Russell

A staunch Gallic Russophile (following his merciless bombardment of the Russian fortress of Bomarsund in the Baltic Sea's Åland Islands during the Crimean War), Alfred-Albert Gervais was promoted to the admiralty of the French Mediterranean fleet and assigned command of the Brennus. Following years of defective results

A. M. Feldman and Y. Stamos, *Zero Sum Political Economy*, World-Systems Evolution and Global Futures, https://doi.org/10.1007/978-3-032-18326-2_6

during sea trials, the newest pre-dreadnought Charles Martel class French battleship (essentially an oft-updated ironclad), Brennus, commanded by Gervais, put to sea in the summer of 1896. The ship was designed as a Mediterranean warship to counterbalance Italian naval strength in the Mediterranean at the turn of the twentieth century, and was therefore named after the famous Gaul who, according to Livy's legend, conquered the Romans ca. 390 BCE. As Brennus himself said to the vanquished Italians as they complained about having to match the weight of his sword on top of their already hefty war reparations—"Vae victis!" ("Woe to the Vanquished!").

Strolling on the Brennus' stern walk on a Corsican summer day in 1896, Gervais fell through the duckboards onto the upper portion of the armor belt of the deck below—and was severely injured and bedridden afterwards. Similarly, no sooner had the original Brennus satiated himself with the curvy spoils of conquest, again according to Livy, Marcus Furius Camillus arrived with a Roman army and, after putting his sword on the opposite end of the scale, replied, "Non auro, sed ferro, recuperanda est patria" ("not with gold, but with iron, will the fatherland be regained"). Brennus was defeated and Camillus was hailed as the refounder of Rome (Caresse, 2019). The passing of 23 centuries may have made a difference in the design and technology of warfare but it meant little for the ultimate justification or logic of war (and the abuse of history to do so): access to the seemingly finite resources of the land and sea. The same law-of-the-jungle logic applied for another generation after the Gauls imposed the same terms on their eastern neighbors, and by the time Gervais died and his beloved battleship *Brennus* was scrapped in 1921–1922, Mussolini's Fascism was already consolidating power in Rome. The use of names as allusions to ancient deeds for irredentist political projects wouldn't end with the *Brennus*: by the early 1930s, Mussolini was using the ancient idea of the *Mare Nostrum* to advocate modern imperial projects (the *Quarta Sponda*, or the "Fourth Shore") to recreate his very own version of the Roman Empire at the zero-sum expense of the French (and many others) (Bernhard, 2013; Kallis, 2003; Knox, 1999; Moore, 1940).

Irredentist (and newly conceived imperialist) political projects were implemented under the guise of concurrent dictatorships and monarchies across the world. Just as their goals were no different from their namesake, neither were their justifications for wars for finite resources. Democracies and autocracies alike, whether nominally liberal capitalist, fascist or communist economies, were all subject to the same zero-sum logic of finite resources to overcome their rivals. Given that a liberal, positive-sum scenario had seemingly failed, the logic which economists like Clark and Marshall and racial theorists like Galton and Spencer used to justify Darwinian winner-take-all economic, financial and racial-national affairs was also used to justify winner-take-all militaristic and geopolitical affairs.

In the 18 years between Sun Yat-sen's 1911 Chinese Revolution and the American crash of 1929, Anglo-American imperial liberalism failed, curdling into neofeudalism and neomercantilism as the world changed beyond all recognition. As sovereign states reorganized themselves away from old models of theocratic monarchy (the ecumenical empires) and oligarchic semi-democracies (the English-speaking countries and their imperial possessions), the failure of liberalism became ever more apparent, as even Robert Kagan (2023) has observed. The new model for sovereign political economy must look unlike anything ever seen before, so statesmen across the world (again, whether they called themselves communists, fascists, or liberal democrats) promptly began building brand new political economies to compete with each other for seemingly finite resources, which they commonly called national self-sufficiency, or autarky. In reality, autarky was a rebranded version of ancient mercantilism and nineteenth-century Malthusianism, where huge corporations were granted gigantic market monopolies which dwarfed the 17th-c. Indian companies, and a few rich, powerful oligarchs cut backroom deals which decided the fates of millions.

The result of this no-quarter-given 1910s–1940s neomercantilism was the same as always: trade wars have always been the economic equivalent of shooting wars. By the time the atomic dust settled in 1945, the casualties reckoned (most historians estimate over 75 million worldwide), the treaties signed and the vanquished occupied, global Keynesian institutions were promptly installed to nominally ensure that unregulated laissez-faire liberal capitalism and its distant oligarchic cousin, autarky couldn't be repeated into the gates of Auschwitz ever again. Instead, such global and national institutions like the Bretton Woods consensus, the UN, IMF, World Bank, WTO, EEC and so on, were meant to maintain the industrial middle classes within their respective countries.

For thirty years after WWII, as wealth was slowly but surely redistributed from the victors to the vanquished and from the rich to the poor, economic miracles occurred in predictable places at the peripheries of Eurasia—like Germany, Japan, Korea, Taiwan, Ireland and Italy—with such regularity that they ceased being miracles. Joe Studwell explained in *How Asia Works* that the ultimate reason for such economic miracles lay with liberal reforms like land redistribution. Others argued that the real reason was urbanization, land clearances and industrialization (Demsas, 2024; Studwell, 2013). Either way, entire working classes were lifted out of poverty by 90% corporate marginal tax rates alongside Keynesian industrial and monetary policies and institutions as the British empire handed the reins off to the Americans, and much of the Global South was freed into yet another era of chaos and civil warfare. Meanwhile, billions remained locked away in the heartlands of Eurasia under the guises of Soviet, Korean, Chinese or Indochinese communism, as Stalinist gulags and guns yielded to Khruschevan bread and butter.

Nevertheless, the post-war global detente between labor and capital was functionally equivalent to the stalemate between the USA and USSR—the uneasy equilibrium sustained the miraculous (at least between Washington and Moscow). However, Keynesian institutions by themselves weren't enough to ensure that middle classes in various countries would remain middle classes when poorer, nonaligned countries in the Global South inherited their colonial legacies and industries due to the lower collective price of their labor and infrastructure. Faced with the choice of whether to continue paying high taxes and making humiliating concessions to ever more powerful organized labor institutions in the industrialized world (partly due to Soviet competition) or moving their factories to poorer (then termed "third world") countries with cheaper labor, by the 1970s, factory-owners chose the latter. Industrialization never ended; it just changed continents when owners saw a chance to free their capital from the legal boundaries of the Keynesian nation-states. Ariñó and Romero (2016) called the transformation since the 1970s "the secession of the rich:" capital abandons the state when it doesn't see itself reflected in it, creating alternative institutions to reflect its interests. At that time the post-war industrial middle-class economic party (fueled by cheap oil) was becoming increasingly unsustainable. Stagnation set in as consistent 4–5% annual economic growth slowed to a crawl, particularly after Nixon's abandonment of the gold standard in 1971 incentivized both inflation and industrial production to move to poorer, non-industrialized countries and the 1973 OPEC oil embargo further underlined the writing on the walls. The West's Seven Sisters of Cold War I lost its energy monopoly when OPEC created its own cartel. With growth plummeting and several rounds of oil and inflation shocks later, by 1980, as stagnation and inflation combined into a political-economic nightmare (imaginatively termed "stagflation"), Keynesianism was all but abandoned in favor of a new economic paradigm—neoliberalism. And so, the gears of history turned yet again, as the zero-sum logic inherent in both production and consumption, supply and demand, wealth and poverty, have and have not, ensured the demise of Keynesianism and the return of laissez-faire "neo"-liberalism and its attendant (and predictably cyclical) consequences.

This chapter charts the story of the rise and fall of the Keynesian middle classes in industrialized countries. And it begins in the aftermath of the failure of liberalism and the zero-sum economic causes of WWII.

Autarky: Corporatism and Blood and Soil

Ideas such as the Great Divergence and Social Darwinism never truly went out of fashion: since their 19th-century creations, nations have frequently, if intermittently, been seen as organisms that grow and mature, while the fittest ones (the most "developed" ones) are sometimes justified to subjugate, enslave and exploit the weakest (the "underdeveloped"). Such a mindset, however, could not but approach the ensuing zero-sum struggle between great powers as natural too. Yet, many public figures, including Carl Jung, apparently had little taste for a major conflict among the "developed" or "civilized" nations, preferring to expand toward the "underdeveloped" or the "last frontier": the vast tracts of "Black Earth" under Slavic/Soviet sovereignty seemingly waiting to be colonized by *Übermenschen* (Snyder, 2016). Colonial subjugation was acceptable in the previous generation when the British, French and American liberals had engaged in racial imperialism, but the new generation would decide that it was no longer acceptable; or at least not where their predecessors had already conquered.

Chapter four of Hitler's (1941) *Mein Kampf* explicitly advocates a corporatist, autarkic and Malthusian approach to German political economy. He begins by laying out the challenges of providing enough resources for a growing population on a finite territory:

> Germany has an annual increase in population of almost 900,000 souls. The difficulty of feeding this army of new citizens would become greater with every year, and was bound some day to end in a catastrophe, provided ways and means were not found to avert this impending danger of hunger-pauperization in time. (p. 168)

For Hitler, the four choices constituted (1) limiting the birth rate following contemporary French policies, (2) improving crop yields on German soil, (3) conquering other nations, or (4) pursuing mercantilist policies to profit from international trade at the expense of foreign nations. After rejecting the first out of hand, deploying a social Darwinist argumentation akin to natural selection (p. 171), Hitler rejected the second choice more circuitously by making the Malthusian argument that, aside from the pernicious effects of large landowners, rent-seeking speculators and Jews, hunger and the demand for food always outstrip supply no matter how well crop yields are managed. Better land distribution would merely be Bolshevism. His arguments against this second choice are simultaneously arguments for the third choice, territorial expansion. In his estimation, the birth rate must increase alongside national territory to strengthen the nation in a zero-sum competition for land, gold, oil and other finite resources against rival nations and empires on a finite planet:

> The size of a people's living area includes an essential factor for the determination of its outward security. [...] In the greatness of the State territory, therefore, lies a reason for the easier preservation of a nation's liberty and independence, whereas, in the reverse case, the smallness of such a formation simply invites seizure. (pp. 174–177)

His fourth choice, increasing the country's commonwealth at the expense of foreigners, was dismissed as compatible either with the second or third options. For Hitler, "the sounder alternative, however, was undoubtedly" conquest (pp. 174–177).

Not all foreign nations were equally in jeopardy, and some actively saw their own safety from fascist regimes as coming at the zero-sum expense of others. Carl Jung, for example, said of Hitler in 1938: "I say let him go East. Turn his attention away from the West, or rather encourage him to keep it turned away. Let him go to Russia. That is the logical *cure* for Hitler." Jung argued that Germany required a "*much larger*" place for its almost eighty-million population than the share of Africa "occupied by any of the other three Western Great Powers" (Britain, France and Italy). Yet, Jung rhetorically asked: "How is she [Germany] going to get that in the West without destroying one or more of the nations which now occupy the West? There is only one field for her to operate in, and that is *Russia*" (Jung, 1987, p. 132). One could easily replace "occupied by" with "apportioned to". For it is not only racism, essentialism and anticommunism that mark Jung's thought; it is also an entire colonialist and orientalist mindset that was widespread in the West before WWII—and in some cases even long after it. As Jung elsewhere stated, the Germans "were too late in the scramble for colonies, where the British and French possessed rich colonies and all that *belongs to* a fully matured nation" (Jung, 1987, p. 137; emphasis added). By this logic, if imperialist nations like France, Britain or America could claim subcontinents or entire continents like Australia, West Africa, India or North America, then surely one could offer Eastern Europe to the Germans (Hamlin, 2017). Or as the Nazi and Soviet armies would soon come to realize, the real zero-sum battle for *Lebensraum* (living or housing space) would occur at the Volga. Hitler's regime promised its landless working soldiers that "*The Volga will be our Mississippi!*" (Coates, 2014; Snyder, 2010, p. 160), while Stalin promised Roosevelt that "*The battle for the Volga is the battle for the Mississippi!*" (Fedin, 2012).

Jung's statements also elucidate the real reason behind the policy of appeasement: the hope that the Nazis would deal with the USSR. Hence the fact that the constant concessions ceased abruptly when the Germans allied with the Soviets in the Molotov-Ribbentrop Pact and both invaded Poland, resulting in its umpteenth partition. The issue with Poland wasn't that German aggression ran up against Anglo-French guarantees. Similar guarantees had been extended to Czechoslovakia, but that didn't stop the guarantors from the Munich Conference (1938), when they encouraged Czechoslovakian authorities to "go gently into the night" of subordination, to paraphrase the famous poem by Dylan Thomas. It was that the shuffling of the geopolitical deck following the Pact meant that a Nazi-Soviet war was no longer on the cards, which struck against London's anti-communist agenda while signifying a new zero-sum game among empires. If Hitler wasn't going full East against the Soviets, then he would eventually go North, West and South, inevitably encroaching on Britain's sphere of influence or its very turf—an especially concerning prospect alongside the 1936 Rome-Berlin Axis and Mussolini's thalassocratic ambitions in the Mediterranean.

Justifying the zero-sum struggle entailed in Italy's imperial aspirations, Italian nationalists and fascists had dubbed their country a "proletarian nation." Rather than another imperial project, Italy's conflict with established Great Powers like Britain, was justified as a proletarian national struggle against "plutocratic" or "bourgeois nations" (Paxton, 2004, pp. 37, 49). Similar racial-national taxonomies and hierarchies could always appear in different forms. Ukrainian nationalist Dmytro Dontsov, for instance, used the example of Italy to illustrate his belief in the existence of historically shifting categories of "master nations" and "plebeian nations" (Armstrong, 1968).

Nonetheless, Axis expansionary ambitions collided with the fact that, like in North America, the land wasn't already empty. The peoples of Africa, the Balkans, East Europe, and East Asia necessitated enslavement or elimination. The Italians committed war crimes via chemical weapons in Libya and Ethiopia before 1939 to permit Italian settlement and the Germans committed innumerable crimes of dispossession against Slavs as White Protestants had done previously to pagan natives in North America (Mineau, 2004, p. 180). Hitler clarified his plans for Eastern Europe in 1942: "As for the ridiculous hundred million Slavs, we will mould the best of them as we see fit, and we will isolate the rest of them in their own pig-styes; and anyone who talks about cherishing the local inhabitant and civilizing him, goes straight off into a concentration camp!" (Trevor-Roper, 1953, p. 617).

The situation of a zero-sum racial slaughter wasn't very different in East Asia and around the Pacific. The relevant antagonisms went beyond the blatant cases of Japanese genocides in Manchuria, southern China, Indochina, Indonesia and the Philippines. In the United States, Japanese and Chinese immigrants were pitted against each other from the late-nineteenth century. Japanese propaganda targeting American exclusion laws of Chinese immigration in light of Japan's "Greater East Asia Co-Prosperity Sphere" against Anglo-American imperialism gained ground with Chinese leaders during WWII (Yellen, 2019). Pearl Buck observed that by continuing to reject Chinese immigration on racial grounds, the United States would be "fighting on the wrong side in this war. We belong with Hitler." Her activism was vindicated when FDR advocated before a congressional debate in October 1943 repealing the original Chinese exclusion laws: "Nations, like individuals, make mistakes. We must be big enough to acknowledge our mistakes of the past and to correct them. By the repeal of the Chinese exclusion laws, we can correct a historic mistake and silence the distorted Japanese propaganda." The Magnuson law passed, allowing limited Chinese immigration to America at the expense of Japanese immigrants still locked in camps (Caspian-Kang, 2021).

In the end, WWII, which was largely a continuation of WWI, was little more than a mindless slaughter concocted by the ruling classes of the Axis and Allied empires to pit the entireties of their imperial working classes against each other in a global, zero-sum, war for land, gold, oil and other finite resources. It was, in other words, a war between incipient and incumbent imperialists, or as observed by the head of Britain's navy in 1934, "We have got most of the world already, or the best parts of it. We only want to keep what we have got and prevent others from taking it away from us" (Overy, 2021).

But even before the war, zero-sum thinking had played a major role in the Nazi regime in several other ways. This should not be surprising if one considers the Manicheanism underlying the National Socialist worldview which saw history as a perennial racial struggle that would ultimately lead to the destruction of either the Aryan (German) or the Semite (Jew). Nazi ideology was built upon the foundation of 19th-c. philological and linguistic research on the Indo-European peoples in a seemingly eternal fight for finite resources against the Semitic peoples (Poliakov, 1974). National Socialist ideologues like Goebbels relished talking about the future in zero-sum terms of complete destruction or complete victory:

> Germany, in any event, has no intention of bowing before this Jewish threat, but rather intends to act at the right moment, using if necessary the most total and radical measures to extermin-, to deal with Jewry. [...] When the Führer ordered the army to attack the East on 22 June 1941, [...] [i]t was two minutes before midnight! Waiting any longer could easily

> have led to the destruction of the Reich and a total Bolshevization of the European continent. (Goebbels, 1944)

According to Susan Neiman (2019, pp. 30–31), American eugenics policies provided the template while Carl Schmitt's books (*Nomos of the Earth* and *Land and Sea*), building on MacKinder's and Mahan's ideas about zero-sum political economies of imperial power over land, sea and finite resources, provided the legal justification via the Nuremberg Laws. Combined with the prevalent (and virulent) forms of pseudo-scientific "racialism" (also imported from the USA), Nazism relied on eugenics to legitimize its zero-sum political program of starving and murdering millions of *Untermenschen* to save millions of Aryans. As it has been pithily remarked, "The Nazis were eugenicists and Malthusians. [...] The Malthusianism told them that millions had to die; the eugenics told them who the victims ought to be" (Caplan, 2012). Outside one Baltic railway station in the early 1940s, one Polish eyewitness clarified that the racial and economic justification for genocide came down to a simple zero-sum calculus for working classes caught in the middle: "For the Germans 300 Jews are 300 enemies of humanity; for the Lithuanians they are 300 pairs of shoes, trousers, and the like" (Heath, 2024). The blood sacrifice demanded by the Nazi flag was ultimately little different than the blood sacrifice demanded by any other flag—the American flag very much included (Marvin & Ingle, 1999).

However, big businesses in Germany, Japan, Britain or America didn't stop trading with each other throughout the 20s–30s. Only in the late 30s, governments started putting pressure on their homegrown corporate oligopolies to cut ties with those of other states. Even IG Farben, the German manufacturer of the genocidal Zyklon B gas (using slave labor from Auschwitz), and the major German arms manufacturer, ThyssenKrupp, traded with the New York Union Banking Corporation via Prescott Bush, who later founded his own political and banking dynasty resulting in two presidents and several state governors, congressmen and ambassadors which led the US to more wars across the turn of the millennium. It wasn't until 1942 that the US government seized Nazi corporate assets based in New York under the "Trading with the Enemy" Act of 1917, revealing yet another way in which trade can be (seen as) an act of war (Aris & Campbell, 2004; Baptista & Travis, 2006; Sutton, 1976; Wilkins, 2004).

Still, German-American big business interests like the American IG Chemical Corporation often found ways to bypass these restrictions, e.g. through shell accounts in Swiss firms and banks, most notably through the Swiss holding corporation Interhandel (LeBor, 1997). In 1950, James Stewart Martin, director of the Division for Investigation of Cartels and External Assets in American Military Government, published an exposé of the thwarted "decartelization" and "deindustrialization" process in post-WWII Germany, despite the determined opposition against his efforts by his commanding officer, an investment banker. According to Martin, the reason that this process wasn't successful was because of US business ties with German industry: "We had not been stopped in Germany by German business. We had been stopped in Germany by American business." Of the 24 indicted

IG Farben industrialists at the Nuremberg Trials, 11 were acquitted and the average prison term of the remaining guilty company men was just over 4 years. Business went on as usual or, as Martin put it, there was strong pushback against the plan of breaking up German industry out of "business necessity;" after all these were "not criminals, but honorable men" (Martin, 1950). The honor of the war profiteers was predicated as much on their portfolios as their pedigrees. The business of war was still just another business, whether the oligarch families who owned them were Axis or Allied, German or American, dynasties or mafias.

The Nazi oligarchy survived the war and remains the bedrock on which Germany's 21st-c. economic power was built. Oligarchic business dynasties from Hugo Boss to Thyssen-Krupp happily enriched themselves with Hitler's contracts, slave labor and murder merchantry. Vehicles now driven by the general population were once driven by the genocidal population (De Jong, 2022; Smith, 2022). To continue profiting from the Nazi war machine, Swiss big business like Nestlé, Ciba and Sandoz (the latter two later merged into Novartis) ignored the lucrative genocides, and even barred Jewish board members from their finite c-suites—the cartels may have been too big to fail, but they were only big enough for Aryans. Swiss banks knowingly accepted Nazi gold looted from conquered countries and Jewish bank accounts (or even dental fillings) in exchange for Swiss arms and coal production sold at discounted rates to the Wehrmacht. It was not until the 1946 Washington agreement that Swiss banks were forced to give up $60 million in gold to a handful of Holocaust survivors. A new 1962 law saw another $15 million handed over, while less than half a million descendants of the survivors represented by the World Jewish Restitution Organization had to wait until a settlement after a 1996 lawsuit for UBS, Credit Suisse and Nestlé to pay another $1.25 billion in genocide gold (Bergier et al., 1998; Bradsher, 1999; Eizenstat, 1998; Filipuzzi et al., 2020; Gribetz & Reig, 2020; Rickman, 2011; Vincent, 1997). Swiss banks have continued to hide the wealth of strongmen, war criminals, terrorists, oligarchs and spies ever since (Drucker & Hubbard, 2022).

Perhaps the starkest example of the zero-sum logic of the ruling classes which commanded the war revealed itself in a small Thuringian salt-mining town in early April 1945, as American soldiers of the 90th Infantry Division found one of the principal deposits of Hitler's sovereign treasury at the Merker's Mine (Busterud, 2001). The genocide gold promptly disappeared into Swiss banks and probably the Vatican, and has been the subject of contentious litigation ever since (the Vatican still denies the Bigelow Report) (Marshall, 1997; Pellegrini, 1997; Phayer, 2008). Valuable artwork was also stored as a different kind of currency serving multiple purposes. The ideology through which it was interpreted kept Nazi officers loyal to the banner and the Fuhrer, while legitimizing a new social pyramid tacked onto the old Prussian traditions of aristocratic (cameralist) potlatch patronage, prestige and status symbolism. However, Nazi collection of artwork was not just about socio-economics, aesthetics and racial ideology; the value of the artwork was predicated on its finitude. The older the artwork or the more unique it was considered by art collectors, the more valuable it became due to the prices it would fetch on the world market. There were only so many works by Michelangelo, Donatello,

Da Vinci, Titian, the Cranachs, Breughel, Dürer and Rembrandt. Vermeer's *The Art of Painting* (the Czernin Vermeer) was sold to Hitler in 1939 for 1.65 million Reichsmarks, or about $640,000, which could have fetched a total value in gold equivalent to over $12.5 million in 2021 US dollars. His subordinates quickly followed suit. Not dissimilar from Napoleon, the Nazi party and its employees (soldiers) looted thousands of objects of art across their expanding Third Reich, kept many of the works deemed "Aryan" for their social and ideological purposes while selling the "Semitic" and other "degenerate" objects on the world market through shell accounts in Swiss or Vatican banks. The proceeds in bullion from such sales would go to fund further conquests—a plainly mercantilist political economy (Petropoulos, 1996).

By 1947, according to the International Monetary Fund (n.d.), "the United States had accumulated 70% of the world's gold reserves." Nevertheless, the allied confiscation of the Nazi war chest was a repeat of the allied coalition soldiers who looted one of the principal deposits of Napoleon's sovereign treasury after the Battle of Vittoria in 1813—crippling Napoleon's mercantilist war machine. Each treasury of gold looted from previous conquests was meant to pay for more conquests, primarily eastern conquests of Russian lands. The span of 132 years meant little for the most basic form of political economy: mercantilism. This has always been the political economy of war. 131 yearsseparated Napoleon's conquests as far east as Moscow by 1812 when the tide turned in the wake of Borodino; Hitler's Wehrmacht reached Moscow and Stalingrad by 1943 when the tide turned at Kursk. On each occasion, the price for mercantilist political economies was paid in ever widening rivers of blood. Over a century separated each failed Western attempt to conquer Russia (always charged with a vein of religious conflict between Western and Eastern Christianity but mostly of civilizational struggle between what was often and commonly considered European culture versus Asian barbarity)—all the way back to Alexander Nevsky's defeat of the Teutons on Lake Peipus in 1242. Sergei Eisenstein knew General Winter well enough to understand that history often moves in seasonal cycles. This idea was developed and deepened by the great Soviet economist Nikolaj Kondratiev before his execution by Stalinist firing squad in 1937, who is usually credited with what later thinkers like Eric Hobsbawm (a Marxist historian) and Joseph Schumpeter (a Keynesian economist) called Kondratiev waves, like the liberal business cycle, which explain cycles of production, consumption, debt, speculation, crisis, scapegoating and destruction (in war) as almost deterministic seasonal cycles of history (Hobsbawm, 1994; Kondratiev, 1925; Schumpeter, 1961). Every winter is followed by a spring, but the golden age is never equally golden for all.

Whose Golden Age?

If the 1950s ignited Cold War I, they began with the liquidation of the old imperial oligarchies from the Japanese zaibatsu, Italian confindustria, German Großunternehmen, French parti colonial and British chartered companies. The US top marginal income tax rate in 1951 was 91% and the corporate income tax slightly over 50% (with the only times that the top tax bracket exceeded 50% being during a war: WWII and Korean War). Although Chrysler wasn't the only multinational (German-American) big business which survived WWII, it was with less blood on its hands. Other pre-WWII German (but multinational) bloodstained makers like BMW, VW or Porsche (Quandt dynasty) were able to maintain their foundations and vertical integrations through potlatch programs to continue into the post-WWII "Golden Age of Capitalism." As the New Deal spread into Europe in the form of the Marshall Plan, not all Nazi collaborators (like these companies or Hugo Boss) would face real consequences for their policies during the War. Oligarchic Nazi industries would remain largely concentrated oligopolies, provided they take the dollars and oppose Soviet expansion (Fear, 2006; Levenstein & Suslow, 2011; United States National Archives, 2016). The attempted de-cartelization of Japan's zaibatsu oligarchic business dynasties, which pushed for and profited from the war, met an analogous result (Chomsky & Herman, 1979, pp. 54–58; Finn, 1992, pp. 130–149; Kaiser, 1980, pp. 241–252; McCoy, 2017, pp. 93–104; Mollin, 2006). A similar happy fate befell Franco's dictatorship in Spain, which after WWII, sold 400 million euros-worth of Nazi-owned industrial capacity to the victorious Allies in order to preserve itself as a bulwark against communism for another generation. These were some of the first results of the new zero-sum struggle with the Soviet-led Eastern Bloc.

By 1945, the monopolization and oligopolization of zero-sum, finite market shares was already recognized as an old problem endemic to laissez-faire liberalism. The Keynesian economist Joan Robinson, in her *Economics of Imperfect Competition* (1933) overturned Marshallian classical liberalism by revealing how it facilitated monopolies, oligopolies and trusts—and revealed liberalism's failure in the Great Depression. Robinson and her colleague Michael Kalecki recognized that liberalism's extreme wealth inequalities were at root not individual but structural problems, which were revealed by the ability of entire imperial budgets (measured in gold), when converted into debt owned by other bankers, oligopolists and monopolists, to cycle through massive amounts of inflation, immiserating entire working classes. They understood that inflation wasn't caused by anything other than the grotesque level of oligarchic capital concentration—inequality itself (the man behind the curtain) (Peterson, 2022).

If the blood-soaked conclusion of the global failure of classical laissez-faire liberalism, consequently autarky, Malthusianism and eugenics resulted in atomic ash, human rights charters, Cold War I and the deaths of previous ecumenical and national empires, the story of the Keynesian phoenix which arose from liberalism's ashes truly began during the interregnum between the presidencies of Hoover and FDR. Hoover, a Republican, refused to help the impoverished American working-class WWI veterans, who could no longer afford to purchase the goods they produced and lost their life savings after the 1929 Crash. So, they marched on Washington demanding their bonuses promised by the federal government for their combat against the German working classes. Hoover tried to vacuum them from their squalid Hoovervilles in the national mall using the brute force happily supplied by bloodthirsty generals like Patton and MacArthur in 1932. There is still debate about just how many American innocents were killed in what *Time* called "the Battle of Washington" (the lowest estimate is two dead and 124 wounded), but the casualties undoubtedly included women and children (Daniels, 1971; Dickson & Allen, 2004; Heroes: Battle of Washington, 1932; Ortiz, 2006; Rawl, 2006). The ensuing general election was a landslide; one Ohio voter told Hoover: "Make it unanimous and vote for Roosevelt." FDR represented little more than an abstract notion of change until he addressed the Bonus Army survivors' demand for their deserved financial relief (1933). Instead of killing their families and burning their hovels, FDR dismissed Patton and MacArthur and gave the veterans the first jobs in the New Deal programs, and later, the Works Progress Administration (WPA).

The original New Deal was as much a new social contract as social construct. In 1933, with the decline of imperial expansion at the zero-sum expense of rival powers (such as Japan, Britain, Germany, France, etc.), ruling classes still needed to fulfill their promises of the benefits of expansion to their working classes. When promises could no longer be fulfilled, expansion could only come at the expense of rival ruling classes (and their respective working classes), or indeed the ruling classes generally (oligopolies/oligarchs and monopolies/monarchs). The New Deal was simply a down payment toward that end. It mirrored Thorvald Stauning's Kanslergade Copenhagen Agreement (1933), a Danish national grand bargain between labor, capital and sovereign which also laid the foundations for the Nordic style social-democratic welfare state (Skou, 2005, pp. 367–368). The same was true of Britain's 1942 Beveridge Report (which outlined a post-war British Welfare State), which was resisted by the chancellor of the Exchequer, Kingsley Wood. Even in America, Harvard president James Conant argued in 1940 that the entirety of American liberal capitalism had devolved into a "hereditary aristocracy of wealth," or even "industrial feudalism" (Conant, 1940; Karabel, 2005). Many of these policies were the result of previous or ongoing zero-sum struggles: between labor and capital, landlord and peasant, Allies and Axis, Western and Eastern Blocs (Reynolds, 2013).

FDR's 1935 address was toward younger generations suffering from the stagnation which followed from the failure of liberal imperial expansion:

> There was a time when the formula for success was the simple admonition to have a stout heart and willing hands. A great, new country lay open. When life became hard in one place it was necessary only to move on to another. But circumstances have changed all that. Today we can no longer escape into virgin territory: we must master our environment. The youth of this generation finds that the old frontier is occupied [...] Your advancement, you hope, is along a broad highway on which thousands of your fellow men and women are advancing with you. You and I know that this modern economic world of ours is governed by rules and regulations vastly more complex than those laid down in the days of Adam Smith or John Stuart Mill. [...] Our concepts of the regulation of money and credit and industrial competition, of the relation of employer and employee created for the old civilization, are being modified to save our economic structure from confusion, destruction and paralysis. (Roosevelt, 1935)

Like the American Liberty League, whose fortunes came from their workers' toil, FDR knew that his economic policies which sought to benefit the workers came at the zero-sum expense of their employers, which was made clear in his Madison Square Garden speech following Smedley Butler's outing of the fascist Business Plot on Halloween, 1936:

> We had to struggle with the old enemies of peace – business and financial monopoly, speculation, reckless banking, class antagonism, sectionalism, war profiteering. They had begun to consider the Government of the United States as a mere appendage to their own affairs. We know now that Government by organized money is just as dangerous as Government by organized mob. Never before in all our history have these forces been so united against one candidate as they stand today. They are unanimous in their hate for me – and I welcome their hatred. (Roosevelt, 1936)

Having defeated the fascists at the ballot box, he introduced programs like the WPA's Federal Writers Project, which employed thousands of starving novelists, poets, scholars and others "better suited to desk labor than, say, draining malarial swampland." They published publicly-funded guidebooks of the American landscape that would "resist those signature American habits of boosterism and aggressive national mythologizing," although some writers like Zora Neale Hurston criticized the program as a federal potlatch scheme (Borchert, 2021).

Having defeated the fascists on the battlefield, Anglo-American ruling classes convened at New Hampshire's Bretton Woods Hotel and birthed a new worldwide financial architecture: the dollar would replace the pound as the preeminent currency, but bound alone to the gold standard and guaranteed by the new World Bank. It was an official recognition that the gold standard's liberal corruption and austerity had created a poverty trap for millions of workers worldwide, as well as a revindication of Keynes (Carter, 2021; Conway, 2015). The elegance of the new Keynesian political economy came as an explicit rejection of and replacement for classical laissez-faire liberalism and simultaneously zero-sum thinking in the birth of Modern Monetary Theory (MMT). Just as liberalism promised potentially unlimited economic growth, Keynes promised potentially unlimited public debt to finance citizens' wellbeing—beginning with the question of how to finance WWII. The proposal was simple in its outline, albeit Faustian in its implications: if the war would be financed by redistribution to facilitate increased demand and debt (principally to the US)—then other sovereign budgets could also be (Keynes, 1940). German economists like Ludwig Erhard came to similar conclusions for Germany. His and his friends' politico-economic ideas (the "social market economy") found a welcome reception in von Mises' and Hayek's Mont Pelerin Society for Catholic aristocracy, where they directly competed with Keynes' (Caciagli, 2006, p. 179; Mierzejewski, 2004).

Beardsley Ruml, the chairman of the New York Federal Reserve Bank, understood how the long-term implications of Keynes' new system of political economy would reshape the world by 1945. Ruml built on the work of Keynes and Alfred Mitchell-Innes shortly before WWI (*What is Money?*) which rejected the entire school of classical liberalism as little different from mercantilism practicing the age-old temptation of coin debasement (Mitchell-Innes, 1914). In a speech to the American Bar Association entitled "Taxes for Revenue Are Obsolete," Ruml explained that taxes prevent too much money from chasing finite resources (the layman's explanation for inflation): "The dollars the government spends become purchasing power in the hands of the people who have received them," he said, while "the dollars the government takes by taxes cannot be spent by the people." Calling their financial concept "functional finance," Keynes, Ruml and their associate Abba Lerner laid the foundations of Modern Monetary Theory—potentially unlimited public debt in order to ensure the purchasing power of Keynesian middle classes (Fiebiger et al., 2012; Lerner, 1947). MMT is still a hotly debated topic among 21st-century economists like Stephanie Kelton (as we'll discuss in chapters 7–8), who writes, "the idea that taxes pay for what the government spends is pure fantasy" (Kelton, 2020, p. 3). Then, with the passage of the 1949 Employment Act, their associate, Leon Keyserling, the chair of the US Council of Economic Advisers, standardized the idea of permanent public debt combined with permanent economic growth: "The maximum employment and production objectives of the Employment Act require an expanding economy from year to year" (Susskind, 2024, p. 76).

It was also ironically the foundation of what later became known as "disaster capitalism"—profiting from destruction, first described in Frédéric Bastiat's, 1850 essay, especially in his "Parable of the Broken Window" (that a glazier ought to hire a boy to break windows for his own profits). Even in Frank Fetter's early-20th-c. Austrian mind (who opposed all things Keynesian from the New Deal to the Marshall Plan), it demonstrated why destruction, and reconstruction, don't benefit society, just profiteers, and this form of liberal capitalism is simply a suction pump which vacuums value from the pyramid's bottom to top, and from the vanquished to the victorious (Fetter, 1915). When *WSJ*'s Henry Hazlitt published his *Economics in One Lesson* in 1946, chapter three was understandably entitled "The Blessings of Destruction."

Nevertheless, for Keynes, to ensure the political stability of a government in the face of fascist or communist agitation, governments required enlargement to guarantee basic health and welfare for citizens. As he wrote in 1936,

> Whilst, therefore, the enlargement of the functions of government, involved in the task of adjusting to one another the propensity to consume and the inducement to invest, would seem to a nineteenth-century publicist or to a contemporary American financier to be a terrific encroachment on individualism, I defend it, on the contrary, both as the only practicable means of avoiding the destruction of existing economic forms in their entirety and as the condition of the successful functioning of individual initiative. (p. 380)

In Britain, that meant nationalizing an empire and aristocracy; in the USA, it meant federalizing big business and oligopoly. The New Deal's biggest ripple effect in America *before* WWII was that it extended into Eurasia *afterward*. The Marshall plan was essentially an American-style New Deal in action—supplied as social engineering to Europe to protect the European ruling classes from Soviet Communist influence spreading among the working classes (Pizzigati, 2012; Sharp, 2009). Ultimately, like the American New Deal, it built other nations' middle classes.

As Anglo-American nations widely implemented Keynesianism following WWII, other nations in the Eurasian rimlands developed similar models. In West Germany, the government's close regulation of a social market economy was called Rhenish Capitalism or Ordoliberalism. In France, with a few more technocratic tweaks, it was called dirigisme. The Scandinavian countries implemented Nordic-style capitalism. After the Korean War, Keynesian policies were implemented in Korea and Japan (the Miracle on the Han River and the Japanese economic miracle), alongside Taiwan, whose regimes also received copious cash transfers from the US for land redistribution policies from rent-seeking landlords to peasant tenant farmers. These 1950s anti-communist dictatorships (Chang-Kai Shek's White Terror mirrored Francisco Franco's earlier White Terror) may have implemented varying amounts of socialist-inspired redistributive policies and large-scale infrastructure projects at times, but they remained capitalist-aligned during the Cold War—in other words, American vassals (Bevins, 2020; Ceballos, 2007; Rodríguez, 2022; Studwell, 2013).

Already in the late 1930s, the term "neoliberalism" was coined by Austrian economists Friedrich von Hayek and Ludwig von Mises. As Keynes was celebrating the promulgation of his political economy in Bretton Woods (1944), both Hayek and von Mises elaborated their respective versions of neoliberalism in their books *The Road to Serfdom* and *Bureaucracy*. The same year saw the publication of Karl Polanyi's magnum opus, *The Great Transformation*, which explained how the first classical era of liberalism, when faced with fulfilling the needs of either democracy or empire, chose the latter at the zero-sum expense of the former, thus replacing democracies with fascist dictatorships. If profit's requirements become deadlocked with democracy's requirements (to shield citizens from profit's nefarious side effects), voters are always pied-piped toward fascism, which promises to balance both requirements by sacrificing liberty (and minorities) (Crain, 2018; Kuttner, 2018).

Thus, before WWII, economic and demographic history were typically generalized spatially—nation-by-nation. After WWII, because of Keynesian globalization (Bretton Woods, Marshall Plans, etc.), they were also generalized temporally—decade-by-decade. What was politically possible in one nation could suddenly be possible in others because they shared the same Keynesian (or social-democratic) political economies—whether it was France, West Germany, England or Italy, they were all part of the same burgeoning NATO/EEC bloc. By pooling their collective sovereignties into these greater economic unions of defensive political economies, the working classes may no longer be able to take pride in their respective present imperialisms (albeit certainly those of their respective pasts), but they could enjoy the fruits of political economies designed to prevent them from agitating for greater concessions from their ruling classes. As George Kennan secretly (albeit famously) wrote back to Washington from Moscow in 1946 about making sure the working classes of the Western blocs were socio-economically and politically healthy:

> World communism is like malignant parasite which feeds only on diseased tissue. This is the point at which domestic and foreign policies meet. Every courageous and incisive measure to solve internal problems of our own society, to improve self-confidence, discipline, morale and community spirit of our own people, is a diplomatic victory over Moscow worth a thousand diplomatic notes and joint communiqués. If we cannot abandon fatalism and indifference in face of deficiencies of our own society, Moscow will profit.

After Churchill's "Iron Curtain" speech in Fulton, Missouri (1946) and the Soviet Union's first successful atomic detonation (1949), the world quickly became divided between the "first world" (capitalist, but nevertheless mostly social democratic nations), the "second world" (communist nations) and the "third world" (all remaining and recently or about to be decolonized "underdeveloped" nations). After the US inherited the British empire amid the 1956 Suez crisis (and the British academic-oligarch Arnold Toynbee's own cheerleading for American imperialism (McNeill, 1989, p. 218)—the Rockefeller Foundation was also instrumental in this development, granting thousands of dollars in 1945–1947), the only remaining zero-sum game seemed to be political, in contrast to the old Leninist understanding of the zero-sum game of economics: the geopolitical struggle of the Cold War. If the competition for third-world alliances between the first and second worlds came as a result of the strategic use of nuclear power, then politics had replaced economics as the dominant arena for the zero-sum struggle for hegemony of nations in the 1950s–60s. Or, as NATO's founding fathers explained their goals: "To keep the Americans in, the Russians out and the Germans down" (Maunders, 2016).

Alongside NATO, the UN, IMF, WHO, World Bank and many other global institutions and governing structures were founded in the immediate post-WWII period, like the multitude of FDR's earlier socio-economic programs in the US (FDIC, TVA, CCC, WPA, etc.). These undercut communism's appeal by redistributing wealth to working classes who would spend their newfound assets on consumer goods ("butter, not guns"), decreasing the likelihood of another war and increasing the likelihood of economic growth. The most notable of these programs was the ERP (the European Recovery Program), or the Marshall Plan. That was the carrot; the stick came in the form of brutal anticommunist policies, suspension of human rights, concentration camps right after WWII in countries like Greece and Operation Gladio throughout Western Europe. Characteristically, the Greek Civil War, which came on the heels of the Greek communists' overcoming of the Nazi occupation, was largely sparked by the victorious Allies—particularly the British, who passed the baton to the US in 1947—who supported former Nazi collaborators, monarchists and old elites, many of whom had left Greece during the Nazi occupation and returned to fight the resistance partisans to stake claims on property rights (Clogg, 2002; Close, 1995; Eudes, 1972; Nachmani, 1990).

The midcentury Keynesian paradigm was ingenious in its simplicity if only because it was equally insidious in its duplicity: in order to maintain an economically equitable middle class based on manufacturing, elastic monetary policy to pay workers an equitable share of the growing economic pie and therefore big government to make it so, industrialized nations required steadily increasing public debts and relative social homogeneity to ensure the social engineering of redistribution. In other words, inflation became a constant economic Sword of Damocles and working-class majorities benefited while minorities were marginalized. Smaller, homogeneous, financially disciplined industrialized countries with negligible minorities (like in Protestant Scandinavia) could maintain the Keynesian paradigm the most equitably and durably while larger, financially less disciplined industrialized countries with more heterogeneity saw comparably more restrictions imposed on their minorities, more social pressure to conform when possible, and more prejudice, discrimination and isolation when impossible. This was the hangover from the eugenics euphoria during the decline and fall of British liberal imperialism. Immigration was strictly regulated by the state, more so than economic activity. In the United States this was an extension of the Jim Crow South and New Deal redlining—or in the vocabulary of the age, segregation (and, in South Africa, apartheid). Thus, "the original American paradox of freedom based on inequality was reestablished [and] relegated people of color to inequality" (Kennedy, 2023; Richardson, 2020). The economic fruits of social democracy were shared with those who fit the majorities' ideals of the social contract and democratic merit (via racial and/or national chauvinism)—a "golden age" for some at the expense of others.

Just as the American New Deal was originally meant for White workers and the European Marshall Plan was meant for Christian workers, such programs were extended to Europeans, Japanese and Koreans, but not to China, the Islamic world, Africa or Latin America. The limit was the earth's northwestern quadrant in the context of the zero-sum struggle against the Soviet Union in the northeastern quadrant. As Henry Wallace predicted in his criticisms of the plan, this had serious consequences within a generation when communist revolutions began breaking out in countries of the southern hemisphere which were never able to carry out Keynesian redistributive policies and middle-class economic miracles. It was only regions most strategic in the Cold War which received redistributive support for Reconstruction. Containing the Eastern Bloc meant that a lot of economic support went to the countries at its border, including the former enemies of Japan and Germany, and Turkey, which hadn't even entered the war.

Unsurprisingly, Alfred Sauvy's new "third world" became ground zero for collateral damage from the Cold War (Sauvi, 1952). Just as innocents in developing nations were murdered in the name of anticapitalism, the same occurred in the name of anticommunism elsewhere by regimes which in turn expected to be supported through some sort of Marshall plan or at least given tacit approval for their ruling classes by the US government (Bevins, 2020, 2021). If the so-called "golden age" was experienced by some newly middle-class people in certain nations, it came at the zero-sum expense of others. As FDR's cabinet member Wallace (1943) also predicted in the midst of WWII, "We shall decide sometime in 1943 or 1944 … whether to plant the seeds of World War III." Viewed from the 2020s, it was truly a self-fulfilling prophecy. Nevertheless, Keynesian political economy was essentially a grand compromise between the forces of the working class and the owning class: the golden age of capital was the tantamount to a golden age of labor (Karabel, 2021).

Stagflation and Zero-Sum Thinking

Samuel Fraser, an impoverished Glaswegian electrician and unionist firebrand, welcomed his Sagittarius son Douglas (1916). Soon, the family fled the British empire, embarked on the newly built RMS Cameronia across the now u-boatless sea, shuffled through Ellis Island and via train on to Detroit (1922–1923). Fleeing from imperial poverty in one town to national poverty in another, young Douglas followed his father's firebrand footsteps, finding fellowship at a Chrysler factory, joining a union and getting fired twice for his "radical" beliefs and agitation for better pay and labor conditions. Fortunately for him, FDR's labor-rights proclivities in his youth lent a hand to strengthening union membership and by the time he was 27, he had served in the US army in the defeat of fascism and was elected the head of UAW local 227 in 1943. After the war, he climbed the UAW ranks, led strikes and negotiations and by the late 1960s was closing in on the UAW presidency, which he achieved by 1977. His career saw the ever-increasing power of the UAW, higher wages, benefits and labor protections for union workers and lower earning gaps between the C-suite suits and the line workers in the factories—mirrored across the labor landscape of the "free world" during the "Golden Age." He understood that so much labor power was making it difficult for Chrysler and other manufacturers to stay in business while otherwise keeping their business model intact. When Chrysler went bankrupt in the late '70s, his voice in Congress even secured a loan and saved the company. Citing the necessary "equality of sacrifice" for workers and management, he later negotiated for reduced wages and waived termination restrictions, allowing Chrysler to lay off 50,000 workers back into destitution (Stuart, 1979). His was the first golden parachute from the golden years of the golden age—he was appointed to Chrysler's board of directors when Reaganism ascended (Turchin, 2023; The issue is not to "save" Chrysler, 1979). If "American elites entered into a fragile, unwritten compact" with the working classes, as Fraser (1978) explained, it was only because "the acceptance of the labor movement, such as it has been, came because business feared the alternatives."

Fraser's story illustrates the era's larger economic forces. Unions' strength after the World Wars marked the peak of labor power. But it was not to last. There was a seemingly finite amount of money to be made in industrialized nations where labor markets were dominated by unions. The factory owners could no longer profit from their workers' toil as much as their grandfathers could. As post-war reconstruction progressed and economies were rebuilt, diminishing returns set in and economic growth slowed to a crawl compared to the earlier boom. In this climate, some corporations, economists and politicians spread fears of economic stagnation in the face of the communist threat, foregrounding labor power rather than the primary issues of oil shocks, the completion of the rebound cycle after the war or policy failures (Huang, 2016; International Monetary Fund, 2000; Jorgenson, 1988). Increasingly, popular free-market liberal economists like Milton Friedman began to ask louder and louder: is there too much economic equality? (Cole, 2008). The ears of the rich and powerful were only too open to hear the question. And some trade union bosses that were now in the pockets of the corporations were there to help them. Thus, the story of the downfall of mid-twentieth century Keynesian political economy began with the Dollar's seemingly ineradicable inflation which set in at the height of the Nixon Shock (Silk, 1973).

The stagnation of the 1970s was combined with aggressive levels of inflation, which many still believe to have been caused by Friedman's narrative of too much economic equality ("a monetary phenomenon") (Henderson, 2021). On the contrary, it was especially concentrated corporate wealth and its combination with government power that created inflation (Hewlett, 1977; Jacobs, 2021; Vicks, 2021). By the end of 1971, the setting of American monetary policy was simply too little too late (leaving the door open for Friedman's famous critique), which set the stage for the remainder of Nixon's tenure, as his Keynesian Fed chairman, Arthur Burns, consistently failed to live up to the monetary moment by pushing for an enlargement of LBJ's Great Society (Hetzel, 1998). This allowed Hayek's critics of Keynesian political economy to claim empirical victory while betraying their principles (Bartlett, 2006).

For Burns, as later Chicago-trained economists explained, it was a moment to step up or step aside (French, 2010). By squatting over the squalid squabbles for too long, he not only resigned himself and his administration, but all of the mid-20th-c. Keynesian policies they represented, to the trashbox of history. According to the Fed official Tom Hoenig, the 1970s were "a decade of too-accommodative monetary policy," since monetary policy which benefited the working classes seemingly came at the zero-sum expense of the managerial and ownership classes (Leonard, 2021). Simultaneously, the economic equality facilitated and sustained by Great Society programs, strong unions and tight labor markets stoked waves of inflation unrecognizable since the Weimar era. Combined, they produced the *béte noir* of every Keynes-skeptical economist: stagflation.

As the dollar was completely and experimentally unmoored from the Gold Standard in 1971, it developed a special relationship with another finite resource. While nominally fiat, between 1971 and 1974, the dollar became the petrodollar, with its value significantly derived from its institutionalized use in the global oil market (Adelman, 1972, ch. 5; McMahon, 2014). Donella and Dennis Meadows, the primary authors of *The Limits of Growth* (1972), argued that economic growth, which always requires population growth to sustain the growth of supply and demand for goods and services, couldn't last forever on a planet with ultimately finite resources like land, gold and fossil fuel. As growth skeptics noted, eventually, the worship of growth would have to give way to new models of political economy which would recognize the eternal finitude of resources—yet Degrowthers' heady birth in the early '70s was nipped in the bud by its own "fatalistic spirit" (Susskind, 2024, p. 236). Such fatalism in the face of crisis was already observed more than a century earlier, when Marx (1993/1857) noted "the violent destruction of capital not by relations external to it, but rather as a condition of its self-preservation" (p. 750). Then, four things happened in the following year, 1973: Roe v Wade, the creation of the international SWIFT financial system, the Yom Kippur War and the OPEC oil embargo.

There has always been a finite amount of holy land to fight over. The establishment of a new Jewish state between Egypt, Syria and Jordan in 1948 at their zero-sum expense was still a bone of contention and the response came in 1967 with the 6-Day War, when Israel conquered even more land at their collective expense. The situation was unsustainable and if the surrounding Islamic-majority nations couldn't answer the affront militarily, they could economically. The Organization of Petroleum Exporting Countries (OPEC) was newly formed when it responded to the American support for Israeli policies of retaining total control of the finite land between the Mediterranean Sea and Jordan River. It cut off the steady supply of cheap petroleum in 1973, followed by another war against Israel during the Jewish Day of Atonement (Yom Kippur), which, once again, didn't succeed.

That year, SWIFT was founded by Swedish banker Carl Reuterskiöld who had previously worked for the Wallenberg banking dynasty. The purpose was simple: to break the global market stranglehold of New York's First National City Bank (FNCB, later Citibank) on international banking through the primitive Telex system. While conscious of geopolitical considerations about American financial imperialism, SWIFT sought to promote its own alternate messaging system (Farrell & Newman, 2019). The move succeeded in breaking New York's financial monopoly by lodging a complaint with the European Commission in Brussels (Scott & Zachariadis, 2013, pp. 119–127). One's financial empire came at the zero-sum expense of another.

Finally, Roe v Wade was decided in 1973, legalizing abortion throughout the United States and perhaps doing as much for the worldwide advocacy of limiting the population as any other policy besides making birth control and female sexual education and autonomy widely available. The immediate consequence strengthened the feminist movement. In the medium term, legalized abortion prevented millions of unwanted pregnancies, unwanted births, and eventually, by the early 1990s, a sudden decrease in juvenile delinquency and crime since millions of unwanted children in the mid-1970s were never born (Donohue III & Levitt, 2001, esp. p. 381). A long-term legacy was a victory for the population control movement, although it seems the jury is still out on that score (Ziegler, 2015).

Then, in 1974, the first UN World Food Conference was held in Rome, and responding to the Meadows' metastasizing Malthusian meanings, Pope Paul IV spoke in opposition to human population limits—better to improve resource distribution than to surrender to Malthusianism. Earl Butz, American delegate to the conference and secretary of agriculture under Nixon, replied: "He no playa de game; he no maka da rules." Butz became notorious for his racist remarks about Black Americans next year, but he wasn't alone in his racist rejection of improved distribution. As secretary of agriculture, he encouraged the growth of large agribusiness and agricultural cartels, which later morphed into titans like Monsanto (Carlson, 2008; Wurtz, 2023). The previous administration's secretary of agriculture, Orville Freeman, was openly beholden to Jamie Whitten, a White supremacist Mississippi congressman who opposed "racial intermingling" and simultaneously pushed for upward redistribution of farmland owned by Blacks to wealthier Whites (Francis, 2022). When these policy choices came into full bloom under Reagan, combined with further Friedman-inspired trickle-down policies, the president of the UAW, Doug Fraser, accused their advocates of engaging in a "one-sided class war" (Cowie, 2003). It didn't stop him from jumping ship to the winning side.

Hayek's trusty law of the jungle was used to justify yet another new/old system which ensured the same basic zero-sum ecology and economy. 19th-c. liberalism wasn't the only political-economic movement being dug from the trashbox of history in the twilight of the golden age of capitalism. By the late 1970s, alongside liberalism, nineteenth-century social Darwinism (eugenics) was also increasingly advocated as the answer to the zero-sum logic of stagflation. Reimplemented eugenics policies and forced sterilizations of impoverished Blacks, Native Americans and Hispanics in the United States of America continued well into the 1970s, in a backlash against minority liberation movements like MLKJ's Civil Rights (and Black Power), the Native American Red Power and the Chicano Movimiento (Kline, 2001; Kluchin, 2009; Stern, 2005; Theobald, 2019). The psychologist Raymond Cattell exemplified the return to the older zero-sum logic, advocating for 19th-century natural-law inspired liberalism and eugenics (as Joseph Schumpeter previously described WWII's "gale of creative destruction"): "Wherever a question of relative reduction of a population is concerned the word 'eugenics' is bandied about as a propaganda term. Nature constantly commits both homicide and genocide" (Cattell, 1972; Schumpeter, 1994, pp. 82–83).

The supply siders like Friedman and Hayek who rose to prominence promising a cure to the stagflation correctly diagnosed that it was a supply-side phenomenon, but attributed it to capacity constraints and therefore to advocate on behalf of capital at the zero-sum expense of labor (Mazzucato, 2020, pp. 82–83). Ironically, Keynesians like Henry Reuss and Jimmy Carter passed the 1977 Federal Reserve Reform Act, which sought to get the stagflation under control by implementing the "NAIRU" (non-accelerating inflation rate of unemployment) system, which would consign millions of working-class folks to perpetual unemployment in order to maintain the Petrodollar's value as the global reserve currency. The faith-based NAIRU decisions about raising and lowering interest rates by successive Fed chairpersons since then largely determine the economic livelihoods for billions of people. Friedman's neoliberal philosophy simply required that large-scale unemployment must be accepted as a *fait accompli* to tamp down on inflation. Stephanie Kelton writes that this is a "doctrine that relies on human suffering to fight inflation." The religious assumption is clear in the zero-sum trade-off between inflation and forced unemployment: "Some slack must be maintained in the form of a human sacrifice—forced idleness—lest we condemn ourselves to the ravages of accelerating inflation" (Kelton, 2020, pp. 48–54). As Stiglitz (2024) argues, this economic inequality and immiseration provided fertile soil for political extremism to flourish. Willie Thompson (2011) further elucidates the connection between the stagflation and zero-sum thinking: "What the economic depression of the 1970s did was to enable fascists to link together more effectively issues of racism and material discontent" (p. 232). The economic turmoil coupled with the specter of the 1968 worldwide protests were the ground on which Far Right movements and parties re-emerged, if only in a more polite, *salonfähig* version than their interwar counterparts (Kurlansky, 2004). The new/old "disaffected unemployed working class youth" wasn't a bug but a feature, specifically of the use of inflation to transition away from Keynesianism and back to the liberal oligarchy (Collins, 1996; Krueger, 1974; Stiglitz, 2024).

Milton Friedman famously said in the 1970s that "inflation is too much money chasing too few goods." Friedman's 1970s theory of inflation implies that the solution for inflation is reducing the amount of money accessible for most people to spend—to reduce demand. Chased to its logical conclusion, it assumes that money must become scarcer in order to boost the value of goods and that market values must above all retain their emphasis on finitude—the less money in circulation means the more value would accrue to those who have access to it (and of course less to those who don't)—and that, therefore, less people could have access to money. In other words, Friedman assumed that the solution to 1970s inflation required more inequality (Fix, 2021; Hatheway & Friedman, 2022).

Thus, 19th-century laissez-faire liberalism, the inevitable failure of which led to the World Wars, would be reborn, dressed up in new clothes and called "neoliberalism."

References

Adelman, M. (1972). *The world petroleum market*. Johns Hopkins University Press.

Ariño, A., & Romero, J. (2016). *La secesión de los ricos*. Galaxia Gutenberg.

Aris, B., & Campbell, D. (2004, September 25). How Bush's grandfather helped Hitler's rise to power. *The Guardian*. https://www.theguardian.com/world/2004/sep/25/usa.secondworldwar

Armstrong, J. (1968). Collaborationism in World War II: The integral nationalist variant in Eastern Europe. *Journal of Modern History, 40*(3), 403–404.

Associated Press. (2023, May 5). U.S. adds a strong 253,000 jobs despite Fed's rate hikes. *Politico*. https://www.politico.com/news/2023/05/05/u-s-adds-a-strong-253-000-jobs-despite-feds-rate-hikes-00095541

Baptista, R., & Travis, A. (2006). I. G. Farben in America: The technologies of General Aniline & Film. *History and Technology, 22*(2), 187–224. https://doi.org/10.1080/07341510600629332

Bartlett, B. (2006). *Impostor: How George W. Bush bankrupted America and betrayed the Reagan legacy*. Doubleday.

Bastiat, F. (1850). *Ce qu'on voit et ce qu'on ne voit pas*. Guillaumin.

Bergier, J. -F., et al. (1998). *Switzerland and gold transactions in the Second World War*. Bergier Commission. http://www.uek.ch/en/publikationen1997-2000/golde.pdf

Bernhard, P. (2013). Borrowing from Mussolini: Nazi Germany's colonial aspirations in the shadow of Italian expansionism. *The Journal of Imperial and Commonwealth History, 41*(4), 617–643. https://doi.org/10.1080/03086534.2013.836358

Bevins, V. (2020). *The Jakarta method: Washington's anticommunist crusade and the mass murder program that shaped our world*. PublicAffairs.

Bevins, V. (2021, September 29). The people with the most to lose in a U.S.-China cold war. *The Atlantic*. https://www.theatlantic.com/international/archive/2021/09/us-china-cold-war/620223

Borchert, S. (2021, June 22). The rich, weird, and frustrating world of depression-era travel guides. *The Atlantic*. https://www.theatlantic.com/culture/archive/2021/06/new-deal-american-guides-federal-writers-project/619255/

Bradsher, G. (1999). Nazi gold: The Merkers mine treasure. *Quarterly of the National Archives and Records Administration, 31*(1). https://www.archives.gov/publications/prologue/1999/spring/nazi-gold-merkers-mine-treasure.html

Busterud, J. (2001). *Below the salt: How the fighting 90th Division struck gold and art treasure in a salt mine*. Xlibris.

Caciagli, M. (2006). *The Cambridge history of twentieth-century political thought*. Cambridge University Press.

Caplan, B. (2012, May 9). Eugenics, Malthusianism, and trepidation. *Econlog: Economic Philosophy, Energy, Environment, Resources, Econlib*. https://www.econlib.org/archives/2012/05/eugenics_malthu.html

Caresse, P. (2019). The French battleship *Brennus*. In J. Jordan (Ed.), *Warship* (pp. 29–46). Osprey.

Carlson, M. (2008, February 4). Earl Butz. *The Guardian*. https://www.theguardian.com/world/2008/feb/04/usa.obituaries

Carter, Z. (2021, June 19). The real problem with globalization. *The Atlantic*. https://www.theatlantic.com/politics/archive/2021/06/globalization-bretton-woods-keynes-history/619232/

Caspian-Kang, J. (2021, October 7). The enduring importance of the 1965 Immigration Act. *The New York Times*. https://nyti.ms/2YyDlDk

Cattell, R. (1972). *A new morality from science: Beyondism*. Pergamon Press.

Ceballos, Á. (2007). El marxismo del Régimen (1940–1960). *Revista de Hispanismo Filosófico, 12*.

Chomsky, N., & Herman, E. (1979). *The political economy of human rights, I: The Washington connection and Third World fascism*. South End.

Clogg, R. (2002). *Greece, 1940–1949: Occupation, resistance, civil war: A documentary history*. Palgrave Macmillan.

Close, D. (1995). *The origins of the Greek civil war*. Longman.

Coates, T. -N. (2014, January 16). Hitler on the Mississippi banks. *The Atlantic*. https://www.theatlantic.com/international/archive/2014/01/hitler-on-the-mississippi-banks/283127

Cole, J. (2008). Milton Friedman on income inequality. *Journal of Markets & Morality, 11*(2), 239–254.

Collins, R. (1996). The economic crisis of 1968 and the waning of the 'American Century.' *The American Historical Review, 101*(2), 396–422. https://doi.org/10.2307/2170396

Conant, J. (1940, May). Education for a classless society. *The Atlantic*. https://www.theatlantic.com/magazine/archive/1940/05/education-for-a-classless-society/305254/

Conway, E. (2015). *The summit: Bretton Woods, 1944: J. M. Keynes and the reshaping of the global economy*. Pegasus.

Cowie, J. (2003). 'A one-sided class war': Rethinking Doug Fraser's 1978 resignation from the labor-management group. *Labor History, 44*(3), 307–314. https://doi.org/10.1080/002365603200012928

Crain, C. (2018, May 7). Is capitalism a threat to democracy? *The New Yorker*. https://www.newyorker.com/magazine/2018/05/14/is-capitalism-a-threat-to-democracy

Daniels, R. (1971). *The Bonus March: An episode of the Great Depression*. Greenwood.

De Jong, D. (2022). *Nazi billionaires: The dark history of Germany's wealthiest dynasties*. Mariner Books.

Demsas, J. (2024, October 8). What really fueled the 'East Asian miracle'? *The Atlantic*. https://www.theatlantic.com/podcasts/archive/2024/10/taiwan-east-asian-miracle-land-reform/680183

Dickson, P., & Allen, T. (2004). *The Bonus Army: An American epic*. Walker & Co.

Donohue, J., III., & Levitt, S. (2001). The impact of legalized abortion on crime. *Quarterly Journal of Economics, 116*(2), 379–420. https://doi.org/10.1162/00335530151144050

Drucker, J., & Hubbard, B. (2022, February 20). Vast leak exposes how Credit Suisse served strongmen and spies. *The New York Times*. https://www.nytimes.com/2022/02/20/business/credit-suisse-leak-swiss-bank.html

Eizenstat, S. (1998, June 2). Eizenstat special briefing on Nazi gold. *United States Department of State*. https://1997-2001.state.gov/policy_remarks/1998/980602_eizenstat_nazigld.html

Eudes, D. (1972). *The Kapetanios: Partisans and civil war in Greece, 1943–1949*. Verso.

Farrell, H., & Newman, A. (2019). Weaponized interdependence: How global economic networks shape state coercion. *International Security, 44*(1), 42–79. https://doi.org/10.1162/isec_a_00351

Fear, J. (2006). Cartels and competition: Neither markets nor hierarchies (Harvard Business School Working Paper No. 07–011). *Harvard Business School*. http://www.hbs.edu/faculty/Publication%20Files/07-011.pdf

Fedin, K. (2012, August 6). Volga—Mississippi. *SovLit*. (Original work published August 6, 1942) http://www.sovlit.net/war/volgamississippi.html

Fetter, F. (1915). *Economic principles*. Century.

Fiebiger, B., Fullwiler, S., Kelton, S., & Wray, L. (2012). Modern monetary theory: A debate (Political Economy Research Institute Working Paper No. wp279). UMass Amherst. https://ideas.repec.org/p/uma/periwp/wp279.html

Filipuzzi, P., Samuels, S., & Gelblung, A. (2020, March 2). Wiesenthal Centre reveals 12,000 names of Nazis in Argentina, many of whom apparently had accounts transferred to Credit Suisse. *Simon Wiesenthal Center*. https://www.wiesenthal.com/about/news/wiesenthal-center-argentina-nazi.html

Finn, R. (1992). *Winners in peace: MacArthur, Yoshida, and postwar Japan*. University of California Press.

Fix, B. (2021, November 24). The truth about inflation: Why Milton Friedman was wrong, again. *Evonomics*. https://evonomics.com/the-truth-about-inflation-why-milton-friedman-was-wrong-again

Francis, D., et al. (2022, May 5). How the government helped White Americans steal Black farmland. *New Republic*. https://newrepublic.com/article/166276/black-farm-land-lost-20th-century-billions

Fraser, D. (1978, July 19). Resignation letter to the labor-management group. *Libcom*. https://libcom.org/article/douglas-frasers-resignation-letter-labor-management-group

French, D. (2010, December 27). Burns' diary exposes the myth of Fed independence. *Mises Institute*. https://mises.org/mises-daily/burns-diary-exposes-myth-fed-independence

Goebbels, J. (1944). Nun, Volk steh auf, und Sturm brich los! Rede im Berliner Sportpalast. In *Der steile Aufstieg* (pp. 167–204). NSDAP.

Gribetz, J., & Reig, S. (2020). Chapter 6: The Swiss banks Holocaust settlement. In *Reparations for victims of genocide, war crimes and crimes against humanity* (pp. 169–202). Brill. https://doi.org/10.1163/9789004377196_008

Hamlin, D. (2017). *Germany's empire in the East: Germans and Romania in an era of globalization and total war*. Cambridge University Press.

Hatheway, L., & Friedman, A. (2022, February 7). Wall Street is wrong about inflation. *Barrons*. https://www.barrons.com/articles/wall-street-is-wrong-about-inflation-51644247964

Hazlitt, H. (1946). *Economics in one lesson*. Harper.

Heath, C. (2024, September 26). A secret diary of mass murder. *The Atlantic*. https://www.theatlantic.com/ideas/archive/2024/09/polish-journalist-kazimierz-sakowicz-holocaust-witness-diary/680020

Henderson, D. (2021, May 20). Inflation: true and false. *Hoover Institution*. https://www.hoover.org/research/inflation-true-and-false

Heroes: Battle of Washington. (1932, August 8). *Time*. https://content.time.com/time/subscriber/article/0,33009,744107,00.html

Hetzel, R. (1998). Arthur Burns and inflation. *Economic Quarterly, 84*(1), 21–44.
Hewlett, S. (1977). Inflation and inequality. *Journal of Economic Issues, 11*(2), 353–368. http://www.jstor.org/stable/4224599
Hitler, A. (1941). *Mein Kampf* (E. Reynal & C. Hitchcock, Trans.). Houghton Mifflin. (Original work published 1925).
Hobsbawm, E. (1994). *The age of extremes: The short twentieth century, 1914–1991.* Knopf.
Huang, K. (2016). *The postwar growth slowdown and the path of economic development* (MPRA Paper No. 80988). Munich Personal RePEc Archive. https://mpra.ub.uni-muenchen.de/80988/1/MPRA_paper_80988.pdf
International Monetary Fund. (2000). The postwar economic achievement. In *World Economic Outlook: Asset Prices and the Business Cycle* (pp. 70–98). International Monetary Fund. https://www.imf.org/external/pubs/ft/weo/2000/02/pdf/chapter4.pdf
International Monetary Fund. (n.d.). *Destruction and reconstruction (1945–1958).* https://www.imf.org/external/np/exr/center/mm/eng/mm_dr_01.htm
Jacobs, M. (2021, December 24). Fighting inflation means taking on corporations. *The New York Times.* https://nyti.ms/3FrzR5T
Jorgenson, D. W. (1988). Productivity and postwar U.S. economic growth. *Journal of Economic Perspectives, 2*(4), 23–41. https://doi.org/10.1257/jep.2.4.23
Jung, C. G. (1987). *C. G. Jung speaking: Interviews and encounters.* Princeton University Press.
Kagan, R. (2023). *The ghost at the feast: America and the collapse of the world order, 1900–1941.* Atlantic Books.
Kaiser, D. (1980). *Economic diplomacy and the origins of the Second World War.* Princeton University Press.
Kallis, A. (2003). To expand or not to expand? Territory, generic fascism and the quest for an 'ideal fatherland'. *Journal of Contemporary History, 38*(2), 237–260. http://www.jstor.org/stable/3180657
Karabel, J. (2005). *The chosen: The hidden history of admission and exclusion at Harvard, Yale, and Princeton.* Houghton Mifflin.
Karabel, J. (2021, September 5) Let's Honor the True Spirit of Labor Day. *The New York Times.* https://nyti.ms/3DTaHwG
Kelton, S. (2020). *The Deficit Myth: Modern Monetary Theory and the birth of the people's economy.* PublicAffairs.
Kennan, G. (1946, February 22). The chargé in the Soviet Union (Kennan) to the Secretary of State [Document 475, FRUS, 1946, Vol. VI]. *National Security Archive.* https://nsarchive2.gwu.edu/coldwar/documents/episode-1/kennan.htm
Kennedy, R. (2023, June 7). The truth is, many Americans just don't want Black people to get ahead. *New York Times.* https://www.nytimes.com/2023/06/07/opinion/resistance-black-advancement-affirmative-action.html
Keynes, J. M. (1936). *The general theory of employment, interest and money.* Cambridge University Press.
Keynes, J. M. (1940). *How to pay for the war: A radical plan for the Chancellor of the Exchequer.* Macmillan.
Kline, W. (2001). *Building a better race: Gender, sexuality, and eugenics from the turn of the century to the baby boom.* University of California Press.
Kluchin, R. (2009). *Fit to be tied: Sterilization and reproductive rights in America, 1950–1980.* Rutgers University Press.
Knox, M. (1999). *Mussolini unleashed, 1939–1941: Politics and strategy in Fascist Italy's last war.* Cambridge University Press.
Kondratiev, N. (1925). Большие циклы конъюнктуры [Big cycles of the conjuncture]. *Вопросы Конъюнктуры, 1*(1), 28–79.
Krueger, A. O. (1974). The political economy of the rent-seeking society. *American Economic Review, 64*(3), 291–303.
Kurlansky, M. (2004). *1968: The year that rocked the world.* Random House.
Kuttner, R. (2018). *Can democracy survive global capitalism?* Norton.

LeBor, A. (1997). *Hitler's secret bankers: The myth of Swiss neutrality during the Holocaust*. Carol Publishing.

Leonard, C. (2021, December 28). The Fed's doomsday prophet has a dire warning about where we're headed. *Politico*. https://www.politico.com/news/magazine/2021/12/28/inflation-interest-rates-thomas-hoenig-federal-reserve-526177

Lerner, A. P. (1947). Money as a creature of the state. *American Economic Review, 37*(2), 312–317. http://www.jstor.org/stable/1821139.

Levenstein, M., & Suslow, V. (2011). Breaking up is hard to do: Determinants of cartel duration. *Journal of Law and Economics, 54*(2), 455–492. https://doi.org/10.1086/657660

Livy. (1924). *The history of Rome* (B. Foster, Ed.). Harvard University Press. (Original work published ca. 1st century BCE).

Loftus, J., & Aarons, M. (1998). *Unholy trinity: The Vatican, the Nazis, and the Swiss banks*. Martin's Press.

Marshall, T. (1997, July 23). U.S. document links Vatican, Nazi gold. *Los Angeles Times*. http://articles.latimes.com/1997/jul/23/news/mn-15484

Martin, J. (1950). *All honorable men*. Little, Brown & Co.

Marvin, C., & Ingle, D. (1999). *Blood sacrifice and the nation: Totem rituals and the American flag*. Cambridge University Press.

Marx, K. (1993). *Grundrisse: Foundations of the critique of political economy* (M. Nicolaus, Trans.). Penguin. (Original work published 1857).

Maunders, J. (2016, October 29). 'Keep the Russians out, the Americans in, and the Germans down': A potted and bloody history of NATO. *Counterfire*. https://www.counterfire.org/articles/history/18584-keep-the-russians-out-the-americans-in-and-the-germans-down-a-potted-and-bloody-history-of-nato

Mazzucato, M. (2020). *Mission economy: A moonshot guide to changing capitalism*. Penguin.

McCoy, A. (2017). *In the shadows of the American century: The rise and decline of U.S. global power*. Haymarket.

McMahon, T. (2014, May 30) Oil, petrodollars & gold. *Inflation Data*. http://inflationdata.com/articles/2014/05/30/oil-petrodollars-gold

McNeill, W. (1989). *Arnold Toynbee: A life*. Oxford University Press.

Mierzejewski, A. (2004). 1957: Ludwig Erhard's annus terribilis. *Essays in Economic and Business History, 22*, 17–27.

Mineau, A. (2004). *Operation Barbarossa: Ideology and ethics against human dignity*. Rodopi.

Mitchell-Innes, A. (1914). *The credit theory of money*. Cosimo.

Mollin, G. (2006). *The American deconcentration policy in Germany, 1945–1948*. Berghahn.

Moore, M. (1940). Fourth shore: Italy's mass colonization of Libya. *African Affairs, 39*(155), 129–133.

Nachmani, A. (1990). Civil war and foreign intervention in Greece: 1946–49. *Journal of Contemporary History, 25*(4), 489–522.

Neiman, S. (2019). *Learning from the Germans: Confronting race and the memory of evil* (pp. 30–31). Farrar, Straus & Giroux.

Ortiz, S. (2006). Rethinking the Bonus March: Federal bonus policy, the Veterans of Foreign Wars, and the origins of a protest movement. *Journal of Policy History, 18*(3), 275–303.

Overy, R. (2021). *Blood and ruins: The last imperial war, 1931–1945*. Viking.

Paxton, R. (2004). *The anatomy of fascism*. Knopf.

Pellegrini, F. (1997, July 22). The Vatican pipeline. *Time*. https://time.com/archive/6930568/the-vatican-pipeline

Peterson, N. (2022, June 7). Class war > rate hikes. *Financial Times*. https://www.ft.com/content/4e3327f5-473a-4e76-b04d-e5d884219deb

Petropoulos, J. (1996). *Art as politics in the Third Reich*. University of North Carolina Press.

Phayer, M. (2008). *Pius XII, the Holocaust, and the Cold War*. Indiana University Press.

Pizzigati, S. (2012). *The rich don't always win: The forgotten triumph over plutocracy that created the American middle class, 1900–1970*. Seven Stories.

Poliakov, L. (1974). *The Aryan myth: A history of racist and nationalist ideas in Europe*. Basic Books.
Rawl, M. (2006). *Anacostia Flats*. Publish America.
Reynolds, D. (2013). *Britannia Overruled: British Policy and World Power in the Twentieth Century*. Taylor & Francis.
Richardson, H. (2020). *How the south won the civil war: Oligarchy, democracy, and the continuing fight for the soul of America*. Oxford University Press.
Rickman, G. (2011). *Conquest and redemption: A history of Jewish assets from the Holocaust*. Routledge.
Rodríguez, E. (2022). *El efecto clase media: Crítica y crisis de la paz social*. Traficantes de Sueños.
Roosevelt, F. D. (1935). Address to the Young Democratic Clubs of America. In P. Lawler & R. Schaefer (Eds.), *American political rhetoric: Essential speeches and writings* (7th ed., pp. 188–189). Rowman & Littlefield.
Roosevelt, F. D. (1936). Address at Madison Square Garden, New York City. In *The public papers and addresses of Franklin D. Roosevelt, Vol. 5: The people approve, 1936* (pp. 635–638). Macmillan.
Sauvi, A. (1952, August 14). Trois Mondes, Une Planète. *L'Observateur*, *118*, 14. http://www.homme-moderne.org/societe/demo/sauvy/3mondes.html
Schumpeter, J. (1961). *Konjunkturzyklen: Eine theoretische, historische und statistische Analyse des kapitalistischen Prozesses* [Business cycles: A theoretical, historical, and statistical analysis of the capitalist process] (Original work published 1939). Vandenhoeck & Ruprecht.
Schumpeter, J. A. (1994). *Capitalism, socialism and democracy* (pp. 82–83). Routledge. (Original work published 1942).
Scott, S., & Zachariadis, M. (2013). *The society for worldwide interbank financial telecommunication (SWIFT): Cooperative governance for network innovation, standards, and community*. Routledge.
Sharp, J. (2009). *Geographies of postcolonialism: Spaces of power and representation*. SAGE.
Silk, L. (1973). *Nixonomics: How the Dismal science of free enterprise became the black art of controls*. Praeger.
Skou, K. (2005). *Dansk politik A–Å*. Aschehoug.
Smith, D. (2022, May 18). 'People should be more aware': The business dynasties who benefited from Nazis. *The Guardian*. https://www.theguardian.com/books/2022/may/18/nazi-billionaires-book-hitler-bmw-porsche
Snyder, T. (2010). *Bloodlands: Europe between Hitler and Stalin*. Vintage.
Snyder, T. (2016). *Black earth: The Holocaust as history and warning*. Crown.
Stern, A. (2005). *Eugenic nation: Faults and frontiers of better breeding in modern America*. University of California Press.
Stiglitz, J. (2024). *The road to freedom: Economics and the good society*. Norton.
Stuart, R. (1979, August 10). 5000 Chrysler salaried employees face layoffs. *The New York Times*. https://www.nytimes.com/1979/08/10/archives/5000-chrysler-salaried-employees-face-layoffs-union-spurns-freeze.html
Studwell, J. (2013). *How Asia works: Success and failure in the world's most dynamic region*. Grove Atlantic.
Susskind, D. (2024). *Growth: A history and a reckoning*. Harvard University Press.
Sutton, A. (1976). *Wall Street and the rise of Hitler*. Arlington House.
The issue is not to "save" Chrysler but to step up the struggle against it! (1979, October 22). *The Workers' Advocate*, 9(9).
Theobald, B. (2019, November 28). A 1970 law led to the mass sterilization of Native American women. That history still matters. *Time*. https://time.com/5737080/native-american-sterilization-history
Thompson, W. (2011). *Ideologies in the age of extremes: Liberalism, conservatism, communism, fascism 1914–91* (p. 232). Pluto Press.
Trevor-Roper, H. R. (Ed.). (1953). *Hitler's table talk, 1941–1944: His private conversations* (R. Manvell & H. Fraenkel, Trans.). Weidenfeld & Nicolson.

Turchin, P. (2023, June 2). America is headed toward collapse. *The Atlantic*. https://www.theatlantic.com/ideas/archive/2023/06/us-societal-trends-institutional-trust-economy/674260/

United States National Archives. (2016, August 15). Trade with the Third Reich bibliography. https://www.archives.gov/research/holocaust/bibliographies/trade-with-third-reich.html

Vicks, A. (2021, November 30). The neoliberal view of inflation is convenient for capitalists—but it's wrong. *Jacobin*. https://www.jacobinmag.com/2021/11/inflation-solutions-neoliberalism-biden-manchin-volcker-shock-economy

Vincent, I. (1997). *Hitler's silent partners: Swiss banks, Nazi gold, and the pursuit of justice*. Morrow.

Wallace, H. (1943, February 15). International: or else? *Time*. https://content.time.com/time/magazine/article/0,9171,796086,00.html

Wilkins, M. (2004). *The history of foreign investment in the United States, 1914–1945*. Harvard University Press.

Wurtz, N. (2023, January 23). Butz's Law of Economics. *Agrarian Trust*. https://www.agrariantrust.org/butzs-law-of-economics/

Yellen, J. (2019). *The Greater East Asia Co-Prosperity Sphere: When total empire met total war*. Cornell University Press.

Ziegler, M. (2015). *After Roe: The Lost History of the Abortion Debate*. Harvard University Press.

Neoliberalism

7

Abstract

This chapter charts the collapse of Keynesian social democracies and the attendant period of stagflation, followed by the rise of neoliberalism, the system of political economy that has proven most adept at pursuing ruthless zero-sum games posing as win–win ones. While replacing Keynesianism, **neoliberalism confronted communism**. The USSR itself eventually collapsed under the weight of its own politico-economic contradictions, and the constituents of the communist bloc either fragmented and/or went bankrupt, often off the back of zero-sum struggles amongst themselves. This enabled the consolidation of TINA (the myth that "There Is No Alternative" to neoliberal political economy), the (in)famous postulation of the End of History and the standardization of neoliberalism. The technocratic principles of this era promised benefits for all, but the **technocratic myth of global free markets and free trade** has basically meant free rein of the wealthy at the zero-sum expense of the poor. In the final analysis, neoliberalism did not represent a tide that lifted all boats but the most aggressive form of trickle-down **disaster capitalism**, accumulating capital for the few at the zero-sum expense of the many and the environment. The increasing financial speculation which this situation engendered eventually culminated in the Global Financial Crisis (GFC) of 2008.

> Where must we go… We who wander this wasteland in search of our better selves.—The First History Man (*Mad Max: Fury Road*)

History plays with a short deck. Economic history, as you might imagine, is even more economical with its offerings. If Keynesianism was all but dead by 1976, the only other model of political economy on offer beside communism would be 19th-c. liberalism, reborn and repackaged for a new century. Or, in the immortal words

A. M. Feldman and Y. Stamos, *Zero Sum Political Economy*, World-Systems Evolution and Global Futures, https://doi.org/10.1007/978-3-032-18326-2_7

lifted from Antonio Gramsci's prison notebooks, "The crisis consists precisely in the fact that the old is dying and the new cannot be born; in this interregnum a great variety of morbid symptoms appear" (Gramsci, 1951, §34, p. 311; 1971, p. 276). Just as the 1930s had been a politico-economic interregnal period between the first failure of liberalism and the birth of Keynesianism, the 1970s were also a politico-economic interregnal period between the failure of Keynesianism and the birth of neoliberalism. The morbid symptoms of both chaotic eras are impossible to miss—since the bloody seeds of every dark period of political contraction are unwittingly planted in every sunny period of economic expansion.

One of the most archetypical (and least known) figures who embodied both interregnums from the failure of liberalism and the birth of Keynesianism to the failure of Keynesianism and the birth of neoliberalism was Paul Cacheux, a French communist resistance fighter. As a member of the greatest generation, the arc of Cacheux's life story stretches from the failure of classical liberalism and the ascendancy of communism and fascism in the early '20s through his activism and resistance during and after WWII. Then he won fame (and assassination attempts by neo-Nazis) after his rumored involvement in the killing of one of the most brutal Nazis, Joachim Peiper (who personally murdered hundreds of innocent civilians as well as American soldiers in the massacres of Malmedy and Boves during WWII), in an arson attack on Bastille Day (14 July) amid the stagflation and discrediting of Keynesianism of 1976. He died in 1998 at the height of neoliberalism (Georges & Kahane, 1979; Grandhay, 2008; Martin, 1994). It was ironic that Peiper's death allegedly at Cacheux's hands came at the same time as Keynesianism's death at neoliberalism's hands. His greatness lay in his punishment of fascism, while neoliberalism's punishment of Keynesianism would eventually lead back to neo-fascism. Three decades after the end of WWII, apparently Cacheux had not forgotten the brutality of fascism, unlike the proponents of neoliberalism who had forgotten what gave rise to fascism in the first place.

The end of the Keynesian experiment effectively came with the Nixon Shock. The structuring of economies around debt became more salient as the practice accelerated at the same time that common political discourse abused it. The same was largely true of homogeneous societies predicated on immigration restriction. Nixon gave up the last vestiges of the Gold Standard (1971) amid his racially-charged Southern Strategy realignment, which won him the presidency in the elections of 1968 and 1972. Between Nixon's suspension of the US Dollar's convertibility to gold to pay for the Vietnam War (1971) and the OPEC oil embargo (1973), the Keynesian social contract between capital and labor came to crisis, and since politicians globally sought to avoid picking sides, they ultimately chose to draw resources at the zero-sum expense of future generations rather than choose between present ones. In the words of Wolfgang Streeck, it was "the first time after the postwar growth period that states took to introducing not-yet-existing future resources into the conflict between labor and capital." For Streeck, "Neoliberalism was, above all, a political-economic project to end the inflation state and free capital from its imprisonment in the postwar settlement" (Caldwell, 2024; cf. Streeck, 2024).

Hence, the American public funding of the construction of the World Trade Center in the early '70s at the cost of future domestic tax revenue is interpretable as a sign of the coming of neoliberalism and the downfall of the USSR—the geopolitical irony of which would be their destruction in 2001 as a sign of the coming of the end of neoliberalism with the conclusion of the seemingly futile American war in Afghanistan (the roots of which began during the Soviet invasion in the late '70s). As the economic historian Gary Gerstle has put it, the failure of international (Soviet) communism in the late 1980s

> removed what had been an imperative in America (and in Europe and elsewhere) for compromise between elites and the working classes. [...] A fear of communism made possible the class compromise between capital and labor that underwrote the New Deal order. American labor was strongest when the threat of global communism was greatest. The apogee of America's welfare state [...] was coterminous with the height of the Cold War. After 1991, the year of the Soviet Union's dissolution, the pressure on capitalist elites and their supporters to compromise with the working class vanished. The dismantling of the welfare state and the labor movement marched in tandem with communism's collapse. (Steinmetz-Jenkins & Gerstle, 2022)

The death of Keynesianism in the mid-1970s which ushered in the rise of neoliberalism based on the ideas and theories of Fredrich Hayek and Milton Friedman ("stockholder/shareholder capitalism"), implemented under Thatcher in the UK ("Thatcherism") and Reagan in the USA ("Reaganomics"), reshaped a collective West designed to outspend and eventually bankrupt the USSR and discredit its particular brand of communism. But in so doing, when the Berlin Wall fell, the very triumph of neoliberalism sowed the seeds of its own collapse. The neoliberal vision of shareholder capitalism created a myopic, short-termist mindset at the expense of the far-sighted Keynesian capitalism which relied more on what became called the "stakeholder view" that includes "workers, the communities and the environment" (Mazzucato, 2020, p. 194). The "voodoo economics" it prescribed as the medicine of the "Washington Consensus" included financial deregulation, asset privatization, public service outsourcing, budget austerity, tax cuts for the wealthy, welfare "reform" for the poor, and created the new moneyed classes of global billionaire oligarchs—post-Soviet in Yeltsin's and Putin's Russian Federation and post-modern in the Bush and Clinton dynasties' American empire. There is infinite irony in the zero-sum calculation that for "homo economicus" to rise, "homo sovieticus" had to fall.

Perhaps another one of the greatest ironies was Francis Fukuyama's claim that the collapse of the USSR heralded *The End of History*. It was widely believed that nominally non-zero-sum neoliberal capitalism, spread around the world as the "Washington Consensus" of the 1990s, predicated on credit, growth, and the transcendence of class antagonisms (that class struggle would become obsolete) would "lift all boats." Nothing could be further from the truth. The lessons of 2008 would eventually reveal themselves as the XYZs of neoliberalism and its tragic, if predictable, results, as this form of political economy unraveled in the 2010s-20s. When Putin invaded Ukraine between 2014–2022, Fukuyama paraded himself on TV with Ukrainian soldiers and declared the necessity to reestablish socialism, making it abundantly clear that the "end of history" had ended—even for the man who formulated it.

Neoliberalism Confronts Communism

In the 1960s–1970s, there were reckonings with capitalism's own various internal strifes throughout the capitalist world. The same was simultaneously true throughout the communist world. Each new sovereign actor rhetorically promoted a different ideological blend, like Stalinism, Maoism or socialist self-management (Titoism). Further east in Eurasia, especially in Southeast Asia, communist religions became even more prone to schisms, spin-offs and proxy battles at the edges of their enforceable jurisdictions (Lewin, 2016).

For decades, the zero-sum game of the capitalist West against the Bolsheviks left little leeway to anti-capitalist socialists; George Orwell, Arthur Koestler and Eric Hobsbawm are notable examples. They would either side with the Soviet Union or (appear to) be on the side of its enemies who had repeatedly put aside their differences ever since 1918 in countless efforts to suffocate the USSR. But after WWII, the Soviet Union was seemingly there to stay while self-determination movements gained traction. Meanwhile, the defense of Stalinism was becoming increasingly untenable, causing even Khrushchev's leadership of the USSR itself to denounce it in 1956 and begin a process of "de-Stalinization." In that changed environment, more and more communists sought to pursue alternative political and economic projects without imitating the Soviet paradigm or succumbing to the pressures of the Soviet government for homogeneity and centralized control throughout the camp.

The USSR's victory in WWII also sowed the seeds of its eventual decline, as cracks had already appeared during the war. Obviously the war accelerated the collapse of the remaining old national empires (France, Britain, Japan, Italy, Germany, Portugal, Holland, etc.) and the process of decolonization. National liberation movements sprung up throughout the world seeking not only to defeat the residues of fascism but to cast away the yoke of the old national imperialisms. Many of these movements were—either from the start or through transformation and realignment along the way—of communist orientation. While this often meant an expanded sphere of influence for the Soviet Union, at times it meant a challenge to its hegemony in the communist camp as the *only* successful revolution that had led to a nominal "workers' state."

The first challenger was Yugoslavia. It boasted the largest partisan movement in WWII-Europe. Unlike the countries that would become part of the Warsaw Pact, Yugoslavia was mainly liberated by its own communist movement (and the retreat of the Wehrmacht in 1944 to defend the homefront of the Reich) rather than by the advancing Red Army. The two Josephs, Stalin and Tito, had titanic disagreements that had an impact on other Balkan communist movements, particularly the one in Greece, whose partisans were refused entry and asylum in Yugoslavia at the height of the Greek Civil War after the split between Tito and Stalin had become official in 1948 and Yugoslavia was suspended from the Cominform. Tito later spearheaded the Non-Aligned movement, with his thesis of a separate "National Road to Socialism" becoming the archetype for other communist parties to pursue their own political plans while maintaining their distinct foreign and domestic policies autonomous from Moscow (Banac, 1988, pp. 130–190; Westad, 2005, pp. 139–142).

The next challenger was the People's Republic of China (PRC). The Sino-Soviet split regarding their shared borders culminated in the late '60s, almost leading to a hot war between the two communist powers over a small island in the Ussuri River. Nixon saw an opportunity to get his foot in the door and make a bipolar world into a multipolar world—twenty-first-century ironies notwithstanding. Thus came China's diplomatic recognition by the West from the 1970s onward at the zero-sum expense of Taiwan's ruling class in the Kuomintang—a policy that would be reversed during the emergence of the twenty-first-century multipolar world, as the Biden administration started dropping the One-China Policy in 2022 (Reuters, 2022). These 1970s developments came on the heels of (and sought to exacerbate) other intra-communist conflicts in Vietnam and other South-East Asian national liberation (and communist) movements like those of Ho Chi Minh and Pol Pot. Their destructions of their respective ancient feudal systems in Vietnam and Cambodia also led to chaos, war (including the US involvement in Vietnam—its own "genocide," according to the International War Crimes Tribunal in 1966 [Bedau, 1974]), and mass murder. Next door in Laos, a concurrent brutal civil war between the royalists and the Lao People's Revolutionary Party during the 1960s-70s resulted in the victory of communist reforms and another round of intra-communist ideological differences with its neighbors and with its native "Kaysone Phomvihane Thought" (Yamada, 2018). Meanwhile, back in Europe, Enver Hoxha's communist dictatorship in majority-Islamic Albania became an outlier (many times over) in the Balkans by espousing Maoism (not to mention its other ethno-linguistic differences from its neighbors). Its increasing isolation, being the only Maoist government on the continent, contributed both to its poverty and to a sense of threat from all sides that resulted in a frenzy of bunker building infrastructure planist projects throughout the country. It did, however, manage to play a significant role in the global Maoist movement by promoting the recognition of the PRC by the UN in 1971 (Ramet, 2023).

Meanwhile, Moscow's heavy-handed responses to protest movements in East Germany (1953), Hungary (1956) and Czechoslovakia (1968) gradually alienated significant portions of the communist movements in Western Europe and fed into the development of a thread of Eurocommunism separate from Moscow; Orwell and his fellow disillusioned socialists were only the tip of the iceberg. Italy already had its very own vibrant communist tradition that did not always align with the Stalinist distortions of democratic centralization (which ended up being centralization without democracy). Within the Eastern Bloc itself, Soviet repression had in some cases the opposite effect, leading even the governments that wanted to exercise some autonomy vis-a-vis Moscow to increased authoritarianism. A case in point is Romania, where the general secretary of the Communist Party, Nicolae Ceaușescu, railed against the Russian crackdown in Prague all the while promoting an autocratic and nationalist variant of Bolshevism in his own country. This has sometimes been termed as "National Communism" (Leustean, 2007; Tismaneanu, 1984) or "National Stalinism" (Tismaneanu, 2012), but in some ways it went even further in its instrumentalization of the country's legendary past in ways that are actually reminiscent of fascism. Typified by "Dacomania", the ethno-nationalist drive to manufacture links between contemporary Romanians and ancient Dacians, this was quite similar to the projects that fascists in various countries had undertaken from the 1920s to the 1940s (Boia, 2001, 2018). Pol Pot's Khmer Rouge was a similar political project in Southeast Asia (Kiernan, 2001).

Ironically, this can be seen as having its roots in Stalin's own proclamation of "Socialism in one country," a doctrine that eventually helped provide legitimacy to Stalin at the zero-sum expense of his internal rivals (Zinovjev, Bukharin, Trotsky) but, most importantly, to posit the defense of the Soviet Union (or the promotion of its interests, as interpreted by Stalin himself) as the primary task of communists worldwide, even at the zero-sum expense of their own best interests. On that basis, Stalin developed an ideological mix that gradually replaced internationalism with Great Russian nationalism (ironically despite him being Georgian) and gave form to "National Stalinism." The Soviet-Russian public's pride in its communist imperialism was realistically little different to its grandparents' pride in its czarist imperialism. Or, in the words of Schmemann (2021): "The Soviet state had denied people freedom, but it had given them something else: the pride of superpower – a force, Izvestia wrote, "equal to nationalism" and capable of uniting "millions of fanatical supporters." In the post-WWII period, communist governments that sought to escape the control of Moscow tended to steer towards doctrines of "national roads to communism" or even "National Communism" rather than adequately fostering the universal purpose of communist internationalism (Bideleux & Jeffries, 2020, pp. 317–319).

On the other hand, one of the communist governments that most advanced internationalism started out as a nationalist one and switched to communism due to external pressures from the United States and the decision to find an ally in the Soviets. Despite its small size, Castro's Cuba actually managed to pursue its own foreign policy, particularly in Africa, disagreeing with Brezhnev's choice of proxies in the various conflicts on the continent. At the same time, it became a revolutionary symbol across the globe, particularly due to the involvement of Che Guevara and the resilience of the new regime for all its proximity to the strongest capitalist state in history (Gleijeses, 2006, esp. pp. 120–125). Cuba relished its autonomy from both Washington *and* Moscow, eventually joining the Non-Aligned Movement.

Yet, for all the fragmentation and the defections elsewhere, the Soviet Union of the 1960s-70s was still a centralized multinational state that largely functioned as a nation-state and the Soviet-led Eastern bloc was still an alliance of nation-states. The system wasn't perfect, but it functioned as long as belief in its justice could be sustained. Nobody got everything, but everybody got something (Brown,

2009, pp. 257–259). It still ran on a manufacturing/industrial base and its economic system had similarities with the by-now old-fashioned Keynesian paradigm that dominated in other states in the industrialized world: tightly regulated fiat currency alongside government interventions, regulations and subsidies for various industries in certain regions.

Despite the challenges from other communist states, the Soviet government maintained a monopoly on Leninism, the same as the Czar previously had a monopoly on Russian Orthodox Christianity. Other nations within the Soviet commonwealth could have their own histories, currencies and spinoffs or sub-genres of Leninism the same way that other nations within the Byzantine Commonwealth could have done with Orthodox Christianity. Peripheral capitals got subsidies for Soviet-style star-topped residential high-rises with garbage chutes and education/indoctrination funding for Leninist doctrines the same way they previously got onion-domed cathedrals, icons and clergies trained in Orthodox Christian doctrine. Ideology has always meant a structure of faith in a system, whether it's faith in a savior, faith in a prophet, faith in an emperor or faith in a premier or political economy. As long as all nations stayed faithful to the original brand, it didn't matter whose faces they put on their bills and coins. And faith in one prophet or another is not confined to continental Eurasia. Faith in the prophet of George Washington or the profit of Adam Smith is no different. The United States was simply another nuclear superpowered nation-state ruled by an elite political machine in Washington, full of peripheral capitals of Jeffersonian architecture, subsidies for high-rises with garbage chutes and funding for officially-approved education/indoctrination running on a manufacturing economy with Keynesian fiat currency. They both invaded or meddled in the affairs of other nations to spread their respective ideologies at ballpoint if they could or at gunpoint if they couldn't. The United States just had more gold reserves in Fort Knox. It had also been left relatively unscathed by the destruction of WWII, in contrast to the horrific casualty figures and the leveling of its productive basis that the USSR experienced (in part due to Stalin's own miscalculations).

But none of this meant that either ruling class (intelligentsia) couldn't read the writing on the walls. Already in 1970, Zbigniew Brzezinski, the mastermind of the late US Keynesian presidencies of LBJ and Carter, and a consummate student of the geopolitical ideas of Halford Mackinder, Carl Schmitt, Józef Piłsudski and Alfred Mahon, wrote *Between Two Ages: America's Role in the Technetronic Era*. Just as Neil Armstrong was returning to earth from the moon, Brzezinski recognized that the nation-state manufacturing economy was quickly disappearing and that a new age had begun:

> The nation-state as a fundamental unit of man's organized life has ceased to be the principal creative force: International banks and multinational corporations are acting and planning in terms that are far in advance of the political concepts of the nation-state. (Brzezinski, 1970, p. 55)

His words heralded decades of schisms and broken promises.

The following year (1971), just as another ideological schism divided Eastern and Western Pakistan (creating Bangladesh), a grander schism in Leninism took place, as we saw, with the Sino-Soviet split. Two years later in 1973, Brzezinski teamed up with financier David Rockefeller to start the Trilateral Commission. Dedicated to "fostering a New International Economic Order," it sought to reject the Keynesian social-democratic paradigm of sovereign political economy which had dominated the post-War world in the early Cold War, and specifically to undermine the Soviet Union's sovereignty and political economy. In fact, the intellectual and economic collusion of these two powerful dynasties portended that the Cold War would switch from a competition of promise making to breaking to each power's populations:

> Though the Cold War began as a race to make promises, it ended as a race to break promises, and democratic capitalism prevailed over state socialism because it proved capable of breaking promises and imposing discipline. Neoliberalism rose as the Cold War ended because it provided ideological justification for acts of breaking promises; it made a virtue out of economic discipline. Combined with electoral democracy, it gave democratic capitalist states a political and ideological tool kit to meet the challenge of breaking promises. Lacking these tools, the states of the Eastern Bloc democratized their political systems and reformed their ideology in the 1980s as a means of imposing economic discipline. It is this process of political change and ideological reform that we now call the collapse of communism and the end of the Cold War. (Bartel, 2022, pp. 332–333)

The financial austerity imposed on both the working classes of the USA and USSR, which began with the Trilateral Commission, was hidden behind a veneer of democracy to ensure that one working class would eventually be able to claim victory at the other's zero-sum expense. In that regard, the birth of neoliberalism was what defeated the USSR (Bockman, 2007; Dale & Fabry, 2018; Pagliarini, 2022; Rutland, 2013; Sakwa, 2013).

Eventually, the Brzezinski and Rockefeller dynasties' foundation of the Trilateral Commission portended three varieties of the bankruptcy of the Soviet design: economic, moral and finally political. Little did the Democrat know that the "New International Economic Order" wouldn't become very different from the Old 19th-century International Economic Order (Andrianopoulos, 1991; Firestone, 1988; Wallis, 2018). Another ideological schism divided Northern and Southern Vietnam, just like Korea, triggering an American attempt to replace the French imperial occupation—itself a replacement of the older form of zero-sum feudalism in Indochina (McMahon, 2013).

The first Soviet bankruptcy, the increasingly apparent failing of its economy, was perhaps best exemplified by the failure of Khruschev's Virgin Lands project, which boosted cotton yields in Transoxiana at the zero-sum expense of the Aral Sea and the livelihoods of its fishermen. By overexploiting the waters of the Syr Darya and Amu Darya Rivers for irrigation for the intensive cotton harvest, the main source of replenishment for the Aral Sea quickly dried up (Mazhitova et al., 2021; Micklin, 1988; United Nations, 2007). The unsustainability and reverse incentivization of increasing yields, production capacities, quotas and/or industrial/agricultural efficiency was obvious even in the early '70s. Western criticisms did have a point: why work harder if you'll never get ahead? The motivational bankruptcy of Soviet labor productivity paved the way for the fiscal bankruptcy of the Soviet Union itself (Filtzer, 2009; Harrison, 1994, pp. 182–183; IMF, 1991, pp. 102–105).

The second Soviet bankruptcy was far more insidious: moral bankruptcy. The ruination of natural resources by mismanaged prestige projects, to say nothing of official lies about the harms of forced collectivization, Stalin's responsibility for the Holodomor, great purges, gulags, and other abuses kept under strict official wraps but partially known, all contributed to a general cynicism which couldn't be swept away, even by the 1960s. Moscow's oppressive interventions against popular protest movements in the Warsaw Pact countries during the 50s-60s also contributed to moral bankruptcy.

By the 1970s–1980s, between the steady stream of official lies disbelieved by the citizenry, the gradual creep of Western propaganda like Radio Free Europe and the foundations of North American Ukrainian Studies departments in Harvard and Toronto (as extensions of Piłsudski's Prometheanism political project), the disastrous War in Afghanistan, and the growing cost of atomic arms races with the West coming at the very real zero-sum expense of all other investments, the Soviet Union of the 1970–80s had encountered the same problems as the Western Keynesian systems (Allen, 1993; Gustafson, 1982, 10–14; Hatzivassiliou, 2018; Radio Free Europe/Radio Liberty, 2004; United Nations, 2000, ch. 3). In fact, from the abandonment of the gold standard and the flotation of their socio-economic policies following 1971, both the USA and the USSR were essentially forced to break the promises of the respective social contracts with their working or middle classes to maintain their living standards (Bartel, 2022). The major difference was that Western nations had a 19th-century economic model to fall back on whereas the Soviet Union could only be maintained in direct opposition to the nineteenth-century liberal paradigm.

In 1978, the PRC chose Western reforms over doubling down on Orthodox Leninism, inaugurating five-decades of liberal economic expansion under the auspices of communist control. However, the USSR, which was ideologically sustained by Orthodox Leninism, was incapable of laissez-faire liberal reforms. As it turned out, the zero-sum political-economic structure was so brittle that reforms rendered the entire system destabilized. With the implementation of glasnost' and perestroika, suddenly the official lies were shown to be what they were (CSIS, n.d.; Zubok, 2007). Since the USSR was largely sustained by the faith of the masses in the system, once the faith was extinguished, the system rapidly unraveled.

Political bankruptcy came last. Chernobyl was simply the last straw. By the time the various nations of Eastern Europe began turning all the separatist hues of the late autumn foliage of the Soviet Union, the color revolutions were little more symbolic than the stark phrase "Winter is coming." The fall of the Berlin Wall, which signaled the collapse of the Soviet Bloc into its constituent ethnic republics, was merely a winter solstice in a long and treacherous journey toward the dominant imposition of Western economic models on Eurasian populations which resisted and eventually succumbed. Gorbachev, vilified as he is today by the majority of the Russian people, was the sacrificial figure in the story of Russian Federation's rebirth from the ashes of the USSR (Church, 1989; Solly, 2022; Talbott, 2017). Or, in the words of US Secretary of State Colin Powell in 2004 (after he lied about alleged Iraqi WMDs to the UN):

> Most of my career was in a zero-sum world –us versus the Russians. Zero-sum kind of takes you to places like Vietnam. The domino theory is a form of zero-sum thinking. My whole life, especially as a senior officer, we were always focusing on having to have the better tank, and they would immediately start working on a better tank than our better tank, and of course then we'd have to have a better tank than their better tank, and everything was zero-sum. [... Now,] There's no longer just the United States versus the Soviet Union, but the whole West and international community against [...] the whole whatever-you-want-to-call-it. (O'Rourke, 2004)

Among millions, two men were born in the worldwide ruins of classical liberalism in the 1930s, as their nations geared up for the largest zero-sum war for seemingly finite resources in the history of the earth. Vladimir Abramovich Raevsky was born to a family of journalists and writers in Moscow. Nicholas Frederick Brady was born to a family of tobacco tycoons and philanthropists in Manhattan (the nicotine addiction of millions of wretches through the Bradys' tobacco business paid for their potlatch dependence through the family's philanthropy). After graduating from their respective nations' prestigious universities, they climbed their respective social pyramids until they arrived at their nations' respective positions as heads of finance: after decades as an investment banker, Brady became the US secretary of the Treasury in 1988 and after decades as an academic economist, Raevsky became the Soviet finance minister in 1991; he would be the last.

After Bretton Woods (1944), the US Dollar replaced the gold standard as half the world's reserve currency, so Brady proposed to sell dollar-denominated bonds and loans to indebted Latin American nations as a form of sovereign debt restructuring to address risks of widespread sovereign defaults and the downstream risks of communist agitation (the Brady Plan, AKA Washington Consensus) to newly categorized LDCs, or Least Developed Countries (Chomsky, 1999; Jones, 2012, pp. 305–312; Shadlen, 2004; Spiegel, 1996). Since nations were required to adopt neoliberal political economies to qualify, it was a financial tool for spreading the prosperity gospel of so-called free-market neoliberalism beyond American borders—basically a twentieth-century American imperial version of the nineteenth-century British imperial policy against trading with sovereign nations whose currencies were not convertible to the gold standard, something that didn't go unnoticed by Raevsky.

The same plan was granted to the new Russian Federation after the liquidation of Raevsky's Soviet finance ministry. Ecuador eventually defaulted anyway, but the first Russian finance minister to replace Raevsky in the intervening period (between 4–19 February, 1991), Egor Timurovich Gaidar, adopted the bonds, market reforms, industrial deregulations, privatizations and trickle-down economic models with the zeal of a convert (what later became called "shock therapy," with the deregulations and privatizations of previously state-owned sectors leading to zero-sum turf wars for the limited number of these behemoths, enriching multinational corporations while creating the first Russian oligarchs). Seemingly overnight, the obligations of sovereign debts were passed onto millions of citizens and taxpayers, making them into consumers and debtors to be milked (like good old-fashioned tax farming) rather than constituents to be pleased. Brady and Raevsky both went on to comfortable retirements as grey elder statesmen; the former as a director, board member or trustee for universities, the Bilderberg Group, offshore hedge funds and various corporations in industries such as international finance, petroleum, automation, war profiteering, pharmaceuticals, meatpacking and thoroughbred horse racing; and the latter returned to academic economics as a member of the post-Soviet International Union of Economists, dying right on the arrival of COVID-19 on 8 December, 2020 (Bilderberg former steering committee members, n.d.; Izutova, 2021; Nicholas Frederick Brady, n.d.; Raevsky, 2014, 2020).

It was ironic that neoliberalism claimed to facilitate a "win–win" structure for George H. W. Bush's "New World Order"—for neoliberalism to rise, the Soviet political economy had to fall.

The Technocratic Myth of Global Free Markets & Free Trade

Remember Herbert Spencer and his 19th-century social Darwinism? Recall his good friend John Galton, Darwin's cousin, who used the same ideas to create eugenics, which was later employed to justify genocide? Recollect that Spencer also pioneered the idea that there could be no real alternative to the classical liberal political economy? (Spencer, 1851, pp. 42, 307). Like every other forgotten science experiment at the back of the fridge and rediscovered decades later by eternally enterprising vested interests, the lid was removed and the mold was scooped out (which had long since parasitically consumed the remaining host paste to resemble an unrecognizable decomposed substance). The remaining primeval ooze was chucked post haste into the microwave to be warmed over for a "new" political-economic program. When the timer dinged and the specter was served, a new label was affixed to the partially melted plastic tupperware container: "There Is No Alternative" (TINA). Recast in the charades of "win–win" solutions and the shrouds of liberty, liberalism, like Lazarus, levitated and lived anew as neoliberalism. Rather than engaging in the dull travails of imagination and perspiration to form a fresh future, from a fridge (or perhaps trash box) full of the fugue figures of failed political economies, the Old Boys Club, represented by the Reagan, Bush, Brady, Cheney, Clinton and Koch dynasties who won the zero-sum competition for political economy in the First Cold War chose as their solution the very system whose inevitable failure led to the world wars in which others' parents and grandparents were forced to fight (their own typically had the equivalent of bone spurs—namely, political connections).

The fact that the rebirth of nineteenth-century liberalism could make strange, if happy, bedfellows of the likes of the Reagan, Bush, Brady, Cheney, Clinton and Koch dynasties was no accident. It promised a great return to Herbert Spencer's social darwinism of individual responsibility (Cooney, 1973). Pick yourself up by your bootstraps is its mantra. After the Roosevelts' and Kennedys' legacy of the War on Poverty wound down and a surrender document was signed in the early '80s—Reagan (1988) famously announced that "poverty won"—the entire charade was recast instead of as a zero-sum class struggle against poverty as a positive-sum individual identitarian struggle for liberty. No wonder two generations of Americans have looked smilingly back at the "great communicator" Reagan's rhetoric of a "beacon of democracy, city on a hill, morning in America" and his legacy of "sunny patriotic optimism;" he told them exactly what they wanted to hear (at the zero-sum expense of the truth). It was all enough to believe the idea that "government isn't the solution; government is the problem." Whereas the actual *un*freedom of the marketplace had been the principal cause of the downfall of liberalism two generations ago, now the market would be its primary springboard. Trade unions were portrayed as collectivist tyrants that impinge on the freedom of the individual (the entrepreneur of the self) and impede the free activity of the market by imposing terms and regulations, by going on strike when their demands would not be met, etc. The worker could now revel in his newfound freedom—until the deluge came for his internment tent. "And then, when he had his fling, when the tent top blew off and he had a good look at the sky, he saw that it wasn't a circus, but an arena, just like everywhere. And a damned grim one" (Miller, 2005, pp. 306–308). It's no surprise that American liberals (and other global citizens) have been nonstop wringing their hands since the global reimposition of the technocratic myth of the free market.

The works of three prominent hand-wringing economists are instructive. Susan Strange, whose works argued that the newly globalizing free market ideology of the 1990s was little more than a mass delusion (Brown, 1999; Strange, 1976, 1988, 1997, 1998; Strange et al., 1991), her friend Robert Rowthorn, whose voluminous Marxian economic works (Rawthorn, 1980, 1981; Rawthorn & Wells, 1987; Rawthorn & Ramaswamy, 1997) she called among the few read in business schools (Strange, 1997, p. 93) and his student, Ha-Joon Chang, whose own books debunk global neoliberalism's myths of free markets and free trade (Chang, 2002, 2008, 2010, 2014, 2023), have been instrumental to revealing the metaphorical man behind the curtain. Together, these three economists have demonstrated that the concepts of free trade and free markets were little more than planned fabrications, much as Karl Polanyi had during the first failure of liberalism. Despite clear warning signs, though, the propaganda of big banks and businesses would meanwhile succeed in turning the belief that There Is No Alternative to so-called "free markets" to common sense. Again in control, big banks and businesses would again lower the veil.

The arc of the story from the politico-economic maturation of Susan Strange and Robert Rowthorn to Ha-Joon Chang thus illustrates the global reimposition of the myth of free trade and free markets in the 1990s. The bottom-up labor movements and top-down Keynesian policies of the 1930s-1940s had created the middle classes (now termed "the Great Compression") (Goldin & Margo, 1991). However, the reimposed myth would now seek to recast the entire story as a nefarious plot to reduce freedom by overextending democracy. The rewriting of economic history during the late '80s, among others by the predictably entitled *Foundation for Economic Education*, didn't just stop in the twentieth century; it sought to go back all the way to the sixteenth century in order to bolster its newfound claims (but no earlier and only to other Protestant powers—the Dutch Republic). Such articles which seek to learn all the wrong lessons from history fail to mention that 16–18th-century Holland was dominated by another dynasty (Orange) whose entire economic policy boiled down to piratical profit at the zero-sum expense of the Catholic Habsburg dynasty (Peterson, 1987). Clearly unsatisfied with such nonsense, other think tanks like the *American Institute for Economic Research* engage in typical intellectually contortionist economic logic when they claim that, as far back as the eighteenth century, there was never any alternative (TINA) to an economic system in which private property rights would always be *absolutely* guaranteed, forgetting that this is precisely what caused the French Revolution (Salsman, 2021). The reversion to nineteenth-century private law beginning in the 1980s, facilitated through the use of Hayek's and Friedman's reborn (neo-)liberal political-economic doctrines toward privatization and deregulation, made it possible for entire swathes of the economy to be self-governed by those who controlled them. This was nowhere more apparent than in banking operations (Brown, 2015; Hayek, 1976; Jones, 2012, pp. 300–315; Slobodian, 2018).

Thus, in recasting the twentieth century, the same contortionists painted FDR's New Deal and victory against fascism as a global infringement on the rights of bankers to operate in so-called "free markets" (Billington & Ridge, 1981, p. 193). Disregarding the many banks that were prevented from failing by FDR's FDIC, the chairman of the Federal Reserve in the 1980s, Alan Greenspan, remarked about the futility and illogic of the FDIC's federal regulation of the banking system: "We are, in effect, attempting to use government to enforce two different prices for the same item –namely, government-mandated deposit insurance. Such price differences only create efforts by market participants to arbitrage the difference" (Sicilia & Cruikshank, 2000, pp. 96–98). Unsurprisingly, by the early '90s, as the new high priests of the new neoliberal religion (Hayek, Friedman and their disciples) sought (and achieved) democratic sacrifices for their new deity at the altar of "liberty," the first on the menu would be defanging the FDIC.

The trouble was that, banks deregulated this way could now, without fear of government, restart risky investing at the zero-sum expense of their clients and critics:

> The F.D.I.C. definitely prevented panics. From its creation until America's entry into World War II, banks failed at a rate of close to 50 per year, not bad considering the economic

> depression in most of that period. And most of the banks that failed were small. By the postwar period, deposit insurance seemed to have been created for an era that no longer existed. Bankers schooled in the 1930s tended toward prudence, and the industry was risk averse. The failure rate was exceptionally low. That all changed in the 1970s and '80s. A combination of financial deregulation, revived animal spirits on Wall Street, and rising inflation led to financial instability and swings in interest rates. Voilà – bank failures returned. (Lowenstein, 2023)

This was related to the "notoriously short" financial memory that Galbraith (1990) described in his *Short History of Financial Euphoria*, published a mere three years after "Black Monday", the banking crisis of 1987 (the cherry on top of the Reagan Revolution that should have come as a warning bell about the vacuity of neoliberalism's utopian promises). It was this short memory that allowed for the myth of the free market to re-entrench itself. The overpromotion of the free market was combined with the claim that it is only organized labor and state regulations that work at the zero-sum expense of the individual. It was conveniently forgotten that, if left unregulated, the business and banking sector organizes its own interests in trusts and cartels, oligopolies and monopolies that operate at the zero-sum expense of everyone else—including the state. The state, which imposes taxes with the supposed aim to provide basic services to all its citizens, when hollowed out of its social function, ends up having neither the power nor the legitimacy to crack down on big business, and instead becomes its handmaid and creditor of last resort. This is the essence of the "Waterbed Effect," the term originally used to refer to the zero-sum economic industrial policy between big business and small business: what suits a big business as it consolidates a market comes at the zero-sum expense of small business. In other words, when markets are "freed," they tend toward oligopolization, and eventually, monopolization (Inderst & Valletti, 2011). Thus, an American bank failed every three days on average during the fourteen years between 1980 and 1994 (FDIC, 1997). And as the process continued, the federal government would later spend tens of billions upon billions of taxpayer dollars to bail out banks which had in the meantime become "too big to fail", all the while leaving millions of ordinary "entrepreneurs of the self" to lose their mortgaged houses. But more on that in the next part.

Yet it was all too little, too late. The intellectual underpinnings of neoliberalism had already been laid as far back as the mid '60s when Milton Friedman helped found the Philadelphia Society. By that point, Friedman had already become the high priest for a rising new movement in the United States (ironically imported from Austria, a small country that had the twofold misfortune of unleashing on the world the leaders of the two biggest ideological afflictions of the last century: nazism and neoliberalism) which sought to deny the government of economic responsibility for its citizens. While Friedman's thesis was at odds with the strong Jewish humanitarian tradition, he used other parts of his heritage to justify his project, presenting the long survival of the Jewish diaspora as a result of the fact that "it was able to carve out for itself a niche in the free market." His proposals, which, once broadly adopted, catalyzed lower-class immiseration, were initially legitimized through the narrative that "the underprivileged and the poor in our own day have far better opportunities to improve their status in a fluid, competitive system than under a paternalistic bureaucracy that preserves the status quo in the name of justice" (Viorst, 1970).

Friedman's ignorance of an earlier Ashkenazi economist who had pointed out that most of history was driven by zero-sum class struggle was no accident. He preferred only to notice his mentor's (Friedrich Hayek's) preference for "economic liberalism" over "political liberalism" without delving into the reasons why hereditary classes (and oligarchies) form in the first place. Hayek and Friedman were quite clear in their preference for using the Pinochet regime's top-down power to implement policies on millions of Chileans in their image:

> As Friedrich Hayek explained in an interview for Chile's *El Mercurio* (April 12, 1981), dictatorship "may be a necessary system for a transitional period. At times it is necessary for a country that there is some form of dictatorial power." When you have the invisible hand on your side, destroying obstacles to the market is just helping Nature (in Adam Smith's words) to remedy the "bad effects of the folly and injustice of man." So, remove all restrictions on the movement of capital, remove all laws that strengthen workers, consumers and citizens against capital, and reduce the power of the state to check capital (while increasing the power of the state to police *on behalf of* capital). In the end, the simple message of neoclassical economics (and the neoliberal policy it supports) is, Let capital be free! (Selwyn, 2015)

Hayek didn't care a whit about democracy. He was delighted to see his free-market fundamentalism adopted by an autocrat as long as it was adopted. Friedman, a bit more circumspect, was equally happy to oblige, though he added in the 1980s (when the military junta in Chile was itself proclaiming its willingness to transfer power to a civilian government) that political freedom may be necessary for the long-term viability of economic freedom (Edwards & Montes, 2020; Friedman, 1990; Valdes, 1995).

It was rather a small step for these implications to lead to what the British sociologist Colin Crouch so fittingly described as "post-democracy." When democracy maintains formal mechanisms and insignia but is emptied of substance (popular will, democratic deliberation, checks and balances), then we have the creepy creature of "post-democracy" where elections are bought and sold on the "free market" according to the dictates of "economic freedom" of Friedman and Hayek (Crouch, 2004). Free-market advocates adore such a creature insofar as (the myth of) democracy itself is maintained as the beautiful facade of a decaying building (how easy is it to question that Westerners are still living in democratic countries?), but it is actually worthless. *Les jeux sont faits.* It doesn't matter how often you go out to vote or protest, the rules of the game are decided beforehand. Oligopolies and elites become the sorcerer's apprentice who seek to control and profit from this creature until it takes on a life of its own.

Even before their hegemony, the famously milquetoast Canadian economist Galbraith (1963) pointed out that the ideas of Hayek and Friedman were relatively easy pickings for those haves who sought to justify their own greed at the zero-sum expense of the have-nots:

> The modern conservative is not even especially modern. He is engaged, on the contrary, in one of man's oldest, best financed, most applauded, and, on the whole, least successful exercises in moral philosophy. That is the search for a superior moral justification for selfishness. It is an exercise which always involves a certain number of internal contradictions and even a few absurdities. The conspicuously wealthy turn up urging the character-building value of privation for the poor. The man who has struck it rich in minerals, oil, or other bounties of nature is found explaining the debilitating effect of unearned income from the state. The corporate executive who is a superlative success as an organization man weighs in on the evils of bureaucracy. Federal aid to education is feared by those who live in suburbs that could easily forgo this danger, and by people whose children are in public schools. Socialized medicine is condemned by men emerging from Walter Reed Hospital. Social Security is viewed with alarm by those who have the comfortable cushion of an inherited income. Those who are immediately threatened by public efforts to meet their needs – whether widows, small farmers, hospitalized veterans, or the unemployed – are almost always oblivious to the danger.

But Galbraith wasn't the only civic-minded public intellectual to survive the new onslaught of old ideas. The neo-Malthusian figure of Ayn Rand is instructive. Born into the Russian aristocracy in early-20th-century St Petersburg, her dynasty fled the October Revolution, coming to New York after WWII, where she lived off American welfare (until her death) and published voluminous fictions (ironically, she called it "objectivism") denigrating the poor working classes as "takers" and glorifying the rich as "makers." Although they were initially dismissed by those who knew better, as such ideas poured forth from the pages of Rand's fiction, they gradually grew in popularity throughout the 1980s banks (think of Gordon Gekko's "greed is good" prosperity gospel). The all-consuming waves of green-eyed avarice were quickly inundating the economic thinking of those "technocrats" who ought to know better. It was not for nothing that William F. Buckley Jr did his best to stem the tide of Ayn Rand's cognitive poison as it slowly but surely submerged the American Republican party (Burns, 2004, 2010, p. 162; Heller, 2009, pp. 246–285).

Propaganda that thematized zero-sum thinking and zero-sum relations between various "identities" (in reality between neoliberalism and any other form of political economy) was instrumental in cementing neoliberalism as the dominant first-world economic model from the 1970s onward and the New World Order that George H. W. Bush declared a bit later. Proponents of the "new" ideology of free market fundamentalism that gradually took hold after the dismantling of the Bretton Woods system and the post-WWII Keynesian arrangement in the 1970s would strive to mask neoliberalism's propensity for ruthless exploitation of labor as well as the resources of a finite planet. Instead, they would sugarcoat it as a catalyst for win–win economic outcomes, while attacking various forms of state planning, regulation and intervention as zero-sum practices.

Examples of neoliberal attacks against other forms of political economy include the many typical 1980s polemics against socialism, communism and Keynesian social democracy as a zero-sum game that leads to internal war or tyranny. In fact, Keynesian welfare states like Sweden or Japan are outright dismissed as engendering zero-sum wars of "all against all" (Douglas, 1980). The same propaganda continued into the '90s with neoliberal polemics against Leninism. The author of such a polemic published in the *Wall Street Journal* in 1999, shortly after the adoption of the Kyoto Protocol (1997), added Malthusianism and "the global warming theory" in his targets. The author, George Gilder, is introduced in his article as "a fellow at Seattle's Discovery Institute," a framing indicative of the technocratic pretensions of the myth of free-market. In reality, he is the co-founder of the Discovery Institute, an offshoot of the libertarian Hudson Institute (founded by Gilder's associate Herman Kahn in Croton-on-Hudson, then a member of the Philadelphia Society along with Friedrich Hayek, Milton Friedman, Victor Davis Hanson, William F. Buckley Jr, etc.). It began operation in the early '90s in a technocratic bid to promote privatization of public services, deregulation of private industry, and later moved to cultural issues, championing the cause of intelligent design. Thus, Gilder's Institute is also an indicative example of the transition of US politics from the economic (class) to the cultural (identity) arena following the consolidation of bipartisan neoliberal unanimity in the '90s. As a scion of the Tiffany jewelry dynasty (his name says it all really), Gilder (1999) felt far more comfortable with making accusations of zero-sum logic in governmental policies rather than reckoning with the harsh realities of finite resources on a finite planet: "Many grasp the zero-sum futility of trade protectionism. But the U.S. intelligentsia is now adopting a posture even more dismal. The Kyoto treaty embodies a new zero-sum theory of ecology as stifling and sterile as the worst excesses of Marx and Malthus." This did not prevent Gilder (2020) from later offering his support to the first US president in generations who would openly pursue an agenda of trade protectionism, the 45th.

These neoliberal arrangements were called the Washington Consensus by leading technocrats like John Williamson, Hernando de Soto, Daniel Yergin and Joseph Stanislaw, who essentially sold a story that the zero-sum conflict was always between business and government—and that the victory of capitalism over communism was coefficient with the victory of business over government (de Soto et al., 1986; Williamson, 1990; Yergin, pp. 10–12). Thus, the publics of Washington-aligned countries were told that throughout the twentieth century, the central conflict was between enterprise as an endeavor exclusively of the private sector versus the state (Pistor, 2025). As long as the Washington Consensus could be a prescriptive set of policy packages which could be delivered, assembled and implemented by neoliberal technocrats in any country, that country too could join the club of economic winners—the so-called "Free World" (Menand, 2021). In fact, though, it became little different from the British empire's 19th-century refusal to trade with any nation from which it could not profit (at their zero-sum expense)—Keynes' original "barbarous relic"—the Gold Standard (Tandon, 2018).

By the late 1980s-early 1990s, the respected American economist Hyman Minsky's implicit critiques of the win–win charade of neoliberalism inherent in the new Washington Consensus was what made his hesitant defense of it the cornerstone of his success (Minsky, 2008). This is why his explicit critiques of more sober-minded economic analyses and proposals like Lester Thurow's *The Zero-Sum Society* were received so well: they supported the consensus at the expense of the reality Thurow sought to demonstrate and address (Minsky, 1986a, 1986b; Thurow, 1985). It didn't matter how many fascist-aligned, pro-corporatist rhetorical sleights of hand could be disguised by the Atlas Network's libertarian think tanks like the John Birch and Federalist Societies, the Hudson Institute, PraegerU or the Heritage Foundation (Mackert et al., 2021). As political theorist Mouffe (2005) has put it, "every consensus is based on acts of exclusion" (p. 11). The excluded were small businesses, middle and working classes, and minority or marginalized communities (Shipler, 2008). The ever widening gap between the rich and poor obviously repeated throughout younger generations as the wealth gaps *within* countries gradually approached the wealth gap *between* countries (Bauluz & Meyer, 2024; OECD, 2008; Matsumoto & Alichi, 2018; Milanovic, 2021; Piketty et al., 2014). As usual, the most marginalized and vulnerable (children) paid the highest price. As chronicled by Kozol (1991): "One searches for some way to understand why a society as rich and, frequently, as generous as ours would leave these children in their penury and squalor for so long – and with so little public indignation."

The new religion of free market fundamentalism preached by its high priests like Friedman and Hayek didn't triumph because of its own inherent superiority to Keynesian social democracy. Rather, it triumphed because of very specific historical events peculiar to the 1970s. When Nixon singlehandedly unmoored the dollar from the gold and set it adrift in a deluge of stagflation, it destroyed the Keynesian democracy's social contract between labor and capital. This came on top of the diminishing returns of post-WWII recovery efforts after almost three decades of high growth. As Professor of English Menand (2023) aptly described it, "The real reason market fundamentalism prevailed was not that it won the war of ideas. It was that the postwar boom came to an end."

Any warnings that this modus operandi would cause western middle classes to sink to qualities of life not seen since nineteenth-century liberalism went unheeded, as the technocrats' mythology had already done its work:

> As both citizen and historian, I took alarm when consensus historians armed the United States for Cold War by purging class from consciousness. Muffling exploitative capital in appealing democratic garb, their mythology of consensual democratic capitalism purged egalitarian meaning from democracy. I winced when Ronald Reagan evoked "democracy" against the Evil Empire though clearly meaning capitalism. I grieved when public discourse translated democracy into "freedom" ("liberty" in the academic mode) – typically meaning freedom to aggrandize yourself without any concern for people who lack the gumption, social advantages, or luck to do the same. (Sellers, 1996, pp. 312–313)

By the mid '90s, economists were essentially forced to choose sides in a new zero-sum struggle within the profession as it transitioned into the Bush dynasty's "New World Order" (winners vs losers). As much as the new orthodoxy cast itself as a "win–win," yet "without alternatives," its own internal contradictions were hard to ignore. So whether or not a technocratic economist got the numbers right, they were still forced to get the ideology right. And the core of the "right ideology" was that economics must focus on numbers rather than humans, based on "mathematical models" and abstract principles that promoted the neoliberal thesis, even when the thesis was proven palpably wrong, like in the 1987 crash in the midst of the Reagan Revolution (cf. Bookstaber, 2023). And yet, the Washington Consensus was immediately challenged by its own proponents (Broad & Cavanagh, 1999). Even neoliberals like Williamson (2000) recognized that, far from reducing poverty, neoliberal market fundamentalism actually increased it—and thus the technocrats over at the World Bank would need to redefine the poverty line in order to disguise the problem and separate "poverty" from "inequality." The more zealously the new orthodoxy was propagated, the more forcefully it was resisted—least of all in the most industrialized nations.

This in turn had broad implications for nations seeking to improve their modes of production. For some, that meant deindustrialization and for others it meant further industrialization. The cases of India, Korea, Japan, Russia and China are instructive. In July, 1991, at the initiative of a new budget of its finance minister, Manmohan Singh, India abandoned its longstanding social market economy for neoliberalism, drastically increasing economic expansion alongside exponentially rising inequality and steady democratic backsliding (India's economy, 2011; Rammanohar-Reddy, 2000). India's non-aligned status during the First Cold War immediately gave way to its adoption of the Washington Consensus and thus reduced India's sovereignty. Regardless of their statuses in the First Cold War, the results were not very dissimilar in Russia, China, Korea and Japan.

In Russia, neoliberalism meant deindustrialization, or at the very least privatization and deregulation. The imposition of Brady's free-market neoliberalism in Russia and Gaidar's shock doctrine in the early '90s led to Russian mafiosos killing each other in the zero-sum struggles for newly privatized government industries and the foundation of the "Russian oligarch" class which Putin began co-opting and subduing by the new millennium, while keeping Gazprom and other key corporations still government-controlled (Bardasz, 2022; Gessen, 2023; Lobacheva, pp. 58–59; Rosalsky, 2022; Rutland, 2013). Thus, Friedman's neoliberal Shock Therapy facilitated yet another era of oligarchy, as Western neoliberal economists flooded Russia in the 1990s to assist in the "liberalization" of its economy at the zero-sum expense of the majority of its people (Service, 2022).

The neoliberalism imposed on Russia was the same model resisted in the PRC. The major difference between Chinese and Soviet economic changes in the late 1980s-early 1990s was that Gaidar's Shock Therapy, advocated by none other than Friedman himself, destroyed Russia's socioeconomic stability and created a caste of oligarchy whose wealth and power could scarcely be checked. Contrastingly, China created a gradual system of market reforms which preserved the underlying status quo and the authority of the CCP, lifted the peasantry into a durable middle class, preserved its patriotism and maintained the fiction of Chinese Communism. It was like a monetary policy of quantitative easing addressed toward social policy. Deng Xiaoping called it "socialism with Chinese Characteristics." Friedman wrote myriad letters to Deng Xiaoping denouncing the pace of reforms as not imposing his ideas quickly or zealously enough (Weber, 2021). What the Chinese learned from the Japanese, Koreans, Indians and Russians in the 1980s-1990s was that growth had to be on their own terms. Wealth without sovereignty would simply consign China's future to being little different from what it saw as Korea's and Japan's vassalage to Washington (Schuman, 2009). Recent works of South Korean economists bear this out: America's promises of free markets were never free—nor is South Korea's own sovereignty (Chang, 2008).

In the EU, it was commonly believed in the 1980s-1990s that expansion into southern and eastern Europe and steady enlargement with incorporation of new member states would always be a win–win scenario for all (Tsoukalis, 1981). What the Czechs found out was that the Czech Republic's switch to a free market laid the groundwork for oligopolization of Czech markets in the late '90s (Greenhouse, 1991; Kočenda & Valachy, 2002). Similar stupefaction was registered elsewhere in Central/Eastern and Southern Europe. This was at the same time that newly minted neoliberal democracies in former Warsaw Pact nations saw economic growth rates skyrocket—and simultaneously the cartelization of homegrown big business interests mutually supported through political dynasties like the Orbans, Kaczyńskis and their respective cronies (and military interests) (Hinshaw & Walker, 2018; MON podsumowuje zmiany kadrowe, 2017; Orbán nem gyanít korrupciót..., 1999; Solska, 2019). Like similar neoliberal triangulation in American and British politics in the '90s, in France it took the form of Jaques Chirac in 1994 technocratically triangulating around the social security crisis caused by the Alain Juppe government reform and union resistance. The schism between Alain Juppe and Jaques Chirac was equivalent to the schism between the left and the right (Girerd et al., 2021; Gualmini & Schmidt, 2013). In Britain, already in 1996, the early results of the neoliberal experiment clearly contradicted free-market ideology:

> Reports by three blue-chip international bodies – the World Bank, the Organisation for Economic Co-operation and Development (OECD) and the United Nations Development Programme (UNDP) – have all roundly condemned rising inequality in Britain, now revealed as the most unequal country in the Western world. And they went on to explode the central rationale of policies pioneered here by Margaret Thatcher and exported, with the willing assistance of Ronald Reagan, to the rest of the world. They made it clear ... that inequality – deliberately promoted by Thatcherism as an aid to economic growth – in fact hinders it. ... For 20 years economists have kowtowed to the idea that there was a necessary trade-off between equality and efficiency. You could have a fast-growing, efficient economy, they said, or a more equal society – but not both. Thatcher and Reagan took this a stage further with their so-called "trickle-down theory" ... that if the rich were encouraged to have plenty of cake, the poor would get to eat it. By this theory, the rich were performing a public service by getting richer still, because their prosperity would automatically "trickle down" to the poor (Lean & Cooper, 1996).

Europe's road to crony capitalism was paved with '90s technocratic myths of free markets (Munger & Villarreal-Diaz, 2019).

In the Global South, since the 1990s (like the "Banana Wars" of the early twentieth century), multinational corporations in collaboration with intelligence services have orchestrated coups and other forms of political interference to control vital resources (minerals, alcohol, cash crops like coffee, cocoa, gold, drugs, oil); the activities of the Cargill dynasty are just the tip of the iceberg (Provost & Kennard, 2024, pp. 207–210). However, the "New World Order" was not that new in the aggressive pursuit of big-capital interests, only more unchecked. Western Big Oil and other monopolistic fossil fuel interests had colluded to mislead the global public about climate change in massive campaigns since the early '50s (McMullen, 2022). In the decades following decolonization during the '50s-80s, the US intervened all over Latin America much like the British had tried, but failed, to reimpose empire in the Suez against Nasser and joint US-UK efforts had earlier found success against Mossadegh in Iran (1953). The same was true for the French in Algeria, Vietnam, Mali, etc., while Australia carried out anti-communist interventions in the peninsulas and islands at the southeastern edges of Eurasia in Malaysia and Indonesia in the '60s (Bevins, 2020). In the same regions, this continues today with US defense of Taiwanese microchip manufacturers against the PRC (Islam, 2025). Similarly, global energy interests have been steadily consolidating since the '90s (GAO, 2004, pp. 1–5, 10–14; Focus on growth, 2001). All these interventions have been carried out under the cover of broad legitimizing campaigns, such as the War on Drugs or the War on Terror alongside efforts to bring "democracy" and "market reforms" to peripheral countries. Even the 2025 Caribbean campaign against Venezuela is unrelated to drugs, as fentanyl is not manufactured in Venezuela and the majority of drug trafficking enters the US from the Pacific (Facts to inform..., 2025). What has often been presented as related to the promotion of free markets and free trade is in reality a well-planned operation by big, powerful players to appropriate limited resources of the global pie at the expense of local businesses and working classes—just as Joan Robinson observed in the 1930s (Carter, 2021).

The myth of "free markets" has become so unignorable as to supercharge renewed interest in early-20th-century economic analyses. It's not for nothing that Zachary Carter's *The Price of Peace: Money, Democracy, and the Life of John Maynard Keynes* came out in the 2010s. As Dean (2009) has observed:

> In neoliberal ideology, the fantasy of free trade covers over persistent market failure, structural inequalities, the prominence of monopolies, the privilege of no-bid contracts, the violence of privatization, and the redistribution of wealth to the "have mores": Free trade thus sustains at the level of fantasy what it seeks to avoid at the level of reality-namely, actually free trade among equal players, that is, equal participants with equal opportunities to establish the rules of the game, access information, distribution, and financial networks, and so forth. Paradoxically, free trade is invoked as a mantra in order to close down possibilities for the actualization of free trade and equality. (pp. 56–57)

Thus, Cowie (2016) interprets the American New Deal era, from the FDR administration to the 1970s, as a speed bump in the long history of oligarchy, effectively a “sustained deviation from some of the main contours of American political practice, economic structure, and cultural outlook.” Hartmann (2020) makes similar observations. The so-called “competitiveness” doctrine foisted on the global working classes from the 1990s was meant to disguise a global zero-sum parlor game. It involved a few major myths: the myth of decreased labor costs as the primary way to become competitive and the myth of the necessity of deindustrialization in previously industrialized countries—to transition to “service” economies (the deindustrial revolution *was* televised—in sitcoms like *Friends* and *Seinfeld*) (McDonald, 2023).

The rapid transition away from Keynesian social democracy after the 1990s and toward neoliberal globalization’s technocratic myth of free markets and free trade was perhaps best encapsulated by the figure most prominently embodying the new “reality.” It was Karl Rove, a senior advisor to GWB and oft-accused war criminal, who derisively referred to the “reality-based community.” As an embodiment of the neoliberal ruling class of the American empire, Rove’s views of his own perceived imperial power came at the expense of reality; or in his own words:

> We’re an empire now, and when we act, we create our own reality. And while you’re studying that reality – judiciously, as you will – we’ll act again, creating other new realities, which you can study too, and that’s how things will sort out. We’re history’s actors... and all of you, will be left to just study what we do. (Suskind, 2004)

It was clear that he spoke for the entirety of the Bush administration—and that American neoliberal imperialism collided with reality in Iraq. The results are even clearer (Engelhardt, 2014; Greenberg, 2010).

By the time the First Cold War was over, the transformation of active political engagement into “There Is No Alternative” was complete. Asimov (1980) warned very early that the combination of the ruling classes’ official lies with TINA would produce the combustible mixture of anti-elitism, willful ignorance and lack of trust in experts. As Skworz and Kapuściński (2006) remarked about the War against Poverty, it was abandoned precisely because of the ruling classes’ own implicit recognition of their reliance on poverty: “We know everything about the global problem of poverty. What we can’t figure out is how to reduce it in practical terms. [The moment we try] there appear obstacles that cannot be surmounted, and interests one cannot go against.” Rather than solving longstanding problems and making everyone better off, the freedom of markets became unfreedom as speculators became rent-seekers chasing monopoly power (America’s concentration crisis, 2019).

Disaster Capitalism: from Creative Destruction to Shampoo Economics

The seeming triumph of neoliberalism and the TINA doctrine went hand in hand with the proliferation of "disaster capitalism": the destruction of value for the profit from rebuilding (Fraser, 2022; Klein, 2007; Loewenstein, 2017). This goes back to Frédéric Bastiat's 19th-c. "Parable of the Broken Window," with examples to be found throughout history and particularly under various capitalist systems. Yet, its ubiquity to the point of normalization is a product of the neoliberal era—the profit from destruction and reconstruction in various neoliberal foreign policies throughout the Third World.

Liberalism's basic Manichaean tendency to reduce everything to zero-sum dichotomies of war and peace, liberty and slavery, has been distilled down to the economic theory of "Creative Destruction" in the decades since WWII (Caballero, 2008). The history of this ideology, however, extends much further back. In the mid-nineteenth century, a pair of critical economists noticed how periods of capital accumulation were invariably associated with capital annihilation—for its own sake. This fundamentally zero-sum idea appeared in many of their publications, and most archetypically in one of the most influential in the history of political economy:

> A large part of the nominal capital of the society, i.e., of the exchange-value of the existing capital, is once for all destroyed, although this very destruction, since it does not affect the use-value, may very much expedite the new reproduction. This is also the period during which moneyed interest enriches itself at the cost of industrial interest. (Marx, 1969, IV.II, pp. 495–496)

The zero-sum logic of creative destruction was repeated in the work of Nietzsche (1924):

> But have you ever asked yourselves sufficiently how much the erection of every ideal on earth has cost? How much reality has had to be misunderstood and slandered, how many lies have had to be sanctified, how many consciences disturbed, how much "God" sacrificed every time? If a temple is to be erected a temple must be destroyed: that is the law – let anyone who can show me a case in which it is not fulfilled!

Then, in 1913, Werner Sombart (the only man who Frederich Engels said truly understood *Das Kapital*), produced a tidy zero-sum explanation of what he called *War and Capitalism* (*Krieg und Kapitalismus*):

> Again, however, *from destruction a new spirit of creation arises;* the scarcity of wood and the needs of everyday life... forced the discovery or invention of substitutes for wood, forced the use of coal for heating, forced the invention of coke for the production of iron. (Sombart, 1913, p. 207)

The overtly religious connotations of creative destruction made it popular among theologically oriented philosophers and writers in the interwar years, including Orthodox thinkers such as Nikolai Berdyaev and Nikos Kazantzakis (Owens, 2003). The term thus floated freely throughout the fields of philosophy, theology, and political economy—especially in Nazi Germany (Harris, 1942, esp. p. 807). It would officially and formally enter the English-speaking economic parlance through Joseph Schumpeter's 1942 treatise, where the author referred to a "gale of creative destruction" (pp. 82–83). Schumpeter himself was not untouched by the term's religious baggage (Nightingale, 2015). As a result, the religious overtones of "creative destruction" and WWII would serve to reunite political, economic and social affairs under the umbrella of theology amid the destruction and reconstruction of the 1940s-70s (Reinert & Reinert, 2006). Even in the 2020s, it is still a zero-sum ideological touchstone which unites the most libertarian and Marxian economists (Aghion & Howitt, 1992; Archibugi & Filippetti, 2000; Berman, 1988; Castells, 2000; Cowen, 2002; de Figueiredo & Kyle, 2006; Harvey, 2007, pp. 200–203; Hart, 2005; Hartshorn et al., 2005; Komlos, 2016; Page, 1999). As Harvey (2010) has noted,

> Both Karl Marx and Joseph Schumpeter wrote at length on the "creative-destructive" tendencies inherent in capitalism. While Marx clearly admired capitalism's creativity he... strongly emphasised its self-destructiveness. The Schumpeterians have all along gloried in capitalism's endless creativity while treating the destructiveness as mostly a matter of the normal costs of doing business. (p. 46)

Ever since WWII, the theological implications of the ideology of "creative destruction" embedded within the discourse of liberal political economy have made various iterations of capitalism, from Keynesianism to actual neoliberalism, into a veritable 20th-21st-century religion.

After WWII, the predominant (and religiously proselytized) form of political economy in the English-speaking world and in the core countries of the emerging European Economic Community (the predecessor of the EU) was Keynesianism, which was still implicated in both the causes and effects of the bloodiest, most destructive war in human history (and one that also created millions of jobs) (Drucker, 1994, pp. xv, 218; Hampton, 1999; Harman, 1999, 2003; Oakes, 1944; Vance, 1950, 1951; Wilson, 1944). As Keynes himself wrote to FDR in 1933:

> A war has always caused intense industrial activity. In the past orthodox finance has regarded a war as the only legitimate excuse for creating employment by governmental expenditure. You, Mr President, having cast off such fetters, are free to engage in the interests of peace and prosperity, the technique which hitherto has only been allowed to serve the purposes of war and destruction.

Throughout the 1950s, at the height of Keynesianism in Western Europe and the Anglo-American World and of Communism in Eurasia (and the height of Cold War I), dissenting thinkers like Cliff (1982, pp. 101–107) noted that the new reality had simultaneously become the new normal: military expansionism (imperialism) in this brave new world was just as true in Washington DC and Moscow as it had been before in London and Berlin. By the late 1950s, the industrial production (and profitability) of weaponry had become a self-justifying loop and an instrument of Creative Destruction—soon termed the "Military-Industrial Complex."

Eisenhower's "Military-Industrial Complex" was first used in his farewell address in 1960, shortly after the widespread use of the sociologically critical phrase "the power elite"—used as much as a rhetorical tool of criticism as admiration (Eisenhower, 1960; Mills, 1956). The utmost point in using this term was to grant to the American public a specific phrase which they could use to refer to the danger of American war-profiteering corporations relying on constant foreign policies of imperialism (Kurth, 2000). It was a cautionary tale about the ways in which corporations could supersede even elected politicians, undermining democracy. But whatever its relation with American democracy, the Military-Industrial Complex became the primary force of disaster capitalism. Like every other form of capitalism, however, the military-industrial complex is a "misnomer," as Noam Chomsky points out: "it's just the industrial system operating under one or another pretext (defense was a pretext for a long time)" (quoted in Best, 2011, p. xvi). Particularly after Eisenhower, Americans and their allies were fed a steady diet of warmongering by legacy media funded by industrial weapon manufacturers like Raytheon, Lockheed Martin, Boeing, etc. (Melman, 1970, 1971; Mollenhoff, 1967). By the time the Vietnam War had been widely recognized in American public discourse of the early 1970s as the debacle it always was, it was too late—American imperialism was already comparable to WWII-era German or British imperialism (Kidron, 1970; Mandel, 1975; Sohn-Rethel, 1978, 1992). Far removed from its prior isolationist and non-interventionist inclinations, the US public was inundated with the agenda of endless war, from Korea to Vietnam to Afghanistan, to the point of not even thinking about the fact that the country has been at war nearly every day since WWII—ironically, the very war that was supposed to end all wars.

Particularly from Reagan's presidency in the 1980s, American foreign policy largely became a war machine that has bred and continues to breed war from war as a means of war profiteering (Adams, 2019; Hartung, 2001; Watry, 2014; cf. Guérin, 1939). In the decades since, war profiteering has become, as various thinkers have pointed out, an acutely American addiction (Andreas, 2024; Johnson, 2004; McCartney & McCartney, 2015; Nelson, 2000). As *Harper's Magazine* aptly puts it: "The military-industrial complex could be said to be concerned, exclusively, with self-preservation and expansion.... The defense budget is not propelled by foreign wars. The wars are a consequence of the quest for bigger budgets" (Cockburn, 2019). This foreign policy is driven expressly by private, for-profit war profiteering corporations like Northrop–Grumman, Lockheed Martin, Boeing, Raytheon, BAE Systems, General Dynamics and Halliburton (Cockburn, 2021; Pierre, 1982; Sampson, 1977; St. Clair, 2005; Sweetman, 2000). Quite understandably so, since much of American foreign policy has been outsourced to think tanks funded by these very corporations (Friedman & Friedman, 1996; Good, 2022; Hossein-Zadeh, 2006; Keller, 1995; Kelly, 1992; Lassman, 2015; Pasztor, 1995;

Thorpe, 2014). As with all weapons, the most powerful and the most exclusive render the highest profits—nuclear weapons very much included (Patterson, 1984). As with all empires, the American empire is paid for by its taxpayers:

> For many years, the United States has increasingly relied on military strength to achieve its foreign policy aims.... We are [...] allocating too large a portion of the federal budget to defense as compared to domestic needs [...] accumulating too much federal debt, and yet not acquiring a forward-looking, twenty-first-century military built around new cyber and space technologies. (Matthews, 2019)

American taxpayers, indebted and impoverished by their requisite subsidies for American war profiteers, also take chauvinistic pride in US global hegemony (Robinson, 2017; Tucker & Dayen, 2020). Just as Russian, Spanish, English or French workers and peasants could take pride in their respective empires (which came at their own zero-sum expense), the same is true for Americans.

The function of this system became more apparent after the fall of the Soviet Union. The supposed "end of history" and the "New World Order" were hailed as the beginning of an era of global peace and stability under the auspices of liberal democracy. What actually happened was that the US war machine and NATO went on overdrive. At the end of his life in 1998, the old geostrategic thinker George Kennan forewarned that eastward NATO expansion would cause "the beginning of a new cold war" in the twenty-first century:

> I think the Russians will gradually react quite adversely and it will affect their policies. I think it is a tragic mistake. There was no reason for this whatsoever. No one was threatening anybody else. This expansion would make the Founding Fathers of this country turn over in their graves. We have signed up to protect a whole series of countries, even though we have neither the resources nor the intention to do so in any serious way. (Friedman, 1998)

But that was too farsighted for Congress at the time. In the meantime, if there was no arch-enemy anymore, then one had to be manufactured. Individuals and groups that had been formerly funded or backed by the US such as Saddam Hussein and the Mujahideen were now declared the enemies. Distorted or completely made-up stories were disseminated to manufacture consent for military intervention. Public relations agencies were enlisted in that effort, first coming up with the "Iraq is killing babies in incubators" hoax (The Kuwaiti incubator hoax, 1994). Instrumental in this was the "Nariyah testimony": a teenage girl, who was later revealed to be the daughter of the Kuwaiti ambassador to the US, testified before Congress that she was a nurse who had witnessed such atrocities committed by Iraqi troops (Regan, 2002). This was more or less the prelude to the "War on Terror," written under George Bush Sr in the early 1990s. The beginning of the main part would be written under George Bush Jr in the early 2000s and the saga would continue to be written for decades with similar lies, sensationalism and manufactured stories, such as Saddam's WMDs (Chernus, 2006). Unsurprisingly, the destruction of the World Trade Center and part of the Pentagon on 9/11 was used as a justification for creating new profits from invasions of Muslim-majority countries (Blum, 2003, 2013). In fact, the so-called "War on Terror" was little more than a global cash cow for war profiteers like Raytheon, Boeing, Lockheed Martin, General Dynamics and Northrop Gumman to swallow up the profits from the latest acquisitions of the American empire—Afghanistan and Iraq (Hartung, 2021a, 2021b, 2021c; Roth, 2025). Whoever benefitted the most from 9/11, it certainly wasn't Al Qaeda or the Taliban, while the American worker paid in taxes and the Afghan and Iraqi worker paid in blood.

It's no surprise that while the *War Profiteering Act* of 2007 was introduced to limit war profiteering from the American invasions of Iraq and Afghanistan by corporate lobbyists, the Act was never passed into law. The wars were simply too profitable for the corporate lobbyists and congresspeople who make up the American ruling class itself (Leahy, 2017). Thus, the expansion of NATO and other American imperial vassal states around Eurasia's edges since the USSR's collapse and the end of Cold War I have provided a ready source of profit through "Military Keynesianism" for ruling-class American politicians, CEOs, investors and war profiteers at the zero-sum expense of working classes from California to Kamchatka (Awaworyi & Yew, 2014; Custers, 2010). The logic of Military Keynesianism is unmistakable in the words of leading neoliberal corporate representative Barney Frank (D—MA):

> These arguments will come from the very people who denied that the economic recovery plan created any jobs. We have a very odd economic philosophy in Washington: It's called weaponized Keynesianism. It is the view that the government does not create jobs when it funds the building of bridges or important research or retrains workers, but when it builds airplanes that are never going to be used in combat, that is of course economic salvation. (Krugman, 2009; cf. Frick, 2009)

Meanwhile, ever since the 1960s, public discourse in the US has been saturated with war rhetoric. For every problem there has always been a war to address it: the "War on Poverty", "War on Drugs", "War on Crime", etc. This doesn't mean that all these "wars" are comparable; but they have helped to normalize a public mentality of being constantly at war and desensitize Americans to the horrors of warfare. At the same time, these domestic "wars" have typically funneled public funds to private corporations, often at the very tangible zero-sum expense of the working class, the poor and communities of color, which feed into various politico-economic complexes such as the "Prison-Industrial Complex", "Military-Entertainment Complex", and the "Politico-Media Complex".

All this amounts to a colonial complex, firmly entrenched since the Global Wars on Terror. As usual, the clear zero-sum nature of the complex has been brushed away through appeals to more sophisticated economic principles that critics of the complex supposedly cannot understand. "The arithmetic of occupation is not the zero-sum game it sometimes appears to President Bush's more radical critics, who insist that every dollar spent in Iraq is a dollar less for American schools of hospitals," writes Niall Ferguson. "On the contrary, success in Iraq could pay significant dividends – and not just to those companies that take the risk of accepting contracts for the country's reconstruction" (Ferguson, 2005, p. 267). Other scholars, like the geographer Derek Gregory (2004), pointed out that the ideology underpinning the Wars on Terror was a renormalization of old colonialism, with its "ethnocentric assumption of Might and Right" and its "split geographies of 'us' and 'them', 'civilization' and 'barbarism', 'Good' and 'Evil'" (pp. 10–11).

Ever since the 1970s, several devices of neoliberal political economy have maintained the zero-sum status quo of disaster capitalism behind the official facade of win–win "growth": inflation, public debt, privatization and deregulation. These devices appear most prominently when they are accompanied by the destruction of infrastructure, the pollution of the environment, the degradation of middle classes, the immiseration of working classes, the diminishment of labor power (which leads to increased accident rates), and the creations of new businesses to address the problems caused by old businesses, thereby continuing the same zero-sum status quo. Initially, debt was used alongside the ideology of "workism" as a primary instrument of Creative Destruction. This is why, for example, Wolfgang Streek wrote in 2012 about the increasing willingness of consumers to work more and to borrow more "for the purchasing power needed to participate in the new paradigm of economic growth." If consumers didn't have good enough work ethics, credit or luck, so be it: the creativity of growth would outshine the destruction of either the products or their producers. It was no surprise that the Degrowthism born in the early '70s went through an appropriate period of stagnation throughout the '80s–00s (Susskind, 2024, p. 137).

The corporate destruction of production from Burberry bags to Bimbo bread has consistently and artificially created scarcity to inflate prices, maintain value and maintain the economic arms race between capital and labor (McCarthy, 2021; UGT dice que…, 2015; Why are Bimbo…, 2018). While the goal is not necessarily broader inflation (and it can even be deflation), part of the surplus must be destroyed (rather than, say, given to poorer countries, communities, or individuals) to retain profit rates. Thus, financial speculators have been the chief advocates for creative destruction. In fact, one famous financial speculator, FDR, eventually became president and his administration subsidized the destruction of crops and the slaughtering of millions of pigs for the same purpose (Blakey, 1967). Even in the 2020s, similar speculative and inflationary policies in response to the Coronavirus recalled memories of the New Deal and the Great Depression (Semuels, 2020).

Rather than this active practice of product destruction, neoliberalism increasingly prefers the practice of "planned obsolescence" (Slade, 2009). This model famously started with a conspiracy of the "Phoebus cartel", i.e. a cartel of lightbulb companies (Krajewski, 2014). Albeit not the fanciest product, it did set a precedent for other commodities with greater profit margins. Accordingly, while technology advances, industrial products, particularly electronics, are made less rather than more durable. This is by design, so that the consumer is forced to spend money every couple of years for a product that could otherwise last for decades. The iconic "centennial bulb," produced decades before the Phoebus Cartel set out to change the market, is still up and running 122 years after it was installed (Live

Cam…, 2025). It's on the back of this practice that Apple can justify its higher prices, as it stands out against all its competitors that pursue planned obsolescence. And this is also an additional reason that the influx of Chinese brands in Western markets caused such a backlash, as Huawei, Xiaomi and others offered cheaper products than Apple without pursuing the aggressive planned obsolescence practices of Samsung, HP, etc. Hence, Higgs (2014) wrote: "Just as immense effort was being devoted to persuading people to buy things they did not actually need, manufacturers also began the intentional design of inferior items, which came to be known as 'planned obsolescence'" (p. 75).

This is criminal corporate profiteering and it gets even more abhorrent when one considers its impact on the environment alongside the farcical climate change policies of Western governments like banning plastic straws and charging for plastic bags and the greenwashing PR campaigns of some of those same corporations. The French government raised taxes on gas, affecting more badly everyday people who had to commute to work or who had to use a car, van, truck or tractor during work, triggering the massive Yellow Vest movement (Holman, 2018). The Dutch government has sought to reduce nitrogen emissions by closing down farms, leading to nationwide farmers' protests and the emergence of a right-wing populist farmers party (Meijer, 2023). It's always policies that harm the average consumer, the workers or small business, but never the big corporations. The latter are even allowed to add to the problem by intentionally producing items that turn to rubbish a few months after their warranty expires.

From the 1970s, public debt and privatization have also been used as politico-economic instruments of creative destruction. "Reaganomics" opened up the way for the ballooning of the financial sector, which would then function, either deliberately or inadvertently, as a means for bringing disaster capitalism to bear. Consider for example how the destruction of the USSR at the behest of neoliberalism ushered in an era of neoliberal "economic shocks" across Eurasia in the form of the Washington Consensus which saw the near-elimination of public debt and the foundations of the first Russian oligarch class (Klein, 2007). Whereas public debt had previously been used to subsidize citizens' demands for basic necessities like education, infrastructure, healthcare and housing, by nearly eliminating or drastically reducing public debts, these government-provided necessities in Soviet social contracts became almost completely unavailable while the buying power of the richest and best-connected political dynasties shot past the cosmonauts. This occurred simultaneously as these dynasties used their wealth and political connections to gain ownership of the newly privatized heavy industries. Oligarchies created in the ruins of the various Soviet Socialist Republics from Kazakhstan to Ukraine were the very real creations wrought by Washington's destruction of the USSR (Åslund, 1995, pp. 45–60; Popov & Sundaram, 2017). By destroying foreign public debts and public ownership of heavy industry, neoliberalism created oligarchs and neo-serfs. At the same time, multinational corporations made a killing, grabbing vital parts of infrastructure, industrial facilities, gas fields, etc., for pennies on the dollar. And so the countries where these corporations were based had every reason to turn a blind eye to the emergence of oligarchies in the post-Soviet space, as these oligarchies (whether in the form of mafias or business dynasties) established symbiotic relationships with their own multinationals, all of them profiting at the expense of the ordinary citizens of the former USSR by destroying what decades of Soviet labor and capital had created (Kotz, 2015).

Deregulation has also been used as a primary instrument of Creative Destruction, which is easily observable in the repeal of the Glass-Steagall Act. This particularly pernicious bit of legislation had catastrophic consequences for the US economy and the world. It created corporate behemoths in the financial sector that, when faced with the destructive chaos they had unleashed, could simply run to the government to save them as they had in the meantime become "too big to fail" (Gould & Lokrou, 2018; Swanepoel et al., 2017; Wilmarth, 2009). By deregulating the banks and the rest of the financial services sector, millions saw their homes and livelihoods destroyed in the aftermath of the 2008's Big Short, while the buying power of the richest and best-connected political dynasties soared. Then, in 2010, shortly after the Citizens' United SCOTUS decision to allow corporations to "freely" speak through their financial political donations, the Dodd-Frank Act became a bandaid on the very gangrene it sought to creatively destroy—by protecting American consumers only enough to keep them hooked on the very banks which had by then become "too big to fail" (Brown, 2015; Morgenson, 2010; Sharma et al., 2022; Skeel, 2011).

A related manifestation of disaster capitalism is short-selling and bets against companies or even entire countries and currencies. Such practices too became entrenched after the Reagan era. A notorious example is "Black Wednesday", basically George Soros's bet against the British Pound Sterling that made him more than a billion while destabilizing an entire country and forcing the UK to leave the European Exchange Rate Mechanism in 1992 (Lee, 2001). Similar gambling with other people's money by the richest bankers continued long after, and became widespread in the first decades of the twenty-first century (Fletcher, 2023). The fact that this practice has become so common in the financial sector has led to any opposition to it being presented as not playing by the rules. Which is exactly what happened in 2021, when ordinary stock traders on Reddit coordinated to raise the stock price of GameStop, as they had realized hedge funds were trying to short it (Stewart, 2021).

"Gain-of-Function" medical research is one of the latest examples of disaster capitalism, this time involving Big Pharma and the military (yet another complex). The goal of "Gain-of-Function" is to modify viruses in order to assist medical professionals (and governments in biological warfare) (European Academies Scientific Advisory Council, 2015; Fears & ter Meulen, 2015; Imperiale et al., 2018; National Research Council et al., 2015; Selgelid, 2016; U.S. Department of Health & Human Services, 2025). However, a virus leak could possibly lead to a global disaster that ends up reaping huge profits for a few corporations. There is a lot of speculation about the origins of the COVID pandemic for instance, but some, amongst them a few US authorities, have claimed that a lab leak could have been the cause (as opposed to a natural source—meat from a wet market) (Gordon & Volz, 2025; U.S. House Committee on Oversight & Accountability,

2023). Whether true or not, the pandemic would line the pockets of Big Pharma all the while lockdowns had a calamitous effect on small businesses and low-class communities. Economic activity was halted in many places, leading to the destruction of value, but some firms profited from this destruction and therefore, unsurprisingly, funded the media and think tanks that pushed for extended lockdowns, remote learning, mandates, etc. (Bundervoet et al., 2022; ICYMI, 2021; Day & Soper, 2020; Nevradakis, 2021; Palomino et al., 2020). Thus, the economic ideology of creative destruction, when embedded within capitalism, typically sees creation for the richest and most powerful and destruction for the weakest and poorest.

The much-touted "Great Reset" (World Economic Forum, 2020) after the COVID pandemic, sought to be imposed top-down by the Davos Elites' World Economic Forum has been a case in point. It represents little more than the "rinse-and-repeat" laundering part of the shampoo economics that has ever more commonly led the world from bubble to burst—at the expense of the many, for the benefit of the few. Like all laundering (financial, reputational, etc.), it requires soap and water—and when combined, it produces bubbles. But bubbles have always been quite useful for neoliberal political economies which rely on ideologies of "creative destruction." Neoliberal capitalism's "revolutionary" force relies on its perpetual overcoming, and the bubbles are its most powerful bullets. The real estate bubble, the financial bubble, the dot.com bubble, the crypto-currency bubble, etc., all exploded a disruptive force which left the many on the pavement while the ruling proponents of neoliberal capitalism could present their system in a new dress In the name of "progress". Bubbles are the expression of neoliberalism's structural precarity: in order to function, it must constantly intervene on, benefit from, and dispose of, the daily life of individuals. It would be useful to recall Peter Sloterdijk's notion of the sphere, as the environment into which human beings are always encompassed, be it the family, society, workplace, etc. Neoliberalism has understood better than other forms of political economy that spheres can be grown, managed, exploited and burst. A clear example that Sloterdijk recalls is precisely the 2008–09 real estate bubble, as "we can see in the US real estate bubble a tangible space, though imaginary, inhabited and yet illusory. This bubble represented a form of collective action carried out by many global actors, who supported it with their actions and thoughts" (Sloterdijk, 2009, p. 189). If bubbles do represent the inhabitable space of the individual, then the shampoo economics we are talking about make for a cyclically insecure, trembling and unsafe socioeconomic structure.

This was noticed even in the 1980s when the economist Hyman Minsky maintained that, for eternal economic growth to be sustained, it required constant bubbles. His famous book was appropriately entitled *Stabilizing an Unstable Economy* (1986). Thus, the creative destruction implicit in the idolatrous worship of economic growth which required constant economic bubbles to sustain and justify itself also carried moral besides economic consequences, which is what the economist Benjamin Friedman observed in the early 2000s (Friedman, 2006). Minsky's repeated warnings about constant bubbles became known as the "Minsky

Moment," when speculative markets were revealed as shams—which of course burst (McCulley, 2009). By the early 2000s, efforts by central bankers like Ben Bernanke to reduce the risks of constant bubble bursts through what was called the "Great Moderation" failed as they ironically tried to moderate the same economic forces which they sought to facilitate (Keen, 2010).

Other economists like Jared Berstein coined the term "shampoo economics" to refer to neoliberalism's structural addiction to the financialization of creative destruction inherent in allowing avaricious big business to essentially regulate itself, ultimately causing ever more obscene levels of inequality and constant economic bubbles bursting (Bernstein, 2014; Magdoff & Foster, 2014). Bernstein (2019) remarks:

> The assumption that self-interested firms would self-regulate gave rise to repeated rounds of deregulation that gave us what I call the "shampoo economy": bubble, bust, repeat. The old economics wrongly claimed we couldn't have persistently low unemployment without spiraling inflation, yet that's precisely what we've enjoyed in recent years. In other words, the new economics isn't arising just because we want "better" outcomes from our markets. It's also arising because a lot of the old stuff has turned out to be just plain wrong.

As we will see in the next part, shampoo economics have become the norm and the bursting of bubbles is not to be expected only periodically but increasingly frequently. This has been recently noted by Quinn and Turner (2020) who studied the longue durée history of boom and bust. And it was presciently (and eerily) described by David Harvey already in the wake of the 2008 Crash:

> the likelihood of more frequent and more violent crises of the sort that have been occurring since 1980 or so will almost certainly increase. The manner, form, spatiality and time of these surface disruptions are almost impossible to predict, but that they will occur with greater frequency and depth is almost certain. The events of 2008 have therefore to be situated in the context of a deeper pattern.... [T]hese stresses are internal to the capitalist dynamic (which does not preclude some seemingly external disruptive event like a catastrophic pandemic also occurring)... (Harvey, 2009)

Some economists were actually anticipating a crisis around 2020, but the eruption of the Covid pandemic on the one hand blurred the roots of the crisis and on the other hand exacerbated it (Cox, 2019; Gopinath, 2019; Varoufakis, 2020). For example, Greece had already entered a recession in the last quarter of 2019 (Hellenic Statistical Authority, n.d.), but the government attributed all economic woes to the pandemic; at the same time, the imposition of authoritarian measures that made little sense from a public-health perspective caused immense damage to the lower strata and small businesses, which again could be "naturalized" as the results of the pandemic rather than of pre-pandemic economic trends and bad policy decisions. Bernstein (2008, 2017), like Minsky (and Keynes before them), has since been touted as a Cassadra-like economist.

The political-economic addiction to shampoo economics culminated in the biggest bank failure since 1929, the Big Short of 2008, when bankers financially bet against the mortgages of millions of homeowners and the economic livelihoods of the small businesses and working classes of entire nations, driving millions of people into desperation, poverty, misery and bankruptcy. Such forces, once unleashed, led to the beginning of the end of neoliberalism in its previous form and the rise of new/old forms of the political economies that characterized the period of the 1910–40s (Harvey, 2023). With the COVID-19 pandemic, neoliberalism would quickly transform into something quite different, leading some analysts to proclaim that it's dead and others that it has taken a new hybrid form. But more on this in the next part.

References

Adams, G. (2019). *The iron triangle: The politics of defense contracting (Original work published 1981).* Routledge.

Aghion, P., & Howitt, P. (1992). A model of growth through creative destruction. *Econometrica, 60*(2), 323–351.

Allen, R. (1993). Resource allocation and growth slowdown in the USSR. *Economic History Review, 46*(2), 290–295.

America's concentration crisis. (2019, June). *Open Markets Institute.* https://concentrationcrisis.openmarketsinstitute.org

Andreas, J. (2024). *Addicted to war: Why the U.S. can't kick militarism* (Updated ed.; Original work published 1993). PMP.

Andrianopoulos, G. (1991). *Kissinger and Brzezinski: The NSC and the struggle for control of U.S. national security policy.* Palgrave Macmillan.

Archibugi, D., & Filippetti, A. (2000). *Innovation and economic crisis: Lessons and prospects from the economic downturn* (Original work published 1996). Routledge.

Asimov, I. (1980, January 21). A cult of ignorance. *Newsweek.* https://aphelis.net/wp-content/uploads/2012/04/ASIMOV_1980_Cult_of_Ignorance.pdf

Åslund, A. (1995). *How Russia became a market economy.* Peterson Institute for International Economics.

Awaworyi, S., & Yew, S. (2014). The effect of military expenditure on growth: An empirical synthesis. *Monash University Economics Discussion Paper*, 25/14. https://www.monash.edu/__data/assets/pdf_file/0008/925685/the_effect_of_military_expenditure_on_growth_an_empirical_synthesis.pdf

Banac, I. (1988). *With Stalin against Tito: Cominformist splits in Yugoslav communism.* Cornell University Press.

Bardasz, N. (2022, March 15). How America helped Russian oligarchs steal billions. *Perfect Union.* https://perfectunion.us/how-america-helped-russian-oligarchs-steal-billions

Bartel, F. (2022). *The triumph of broken promises: The end of the Cold War and the rise of neoliberalism.* Harvard University Press.

Bauluz, L., & Meyer, T. (2024). The wealth of generations. *World Inequality Database.* https://wid.world/news-article/the-wealth-of-generations

Bedau, H. (1974). Genocide in Vietnam? The line between legal argument and moral judgment. *Worldview, 17*(2), 40–45. https://doi.org/10.1017/S0084255900018623

Berman, M. (1988). *All that is solid melts into air: The experience of modernity.* Viking Penguin.

Bernstein, J. (2008, August 4). The "Shampoo economy": Bubble, bust, repeat. *Economic Policy Institute.* https://www.epi.org/publication/webfeatures_viewpoints_shampoo_economy/

Bernstein, J. (2014, November 14). Inequality & the economic 'shampoo cycle': Bubble, bust, repeat.... *The Washington Post*. https://www.washingtonpost.com/posteverything/wp/2014/11/14/inequality-and-the-economic-shampoo-cycle-bubble-bust-repeat/
Bernstein, J. (2017, December 11). The bubble economy, explained. *The New York Times*. https://www.nytimes.com/2017/12/11/opinion/bubble-economy-financial-regulation.html
Bernstein, J. (2019, September 13). A generation of economists helped get us into this mess. A new generation can get us out. *Vox*. https://www.vox.com/policy-and-politics/2019/9/13/20862607/economics-inequality-deregulation-wealth-taxes-policy
Best, S. (2011). *The global industrial complex: Systems of domination*. Rowman & Littlefield.
Bevins, V. (2020). *The Jakarta method: Washington's anticommunist crusade and the mass murder program that shaped our world*. PublicAffairs.
Bideleux, R., & Jeffries, I. (2020). *A history of Eastern Europe: Crisis and change* (6th ed.). Routledge.
Bilderberg former steering committee members. (n.d.). *Bilderberg*. https://web.archive.org/web/20140202095633/http://www.bilderbergmeetings.org/former-steering-committee-members.html
Billington, R., & Ridge, M. (1981). *American history after 1865*. Rowman & Littlefield.
Blakey, G. (1967). Ham that never was: The 1933 emergency hog slaughter. *The Historian, 30*(1), 41–57. http://www.jstor.org/stable/24440624
Blum, W. (2003). *Rogue state: A guide to the world's only superpower* (2nd ed.). Zed Books.
Blum, W. (2013). *America's deadliest export: Democracy*. Zed Books.
Bockman, J. (2007). The origins of neoliberalism between Soviet socialism and Western capitalism: "A galaxy without borders." *Theory & Society, 36*(4), 343–371. http://www.jstor.org/stable/40213586
Boia, L. (2001). *History and myth in Romanian consciousness*. Central European University Press.
Boia, L. (2018). *De la Dacia antică la Marea Unire, de la Marea Unire la România de azi*. Humanitas.
Bookstaber, R. (2023, March 27). The slow-motion tidal wave consuming our economy. *The New York Times*. https://nyti.ms/3npITft
Broad, R., & Cavanagh, J. (1999). The death of the Washington Consensus? *World Policy Journal, 16*(3), 79–88. http://www.jstor.org/stable/40209648
Brown, A. (2009). *The rise and fall of communism*. HarperCollins.
Brown, C. (1999). Susan Strange—A critical appreciation. *Review of International Studies, 25*(3), 531–535. https://doi.org/10.1017/S0260210599005318
Brown, W. (2015). *Undoing the demos: Neoliberalism's stealth revolution*. Zone Books.
Brzezinski, Z. (1970). *Between two ages: America's role in the technetronic era*. Viking Press.
Bundervoet, T., Dávalos, M. E., & Garcia, N. (2022). The short-term impacts of COVID-19 on households in developing countries: An overview based on a harmonized dataset of high-frequency surveys. *World Development, 153*, 105844. https://doi.org/10.1016/j.worlddev.2022.105844br
Burns, J. (2004). Godless capitalism: Ayn Rand and the conservative movement. *Modern Intellectual History, 1*(3), 359–385.
Burns, J. (2010). *Goddess of the market: Ayn Rand and the American right, 1930–1980*. Oxford University Press.
Caballero, R. (2008). Creative destruction. In S. Durlauf & L. Blume (Eds.), *The New Palgrave dictionary of economics II* (2nd ed., pp. 307–311). Palgrave Macmillan.
Caldwell, C. (2024, November 28). Opinion | This Maverick Thinker Is the Karl Marx of Our Time. *The New York Times*. https://www.nytimes.com/2024/11/28/opinion/wolfgang-streeck-populism.html
Carter, Z. (2021, April 24). The woman who shattered the myth of the free market. *The New York Times*. https://nyti.ms/3vfa0IL
Castells, M. (2000). *The rise of the network society* (2nd ed.). Blackwell. (Original work published 1996).

CSIS. (n.d.). Soviet lessons for China watching. *Center for Strategic & International Studies.* https://www.csis.org/analysis/soviet-lessons-china-watching

Chang, H. -J. (2002). *Kicking away the ladder: Development strategy in historical perspective.* Anthem Press.

Chang, H. -J. (2008). *Bad Samaritans: The myth of free trade and the secret history of capitalism.* Bloomsbury.

Chang, H.-J. (2010). *23 things they don't tell you about capitalism.* Penguin.

Chang, H. -J. (2014). *Economics: The user's guide.* Bloomsbury.

Chang, H. -J. (2023). *Edible economics: A hungry economist explains the world.* PublicAffairs.

Chernus, I. (2006). *Monsters to destroy: The neoconservative war on terror and sin.* Paradigm.

Chomsky, N. (1999). *Profit over people: Neoliberalism and global order.* Seven Stories Press.

Church, G. (1989, November 20). Freedom! The Berlin Wall. *Time.* https://time.com/3558854/freedom-the-berlin-wall

Cliff, T. (1982). *Neither Washington nor Moscow.* Bookmarks.

Cockburn, A. (2019). The military-industrial virus: How bloated budgets gut our defenses. *Harper's Magazine, 338*(2029), 61–67.

Cockburn, A. (2021). Why America goes to war: Money drives the US military machine. *The Nation, 313*(6), 24–27.

Cooney, R. (1973). Herbert Spencer: Apostle of liberty. *The Freeman, 23*(1), 54–60.

Cowen, T. (2002). *Creative destruction.* Princeton University Press.

Cowie, J. (2016). *The great exception: The New Deal and the limits of American politics.* Princeton University Press.

Cox, J. (2019, October 8). Inverted yield curve guru Campbell Harvey: Prepare for recession. *CNBC.* https://www.cnbc.com/2019/10/08/inverted-yield-curve-guru-campbell-harvey-prepare-for-recession.html

Crouch, C. (2004). *Post-democracy: Themes for the 21st century.* Polity.

Custers, P. (2010). Military Keynesianism today: An innovative discourse. *Race & Class, 51*(4), 79–94. https://doi.org/10.1177/0306396810363049

Dale, G., & Fabry, A. (2018). Neoliberalism in Eastern Europe and the former Soviet Union. In D. Cahill et al. (Eds.), *The SAGE handbook of neoliberalism* (pp. 234–247). SAGE. https://doi.org/10.4135/9781526416001.n19

Day, M., & Soper, S. (2020, May 27). Amazon writes its own TV news segments to Laud virus response. *Bloomberg.* https://www.bloomberg.com/news/articles/2020-05-27/amazon-writes-its-own-tv-news-segments-to-laud-virus-responsebr

de Figueiredo, J., & Kyle, M. (2006). Surviving the gales of creative destruction: The determinants of product turnover. *Strategic Management Journal, 27*(3), 241–264. https://doi.org/10.1002/smj.512

de Soto, H., et al. (1986). *El otro sendero: La revolución informal.* Barranco.

Dean, J. (2009). *Democracy and other neoliberal fantasies: Communicative capitalism and left politics.* Duke University Press.

Douglas, J. (1980, July 1). The welfare state as a zero-sum game. Foundation for Economic Education. https://fee.org/articles/the-welfare-state-as-a-zero-sum-game

Drucker, P. (1994). *Max Schachtman and his left: A socialist odyssey through the "American Century".* Humanities Press.

Edwards, S., & Montes, L. (2020). Milton Friedman in Chile: Shock therapy, economic freedom, and exchange rates. *Journal of the History of Economic Thought, 42*(1), 105–132. https://doi.org/10.1017/S1053837219000397

Eisenhower, D. (1960). Farewell address. In *Public papers of the presidents* (pp. 1035–1040). National Archives.

Engelhardt, T. (2014, June 19). Karl Rove unintentionally predicted the current chaos in Iraq. *Mother Jones.* https://www.motherjones.com/politics/2014/06/us-karl-rove-iraq-crisis

European Academies Scientific Advisory Council. (2015). *Gain-of-function: Experimental applications relating to potentially pandemic pathogens* (EASAC Policy Report 27). https://web.archive.org/web/20230330163742/https://easac.eu/fileadmin/PDF_s/reports_statements/Gain_of_Function/EASAC_GOF_Web_complete_centred.pdf

Facts to inform the debate about the U.S. government's anti-drug offensive in the Americas. (2025, November 3). IDPC. https://idpc.net/news/2025/11/facts-to-inform-the-debate-about-the-u-s-government-s-anti-drug-offensive-in-the-americas

FDIC. (1997). *History of the Eighties: Lessons for the Future, I: An examination of the banking crises of the 1980s and early 1990s*. Federal Deposit Insurance Corporation. https://www.fdic.gov/bank/historical/history/3_85.pdf

Fears, R., & ter Meulen, V. (2015). European academies advise on gain-of-function studies in influenza virus research. *Journal of Virology, 90*(5), 2162–2164. https://doi.org/10.1128/JVI.03045-15

Ferguson, N. (2005). *Colossus: The rise and fall of the American empire*. Penguin.

Filtzer, D. (2009). Labor discipline and the decline of the Soviet system: The use of work time and the decline of the Soviet system, 1928–1991. *International Labor & Working-Class History, 75*, 51–78.

Firestone, T. (1988). Four Sovietologists: A primer. *National Interest, 14*, 102–107. https://www.jstor.org/stable/24027135

Fletcher, L. (2023, April 5). Hedge funds made $7bn from betting against banks during turmoil. *Financial Times*. https://www.ft.com/content/a8a56860-6092-4b55-aa50-78d989601bab

Focus on growth vs. costs key to oil company merger success. (2001, March 5). *Oil & Gas Journal*, 172. https://www.ogj.com/general-interest/companies/article/17220492/focus-on-growth-vs-costs-key-to-oil-company-merger-success

Fraser, N. (2022). *Cannibal capitalism: How our system is devouring democracy, care, and the planet—and what we can do about it*. Verso.

Frick, A. (2009, June 23). Barney Frank: GOP thinks $2 billion F-22 project is funded by Monopoly money. *ThinkProgress*. https://archive.thinkprogress.org/barney-frank-gop-thinks-2-billion-f-22-project-is-funded-by-monopoly-money-a364c9c9320c

Friedman, B. M. (2006). *The moral consequences of economic growth*. Knopf Doubleday.

Friedman, G., & Friedman, M. (1996). *The future of war: Power, technology and American world dominance in the 21st century*. Crown.

Friedman, M. (1990). *Free to choose 5: Created equal*. Collected Works of Milton Friedman Project Records. Hoover Institution Library & Archives. https://miltonfriedman.hoover.org/objects/57882/volume-5-created-equal

Friedman, T. (1998, May 2). Foreign affairs: Now a word from X. *The New York Times*. https://www.nytimes.com/1998/05/02/opinion/foreign-affairs-now-a-word-from-x.html

Friedman, T. (2023, April 14). America, China and a crisis of trust. *The New York Times*. https://nyti.ms/3MHnw3K

Galbraith, J. K. (1963, December 13). *Wealth and poverty* [Speech to the National Policy Committee on Pockets of Poverty].

Galbraith, J. K. (1990). *A short history of financial euphoria: Financial genius is before the fall*. Whittle Direct Books.

GAO (U.S. Government Accountability Office). (2004). *Energy markets: Effects of mergers and market concentration in the U.S. petroleum industry* (GAO-04-96). https://www.gao.gov/products/gao-04-96

Georges, A., & Kahane, R. (1979). *L'affaire Peiper*. Poche.

Gessen, K. (2023, June 12). How Russia went from ally to adversary. *The New Yorker*. https://www.newyorker.com/magazine/2023/06/19/how-the-west-lost-the-peace-philipp-ther-book-review

Gilder, G. (1999, May 6). Zero-sum folly, from Kyoto to Kosovo. *The Wall Street Journal*. https://www.wsj.com/articles/SB925935310251421950

Gilder, G. (2020, April 12). We need politicians in a pandemic. *The Wall Street Journal*. https://www.wsj.com/articles/we-need-politicians-in-a-pandemic-11586710824

Girerd, L., et al. (2021). Neoliberal ideology in France: A qualitative inquiry. *Frontiers in Psychology, 12*, Article 686391. https://doi.org/10.3389/fpsyg.2021.686391

Gleijeses, P. (2006). Moscow's proxy? Cuba and Africa, 1975–1988. *Journal of Cold War Studies, 8*(4), 98–146. https://www.jstor.org/stable/26925953

Goldin, C., & Margo, R. (1991). *The great compression: The wage structure in the United States at mid-century* (NBER Working Paper No. 3817). National Bureau of Economic Research. https://www.nber.org/papers/w3817

Good, A. (2022). *American exception: Empire and the deep state.* Skyhorse.

Gopinath, G. (2019, October 15). The world economy: Synchronized slowdown, precarious outlook. *IMF Blog.* https://www.imf.org/en/Blogs/Articles/2019/10/15/the-world-economy-synchronized-slowdown-precarious-outlook

Gordon, M., & Volz, D. (2025, January 25). COVID most likely originated in lab leak, concludes U.S. Energy Department. *The Wall Street Journal.* https://www.wsj.com/articles/covid-origin-china-lab-leak-807b7b0a

Gould, A., & Lokrou, M. (2018). Paved with good intentions: Misdirected idealism in the lead-up to 2008's GFC. *Economic and Labour Relations Review, 29*(4), 394–409.

Gramsci, A. (1951). *Quaderni del carcere III: Passato e presente.* Einaudi.

Gramsci, A. (1971). *Selections from the prison notebooks* (Q. Hoare & G. Smith, Eds. & Trans.). International Publishers.

Grandhay, J. -C. (2008, June 30*). Cacheux, Paul. Le Maitron.* https://maitron.fr/cacheux-paul-cacheux-celestin-octave-paul

Greenberg, D. (2010). Creating their own reality: The Bush administration and expertise in a polarized age. In J. Zelizer (Ed.), *The presidency of George W. Bush: A first historical assessment* (pp. 199–200). Princeton University Press.

Greenhouse, S. (1991, January 1). Czechs begin shift to a free market. *The New York Times.* https://www.nytimes.com/1991/01/01/world/czechs-begin-shift-to-a-free-market.html

Gregory, D. (2004). *The colonial present: Afghanistan, Palestine.* Blackwell.

Gualmini, E., & Schmidt, V. (2013). State transformation in Italy and France: Technocratic versus political leadership on the road from non-liberalism to neo-liberalism. In V. Schmidt & M. Thatcher (Eds.), *Resilient liberalism in Europe's political economy* (pp. 346–373). Cambridge University Press.

Guérin, D. (1939). *Fascism and big business.* Pioneer.

Gustafson, T. (1982). *The Soviet economy in the 1980s.* RAND Corporation.

Hampton, P. (1999). Trotskyism after Trotsky? C'est moi! *Workers Liberty, 55*, 38.

Harman, C. (1999). *Explaining the crisis—A Marxist re-appraisal.* Bookmarks.

Harman, C. (2003). Analysing imperialism. *International Socialism, 2*(99).

Harris, A. (1942). Sombart and German (National) Socialism. *Journal of Political Economy, 50*(6), 805–835. https://doi.org/10.1086/255964

Harrison, M. (1994). *The Soviet economy: Growth and transition.* Routledge.

Hart, S. (2005). Innovation, creative destruction and sustainability. *Research Technology Management, 48*(5), 21–27. https://doi.org/10.1080/08956308.2005.11657334

Hartmann, T. (2020). *The hidden history of monopolies: How big business destroyed the American dream.* Berrett-Koehler.

Hartshorn, J., Zervos, C., & Seager, T. (2005). Creative destruction: Building toward sustainability. *Canadian Journal of Civil Engineering, 32*(1), 170–180. https://doi.org/10.1139/l04-119

Hartung, W. (2001). Eisenhower's warning: The military–industrial complex forty years later. *World Policy Journal, 18*(1), 39–44. http://www.jstor.org/stable/40209730

Hartung, W. (2021, September 13). Profits of war: Corporate beneficiaries of the post-9/11 Pentagon spending surge. *Watson Institute for International & Public Affairs.* https://watson.brown.edu/costsofwar/files/cow/imce/papers/2021/Profits%20of%20War_Hartung_Costs%20of%20War_Sept%2013%2C%202021.pdf

Hartung, W. (2021, September 21). How corporate profiteers won the war on terror. *Countercurrents.* https://countercurrents.org/2021/09/how-corporations-won-the-war-on-terror

Hartung, W. (2021, September 24). Corporate America cashed in on 9/11. *The Nation.* https://www.thenation.com/article/world/corporations-war-spending

Harvey, D. (2007). *Limits to capital* (2nd ed.). Verso. (Original work published 1982).

Harvey, D. (2009, February 12). Why the U.S. stimulus package is bound to fail. *Reading Marx's Capital with David Harvey*. https://davidharvey.org/2009/02/why-the-us-stimulus-package-is-bound-to-fail/
Harvey, D. (2010). *The enigma of capital and the crises of capitalism*. Profile.
Harvey, D. (2023). *A companion to Marx's Grundrisse*. Verso.
Hatzivassiliou, E. (Ed.). (2018). *Pointing to the emerging Soviet dead ends: NATO analysis of the Soviet economy, 1971–1982* (CWIHP Working Paper 87). Wilson Center.
Hayek, F. A. (1976). *The denationalization of money*. Institute of Economic Affairs.
Hellenic Statistical Authority. (n.d.). Quarterly GDP—Seasonally adjusted, chain-linked volumes, percentage change against previous quarter. *ELSTAT*. https://www.statistics.gr/en/statistics/-/publication/SEL84/2019-Q4
Heller, A. (2009). *Ayn Rand and the world she made*. Doubleday.
Higgs, K. (2014). *Collision course: Endless growth on a finite planet*. MIT Press.
Hinshaw, D., & M. Walker (2018, January 22). Poland's new nationalist rulers are erasing Lech Walesa from history. *Wall Street Journal*. https://www.wsj.com/articles/polands-new-nationalist-rulers-are-erasing-lech-walesa-from-history-1516636420
Holman, R. (2018, November 13). France angry drivers block roads to protest tax increase on diesel fuel. *France 24*. https://www.france24.com/en/20181113-france-angry-drivers-block-road-protest-tax-increase-diesel-fuel
Hossein-Zadeh, I. (2006). *The political economy of U.S. militarism*. Palgrave Macmillan.
ICYMI. (2021, October 27). New study finds Big Pharma spent more on sales and marketing that R&D during pandemic. CSRxP. https://www.csrxp.org/icymi-newstudy-finds-big-pharma-spent-more-on-sales-and-marketing-than-rd-during-pandemic/br
Imperiale, M., Casadevall, A., Relman, D. A., & Engel, L. S. (2018). The silver lining in gain-of-function experiments with pathogens of pandemic potential. In S. I. Miller (Ed.), *Methods in Molecular Biology* (Vol. 1836, pp. 575–587). Springer. https://doi.org/10.1007/978-1-4939-8678-1_28
Inderst, R., & Valletti, T. (2011). Buyer power and the 'waterbed effect.' *Journal of Industrial Economics, 59*(1), 1–20.
India's economy: One more push. (2021, July 21). *Economist*. https://www.economist.com/leaders/2011/07/21/one-more-push.
IMF. (1991). *A study of the Soviet economy I*. International Monetary Fund.
Islam, F. (2025, May 18). The secretive US factory that lays bare the contradiction in Trump's America First plan. *BBC News*. https://www.bbc.com/news/articles/cwywj0zgzwxo
Izutova, O. (2021). От простого экономиста до министра СССР. *Бюджет*. https://bujet.ru/article/416553.php
Johnson, C. (2004). *The sorrows of empire: Militarism, secrecy, and the end of the republic*. Metropolitan.
Jones, D. (2012). *Masters of the universe: Hayek, Friedman, and the birth of neoliberal politics*. Princeton University Press.
Keen, S. (2010). A monetary Minsky model of the Great Moderation and the Great Recession. *Journal of Economic Behavior & Organization, 86*, 221–235. https://doi.org/10.1016/j.jebo.2011.01.010
Keller, W. (1995). *Arm in arm: The political economy of the global arms trade*. Basic Books.
Kelly, B. (1992). *Adventures in porkland: How Washington wastes your money and why they won't stop*. Villard.
Keynes, J. M. (1933, December 31). An open letter to President Roosevelt. *The New York Times*. https://www.nytimes.com/1933/12/31/archives/from-keynes-to-roosevelt-our-recovery-plan-assayed-the-british.html
Kidron, M. (1970). *Western capitalism since the war*. Penguin.
Kiernan, B. (2001). Myth, nationalism and genocide. *Journal of Genocide Research, 3*(2), 187–206.
Klein, N. (2007). *The shock doctrine: The rise of disaster capitalism*. Holt.

Kočenda, E., & Valachy, J. (2002). Secondary privatization in the Czech Republic: Changes in ownership structure and corporate control (CASE Report No. 45). Center for Social and Economic Research.

Komlos, J. (2016). Has creative destruction become more destructive? *B.E. Journal of Economic Analysis & Policy, 16*(4). https://doi.org/10.1515/bejeap-2016-0179

Kotz, D. M. (2015). *The rise and fall of neoliberal capitalism.* Harvard University Press.

Kozol, J. (1991). *Savage inequalities: Children in America's schools.* Crown.

Krajewski, M. (2014). The great lightbulb conspiracy. *IEEE Spectrum, 51*(10), 56–61. https://spectrum.ieee.org/the-great-lightbulb-conspiracy

Krugman, P. (2009, June 24). Weaponized Keynesianism. *The New York Times.* https://krugman.blogs.nytimes.com/2009/06/24/weaponized-keynesianism

Kurth, J. (2000). Military–industrial complex. In J. Chambers (Ed.), *The Oxford companion to American military history* (pp. 440–442). Oxford University Press.

Lassman, T. C. (2015). Putting the military back into the history of the military-industrial complex: The management of technological innovation in the U.S. army, 1945–1960. *Isis, 106*(1), 94–120.

Leahy, P. (2017, February 14). S. 119—110th Congress: War Profiteering Prevention Act of 2007. *GovTrack.* https://www.govtrack.us/congress/bills/110/s119

Lean, G. & Cooper, Y. (1996, July 21). Not enough for us. *The Independent.* https://www.independent.co.uk/news/uk/not-enough-for-us-1329728.html

Lee, S. (2001). Black Wednesday. In R. Jones (Ed.), *Routledge encyclopedia of international political economy* (Vol. I, p. 87). Routledge.

Leustean, L. (2007). Between Moscow and London: Romanian Orthodoxy and national communism, 1960–1965. *Slavonic & East European Review, 85*(3), 491–521. https://www.jstor.org/stable/25479106

Lewin, M. (2016). *The Soviet century.* Verso.

Live cam of the Centennial Light Bulb. (2025, July 27). *Livermore's Centennial Bulb.* http://www.centennialbulb.org/cam.htm

Lobacheva, K. (2012). *Экономическая теория: учебник для бакалавром.* Юрайт.

Loewenstein, A. (2017). *Disaster capitalism: Making a killing out of catastrophe.* Verso.

Lowenstein, R. (2023, March 15). The Silicon Valley Bank rescue just changed capitalism. *The New York Times.* https://nyti.ms/3FqOnNf

Lukács, G. (1967). *History and class consciousness.* MIT Press.

Luxemburg, R. (1913). *The accumulation of capital.* Routledge.

Mackert, J. et al., (Eds.). (2021). *The condition of democracy, I: Neoliberal politics and sociological perspectives.* Routledge.

Magdoff, F., & Foster, J. B. (2014). Stagnation & financialization: The nature of the contradiction. *Monthly Review, 66*(1), 1–24. https://monthlyreview.org/2014/05/01/stagnation-and-financialization/

Mandel, E. (1975). *Late capitalism.* Verso.

Martin, R. (1994). *L'Affaire Peiper*. Dagorno.

Marx, K. (1863–1867). *Capital: Volumes I–IV.* Penguin Classics.

Mathews, J. (2019). America's indefensible defense budget. *New York Review of Books, 66*(12), 24.

Matsumoto, M., & Alichi, A. (2018). *Inequality and poverty across generations in the European Union* (IMF Staff Discussion Note 18/01). International Monetary Fund. https://www.elibrary.imf.org/view/journals/006/2018/001/article-A001-en.xml

Mazhitova, Zh., et al. (2021). Environmental consequences of Khrushchev's Virgin Land Campaign in Kazakhstan (1950s–1960s). *E3S Web of Conferences, 258*, 1–9. https://doi.org/10.1051/e3sconf/202125805036

Mazzucato, M. (2020). *Mission economy.* Penguin.

McCarthy, N. (2021, March 5). The enormous scale of global food waste [Infographic]. *Forbes.* https://www.forbes.com/sites/niallmccarthy/2021/03/05/the-enormous-scale-of-global-food-waste-infographic/?sh=5ce79e9926ac

McCartney, J., & McCartney, M. (2015). *America's war machine: Vested interests, endless conflicts*. Dunne.
McCulley, P. (2009, May 26). The shadow banking system and Hyman Minsky's economic journey. *Global Central Bank Focus, PIMCO*. https://www.pimco.com/en-us/insights/economic-and-market-commentary/global-central-bank-focus/the-shadow-banking-system-and-hyman-minskys-economic-journey
McDonald, S. (2023, August 10). 'Seinfeld' and 'Friends' reflected the atomized US of the '90s—and today. *Current Affairs*. https://www.currentaffairs.org/news/2023/08/seinfeld-and-friends-reflected-the-atomized-u-s-of-the-90s-and-today
McMahon, R. (2013). *Colonialism and cold war: The United States and the struggle for Indochina*. Cambridge University Press.
McMullen, J. (2022, July 23). The audacious PR plot that seeded doubt about climate change. *BBC News*. https://www.bbc.com/news/science-environment-62225696
Meijer, B. (2023, March 16). Dutch farmers' protest party scores big election win, shaking up Senate. *Reuters*. https://www.reuters.com/world/europe/farmers-protest-party-set-shake-up-dutch-political-landscape-2023-03-15/
Melman, S. (1970). *Pentagon capitalism: The political economy of war*. McGraw Hill.
Melman, S. (Ed.). (1971). *The war economy of the United States: Readings in military industry and economy*. St. Martin's Press.
Menand, L. (2021). *The free world: Art and thought in the Cold War*. Farrar, Straus & Giroux.
Menand, L. (2023, July 17). The rise and fall of neoliberalism. *New Yorker*. https://www.newyorker.com/magazine/2023/07/24/the-rise-and-fall-of-neoliberalism
Micklin, P. (1988). Desiccation of the Aral Sea: A water-management disaster in the Soviet Union. *Science, 241*, 1172–1175.
Milanovic, B. (2021). More or less: Income inequality has risen over the past quarter-century, *IMF Finance & Development*, *48*/3, https://m.elibrary.imf.org/view/journals/022/0048/003/article-A003-en.xml
Miller, H. (2005). *Tropic of Cancer* (Original work published 1934). Harper.
Mills, C. W. (1956). *The power elite*. Oxford University Press.
Minsky, H. P. (1986a). *Stabilizing an unstable economy*. Yale University Press.
Minsky, H. (1986). Review of: *The Zero-Sum Solution: Building a World-Class American Economy*, by L. Thurow. *Challenge*, *29*/3, 60–64, http://www.jstor.org/stable/40721032
Mollenhoff, C. (1967). *The Pentagon: Politics, profits and plunder*. Putnam.
MON podsumowuje zmiany kadrowe: Coraz większa armia, szeroka wymiana kadr. (2017, February 22). *Gazeta Prawna*. http://www.gazetaprawna.pl/artykuly/1021852,mon-liczniejsza-armia-szeroka-wymiana-kadr.html
Morgenson, G. (2010, June 25). Strong enough for tough stains? *The New York Times*. https://www.nytimes.com/2010/06/27/business/27gret.html
Mouffe, C. (2005). *On the political*. Routledge.
Munger, M., & Villarreal-Diaz, M. (2019). The road to crony capitalism. *The Independent Review, 23*(3), 331–344. https://www.independent.org/publications/tir/article.asp?id=1343
Nelson, L.-E. (2000). Military–industrial man. *New York Review of Books, 47*(20), 6.
Nevradakis, M. (2021, November 2). 'Brought to You by Pfizer': Pharma giant spends more on Ads, news sponsorships, than research. *Children's Health Defense*. https://childrenshealthdefense.org/defender/pfizer-vaccination-ads-news-sponsorships-research/br
Nicholas Frederick Brady—Holowesko Partners Ltd. (n.d.). *Private Fund Data*. https://privatefunddata.com/fund-employees/nicholas-frederick-brady-28503
Nietzsche, F. (1924). *A genealogy of morals* (W. Haussmann, Trans.). Macmillan.
Nightingale, P. (2015). Schumpeter's theological roots? Harnack and the origins of creative destruction. *Journal of Evolutionary Economics, 25*(1), 69–75. https://doi.org/10.1007/s00191-014-0360-x
Oakes, W. (1944). Towards a permanent arms economy? *Politics*, 11–17.
OECD. (2008). *Growing unequal? Income distribution and poverty in OECD Countries*. OECD. https://www.oecd.org/en/publications/2008/10/growing-unequal_g1gh8dfb.html

Orbán nem gyanít korrupciót a Lockheed-botrány mögött (1999, May 26). *Origo*, http://www.origo.hu/itthon/19990526orban.html

O'Rourke, P. (2004, September). *A conversation with Colin Powell. The Atlantic*. https://www.theatlantic.com/magazine/archive/2004/09/a-conversation-with-colin-powell/303436

Owens, L. (2003). *Creative destruction: Nikos Kazantzakis and the literature of responsibility*. Mercer University Press.

Page, M. (1999). *Creative destruction of Manhattan, 1900–1940*. University of Chicago Press.

Pagliarini, A. (2022, September 29). Capitalism triumphed in the Cold War, but not by making people better off. *New Republic*. https://newrepublic.com/article/167888/capitalism-triumphed-cold-war-broken-promises-fritz-bartel-review

Palomino, J. C., Rodríguez, J. G., & Sebastian, R. (2020). Wage inequality and poverty effects of lockdown and social distancing in Europe. *European Economic Review, 129*, 103564. https://doi.org/10.1016/j.euroecorev.2020.103564

Pasztor, A. (1995). *When the Pentagon was for sale: Inside America's biggest defense scandal*. Scribner.

Patterson, W. (1984). *The plutonium business & the spread of the bomb*. Sierra Club.

Peterson, R. (1987, July 1). *Lessons in liberty: The Dutch Republic, 1579–1750*. Foundation for Economic Education. https://fee.org/articles/lessons-in-liberty-the-dutch-republic-1579-1750

Pierre, A. J. (1982). *The global politics of arms sales*. Princeton University Press.

Piketty, T., Zucman, G., & Saez, E. (2014). Capital is back: Wealth-income ratios in rich countries 1700–2010. *Quarterly Journal of Economics, 129*(3), 1255–1310. https://doi.org/10.1093/qje/qju018

Pistor, K. (2025, January 28). The new Washington Consensus. *Project Syndicate*. https://www.project-syndicate.org/commentary/trump-business-controls-government-means-autocracy-instead-of-democracy-by-katharina-pistor-2025-01

Polanyi, K. (1944). *The great transformation*. Beacon Press.

Popov, V., & Sundaram, J. (2017, July 19). What explains the post-Soviet Russian economic collapse? *The Wire*. https://thewire.in/economy/post-soviet-russian-economic-collapse

Provost, C., & Kennard, M. (2024). *Silent coup: How corporations overthrew democracy*. Sage.

Quinn, W., & Turner, J. D. (2020). *Boom and bust: A global history of financial bubbles*. Cambridge University Press.

Radio Free Europe/Radio Liberty. (2004). Cold war archives. In A. Puddington et al. (Eds.), *Cold war broadcasting impact*. Hoover Institution Press.

Raevsky, V. (2014). *На перекрёстке и до него*. Экономическая летопись.

Raevsky, V. A. (2020). *Экономика и жизнь, 49*(9865). https://www.eg-online.ru/article/431392/

Ramet, S. (2023). *East Central Europe and communism: Politics, culture, and society, 1943–1991*. Routledge.

Rammanohar-Reddy, C. (2000). India, the Washington Consensus and the East Asian Crisis. *International Social Science Journal, 52*(166), 505–516. https://doi.org/10.1111/1468-2451.00280

Rasky, S. (1987, October 23). Man in the news: Blue-chip leader for task force: Nicholas Frederick Brady. *The New York Times*. https://www.nytimes.com/1987/10/23/business/man-in-the-news-blue-chip-leader-for-task-force-nicholas-frederick-brady.html

Reagan, R. (1988, January 25). *State of the Union Address*. National Archives. https://www.reaganlibrary.gov/archives/speech/address-joint-session-congress-state-union-1988

Regan, T. (2002, September 6). When contemplating war, beware of babies in incubators. *Christian Science Monitor*. https://www.csmonitor.com/2002/0906/p25s02-cogn.html

Reinert, H., & Reinert, E. (2006). Creative destruction in economics. In J. Backhaus & W. Drechsler (Eds.), *Friedrich Nietzsche (1844–1900), III* (pp. 55–85). Springer. https://doi.org/10.1007/978-0-387-32980-2_4

Reuters. (2022, May 10). China rebukes U.S. for changing Taiwan wording on State Department website. *Reuters*. https://www.reuters.com/world/china-slams-us-changing-taiwan-wording-state-department-website-2022-05-10/

Robinson, N. (2017, April 18). What happened to war tax protests? *Current Affairs*. https://www.currentaffairs.org/2017/04/what-happened-to-war-tax-protests

Rodríguez, J. -P. (2021). The politics of neoliberalism in Latin America: Dynamics of resilience and contestation. *Sociology Compass, 15*(3), Article e12854. https://doi.org/10.1111/soc4.12854

Rosalsky, G. (2022, August 2). How 'Shock Therapy' created Russian oligarchs and paved the path for Putin. *NPR*. https://www.npr.org/sections/money/2022/03/22/1087654279/how-shock-therapy-created-russian-oligarchs-and-paved-the-path-for-putin

Roth, A. (2025, July 8). Pentagon provided $2.4tn to private arms firms to 'fund war and weapons', report finds. *The Guardian*. https://www.theguardian.com/us-news/2025/jul/08/pentagon-military-spending

Rowthorn, B. (1980). *Capitalism, conflict, and inflation: Essays in political economy*. Lawrence & Wishart.

Rowthorn, B. (1981). *Demand, real wages and economic growth*. Thames Polytechnic.

Rowthorn, B., & Ramaswamy, R. (1997). *Deindustrialization—Its causes and implications* (IMF Working Paper 97/42). International Monetary Fund. https://www.imf.org/external/pubs/ft/issues10/issue10.pdf.

Rowthorn, B., & Wells, J. (1987). *De-industrialization and foreign trade*. Cambridge University Press.

Rutland, P. (2013). Neoliberalism and the Russian transition. *Review of International Political Economy, 20*(2), 332–362. http://www.jstor.org/stable/42003296

Sakwa, R. (2013). The Soviet collapse: Contradictions and neo-modernisation. *Journal of Eurasian Studies, 4*(1), 65–77. https://doi.org/10.1016/j.euras.2012.07.003

Salsman, R. (2021, May 25). Supply-side neoliberalism sure beats the alternative. *AIER—Daily Economy News*. https://www.aier.org/article/supply-side-neoliberalism-sure-beats-the-alternative

Sampson, A. (1977). *The arms bazaar: From Lebanon to Lockheed*. Bantam.

Schmemann, S. (2021, December 31). The day the Soviet flag came down. *The New York Times*. https://nyti.ms/340Y1pM

Schuman, M. (2009). *The miracle: The epic story of Asia's quest for wealth*. HarperCollins.

Schumpeter, J. (1994). *Capitalism, socialism & democracy (Original work published 1942)*. Routledge.

Selgelid, M. J. (2016). Gain-of-function research: Ethical analysis. *Science and Engineering Ethics, 22*(4), 923–964. https://doi.org/10.1007/s11948-016-9810-1

Sellers, C. (1996). Capitalism and democracy in American historical mythology. In M. Stokes & S. Conway (Eds.), *The market revolution in America: Social, political, and religious expressions, 1800–1880* (pp. 312–330). University of Virginia Press.

Selwyn, B. (2015, June 9). Friedrich Hayek: In defence of dictatorship. *OpenDemocracy*. https://www.opendemocracy.net/en/friedrich-hayek-dictatorship

Semuels, A. (2020, May 11). Why farmers are dumping milk, destroying eggs and leaving produce to rot in the fields. *Time*. https://time.com/5843136/covid-19-food-destruction

Service, R. (2022, October 31). Back in the U.S.S.R. *The Atlantic*. https://www.theatlantic.com/ideas/archive/2022/10/how-putin-brought-sovietology-back-life/671925/

Shadlen, K. (2004). Debt, finance and the IMF: Three decades of debt crises in Latin America. In *South America, Central America & the Caribbean* (pp. 8–12). Routledge.

Sharma, B., Ghosh, C., & Shivdasani, A. (2022). Unintended consequences of the Dodd-Frank Act on credit rating risk and corporate finance. *Journal of Financial and Quantitative Analysis, 57*(6), 2286–2323. https://doi.org/10.1017/S0022109021000831

Shipler, D. (2008). *The working poor*. Vintage.

Sicilia, D., & Cruikshank, J. (2000). *The Greenspan effect*. McGraw-Hill.

Skeel, D. (2011). *The new financial deal: Understanding the Dodd–Frank Act and its (unintended) consequences*. Wiley.

Skworz, A., & Kapuściński, R. (2006). *Antyciała: Z Ryszardem Kapuścińskim rozmawia Andrzej Skworz. Press, 2*(121), 25–28. https://web.archive.org/web/20120320035151/http://www.press.pl/miesiecznik-press/pokaz/943,Antyciala

Slade, G. (2009). *Made to break: Technology and obsolescence in America*. Harvard University Press.
Slobodian, Q. (2018). *Globalists: The end of empire and the birth of neoliberalism*. Harvard University Press.
Sloterdijk, P. (2009). *Bubbles* (W. Hoban, Trans.). MIT Press. (Original work published 1998).
Sohn-Rethel, A. (1978). *Economy and class structure of German fascism*. CSE Books.
Sohn-Rethel, A. (1992). *Industrie und Nationalsozialismus*. Wagenbach.
Solly, M. (2022, August 30). The contradictory legacy of Mikhail Gorbachev. *Smithsonian Magazine*. https://www.smithsonianmag.com/history/the-contradictory-legacy-of-mikhail-gorbachev-180980694
Solska, J. (2019). Polityka. *Państwo Prywatne, 6*(3197), 9.
Sombart, W. (1913). *Krieg und Kapitalismus*. Duncker & Humblot.
Spencer, H. (1851). *Social statics*. Chapman.
Spiegel, M. (1996, August 23). Collective action difficulties in foreign lending: Banks and bonds. *FRBSF Economic Letter, 24*. https://www.frbsf.org/economic-research/publications/economic-letter/1996/august/collective-action-difficulties-in-foreign-lending-banks-and-bonds
St. Clair, J. (2005). *Grand theft Pentagon: Tales of corruption and profiteering in the War on Terror*. Common Courage Press.
Steinmetz-Jenkins, D., & Gerstle, G. (2022, April 13). Has neoliberalism really come to an end? *The Nation*. https://www.thenation.com/article/politics/neoliberalism-gary-gerstle
Stewart, E. (2021, January 27). The GameStop stock frenzy, explained. *Vox*. https://www.vox.com/the-goods/22249458/gamestop-stock-wallstreetbets-reddit-citron
Strange, S. (1976). *International economic relations of the Western world, 1959–1971: International monetary relations*. Oxford University Press.
Strange, S. (1988). *States and markets*. Pinter.
Strange, S. (1996). *The retreat of the state: The diffusion of power in the world economy*. Cambridge University Press.
Strange, S. (1997). *Casino capitalism*. Manchester University Press. (Original work published 1986).
Strange, S. (1998). *Mad money: When markets outgrow governments*. Manchester University Press.
Strange, S., Stopford, J., & Henley, J. (1991). *Rival states, rival firms: Competition for world market shares*. Cambridge University Press.
Streeck, W. (2012). Citizens as customers: Considerations on the new politics of consumption. *New Left Review, 76*, 27–47.
Streeck, W. (2024). *Taking Back Control? States and State Systems After Globalism* (B. Fowkes & J. Rahtz, Trans.). Verso.
Susskind, D. (2024). *Growth: A history and a reckoning*. Penguin.
Susskind, R. (2004, October 17). Faith, certainty and the presidency of George W. Bush. *The New York Times Magazine*. https://www.nytimes.com/2004/10/17/magazine/faith-certainty-and-the-presidency-of-george-w-bush.html
Swanepoel, E., Smit, E., & Grobler, W. (2017). Dodd-Frank and risk-taking: Reputation impact in banks. *Banks and Bank Systems, 12*(1), 36–43.
Sweetman, B. (2000). In search of the Pentagon's billion-dollar hidden budgets. *Jane's International Defence Review, 33*, 24–32.
Talbott, S. (2017, December 7). *The man who lost an empire. Brookings Institution*. https://www.brookings.edu/articles/the-man-who-lost-an-empire
Tandon, Y. (2018). *Trade is war: The West's war against the world*. OR Books.
The Kuwaiti incubator hoax. (1994, February 25). *The Washington Post*. https://www.washingtonpost.com/archive/opinions/1994/02/26/the-kuwaiti-incubator-hoax/35b1e882-f796-4acb-a106-9280a7dda521
Thorpe, R. (2014). *The American warfare state: The domestic politics of military spending*. University of Chicago Press.
Thurow, L. (1985). *The Zero-sum solution: Building a world-class American economy*. Simon & Schuster.

Tismaneanu, V. (1984). The ambiguity of Romanian national communism. *Telos, 60*, 65–79. https://doi.org/10.3817/0684060065

Tismaneanu, V. (2012). What was national Stalinism? In D. Stone (Ed.), *Oxford handbook of postwar European history* (pp. 462–479). Oxford University Press. https://doi.org/10.1093/oxfordhb/9780199560981.013.0023

Tsoukalis, L. (1981). *The European Community and Mediterranean enlargement*. Allen & Unwin.

Tucker, T., & Dayen, D. (2020, October 2). Just put it on our tab. War financing and the decline of democracy. *War on the Rocks*. https://warontherocks.com/2020/10/just-put-it-on-our-tab-war-financing-and-the-decline-of-democracy

U.S. Board on Life Sciences, Division on Earth and Life Studies, Committee on Science, Technology, and Law, Policy and Global Affairs, Board on Health Sciences Policy, National Research Council, & Institute of Medicine. (2015). *Potential risks and benefits of gain-of-function research: Summary of a workshop*. National Academies Press. https://www.ncbi.nlm.nih.gov/books/NBK285579/

U.S. Department of Health & Human Services, ASPR. (2025, May 5). *Enhanced potential pandemic pathogen oversight framework: S3 Science Safety Security*. https://www.phe.gov/s3/dualuse/Documents/P3CO-FinalGuidanceStatement.pdf

U.S. House Committee on Oversight & Accountability. (2023, March 8). *COVID origins hearing wrap up: Facts, science, evidence point to a Wuhan lab leak* [Press release]. https://oversight.house.gov/release/covid-origins-hearing-wrap-up-facts-science-evidence-point-to-a-wuhan-lab-leak%EF%BF%BC/

UGT dice que intentará evitar el cierre de la fábrica de Bimbo y que el ERE sea lo menos dramático para los trabajadores. (2015, October 1). *20 Minutos*. https://www.20minutos.es/noticia/2657624/0/ugt-dice-que-intentara-evitar-cierre-fabrica-bimbo-que-ere-sea-lo-menos-dramatico-para-trabajadores

United Nations. (2000). *Culture of peace: The cold war cultural offensive*. UNESCO.

United Nations. (2007). Dry tears of the Aral. *The United Nations Chronicle*.

Valdes, J. -G. (1995). *Pinochet's economists: The Chicago School of economics in Chile*. Cambridge University Press.

Vance, T. (1950). After Korea what? An economic interpretation of U.S. perspectives. *New International*, 323–333.

Vance, T. (1951). The permanent arms economy. *New International*, 29–44.

Varoufakis, Y. (2020, August 21). Something remarkable just happened this August: How the pandemic has sped up the passage to postcapitalism. *YanisVaroufakis.eu*. https://www.yanisvaroufakis.eu/2020/08/21/something-remarkable-just-happened-this-august-how-the-pandemic-has-sped-up-the-passage-to-postcapitalism-lannan-institute-virtual-talk/

Viorst, M. (1970, January 25). Friedmanism, n. Doctrine of most audacious U.S. economist; esp., theory "only money matters." *The New York Times*. https://nyti.ms/1LJHsJM

Wallis, C. (2018). *The thinker, the doer and the decider: Zbigniew Brzezinski, Cyrus Vance and the bureaucratic wars of the Carter administration* (PhD thesis, Northumbria University). https://researchportal.northumbria.ac.uk/en/studentTheses/the-thinker-the-doer-and-the-decider-zbigniew-brzezinski-cyrus-va-3

Watry, D. (2014). *Diplomacy at the brink: Eisenhower, Churchill, & Eden in the Cold War*. Louisiana State University Press.

Weber, I. (2021). *How China escaped Shock Therapy: The market reform debate*. Routledge.

Westad, O. (2005). *The global Cold War: Third World interventions and the making of our times*. Cambridge University Press.

Why are Bimbo and other global brands so big in Mexico? (2018, July 20). *BBC News*. https://www.bbc.com/news/business-44885983

Williamson, J. (1990). What Washington means by policy reform. In J. Williamson (Ed.), *Latin American adjustment: How much has happened?* (pp. 7–20). Institute for International Economics.

Williamson, J., (2000). What should the World Bank think about the Washington Consensus? *World Bank Research Observer 15*/2, 251–264, http://www.jstor.org/stable/3986418

Wilmarth, A. E. (2009). The dark side of universal banking: Financial conglomerates and the origins of the subprime financial crisis. *Connecticut Law Review, 42*(4), 963–1050.

Wilson, C. (1944). For the common defense: A plea for a continuing program of industrial preparedness. *Army Ordnance, 26*(143), 285–288. http://www.jstor.org/stable/45471359

World Economic Forum. (2020, June 3). How the world can 'reset' itself after COVID-19—According to these experts. *World Economic Forum.* https://www.weforum.org/agenda/2020/06/covid19-great-reset-gita-gopinath-jennifer-morgan-sharan-burrow-climate

Yamada, N. (2018). Legitimation of the Lao People's Revolutionary Party: Socialism, Chintanakan Mai (New Thinking) and Reform. *Journal of Contemporary Asia, 58*(5), 717–738. https://doi.org/10.1080/00472336.2018.1439081

Yergin, D., & Stanislaw, J. (1998). *The commanding heights: The battle for the world economy that is remaking the modern world.* Free Press.

Zubok, V. (2007). *Collapse: The fall of the Soviet Union.* Yale University Press.

Part IV

Refeudalization: The World Since 2008

The NeoFailure of Neoliberalism

8

Abstract

This chapter explains how, in the years since the GFC, the new (old) promises that rising tides lift all boats and eternal growth is not only desirable but downright imperative have returned in the form of yet more trickle-down **myths of eternal economic growth**. Additionally, **social Darwinism** has taken hold again, this time in the form of **meritocracy**, while the old 1980s politico-economic maxim that **There Is No Alternative (TINA) struck back**. Thus, middle classes and democracies are slowly but surely liquidated by the forces of speculation, inequality and corruption, and the trajectories of the haves, hopes and heards are separated from the have-nots, hope-nots and heard-nots. The blame for the ever-rising inequality and costs of life, liberty and security has predictably fallen on the poor, foreign and marginalized. Subsequently, what was once neoliberalism has curdled into something more akin to **neofeudalism:** another **highway to serfdom**, where the division between global ruling/owning and working/renting classes ensures that social, political and economic agency grows only wider and more concentrated.

> Neoliberalism ... is in its death throes ... Neoliberalism as an ideology is being left behind - because it failed... The question is, as neoliberalism dies, what's going to replace it? (Stiglitz & Guru-Murthy, 2024, 30:44–31:22)

The cultural consultant Lawrence R. Samuel explains that, in the mid-twentieth century, FDR's socioeconomic successes in his New Deal and geopolitical victory in WWII "worked together to create what many historians consider to be the first mass middle class in history." After WWII, he writes, "the vast majority of Americans were, or acted as if they were middle class, a remarkable transformation in national identity" (Samuel, 2014, p. 32). Yet as Keynesianism died in the jungles

A. M. Feldman and Y. Stamos, *Zero Sum Political Economy*, World-Systems Evolution and Global Futures, https://doi.org/10.1007/978-3-032-18326-2_8

of Vietnam, American middle-class attitudes toward foreign policy reached a crisis point amid Cold War I, and went from being idealistic to transactional. Nothing showed this clearer than Reagan's victory in 1980 using a manufactured Iranian hostage crisis, followed up with illegally funding Nicaragua's Contras through arms sales to an officially embargoed Iran and accelerating the financialization of the American political economy. If the way out of the 1970s crises became the way into 2008's Big Short, the aftermath was a financial hangover which lasted over a decade until COVID-19. This was no accident: as power shifted from legislatures to markets and central banks, the language of democracy gave way to technocratic euphemisms of "quantitative easing" and "fiscal responsibility." If Henry Ford really did utter the famous quote, "It is well enough that people of the nation do not understand our banking and monetary system, for if they did, I believe there would be a revolution before tomorrow morning," it would be just as true over a century later. The fact was, after 2008, capital was free, but labor was not; its only "liberty" was precarious international migration. The financial architecture necessary to prevent the grand illusion's exposure as fraudulence rested on collective dissonance: the shift to "post-truth" political discourse, "post-democracy" and "neo-feudalism."

2008's Big Short has typically been described as the twenty-first-century version of 1929's Crash. The big difference was that, after '29, the big banks were allowed to fail, but after '08, they were declared "too big to fail." The implication was that when scale is big enough, market consolidation and oligopolization would once again be perfectly legal, leading to another financial arms race to privatize profits and socialize losses. Soon, entire sectors operated as private protected markets—with compliant politicians and judges to legitimize them (Sorkin, 2010). Such failures could be equally observed in ostensibly democratic elections and so-called "free markets." This was increasingly explained by "Market Failure Theory" (MFT), which, as Mazzucato (2020) writes, maintains that governments must fix these failures, not double down on them: "real markets … will often be oligopolistic or characterized by monopoly power … MFT argues that … perfectly competitive markets don't exist" (p. 172).

We can imagine postindustrial liberal "democracies" as a couple on a road trip, arguing whether to keep the car windows up or down. One party craves air conditioning, aiming for cooler, controlled conditions (lower immigration and higher taxes/redistribution), while the other desires open windows with the freedom of the wind (higher immigration and lower taxes). Initially, the trip goes smoothly with a full tank and a new engine. However, as resources deplete and maintenance is ignored, internal conflicts heat up. The working class, symbolized by the driver's overheating feet, grows resentful towards the detached elite at the helm, leading to fights over control rather than cooperative resolution. The Fed's solution? Treat unemployment as a coolant, throwing workers out of the car: when Fed chairpersons talk of the economy "overheating," they recall a 1970s-style fear of inflation which requires that "the Fed uses unemployed human beings as its primary weapon against inflation" (Kelton, 2020, pp. 50–52).

This tension is reflected in politics dominated by supply-side economics, defined by low taxes for capital, high immigration and unemployment, concentration of market shares and market saturation, a system where privatization, deregulation and generous public subsidies for the wealthy coexist with high—often indirect—taxes and austerity for the poor. While frequently framed as a conflict between industrialized and industrializing nations, this is largely a mirage. In reality, the middle classes in industrialized countries are left to contend with declining living standards not because their counterparts in industrializing countries are the primary beneficiaries, but because the lion's share of economic gains is captured by international oligopolistic corporations and cartels.

Corporate capture proceeded alongside a new political paradigm. The neoliberal turn first emerged in two distant but telling locations: Chile, stretching south from the US mainland, and Britain, lying east across the ocean. These peripheral laboratories, positioned almost orthogonally to the US, tested the policies and discourses that would later consume the center. Thus, although the American federal government did not initiate this transformation, by the Cold War's end, it had become neoliberalism's global enforcer, repurposing its Bretton Woods system to that end and codifying the erstwhile fringe Chicago School theories through the Washington Consensus. Ever since the 1970s stagflation crisis, Western elites abandoned Keynesian class compromise and promoted laissez-faire economics, identity politics and the myth of meritocracy in its stead. By the 1990s, the Washington Consensus had also recast the "two-party model" as a franchise operation for capital.

In replacing class politics with identity politics, we've also gradually replaced the middle class with the myth of social mobility and the hyperindividualism of the cult of the self. In the beginning everything seemed promising: after a brief shock to workers and the obsolescence of unions, employment rose, growth returned to ~4% annually and the Berlin Wall crumbled. But after 40 years of neoliberalism, justice, growth and economic stability are illusory while hyperinflation and the nefarious effects of big money in politics go unchecked. Identity politics and steadily increasing intergenerational inequality now resemble medieval feudalism with smartphones: a world of overabundance of cheap consumer goods and artificial scarcity of finite essential resources like housing, where the rich own nearly everything, the poor depend on their potlatch philanthropy and middle classes have evaporated. The model of *Homo Oeconomicus*, the theory of rational actors and optimal distribution of finite resources, now merely serves to justify extraction (Klein & Thompson, 2025).

This rise-and-fall arc used to unfold over centuries; now it comes full circle over decades. As emblematic novelist Ernest Hemingway wrote in *The Sun Also Rises*, bankruptcy happens "gradually and then suddenly." The profound socioeconomic forces which undergirded the rise of Anglo-American liberal democracy and big business at the outset of the twentieth century were dependent on the bankruptcies, slow declines and sudden falls of the Eurasian imperial dynasties (ironically including the Hannoverian-Windsor empire itself). By the 2020s, these forces move in reverse: It is Anglo-American ecumenical ideologies which have been in slow decline ever since the corruption and consolidation of wealth and power into ever fewer hands at the expense of democracy itself. According to Barack Obama's national security advisor Rhodes (2024), "neoliberalism – that blend of free trade, deregulation and deference to financial markets – hollowed out communities while enriching a global oligarchy." After the USSR's collapse, neoliberalism went on overdrive and consumed the globe under the dogma that There Is No Alternative (TINA). Neoliberalism's grip on the global political economy led to the crisis of 2008. And yet, as a morbid symptom of neoliberalism's parasitic attachment to a system it had already hollowed out, TINA came back with a vengeance after the crisis. Every failure became justification for deeper entrenchment. What Hemingway observed as a temporal arc has morphed into a structural condition: neoliberalism doesn't just collapse; it institutionalizes collapse as a means of survival (Crouch, 2011; Fraser, 2022).

The culture wars fueled by fetishized identity politics and grotesque inequalities (frequently involving literal privileges, derived from blatant corruption) are a combustible mix. Turchin (2023) calls it a "wealth pump" powered by a mixture of "popular immiseration and elite overproduction." The last time this happened was when the first round of laissez-faire liberalism failed and led to the World Wars in Eurasia, when identity politics, extreme corruption, inequality and zero-sum logic combined to produce trenches, tanks and hundreds of millions dead. This is what first engendered Keynesianism. The NeoFailure of NeoLiberalism is unlikely to differ from the first Failure of Laissez-faire Liberalism.

The Myth of Eternal Economic Growth—Part 2

Since the dawn of the Anglo-American-led industrial revolutions two-and-a-half centuries ago, the world's GDP has skyrocketed. The aggregate supply of food, water, shelter and every other human commodity, from base requirements to sexual pleasure and luxury goods, has increased exponentially. Regimes, particularly thalassocratic ones, have risen and fallen the world over in variously doomed efforts to enact their own versions of 1776. Inside of 250 years, a mere blip in human history, let alone geological history, our numbers look like a schoolkid's hyperbolic graph: we have gone from less than a billion to approaching ten. This unprecedented growth has come at a severe cost. Now, the oceans are filled with our waste, the forests, jungles, rivers and mountains are the last besieged and befallen habitats for wildlife, and ever more biodiversity is extinguished with more species going extinct every day. All by itself, this environmental devastation should have been a wake-up call for the zero-sum character of liberal economic expansion.

Although the myth of eternal economic growth has nonetheless endured, cracks in its facade have started multiplying ever since 2008. More than just another economic downturn in the predictable history of financial crises caused by speculation, the Global Financial Crisis (GFC) of 2008 was an indictment of the entire mythology of eternal economic growth. Quite fittingly, just as private banks worldwide were writing down their holdings of subprime related securities and mortgages, the very first international academic conference on *Degrowth*(ism) convened on

18–19 April in Paris. Had the contamination of the global financial industry been confined to the legalized speculative practices of banks, the damage could have been contained. But like the Crash of 1929, the 2008 Crisis wasn't limited to finance and instead exposed the hubris of the growth paradigm itself (Susskind, 2024, p. 137).

The fact that hundreds of millions of individuals and families across scores of nations lost their homes and livelihoods due to economic forces beyond their control and were then told it was due to their own choices was only part of the story. The fallout from 2008's Big Short arrived differently in different parts of the world. One thing was common though: middle classes evaporated, a few saw their wealth explode while millions became impoverished and homeless. 2008 was a global suction pump which vacuumed the wealth of the lower and middle classes into the offshore bank accounts of the ruling classes—all in the name of austerity, fiscal responsibility and job creation.

In the US, the crisis was followed by a familiar script for those at the bottom: individual victim-blaming, eviction, re-/dispossession and jail for the poorest. But it was also followed by unprecedented measures for those at the top. In 2010, the Fed voted on quantitative easing, essentially producing free money and giving it to the wealthiest banks considered too big to fail in the wake of 2008. The decision was not without its critics. Richard Fisher, the Dallas Fed president, expressed serious reservations: "I see considerable risk in conducting policy with the consequence of transferring income from the poor, those most dependent on fixed income, and the saver, to the rich" (Leonard, 2021). But he wasn't the only one. Clearly, there was considerable debate within the smoke-filled unanimity of the Fed's deliberations, where some members tacitly recognized that the price to be paid for free money for the rich would be borne by the poor either immediately or in the future.

In the EU, entire sets of countries where millions of previously middle-class citizens paid taxes were effectively debt-imprisoned. The European South bore the brunt and was simultaneously slandered with the acronym PIGS (Portugal, Italy, Greece, Spain—sometimes with Catholic Ireland thrown in for good measure), echoing familiar tactics of dehumanizing the victims of exploitation in an effort to justify said exploitation (Boucher, 2019; van Vossole, 2016). Greece especially, a small country of around 11 million, was made into a scapegoated, drawn-and-quartered national example of debt peonage overnight, effectively becoming, in financial journalist Michael Lewis' words (2011), "*The New Third World*." This turn of events brought to many people's minds ideas about debt colonialism like the quote commonly misattributed to John Adams: "There are two ways to conquer and enslave a nation. One is by sword. The other is by debt." The fact that the misquote first appeared in 2002 is perhaps telling about the euro's expansion and the EU's monetary policy between 2001 and 2008. As few heterodox economists had warned, sovereign debt in some EU countries was becoming unsustainable already in the early 2000s (Popik, 2009; Vergopoulos, 2005).

While many European nations struggled, core Eurozone countries and especially Germany seemed to fare much better, actually profiting from the crisis.

As economist Milton Ezrati argues (2018), the euro's design mostly benefited Germany while holding other European economies back. Germany's focus on efficiency also widened economic gaps, with its pricing advantage, already at 6% when it adopted the euro, doubling to 12% by 2017, according to IMF reports. The initial structural imbalance was made even worse with the financial crisis, which increased Germany's export advantages globally by devaluing the euro all the while disincentivizing investment in austerity-ridden countries. "The German economy, most especially the German elite, has done very well for itself because of the union and the euro, not a little of it at the expense of the rest of Europe," Ezrati notes.

Much like the GFC divided the EU in winners and losers, reputed benefactors and scapegoats, the "Old Third World", the more heavily populated countries of Latin America, Africa and Asia, experienced a bifurcation in its wake. Some countries successfully converted their political economies into tax havens for the Davos-doting global elite. Panama, Bermuda, the Cayman Islands and Singapore are prime examples of this transformation. According to the political scientist Hall (2023), most other nations faced increased instability, leading to the Arab Spring, more Sub-Saharan African civil warfare, the flourishing of Latin American drug cartels and, lastly, increasing authoritarianism in the up-and-coming BRICS countries with the biggest populations.

As the 2010s continued to pass, economists gradually acknowledged once more that economic growth benefits the wealthy few—the theoretical trickle down effect does not materialize in practice. The realization wasn't new; it had been noted in the 1980s by economists like Thurow (1981), Magdoff and Sweezy (1987), but was largely overlooked. By the second decade of the twenty-first century, market neoliberalization clearly produced results opposite to the promised ones. Rather than fostering competition and growth, it reduced market freedom and expansion and created oligopolies and oligarchies.

The failure of neoliberalization to deliver on its promises is particularly evident in the food and drink market—perhaps the most relatable example given its direct impact on daily life. As Stacy Mitchell, executive director of the Institute for Local Self-Reliance, writes in the *New York Times*, major retailers' control over suppliers undermines competition and distorts the whole food system. This dominance has resulted in the collapse of smaller grocery businesses, reduced food access in some areas and increased industry consolidation. At the same time, it negatively impacted farmers' earnings, created supply chain vulnerabilities and raised food prices for consumers (Howard, 2021; Mitchell, 2023). In other words, neoliberalization engendered a zero-sum configuration against producers, small businesses and consumers to the sole benefit of large corporations.

Another false promise of neoliberalism that masked, distorted and/or deflected its zero-sum nature through ideology is linked to the notion of competitiveness promoted by institutions like the IMF. Much touted as a panacea, the IMF's—and McKinsey's—approach rests on the zero-sum equation "decreased labor costs = increased competitiveness" (Bogdanich & Forsythe, 2022; Stiglitz, 2024). It is export-oriented, seeking to make a national economy more competitive in the global market simply by way of cheaper products and services. Quality standards and working conditions are left out of the equation. Both the domestic and transnational rationales of IMF adjustment programs do not contribute to market growth. There are no considerations for win–win outcomes or larger economic pies. It's just a race to the bottom: A rat race between employees, pushed to accept ever lower wages to take a set—or, in some cases, decreasing—number of jobs; and a rat race between state economies, with those willing to sell cheaper taking a bigger share in a fixed market at the zero-sum expense of other states—little different from the eighteenth-century "beggar-thy-neighbor" policies warned against by Adam Smith.

Although it became clear already in the Asian crises of the late '90s that IMF policies and McKinsey proposals make problems worse, the post-2008 era saw a doubling-down on this emphasis on global competitiveness. This has accelerated trends of cutting labor costs, offshoring manufacturing and taxing, reducing corporate taxes and worsening working conditions at home. It has also given rise to the "New Taylorism" or "Digital Taylorism" exemplified in Amazon and other retail warehouses, where surveillance is coupled with machine-like performance requirements, with employees pressured to relieve themselves in bags and bottles to preserve their employment (Gautié et al., 2020; Fuchs et al., 2021; Kassem, 2023, pp. 67–79; Salame, 2018). As part of the same trend, companies even manipulate job titles to avoid paying overtime, further exploiting workers in the name of efficiency and competitiveness (Cohen et al., 2023).

The zero-sum nature of current growth-related policies is also evident in the approach to redistribution. Despite the proclamations to the contrary, the ruling-class idea is that there's a largely zero-sum economic pie, and the more it's redistributed, the more zero-sum it gets. As the economist Mankiw (2021) notes, "Policymakers want to maximize the economic pie while slicing it equally. But these goals often conflict. As policymakers attempt to rectify the market's outcome by equalizing the slices, the pie tends to shrink." This familiar perspective functions to justify policies that favor the wealthy, cautioning that attempts to redistribute wealth will inevitably lead to economic contraction. Such thinking has contributed to a situation where, as even the Editorial Board (2023) of the multi-millionaire-dynasty-owned *New York Times* remarks, "Rather than collecting taxes from the wealthy, the government is paying the wealthy to borrow their money," thereby amplifying wealth disparities and adding to state debt. The ruling-class idea of a largely zero-sum economic pie thus acts as a self-fulfilling prophecy, with redistribution efforts viewed as inherently detrimental to overall economic health, "predistribution" policies largely unthinkable and zero-sum parasitic partnerships between government and big business completely normalized (Mazzucato, 2020, pp. 167–168).

Perhaps nothing was associated more with the myth of eternal economic growth of the neoliberal era than the project of globalization, which promised prosperity for all without redistribution. In reality though, the 2008 crisis was dealt with in most Western countries by means of upward redistribution without much critique analogous to the discourse on the alleged disincentivizing function of downward redistribution. This built on earlier neoliberal habits: "For decades, America delivered economic development subsidies without strings attached. Wall Street–fueled private corporations were first in line for those gifts, and they hoarded them" (Dayen, 2023). While the dominant response to 2008 reinforced this kind of upward redistribution and state-business cohabitation, globalization began to unravel after the Crash, picking up steam on the back of the Trump administration's mercantilist policies and the contraction of global trade during the COVID pandemic. Even if, for liberal commentators like Draper (2023), the "zero-sum brand of politics" that gave rise to Trumpism go back to 1990s Republican tactics, right-wing populism cannot be understood apart from systemic dysfunction and popular disenfranchisement (Berman, 2019; Fitzi, 2018; Millman, 2024). If any of its origins can be definitely traced in the 1990s, it is in the production offshoring and other aspects of globalization heralded by deals such as NAFTA (Rodrik, 2021).

The failures of neoliberal globalization are illuminated precisely by discussions surrounding international trade and labor markets. In a notable exchange between Sanders and Klein (2015), Sanders challenged the notion of open borders as a progressive policy, instead framing it as a "right-wing proposal". The main beneficiaries of globalization have been big corporations rather than local workers or migrants. Sanders argued that the issue "has to do with the greed of corporate America who sold out American workers and essentially moved manufacturing to China and other low-wage countries". The conversation repeatedly approached globalization in zero-sum terms, with Klein questioning if US-China relations are "a zero-sum competition" and Sanders rebuffing the idea that improving Chinese living standards should come "at the expense of the American worker." Sanders firmly reiterated his positions during the controversy surrounding visa exceptions for high-skilled immigrants at the outset of the second Trump administration (Karma, 2025).

Just as free markets in capital and labor, so too for taxation. Biden's treasury secretary Yellen (2021) famously talked about the false promise of a "damaging" and "global race to the bottom on corporate taxation" which has tacitly been accepted since the 1980s. The constant dull throb of tax evasion scandals of self-appointed "Davos men" has resulted in accumulated scoops of papers indicting political and economic dynasts, mafiosos and their oligarchic servants in the global jet-setting class in such explosions as the Panama Papers, Pandora Papers, Paradise Papers, etc.—so much so that an entire internet database has been created to catalog them by the International Consortium of Investigative Journalists (ICIJ, 2025). Accordingly, scholars like Turchin (2023, p. 134) have come to unequivocally conclude that "globalization is wielded by the governing elites to increase their power at the expense of the non-elites. It's another wealth pump that takes from the workers and transfers wealth from the developing world to rich regions."

Thus, economic policies (monetary, fiscal, commercial, etc.) remained decided by bankers and failed to reform after 2008. The only reforms were token measures to forestall widespread working-class unrest: endlessly low interest rates and quantitative easing. Such policies dominated and were defended as technocratic solutions by so-called economic experts, but really bolstered the fortunes of the bankers themselves and their top clients. In his essay "Against Economics," Graeber (2019) discussed how mainstream economic education emphasizes the government's primary role as maintaining price stability and combating inflation. This monetarist approach, popularized in Friedman's 1980s, advocates for limited government intervention beyond money supply management. The approach remains a dominant doctrine, despite post-2008 (largely failed) efforts by central banks to stimulate inflation and productive investment through quantitative easing. In every instance, Friedman's logic that inflation is always caused by too much money chasing too few goods is reprised to justify both austerity and artificially keeping labor markets loose and wages low (without acknowledging that this is also to compete with China).

Failing both, neoliberal propaganda sought to convince the public that the inevitable inflation is *not* the result of corporate price gouging (DePillis, 2022). Yet, talk of anticipated inflation which dominates the debate also reveals the problem: big businesses which artificially inflate their consumer prices in anticipation of inflation cause the very inflation they decry. Like legalized bribery termed lobbying, which requires a conflation of vested political and economic interests, this anticipated inflation is both a cause and a result of price gouging by corporate interests in alliance with their political proxies (Tulip & Bishop, 2017). Thus, the issue of inflation is an illustration of the Manichaean relationship between labor and capital (rich vs poor): whoever gets credit—or blame—for it comes at the expense of the other (Kelley, 2023; Meadway, 2023). By 2023, it became so manifest that the resulting working-class immiseration could no longer be chalked up to fiscal lenience, that even the *Wall Street Journal* acknowledged that inflation was truly caused not by raising wages but predominantly by corporate profiteering and price gouging (Hannon, 2023).

The persistent belief in eternal economic growth has not only perversely affected attitudes towards the distribution of resources but the very source of all resources: Nature. Yet, even though now pretty much every major government and corporation accepts the existence and perils of man-made climate change, the reaction in the direction of averting a move beyond the point of no return can be described as slow and timid at best. This inaction—or often, action in the opposite direction—is partly because of zero-sum competition: governments and corporations won't back off fossil fuel extraction, natural gas fracking and other climate-wrecking economic activities so long as this is a game where they fear missing out while other players may surpass them. This dynamic is little different from the national-imperial competitions for land and gold which resulted in the early-twentieth-century World Wars. The tensions of the late 2010s and the 2020s in the Eastern Mediterranean, involving Libya, Egypt, Israel, Greece, Cyprus and Turkey, are an expression of the fact that the region's offshore oil and natural gas fields have become an arena for competition among great powers and their monopolistic corporations. Meanwhile, climate change is increasingly recognized even by the UN as a zero-sum affair of rich nations at the expense of poor nations, leading to military confrontations across the Global South throughout the 2010s (Borenstein et al., 2022; Bove & Sekeris, 2015; Jordans, 2023).

Alongside climate concerns, Malthusian thinking has resurged, reviving overpopulation and famine anxieties along with sustainability ideas. As it happens, the Obama administration fused the fashion for sustainability with neo-Malthusian one-child policies in official research, while "liberals" of that era would openly champion neo-Malthusianism in the 2020s (Bradshaw & Brook, 2014; Bradshaw et al., 2021; Henderson, 2024). Even Paul Ehrlich's works, particularly *The Population Bomb*, were repopularized after 2008. "If I were a gambler," Ehrlich wrote in the 1970s, "I would take even money that England will not exist in the year 2000 and give ten to one that the life of the average Briton would be of distinctly lower quality than it is today" (Gardner, 2023). While the former gamble was ill-advised, the latter was largely accurate, so his takings would still be good (Helmore, 2021). Such are the critiques of beliefs in economic growth for its own sake that have lately given rise to the activist movements for "Degrowth" and "Extinction Rebellion" (Naudé, 2023). Mann (2018) interpreted this scaremongering over overpopulation into a diachronic ideological war between the forces of "prophets" seeking to ring the alarm bells of the problems of overpopulation against "wizards" seeking to ring the liberty bells of solutions for overpopulation. The zero-sum presuppositions of finite earthly resources were never seriously questioned.

In short, the growth mythology promised we could infinitely expand GDP without exhausting finite resources. Yet, the bleak reality that is increasingly coming into view is dominated by zero-sum transfers, and indeed not only spatial (the Global South ransacked for Global North consumption) but also temporal (future generations robbed for present profits). Just as 2008 revealed economic "growth" was wealth transfer from the poor to the rich, ecological collapse shows that growth was resource transfer from the future to the present. The same competitiveness doctrine that forces workers to accept lower wages compels nations to strip-mine their environments to stay "competitive." Climate change brings this into sharp relief: rich nations have enjoyed centuries of carbon-fueled growth, then when the bill comes due, poor nations pay through droughts, floods, famines (and green-washing lecturing by the rich). The growth myth's trickery was that we could create value from nothing, that unregulated markets would generate new wealth but stop short of merely extracting or moving it around. In reality, every dollar of GDP growth has involved either extraction from workers (through wage suppression), from other nations (through "competitiveness"), from the earth itself (through resource depletion) or from future generations (through debt). The ruling class uses complexity to obscure these transfers, but they are always there—there's always someone, somewhere, at some point who pays.

Thus, no escape appeared from the zero-sum logic of "the economy" as a finite household—that in order for the economy to grow or for a sector to improve there have to be cuts elsewhere. By promoting a belief in market superiority and turning public welfare into budgetary liabilities, the neoliberal paradigm since the 1980s has sidelined ESCRs (Economic, Social and Cultural Rights), transforming these rights from "material entitlements" to "formal guarantees" (Berrada, 2022, p. 64).

In 2015, the American Economic Policy Institute concluded: "Wage stagnation for the vast majority was not created by abstract economic trends. Rather, wages were suppressed by policy choices made on behalf of those with the most income, wealth and power" (Mishel et al., 2015). But the dire reality of zero-sum transfers in favor of the wealthy and the powerful is not an easy story to sell. Things are quite different, though, when the road to ESCRs is atomized and commodified, while wealth and poverty are naturalized as mere results of personal responsibility.

Social Darwinism Part 2: Meritocracy

Some ideas evolve from serious proposals to objects of satire as their flaws increasingly become apparent. Others go in the opposite direction. Meritocracy gained prominence as satire in Michael Young's 1958 dystopian book *The Rise of the Meritocracy* and transformed into a serious ideology later, coinciding with the rise of neoliberalism in the late '70s (Littler, 2017). This reversal is in line with the sweeping shift in social values under neoliberalism. It also reminds us that historical movement is not always linear; societies can adopt ideas that were once considered absurd, particularly if these are promoted top-down to justify power structures. Just as the "bootstraps" self-made success story began as a nineteenth-century caricature and morphed into a serious ideal in the early twentieth century to suit the vested interests of the wealthy and powerful, meritocracy has become the dominant justification for inequality in the early twenty-first century, perpetuating the zero-sum status quo that favors those already privileged (Markovits, 2019a, 2019b).

In the wake of 2008's GFC, ŽiŽek (2009, p. 51) aptly described how ideology often functions: "nobody takes democracy or justice seriously, we are all aware of their corrupted nature, but we participate in them, we display our belief in them, because we assume that they work even if we do not believe in them." Similar to democracy or justice, meritocracy is a widely touted belief system within liberal democracies that is little more than a new form of Social Darwinism. Like its predecessor, meritocracy justifies social hierarchies through seemingly objective criteria, in this case individual merit rather than genetic fitness. But after 2008's Big Short, the jury retreated when the question was raised: does the discourse of meritocracy reflect the socioeconomic reality on the ground or just serve to underpin a morality play for the privileged?

This seemingly fair system operates on a fundamentally zero-sum premise: for every winner, there must be losers, as it creates a finite "pie" of success. For Markovits (2019a, p. ix), meritocracy prevents the very social mobility it claims to uphold by exclusivizing education. It simultaneously blames the losers for their failure, although, "even when everyone plays by the rules, only the rich can win." Education, once viewed as the great equalizer, has become a principal battleground of meritocratic competition. Elite universities, transformed into businesses profiting from student debt, proudly advertise their low acceptance rates and serve as gatekeepers to opportunity by manufacturing exclusivity as their main product.

Simultaneously, neoliberal higher education promotes a type of studies geared toward that competition, with little real interest in the common good, its greatest utility lying in the perpetuation of market worship. Thus, higher education now produces workers fluent in market logic but illiterate in social responsibility (Giroux, 2014, p. 13).

In this hypercompetitive environment, students are pitted against each other for a limited number of spots, with the winners gaining access to privileged networks and career opportunities, while the losers are left with mounting debt and diminished prospects (Lampert, 2012). Scandals surrounding the zero-sum implications of rigged admissions and scoops like the 2019 Varsity Blues exposé are just the tip of the iceberg (Golden & Burke, 2019; Smith, 2019). And even them are indicative of the lack of accountability that accompanies neoliberal meritocracy, as, in the rare instances when such schemes are revealed, sentences are either extremely lenient or those convicted can easily pay their way out (Taylor, 2019). Meanwhile, parents are forced to collude with a system which implicates them in pressuring their children to compete ever harder in a zero-sum game of merit that sickens, exhausts and impoverishes both parents and their increasingly younger children (Bianchi, 2011; Miller, 2024).

The higher education system has devolved into little more than a degree industry, from barely-accredited "diploma mills" at the bottom to the Ivy League on top, each offering their "educations" as formal tickets to already foreclosed domains. Colleges maintain the facade of meritocracy while actually functioning as nodes in a broader "CV industry." High-status jobs in corporate, legal and government sectors are offered to the well-off and the well-connected to help them create a shiny resumé that is then leveraged to secure even more prestigious jobs and accumulate socioeconomic capital. Professional politicians, increasingly functioning like "professional managers" appointed by special interests rather than public servants, are prime examples (Livingstone et al., 2021, p. 51). Hillary Clinton's appointment as US Secretary of State allowed her to subsequently pose as the most qualified candidate for the presidency. Similarly, Kamala Harris, who failed to gain traction and dropped out from the 2020 primaries, was appointed as Biden's VP in 2020 and then anointed as the party's 2024 presidential candidate. J. D. Vance's transformation from calling Trump "cultural heroine" to his VP in 2024 ran through stints in Yale Law School and a venture capital firm while cashing in on his matriarchs' accumulated pain in his *Hillbilly Elegy*. In these and many other cases in the era of neoliberalism, politicians were the choices of special interests and party establishments, but their manufactured CV credentials allowed their nominations for various positions in the executive branch to appear as the results of merit.

In this context, diversity initiatives serve more as marketing than meaningful structural change. As journalist Kang (2022) has aptly put it, "schools themselves [...] have turned college admissions into a brutal, zero-sum game in which each minority applicant must also double as a racial statistic" (cf. Fattal, 2022). While the model of artificial scarcity and the tremendous imbalance of funds for administration and shareholders versus lecturers and students remain unchallenged, this is a convenient tokenistic strategy that doubles as marketing for the schools' supposed progressivism and social responsibility. Affirmative action also served to obfuscate that too many Ivy League students are admitted due to family connections with the university (donations, alumnus status, etc.) or family wealth that allowed them to prepare for college admission since early childhood and outcompete most members of the very groups that affirmative action allegedly cared for. *The Economist* (2022) has noted that "43% of white students admitted to Harvard enjoy some kind of non-academic admissions preference," and advised a "less socially divisive system based on income." This would in any case disproportionally help minority children because of their family's low income. However, as even the neoliberal commentator Brooks (2023) puts it, "Elite institutions have become so politically progressive in part because the people in them want to feel good about themselves as they take part in systems that exclude and reject." This weaponization of identity within competitive admissions processes essentially reflects a broader pattern in how meritocracy operates. Though it may deploy newfangled frameworks, it seeks to preserve hierarchies, pitting individuals and identity groups against each other.

As elite universities have transformed into "credentialing institutions" of meritocracy, they don't educate students so much as certify them, providing a limited number of credentials that open the doors to the most privileged positions while maintaining the facade of meritocracy (Koganzon, 2023, p. 53). Their graduates then go on to monopolize the best jobs and create technologies that add to the gap between top earners and everyone else (Markovits, 2019a, p. 27). The result is an extreme winner-take-all dynamic in the labor market, which spills over to social stratification. The middle class, once the backbone of many Western economies, and particularly of the United States, is rapidly shrinking, as the benefits of meritocratic policies are increasingly accruing to a small elite at the expense of the majority. The central promise of meritocracy—that hard work will be rewarded—often comes up empty in a system where connections, prestige and elite education matter much more than actual skills or effort.

Turchin (2023, pp. 149–155) explicitly equates "ideas of Social Darwinism and what we would now call market fundamentalism," pushed by elites intent on retaining and expanding their advantage at the expense of the subaltern. Much like the original Social Darwinism, these ideas are pseudo-scientific at best, meant to provide a technical veneer for self-interest. In reality, there is no correlation between wealth and merit. Some economists like John Kenneth Galbraith have long warned against the "specious association of money and intelligence", as we saw in Chap. 5—and a recent study shows that average intelligence among the rich is the same as among the poor, or even less (Keuschnigg et al., 2023; Kuper, 2023). This is particularly striking if one takes into account the significant impact that poverty—and its repercussions such as bad nutrition or the stress of always being on edge to make ends meet—has on intelligence (al-Shargie et al., 2024; Dean et al., 2019; Desmond, 2023; Dickerson & Popli, 2016; Mani et al., 2013). But it is the condition of poverty that puts a strain on cognitive function and not diminished cognitive ability that leads to poverty. In fact, the main driver for economic success or failure is whether individuals are set in environments of abundance or scarcity (Ruggeri et al., 2022, 2023).

Yet for commentators like Lowrey (2023a, 2023b), the starkest questions bear the starkest answers: "Why do so many Americans live in poverty? Because so many rich people benefit from it." And from the perspective of analyst Appiah (2018), "a significant portion of what we call the American white working class has been persuaded that, in some sense, they do not deserve the opportunities that have been denied to them." Yesterday's middle classes, trained to believe in the ultimate righteousness of capital, have become today's proletarians and are often the most ardent defenders of the status quo. Ironically, the more meritocracy is shown to be a false god, the more its worshippers sacrifice themselves at its altar, as "income inequality and belief in meritocracy go hand in hand" (Mijs, 2021).

One of the main causes for this is America's cultural values that champion individual responsibility for success and failure. A pervasive if often implicit belief persists that it is some sort of cosmic justice that bestows riches upon the worthy while condemning the unworthy to destitution (Reich, 2022a, 2022b). For instance, David Kelly, the chief global strategist at J. P. Morgan Asset Management, cautions that "it's not a matter of just taxing the wealth of the richest and handing it out to everybody else. … The real question is not 'why are the rich rich?' or what to do about that. It is 'why are the poor poor?' and what to do about that" (Smith & Russell, 2023). This is the ultimate distillation of "you've-done-it-to-yourself" individualized victim-blaming (Freeman, 2021). Much like the Poor Laws of the nineteenth-century British empire, libertarianism has informed twenty-first-century American poverty policy through legal structures which force the poor to work for low pay to continue to receive welfare, a situation which is described by its proponents in explicitly zero-sum terms of morality versus growth: "helping people who are truly in need, while also not weakening the broader economy" (Miron, 2011).

This confluence of meritocracy and individualism has pernicious zero-sum effects on society. As the success of the well-to-do and the well-connected few comes at the expense of the many, it creates "stressed societies", i.e. conditions of "acute social abnormality and existential disorientation" like the ones identified in the fascist epoch (Griffin, 2007, p. 269). Such conditions are fertile ground for violence and illness (both mental and physical) as they lead to subjective violence in response to systemic violence and chronic stress, which is a further cause of disease, violence and poor decision-making (constant fight-or-flight mode, IQ reduction). Stressed societies are where extremist movements premised on violence and irrationalism thrive, exacerbating zero-sum dynamics even to the material detriment of their own followers. But the zero-sum social chaos appears inescapable when social Darwinism in the form of meritocracy is tied to a system of political economy naturalized to the point of not allowing for any alternatives.

TINA Strikes Back

After years of undisputed hegemony, the system hailed as the bearer of eternal, increasing prosperity started to unravel. The alleged incremental move forward patently came to a halt. All the calls for market forces to be kept out of the reach of the government were supplanted with calls for the government to intervene to save the pillars of the market which had become "too big to fail". As the inherent contradictions of the system veered into the open with the 2008 GFC, some critics of neoliberalism hoped that it would indeed collapse and give way to something new—or at least to a rebranded version of something old that had worked better for the many, such as Keynesianism. But instead of the dismantling of the myth, what we got was a doubling-down on neoliberalism.

As we saw at the beginning of the chapter, the rule for policy responses to the GFC consisted of transferring wealth upward (QE), forcing workers and nations to undercut each other (competitiveness) and framing any downward redistribution as economically destructive while offering no such critique for upward redistribution—or rather diverting from the fact that such a redistribution was even taking place. This is because the narratives of eternal economic growth were always a myth: The objective was not to generate win–win growth but rather to obscure zero-sum transfers through complexity and ideology (and the saturation of public discourse with economistic jargon helped with that by producing noise rather than clarity). When 2008 caused fractures to the myth, policymakers didn't attempt to restore positive-sum dynamics but doubled down on zero-sum extraction, revealing what was always the game. The competitiveness doctrine particularly damns the growth mythology: if the latter was true, nations wouldn't need to cannibalize each other's wages. The fact that post-crisis "recovery" meant intensifying beggar-thy-neighbor policies proves that the point was never to expand the pie—just to redistribute it upward through wage suppression, offshore tax havens and financial engineering.

But how can we understand the resilience of TINA after 2008? This is more than the preservation of the grim zero-sum reality hidden underneath the euphoric myth of eternal growth. Just as we thought we were witnessing the death throes of TINA, its specter struck back with the ferocity that only myths which have taken on a life of their own can achieve. In its global diffusion and naturalization as the only possible system of political economy, neoliberalism has transformed even its most abject failures into arguments for its necessity—a result of its practice of marketizing the entirety of society to preserve market economy.

TINA's detachment from reality seemed to enhance rather than diminish its power, suggesting that we were witnessing not merely the persistence of an economic doctrine but the manifestation of something more akin to religious zealotry. Like a religious doctrine facing disconfirmation, TINA deployed typical belief-preservation mechanisms identified in Festinger et al. classic *When Prophecy Fails* (1956, pp. 4, 126). It met perfectly the five conditions the study outlined as necessary for increased fervor after disconfirmation. The first (deep conviction and action relevance) could be evinced in the fact that market fundamentalism had become deeply embedded in policy, education and culture, shaping the behavior of politicians, educators and the public. The second (commitment through action) was reflected in how entire institutions and careers were built on—and identified with—neoliberal principles, often in ways hard to reverse. Third came the clear contradiction to the specific promise of market efficiency and self-regulation (amenability to unequivocal disconfirmation) and fourth the impossibility to ignore the contradiction due to the scale of the crash (occurrence of unequivocal disconfirmation). Finally, the extensive network of think tanks, academic departments, media outlets and so on provided crucial social support for maintaining belief despite evidence (availability of social support following disconfirmation). This extensive network in fact made it possible to promote TINA to the public, reflecting Festinger et al.'s emphasis on proselytizing following disconfirmation.

This religious dynamic manifested in two interconnected defensive mechanisms based on cognitive dissonance (Harmon-Jones, 2019; Jenkins, 2013). One was the reframing of the crisis itself: the problem, believers insisted, was not too much neoliberalism but too little of it. This doubling-down logic turned market failures into arguments for further marketization, much like medieval doctors might prescribe more bloodletting when the first round failed to cure the patient. Simultaneously, believers engaged in systematic blame displacement. Narratives of blame were manufactured and disseminated by politicians and corporate/oligarch-owned media that presented the crisis as the result of (a) a zero-sum game of parasitic foreigners within and outside the borders at the expense of the national body and/or (b) a zero-sum game of parasitic socialism, welfarism or statism at the expense of free markets, healthy entrepreneurship and fiscal responsibility.

The welfare state emerged as one of TINA's main targets. Naturally so, as collective responsibility, universal protections and investments in public welfare stood in direct contradiction to the neoliberal worship of individualism and market supremacy. Yet, instead of through an outright attack, the welfare state was taken apart piecemeal, its dismantling often framed as necessary reforms to "save" or "modernize" it. Cuts and privatization were the primary means of these so-called reforms, and those who pursued them did not hesitate to portray themselves as saviors of the welfare state through means-testing, exclusions, and austerity measures. They thereby contaminated the welfare state with the TINA faith, embedding market logic into its institutions and policies. Characteristically, they normalized the practice of outsourcing services and provisions and thus made welfare yet another conduit for the transfer of public funds to the private sector ("privatization through the back door"). By presenting these changes as natural inevitabilities, as necessary adjustments of a relic of a foregone era to modern conditions, rather than as political choices serving specific interests, they misidentified modernization with neoliberalization and promoted the maxim that There Is No Alternative to reshaping the welfare state into a mechanism for market discipline and private profit. In this way, the welfare state was hollowed out, its collective ethos replaced by a logic of individual responsibility and market efficiency, while austerity (i.e. upward redistribution of wealth) was wrapped in "common-sense", zero-sum terms. The result is an obscene inversion: a welfare state that serves less and less as a protection against the most destructive aspects of market forces but as their extension, reinforcing the hegemony, the self-evidence, of TINA (Farnsworth & Irving, 2018; Loxbo, 2022; Perocco & della Puppa, 2023; Sahdan & Gregorius, 2023).

Building on the same logic that presents inequality as meritocratic justice, politicians and media framed poverty as a moral failing. The 2014 reality series *Benefits Street* is an illustrative case, as the show became a propaganda arm for this ideology in the UK. *Benefits Street* did not merely reflect existing prejudices but actively produced neoliberal "commonsense" that assumed a direct link between welfare dependency and personal responsibility rather than structural inequality or other difficulties beyond people's control (e.g. health issues) (Jensen, 2014). Its sensationalized portrayal of welfare recipients mirrored Conservative rhetoric about "skivers vs strivers" while aligning perfectly with neoliberal reforms like Iain Duncan Smith's Universal Credit (Dean, 2012; Valentine & Harris, 2014; Wiggan, 2012; Williams, 2013). The show's manufactured outrage provided Conservative MPs with ammunition for political theater in the House of Commons. Philip Davies, infamous for his filibustering antics (Stone, 2016), staged a performance of faux-populist outrage, posing as the voice of hardworking taxpayers while questioning Duncan Smith:

> Have you managed to watch programmes like *Benefits Street* and *On Benefits and Proud*? If so, have you, like me, been struck by the number of people on there who manage to combine complaining about welfare reforms whilst being able to afford being able to buy copious amounts of cigarettes, have lots of tattoos done, watch Sky TV on the obligatory wide-screen television? Do you understand the concerns and irritations of many of the people who go out to work every day, pay their taxes, who cannot afford those kinds of luxuries themselves? (McTague, 2014)

This choreographed exchange allowed Duncan Smith to play his part, presenting predecided benefit cuts as a righteous response to public demand: "We will keep the policy under review but the one thing we should celebrate is we are reforming welfare to ensure those who need the money get it, and those who don't make sure they go back to work" (McTague, 2014). This cynical circus—Davies pretending to pressure a minister who was already eager to cut benefits, both citing a show designed to profit from "poverty porn" and public knee-jerk reactions that would justify those very cuts—is a prime example of how the media and politicians have worked in tandem to manufacture consent for austerity, furthering a zero-sum framework that pitted "hardworking families" against "welfare queens" (Feltwell et al., 2017; Macdonald et al., 2014). It was straight out of the same playbook used by Margaret Thatcher in the 1980s, Benjamin Disraeli in the 1880s and Joseph Priestley in the 1780s. In the United States, the same zero-sum logic manifested itself in Matt Gaetz' dichotomy (following Reagan's logic) of "couch potatoes over hard-working Americans" (Noah, 2023). It was no surprise that by 2016, these discourses of Duncan Smith and Gaetz coincided with the elections of their policy preferences in Brexit and Trump.

Privatization mania, a natural extension of TINA's victory, found its natural habitat in this ideological climate. As long as even nominally left-wing political forces bought into TINA and sold it to their followers, private companies—particularly those operating natural monopolies such as energy grids and transportation systems—continued to profit at the public's expense. The moralization of economic relations provided cover for an accelerated wave of privatization, even as the failure of neoliberalism became increasingly palpable. Despite privatization delivering neither efficiency nor better service—let alone the cheaper options for the citizen-customer that Thatcher, Reagan and their disciples worldwide had promised—the process only intensified. From energy grids to public transport, from healthcare to education, everything was marked for sale. The logic was circular: neoliberal governments would underfund and run public services down, then cite inefficient public services to justify privatization. Subsequently, private companies would create artificial scarcity, continue underfunding infrastructure and hike prices to maximize profits. Privatization would thus, predictably, deliver the opposite results, but TINA would allow it to continue unabated.

The moment a challenger to TINA arose, private companies would adapt to undermine the case for public ownership. For example, when faced with the prospect of a Corbyn-led Labour government in the 2019 UK elections, whose manifesto included renationalization of key public utilities, water companies launched extensive public relations campaigns to highlight the supposed benefits of privatization, among other things by spinning bill reductions mandated by the regulator (Ofwat) as evidence of their efficiency and customer focus. They engaged in lobbying efforts to influence policymakers and the public, arguing that nationalization would be costly and disruptive. Simultaneously, they sought to deflect criticism of their record (excessive executive pay and dividend payouts, environmental ruination, rising bills) by emphasizing their investments in infrastructure and ecological initiatives (Lea, 2019; Ofwat, 2019). Despite these claims, though, the state (i.e. taxpayers) continued to shoulder significant costs for infrastructure maintenance and environmental remediation, in yet another iteration of the familiar zero-sum scenario of privatized profits and socialized risks. And once the threat of a Corbyn government passed, the familiar zero-sum game of profit maximization and underinvestment in (or cannibalization of) public goods resumed; business as usual indeed (Corfe, 2022; Horton, 2024; Smith, 2024; Williams & Mustoe, 2024).

It is especially evocative of TINA's obfuscating character that it is so often applied to the commodification of the commons. Yet, the process of commodification is by definition zero-sum because it subjects public goods and services to market competition and corporate profit maximization (Palley, 2022; Spicker, 2024). This often means that for one entity (typically a private corporation) to gain, another (often local communities or consumers) must lose. When health or education becomes highly commodified, those who can afford to pay more get better services, while those who cannot afford these increasingly higher expenses get worse services or none at all (Perry et al., 2024; Viana & Silva, 2018). Thus, the gains of few (corporate profits) come at the direct loss of many (reduced access and quality for lower-income individuals), constituting a zero-sum transfer of value from the public to the private sector and from the bottom to the top (Bayliss et al., 2021; Goodair & Reeves, 2024). Moreover, the intensification of market forces in traditionally non-market areas often diverts resources away from public welfare toward private accumulation, creating a self-perpetuating cycle of public losses and private gains. This, of course, exacerbates inequalities and shifts a society's focus from collective well-being to individual or corporate profit, further entrenching the zero-sum game where the success of the few comes at the disadvantage of the many.

TINA's religious character thus extends beyond defensive mechanisms: through economic and financial policy after the predictable crash, a belief turned into what the sociologist Merton (1948) defined as a "self-fulfilling prophecy." When governments chose to bail out banks while imposing austerity on populations (including by privatizing public services), central banks provided unlimited liquidity to financial markets while public services were cut, big financial criminals were not prosecuted while millions of ordinary citizens were punished to lose their houses, jobs and livelihoods and accept declines in their living standards, their health (physical and mental) and their hopes for the future, these policies actively created conditions that made alternatives hard to even imagine (Chwieroth & Walter, 2022; McKee et al., 2012; Rex, 2019). Like a prophecy that comes true because believers act in ways to ensure its fulfillment, TINA's adherents in positions of power implemented policies that foreclosed other possibilities. The "too big to fail" doctrine, for instance, didn't just *describe* reality—in fact, it contradicted the professed foundations of free-market ideology—but *prescribed* actions that made financial institutions even bigger and more essential to the system's functioning. Post-2008 policy choices did not just fail to solve the problem but actually hardwired it into the system, making its future repetition inevitable and the pursuit of similar policies when that happens almost inescapable. It's like an obscene paraphrasis of Samuel Beckett's famous dictum: "Fail Again. Fail worse."

Nowhere were these defense mechanisms, along with the transformation of belief into self-fulfilling prophecy, more evident than in Greece. Internally, blame was directed at multiple "others": the Keynesian "heresy" of 1980s PASOK rather than the neoliberal "orthodoxy" that followed; immigrants and refugees who supposedly drained state resources; and the usual suspects of "lazy" public sector workers and "tax-evading" self-employed professionals and small businesses. This internal blame-game created a feedback loop with a rising Far Right and the nominally center-right New Democracy's increasingly xenophobic rhetoric about "illegal migrants" while promoting the militarization and fetishization of the border (Tsimouris, 2015). At the European federal level, Greece itself became the ultimate scapegoat, embodying the "profligate" South that threatened the stability of the "prudent" North. This narrative conveniently ignored how Northern European banks and businesses had profited from Greek debt and how the Eurozone's structural imbalances had exacerbated the crisis (De Grauwe & Ji, 2018; Lapavitsas et al., 2010), leading even German neoliberal scholars Rocholl and Stahmer (2016) to proclaim: "It is reasonable to assume that the public debate would have taken a different direction if losses had been borne by Germany and France right away, making it more difficult in public sentiment to seek responsibility in Greece alone" (p. 17). But the ethics of debt transformed an economic crisis into a morality play, with Greece cast as the sinner—much has been said in this context about the double meaning of the German word *Schuld* as both debt and guilt/sin—who needed punishment through austerity (Graeber, 2011, p. 77; Hasan et al., 2024; Kloeckner, 2020).

The perversion of "European solidarity" during the Greek crisis eerily echoed religious inquisitions of the past. Just as the Inquisition claimed to "save souls" through bodily torture and punishment, European institutions and politicians from the Union's core countries spoke of "solidarity" while imposing devastating austerity. The public posturing and language of Troika functionaries and like-minded EU politicians was tellingly similar: Greece needed to be "purified" through suffering, "reformed" through structural adjustment, "saved" through the destruction of its social fabric. Bailouts came with conditions that resembled penitence rituals: public confessions of fiscal sin, acceptance of external monitoring, prescribed acts of economic self-flagellation. But then again the vicious circle of self-fulfilling prophecy emerged. When austerity measures shrank the economy, the resulting decline in tax revenues was not treated as the predictable outcome of these policies but as evidence of Greece's continuing fiscal sinfulness, requiring even harsher measures. When fire-sale privatizations failed to generate predicted revenues, this was presented not as a flaw in the policy but as proof that Greece needed to privatize more assets at even lower prices—indeed, to transfer all state property to a fund essentially controlled by the Troika (Vlachogiannis, 2019). This cycle of punishment and prophecy reached its apotheosis in the notorious multiplier miscalculation. The IMF later admitted it had severely underestimated austerity's negative impact on growth, but this confession of technical error did nothing to change the prescribed penitence. The "extend-and-pretend" approach to Greek debt continued, with each new bailout supposedly putting Greece on a path to sustainability while actually making its debt burden less sustainable (Gordon et al., 2013; International Monetary Fund, 2017; Lennard, 2013; Mody, 2015; Morris, 2015; The Toc Team, 2013; Varoufakis, 2023). Yet, this obvious contradiction only strengthened the conviction that Greece needed more of the same medicine—the failure of the treatment perversely becoming the justification for its intensified continuation. Like all fundamentalist religious beliefs, TINA keeps finding ways to reinterpret or ignore reality when reality contradicts the belief.

This framework of political theology and economy produced its own ideal subject: *homo neoliberalus*, the individual believer who internalizes market logic as moral or transhistorical truth. Just as religious devotees may interpret personal setbacks as tests of faith, *homo neoliberalus* views market failures as evidence of insufficient devotion to market principles. Hence why policies that objectively harm most people's interests—from austerity to privatization—can still command popular support. The believer interprets economic suffering not as systemic failure but as personal inadequacy or, worse, as punishment for deviating from market orthodoxy. The commodification of everything and the politics of division work not just through institutional force but through willing participation of subjects who have learned to see market "solutions" as sacred and collective alternatives as heretical (Blakeley, 2021; Hamann, 2009; Ramey, 2015; Read, 2022; Teo, 2018). And so, underneath the most secular economic ideology lies another religious zero-sum understanding of economic affairs—just as from within the most modern political economy there re-emerges an ancient zero-sum system of economic arrangements.

Neo-Feudalism: Highway to Serfdom

Refeudalization, new feudalization, neo-feudalism, technofeudalism... Whichever term is used, a growing number of scholars and commentators are acknowledging a fundamental change in the dominant system of political economy after 2008. Throughout its history, capitalism has experienced many transformations and different variants (e.g. merchant, industrial, ordoliberal etc.). Having been unshackled in its neoliberal variant, which intensified after the GFC, capitalism is increasingly being hybridized with hyper-modern features that are eerily reminiscent of the pre-industrial past (Kotkin, 2020).

An emblematic feature of this old-but-new system is its treatment of land. Land is increasingly accumulated in fewer hands as the primary store of value and source of rent extraction. There is a profound shift from profits from producing theoretically non-finite goods to rents from controlling access to practically finite resources. The most visible manifestation of this shift is the 2020s housing crisis. As existing real estate is scooped up by the wealthy, housing stock is depleted and governments beholden to neoliberal dogma refuse to subsidize or undertake housing construction, more and more low-income people can't afford to rent (let alone to buy) a house. As a result, homelessness hit record-high rates in the mid-2020s (Frost, 2024; Herre & Arriagada, 2024; Horowitz et al., 2023; Kamp & Najmabadi, 2023). Given the intensified sacralization of property and profanation of human life under neoliberalism—and, subsequently, neofeudalism—it is perfectly acceptable to have millions of vacant properties owned by absentee landlords as stores of value while millions of people go homeless. During the pandemic, some mega-rich conservatives like Charles Koch even channeled money to both legal fights against eviction moratoria and real estate investments (Perez & Sirota, 2021).

Given the gravity of the problem, the housing crisis has become the focal point of many researchers and commentators. The zero-sum nature of the housing status quo is illustrated already in the online ad for a collection of essays by *The Atlantic*'s Jerusalem Demsas: "local democracies have become coconspirators in the anti-development aspirations of the very few, at the hefty expense of the many" (Zando, 2025). In one essay, Demsas (2022) critiques "shortage denialism" and "supply skepticism" as false narratives which allow people to avoid addressing difficult issues like NIMBYism (Not In My Back Yard) and construction costs, while pointing out the contradiction in voter demands for affordable housing without new construction. In another essay, she claims that local zoning policies frequently hinder affordable housing development, as public sentiment in favor of addressing homelessness and housing costs clashes with individual interests like parking and views. As Demsas (2023) notes, though, "Everyone has a little NIMBY in them. It doesn't have to be the part that wins."

The zero-sum nature of the housing crisis is not confined to the attempts at preserving current neighborhoods at the expense of broader housing accessibility. Another aspect is hedge funds (including pension funds) buying houses, speculating prices up and turning most people into renters (Dezember, 2021). For most twenty-first-century prospective homeowners, the American Dream seems likely to remain just that: a dream. This trend in real estate prices is also partly behind the generational clash between Baby Boomers and Millennials. More than an ordinary generational conflict, what we are witnessing in the 2010s and 2020s appears to be an ever-expanding ideological rift driven by ever-increasing material discrepancies. It is not just conformism, the predilection of old age for order or pure nostalgia for the "good old days" that makes boomers support reactionary politicians who call themselves conservatives or promise "retrotopias" (Bauman, 2017). It is also because they are the last generation containing a mass of homeowners. They thus usually have limited sympathy for the redistributive policies that would benefit Millennials—and Zoomers (Kolomatsky, 2021). And it is no surprise that they often have very little sympathy for younger folks striving to buy a house when boomers find themselves sitting atop properties whose value is going up without them having to do anything; nor that it is among them that one usually finds the most fervent advocates of neoliberalism (or neofeudalism).

This is the central question: if the inaccessible cost of housing is an expression of the finitude of land ownership, then how is the early-21st-c. landlords-dominated housing market any different from 18–19th-c. (or 8–9th-c.) feudalism? For housing scholars like Myers et al. (2021), the inaccessibility and unaffordability of land (and house) ownership has become the central fact causing the deterioration of democracy, and all other zero-sum structural problems downstream from that. Relying on Piketty's idea of a "housing theory of everything", they also account for the growing generational divide, with young people struggling to afford homes and start families while older generations benefit from property value increases (which obviously fosters resentment and zero-sum thinking). As neo-feudalism progressively engulfs the world, the rentierization of housing is mirrored in several other countries, like Australia (Ryan-Collins & Murray, 2021).

Schemes like the EU's Golden Visa are similarly impacting the housing market, adding to the trend of transforming a vital consumer product into a rent-seeking asset. The scheme merely sets a minimum investment threshold, defined separately by each member state, but does not differentiate between productive investments and purchases of real estate. As a result, scores of wealthy individuals from outside the EU have opted for buying up rental property, mostly in the tourism-driven economies of the South. Rather than contributing to the collective wellbeing of those member states' citizens, they only extract rents, creating much larger mid- or long-term wealth outflows than the initial inflows. Rent-seeking investments also tend to have minimal multiplying effects, and thus do not do much to boost the local economy indirectly (Bocková, 2023; Foremny et al., 2025; Holleran, 2021; Mendes, 2021).

The situation is similar when it comes to agricultural land. Many billionaires, like Thomas Peterffy, have scooped up U.S. farmland as a store of value, but Bill Gates stands out as he has become the country's biggest farmland owner. Ironically, RFK Jr, among others, points out how Gates has amassed huge stretches of land in multiple federal states, in a bid to control not just finite land but also agricultural production along with food and climate policy—domestically but also globally (Estes, 2021; Kennedy, 2021; Lee, 2021; Meigs, 2021). These kinds of tactics demonstrate how land ownership increasingly translates to all sorts of political power. Simultaneously, they can only exacerbate inequality in rural communities, as farmland prices keep rising and younger farmers are finding it increasingly difficult to own land (Minter, 2022; Schafer, 2021). Meanwhile, there have been verified reports in some states that the rate of absentee landlords is rising (Prairie-Farmer, 2022). Wealthy investors, bankers, tech CEOs and speculative developers are also obtaining vast tracts of land in the US in order to rent it out to tenant farmers, quickly rendering the entire situation in the US, in the words of Tennessee agricultural consultant Nathaniel Bankhead, akin to "digital feudalism," where the rich, who buy up the finite land and pay tenants to work it, "lock that person to this new flavor of serfdom where you might be decently paid, you've got access to it, but it will never be yours" (Qiu, 2022). And yet, their farm acquisition practices and the mobilization of PR perversely allow billionaires to pose as philanthro-capitalists who care about ecology and agricultural sustainability while creating "a modern-day feudal system, gussied up for Instagram" (Dunn, 2022).

Things are not that different in other parts of the world. Farmland-centered refeudalization (especially by Cargill) has actually been most pronounced in Latin America. Particularly in the country where neoliberalism was first tested at scale, Chile, the process was observed already in the 2000s, providing further hints about the causal relationship between neoliberalism and neofeudalism (Murray, 2006; Oxfam, 2013). It is now becoming evident in countries like Canada, while in the EU the problem is exacerbated by the rigging of its farm subsidies scheme, which often ends up benefitting corrupt oligarchs, local clientelistic networks, mafias and illiberal politicians (Apuzzo, 2020; Atlas, 2021; Boffey, 2021; Gebrekidan et al., 2019; Magnan & Desmarais, 2023; Reuters, 2025; Wax, 2021).

Physical and digital commons both have their own histories of enclosures. Quasi-feudal land arrangements are an inherent tendency in neoliberalism, caused by the drive to privatize and commodify everything, including all public land—the tragedy of the commons. Enclosures, the very symbol of the inception of the system of capitalism, are becoming the means for its return to the system that preceded it (Christophers, 2018). Digital space too is increasingly commodified, privatized and utilized in a zero-sum way for rent extraction while tech overlords are shifting from one domain to the other, hoarding rent-extracting wealth in both. Similarly, the zero-sum jungle morals of the AI gold rush are driven largely by manufactured precarity and Manichaean preferences between ownership or slavery: "even more important in Silicon Valley than a messianic belief in AI is a terrible fear of missing out" (Wong, 2024). For the commentator Bridle (2023a, 2023b), AI-generated content represents a modern form of primitive accumulation, where tech giants expropriate collective human endeavor for their own profit. These companies have monetized personal aspects of life and effectively "enclosed our imaginations" like historical land enclosures. Despite promises of expanding human experience, knowledge and connectivity, they're now commodifying our own ideas as machine products. In the process, the AI industry is growing into a massive bubble that coincides with speculative cryptocurrency bubbles, repeating familiar historical patterns.

This started much earlier, as the internet congealed into a specific economy in its own right in the early twenty-first century and data became its lifeblood. The datafication of the internet economy (and private markets of terabytes worth of data) directly led to the rise of big tech, dot.com bubbles and the movement of the sector of services to the sector of data. The once worst-off are now integrated into the economic system since they don't need to "consume" physical goods and products anymore. That images, spectacles and commodity fetishes are the new goods was highlighted as early as the 1960s, but it has become unavoidable ever since (Debord, 1967). Whereas the worker once did a job to pay his debts to his employer, the business baron (in the form of time) or landlord/bank (in the form of rent/mortgage), now, as time and space—like liberty or security—have been commodified/gamified and privatized, chasing data is the new gold—only better, since it's theoretically an infinite resource (Caparini, 2006; Loader, 1999). Ultimately, that data and platform rents are the revenues of the tech age demonstrates the theory of digital feudalism (Braithwaite, 2000; Evans, 2018; López Godoy, 2024).

While refeudalization became apparent in the oligopolization of traditional big business markets after 2008 (big pharma, big energy, big real estate, big banks, big chemical, big agribusiness, big media, big alcohol, etc.), it was driven by the privatization and oligopolization of big tech (Dean, 2020). The shift had already begun to reveal itself in the aftermath of the 1998 federal antitrust trial against Microsoft. Milton Friedman predicted in 1999: "From now on the computer industry, which has been very fortunate in that it has been relatively free of government intrusion, will experience a continuous increase in government regulation" (Crovitz, 2013). Like Friedman's other predictions, it hasn't come true. Instead, it simply allowed a small number of competitors into a tight market which then contracted into a handful of megacorporations controlling a world increasingly alienated and depressed by infotainment and addicted to the smartphone-driven attention economy (Burton, 2023; Spencer, 2018). After 1998, as Bill Gates lost more market share to other feudal tech lords, he increasingly became the biggest landowner in the US. And he hasn't been the only tech billionaire aiming at vast landholdings. The oligarchs controlling the physical commons are often the same controlling the digital commons, sinking both rural and urban workers alike into debt peonage (Bedford, 2021; Ratliff, 2015; Warner, 2013). It is thus instructive that publications and writers long known for their market fetishisms have acknowledged their limits. The Economist (2016) and *ProMarket*'s Chicago business professor

Rolnik (2016) admit that neoliberal profitability has become little more than speculative rent-seeking extraction and exploitation. Even Irwin (2019), the apologist for winner-take-all neoliberalism, acknowledges that corporate consolidation reveals a stunning zero-sum mindset: "In thinking about the rise of winner-take-all effects in the corporate world, [...] we need to separate the broad shifts in the economics of an industry from pernicious deployment of corporate power."

The works of four economists, Mariana Mazzucato, Joseph Stiglitz, Daniel Susskind and Yanis Varoufakis, on big tech oligopolies clarified the nature of the transformation from neoliberalism to technofeudalism. Mazzucato (2020, p. 197) explained digital predatory capitalism: "The problem is they have increasingly used this power to extract what I have called 'algorithmic rents' in a modern capitalist system that looks more like 'digital feudalism' – the ability to manipulate what people see and what they want." Stiglitz (2024) gave a bird's-eye view of how neoliberal beliefs in "free markets" actually consumed themselves by constraining freedom to only those who controlled the markets: the biggest tech titans. Susskind (2024, pp. 158–167) demonstrated that the same titans who worship innovation and growth prevent it by oligopolizing and hoarding intellectual property at the zero-sum expense of everyone else—and their own long-term futures (hence doomsday bunkers). It resulted in Varoufakis' synthesis on *technofeudalism* (2023) and more fodder for critiques and tweaks of technofeudalism (Gane, 2024; Morozov, 2022; Napoleoni, 2024).

While the tech industry is leading the charge, a major neo-feudal trait of the economy across the board in recent decades has been the obscene concentration of wealth. The world's top five billionaires doubled their wealth between 2020 and 2023 while five billion people saw theirs decline (Oxfam, 2024; Riddell et al., 2024), and then, in late 2025, the stage was set for Elon Musk to become the first trillionaire (Lauria, 2025). As wealth leads to more wealth (and power), the promise of socioeconomic mobility falls flat. There is an ever more rigid social stratification that directly translates to power or lack thereof. As Krugman (2020) writes, "America is less of a democracy and more of an oligarchy than we like to think." Similarly, Turchin (2023) portrays America as a plutocracy where politicians, judges and entire elections are simply traded like baseball cards among oligarchs—and the economic statistics support him. Goldman (2021) argues that "America has a ruling class," while others are speaking about the "birth of a new American aristocracy" and the need to examine the problem of "America's oligarchs" rather than facilely talking solely about oligarchs in countries that are America's enemies (BBC, 2014; Gilens & Page, 2014; Osnos, 2022; Persson & Sundell, 2024; Stewart, 2018). This is what oligarchy has always been about, argues Kelton (2020, pp. 226–227): "Many of our firms are now feudal economic fiefdoms, in which a small group of wealthy owners give orders to-and extract value from-the labor of vast numbers of everyday Americans."

Like feudal lords, big businesses have their own domains of absolute authority. These are not only explicitly codified through international free-trade agreements (private law) or financial deregulation (private money) but also implicitly accepted:

corporations have their own sets of laws and they enforce them through their political power and their armies of attorneys and PR consultants. Even if they routinely break common law, good luck bringing them to justice. According to former US federal prosecutor Pelletier (2021),

> Practically everyone knows, on some level, that the rich get better treatment than the poor. But I saw it so clearly: The wealthy live in a different legal reality entirely, one in which blatant financial fraud routinely goes unpunished. For the poor, even the merest transgression can lead to ruined lives. This problem has always existed, but it has gotten worse – far worse – in recent years.

The rich can influence the law through lobbying but they can also bypass it, having their lawyers and accountants use loopholes and elaborate tax evasion schemes to continue hoarding (Collins, 2021; Kaiser-Schatzlein, 2021; Pistor, 2019).

In their pioneering 2020 essay "The Rise of Neo-Feudalism", legal scholar Katherine Stone and journalist Robert Kuttner recount multiple cases where exclusive domains of private law have been created. One is in the financial derivatives market, which has been largely self-regulated since its inception in the 1980s by the International Swaps and Derivatives Association (ISDA) rather than government agencies. For Stone and Kuttner (2020), "this is neo-feudalism, par excellence. The democratic state plays no role whatever, except to bless the privatized realm of law." During the housing bubble, a private entity called Mortgage Electronic Registration Systems (MERS) was frequently listed on U.S. mortgages, circumventing public recording fees. This system's flaws became apparent during the subprime crisis when MERS made dubious claims on mortgages or improperly reassigned them. The company designated numerous low-ranking employees to sign questionable documents, which were then used in countless foreclosure cases. Despite some judicial challenges, as Stone and Kuttner (2020) detail, most of these foreclosures proceeded, with very real consequences for indebted homeowners. "The industry's creation of a proprietary fiefdom of law – a private property records system created with no public debate or legislative approval – was richly rewarded. MERS still exists." "Another emblematic case of neo-feudalism" is detected by Stone and Kuttner (2020) in the practice of compulsory arbitration, which shifts disputes from public courts to private systems. This change, relying on reinterpretations of the Federal Arbitration Act (FAA), has eroded consumer and worker rights that were gained in previous decades. The Supreme Court's 2011 decision to allow bans on class actions in arbitration further disadvantages individuals with small claims. This way, the Supreme Court effectively shields corporations from accountability for minor but widespread infractions.

Such decisions are no coincidence, though: Across the political spectrum, from academic researchers to media commentators to elected officials, there's growing recognition that Washington operates under the influence of big money (Brennan Center for Justice, 2025; Eisenbrey, 2012; Pew Research, 2023; Whitehouse & Stinnett, 2017). This applies to all branches of government, effectively suspending the much-touted system of checks and balances: there is no separation of powers when the executive, the legislative and the judicial power are captured by the same ultrarich individuals and corporations. While previously this process seemed to mostly involve politicians, the Supreme Court of the United States became a focal point of power capture in the 2020s (Greenhouse, 2023; Harrington, 2023; van Sickle & Eder, 2023).

The public dissatisfaction with the status quo which brought Brexit and Trump in 2016 also revered and reviled the new tech monopolists that made it possible, in what journalists began to increasingly call a "new gilded age" for the sheer level of inequality and open corruption between Washington and "Silicon Valley as a Giant Fiefdom." As the monopolies created their own laws, bought up or beggared their competitors and/or avoided public regulation and oversight, "companies such as Google, Apple, and Amazon have invented their own jurisprudence, hidden in obscure terms of service, to govern the consent of users to the commercial use of personal data" (Stone & Kuttner, 2020). It wasn't long before men like Musk, Branson and Bezos switched their business models from innovating to renting, "becoming neo-feudal barons of the nation's expanding industrial infrastructure and reaping the financial rewards" (Savage, 2021).

During the Obama years, so long as they could expand their attention-economy businesses worldwide, big tech companies were happy to play a big part in the American culture wars (guns, abortion, etc.). By 2016, as tech lords were faced with the first Trump presidency, wringing their hands at his rhetoric while licking their chops at his tax cuts and trying to assuage his histrionics, historians, economists, journalists and sociologists increasingly sounded dire warnings about a growing digital form of neofeudalism especially in the realms of tax, labor and class (Kellner, 2021; Suarez-Villa, 2012). Ever since, American tax policy has, especially in the financial and tech sectors "become so skewed in favor of the wealthy, at the expense of just about everyone else" (Drucker & Hakim, 2021). The creation of tech dynasties is made possible through legal instruments called GRATs (like taxless trusts for heirs) (Paulden, 2021). Ultimately, labor pays the price for capital automation, or in the words of Susskind (2024, p. 211), "The US tax regime has created a very strong incentive for employers faced with the choice between a human being and an equally productive machine to choose the latter—in part because it comes with a lower tax attached." This can be seen clearly in stories about Amazon employees being forced to pee in water bottles, so odiously representative that even the *Wall Street Journal* grimaces with the vernacularization of the term "Bezosism" referring to the man's demeaning of his own labor force (Mims, 2021).

At the same time, such neo-feudal lords are seeking to entrench neo-potlatch dependence on trickle-down charity (Maxey, 2021). "Philanthrocapitalists", the ultrarich who openly combine philanthropy with market ideology and praxis, portray themselves as benevolent lords solving problems for their subjects, in a reflection of classic feudal patronage structures. Simultaneously, they position themselves as more efficient than governments at solving social problems, reinforcing the drive for a "minimal state", i.e. a state that is absent for everyday people but ever-present for themselves, being "too-big-to-fail" as they are. Although it is the exploitation of the majority by the ultrawealthy and their relentless push for the unravelling of the welfare state that make philanthropic intervention necessary, this can all be obscured behind PR campaigns. Philanthrocapitalism is thus moving us further into neofeudalism, as material inequality is coupled with the idea that the subaltern should be thankful to their neofeudal overlords for what they give, oblivious of what they take (Caldas, 2021; Haydon et al., 2021; Hites, 2019; McGoey, 2021). In another instance of wealth allowing the manufacturing of complexity to reproduce itself, philanthropy is even deployed as a tactic to bypass insider trading prosecutions. Stockholders with apparent inside knowledge dump stocks that are about to lose value by donating them to charities and then claim tax deductions for their price at the time of the donation—or even backdate their donations to claim even larger deductions (Avci et al., 2021).

While oligarchs engage in Potlatch philanthropy to legitimize their position at the top of the meritocratic pyramid, they pursue the other side of Potlatch to augment their status: competition amongst themselves. Every other multi-billionaire today engages in well-advertised, vainglorious projects like private, for-profit space travel while a whole host of extremely rich individuals have turned superyachts into competitive displays of conspicuous consumption. As Krugman (2023a) puts it: "Rarely in the course of modern history has so much wealth been concentrated in the hands of so few, yet much of that wealth is being expended on zero-sum games of one-upmanship."

The pervasive flaunting of philanthropy coupled with overexploitative and undignified treatment of employees is another sign of restratification along two main classes: lords and serfs. The erstwhile large middle class which was hailed as a defining feature of liberal democracies is eroding (Buchholz, 2023; Kochhar & Sechopoulos, 2022). Next to the two new main classes, reappears a third, complementary class, which, according to the historian Patrick Whyman, has been a common feature in steeply hierarchical societies throughout history. This is the gentry class, whose members serve as local elites distinct from the highest political and economic echelons. This class, often hereditary, has varied in its roles and relationships to power, from Roman civic elites to medieval European landowners to the American South's planter class. The modern American gentry, while allowing some social mobility, is also largely hereditary. They inherit significant assets and maintain their status through property ownership and generational wealth. But the ideology of meritocracy conceals this: "Equating wealth, especially generational wealth, with virtue and ability is a deeply American pathology. This country loves to believe that people get what they deserve, despite the abundant evidence to the contrary. Nowhere is this more obviously untrue than with our gentry class" (Wyman, 2021).

Some academics are part of this class. In general, academics are 25 times likelier to have parents with a PhD, 50 times if employed in what we've called the leading "credentialing institutions of meritocracy." As stated in the study that demonstrates this, their privileged background "is likely to deeply shape their scholarship and their reproduction" (Morgan et al., 2022). Given the frequent correlation of wealth rather than merit with these credentials, it is little wonder that many academics are part of the "clerisy," another relevant term that Kotkin (2020, pp. 49–72) uses to describe those who legitimize the neofeudal arrangement through ideological work. Even if they do not come from wealth, academics may sometimes acquire it precisely by running cover for big business (Coy, 2024). It is probably no coincidence that the "progressive" complement of TINA, i.e. hand-wringing identity politics, is largely a product of US academia. Meanwhile, most younger academics are subjected to a regime of precarity and dependence that amounts to little more than "academic serfdom" (Mikhailova, 2020).

The fixation on capturing and exploiting finite wealth, as opposed to the liberal promises of growth, is paired with a burgeoning trend towards distributive rather than creative activities, i.e. zero-sum competition in non-productive domains such as legal and PR services for corporations (Reich, 2022a, 2022b; Turner, 2018). Many of these are what Graeber has termed *Bullshit Jobs* (2018), defining them as an integral component of "managerial feudalism." Academics who engage in refeudalization apologia are part of this managerial feudalism, as much as they are members of the gentry and the clerisy. And so are bosses of the Bank of England who claimed the reason for inflation is greedy workers as opposed to greedy corporations and called for "restraint in pay bargaining, otherwise it will get out of control" (Partington, 2022).

According to the chief BOE economist, Huw Pill, the UK was facing an inflationary cycle in 2022 fueled by widespread resistance to accepting reduced spending power. As various groups attempted to maintain their economic status, costs were continually passed on. While there is some truth in that, Pill tries to frame greedflation and justified labor demands after more than a decade of austerity as two sides of the same zero-sum coin. On the contrary, if only corporations for once took the brunt of this economic downturn by accepting some losses—as workers and consumers are so readily asked to do—instead of seeking to maintain their profit margins—or even expand them on the back of another disaster capitalism scenario—inflation could be brought under control. Pill's statements are indicative of his role in the Bank of England, which is there to protect the interests of the well-off masquerading them as the national interest—hence his wording that "we're *all* worse off, and we *all* have to take *our share*, to [not] try and pass that cost on to one of our *compatriots*" (emphasis added). By suggesting that the renewed labor militancy and industrial action in the UK in 2022–2023 was a zero-sum game against the rest of society, Pill was subtly but surely employing a usual tactic of deflection from the ghastly zero-sum game played for decades by those whose interests he represents (Authers, 2023). Other economists like Krugman (2023b) identified the tactic and criticized his use of the "classic wage-price-spiral story."

In terms of labor and class, increasing analysts see generational overtones at work amidst "a zero-sum struggle between a swollen retired population and the overburdened young" (Douthat, 2023). Yet the privileged few heirs can look forward to "a neo-feudal dystopia" through the massive inheritances of "the great wealth transfer" sparking a "millennial civil war," since, of course, "for labor's share of income to rise, capital's must fall" (Eisen & Tergesen, 2021; Levitz,

2021). As Susskind (2024, p. 213) wrote, "It should come as no surprise when technological progress is biased toward substituting, rather than complementing, workers… [that] social narratives and norms appear to be strengthening, rather than weakening, the tradeoff between growth and a healthy labor market." One Berkeley law professor wrote: "The rich understand that maintaining their absolute and relative position as a minority elite requires a low rate of upward mobility [… demonstrating] the zero-sum logic of class conflict" (Krishnamurthy, 2021). And another described the way 21st-c. American imperial elitism has evolved into a system little different from 19th-c. British imperial elitism:

> These politicians were bred to be leaders, you see, and having to gouge some votes out of the hayseeds back home requires a bit of performance art now and then, a small price to pay so that the sons and daughters of Harvard and Yale, Princeton and Stanford, can live in the imperial capital and rule as is their due and their right. (Nichols, 2023)

Ultimately, the individualistic failure of digital markets which generated technofeudalism made obsolete the very social mobility it promised to liberate (Panferova et al., 2024).

Low socioeconomic mobility for most combined with the accumulation of finite resources for the very few creates a situation where hereditary privilege rules. The journalist Cohan (2023) claims that corporate America embraces dynastic succession, as evidenced by Lachlan Murdoch's defense of Fox News following the Dominion settlement. This is also seen in other family-controlled companies like Comcast and Paramount Global but often leads to subpar decision-making and financial performance. The dual-class stock structure amplifies the issue, as it gives families disproportionate voting power, in contrast with the century-old concept of professional management, which is supposed to create objectivity and accountability through a board of directors. While imperfect, Cohan argues, this system has proven more effective in generating long-term wealth than family-controlled enterprises. Yet, we would argue that this is not paradoxical, as the point is not optimal wealth creation but its zero-sum concentration through the impoverishment of others and the legitimization of the will of the family heir as the main arbiter. The era of dynasties is back.

References

Appiah, K. A. (2018, October 19). The myth of meritocracy: Who really gets what they deserve? *The Guardian*. https://www.theguardian.com/news/2018/oct/19/the-myth-of-meritocracy-who-really-gets-what-they-deserve

al-Shargie, F., Taresh, S. M., & Al-Ezzi, A. (2024). Mental stress and cognitive deficits management. *Brain Sciences*, *14*(4), Article 4. https://doi.org/10.3390/brainsci14040316

Apuzzo, M. (2020, January 23). E.U. farm chief pledges to tackle corruption in subsidy program. *The New York Times*. https://www.nytimes.com/2020/01/23/world/europe/farm-subsidies-corruption.html

Atlas, M. (2021, May 24). MEPs target Babis and Orban over EU farm funds. *Prague Business Journal*. https://praguebusinessjournal.com/meps-target-babis-and-orban-over-eu-farm-funds/
Authers, J. (2023, April 26). *How not to sell burden-sharing to fight inflation*. Bloomberg. https://www.bloomberg.com/opinion/articles/2023-04-26/uk-inflation-boe-s-chief-economist-fails-find-the-right-words
Avci, S. B., Schipani, C. A., Seyhun, H. N., & Verstein, A. (2021). Insider giving. *Duke Law Journal, 71*(3), 619–700.
Bauman, Z. (2017). *Retrotopia*. Polity.
Bayliss, K., Mattioli, G., & Steinberger, J. (2021). Inequality, poverty and the privatization of essential services: A 'systems of provision' study of water, energy and local buses in the UK. *Competition & Change, 25*(3–4), 478–500. https://doi.org/10.1177/1024529420964933
BBC. (2014, April 17). Study: US is an oligarchy, not a democracy. *BBC News*. https://www.bbc.com/news/blogs-echochambers-27074746
Bedord, L. (2021, September 27). *Tillable, Compeer Financial partner to offer digital finance for farmland*. Successful Farming. https://www.agriculture.com/tillable-compeer-financial-partner-to-offer-digital-finance-for-farmland
Berman, S. (2019). Populism is a symptom rather than a cause: Democratic disconnect, the decline of the center-left, and the rise of populism in Western Europe. *Polity, 51*(4), 654–667.
Berrada, M. (2022, December). Demanding what is rightfully theirs: The link between social justice protests and economic, cultural, and social rights. *Deusto Journal of Human Rights, 10*, 55–75. https://doi.org/10.18543/djhr.2621
Bianchi, S. M. (2011). Family change and time allocation in American families. *The Annals of the American Academy of Political and Social Science, 638*(1), 21–44. https://doi.org/10.1177/0002716211413731
Blakeley, G. (2021, January 22). How neoliberalism created a society of individuals. *Tribune*. https://tribunemag.co.uk/2021/01/how-neoliberalism-created-a-society-of-individuals
Bocková, L. (2023). Golden visas and golden passports policy crisis in the European Union. *The Journal of Cross-Regional Dialogues/La Revue de Dialogues Inter-Régionaux*. https://doi.org/10.25518/2593-9483.292
Boffey, D. (2021, June 25). Environmental claims of new EU farm subsidy policy are questioned. *The Guardian*. https://www.theguardian.com/environment/2021/jun/25/environmental-claims-of-new-eu-farm-subsidy-policy-are-questioned
Bogdanich, W., & Forsythe, M. (2022). *When McKinsey comes to town: The hidden influence of the world's most powerful Consulting firm*. Knopf Doubleday
Borenstein, S., Magdy, S., & Jordans, F. (2022, November 20). UN climate deal: Calamity cash, but no new emissions cuts. *Associated Press*. https://apnews.com/article/united-nations-john-kerry-climate-and-environment
Boucher, D. (2019). Reclaiming history: Dehumanization and the failure of decolonization. *International Journal of Social Economics, 46*(11), 1250–1263. https://doi.org/10.1108/IJSE-03-2019-0151
Bove, V., & Sekeris, P. G. (2015, March 5). *Fueling conflict: The role of oil in foreign interventions*. International Peace Institute Global Observatory. https://theglobalobservatory.org/2015/03/civil-wars-oil-above-water-military-intervention
Bradshaw, C. J. A., & Brook, B. W. (2014, November 18). Human population reduction is not a quick fix for environmental problems. *Proceedings of the National Academy of Sciences, 111*(46), 16610–16615. https://doi.org/10.1073/pnas.1410465111
Bradshaw, C. J. A., Ehrlich, P. R., Beattie, A., et al. (2021, January 13). Underestimating the challenges of avoiding a ghastly future. *Frontiers in Conservation Science, 1*, Article 615419. https://doi.org/10.3389/fcosc.2020.615419
Braithwaite, J. (2000). The new regulatory state and the transformation of criminology. *The British Journal of Criminology, 40*(2), 222–238. https://doi.org/10.1093/bjc/40.2.222
Bridle, J. (2023a). *New dark age: Technology and the end of the future*. Verso.
Bridle, J. (2023b, March 16). The stupidity of AI. *The Guardian*. https://www.theguardian.com/technology/2023/mar/16/the-stupidity-of-ai-artificial-intelligence-dall-e-chatgpt

Brennan Center for Justice. (2025). *Influence of big money*. Brennan Center for Justice. https://www.brennancenter.org/issues/reform-money-politics/influence-big-money
Brooks, D. (2023, August 2). What if we're the bad guys here? *The New York Times*. https://www.nytimes.com/2023/08/02/opinion/trump-meritocracy-educated.html
Buchholz, K. (2023, April 21). How America's middle class is shrinking [Infographic]. *Forbes*. https://www.forbes.com/sites/katharinabuchholz/2023/04/21/how-americas-middle-class-is-shrinking-infographic/
Burton, T. I. (2023, June 27). How to escape "the worst possible timeline". *The Atlantic*. https://www.theatlantic.com/ideas/archive/2023/06/doom-pessimism-worst-possible-timeline/674441/
Caldas, J. (2021, October 11). Philanthropy is a scam. *Jacobin*. https://www.jacobinmag.com/2021/10/philanthropy-is-a-scam
Caparini, M. (2006). Applying a security governance perspective to the privatisation of security. In A. Bryden & M. Caparini (Eds.), *Private actors and security governance* (pp. 263–282). LIT Verlag.
Christophers, B. (2018). *The new enclosure: The appropriation of public land in neoliberal Britain*. Verso.
Chwieroth, J. M., & Walter, A. (2022). Neoliberalism and banking crisis bailouts: Distant enemies or warring neighbors? *Public Administration, 100*(3), 600–615. https://doi.org/10.1111/padm.12774
Cohan, W. D. (2023, July 4). No one can stop Rupert Murdoch. That's increasingly a problem. *The New York Times*. https://www.nytimes.com/2023/07/04/opinion/rupert-murdoch-fox-news-dual-class-corporate-governance.html
Cohen, L., Gurun, U., & Özel, N. B. (2023, January). *Too many managers: The strategic use of titles to avoid overtime payments* (National Bureau of Economic Research Working Paper Series, 30826). https://doi.org/10.3386/w30826
Collins, C. (2021). *The wealth hoarders: How billionaires pay millions to hide trillions*. Polity.
Corfe, O. (2022, August 24). *Water companies dumped 1,000 years worth of sewage into Britain's seas in just FIVE YEARS*. Express. https://www.express.co.uk/news/uk/1659927/uk-sewage-water-companies-britain-beaches-spt
Coy, P. (2024, September 20). For economists, defending big business can be big business. *The New York Times*. https://www.nytimes.com/2024/09/20/opinion/economists-conflict-interest-kanter.html
Crouch, C. (2011). *The strange non-death of neoliberalism*. Polity Press.
Crovitz, L. G. (2013, January 28). Silicon Valley's 'suicide impulse'. *Wall Street Journal*. https://www.wsj.com/articles/SB10001424127887323539804578266290231304934
Dayen, D. (2023, May 25). A liberalism that builds power. *The American Prospect*. https://prospect.org/economy/2023-05-25-liberalism-that-builds-power
Dean, E. B., Schilbach, F., & Schofield, H. (2019). Poverty and cognitive function. In C. B. Barrett, M. R. Carter, & J.-P. Chavas (Eds.), *The economics of poverty traps* (pp. 57–118). University of Chicago Press. https://doi.org/10.7208/chicago/9780226574448.001.0001
Dean, H. (2012). The ethical deficit of the United Kingdom's proposed Universal Credit: Pimping the precariat? *The Political Quarterly, 83*(2), 853–859. https://doi.org/10.1111/j.1467-923X.2012.02292.x
Dean, J. (2020, May 12). Neofeudalism: The end of capitalism? *Los Angeles Review of Books*. https://lareviewofbooks.org/article/neofeudalism-the-end-of-capitalism/
Debord, G. (1967). *La société du spectacle*. Buchet/Chastel.
De Grauwe, P., & Ji, Y. (2018). Core-periphery relations in the Eurozone. *The Economists' Voice, 15*(1), 20180027. https://doi.org/10.1515/ev-2018-0027
Demsas, J. (2022, November 23). Housing breaks people's brains. *The Atlantic*. https://www.theatlantic.com/ideas/archive/2022/11/us-housing-supply-shortage-crisis-2022/672240/
Demsas, J. (2023, March 25). Colorado's ingenious idea for solving the housing crisis. *The Atlantic*. https://www.theatlantic.com/magazine/archive/2023/07/local-government-power-nimby-denver/674164/

DePillis, L. (2022, June 3). Is 'greedflation' rewriting economics, or do old rules still apply? *The New York Times*. https://www.nytimes.com/2022/06/03/business/economy/price-gouging-inflation.html

Desmond, M. (2023). *Poverty, by America*. Crown.

Dezember, R. (2021, April 4). If you sell a house these days, the buyer might be a pension fund. *The Wall Street Journal*. https://www.wsj.com/articles/if-you-sell-a-house-these-days-the-buyer-might-be-a-pension-fund-11617544801

Dickerson, A., & Popli, G. K. (2016). Persistent poverty and children's cognitive development: Evidence from the U.K. Millennium Cohort Study. *Journal of the Royal Statistical Society Series A, 179*(2), 535–558. https://doi.org/10.1111/rssa.12128

Douthat, R. (2023, January 21). Five rules for an aging world. *The New York Times*. https://www.nytimes.com/2023/01/21/opinion/aging-climate-change-demographics.html

Draper, R. (2023, January 7). From Gingrich to McCarthy, the roots of governance by chaos. *The New York Times*. https://nyti.ms/3ItbPvp

Drucker, J., & Hakim, D. (2021, September 19). How top accounting firms help their clients sidestep taxes. *The New York Times*. https://www.nytimes.com/2021/09/19/business/accounting-firms-tax-loopholes-government.html

Dunn, E. (2022, June 9). How 'fairy tale' farms are ruining Hudson Hudson Valley agriculture. *The New York Times*. https://www.nytimes.com/2022/06/09/nyregion/hudson-valley-farms.html

Economist. (2016, March 26). The problem with profits. *The Economist*. https://www.economist.com/leaders/2016/03/26/the-problem-with-profits

Economist (2022, November 5). Making a meritocracy. American society is so focused on race that it is blind to class. *The Economist*. https://www.economist.com/leaders/2022/11/02/american-society-is-so-focused-on-race-that-it-is-blind-to-class

Editorial Board (2023, July 5). America is living on borrowed money. *The New York Times*. https://www.nytimes.com/2023/07/05/opinion/debt-crisis.html

Eisen, B., & Tergesen, A. (2021, July 2). Older Americans stockpiled a record $35 trillion. The time has come to give it away. *The Wall Street Journal*. https://www.wsj.com/personal-finance/older-americans-35-trillion-wealth-giving-away-heirs-philanthropy-11625234216

Eisenbrey, R. (2012, September 26). *Rare conservative-progressive agreement: Corporate capture of the government is a bad thing*. Economic Policy Institute. https://www.epi.org/blog/rare-conservative-progressive-agreement/

Estes, N. (2021, April 5). Bill Gates is the biggest private owner of farmland in the United States. Why? *The Guardian*. https://www.theguardian.com/commentisfree/2021/apr/05/bill-gates-climate-crisis-farmland

Evans, M. (2018, March 12). Why data is the most important currency used in commerce today. *Forbes*. https://www.forbes.com/sites/michelleevans1/2018/03/12/why-data-is-the-most-important-currency-used-in-commerce-today

Ezrati, M. (2018, January 23). The German Swindle Built into the Euro. *Forbes*. https://www.forbes.com/sites/miltonezrati/2018/01/23/the-german-swindle-built-into-the-euro

Farnsworth, K., & Irving, Z. (2018). Austerity: Neoliberal dreams come true? *Critical Social Policy, 38*(3), 461–481. https://doi.org/10.1177/0261018318762451

Fattal, I. (2022, November 4). America after affirmative action. *The Atlantic*. https://www.theatlantic.com/newsletters/archive/2022/11/americas-college-admissions-myth/672011/

Feltwell, T., Vines, J., Salt, K., Blythe, M., Kirman, B., Barnett, J., Brooker, P., & Lawson, S. (2017). Counter-discourse activism on social media: The case of challenging "poverty porn" television. *Computer Supported Cooperative Work, 26*(3), 345–385. https://doi.org/10.1007/s10606-017-9275-z

Festinger, L., Riecken, H. W., & Schachter, S. (1956). *When prophecy fails: A social and psychological study of a modern group that predicted the destruction of the world*. HarperTorch.

Fisher, I. (1910). *Introduction to economic science*. Macmillan.

Fitzi, G. (2018). Introduction: Political populism as a symptom of the great transformation of democracy. In G. Fitzi, J. Mackert, & B. S. Turner (Eds.), *Populism and the crisis of democracy, Vol. 2: Politics, social movements and extremism* (pp. 1–8). Routledge.

Foremny, D., Li, Z., Martinez-Toledano, C., & Segu, M. (2025). *Golden Visas and real estate markets* (SSRN Scholarly Paper No. 5347820). Social Science Research Network. https://doi.org/10.2139/ssrn.5347820

Fraser, N. (2022). *Cannibal capitalism: How our system is devouring democracy, care, and the planet—And what we can do about it*. Verso.

Freeman, J. (2021, September 20). Income inequality is often by choice. *The Wall Street Journal*. https://www.wsj.com/articles/income-inequality-is-often-by-choice-11632173182

Frost, R. (2024, February 12). *Record homelessness amid ongoing affordability crisis*. Joint Center for Housing Studies of Harvard University. https://www.jchs.harvard.edu/blog/record-homelessness-amid-ongoing-affordability-crisis

Fuchs, M., Dannenberg, P., & Wiedemann, C. (2021). Big Tech and labour resistance at Amazon. *Science as Culture, 31*(1), 29–43. https://doi.org/10.1080/09505431.2021.1937095

Gane, N. (2024). Capitalism is capitalism, not technofeudalism. *Journal of Classical Sociology, 25*(4), 1–16. https://doi.org/10.1177/1468795X241269293

Gardner, D. (2023, January 7). *What we can learn from Paul Ehrlich*. Substack. https://dgardner.substack.com/p/what-we-can-learn-from-paul-ehrlich

Gautié, J., Jaehrling, K., & Perez, C. (2020). Neo-Taylorism in the digital age: Workplace transformations in French and German retail warehouses. *Relations Industrielles/Industrial Relations, 75*(4), 774–795. https://doi.org/10.7202/1074564ar

Gebrekidan, S., Apuzzo, M., & Novak, B. (2019, November 3). The money farmers: How oligarchs and populists milk the E.U. for millions. *The New York Times*. https://www.nytimes.com/2019/11/03/world/europe/eu-farm-subsidy-hungary.html

Gilens, M., & Page, B. (2014). Testing theories of American politics: Elites, interest groups, and average citizens. *Perspectives on Politics, 12*(3), 564–581. https://doi.org/10.1017/S1537592714001595

Giroux, H. A. (2014). *Neoliberalism's war on higher education*. Haymarket Books.

Golden, D., & Burke D. (2019, October 8). *An unseen victim of the college admissions scandal: The high school tennis champion aced out by a billionaire family*. ProPublica. https://www.propublica.org/article/an-unseen-victim-of-the-college-admissions-scandal-the-high-school-tennis-champion-aced-out-by-a-billionaires-family

Goldman, S. (2021, March 30). America has a ruling class. *The New York Times*. https://nyti.ms/2PjLE1c

Goodair, B., & Reeves, A. (2024). The effect of health-care privatisation on the quality of care. *The Lancet Public Health, 9*(3), e199–e206. https://doi.org/10.1016/S2468-2667(24)00003-3

Gordon, J., Karpowicz, I., Lanau, S., Manning, J., McGrew, W., Nozaki, M., & Shamloo, M. (2013). *Greece: Ex post evaluation of exceptional access under the 2010 stand-by arrangement* (No. 13/156; IMF Country Report). International Monetary Fund. https://elibrary.imf.org/openurl?genre=journal&issn=1934-7685&volume=2013&issue=156

Graeber, D. (2011). *Debt: The first 5,000 years*. Melville House.

Graeber, D. (2018). *Bullshit jobs: A theory*. Penguin.

Graeber, D. (2019, December 5). *Against economics*. The New York Review of Books. https://www.nybooks.com/articles/2019/12/05/against-economics

Greenhouse, L. (2023, July 9). Look at what John Roberts and his court have wrought over 18 years. *The New York Times*. https://www.nytimes.com/2023/07/09/opinion/supreme-court-conservative-agenda.html

Griffin, R. (2007). *Modernism and fascism. The sense of a beginning under Mussolini and Hitler*. Palgrave Macmillan.

Hall, S. G. F. (2023). *The authoritarian international: Tracing how authoritarian regimes learn in the post-Soviet space*. Cambridge University Press.

Hamann, T. H. (2009). Neoliberalism, governmentality, and ethics. *Foucault Studies, 6*, 37–59. https://doi.org/10.22439/fs.v0i0.2471

Hannon, P. (2023, May 2). Why is inflation so sticky? It could be corporate profits. *The Wall Street Journal*. https://www.wsj.com/articles/why-is-inflation-so-sticky-it-could-be-corporate-profits-

Harmon-Jones, E. (Ed.). (2019). *Cognitive dissonance: Reexamining a pivotal theory in psychology* (2nd ed.). American Psychological Association.
Harrington, B. (2023, May 7). Mob justice. *The Atlantic.* https://www.theatlantic.com/ideas/archive/2023/05/clarence-thomas-supreme-court-ethics-neil-gorsuch-john-roberts/673967/
Hasan, I., Noth, F., & Kiesel, K. (2024). 'And forgive us our debts': Christian moralities and over-indebtedness. *Journal of Financial Research,* 1–19. https://doi.org/10.1111/jfir.12436
Haydon, S., Jung, T., & Russell, S. (2021). 'You've Been Framed': A critical review of academic discourse on philanthrocapitalism. *International Journal of Management Reviews, 23*(3), 353–375. https://doi.org/10.1111/ijmr.12255
Helmore, E. (2021, July 25). Yep, it's bleak, says expert who tested 1970s end-of-the-world prediction. *The Guardian.* https://www.theguardian.com/environment/2021/jul/25/gaya-herrington-mit-study-the-limits-to-growth
Henderson, D. (2024, January 11). *How Malthus got it wrong.* The Hoover Institution. https://www.hoover.org/research/how-malthus-got-it-wrong
Herre, B., & Arriagada, P. (2024). *Homelessness.* Our World in Data. https://ourworldindata.org/homelessness
Hites, S. (2019). Between social duty and the greed of giving: On philanthrocapitalism and gift-patriotism. *Comparative Literature Studies, 56*(3), 469–486. https://doi.org/10.5325/complitstudies.56.3.0469
Holleran, M. (2021). Buying up the semi-periphery: Spain's economy of 'Golden Visas.' *Ethnos, 86*(4), 730–749. https://doi.org/10.1080/00141844.2019.1687548
Horowitz, A., Hatchett, C., & Staveski, A. (2023, August 22). *How housing costs drive levels of homelessness.* The Pew Charitable Trusts. https://www.pew.org/en/research-and-analysis/articles/2023/08/22/how-housing-costs-drive-levels-of-homelessness
Horton, H. (2024, March 15). Water firms' profits in England and Wales almost double since 2019, find Lib Dems. *The Guardian.* https://www.theguardian.com/business/2024/mar/15/water-firms-profits-england-wales-almost-double-since-2019;
Howard, P. H. (2021). *Concentration and power in the food system: Who controls what we eat?* Bloomsbury Academic.
ICIJ (International Consortium of Investigative Journalists). (2025). *Offshore leaks database.* https://offshoreleaks.icij.org/
International Monetary Fund. (2017). Greece: Ex-post evaluation of exceptional access under the 2012 extended arrangement-press release; Staff Report; and Statement by the Executive Director for Greece. *IMF Staff Country Reports, 17*(44). https://doi.org/10.5089/9781475576252.002
Irwin, N. (2019, June 24). It's a winner-take-all world, whether you like it or not. *The Atlantic.* https://www.theatlantic.com/ideas/archive/2019/06/its-a-winner-take-all-world-heres-how-to-get-ahead/591700
Jenkins, T. (2013). *Of flying saucers and social scientists: A re-reading of when prophecy fails and of cognitive dissonance* (1st ed.). Palgrave Pivot.
Jensen, T. (2014). Welfare commonsense, poverty porn and doxosophy. *Sociological Research Online, 19*(3), 277–283. https://doi.org/10.5153/sro.3441
Jordans, F. (2023, March 19). Nations approve key UN science report on climate change. *Associated Press.* https://apnews.com/article/un-climate-change-science-report-ipcc-meeting5cb018f
Kaiser-Schatzlein, R. (2021, September 24). This is how America's richest families stay that way. *The New York Times.* https://www.nytimes.com/2021/09/24/opinion/biden-tax-loophole.html
Kamp, J. & Najmabadi, S. (2023, August 14). More Americans are ending up homeless—At a record rate. *The Wall Street Journal.* https://www.wsj.com/articles/homelessness-increasing-united-states-housing-costs-e1990ac7
Kang, J.-C. (2022, January 27). It's time for an honest conversation about affirmative action. *The New York Times.* https://www.nytimes.com/2022/01/27/opinion/affirmative-action-harvard.html
Karma, R. (2025, January 11). What the H-1B visa fight is really about. *The Atlantic.* https://www.theatlantic.com/ideas/archive/2025/01/trump-musk-sanders-immigration/681274

Karp, A. (2023, March 8). The U.S. military has a lot of stuff. *Foreign Policy*. https://foreignpolicy.com/2023/03/08/pentagon-excess-surplus-property-military-spending
Kassem, S. (2023). *Work and alienation in the platform economy*. Bristol University Press.
Kelley, L. (2023, June 16). Why it matters who caused inflation. *The Atlantic*. https://www.theatlantic.com/newsletters/archive/2023/06/why-it-matters-who-caused-inflation/674448
Kellner, D. (2021). *Technology and democracy: Toward a critical theory of digital technologies, technopolitics, and technocapitalism*. Springer.
Kelton, S. (2020). *The deficit myth: Modern monetary theory and the birth of the people's economy*. PublicAffairs.
Kennedy, R. F. (2021, February 23). Bill Gates and Neo-feudalism: A closer look at Farmer Bill. *The Defender (Children's Health Defense)*. https://childrenshealthdefense.org/defender/bill-gates-neo-feudalism-farmer-bill
Keuschnigg, M., van de Rijt, A., & Bol, T. (2023). The plateauing of cognitive ability among top earners. *European Sociological Review, 39*(5), 820–833. https://doi.org/10.1093/esr/jcac076
Klein, E., & Thompson, D. (2025). *Abundance*. Avid Reader Press.
Klein, E. (2015, July 28). Bernie Sanders. *Vox*. https://www.vox.com/2015/7/28/9014491/bernie-sanders-vox-conversation
Kloeckner, C. (2020). *Schuld/en*, or: Renegotiating debt and guilt in US culture after the 2007/08 financial crisis. *KulturPoetik, 20*(1), 108–122.
Kochhar, R., & Sechopoulos, S. (2022, April 20). How the American middle class has changed in the past five decades. *Pew Research Center*. https://www.pewresearch.org/short-reads/2022/04/20/how-the-american-middle-class-has-changed-in-the-past-five-decades
Koganzon, R. (2023). The inescapable meritocracy. In C. McNamara & T. Shelley (Eds.), *Renewing America's civic compact*. Lexington Books.
Kolomatsky, M. (2021, July 8). Baby boomers: Rich with real estate and not letting go. *The New York Times*. https://nyti.ms/3dWDk0u
Kotkin, J. (2020). *The coming of neo-feudalism: A warning to the global middle class*. Encounter.
Krishnamurthy, P. (2021, September 27). The Great Gatsby curve and a glimpse of America's dystopian future. *The Hill*. https://thehill.com/opinion/finance/574029-the-great-gatsby-curve-and-americas-dystopian-future
Krugman, P. (2020, July 1). Why do the rich have so much power? *The New York Times*. https://www.nytimes.com/2020/07/01/opinion/sunday/inequality-america-paul-krugman.html
Krugman, P. (2023a, April 11). Inequality ahoy! On the meaning of the superyacht. *The New York Times*. https://nyti.ms/3o3okG1
Krugman, P. (2023b, April 28). The perils of tough-guy economics. *The New York Times*. https://www.nytimes.com/2023/04/28/opinion/inflation-wages-unemployment.html
Kuper, S. (2023, February 16). The one per cent are not as clever as they think. *Financial Times*. https://www.ft.com/content/f716bea0-21eb-4ac5-923e-e268d307f3e6
Lampert, K. (2012). *Meritocratic education and social worthlessness*. Palgrave Macmillan.
Lapavitsas, C., Kaltenbrunner, A., Lindo, D., Michell, J., Painceira, J. P., Pires, E., Powell, J., Stenfors, A., & Teles, N. (2010). Eurozone crisis: Beggar thyself and thy neighbour. *Journal of Balkan and Near Eastern Studies, 12*(4), 321–373. https://doi.org/10.1080/19448953.2010.510012
Lauria, M. (2025, November 7). How Tesla shareholders put Elon Musk on path to be world's first trillionaire. *The Guardian*. https://www.theguardian.com/technology/2025/nov/06/how-tesla-shareholders-elon-musk-trillionaire
Lea, R. (2019, April 12). Water bills cut as Corbyn threat looms. *The Times*. https://www.thetimes.com/article/water-bills-cut-as-corbyn-threat-looms-k80qzf73t
Lee, J. (2021, August 20). Here's why the ultra-wealthy like Bill Gates and Thomas Peterffy are investing in U.S. farmland. *CNBC*. https://www.cnbc.com/2021/08/20/heres-why-the-ultra-wealthy-like-bill-gates-investing-to-farmland.html
Leonard, C. (2021, 28 December). The Fed's doomsday prophet has a dire warning about where we're headed. *Politico*. https://www.politico.com/news/magazine/2021/12/28/inflation-interest-rates-thomas-hoenig-federal-reserve-526177

Lennard, N. (2013, January 5). IMF economists apologize for austerity forecasts. *Salon*. https://www.salon.com/2013/01/04/imf_economists_apologize_for_austerity_forecasts
Levitz, E. (2021, July 1). Will the great wealth transfer spark a millennial civil war? *Intelligencer*. https://nymag.com/intelligencer/2021/07/will-the-great-wealth-transfer-spark-a-millennial-civil-war.html
Lewis, M. (2011). *Boomerang: Travels in the new Third World*. Norton.
Livingstone, D. W., Adams, T. L., & Sawchuk, P. H. (2021). *Professional power and skill use in the 'knowledge economy': A class analysis*. Brill.
Littler, J. (2017). *Against meritocracy: Culture, power and myths of mobility*. Routledge.
Loader, I. (1999). Consumer culture and the commodification of policing and security. *Sociology, 33*(2), 373–392. https://doi.org/10.1177/S003803859900022X
López Godoy, A. P. (2024). The rule of digital rent: An aftermath of neoliberal globalization. In F. Ubierna (Ed.), *Estudios multidisciplinares en universidad, empresa y sociedad* (pp. 117–132). Fragua.
Lowrey, A. (2023a, May 14). The war on poverty is over. Rich people won. *The Atlantic*. https://www.theatlantic.com/ideas/archive/2023/05/poverty-in-america-book-matthew-desmond-interview/674058
Lowrey, A. (2023b, March 14). The U.S. housing market has become deeply unfair. *The Atlantic*. https://www.theatlantic.com/ideas/archive/2023/03/housing-market-affordability-zoning-homeownership/673374
Loxbo, K. (2022). The varying logics for supporting populist right-wing welfare politics in West European welfare regimes. *European Political Science Review, 14*(2), 171–187. https://doi.org/10.1017/s175577392200011x
Macdonald, R., Shildrick, T., & Furlong, A. (2014). 'Benefits Street' and the myth of workless communities. *Sociological Research Online, 19*(3), 263–268. https://doi.org/10.5153/sro.3438
Magdoff, H., & Sweezy, P. (1987). *Stagnation and the financial explosion*. Monthly Review Press.
Magnan, A., & Desmarais, A. (2023, February 28). Growing farmland inequality in the Prairies poses problems for all Canadians. *The Conversation*. https://theconversation.com/growing-farmland-inequality-in-the-prairies-poses-problems-for-all-canadians-196777
Mani, A., Mullainathan, S., Shafir, E., & Zhao, J. (2013). Poverty impedes cognitive function. *Science, 341*(6149), 976–980. https://doi.org/10.1126/science.1238041
Mankiw, N. G. (2021, September 15). Can America afford to become a major social welfare state? *The New York Times*. https://nyti.ms/2VP2Sa4
Mann, C. C. (2018, March). How will we feed the new global middle class? *The Atlantic*. https://www.theatlantic.com/magazine/archive/2018/03/charles-mann-can-planet-earth-feed-10-billion-people/550928
Markovits, D. (2019a). *The meritocracy trap: How America's foundational myth feeds inequality, dismantles the middle class, and devours the elite*. Penguin.
Markovits, D. (2019b, September). How life became an endless, terrible competition. *The Atlantic*. https://www.theatlantic.com/magazine/archive/2019/09/meritocracys-miserable-winners/594760
Maxey, D. (2021, July 12). Improper 'insider charitable giving' is widespread, study says. *The Wall Street Journal*. https://www.wsj.com/finance/investing/insider-charitable-giving-11625418315
Mazzucato, M. (2020). *Mission economy: A moonshot guide to changing capitalism*. Penguin.
McCarthy, N. (2023, May 3). The U.S. cities where the rich are richer and the poor are poorer. *Statista*. https://www.statista.com/chart/16063/income-inequality-in-us-cities
McGoey, L. (2021). Philanthrocapitalism and the separation of powers. *Annual Review of Law and Social Science, 17*(1), 391–409. https://doi.org/10.1146/annurev-lawsocsci-120220-074323
McKee, M., Karanikolos, M., Belcher, P., & Stuckler, D. (2012). Austerity: A failed experiment on the people of Europe. *Clinical Medicine, 12*(4), 346–350. https://doi.org/10.7861/clinmedicine.12-4-346
McTague, T. (2014, January 13). Iain Duncan Smith suggests hit show Benefits Street justifies savage welfare cuts. *Mirror*. https://www.mirror.co.uk/news/uk-news/benefits-street-iain-duncan-smith-3019449

Meadway, J. (2023, March 24). The dirty secret behind the cost-of-living crisis. *New Statesman*. https://www.newstatesman.com/comment/2023/03/dirty-secret-cost-of-living-crisis
Meigs, J. B. (2021, February 27). Why Bill Gates is now the US' biggest farmland owner. *New York Post*. https://nypost.com/2021/02/27/why-bill-gates-is-now-the-us-biggest-farmland-owner
Mendes, L. (2021). Transnational gentrification and the housing market during pandemic times, Lisbon Style. *Urban Geography, 42*(7), 1003–1010. https://doi.org/10.1080/02723638.2021.1949832
Merton, R. K. (1948). The self-fulfilling prophecy. *The Antioch Review, 8*(2), 193–210. https://doi.org/10.2307/4609267
Mijs, J. J. B. (2021). The paradox of inequality: Income inequality and belief in meritocracy go hand in hand. *Socio-Economic Review, 19*(1), 7–35. https://doi.org/10.1093/ser/mwy051
Mikhailova, Y. (2020, January). Abolishing academic serfdom. *Newsnet*, 13–16. https://aseees.org/wp-content/uploads/2015/02/january-2020.pdf
Miller, C. (2024, September 16). Today's parents: 'Exhausted, burned out and perpetually behind'. *The New York Times*. https://www.nytimes.com/2024/09/14/upshot/parents-stress-murthy-warning.html
Millman, N. (2024, September 5). Trump-Vance is making something very clear about Trumpism. *The New York Times*. https://www.nytimes.com/2024/09/05/opinion/trump-vance-populism.html
Mims, C. (2021, September 11). The way Amazon uses tech to squeeze performance out of workers deserves its own name: Bezosism. *The Wall Street Journal*. https://www.wsj.com/articles/the-way-amazon-uses-tech-to-squeeze-performance-out-of-workers-deserves-its-own-name-bezosism-11631332821
Minter, A. (2022, May 29). *US farmland is a hot commodity. That's not great for farms*. Bloomberg. https://www.bloomberg.com/opinion/articles/2022-05-29/millennial-farmers-can-t-afford-to-buy-us-agricultural-land
Miron, J. A. (2011). Rethinking redistribution. *National Affairs*. https://www.nationalaffairs.com/publications/detail/rethinking-redistribution
Mishel, L., Gould, E., & Bivens, J. (2015, January 6). *Wage stagnation in nine charts*. Economic Policy Institute. https://www.epi.org/publication/charting-wage-stagnation
Misra, T. (2024, February 29). *Cities can't solve the housing crisis alone*. Bloomberg. https://www.bloomberg.com/news/articles/2024-02-29/cities-can-t-solve-the-housing-crisis-alone
Mitchell, S. (2023, May 29). The real reason your groceries are getting so expensive. *The New York Times*. https://www.nytimes.com/2023/05/29/opinion/inflation-groceries-pricing-walmart.html
Mody, A. (2015, July 15). *What does the IMF's Greek defence tell us?* World Economic Forum. https://www.weforum.org/stories/2015/07/what-does-the-imfs-greek-defence-tell-us/
Morgan, A. C., LaBerge, N., Larremore, D. B., Galesic, M., Brand, J. E., & Clauset, A. (2022). Socioeconomic roots of academic faculty. *Nature Human Behaviour, 6*(12), 1625–1633. https://doi.org/10.1038/s41562-022-01425-4
Morozov, E. (2022). Critique of Techno-Feudal reason. *New Left Review, 133/134*, 89–126. https://newleftreview.org/issues/ii133/articles/evgeny-morozov-critique-of-techno-feudal-reason
Morris, C. (2015, July 15). Greece debt crisis: IMF says bailout numbers don't add up. *BBC News*. https://www.bbc.com/news/blogs-eu-33545416
Murray, W. E. (2006). Neo-feudalism in Latin America? Globalisation, agribusiness, and land re-concentration in Chile. *The Journal of Peasant Studies, 33*(4), 646–677. https://doi.org/10.1080/03066150601152281
Myers, J., M., Bowman, S., & Southwood, B. (2021, September 14). *The housing theory of everything*. Works in Progress. https://worksinprogress.co/issue/the-housing-theory-of-everything
Napoleoni, L. (2024). *Techno-capitalism: The rise of the new Robber Barons and the fight for the common good*. Seven Stories.
Naudé, W. (2023, May). *Melancholy hues: The futility of green growth and degrowth, and the inevitability of societal collapse* (IZA Institute of Labor Economics Discussion Paper Series, 16139). https://docs.iza.org/dp16139.pdf

Nichols, T. (2023, March 9). The ugly elitism of the American right. *The Atlantic*. https://www.theatlantic.com/newsletters/archive/2023/03/the-ugly-elitism-of-the-american-right/673350

Noah, T. (2023, April 27). Why Republicans hate it when poor people have food to eat. *The New Republic*. https://newrepublic.com/article/172242/republicans-hate-poor-people-food-eat

Ofwat. (2019, July 18). *PN 16/19 2019 price review: Ofwat unveils programme of huge investment, service improvements and lower bills for water customers*. Ofwat. https://www.ofwat.gov.uk/pn-16-19-2019-price-review-ofwat-unveils-programme-of-huge-investment-service-improvements-and-lower-bills-for-water-customers

Osnos, E. (2022, March 7). Turning the focus on America's oligarchs. *The New Yorker*. https://www.newyorker.com/news/daily-comment/turning-the-focus-on-americas-oligarchs

Oxfam. (2013). *Divide and purchase: How land ownership is being concentrated in Colombia*. https://web.archive.org/web/20171114100522/.../rr-divide-and-purchase-land-concentration-colombia-270913-en_0.pdf

Oxfam. (2024, January 15). *Wealth of five richest men doubles since 2020, as wealth of five billion people falls*. Oxfam. https://www.oxfam.org.uk/media/press-releases/wealth-of-five-richest-men-doubles-since-2020-as-wealth-of-five-billion-people-falls/

Palley, T. (2022). Theorizing varieties of capitalism: Economics and the fallacy that "there is no alternative (TINA)." *Review of Keynesian Economics, 10*(2), 1–38.

Panferova, E., Schaapherder, N., Sharova, S., & Theseira, T. D. (2024). The emergence of neo-feudalism and its distortion of Maslow's hierarchy of needs. In F. Ubierna (Ed.), *Estudios multidisciplinares en universidad, empresa y sociedad* (pp. 211–223). Fragua.

Paulden, P. (2021, September 28). *America's richest use GRATs to avoid estate tax*. Bloomberg. https://www.bloomberg.com/news/articles/2021-09-28/america-s-richest-use-grats-to-avoid-estate-tax-propublica

Partington, R. (2022, February 4). Bank of England boss criticised for asking workers not to demand pay rise. *The Guardian*. https://www.theguardian.com/business/2022/feb/04/bank-of-england-boss-calls-for-wage-restraint-to-help-control-inflation

Pelletier, P. E. (2021, May 10). How to actually prosecute the worst financial crimes. *The Atlantic*. https://www.theatlantic.com/ideas/archive/2021/05/prosecute-tax-fraud-financial-crimes-garland/618914

Perez, A. & Sirota, D. (2021, May 21). Charles Koch Foundation funded eviction push while investing in real estate companies. *The Guardian*. https://www.theguardian.com/us-news/2021/may/21/charles-koch-foundation-eviction-real-estate

Perocco, F., & della Puppa, F. (2023). The racialized welfare discourse on refugees and asylum seekers: The example of "Scroungers" in Italy. *Social Sciences, 12*(2), 59. https://doi.org/10.3390/socsci12020059

Perry, L. B., Yoon, E.-S., Sciffer, M., & Lubienski, C. (2024). The impact of marketization on school segregation and educational equity and effectiveness: Evidence from Australia and Canada. *International Journal of Comparative Sociology*, 00207152241227810. https://doi.org/10.1177/00207152241227810

Persson, M., & Sundell, A. (2024). The rich have a slight edge: Evidence from comparative data on income-based inequality in policy congruence. *British Journal of Political Science, 54*(2), 514–525. https://doi.org/10.1017/S0007123423000066

Pew Research. (2023, September 19). Money, power and the influence of ordinary people in American politics. *Pew Research Center*. https://www.pewresearch.org/politics/2023/09/19/money-power-and-the-influence-of-ordinary-people-in-american-politics

Piketty, T. (2014). *Capital in the twenty-first century* (A. Goldhammer, Trans.). Harvard University Press.

Pistor, K. (2019). *The code of capital: How the law creates wealth and inequality*. Princeton University Press.

Popik, B. (2009, December 8). *There are two ways to conquer and enslave a nation. One is by the sword. The other is by debt*. The Big Apple. https://www.barrypopik.com/index.php/new_york_city/entry/there_are_two_ways_to_conquer_and_enslave_a_nation_one_is_by_the_sword_the

PrairieFarmer. (2022, May 17). *Who are the biggest absentee landowners in Illinois?* FarmProgress. https://www.farmprogress.com/commentary/who-are-biggest-absentee-landowners-illinois

Qiu, L. (2022, November 13). Farmland values hit record highs, pricing out farmers. *The New York Times*. https://www.nytimes.com/2022/11/13/us/politics/farmland-values-hit-record-highs-pricing-out-farmers.html

Ramey, J. (2015). Neoliberalism as a political theology of chance: The politics of divination. *Palgrave Communications, 1*(1), 15039. https://doi.org/10.1057/palcomms.2015.39

Ratliff, L. (2015, July 21). *Seven massively sprawling ranches from around the world*. Bloomberg. https://www.bloomberg.com/news/articles/2015-07-21/7-massively-sprawling-ranches-from-around-the-world

Read, J. (2022). A genealogy of homo-economicus: Neoliberalism and the production of subjectivity. In *The production of subjectivity: Marx and philosophy* (pp. 311–322). Brill. https://doi.org/10.1163/9789004515277_017

Reich, R. (2022a, December 16). America's growing zero-sum economy. *Substack*. https://robertreich.substack.com/p/the-economys-large-and-growing-unproductive

Reich, R. (2022b, October 2). The US ultra-rich justify their low tax rates with three myths—All of them rubbish. *The Guardian*. https://www.theguardian.com/commentisfree/2022/oct/02/ultra-rich-low-tax-rates-economy-myths

Reuters. (2025, June 17). EU hits Greece with record fine over farmers subsidy fraud. *Reuters*. https://www.reuters.com/business/finance/eu-hits-greece-with-record-fine-over-farmers-subsidy-fraud-2025-06-17

Rex, J. (2019). Criminal prosecutions and the 2008 financial crisis in the U.S. and Iceland: What can a small town Icelandic Police Chief teach the U.S. about prosecuting Wall Street? *Concordia Law Review, 4*(1), 101–146.

Rhodes, B. (2024, November 8). I study guys like Trump. There's a reason they keep winning. *The New York Times*. https://www.nytimes.com/2024/11/08/opinion/republicans-democrats-trump.html

Riddell, R., Ahmed, N., Maitland, A., Lawson, M., & Taneja, A. (2024). *Inequality Inc. How corporate power divides our world and the need for a new era of public action*. Oxfam International. https://doi.org/10.21201/2024.000007

Rocholl, J., & Stahmer, A. (2016). *Where did the Greek bailout money go?* (ESMT White Paper Nr. WP–16–02). http://static.esmt.org/publications/whitepapers/WP-16-02.pdf

Rodrik, D. (2021). Why does globalization fuel populism? Economics, culture, and the rise of right-wing populism. *Annual Review of Economics, 13*(1), 133–170. https://doi.org/10.1146/annurev-economics-070220-032416

Rolnik, G. (2016, April 16). Are we all rent-seeking investors? *ProMarket*. https://promarket.org/2016/04/16/are-we-all-rent-seeking-investors

Ruggeri, K., Panin, A., Vdovic, M., Većkalov, B., Abdul-Salaam, N., Achterberg, J., Akil, C., Amatya, J., Amatya, K., Andersen, T. L., Aquino, S. D., Arunasalam, A., Ashcroft-Jones, S., Askelund, A. D., Ayacaxli, N., Sheshdeh, A. B., Bailey, A., Barea Arroyo, P., Mejía, G. B., … García-Garzon, E. (2022). The globalizability of temporal discounting. *Nature Human Behaviour*, *6*(10), 1386–1397. https://doi.org/10.1038/s41562-022-01392-w

Ruggeri, K., Ashcroft-Jones, S., Abate Romero Landini, G., Al-Zahli, N., Alexander, N., Andersen, M. H., Bibilouri, K., Busch, K., Cafarelli, V., Chen, J., Doubravová, B., Dugué, T., Durrani, A. A., Dutra, N., Garcia-Garzon, E., Gomes, C., Gracheva, A., Grilc, N., Gürol, D. M., … Stock, F. (2023). The persistence of cognitive biases in financial decisions across economic groups. *Scientific Reports, 13*(1), 10329. https://doi.org/10.1038/s41598-023-36339-2

Ryan-Collins, J., & Murray, C. (2021). When homes earn more than jobs: The rentierization of the Australian housing market. *Housing Studies, 38*(10), 1888–1917. https://doi.org/10.1080/02673037.2021.2004091

Sahdan, F., & Gregorius, J. (2023). Neoliberalism and the retraction of welfare law: A theoretical critique. *Interdisciplinary Studies in Society, Law, and Politics, 2*(1), 16–23. https://doi.org/10.61838/kman.isslp.2.1.3

Salame, R. (2018, February 20). The new taylorism. *Jacobin*. https://www.jacobinmag.com/2018/02/amazon-wristband-surveillance-scientific-management

Samuel, L. (2014). *The American middle class: A cultural history*. Routledge.

Savage, L. (2021, July 14). The billionaire space race is the ultimate symbol of capitalist decadence. *Jacobin*. https://jacobinmag.com/2021/07/billionaire-space-race-richard-branson-bezos-musk

Schafer, S. (2021, September 16). Rural bankers: Farmland prices at record highs. *Agweb*. https://www.agweb.com/news/business/farmland/rural-bankers-farmland-prices-record-highs

Smith, A. (1776). *The wealth of nations*. Straughn & Cadell.

Smith, R. (2024, April 5). Thames Water's parent company defaults on debt. *Financial Times*. https://www.ft.com/content/58834a3a-8754-41b9-bd40-938e62fd662c;

Smith, T. J., & Russell, K. (2023, May 14). The greatest wealth transfer in history is here, with familiar (rich) winners. *The New York Times*. https://nyti.ms/43bR7HR

Sorkin, A. R. (2010). *Too big to fail: The inside story of how Wall Street & Washington fought to save the financial system—And themselves*. Viking.

Smith, L. (2019, March 12). College admissions bribery scheme affidavit. *Washington Post*. https://www.washingtonpost.com/context/college-admissions-bribery-scheme-affidavit

Spencer, K. A. (2018). *A people's history of Silicon Valley: How the tech industry exploits workers, erodes privacy and undermines democracy*. Eyewear.

Spicker, P. (2024). The effect of treating public services as commodities. *Public Money & Management, 44*(4), 281–288. https://doi.org/10.1080/09540962.2023.2240641

Standing, G. (2011). *The precariat: The new dangerous class*. Bloomsbury Academic.

Stewart, M. (2018, June). The 9.9 percent is the new American aristocracy. *The Atlantic*. https://www.theatlantic.com/magazine/archive/2018/06/the-birth-of-a-new-american-aristocracy/559130

Stiglitz, J. E., & Guru-Murthy, K. (2024, May 7). Economist Joseph Stiglitz on pro-Palestine campus protests, Trump and rethinking freedom [Video]. *Channel 4 News*. https://youtu.be/ie5GX8e3FbA?si=KfAJSDbAoUOOSeIx

Stiglitz, J. E. (2024). *The road to freedom: Economics and the good society*. Penguin.

Stone, J. (2016, December 16). Here are some of the bills Tory MP Philip Davies has filibustered. *Independent*. https://www.independent.co.uk/news/uk/politics/philip-davies-filibuster-domestic-violence-a7479266.html

Stone, K., & Kuttner, R. (2020, April 8). The rise of neo-feudalism. *The American Prospect*. https://prospect.org/economy/rise-of-neo-feudalism

Suarez-Villa, L. (2012). *Globalization and technocapitalism: The political economy of corporate power and technological domination*. Ashgate.

Susskind, D. (2024). *Growth: A history and a reckoning*. Harvard University Press.

Taylor, K. (2019, October 3). Parents paid to open college doors. Now they're spending to limit prison time. *The New York Times*. https://www.nytimes.com/2019/10/03/us/college-admissions-scandal-consultants.html

Teo, T. (2018). Homo neoliberalus: From personality to forms of subjectivity. *Theory & Psychology, 28*(5), 581–599. https://doi.org/10.1177/0959354318794899

The Toc Team. (2013, December 11). IMF's admission of error on fiscal multipliers for Greece 'a matter of honour,' Lagarde says. *The TOC*. https://www.thetoc.gr/eng/politics/article/imfs-admission-of-error-on-fiscal-multipliers-for-greece-a-matter-of-honour-lagarde-says

Thurow, L. (1981). *The zero-sum society: Distribution and the possibilities for economic change*. Penguin.

Tsimouris, G. (2015). From mainstream to extreme: Casino capitalism, fascism and the re-bordering of immigration in Greece. *Intersections: East European Journal of Society and Politics, 1*(1), 83–99. https://doi.org/10.17356/ieejsp.v1i1.27

Tulip, P., & Bishop, J. (2017, May 22). *Anticipatory monetary policy and the price puzzle* (Reserve Bank of Australia Research Discussion Papers, 2017-02). https://doi.org/10.2139/ssrn.2971775

Turchin, P. (2023). *End times: Elites, counter-elites, & the path of political disintegration*. Penguin.

Turner, J. A. (2018, August 21). *We're living in the age of the zero-sum economy*. World Economic Forum. https://www.weforum.org/agenda/2018/08/were-living-in-the-age-of-the-zero-sum-economy

Valentine, G., & Harris, C. (2014). Strivers vs skivers: Class prejudice and the demonisation of dependency in everyday life. *Geoforum, 53*, 84–92. https://doi.org/10.1016/j.geoforum.2014.02.007

van Sickle, A., & Eder, S. (2023, July 9). Where Clarence Thomas entered an elite circle and opened a door to the court. *The New York Times*. https://www.nytimes.com/2023/07/09/us/clarence-thomas-horatio-alger-association.html

Varoufakis, Y. (2023). *Technofeudalism: What killed capitalism*. Random House.

Vergopoulos, K. (2005). *Η αρπαγή του πλούτου: Χρήμα – Εξουσία – Διαπλοκή στην Ελλάδα*. Λιβάνης.

Viana, A. L. D. Á., & Silva, H. P. D. (2018). Neoliberal meritocracy and financial capitalism: Consequences for social protection and health. *Ciência & Saúde Coletiva, 23*(7), 2107–2118. https://doi.org/10.1590/1413-81232018237.07582018

Vlachogiannis, A. (2019). The Greek experience of privatisation through the Hellenic Republic Asset Development Fund. *International Journal of Public Policy, 15*(1–2), 76–91. https://doi.org/10.1504/IJPP.2019.099053

van Vossole, J. (2016). Framing PIGS: Patterns of racism and neocolonialism in the Euro crisis. *Patterns of Prejudice, 50*(1), 1–20. https://doi.org/10.1080/0031322X.2015.1128056

Warner, J. (2013). The new refeudalization of the public sphere. In M. P. McAllister & E. West (Eds.), *The Routledge companion to advertising and promotional culture* (pp. 285–297). Routledge.

Wax, E. (2021, May 23). MEPs seek to tackle Orbán and Babiš over EU farm funds. *Politico*. https://www.politico.eu/article/european-parliament-viktor-orban-andrej-babis-eu-farm-funds-common-agricultural-policy

Whitehouse, S. & Stinnett, M. (2017). *Captured: The corporate infiltration of American Democracy*. New Press.

Wiggan, J. (2012). Telling stories of 21st century welfare: The UK Coalition government and the neo-liberal discourse of worklessness and dependency. *Critical Social Policy, 32*(3), 383–405. https://doi.org/10.1177/0261018312444413

Williams, H. & Mustoe, H. (2024, November 21). Water firms blocked from using customer cash for 'undeserved' £6.8m boss bonuses. *Independent*. https://www.independent.co.uk/business/thames-water-companies-pollution-bonuses-ofwat-b2651118.html

Williams, Z. (2013, January 9). Skivers v strivers: The argument that pollutes people's minds. *The Guardian*. https://www.theguardian.com/politics/2013/jan/09/skivers-v-strivers-argument-pollutes

Wong, M. (2024, July 29). Silicon Valley's trillion-dollar leap of faith. *The Atlantic*. https://www.theatlantic.com/technology/archive/2024/07/ai-companies-unprofitable/679278

Wyman, P. (2021, September 23). American gentry. *The Atlantic*. https://www.theatlantic.com/ideas/archive/2021/09/trump-american-gentry-wyman-elites/620151

Yellen, J. L. (2021, October 30). Statement on the global minimum tax agreement. *U.S. Department of the Treasury*. https://home.treasury.gov/news/press-releases/jy0447

Zando (2025). Atlantic editions. *The Atlantic*. https://www.theatlantic.com/atlantic-editions/#on-the-housing-crisis

ŽiŽek, S. (2009). *First as tragedy, then as farce*. Verso.

Unipolarity, Multipolarity and Zero-Sum Thinking

9

Abstract

In the wake of 2008 and 2016, the conflicts over finite resources reached a new level since zero-sum competition for the accumulation of sovereignty roared into the open. The peculiar economic system which reappeared, what Naomi Klein calls **disaster capitalism**, spread through the tax write-downs, lockdowns and shutdowns of the **COVID-19 Pandemic** and its attendant financial handouts to global pharmaceutical corporations from taxpayer coffers. Both the problem of inflation and the collapse of supply chains that were brought about by the pandemic were exacerbated soon after COVID restrictions started loosening, as Russia invaded mainland Ukraine in 2022. Building on trajectories set after the GFC, political economies rapidly switched from neoliberalism to **Autarky part 2: Neo-Mercantilism**. In its wake, the zero-sum Climate Change crisis of **the Anthropocene** is quickly entangling the entirety of humanity in yet another **Cold War II** and threatens to cast it in a global hot conflict on land and sea **between Thalassocracy and Tellurocracy**.

> The time has come for the U.S. foreign policy establishment to recognize that the liberal international order was a failed enterprise with no future. (Mearsheimer, 2019, p. 50)

By the time that Ukraine, Gaza, Sudan, Myanmar, Haiti, Tigray, Yemen and Syria were smoldering in mid-2025, tensions were flaring up from Taiwan to Greenland, risking more wars involving nuclear-armed powers. As trillions of dollars had since 2008 been piled high in 21st-c. tax havens from Panama to Ireland to Switzerland to Malta, Reagan's "shining city on a hill" was now a washed up imitation of the very nations like Iraq or Afghanistan it had previously sought to subdue: "Trump vowed to 'make America great again' with the same predatory methods he used in business… His plan for enriching America was predicated on dominating and

A. M. Feldman and Y. Stamos, *Zero Sum Political Economy*, World-Systems Evolution and Global Futures, https://doi.org/10.1007/978-3-032-18326-2_9

wronging others" (Frum, 2025). It had taken since the 1970s for the zero-sum nature of American imperial foreign policy to become so plain to see (Piketty, 2014; Reich, 2013; Zucman, 2015).

In the wake of the debacle of Vietnam and the Nixon Shock, it was clear to the economist Michael Hudson (2021) that the political economy of American imperialism was little different than any other previous empire: the blood of conquest was transformed into the gold of spoils, just as John Hobson, Vladimir Lenin, Rosa Luxemburg and Hannah Arendt had earlier observed of empires on the opposite side of the Atlantic. The fact that the coup and resulting Soviet invasion of Afghanistan in the late 1970s precipitated the very same series of wars and crises which would lead to September 11th and end with the repetition of the fall of Saigon but with a C-17 instead of a Huey would portend the fall of not one but two empires (Maley, 2021). Wang Huning came to the US as a student in the late 1980s and observed the paradoxes, ironies and contradictions of American-style liberal democracy, predicted its eventual decadence and implosion. A generation later, Wang became Jinping's chief ideologue and has been pushing the CCP's "Just World Order" (1991). In other words, if Fukuyama's *End of History* began with the fall of the Berlin Wall in the late 1980s, it ended with the rise of the Crimean Bridge in the late 2010s (Hochuli et al., 2021).

The academic field of World Systems is to the twenty-first century what Geopolitics was to the twentieth century. While the concept of the "balance of power" was used by men like Churchill, Hitler, Mussolini and Stalin (and Metternich, Talleyrand, Castlereagh and Nesselrode before them), in the twenty-first century, such terms have transformed into "polarity"—unitary or multiple. To subscribe to one single truth or hegemon or to acquiesce to multiple may itself be a zero-sum calculation. As Klyszcz (2023) writes, "'multipolarity' fits into the inherent pessimism of Russian messianism. In the Kremlin's version, 'multipolarity' concerns different civilisations of 'traditional societies', on which the West attempts to impose its 'globalist' values and its 'unipolar' and 'colonial' order." Analogous narratives can be found emanating from the White House or Zhongnanhai.

Walter Scheidel (2017, figs. 3.1–3.5) argued that "Death is the great leveler" when he summarized what the World Wars did to Eurasia, destroying the old imperial classes (both ruled and ruling) from 1899 to 1949. David Fischer's *Great Wave* (1996)—especially showing the Price of Consumables in England, 1201–1993—pointed to similar long-term cycles of economic upheaval and concomitant sociopolitical change. Like the early 20th-c. European imperial ruling classes, the same unstable level of inequality and elite overproduction was true in the United States, but the destruction was avoided by the Keynesian Grand Bargain, which reformed the old feudal systems without allowing reform to become revolution. The grand question of the profoundly unstable inequality and elite overproduction of the twenty-first century is, will the next period of great leveling, or as Turchin calls it, the "Great Compression," be violent or nonviolent; or rather, how violent will it be?

Pandora's Pandemic: Disaster Capitalism and COVID-19

For decades, worldwide public health researchers chronicled patterns of zoonotic viral outbreaks from Asia and Africa back to the turn of the millennium in scientific journals—AIDS, Bird Flu, SARS, MERS, Ebola, Zika, etc. And for decades, policymakers frequently ignored them (Farmer, 2001; Hunter, 2016; Reperant & Osterhaus, 2017; Woo et al., 2006). By late 2019 and early 2020, the warnings of new viral outbreaks had moved to legacy media and newsmagazines. And by the time the first books were being written on the outbreak, it had become the first genuinely global pandemic to spread via airports (Koley & Dhole, 2020; Kuchipudi, 2020; Wickramasinghe et al., 2022).

If the 2010s were the reverse of the 1920s (the latter began with a pandemic *and* an economic crisis, and ended with a bigger economic crisis, while the former began with an economic crisis, and ended with a bigger economic crisis *and* a pandemic), then it seemed that Piotr Stolypin's old quip was new again: in a decade, everything changed, but in a century, nothing changed (Barro et al., 2020). This inverse mirroring is coincidental but also eerie, especially when one considers that we seem to be fast approaching what preceded the 1920s: a world war. The similarities between 1918–1929 and 2008–2020 are striking in that they demonstrate the zero-sum thinking of Austrian economics—a second time (Krugman, 2021a, 2021b). The legacy of 2008s global financial austerity never disappeared—it simply fostered enough resentment to elect Brexit and Trump, the negative-sum policies of which exacerbated the immiserations of their respective constituencies (Barnett, 2017; Mair et al., 2017; Norris & Inglehart, 2019; Tudoroiu, 2018).

One instructive case is Dr. Jihad Mustapha, who fled the Lebanese civil war (exacerbated by Reagan's policies) and came to New York as an umbrella salesman. Working his way up through medical school in the 1980s–1990s until he landed a post at Metro Health Hospital in Grand Rapids, Michigan, his story reads like one of Horatio Alger's: "Dr. Mustapha's ascent through vascular medicine is a rags-to-riches story that he has told frequently, including in promotional materials produced by G.E. Healthcare, which makes equipment used in vascular clinics." Calling himself "the leg saver," his success was predicated on incessant billing of medicare, a "symbiotic relationship" with insurance and healthcare companies and an "assembly line" pace. Above all, he worked a sick system to his benefit, while his patients lost their limbs. The vascular industry in the US alone is a "self-sustaining ecosystem worth $2 billion a year" (Thomas et al., 2023). It was also representative of the disinvestment in public health and the entire for-profit healthcare industry in America and to a lesser extent in other Anglophone nations (Kamaruzaman et al., 2022; Pu et al., 2023; Rotteveel, 2022).

Beside the obvious disinvestment in public health, structural problems had been worsening due to being ignored for decades: growing opioid epidemics, large-scale sickness and predatory insurance/pharma businesses (Hoffman, 2003; Rosenthal, 2017; Wolff, 2020). Americans' 21st-c. addiction to big pharma's opioids and fentanyl is powered by neoliberal public policies (mirrored in China and Mexico), which repeat the Anglo-American opium addiction public policies in 19th-c. China

(Felbab-Brown, 2022). Big Pharma, like Big Tech, operates within a parasitic system of privatized law despite relying heavily on public funding for innovations. It manipulates patent laws to stifle competition, inflates prices through minor drug modifications and forces medical systems to choose its pricier variants. "The industry also keeps well-established and cheap drugs artificially scarce and expensive by driving out generic producers or merging and carving up markets so that even many drugs that are off-patent have only one producer." All these practices are enabled by the industry's market power and political influence, which allow it to create its own regulatory environment, effectively becoming "a law unto itself" (Stone & Kuttner, 2020). Deregulation simply fosters the conditions for "bad actors" to engage in a zero-sum game at the expense of public health and consumer affordability, but also of smaller producers and innovation. Without comprehensive and strict regulation and accountability, the wealth of big corporations will always tend to expand in a way detrimental to everyone else and will easily translate into political power, ensuring that authorities like the FDA will be bent to their will. (Economic) oligopolies will ultimately always engender (political) oligarchies.

While it is American Big Pharma that has manufactured and promoted the drugs by any means possible (including bribery of doctors and other illegal or unethical practices), the epidemic has even been framed as an "attack" from China—and one may expect more of this framing as tensions with China escalate. The embedding of the epidemic in a zero-sum antagonism between the United States and its main rival has only fostered ideas of retaliation. Even if China really was behind the problem, the zero-sum framework is counter-productive in that it does not promote solutions focused on saving American lives but prefers responses that will create a problem for the other side, so that Chinese lives will be somehow harmed as well. The sanctity of life is relativized as something to be measured and counterweighted by destroying more lives (Coates, 2025a, 2025b; Graci, 2023; Hawkins, 2025; Keating, 2025; Martina & Slodkowski, 2024).

Many fentanyl and oxycontin addicts were made homeless or died on the streets as a result of entirely preventable addictions which enriched corporate shareholders (particularly the Sackler dynasty's Purdue Pharma). When the Sackler dynasty was ultimately found guilty of a major portion of the opioid epidemic, none went to jail and they attempted to turn their $4.5b settlement payout into a potlatch initiative with 15 American states (Hoffman, 2021). So the zero-sum strategy was always the same: enrich the corporation/dynasty by impoverishing, addicting and ultimately killing others, blaming it on internal or external foreigners and then laundering one's reputation by donating to charities, museums and super PACs. If the external 21st-c. Wars on Terrorism in Iraq and Afghanistan were to the 20th-c. War on Communism in Vietnam what the internal 21st-c. War on Drugs was to the 20th-c. War on Poverty, then American working-class soldiers, patients and the poor were sacrificed as collateral in each (Cruz, 2022; Dolphin-Krute, 2018; Hampton, 2024; John et al., 2023; Keefe, 2021; Lockwood, 2006; Phillips et al., 2017). Whether the market was in weapons, drugs or ideology, justifications for greed and potlatch philanthropy were one and the same (Jin & Ryu, 2022).

Finally, the racket required stashing the proceeds in overshore tax havens to prevent it from being used to heal the victims—and dynasties like the Sacklers evaded taxes "on an industrial scale" (Cohen, 2018). Throughout the 2010s, a worldwide set of journalistic investigations exposed a series of papers detailing which dynasties were stashing their money and where—the Panama/Paradise/Pandora Papers (2016/2017/2021) (Guardian Investigations Team, 2021; Janda, 2021; Starkman et al., 2021).

As the global oligarchies were dodging taxes, donating to charities and sipping champagne on their yachts, the first cases of the novel COVID-19 virus spread beyond Wuhan and arrived in airports worldwide, from which the virus spread outward. By mid-March 2020, the entire Eastern Seaboard of the United States was engulfed, and by April, there were mask mandates and enforced shutdowns of economic activity. With the shutdowns, mask mandates and other public health measures imposed on publics long accustomed to individualized, DIY healthcare, came the official story of the COVID outbreak and the predictable backlash to it, among other stories in the form of the so-called "plandemic" (CDC Museum, 2024). The dueling narratives boiled down to two theories: the wet-market theory versus the lab-leak theory. The former became the authorized version, holding that the virus began in the Wuhan Huanan Seafood Wholesale Market from a diseased bat or pangolin virus which spontaneously jumped into humans; the latter held that it was leaked from the Wuhan Institute of Virology. Between the secretive information hoarding of the CCP and the conflicting stories circulated by US, UK and EU authorities at different times, no definitive theory has been proven correct or incorrect.

Yet, it didn't matter which theory was authorized or unauthorized, because it was drowned out by the I-told-you-so warnings in the midst of the global outbreak (Levitt, 2020; Lopreite et al., 2021; Pustake et al., 2022; Zhao et al., 2022). The narratives were politicized by governments, Peta, Indo-Pacific Defense Forum and so forth (IPD Forum Staff, 2020). With each politicization came more backlash, cementing them into the broader culture wars (Horton, 2022; Morone, 2024; Perry et al., 2020). It didn't help that the politicians who imposed mark mandates, curfews and shutdowns on their constituents during the pandemic were vacationing, partying and flouting their own rules (Goldmacher & Fandos, 2021; McTague, 2022; Mimbs Nyce, 2021; Parker & Stern, 2022; Weaver, 2020). Then, they politically exploited the confusion over the pandemic's origins to distract from their own scandals and feed into the broader zero-sum antagonism toward China and migrants at home; the US president called it the "China virus" and even "kung flu" (Itkowitz, 2020; Reuters, 2020; Wang & Catalano, 2023; Zheng & Zompetti, 2023).

A temporary discrediting of austerity economics came when the "win–win" scenarios falsely promised by liberals were actually kept in 2020—by Trump's appointee for Fed chairman no less. While other central bankers were preparing to implement neo-mercantilist capital controls in response to COVID-19, Jerome Powell swung back toward Keynesian monetary policy. In March 2020, the Federal Reserve took unprecedented action to stabilize global financial markets by providing unlimited dollar liquidity and purchasing massive amounts of securities. This intervention, while stabilizing markets and benefiting wealthy stakeholders, created a stark contrast with the economic struggles faced by billions worldwide. The scale and speed of central bank actions also reflected a growing comfort with radical monetary policy that blurs the line between emergency measures and normal operations (Tooze, 2021). But Powell realized that shutdowns could not be successfully implemented without sending cash directly to American citizens and that he would need to borrow vastly more to bail out American citizens (not just banks for once). The first checks went out between April-June 2020. The sudden loosening of monetary and therefore fiscal policy had dramatic knock-on effects because, with the Dollar as the world's reserve currency, as goes the Fed, so goes the rest of the world. Overnight, the Bank of England, the Bank of Japan, the European Central Bank and all major central banks followed suit in borrowing and spending with abandon. Then came the private banks from the biggest to the smallest. Amid Trump's "Operation Warp Speed" to kickstart vaccine research and production, with the biggest pharmaceutical corporations suddenly set to deliver actual health benefits to people, and the colossal subsidies to the pleading service and tourism sectors, it seemed the world had turned upside down: it wasn't just big business getting bailed out with taxpayer money; it was also the taxpayers themselves.

But this was only ephemeral and superficial. With shutdowns failing repeatedly, healthcare and other "essential workers" were applauded, but still paid peanuts. The fetishization of those at the top of the meritocratic ladder has long meant that workers in sectors like healthcare, education and service industries find their contributions greatly undervalued and underpaid, despite their critical role in society's functioning. This role was momentarily brought to the fore during the COVID-19 pandemic, only to be recompensed with symbolic and—particularly when coordinated by governments glorifying meritocracy, austerity and privatization like the Tories—insidiously insulting gestures of gratitude, such as the clapping for healthcare staff initiatives that were launched in various countries across the world (Booth et al., 2020; Hurst, 2020; Jones, 2020; Lockwood, 2021; McCarthy, 2024; Mitchell, 2021). Then it receded into its usual invisible position.

This absurdity led to the post-pandemic "great resignation" and resulting "labor shortage" across developed nations (Cook, 2021; Krugman, 2022; Parker & Horowitz, 2022; Serenko, 2023). The same patterns in developed nations also led to the COVID-19 baby bust (Aassve et al., 2021). The entire global post-Cold-War order was failing since "it benefited Western consumers and multinational corporations, who got access to inexpensive labor overseas. Workers, not so much" (Acemoglu, 2024). For some, the pandemic revealed that not only was *Freakonomics* wrong (it protected the neoliberal status quo and advocated against reform), but that the status quo itself was ultimately *Wall Street's War on Workers* (Economist, 2024; Leopold, 2024). The UN reported that inequality was structurally embedded worldwide: "the interconnected crises the world is facing – from the COVID-19 pandemic to environmental degradation and deep-seated economic inequality" require methods to "reform the international financial architecture"

(ECOSOC, 2023). Worse, the entire global structure (the American-led "liberal international order") was shown as no different from the old British imperial model: "This model – the import of expensive goods and the export of cheap resources – characterized the colonial system" (Cohen, 2023).

While extraordinary measures were justified on the basis of the public health crisis, pre-existing trends of approaching health as the domain of private profit and individual responsibility continued and actually intensified. The inflation and increased inequality that followed were a side effect of the "privatization" of the pandemic (Mukherjee, 2025), where corporations enjoyed both state subsidies and huge profits while refusing to cooperate for faster and more effective vaccines. The mortality rates speak for themselves: in total, according to the WHO (2025, May), 1,223,101 have been reported as fatalities from COVID in the USA alone. The real story was the pandemic's disaster capitalism. The spiralling worldwide cost of living crises, especially in the most highly developed economies, led to protests, demonstrations, manifestations, riots and so forth. Legacy media outlets belonging to the Democratic Party's donor class trotted out headlines like "Joe Biden has presided over the fastest and steepest unemployment reduction in U.S. economic history," but this was only because much of that unemployment was caused by the greatest shutdown of economic activity in US history; just doing away with lockdowns drastically boosted employment on its own (Frum, 2023).

In truth, the monetary policies of the 2010s continued to impact the economy of the 2020s, arguably playing a role in the COVID-associated stagflation and the ongoing socio-economic re-stratification along two classes—i.e. "Neo-Feudalism". Interest-free access to capital for big players and an overall trend of upward wealth transfer created the conditions for the same more or less individuals and entities to gain at the expense of everyone else when the Fed started raising interests in response to inflationary pressures. Higher interest rates meant higher values for financial and real estate assets but higher costs for debts, mortgages and rents; in short, another zero-sum bonanza of the owners class at the expense of the renters class. In what Baines and Hager term "the great debt divergence" (2021), big businesses over the past few decades increased their leverage and decreased their debt servicing costs due to policies such as zero interests, whereas small businesses had to contend with the opposite scenario. A similar contrast is witnessed with regard to net gains and losses. The result has been increasing market consolidation, inequality and deployment of financial leverage as political power. Baines and Hager predicted in 2021 that COVID would only exacerbate this trend, something that indeed turned out to be the case as multiple later studies demonstrated.

Autarky Part 2: 21st-c. Neo-Mercantilism

As the world was emerging from lockdowns and mask mandates in early 2022, it was clear that the free market orthodoxy of neoliberal globalism was curdling into something else. The postmodern mixture of grotesque levels of corruption, inequality and oligopoly inherent in AI-driven technofeudalism, the milquetoast neo-Keynesian social spending and worsening international relations increasingly blurred the lines between truth and lies (Elliott, 2022). With neoliberalism itself gravely injured, "security, resilience and self-sufficiency were pushed to the front of the list of economic policy goals along with growth and efficiency" (Cohen, 2024a, 2024b).

And so establishment commentators called for a new bipartisan consensus or paradigm—Edward Luce labelled it the new Washington Consensus whereas David Leonhardt denoted it as a "new centrism." This was to be a departure from the post-Cold-War-I Washington Consensus, which worshiped free markets and promised prosperity through free trade and limited government. For Leonhardt (2024), the old consensus failed to deliver, resulting in slow income growth for most Americans, declining life expectancy and global challenges like China's economic rise alongside increased authoritarianism. For Luce (2023), however, "The old consensus was a positive sum game; if one country got richer others did too. The new one is zero sum; one country's growth comes at the expense of another's."

That, at least, was the assumption behind the broadening great-power competitions and mutual recriminations between Beijing and Washington, especially in regard to growing espionage accusations in the early 2020s. Since WWII, the United States had established a global surveillance network with its Anglophone allies in the Atlantic and Oceania called the "Five Eyes," launching multiple programs like PRISM and ECHELON that allow them to bypass privacy laws. Yet China had its own perfectly legal data collection programs in the Anglophone nations. Official or practical US embargoes on Chinese state-oligopoly telecommunication corporations like Huawei were put in place starting with the first Trump term (Davidson et al, 2021). However, the state-business ties accusation for these Chinese companies is largely a pretext, serving both to justify decisions that have to do with the zero-sum geopolitical game of US elites against Chinese elites and to obscure the fact that US corporations have similar relations with each other and with the government. Google hands over data to intelligence services, Amazon Web Services, Microsoft, etc., provide the IT infrastructure for the CIA, the Facebook app comes with every non-Chinese phone and it has often been impossible to delete as if it's a system file. Such things had been going on long before *TikTok* entered the scene. But *TikTok* would later be cynically used to intensify US government spying through its tech corporations (Hale, 2023). Thus, in 2023, the US Congress began a process to ban the most popular social media app (still, no less or more problematic, especially for underage users, than Meta-owned apps like Instagram), Chinese-owned *TikTok*. As American cybersecurity company Malwarebytes explained though, "Until proof is provided that *TikTok* is worse than other social media apps, there is no compelling reason to treat it differently" (Arntz, 2023).

According to Fomenko (2023a), US opposition to TikTok stemmed from its inability to control the platform for its own espionage purposes rather than genuine privacy concerns: "it's a matter of hegemony". While waging their anti-TikTok campaign, American politicians of both parties continued greenlighting the business-as-usual US spying activities, such as Section 702 of the Foreign Intelligence Surveillance Act (FISA). And if America's "monopoly over the means of information and data gathering" due to its jurisdiction over the leading tech companies was not enough, there are also all sorts of covert operations like the CIA secretly acquiring a Swiss cryptography company or spying on both allies and adversaries, including German chancellor Angela Merkel. Therefore, the author suggests, having non-US-controlled platforms might actually increase individual privacy worldwide. After all: "Even if one has their suspicions about China, how can Washington's claims about TikTok, and the motives behind the mounting pressure on the social media platform, be taken at face value?"

As Fomenko has moreover argued (2023b), US actions against TikTok and other Chinese companies are driven by "Washington's inability to accept competition" rather than genuine security concerns. He portrays Washington's approach as akin to gangster tactics, using threats to maintain dominance. According to Fomenko, the US consistently targets successful Chinese products and services with dubious "national security" claims or unsubstantiated allegations of human rights abuses. This strategy, applied across various sectors, from technology to manufacturing, "is always about market share and American dominance, and the outrage is manufactured as a way of creating support for sanctions." Ironically, an American tech monopoly, Apple, spent decades and tens of billions of heavily taxpayer-subsidized dollars enriching itself and China while impoverishing Americans. This brings to the fore the zero-sum mentality dominating U.S. foreign policy, where Chinese success is viewed as inherently threatening to American interests: "The US claims that it seeks to outcompete China but does not seek conflict," Chinese Foreign Minister Qin Gang said at his first news briefing since taking office at the end of 2022. "Yet in reality, its so-called competition aims to contain and suppress China in all respects and get the two countries locked in a zero-sum game" (Bloomberg News, 2023).

The ever-accelerating disintegration of "Chimerica" and rivalry between America and China after 2008 is itself primarily the result of zero-sum thinking. For world-renowned Singaporean diplomat Kishore Mahbubani (2020), the "great geopolitical contest" between the two super powers is avoidable as they actually have more to win by cooperating, at least on some key areas such as open maritime trade routes. However, he argues that it is also inevitable "because many of the policymakers who will make the tactical decisions that will drive this contest are possessed by a psychology that sees all competition among great powers as a zero-sum game." Another Singaporean geopolitical thinker, professor Yuen Yuen Ang, similarly argues that the competition between the two countries should not be zero-sum—but it currently is:

> And this idea of a zero-sum competition, where if China has the Belt and Road, the U.S. is going to double that. If China's industrial policies, we are going to double that.... What the U.S.-China competition is really about, if there is one, is which of these two countries are going to make use of their political system to solve problems of capitalism. That is the real competition. But it's not a zero-sum competition of, you are doing this, so I'm going to double you on that. (Ang & Klein, 2023)

The zero-sum character of this competition becomes even clearer when one realizes that the response of the United States is not so much to double China on its growth policies but rather to undermine them. The only truly global empire the world has ever witnessed is using China's alleged plan for world domination as a justification to do everything it can to oppose China's project of development through connectivity with the rest of the world by building blocs and barriers around it. Simultaneously, a sovereign that has time and again been accused by the West for its isolationism, whose markets were in the past pried open by Anglo-Americans "by any means necessary," is now blamed for the exact opposite. Clearly, then the issue was never free trade, liberalization, participation in the global market, etc. All these are only acceptable when they occur on the terms and to the benefit of the West—just code words for Western domination. When a country attempts to participate in the global market on its own terms, it has to be isolated and/or destroyed—not just for its own sake but lest other countries that have been on the losing side of the zero-sum charade follow its example or corral around it to form a counter-hegemonic bloc.

It is even more illuminating that the competition has most openly taken place in the field of science and technology, areas that have long been an integral part of Western positive-sum narratives. The liberal idealizations of technological progress as a gift to the whole of humanity are undercut by the devastation it has wrought upon ecosystems and by the dire reality that mechanization did not and cannot on its own liberate workers. The question will always be how the machines are used and—relatedly and most importantly—who controls them. Likewise, the scientific and technological race that is picking up steam between the United States and China as well as the American endeavors to prevent China from learning and building on Western science and technology make the postcolonial critique of knowledge accumulation as a means to subjugation applicable again. The 21st-c. US approach to the issue shows the continuity of Western patterns of colonization. Knowledge is power, and as such its existence may be vaunted for prestige (to justify one's position at the top of the pyramid) but its content must be stringently protected to retain the edge in the zero-sum game (to maintain that top position). Science in this respect does not differ much from the sacred knowledge of foregone eras. In this light, JFK's (1961) speech to the UN can only be read as an ironic contrast: "Development can become a cooperative and not a competitive enterprise—to enable all nations, however diverse in their systems and beliefs, to become in fact as well as in law free and equal nations." In contrast, in his State of the Union Address, Trump (2019) tagged the development of China's economy and technology in recent years as "the theft of American jobs and wealth," even though it was a largely American elite effort to addict or impoverish its own working classes. According to Bernie Sanders (2024), it is the American ruling class that "frames the U.S.-Chinese relationship as a zero-sum struggle."

Between 2020 and 2022, the increasing climate of confrontation from Nagorno-Karabakh between Armenia and Azerbaijan conflict to the nationally-directed cyberattacks, weaponization of immigration crises and hypersonic missile tests signalled to the NYU economist Roubini (2023) (better known as Dr Doom) that the great powers were bound to collide:

> The new cold war between them may eventually turn hot over the issue of Taiwan. The "Thucydides trap" – in which a rising power seems destined to clash with an incumbent hegemon – looms ominously. … US anxiety about China's economic rise is reminiscent of its attitude toward the rise of Germany and Japan decades ago.

Like all previous escalations in geopolitical tensions, US foreign policy turned to imperial domination of the entire western hemisphere. Trump talked about reclaiming the "Gulf of America", annexing Panama, Greenland, Canada, imposing sanctions on Cuba, Colombia, etc. In January 2026, his regime invaded Venezuela, openly recognizing that it was to take the oil. Simultaneously the whole vassalage ecosystem the United States created after WWII in Europe, Oceania and East Asia would be cannibalized—a process that started timidly in Trump's first term and accelerated under Biden (Roa, 2025). Ever since Trump renegotiated NAFTA, eventually replacing it with the more protectionist USMCA in 2020, Biden kept and even expanded the former's "mercantilist" trade policies with Latin America (Schake, 2021). As NAFTA "broke American politics," 30 years later both Republicans and Democrats supported protectionist policies. If in 1994 the enrichment of business came through free trade, then the pendulum swings back (Kaufman & Barbaro, 2024).

How did neoliberal globalism shift to economic nationalism (neomercantilism) by the early 2020s? First, it should be noted that the traditional capitalism vs. socialism narrative was always simplistic: both private and state forms of economic systems have coexisted throughout history (slavery, feudalism, capitalism). In recent years, the United States increasingly adopted a hybrid model, combining private and state capitalism, similar in some ways to China's approach, which was seen as more effective for economic growth than purely private or public systems, allowing finance to oligopolize business and implement regulatory races "to the bottom" into protected, private markets (Foroohar, 2016; Stiglitz, 2019). Economist Richard Wolff (2023) predicted a new global order characterized by economic nationalism and state-private hybrids, alongside a growing global working-class movement, particularly in the East and Global South. This shift is indicative of an intensifying zero-sum game between Western and Eastern economic powers, with Western oligarchs struggling to maintain dominance in the face of emerging Eastern economic strength. The ensuing international trade wars and class wars utilize America's lone remaining domestically-produced industry to ultimate effect: Eisenhower's military-industrial complex (Lighthizer, 2023). It was therefore understandable that Chomsky et al. (2021) agreed with McKinsey's "2020 business book of the year," *Trade Wars are Class Wars* (Klein & Pettis, 2020), since both explain how the real disciples of Marx are the liberal business elites who wage class warfare from the top-down, and then claim the opposite, causing the very military confrontations they purportedly seek to prevent.

The early 2020s witnessed growing calls for "reshoring" or "friendshoring" in a combination of protectionist subsidies, tariffs, sanctions and industrial sabotage (e.g. Nord Stream 2) seeking to attract corporations (back) to the United States at the expense of everyone else—including its allies in the EU (Posen, 2023). It was for this reason that the *New Statesman* proclaimed after an interview that "Joe Biden has broken with neoliberalism" (Eaton, 2021). He wasn't the only Democrat either; for the Connecticut senator Murphy (2022), "actionable economic nationalism" was to be "the antidote to the failures of neoliberalism." Democrats led by Joe Biden increasingly rejected neoliberalism as we knew it and embraced a twenty-first-century version of autarky ("economic nationalism") which would be as aggressive toward adversaries as toward allies. This arguably began with Obama's disparagement of NATO members and European allies as "free riders" beneath the American nuclear umbrella (Goldberg, 2016). His administration's NSA continued policies of spying on EU politicians, which caused mutual recriminations between the transatlantic allies (Bermingham, 2021; Reuters in Berlin, 2015; Spiegel Staff, 2013).

It was a remarkable return of autarkic, mercantilist logic not seen since the 1940s (Helleiner, 2021). The protectionist wave has been predicted to be even worse for poorer nations: "This kind of zero-sum thinking would sharply curtail development opportunities for countries with living standards far below those in the West" (Aiyar, 2024). Along with the profound change away from cheap credit, the pandemic was followed by the disruption of supply chains and increasing predilection for self-sufficiency (Farrer, 2021). But the demise of free markets and the rise of autarky had major effects on rich countries too, most emblematically in the bankruptcy of Angela Merkel's "Wandel durch Handel" policies (Edgerton, 2020). The end of Merkel and her party's dominance is equivalent to the end of the social market economy in the EU's most important member state (ordoliberalism). The journalist Caldwell (2021) eulogized Merkel's leadership as balancing Germany's efficient economy with social responsibility, implementing policies like minimum wage and immigrant integration while steering clear of nuclear power, an approach which he presented as virtuous but also prone to induce instability and class conflict. Although major crises were averted, according to Caldwell who overlooked Merkel's disastrous role in the Eurocrisis, "the shrinking of Germany's great stabilizing bourgeois party is bound to reduce her successors' room for error." This was especially true since, as the financial fallout from the pandemic and the Ukraine war revealed, the euro was plainly subservient to the dollar.

Yet the warning signs of currency dominance were clear. The analyst Sharma (2022) warned that, despite the petrodollar reaching a 20-year high, its reign as global reserve currency may end soon, having outlasted historical averages. Sharma dismissed TINA thinking (that there is no alternative to the dollar), citing weakening fundamentals, and predicted the advent of "the post-dollar world." For Elliott (2023), the global financial system, established post-World-War-II, heavily favored the US dollar, in an arrangement that allows America to maintain large trade and budget deficits without facing the economic constraints of other nations. The dollar's dominance in commodity pricing and international lending gives the

US uncommon economic advantages which, however, face growing opposition. As Elliott explains, the euro's creation was partly motivated by a desire to challenge the dollar's supremacy, while the 2023 BRICS meeting in Johannesburg represents another attempt to counter US financial hegemony and reshape the international economic order. Nevertheless, although Elliott's description is largely accurate, this was not so much the case since WWII, as he claims, but since the Nixon Shock and the creation of the petrodollar. It's only in the neoliberal era that the United States became a truly deficit country and therefore relied on this global mechanism of dollar recycling to sustain its trade and fiscal deficits (Varoufakis, 2011). As a matter of fact, in the '60s–'70s, the US ran surpluses or only small deficits. It was under Reagan, who promised small government, that government deficits ballooned—an ironic yet common feature of actually-existing neoliberalism (see Chap. 6). The capital controls and currency manipulation utilized by up-and-coming nations like China enabled them to use America's hegemonic policies against it, thereby creating the very conditions for America to reimplement autarkic mercantilism, the same capital controls and currency manipulation, which would result in a new Cold War (II). This was the backdrop against which Nouriel Roubini predicted the nuclear annihilation of New York by 2042: "In some sense, World War III has already started" (Spitznagel, 2022).

The tensions rose fastest amid the realignments occurring in long-festering hotspots in places like Ukraine, Gaza and Taiwan. Biden's semiconductor chip warfare against China, escalating in October 2022 and codified in the CHIPS Act of 2022, also sought to move Taiwanese chip expertise and manufacturing to the US from Taiwan Semiconductor Manufacturing Company (TSMC). This was answered by China's "Supply Chain Warfare" against Biden and then Trump in 2024–2025, which produced a combined tariff regime against each other of nearly 300% by 2025 (Stevenson & Mozur, 2024; Chan, 2025). Then came the cascade of declarations of sovereignty over the ocean floor: claims of jurisdiction over sea lanes and sea beds for the purposes of controlling commerce and mining/drilling rights (continental shelves & exclusive economic zones). The last marine frontiers on earth were claimed, carved up and disputed between nations like Australia, New Zealand, Greece, Cyprus, Turkey, Israel, Egypt, Libya, China, Russia, Italy, Canada, the entire EU, UK, USA, etc.

On February 24, 2022, the full-scale Russian invasion of Ukraine from three sides began: Crimea from the south, Russia from the east and Belarus from the north. An analysis of the Ukraine War, its prehistory and its consequences thus far reveals multiple zero-sum games being played at once. But more than the military confrontation on the Black Sea steppe at the borderlands between Europe and Asia, these zero-sum antagonisms are economic and geopolitical and span the whole world. Rather than a regional conflict with global consequences, the Russo-Ukrainian War has largely been a proxy war and a local eruption of a global struggle for hegemony. And both the leadup to it and its consequences—intended or not—provide ample examples of the accelerating replacement of globalization with neo-mercantilism (Mearsheimer, 2022; Orhan, 2022; Tong, 2024).

Just in the early 2000s, Ukraine was a major component of the Moscow-led bloc that Putin's Russian Federation was attempting to consolidate under the "Eurasian Economic Union." The bloc would largely reintegrate the former Soviet Republics and play both a plainly economic and a geostrategic role, allowing Russia to occupy the hegemonic position in an enlarged sphere of influence while simultaneously providing a buffer zone around the country's immense borders. In that effort, Ukraine was of tremendous significance to Russia for multiple reasons. It had rich natural resources and had historically been a huge source of grain not only for the sovereigns that controlled it over the centuries but for Europe and other parts of the world as well. It was the main passageway for the transfer of oil and natural gas from Russia to the EU. It was the base of the Russian Black Sea Fleet following bilateral agreements that had been in effect since 1997—the same year that the Union State of Belarus and Russia was signed into a treaty (Subtelny, 2009, pp. 599–600). More generally, it made it possible for Russia to maintain increased access to the Black Sea, an objective that has plagued Russian statesmen (and stateswomen like Catherine the Great) for centuries, and which was and remains of vital importance for a country whose ports largely freeze during the winter (LeDonne, 2006).

Ukraine is also the corridor through which most major Western invasions of Russia have been launched, from the Teutons, the Lithuanians and the Polish to the Swedish, the French and the Germans. Then there are the historical links between the two countries, stretching all the way back to their origin myths in the 8–13th-c. Kievan Rus. Add to that the cultural links back to the 14th-c. Byzantine-Roman creations of the "Little," "White" and "Great" Russias, the fact that most Ukrainians would also speak Russian and that Ukraine included large communities that identified as ethnically Russian as well as territories that were considered historically Russian and metropolises that had been built by Russian rulers such as Catherine. All these and other factors made it so that Ukraine was largely seen as belonging to the "Russian World" until the early 2010s, and there were even thoughts to ultimately establish a confederation encompassing Russia, Ukraine and Belarus on the basis of the Union State. However, Ukraine never joined and the Union State has not yet become a full-fledged confederation despite the close cooperation between Russia and Belarus (Mychajlyszyn, 2008; Szporluk, 1993; White et al., 2008). In the immediate wake of the disintegration of the Soviet Union, tensions had lit between Ukraine and Russia, primarily revolving around the questions of the Black Sea Fleet in Crimea and Soviet nuclear weapons in Ukraine. It was in those backs and forths in the few years that preceded the 1997 treaties that a Ukrainian government first put forward the NATO option as a response to Russian territorial claims (Solchanyk, 2001). Closer Ukrainian relations with NATO and the EU were seen both in Russia and the Ukraine itself as a zero-sum affair at the expense of the special relationship with Russia. They have also been a recurring building block in the project of Ukrainian nation-building as a "European" nation seeking to break with its Soviet and Slavic past. Nonetheless, Ukrainian "European" identity was declining until the late 2000s in parallel with "Soviet nostalgia", while public sentiment in Ukraine, Belarus and Russia favored further integration within the Commonwealth of Independent States (CIS) that succeeded the Soviet Union (White et al., 2010).

But while support for integration with Russia remained very strong in the "historically" Russian or the Russian-speaking regions of the country in the East and South (in the Donbas and around the Black Sea), northwestern Ukraine had a long tradition of anti-Russian nationalism. Volhynia and Galicia were the main areas of operation of the Organization of Ukrainian Nationalists (OUN) in the 1930s and 1940s, a fascist group that was responsible for the mass murders of Jews, Poles and Russians led by figures like Stepan Bandera (Kuromiya, 2008; Rossoliński-Liebe, 2015). In their effort to drive Ukraine into the Western sphere at the zero-sum expense of Russia, US neocons cooperated with Ukrainian political and paramilitary groups that had the OUN as their model, which were happy to turn the Euromaidan demonstrations of 2014 into a violent coup against the pro-Russian (Donbas-born) president of Ukraine, Viktor Yanukovych, shooting even at other protestors and the police in a ruthless false flag operation (Ishchenko, 2016; Katchanovski, 2024, 2026; Snider, 2022; Tsygankov, 2024).

Thus, the internal cold war within Ukraine exploded into a civil war in 2014 as NATO weapons manufacturers and their political representatives watched. The hundreds killed waving the Ukrainian and European Union flags were the only to do so until that time. And when the demonstrators chased Yanukovych from his palace, Putin announced the entire mess had been an "anti-constitutional coup and armed seizure of power" while Obama responded: "Putin seems to have a different set of lawyers, maybe a different set of interpretations" (Agence France-Presse, 2014; Brennan, 2014). So it was little surprise that NATO chief Jens Stoltenberg wrote (2023a) that Putin's ambitions threaten democracy and international law beyond Ukraine. He argued that any Russian territorial gains would encourage other authoritarian regimes, especially China, to use force. Stoltenberg stressed the need to show that aggression has consequences. In a testimony to the EU Parliament just two months later (2023b), Stoltenberg reiterated some of the same talking points while contradictorily recounting how it was the relentless push to enlarge NATO to Ukraine that was the real cause of the war and its perpetuation. The tortured, zero-sum logic of a militarist justifying militarism needs little explanation (Damon, 2023; Sachs, 2023).

In its continuing insistence to use Ukrainians as pawns and Ukraine as the chessboard for its zero-same game against Russia and China, the US empire was also increasingly pushing the cost onto the shoulders of its EU "vassal", as even the French president Emmanuel Macron has called it (Rankin, 2023; Trebesch, 2023). In typical inversion-of-reality propaganda, advocates of this policy like Max Boot moreover maintain that a war provoked to satisfy the zero-sum agenda of the global hegemon was not only unprovoked but has to continue for the sake of both Ukrainian and European security. Much like the sophistry that a Russian victory in Ukraine would make Putin more likely to use his country's nuclear arsenal (rather than in the imaginary scenario of Ukraine repelling the Russian army and launching a successful counter-invasion to take down the Russian government in Moscow), this presented the dangerous deterioration of European security and the slaughter of Ukrainians as a gift by the benevolent ally from the other side of the pond. It would also put ever more pressure on the EU to fund the US proxy war against Russia that has cut it off from its cheap energy source, has caused inflation to soar, leading to the dismantling of its industrial capacity and making it less secure and more one-sidedly dependent on the US (Larsen, 2025). Meanwhile, wheat speculation skyrocketed in 2022 after the invasion of Ukraine—just like Anglo-American corporate wheat speculation during 1930s–1940s and British oligarchs' wheat speculation during the French revolution (Trading Economics, n.d.).

By the dawn of 2024, it didn't matter whether they paid fealty to Washington, Beijing or Moscow (because they certainly didn't pay taxes), it was growing clear that the billionaires and oligarchs were causing trouble—on a global scale. Turchin (2023, pp. 188–189) blames the predictable short-term success and long-term failure of neoliberalism for the trajectory of Ukraine since the collapse of the Soviet Union: "Massive privatization of the state-owned corporations in Ukraine created a wealth pump that resulted in overproduction of oligarchs, inter-oligarch conflict, and repeated state collapses." Zhu (2022) notes that the highest echelons of the Chinese Communist Party are comprised of China's own oligarchs:

The combination of single-party authoritarianism and state capitalism gave rise to ruling oligarchs in China who utilized their political power as the primary foundation for engaging in a defense of both political power and material wealth in the reform era to protect their existing status and expand their influence.

Even *The Atlantic*'s Jeffrey Goldberg complained about "the oligarchic class" in America (Rosin & Goldberg, 2024). No matter the official ideology, in each case, whether in China, Russia or America, wealth would buy power, vice versa and justify it with zero-sum logic. Nothing made this clearer in 2024 than the US general election.

The most apparent aspect was the fashion among billionaires like Donald Trump and Elon Musk to present themselves as populists, promising tariffs and trade wars against foreign nations in the zero-sum service of the "America First" agenda to "Make America Great Again" (Harford, 2017). As the American tech elite attended the second inauguration in January, 2025, the new/old president said:

> Instead of taxing our citizens to enrich other countries, we will tariff and tax foreign countries to enrich our citizens. For this purpose, we are establishing the External Revenue Service to collect all tariffs, duties and revenues. It will be massive amounts of money pouring into our Treasury, coming from foreign sources.

If David Brooks equated 2025's "balance between Big Tech feudalism and the politics of protectionism," then for another, Trump's second electoral victory represents "a turn away from the postwar internationalism and back toward mercantilist nationalism." He and the rest of the beltway pundits immediately jumped on the phrase "zero-sum" to describe Trump's entire worldview and geopolitical agenda—revealed in his Norquist-inspired idealization of 19th-c. American foreign policy (Brooks et al., 2025; Greider, 2003; Miller, 2024).

Even Larry Summers conceded that the trade war would further enrich the investors by further impoverishing the workers. As one analyst summarizes Summers' zero-sum views of Trump's tariff proposals, they "would stifle international competition, raise consumer costs and increase corporate profits at the expense of falling inflation-adjusted wages in the American work force." Even more ironically, after calling his opponent Kamala Harris a Marxist, Trump modelled his own pitch directly after the CCP's mercantilist political economy: "China was built on doing exactly what we're going to be doing" (Weisman, 2024). As Kelton (2020, p. 151) writes,

> We have to stop treating trade as something we 'beat' other countries at by running a trade surplus. One country's surplus is another country's trade deficit, so by definition not everyone can win in that way at once. But it doesn't follow that the deficit country has to sustain real economic loss if it gets its policy matrix right. The Trumpian approach to trade creates strife and a zero-sum race to the bottom over too few globally available jobs... All in subservience to the trade deficit myth.

Other economists like Susskind (2024, pp. 131–132) have similarly warned that fixation with the GDP at the expense of other parameters inevitably leads to a parasitic, zero-sum form of political economy. What prevails in every case is a war of all against all.

Cold War II: the Anthropocene Between Thalassocracy and Tellurocracy

Empires are famously expensive to maintain, whether paid in blood or in gold. The old Eurasian ecumenical dynastic regimes like the Habsburgs, Ottomans, Romanovs and Bourbons weren't very efficient—they paid heavily in both. By contrast, the 19–20th-c. British Windsors famously ran their empire on a shoestring budget to outlast their German, Italian and Japanese rivals. Yet they all undoubtedly were structured as Wallerstein classically categorized: cheap labor and raw materials imported to the core and expensive finished goods exported to the periphery. The difference with the American empire is that, aside from its official nonexistence, by the 21st c., everything was outsourced—except for weapons and finance (Barnett, 2004; Immerwahr, 2019; Stiglitz, 2003). The American business with the best guarantee of long-term economic security was the security business itself. One representative plainly stated that "periodically culling the work force is actually good for a healthy organization" (Bumiller, 2025). According to another sector analyst, the American firearms industry, represented by the NRA (led by business dynasties like the Mercers, Daniels, Barretts, Mossbergs, etc.), is interested above all in murder profiteering, as "fascist billionaires like Rebekah Mercer have bankrolled and fueled the rise of violent white supremacist and authoritarian forces in this country" (Cunningham-Cook, 2021). Nothing guarantees good business for the arms industry quite like war and no political game is as ungovernable as war. In the era of the Anthropocene, the empire model is both constrained by and conducive to planetary transformations.

The increasing worldwide consolidation of neo-mercantilism has to be placed within processes of decoupling of national economies and a broader realignment of the world economy alongside geopolitical bloc formations in preparation for an all-out conflict in a new multipolar world (O'Sullivan, 2024). First of all, there are the big blocs, or, as Carl Schmitt called them, "Großräume" and, as commonly called in the 21st-c. geopolitical jargon of Moscow, New Delhi and Beijing, "civilization states." As it happened before every major confrontation, as well as during every such confrontation (think of the Italians changing sides in both World Wars), the blocs are volatile and beset by internal tensions that make bloc consolidation difficult and open to fissures or even breakdown. By the early 2020s, the Great Powers around which the blocs were formed were the United States, the EU, Russia, China, and to a lesser extent Turkey, Saudi Arabia and Iran. In yet another era of geopolitical realignment, the lesser blocs would be subject to ever shifting fealty regimes—much like the medieval dukes and other feudal lords that joined the banners of this or that emperor or king—with zero-sum fealty games played among many of them as well. Instead of seeing the global geopolitical and economic arena as monolithic, we have to understand it as a field in flux, with both mobility within the big blocs and peripheral antagonisms that further complicate the scene (Ikenberry, 2024; Fontaine & Kendall-Taylor, 2023).

The first old and wealthy alliance, between the EU, the United States and the other Anglophone nations was called into question during Trump's first presidency and fell into crisis during the beginning of his second. Beginning 2025 with yet another renegotiation of NAFTA (his 2017–2020 renegotiation wasn't rapacious enough) and insistences to buy Canada and Greenland, he clearly signalled a new era of geopolitical confrontation. In May 2025, after a formal speech about Canadian sovereignty by the British king Charles in Ottawa, blustering about his new "Golden Dome" missile shield over the continental 48 states, Trump offered $61b/year for Canadian protection—or free of charge in exchange for formal annexation. While the Canadians, British and Europeans were rebuilding their common military capabilities, Trump also threatened 50% tariffs to renegotiate EU-US trade agreements. Renegotiating NATO came next.

21st-c. American presidents back to GWB (2006) talked about European nations needing to shoulder the weight of NATO; it was a bone of contention. That year the US had 281 naval ships and 12 aircraft carriers but no universal healthcare, while Europeans (including the UK) had universal healthcare but only six carriers (Naval History & Heritage Command, 2010). The old Cold War's zero-sum dichotomy between "guns and butter" never left. The feeling was common that NATO benefitted Europeans more than Americans, but it didn't stop liberal interventionists in Washington (like Madeleine Albright, Zbigniew Brzezinski, Damon Wilson, together called "the blob") from pushing for NATO expansion funded by American taxpayers (Haslam, 2021; Mearsheimer, 2018; Sarotte, 2021; Walt, 2018). Ironically, after the accession of former Warsaw Pact members like Poland, Romania and the Baltics, it was the Europeans themselves who refused to comply with America's plan to have Ukraine join NATO. France and Germany opposed the 2008 Bucharest Agreement. They eventually backed down and went along with offering Georgia and Ukraine NATO membership but without a MAP (Membership Action Plan) (Wertheim, 2023). The Eurocrats thus engaged in their favorite mode of politics: can-kicking, namely playing a zero-sum game against the future by allowing serious problems to fester instead of taking a clear and principled position. Their steadfastness seems to chiefly appear in enforcing and embellishing zero-sum policies against the European working classes and the Global South, some areas of which they still exploit, destroy, and destabilize while repelling refugees fleeing from these same areas ("Fortress Europe") (Carr, 2015; Jünemann et al., 2017; Pérez, 2020).

Since the mid-2010s, the French President Macron repeatedly resorted to the discourse of "European strategic autonomy", mobilizing an idea that harks back to the origins of the EU project and has a prominent tradition in French politics (Česnakas, 2023). He even talked about an independent European policy vis-a-vis China that does not succumb to US pressures for the EU to get involved in its zero-sum antagonism with China (Anderlini & Caulcutt, 2023; Yan, 2023). However, France is not proposing neutrality but vainly trying to carve out a distinct role that allows for some autonomy while still generally aligning with the United States (Pajon, 2023). Thus, the discourse of strategic autonomy has not been translated into much materially—at least in relation to the United States—and, as the EU gets ever more entangled in US geopolitical prerogatives to reshuffle the global order, one assumes that it won't be long before this discourse is either silently relinquished or completely hollowed out and distorted to mean something else, such as European militarization on overdrive. The launching of the Weimar+ geopolitical alliance and the "ReArm Europe" project alongside the increase in NATO military spending, all initiated or endorsed by France in the first half of 2025 suggests the latter (Clapp et al., 2025; France Diplomacy, 2025; Kayali, 2025).

In this context, when Kyiv's Euromaidan crisis erupted in 2014, Brussels preferred not to sanction Yanukovych and instead maintained ties with Russia to secure Europe's energy needs and have some degree of independence from the United States. That was when Victoria Nuland, while giving instructions on who should be part of the Ukrainian cabinet (so much for Ukraine being a "sovereign country"), said: "fuck the EU" (Pilkington, 2014). The United States was repeatedly forcing the hand of the Germans to shoot themselves in the foot: first made them suspend the Nord-Stream 2 project, then likely sabotaged Nord-Stream pipelines, meanwhile convincing them to send weapons and tanks to Ukraine that the Germans initially objected to sending. As late as February 2022, Germany had avoided explicitly putting Nord-Stream 2 on the table when it came to sanctions on Russia (Batzella, 2024; DW, 2022; Hersh, 2023; Marsh & Chambers, 2022; Orozco, 2023; Terajima, 2025).

After the Ukraine War erupted, the USA "promised" to sell liquified gas to the EU, all the while the limited supply in its domestic market alongside the preexisting problem of inflation caused fossil fuel prices to soar. But confrontation with Russia and China was long in the making, and US elites had been preparing by making the US self-sufficient energy-wise through the worst method of oil extraction: fracking, which intensified under Obama, turning the United States into a huge player in the energy market (Bove et al., 2015; Clemente, 2019; Richardson, 2018). The lack of US energy self-sufficiency was only dealt with after 2008 but it was a major conundrum in the United States after the previous crisis, in the 1970s, extensively discussed in Thurow's *Zero-Sum Society* (2001). Obama oversaw this transition toward energy autarky just as Hillary Clinton (2011) was making announcements about America's "pivot to Asia"—codeword for containment of and, eventually, confrontation with China.

Ukraine itself was being saddled with unsustainable debt to fight a proxy war—the assistance packages from the West were rather purchases than gifts, only that the time of payment would be pushed into the future. In the meantime, Ukraine was indebted to pretty much all the parts of the US-led global financial architecture, including the IMF, which has (again) violated its own articles of agreement, this time by lending to a country at war. Some years back, in another great zero-sum stunt of the twenty-first century, the IMF had lent billions to the Greek state, although its constitution prohibits it from lending to countries with unsustainable debt under certain conditions. Greek state debt was not simply unsustainable, but the IMF forced consecutive governments to pursue policies that would ensure and worsen the level of unsustainability (along with dramatically increasing the ratio of debt to GDP), all to save few institutions and investors at the expense of the average Greek citizen. In this case, while Ukraine is allegedly being helped to liberate itself from an aggressor from the East, it is being subjugated to vulture funds and other forms of economic aggression from the West, made to sell off its natural resources and agricultural lands to companies such as Chevron. As if the involvement of the IMF wasn't enough to get a glimpse of the hardcore neoliberal path that Ukraine will be forced to take after the war, Zelensky's agreements with Blackrock have sealed its neoliberal future (Dixit, 2023). Behind the rhetoric of unconditional support for Ukraine, multinational corporations and the US military-industrial complex (primarily of the US but also of some of its allies such as the UK and even Germany) profit at the zero-sum expense of Ukrainians (Schwartz, 2023).

Western policy vis-a-vis Russia did not change with the invasions and counterinvasions of Ukraine and Russia but rather intensified and found a post-factum justification; the continuing expansion of NATO after the collapse of the USSR had no other point than to encircle Russia and make sure it would never again pose a threat to the United States. It was a plainly zero-sum approach to the relations between the two competing super powers of Cold War I—one made particularly perspicuous in RAND's 2018 study *Extending Russia*, which was intended as a manual for the creation of problems and multiple fronts for the Russian state (Dobbins, et al., 2019). Despite initial denial, public figures in support of (the war in) Ukraine increasingly normalized the notion that this was indeed a proxy war. Boot (2023; emphasis added) for instance claimed: "The war in Ukraine also stacks up impressively compared with *other proxy wars* that Republicans, under the Reagan administration, did so much to support." Russian Studies professor Stephen Cohen had summed up the zero-sum mindset of the US foreign policy apparatus three years before the war: "their perspective is what's bad for Russia is good for us" (Maté, 2019; cf. Cohen, 2019).

The Ukraine War would moreover be a way to funnel American tax dollars into its military industrial complex to spend foreign blood, impoverish domestic taxpayers and enrich wartime shareholders (Hartung et al., 2023; Savage, 2023). As the eternal Republican Senator justified American investment in the Ukraine War: "A significant portion of it is being spent in the United States in 38 different states, replacing the weapons that we sent to Ukraine with more modern weapons. So we're rebuilding our industrial base." Mitch McConnell then summarized all the reasons this was a win for the US: "No Americans are getting killed in Ukraine. We're rebuilding our industrial base. The Ukrainians are destroying the army of one of our biggest rivals" (CBS, 2023). The Ukraine war became part of the wider neomercantilist "reshoring" project.

It was little different in Russia's own military-industrial complex. After over three years of seemingly endless war in Ukraine's Donbas, Russian oligarchs sought short-term cheap-money profit over long-term stable investment, threatening the foundations of Putin's monetary and fiscal regime. According to Alexandra Prokopenko, a fellow at the Carnegie Russia Eurasia Center in Berlin and a former official at the Russian central bank, "If a warring nation can't present to its people an idea of a bright future, then it makes sense to stuff yourself while the party lasts. You may not have that chance later" (Kurmanaev, 2024). In the meantime, Putin's autarkic trade policies allowed Russia to pay for the war in Ukraine by replacing Western clients of Russian fossil fuel with Chinese and Indian clients. Russia's own neo-Keynesian war economy could additionally funnel subsidies directly back to Russian taxpayers for their war dead (Ishchenko et al., 2024).

While the Ukraine war after February 2022 fractured Eurasia along the northern corridor, widespread warfare in the Middle East after October 2023 wrought havoc on the southern corridor, accelerating decoupling processes between Western and Eastern Eurasia. The violence of October 7 in the southern Levant erupted not merely as a clash between Likud and Hamas but as another flashpoint in the zero-sum contest between an emergent and unstable Eurasian bloc led by Russia and China (popularly called BRICS) and the hegemonic but declining US-led Atlanticist bloc. The Hamas attack was a calculated reaction to the normalization of Arab–Israeli relations that started with the 2020 Abraham Accords and was meant to lead to a large-scale swap of hostage Israelis with some of the thousands of detained Palestinians. It initiated an iconically dark chapter in the long history of the Israeli-Palestinian conflict, ultimately leading to tens of thousands of Palestinian dead in what even B'tselem, Israel's Human Rights observatory, labelled a genocide, all made possible by Western diplomatic cover and continuous unconditional US support for Israel—as Biden had stated in 1986: "Were there not an Israel, the United States of America would have to invent an Israel to protect her interest in the region" (Ayyash, 2023). Liberal narratives of win–win settlements were again shattered by the zero-sum logics and actions of the most cynical political operators involved.

Benjamin Netanyahu, the Israeli prime minister of the Likud party, whose duplicitous divide-and-rule policies between Ramallah and Gaza had exacerbated the situation for decades, was already under immense pressure to resign on corruption charges. Bombarded for months by anticorruption demonstrations attended by tens of thousands of Israelis, Netanyahu was caught flat-footed and blamed for the intelligence failure (in more ways than one). In order to stay in power, Netanyahu made a deal with the most powerful far-right Jewish supremacists in the Knesset, Itamar ben-Gvir and Bezalel Smotrich, appointing them to cabinet roles to keep him out of jail. In return, they demanded the eventual conquest and ethnic cleansing of Gaza and Netanyahu happily obliged (Abu Ras, 2025; Kingsley et al., 2025).

Israel's intensified militarism since 2023 both fuels and is fueled by the increasing economic competition and geopolitical realignment. Through its military, intelligence and sabotage operations, Israel has largely destroyed the Iran-backed "Axis of Resistance." Hezbollah was downgraded as southern Lebanon was transformed into another battlefield. Syria has been neutralized after the ousting of Assad, with the primary beneficiaries (and likely contributors) being Turkey and Israel. Iran itself and the most steadfast anti-Israeli militants, the Houthis in Yemen, have been repeatedly attacked with open US participation. All these are not only conducive to the consolidation of Israel as the main regional power and the advancement of the project of "Greater Israel" at the zero-sum expense of neighboring Arab and Muslim states but also vital in the decoupling processes underway, as the US-led bloc seeks to counter the (risk of a) Eurasian coalition.

Simultaneously, the BRICS would expand, with ever more countries expressing interest in joining or officially filing for membership. Among the official applicants were both the arch-rivals of the Muslim world, Saudi Arabia and Iran, though only Iran acceded in early 2024. The two countries had taken the world by surprise in signing a China-brokered deal in March 2023 portrayed by many Western journalists as an American defeat in its zero-sum competition with China (e.g. Baker, 2023; CNBC, 2023). The BRICS bloc, which already surpassed the G7 in terms of combined GDP, prepared to launch a new trade currency, further fanning the flames of dedollarization (Sullivan, 2023). By the time the Donbas had firmly become ground zero in Cold War II when Putin hosted the BRICS summit in October, 2024, the power bloc would include "Egypt, Ethiopia, Iran and the United Arab Emirates. Together, the group represents almost half the world's population and more than 35 percent of global economic output, adjusted by purchasing power." With Saudi Arabia scheduled to join as well, the talk was of yet another New World Order, Trump as America's Gorbachev figure and a new reserve currency largely based on the yuan and ruble (Cocks, 2023; Hopkins & Pierson, 2024; Wilson, 2003). The fact that, by the end of 2024, gold had again become a highly demanded commodity by national bankers is telling. As one European central banker lamented: "It's a sign of impending wars" (Boffa & Munster, 2024).

The Saudi application is emblematic of this geopolitical reshuffling moment, given that it was the Saudis who had enabled the absolute domination of Nixon's petrodollar in global trade. Unlike its previous compliance to similar demands, Saudi Arabia disregarded the wishes of the United States and cut down on oil production during the first year of the Ukraine war. At that time the Biden administration was so desperate to keep soaring prices under relative control that it started pumping oil out of the country's strategic reserves into the market, nearly halving the reserves within a few months (USEIA, 2025). Still, Saudi Arabia and the rest of OPEC proceeded to announce further production cuts in the second year of the war. By the time the Trump and Putin governments were invited to Riyadh in February 2025, it was understood that a grand global bargain was to be struck in "a meeting of two big powers dividing up areas of dominance, a modern-day Congress of Vienna or Yalta Conference" (Baker, 2025). The country has also developed trilateral relations with India and Russia while continuing to stall on BRICS accession, and by late 2025 it seemed to be reembedding itself in the Washington-led bloc with a renewed role as a regional player with increased autonomy—encapsulated in its doctrine of "positive neutrality" (Fernández & Figueiredo dos Santos, 2025; Reuters, 2025; Malhotra, 2025; cf. Jon Alterman's statements about the Saudi-Iran deal in CNBC, 2023).

Like previous 19-20th-c. imperial carve-ups, Africa was back on the menu. The new scramble for Africa however was largely an overt reaction against 19–20th-c. European colonial rapacity and occurred within the African Union's own sub-blocs as well as between the US-EU bloc and BRICS (Polakow-Suransky, 2023). Africa would become fertile ground for China's answer to the American Marshall Plan: the Belt-and-Road Initiative. China would create transnational links through commercial infrastructure projects and sponsor archaeological excavations to search for traces of Chinese commerce along ancient silk roads in central Eurasia, maritime links in the 15th-c. South China Sea, and in East Africa (famously visited by Zheng He). Thus, archaeology would again be utilized by the great imperial powers of the twenty-first century, as it was in the twentieth century, to bolster claims of sovereignty, legitimacy, authority and spheres of influence (Hua & Parkyn-Smith, 2024). Meanwhile, the United States and France would try to retain their military presence and practices of resource extraction. This was particularly the case with France, whose residual gold reserves, banking and energy systems from the age of colonialism (based on uranium-fueled nuclear plants) were a glaring example of zero-sum neocolonialism at the expense of West Africa (Adamu, 2024; Ndongo & Pigeaud, 2020; TJN, 2021). Through Wagner mercenaries, Russia would infiltrate the continent, foment coups and interventions, be paid with control over natural resource extraction deals (little different from the French), and be increasingly celebrated by ordinary Africans for its insubordination to the West—with the same zero-sum logic of "the enemy of my enemy is my ally" (Gopaldas, 2023; Serwat et al., 2023).

The region of the Sahel between the Sahara and sub-Saharan Africa would become the primary area for the Franco-Russian intrigue of a new Great Game. Like other geographical/political regions, West African Sahel nations had also cohered their own bloc in Cold War I, the largely French-aligned Economic Community of West African States (ECOWAS). Yet at the outset of Cold War II, due to the endemic (and worsening) violence, corruption and inequality, the "coup belt" quickly splintered and several nations cohered a more pro-Russian emerging bloc against ECOWAS, the Alliance of Sahel States (Mali, Guinea, Burkina Faso, Niger), including the involvement of Libya and Algeria (Mednick, 2023). Niger, finding itself at the center of the geopolitical intrigue in West Africa, became an example when a 2023 coup backed by Russian Wagner mercenaries moved in at the expense of the West (and because of Western arrogance and negligence).

The coup belt stretched much further east than Niger. Something similar was going on in Sudan simultaneously, where worsening violence, corruption and inequality also allowed Wagner to infiltrate and play a role in yet another Sudanese civil war in the early 2020s (Magdy, 2023; News Wires, 2023; Rickett & Amin, 2024; Wilkins, 2023). From across the Red Sea, Saudi Arabia and particularly the UAE got even more involved, exploiting Sudan's gold and seeking to tap its vast agricultural lands for their own food security (UAE imports ~90% of its food) (Bhattacharya & Lathif, 2024; Coloma, 2025; Environmental Justice Atlas, n.d.; SwissAid, 2025). According to Amgad Fareid Eltayeb, adviser to Sudan's deposed prime minister, Abdalla Hamdok, the Biden administration's senior diplomats in Sudan "made the mistake of coddling the generals, accepting their irrational demands and treating them as natural political actors. This fed their lust for power and their illusion of legitimacy." They were never pushed to compromise and give up certain demands to have peace (Wong, et al., 2023). It was little surprise that amidst some of the most brutal wartime death tolls of the early 2020s, the civil war in Sudan, a majority Black and Islamic nation received some of the most minimal attention from the West. Referring to US policy, as a former adviser to the US special envoy for Sudan wrote, "the violence in Sudan is partly our fault" (Burns, 2023).

Alongside the new scramble for Africa, as more mineral wealth is discovered beneath the melting sea ice of the Arctic Ocean, a new 21st-c. scramble for the Arctic would heat up (Claes, 2017; Denning, 2023; Markowitz, 2023; Milne, 2023; Staun, 2017). After Cold War I, confusion over the US-Russia sea border, and apparent control over maritime resources, due to differing cartographic interpretations presaged questions about access to fishing and mineral rights in the high north (Edvardsen, 2024; USA-USSR Maritime Boundary Treaty, 1990). Crossing between the United States and Russia in the Bering Strait's Diomede Islands has been impossible since 2012 while Trump's US later pushed to expand its Thule military base by annexing all of Greenland (Paige, 2025; Roth, 2012). Following the 2010 resolution of a Russian-Norwegian border dispute, one of the byproducts would be increasing East–West spy games in the Arctic—which would threaten to consume the very radar intelligence to be produced (Nilsen, 2019; O'Connor, 2019; Standish, 2018; Taub, 2024).

Another hotspot is between the two most populous countries on the planet, China and India. Despite their co-membership in BRICS, there are historic tensions between the two nations which US foreign policy has sought to tap into. Even though India was one of the first countries to recognize the PRC in 1950, there were several small-scale military confrontations between them from the 1960s to the 1980s. Border disputes reignited passions since the 2010s, with skirmishes in the Himalaya leading to a few dozen deaths on both sides. Indian media are keen on venting anti-Chinese sentiment, an attitude discernible, for instance, on the English-speaking programs and articles of *WION* and *Hindustan Times*, while India preceded even the United States in the expulsion of Chinese software from its digital public space, banning TikTok and hundreds of other China-linked apps since 2020 (Mishra et al., 2022; Sherman, 2023). China is also a major ally of India's most hated neighbor, Pakistan—a hatred that had been masterfully stoked by the British decades earlier in their usual divide-and-rule tactic of entrapping their enemies and their subordinates in zero-sum struggles against each other (Krishnan, 2020; Stacey, 2020). Nevertheless, China has become India's largest trading partner along with the US and the single biggest contributor to India's huge trade deficit (India's deficit was only behind the US and the UK in 2023) (Hindu, 2024; Workman, 2023–2024). Trump's first administration had already played up this antagonism, making deals with India against China (mostly in the context of QUAD), with former CIA director and then secretary of state Mike Pompeo urging tighter alignment to counter the CCP. Chinese authorities openly criticized Pompeo's zero-sum logic: "We urge Pompeo to abandon his Cold War mentality, zero-sum mindset, and stop harping on the 'China threat'" (Arora & Miglani, 2020; Hindu, 2020; Ibrahim, 2020). The US strategy vis-a-vis India additionally involved economic incentives and relocation of production from China to India—as part of a wider process of decoupling with China and "friendshoring" production in the US and key allies like Taiwan, Korea and the QUAD members (Goodman, 2024).

Contrary to China, India boasts a "unique" and "privileged" relationship with Russia that continues uninterrupted from the time of the former's declaration of independence. After all, although it was Tito who officially launched the Non-Aligned Movement with the 1961 Belgrade Conference, the origins of the movement (which reflected a desire for other sovereign states to avoid getting too entangled in the zero-sum games played between the USSR and the USA, maintaining relations with any of the two if they wished so) can be traced back to the 1947 Asian Relations Conference organized in New Delhi by the interim Indian government and the soon-to-be first Prime Minister of independent India Jawaharlal Nehru. This became the foundation for India's "strategic autonomy" principle and its preference for multipolarity (Ganguly, 2024; Joshi & Sharma, 2017; Pandya, 2024; Sibal, 2023).

Like at the outset of the previous Cold War, the two superpowers restarted in earnest the competition for allies and clients in a new "third world"—now termed the "Global South." In 2022, Mexico's president, AMLO, spoke for the entire Global South in his criticisms of the crass corruption, profound inequality and structural unsustainability of the current crop of global oligopolies, most notably the arms industries, in pushing for the war in Ukraine for profit from

NATO expansion (Hackbarth, 2022). Then, in 2023, Brazil's president, Lula, similarly emphasized global South-South cooperation, especially in regard to Africa and Latin America, while criticizing neoliberal global institutions like the IMF and the World Bank as perpetuating international inequalities and injustices (da Silva, 2023; cf. Krugman, 2021a, 2021b). Across the Atlantic, similar remarks were made in South Africa upon Putin's 2023 visit for the BRICS conference, although he spoke of "the global majority" instead, seeking international support for Russia's invasion of Ukraine (DW, 2023; Higham, 2023; Sorman, 2023). For most of the Global South, the Ukraine War would be regarded as another proxy war within another Cold War between the West and the Chinese-Russian alliance. It would also largely be considered as a case of a "pox on both houses" (Askew, 2023). So the 2024 "neocolonial" EU-Mercosur trade deal seemed somewhat out of place given the growing skepticism of free trade in the waning days of neoliberalism (Bieler, 2023).

In its zero-sum contest with China, the United States also sought to tap into and modify the international security and economic arrangements it had enshrined after WWII, which had enabled it to remain the global financial hegemon for almost a century. While pushing for the expansion and military bolstering of NATO and lining up the QUAD of major Indo-Pacific nations (Australia, India, Japan and the US), both major bonanzas for its military-industrial complex, it renegotiated its economic relations with its allies, particularly through Trump's tariff incursions. It made Europeans absorb the brunt costs of the economic war on Russia and Australians fund the modernization of the US submarine fleet (Butler, 2023). It therefore seemed to be increasingly "re-vassalizing" its partners, boosting its zero-sum edge over its Chinese rival at the zero-sum expense of its various allies.

The wistful, almost nostalgic way that American pundits speak of "a time of hope and progress that began in the late 1980s [which] was somehow derailed," bespeaks a clear Western hubristic expression of arrogance—the same smug dismissal of war as when pundits talk about being "on the right side of history" (Nichols, 2022). It also becomes convenient fodder for critics who easily note the "cruelty, slavery and disenfranchisement" in the histories and paradoxes of liberal democracy as (neo)liberalism consumes democracy: "Fear, cynicism, nihilism, and apathy, coupled with disgust and disdain for democracy: This is what modern autocrats sell to their citizens and to foreigners, all with the aim of destroying what they call 'American hegemony'" (Applebaum, 2024; Whitham, 2022). This also is how liberalism goes from yearning for peace to war—creative destruction, or as the economic anthropologists Andersson and Keen (2023) call it, *Wreckonomics*. And so it's little surprise (and cold comfort) that Roger Wicker (2024), chairman of the US Senate armed services committee writes that world peace requires a "generational investment to help us prevent another world war." Similarly, the French historian Emmanuel Todd prophesies the defeat of the West (Caldwell, 2024).

It's understandable that for the Global South, BRICS has become an increasingly attractive way to avoid vassalage to the American imperium: BRICS expansion challenges Washington's traditional zero-sum approach of exploiting regional divisions to maintain global dominance. By fostering cross-continental cooperation, BRICS offers middle powers an alternative to "There Is No Alternative." While signaling declining U.S. hegemony, this shift doesn't necessarily indicate anti-American sentiment. For Shidore (2023), the US should view this not as a threat, but as an opportunity to reassess its global role and address its domestic issues. This perspective challenges the zero-sum view of the political economies inherent in international relations, suggesting that a more balanced global order could benefit both the US and the wider world. The Norwegian sociologist Johann Galtung (2009) made a similar claim—that new civilization states can coexist peacefully without hegemonically imposing one's zero-sum political economy on another.

Yet the so-called "civilization states" of the twenty-first century defy easy descriptions (Coker, 2019; Economist, 2020; Maçães, 2020). The interests of one civilizational bloc could easily come at the expense of another. Whether discussing the Islamic, Orthodox Russian or Confucian Chinese civilizational blocs, the outright rejection of American-led neoliberal globalism would invite the very backlash that would realistically re-partition the world by the United States and exclude/embargo/etc., its antagonists (all the while connecting to the myths of free trade, non-interference, respect of sovereignty, etc.). If Putin had been working toward a new Yalta-style carve-up for a quarter century, the US plan would be to Balkanize Russia or in some way or form return it to its 1990s state of impotence in order for America to handle China, North Korea, Iran and its other traditional adversaries (of course any leeway for US-aligned corporations into the vast reserves of valuable natural resources of an impotent Eurasian sphere would be a bonus) (Ballard, 2023).

The host of new wars proliferating like nuclear weapons at the outset of Cold War II this would obviously engender would be truly unprecedented. Or as Friedman (2024) described the significance of the fall of Syria's Assad regime: "We have never been here before in the post-World War II era—a moment when so many countries have descended into this Hobbesian state of nature, but in a much more connected world." It was in this context that the French president Emmanuel Macron justified the official shift of his foreign policy from liberal multilateralism to zero-sum militarism in November, 2024:

> The world is made up of herbivores and carnivores. If we decide to remain herbivores, then the carnivores will win and we will be a market for them.... I think, at the very least, we should choose to become omnivores. I don't want to be aggressive, just that we know how to defend ourselves on all these subjects. (Reuters, 2024)

A few months later, in September 2025, Trump issued an executive order "restoring the United States Department of War" (Trump, 2025), while various EU bureaucrats as well as senior political and military figures across EU member states would ever more frequently make statements about the need to prepare for an almost inevitable war with Russia and get used to the idea of dead European soldiers, thereby manufacturing consent for such a war (e.g. Dendias' stark message..., 2025; dpa, 2025; Le Monde with AFP, 2025).

And so at global peace summits in recent years, "world leaders troop to the meeting of the General Assembly of the United Nations, where the Security Council is largely paralyzed by Russian vetoes over any Ukraine-related resolutions and American vetoes over Israel-related resolutions" (Cohen, 2024a, 2024b). In late 2025, negotiations over ceasefires, security guarantees and reconstruction packages in Ukraine and Gaza continue in fits and starts, but function less as pathways to real peace than as weapons in the broader fight to lock in spheres of influence and domestic political advantage, to profit at the zero-sum expense of afflicted populations, adversaries and allies, to engage in ever more rounds of disaster capitalism. Without any guardrails on their militaristic foreign policy, with nuclear weapons proliferation treaties expiring and a toothless ICC and UN, the only impediment to a nuclear three-body problem would be the taboo against using nuclear weapons in war.

Although the Anthropocene was rejected as a formal unit of Geologic Time Scale in 2024 by the International Commission on Stratigraphy (ICS) and the International Union of Geological Sciences (IUGS), they still acknowledged that it "will nevertheless continue to be used not only by Earth and environmental scientists, but also by social scientists, politicians and economists, as well as by the public at large. It will remain an invaluable descriptor of human impact on the Earth system" (International Union of Geological Scientists, 2024). It's a good thing too, because the Anthropocene is both a highly ironic name and an implicit corrective. Even if informally, we have named a geological era after our species not because of our achievements but because of the damage we inflict on the planet. Despite the shallowness (both literal and metaphorical) of the anthropogenic plastic in the earth sediment, garbage continents floating in the oceans and massive carbon emissions in the skies, the term also indicates that, with a bit of self-deprecation, we can still make better decisions to protect and share this finite planet among all of us. That's what Human Rights are about after all. Hope without illusion. Realism without resignation.

References

Aassve, A., Alfani, G., Gandolfi, F., Le Moglie, M., & Ødegård, G. (2021). Early assessment of the relationship between the COVID-19 pandemic and births in high-income countries. *Proceedings of the National Academy of Sciences, 118*(36), e2105709118. https://doi.org/10.1073/pnas.2105709118

Abu Ras, T. (2025, November 19). *A calculus of conflict: Netanyahu's political survival through extended war*. Arab Center Washington DC. https://arabcenterdc.org/resource/a-calculus-of-conflict-netanyahus-political-survival-through-extended-war/

Acemoglu, D. (2024, October 17). America is sleepwalking into an economic storm. *The New York Times*. https://www.nytimes.com/2024/10/17/opinion/economy-us-aging-work-force-ai.html

Adamu, T. (2024, December 24). French monetary imperialism in Africa. *The Guardian*. https://guardian.ng/opinion/french-monetary-imperialism-in-africa

Agence France-Presse (2014, March 5). Obama says Putin 'not fooling anybody' over Ukraine. *Hurriyet Daily News*. https://www.hurriyetdailynews.com/obama-says-putin-not-fooling-anybody-over-ukraine-63221

Aiyar, S. (2024, August 30). The cost of protectionism will be paid by the world's poorest. *The New York Times*. https://www.nytimes.com/2024/08/30/opinion/tariffs-us-india-china.html

Anderlini, J. & Caulcutt, C. (2023, April 9). Europe must resist pressure to become 'America's followers,' says Macron. *Politico*, https://www.politico.eu/article/emmanuel-macron-china-america-pressure-interview

Andersson, R., & Keen, D. (2023). *Wreckonomics: Why it's time to end the war on everything*. Oxford University Press.

Ang, Y., & Klein, E. (2023, January 24). Ezra Klein interviews Yuen Yuen Ang. *The New York Times*. https://nyti.ms/3j2MkGY

Applebaum, A. (2024, May 6). The new propaganda war. *The Atlantic*. https://www.theatlantic.com/magazine/archive/2024/06/china-russia-republican-party-relations/678271

Arntz, P. (2023, April 3). *TikTok: What's going on and should I be worried?* Malwarebytes. https://www.malwarebytes.com/blog/news/2023/04/tiktok-whats-going-on-and-should-i-be-worried

Arora, N. & Miglani, S. (2020, October 27). *U.S. warns of threat posed by China, signs military pact with India*. Reuters. https://www.reuters.com/article/usa-asia-india-idUSKBN27C0OF

Askew, J. (2023, March 29). Why does so much of the Global South support Russia, not Ukraine. *Euronews*. https://www.euronews.com/my-europe/2023/03/29/why-does-so-much-of-the-global-south-support-russia-not-ukraine

Ayyash, M. (2023, July 25). Biden says the U.S. would have to invent an Israel if it didn't exist. Why? *The Conversation*. https://theconversation.com/biden-says-the-u-s-would-have-to-invent-an-israel-if-it-didnt-exist-why-210172

Baines, J., & Hager, S. B. (2021). The great debt divergence and its implications for the Covid-19 crisis: Mapping corporate leverage as power. *New Political Economy, 26*(5), 885–901. https://doi.org/10.1080/13563467.2020.1865900

Baker, P. (2023, March 11). Chinese-brokered deal upends Mideast diplomacy and challenges U.S. *The New York Times*. https://www.nytimes.com/2023/03/11/us/politics/saudi-arabia-iran-china-biden.html

Baker, P. (2025, February 18). Trump's pivot toward Putin's Russia upends generations of U.S. policy. *The New York Times*. https://www.nytimes.com/2025/02/18/us/politics/trump-russia-putin.html

Ballard, E. (2023, August 14). The economic losers in the new world order. *The Wall Street Journal*. https://www.wsj.com/articles/global-economy-economic-losers-fba30b53

Barnett, A. (2017). *The lure of greatness: England's Brexit & America's Trump*. Unbound.

Barnett, T. (2004). *The Pentagon's new map: War and peace in the twenty-first century*. Putnam.

Barro, R., Ursúa, J. F., & Weng, J. (2020). *The coronavirus and the Great Influenza Pandemic: Lessons from the "Spanish Flu" for the coronavirus's potential effects on mortality and economic activity* (*NBER* Working Paper No. 26866). https://doi.org/10.3386/w26866

Batzella, F. (2024). Slowly but surely? Assessing EU actorness in energy sanctions against Russia. *Energy Policy, 192*, 114233. https://doi.org/10.1016/j.enpol.2024.114233

Bermingham, P.-P. (2021, May 31). Denmark's secret service helped NSA spy on Merkel, EU officials: Report. *Politico*. https://www.politico.eu/article/press-report-merkel-and-eu-leaders-spied-on-by-nsa-via-denmark/

Bhattacharya, S., & Lathif, A. F. (2024, July 26). *UAE and Saudi Arabia's agricultural diplomacy in Africa: Competition, cooperation and its strategic implications*. Observer Research Foundation (ORF) Middle East. https://orfme.org/expert-speak/uae-and-saudi-arabias-agricultural-diplomacy-in-africa-competition-cooperation-and-its-strategic-implications

Bieler, A. (2023, September 5). *Cementing neo-colonial relations: The EU–Mercosur 'free' trade deal*. Progress in Political Economy. https://www.ppesydney.net/cementing-neo-colonial-relations-the-eu-mercosur-free-trade-deal

Bloomberg News. (2023, March 7). *China warns US risks catastrophe with moves to 'contain' Beijing*. Bloomberg. https://www.bloomberg.com/news/articles/2023-03-07/qin-warns-that-us-zero-sum-game-with-china-risks-catastrophe

Boffa, C., & Munster, B. (2024, December 31). 'It's a sign of impending wars': Why a tense world is betting on gold. *Politico.* https://www.politico.eu/article/sign-impending-war-tense-world-bet-gold-bank

Boot, M. (2023, October 2). This is what the U.S. is getting by aiding Ukraine. *The Washington Post.* https://www.washingtonpost.com/opinions/2023/10/02/ukraine-aid-great-investment/

Booth, W., Adam, K., & Rolfe, P. (2020, March 26). In fight against coronavirus, the world gives medical heroes a standing ovation. *Washington Post.* https://www.washingtonpost.com/world/europe/clap-for-carers/2020/03/26

Bove, V., Gleditsch, K. S., & Sekeris, P. G. (2015). "Oil above Water": Economic Interdependence and third-party intervention. *Journal of Conflict Resolution, 60*(7), 1251–1277. https://doi.org/10.1177/0022002714567952

Brennan, C. (2014, March 5). Putin sees no political future for Yanukovych. *The Moscow Times.* https://www.themoscowtimes.com/archive/putin-sees-no-political-future-for-yanukovych

Brooks, D., Douthat, R., & Goldberg, M. (2025, January 19). 'We'd have been better off if Trump won in 2020': Three columnists brace for the first 100 days. *The New York Times.* https://www.nytimes.com/2025/01/19/opinion/trump-second-term.html

Bumiller, E. (2025, March 6). 'People are going silent': Fearing retribution, Trump critics muzzle themselves. *The New York Times.* https://www.nytimes.com/2025/03/06/us/politics/trump-democracy.html

Burns, J. (2023, April 23). The violence in Sudan is partly our fault. *The New York Times.* https://nyti.ms/3N7pACC

Bush, G. W. (2006, November 28). President Bush discusses the Global War on Terror. *The White House.* https://georgewbush-whitehouse.archives.gov/news/releases/2006/11/20061128-11.html

Butler, J. (2023, March 17). Peter Garrett says nuclear submarine deal 'most costly and risky' action ever taken by an Australian government. *The Guardian.* https://www.theguardian.com/world/2023/mar/17/peter-garrett-says-nuclear-submarine-deal-most-costly-and-risky-action-ever-taken-by-an-australian-government

Caldwell, C. (2021, October 4). A pillar of the European order has collapsed. *The New York Times.* https://nyti.ms/3FfNfdy

Caldwell, C. (2024, March 9). This prophetic academic now foresees the West's defeat. *The New York Times.* https://www.nytimes.com/2024/03/09/opinion/emmanuel-todd-decline-west.html

Carr, M. (2015). *Fortress Europe: Inside the war against immigration.* Hurst.

CBS. (2023, October 22*). Transcript: Senate minority leader Mitch McConnell on 'Face the Nation.'* CBS News. https://www.cbsnews.com/news/mitch-mcconnell-senate-minority-leader-face-the-nation-transcript-10-22-2023

CDC Museum. (2024, July 8). COVID-19 timeline. *Centers for Disease Control & Prevention.* https://www.cdc.gov/museum/timeline/covid19.html

Česnakas, G. (2023). European strategic autonomy: The origin story. In G. Česnakas & J. Juozaitis (Eds.), *European strategic autonomy and small states' security: In the shadow of power* (pp. 14–33). Routledge.

Chan, K. (2025, May 19). In the future, China will be dominant. The U.S. will be irrelevant. *The New York Times.* https://www.nytimes.com/2025/05/19/opinion/china-us-trade-tariffs.html

Chomsky, N., Kasparian, A., & Vila, N. (2021, June 10). *Noam Chomsky: The elites are fighting a vicious class war all the time.* Jacobin. https://jacobin.com/2021/06/noam-chomsky-class-war-universal-health-care-climate-justice-denuclearization

Claes, D. (2017). The scramble for Arctic oil and natural gas. In T. Lehmann (Ed.), *The geopolitics of global energy: The new cost of plenty* (pp. 85–104). Lynne Rienner Publishers.

Clapp, S., et al. (2025). *ReArm Europe Plan/Readiness 2030* (Briefing No. PE 769.566). European Parliamentary Research Service.

Clemente, J. (2019, December 31). President Obama's support for America's shale oil and natural gas. *Forbes.* https://www.forbes.com/sites/judeclemente/2020/12/31/president-obamas-support-for-americas-shale-oil-and-natural-gas

Clinton, H. R. (2011, October 11). America's Pacific century. *Foreign Policy*. https://foreignpolicy.com/2011/10/11/americas-pacific-century

CNBC. (2023, March 13). *Saudi-Iranian deal: Saudis demonstrating they're 'in control of their own destiny,' think tank says [Video]*. CNBC. https://www.cnbc.com/video/2023/03/13/csis-jon-alterman-discusses-deal-between-saudi-arabia-and-iran.html

Coates, R. (2025, January 27). Why Trump's tariffs can't solve America's fentanyl crisis. *The Conversation*. https://theconversation.com/why-trumps-tariffs-cant-solve-americas-fentanyl-crisis-245978

Cocks, T. (2023, July 20). *More than 40 nations interested in joining BRICS, South Africa says*. Reuters. https://www.reuters.com/world/more-than-40-nations-interested-joining-brics-south-africa-2023-07-20

Cohen, D. (2018, May 11). *The Sackler files: Billionaire liked to parade as philanthropist... in fact he was tax avoider on industrial scale*. The Standard. https://www.standard.co.uk/news/uk/the-sackler-files-billionaire-likes-to-parade-as-philanthropist-in-fact-he-was-tax-avoider-on-industrial-a3836371.htm

Cohen, S. F. (2019). *War with Russia? From Putin and Ukraine to Trump and Russiagate*. Skyhorse Publishing Company, Incorporated.

Cohen, P. (2023, September 18). Crisis and bailout: The tortuous cycle stalking nations in debt. *The New York Times*. https://www.nytimes.com/2023/09/18/business/economy/ghana-debt-imf.html

Cohen, P. (2024, April 17). The global turn away from free-market policies worries economists. *The New York Times*. https://www.nytimes.com/2024/04/17/business/economy/industrial-policies-global-economy.html

Cohen, R. (2024, September 29). Why the world's biggest powers can't stop a Middle East war. *The New York Times*. https://www.nytimes.com/2024/09/29/world/middleeast/middle-east-war-peace-nasrallah.html

Coker, C. (2019). *The rise of the civilizational state*. Wiley.

Coloma, T. (2025, March). Smuggled gold fuels Sudan war. *Le Monde diplomatique* (English edition). https://mondediplo.com/2025/03/10sudan

Cook, I. (2021, September 15). Who is driving the great resignation? *Harvard Business Review*. https://hbr.org/2021/09/who-is-driving-the-great-resignation

Cruz, S. (Ed.). (2022). *Opioids: Pharmacology, abuse, & addiction*. Springer.

Cunningham-Cook, M. (2021, January 27). *Rebekah Mercer raised specter of 'armed conflict' in 2019 book*. The Intercept. https://theintercept.com/2021/01/27/rebekah-mercer-book-capitol-riot

Damon, A. (2023, May 11). *The narrative of the 'unprovoked war' in Ukraine falls apart*. World Socialist Web Site. https://www.wsws.org/en/articles/2023/05/11/gfgh-m11.html

da Silva, L. I. L. (2023, September 19). *Speech by President Luiz Inácio Lula da Silva at the opening of the 78th U.N. General Assembly*. Government of Brazil. https://www.gov.br/planalto/en/follow-the-government/speeches-statements/2023/speech-by-president-luiz-inacio-lula-da-silva-at-the-opening-of-the-78th-un-general-assembly

Davidson, H., Ni, V., & Cecco, L. (2021, August 19). Meng Wanzhou: 'princess of Huawei' who became the face of a high-stakes dispute. *The Guardian*. https://www.theguardian.com/technology/2021/aug/19/meng-wanzhou-huawei-profile-china-canada-us-dispute

Dendias' stark message on war casualties alarms Europe. (2025, November 19). *Ta Nea: The Hellenic Australian Insight*. https://tanea.com.au/en/dendias-stark-message-on-war-casualties-alarms-europe/

Denning, L. (2023, June 4). *Hiding an army at the top of the world*. Bloomberg. https://www.bloomberg.com/graphics/2023-opinion-arctic-geopolitics-resources/army-training.html

Dixit, P. (2023, May 6). 'Is Ukraine being privatised': Netizens fume over President Zelensky's meet with BlackRock management. *Business Today*. https://www.businesstoday.in/latest/world/story/is-ukraine-being-privatised-netizens-fume-over-president-zelenskyys-meet-with-blackrock-management-380295-2023-05-06

Dobbins, J., et al. (2019, April 24). *Extending Russia: Competing from advantageous ground.* RAND Corporation. https://www.rand.org/pubs/research_reports/RR3063.html

Dolphin-Krute, M. (2018). *Opioids: Addiction, narrative, freedom.* Punctum Books.

dpa. (2025, October 16). EU unveils rearmament plan, warns continent 'at risk' from Russia. *European Newsroom.* https://europeannewsroom.com/eu-unveils-rearmament-plan-warns-continent-at-risk-from-russia/

DW. (2022, February 22). Germany halts Nord Stream 2 approval. *Deutsche Welle.* https://www.dw.com/en/ukraine-crisis-germany-halts-nord-stream-2-approval/a-60867443

DW. (2023, August 23). BRICS Summit Day One: Leaders eye expansion, common currency. *Deutsche Welle.* https://www.dw.com/en/brics-summit-day-one/live-66598906#liveblog-post-66603293

Eaton, G. (2021, September 22). Michael Sandel interview: "Joe Biden has broken with neoliberalism." *The New Statesman.* https://www.newstatesman.com/encounter/2021/09/michael-sandel-joe-biden-has-broken-with-neoliberalism

Economist. (2020, January 2). Huntington's disease and the clash of civilisation-states. *The Economist.* https://www.economist.com/europe/2020/01/02/huntingtons-disease-and-the-clash-of-civilisation-states

Economist. (2024, March 21). Why "Freakonomics" failed to transform economics. *The Economist.* https://www.economist.com/finance-and-economics/2024/03/21/why-freakonomics-failed-to-transform-economics.

ECOSOC [UN Economic & Social Council]. (2023, January 24). *Economic and Social Council adopts decision setting dates of financing for development follow-up, youth forum in 2023* [Press release]. United Nations. https://press.un.org/en/2023/ecosoc7118.doc.htm

Edgerton, D. (2020, June 10). The new age of autarky. *The New Statesman.* https://www.newstatesman.com/uncategorized/2020/06/new-age-autarky

Edvardsen, A. (2024, February 19). Lavrov stands firm on maritime border agreements with Norway and the US. *High North News (Arctic Today).* https://www.highnorthnews.com/en/lavrov-stands-firm-maritime-border-agreements-norway-and-us

Elliott, L. (2022, March 13). Incessant crises show old economic model is running on empty. *The Guardian.* https://www.theguardian.com/business/2022/mar/13/incessant-crises-show-old-economic-model-is-running-on-empty-financial-crisis-covid-inflation-war

Elliott, L. (2023, August 27). In a multipolar world the dollar's dominance won't last forever. *The Guardian.* https://www.theguardian.com/business/2023/aug/27/multipolar-world-dollars-dominance-wont-last-forever-brics

Environmental Justice Atlas. (n.d.). *Land grabbing in Sudan.* Global Atlas of Environmental Justice. https://ejatlas.org/conflict/land-grabbing-sudan

Farmer, P. (2001). *Infections and inequalities: The modern plagues.* University of California Press.

Farrer, M., (2021, October 2). 'A perfect storm': Supply chain crisis could blow world economy off course. *The Guardian.* https://www.theguardian.com/business/2021/oct/02/supply-chain-world-economy-energy-labour-transport-covid

Felbab-Brown, V. (2022, March). *China & synthetic drugs control: Fentanyl, methamphetamines, & precursors.* Brookings Institution. https://www.brookings.edu/research/china-and-synthetic-drugs-control-fentanyl-methamphetamines-and-precursors

Fernández, M., & Figueiredo dos Santos, M. L. (2025). A Arábia saúdita e o BRICS: neutralidade positiva e liberança diplomática em tempos multipolares. *BPC Papers, 15*(4). https://bricspolicycenter.org/en/publications/saudi-arabia-and-the-brics-positive-neutrality-and-diplomatic-leadership-in-multipolar-times/

Fischer, D. H. (1996). *The great wave: Price revolutions and the rhythm of history.* Oxford University Press.

Fomenko, T. (2023a, April 4). *US efforts to ban TikTok are pure projection by the world's biggest spy power.* RT. https://www.rt.com/news/574164-us-efforts-ban-tiktok

Fomenko, T. (2023b, March 20). *US demands to sell TikTok are a political extortion scheme.* RT. https://www.rt.com/news/573257-us-china-tiktok-demands

Fontaine, R., & Kendall-Taylor, A. (2023, May–June). The axis of upheaval. *Foreign Affairs.* https://www.foreignaffairs.com/world/axis-upheaval

Foroohar, R. (2016). *Makers and takers: The rise of finance and the fall of American business.* Crown.

France Diplomacy. (2025, February 12). *Weimar+ statement (France, Germany, Poland, Italy, Spain, United-Kingdom, Ukraine, HRVP, European Commission).* Ministry for Europe and Foreign Affairs. https://www.diplomatie.gouv.fr/en/country-files/ukraine/news/article/weimar-statement-france-germany-poland-italy-spain-united-kingdom-ukraine-hrvp

Friedman, T. L. (2024, December 8). Five quick takes on regime change in Syria. *The New York Times.* https://www.nytimes.com/2024/12/08/opinion/friedman-syria-iran-future.html

Frum, D. (2023, April 26). The coming Biden blowout. *The Atlantic.* https://www.theatlantic.com/ideas/archive/2023/04/gop-republicans-2024-election-biden-trump/673856

Frum, D. (2025, April 25). The coming economic nightmare. *The Atlantic.* https://www.theatlantic.com/magazine/archive/2025/06/trump-economy-tariffs-stagflation/682572/

Galtung, J. (2009). *The fall of the US empire—And then what?* Transcend University Press.

Ganguly, S. (2024). India, Russia and the Ukraine crisis. *Washington Quarterly, 47*(2), 55–69. https://doi.org/10.1080/0163660X.2024.2366108

Goldberg, J. (2016, March 10). Obama unhappy with allies, upset at free riders. *Atlantic Council.* https://www.atlanticcouncil.org/blogs/natosource/obama-unhappy-with-allies-upset-at-free-riders/

Goldmacher, S., & Fandos, N. (2021, February 18). Ted Cruz's Cancun trip: Family text messages detail his political blunder. *The New York Times.* https://www.nytimes.com/2021/02/18/us/politics/ted-cruz-storm-cancun.html

Goodman, P. (2024, June 26). For American brands worried about China, is India the future? *The New York Times.* https://www.nytimes.com/2024/06/26/business/india-us-manufacturing.html

Gopaldas, R. (2023, April 26). *Will the invasion of Ukraine change Russia-Africa relations?* Carnegie Endowment for International Peace. https://carnegieendowment.org/research/2023/04/will-the-invasion-of-ukraine-change-russia-africa-relations

Graci, G. (2023, December 4). *The fentanyl blame game: How Mexico, the United States, & China avoid coordinated efforts.* Stanford International Policy Review. https://fsi.stanford.edu/sipr/fentanyl-blame-game

Greider, W. (2003, May 12). Rolling back the twentieth century. *The Nation.*

Guardian Investigations Team. (2021, October 3). Pandora Papers: Biggest ever leak of offshore data exposes financial secrets of rich & powerful. *The Guardian.* https://www.theguardian.com/news/2021/oct/03/pandora-papers-biggest-ever-leak-of-offshore-data-exposes-financial-secrets-of-rich-and-powerful

Hackbarth, K. (2022, September 29). AMLO is calling for peace in Ukraine, but more military in Mexico. *Jacobin.* https://jacobin.com/2022/09/amlo-mexico-ukraine-peace-military-internal-security

Hale, E. (2023, March 28). US says China can spy with TikTok. It spies on world with Google. *Al Jazeera.* https://www.aljazeera.com/economy/2023/3/28/bid-to-ban-tiktok-raises-hypocrisy-charge-amid-global-spying

Hampton, R. (2024). *Fentanyl nation: Toxic politics and America's failed war on drugs.* Martin's Press.

Harford, T. (2017, August 25). Trump, Bannon and the lure of zero-sum thinking. *Financial Times.* https://www.ft.com/content/381f5888-88b0-11e7-bf50-e1c239b45787

Hartung, W., Gamio, L., & Swanson, A. (2023, March 13; 2022, October 30). US dominates global arms trade as exports to Europe surge/How Russia pays for war. *Responsible Statecraft & The New York Times.* https://responsiblestatecraft.org/2023/03/13/us-dominates-global-arms-trade-as-exports-to-europe-surge/; https://www.nytimes.com/interactive/2022/10/30/business/economy/russia-trade-ukraine-war.html

Haslam, J. (2021). *The spectre of war: International communism and the origins of World War II.* Princeton University Press.

Hawkins, A. (2025, February 4). Is the China-US fentanyl pipeline really responsible for the US opioid crisis? *The Guardian*. https://www.theguardian.com/society/2024/nov/26/is-the-china-us-fentanyl-pipeline-really-responsible-for-the-us-opioid-crisis

Helleiner, E. (2021). The return of national self-sufficiency? Excavating autarkic thought in a de-globalizing era. *International Studies Review, 23*(3), 933–957. https://doi.org/10.1093/isr/viaa092

Hersh, S. (2023, February 8). *How America took out the Nord Stream pipeline*. Substack. https://seymourhersh.substack.com/p/how-america-took-out-the-nord-stream

Higham, A. (2023, September 29). Russian state TV lays out plans for new empire. *Newsweek*. https://www.newsweek.com/russian-state-tv-russian-empire-restore-sergey-mardan-1830854

Hindu. (2020, October 6). Pompeo Tears into 'Rogue Actor' China for escalating Border Tension with India. *The Hindu*. https://www.thehindu.com/news/international/pompeo-tears-into-rogue-actor-china-for-escalating-border-tension-with-india/article61666652.ece

Hindu. (2024, May 26). India in trade deficit with nine of top 10 trading partners in 2023–24. *The Hindu*. https://www.thehindu.com/business/Economy/india-in-trade-deficit-with-nine-of-top-10-trading-partners-in-2023-24/article68217897.ece

Hochuli, A., Hoare, G., & Cunliffe, P. (2021). *The end of the end of history*. Zero Books.

Hoffman, B. (2003). *The wages of sickness: The politics of health insurance in progressive America*. University of North Carolina Press.

Hoffman, J. (2021, July 8) 15 states reach a deal with Purdue Pharma Over Opioids. *The New York Times*. https://nyti.ms/3dYur6G

Hopkins, V., & Pierson, D. (2024, October 22). Seeking to elude sanctions, Putin and Xi Promise 'A Just World Order.' *The New York Times*. https://www.nytimes.com/2024/10/22/world/asia/putin-brics-summit-xi-modi.html

Horton, R. (2022). Offline: COVID-19 as culture war. *The Lancet, 399*(10322), 346. https://www.thelancet.com/journals/lancet/article/PIIS0140-6736(22)00093-9/fulltext

Hua, S., & Parkyn-Smith, A. (2024, July 29). China reaches back in time to challenge the West. Way, way back. *The Wall Street Journal*. https://www.wsj.com/science/archaeology/china-reaches-back-in-time-to-challenge-the-west-way-way-back-236c4e90

Hudson, M. (2021). *Super imperialism: The economic strategy of American empire* (3rd ed.). Islet.

Hunter, E. (2016). Politics and public health—Engaging the third rail. *Journal of Public Health Management and Practice, 22*(5), 436–441. https://doi.org/10.1097/PHH.0000000000000446

Hurst, L. (2020, March 24). Coronavirus: Health workers clapped across the world for battling on the COVID-19 frontline. *Euronews*. https://www.euronews.com/2020/03/24/coronavirus-health-workers-clapped-across-the-world-for-battling-on-the-covid-19-frontline

Ibrahim, T. (2020, October 28). India-USA BECA: Another pact to turn Indians into the US's cannon fodder. *People's Review*. https://www.peoplesreview.in/politics/2020/10/india-usa-beca-another-pact-to-turn-indians-into-the-uss-cannon-fodder

Ikenberry, G. (2024). The return of geopolitical blocs. *Survival, 66*(2), 7–24. https://doi.org/10.1080/00396338.2024.2332056

Immerwahr, D. (2019). *How to hide an empire*. Random House.

International Union of Geological Scientists. (2024, March 20). *The Anthropocene: IUGS-ICS statement*. https://www.iugs.org/_files/ugd/f1fc07_ebe2e2b94c35491c8efe570cd2c5a1bf.pdf

IPD Forum Staff. (2020, March 21). *China a hotbed for pandemics historically, experts say*. IPDefense Forum. https://ipdefenseforum.com/2020/03/china-a-hotbed-for-pandemics-historically-experts-say/

Ishchenko, V. (2016). Far right participation in the Ukrainian Maidan protests: An attempt of systematic estimation. *European Politics and Society, 17*(4), 453–472. https://doi.org/10.1080/23745118.2016.1154646

Ishchenko, V., et al. (2024, January 23). *Russian military Keynesianism: Who benefits from the war in Ukraine?* Links. https://links.org.au/russian-military-keynesianism-who-benefits-war-ukraine

Itkowitz, C. (2020, June 23). Trump again uses 'kung flu' to describe coronavirus. *The Washington Post*. https://www.washingtonpost.com/politics/trump-again-uses-kung-flu-to-describe-coronavirus/2020/06/23/0ab5a8d8-b5a9-11ea-aca5-ebb63d27e1ff_story.html

Janda, M. (2021, October 5). *Pandora, Paradise & Panama Papers: Offshore structures exposed by leaks explained*. ABC News. https://www.abc.net.au/news/2021-10-05/offshore-companies-trusts-tax-and-secrecy-explained/100514250

Jin, S., & Ryu, E. (2022). "The greedy I that gives"—The paradox of egocentrism & altruism: Terror management & system justification perspectives on the interrelationship between mortality salience & charitable donations amid the COVID-19 pandemic. *Journal of Consumer Affairs, 56*(1), 414–448. https://doi.org/10.1111/joca.12381

John, S., et al. (2023). Editorial: Opioids in the time of the COVID-19 pandemic: From cellular mechanisms to public health policy. *Frontiers in Pharmacology, 14*, Article 1251958. https://doi.org/10.3389/fphar.2023.1251958

Jones, O. (2020, April 23). While the UK's key workers lack PPE, ministers clapping for them is an insult. *The Guardian*. https://www.theguardian.com/commentisfree/2020/apr/23/uk-key-workers-ppe-ministers-clapping-protect-nhs

Joshi, N., & Sharma, R.-K. (2017). India-Russia relations in a changing Eurasian perspective. *India Quarterly, 73*(1), 36–52. https://doi.org/10.1177/0974928416683056

Jünemann, A., et al. (Eds.). (2017). *Fortress Europe? Challenges and failures of migration and asylum policies*. Springer Fachmedien.

Kamaruzaman, H., Ahmad, M. H., Suriyamoorthy, S., Hassan, M. F., & Zakaria, A. S. (2022). Disinvestment in healthcare: A scoping review of systematic reviews. *International Journal of Technology Assessment in Health Care, 38*(1), e69. https://doi.org/10.1017/S0266462322000514

Katchanovski, I. (2024). *The Maidan Massacre in Ukraine: The mass killing that changed the world*. Springer Nature.

Katchanovski, I. (2026). *The Russia-Ukraine War and its origins: From the Maidan to the Ukraine war*. Palgrave Macmillan.

Kaufman, D., & Barbaro, M. (2024, October 8). How NAFTA broke American politics. *The New York Times*. https://www.nytimes.com/2024/10/08/podcasts/the-daily/american-politics-trade.html

Kayali, L. (2025, July 13). Macron promises billions more for French defense budget. *Politico*. https://www.politico.eu/article/emmanuel-macron-france-defense-budget/

Keating, J. (2025, March 31). *Are China, Canada, and Mexico really to blame for fentanyl?* Vox. https://www.vox.com/politics/406336/fentanyl-china-canada-mexico-trump

Keefe, P. (2021). *Empire of pain: The secret history of the Sackler dynasty*. Macmillan.

Kelton, S. (2020). *The deficit myth: Modern monetary theory & the birth of the people's economy*. Public Affairs.

Kennedy, J. F. (1961, September 25). *Address before the General Assembly of the United Nations*. In *Public Papers of the Presidents of the United States: John F. Kennedy, 1961* (pp. 619–626). US Government Printing Office.

Kingsley, P., Bergman, R., & Odenheimer, N. (2025, July 11). How Netanyahu prolonged the war in Gaza to stay in power. *The New York Times*. https://www.nytimes.com/2025/07/11/magazine/benjamin-netanyahu-gaza-war.html

Klein, M. C., & Pettis, M. (2020). *Trade wars are class wars: How rising inequality distorts the global economy and threatens international peace*. Yale University Press.

Klyszcz, I. (2023, April 6). *Messianic multipolarity: Russia's resurrected Africa doctrine*. Riddle. https://ridl.io/messianic-multipolarity-russia-s-resurrected-africa-doctrine

Koley, T., & Dhole, M. (2020). *The COVID-19 pandemic: The deadly coronavirus outbreak*. Routledge.

Krishnan, A. (2020, July 10). China's state media attacks Indian channels like WION and Times Now for Anti-China coverage. *The Hindu*. https://www.thehindu.com/news/international/chinas-state-media-attacks-indian-channels-like-wion-and-times-now-for-anti-china-coverage/article32035338.ece

Krugman, P. (2021, September 2). Corporate America is lobbying for climate disaster. *The New York Times*. https://nyti.ms/3jESVFf

Krugman, P. (2021, September 3). Wonking out: A very Austrian pandemic. *The New York Times*. https://nyti.ms/3DMIzez

Krugman, P. (2022, April 5). What ever happened to the great resignation? *The New York Times*. https://www.nytimes.com/2022/04/05/opinion/great-resignation-employment.html

Kuchipudi, S. (2020, March 4). Why so many epidemics originate in Asia and Africa – and why we can expect more. *The Conversation*. https://theconversation.com/why-so-many-epidemics-originate-in-asia-and-africa-and-why-we-can-expect-more-131657

Kurmanaev, A. (2024, December 2). Tensions rise among Russia's elite as economic growth slows. *The New York Times*. https://www.nytimes.com/2024/12/02/world/europe/russia-economy-war-ukraine.html

Kuromiya, H. (2008). "The Donbas—The Last Frontier of Europe?" In O. Schmidtke & Yekelchyk, S. (Eds.) *Europe's last frontier? Belarus, Moldova, and Ukraine between Russia and the European Union* (pp. 97–114). Palgrave Macmillan.

Larsen, P. (2025, March 5). *Europe will struggle to Slip U.S. Economic Chokehold*. Reuters. https://www.reuters.com/breakingviews/europe-will-struggle-slip-us-economic-chokehold-2025-03-05.

LeDonne, J. P. (2006). Geopolitics, logistics, and grain: Russia's ambitions in the Black Sea Basin, 1737–1834. *International History Review, 28*(1), 1–41. https://doi.org/10.1080/07075332.2006.9641086

Le Monde with AFP. (2025, November 20). French army chief warns France should be "prepared to lose children" in face of Russian threat. *Le Monde*. https://www.lemonde.fr/en/france/article/2025/11/20/outcry-after-french-army-chief-s-prepared-to-lose-children-warning_6747661_7.html

Leonhardt, D. (2024, May 19). A new centrism is rising in Washington. *The New York Times*. https://www.nytimes.com/2024/05/19/briefing/centrism-washington-neopopulism.html

Leopold, L. (2024). *Wall Street's war on workers: How mass layoffs and greed are destroying the working class and what to do about it*. Chelsea Green.

Levitt, T. (2020, September 15). Covid and farm animals: 9 pandemics that changed the world. *The Guardian*. https://www.theguardian.com/environment/ng-interactive/2020/sep/15/covid-farm-animals-and-pandemics-diseases-that-changed-the-world

Lighthizer, R. E. (2023). *No trade is free: Changing course, taking on China, and helping America's workers*. Broadside.

Lockwood, B. (2006). *OxyContin: From pain relief to addiction*. Rosen.

Lockwood, T. (2021, January 7). 'Claps don't pay the bills': Readers react to Clap for Carers, returning TONIGHT amid Covid lockdown. *Northern Echo*. https://www.thenorthernecho.co.uk/news/18993265.claps-dont-pay-bills-readers-react-clap-carers-returning-tonight-amid-covid-lockdown

Lopreite, M., Marozzo, F., Manca, M., & Quattrociocchi, W. (2021). Early warnings of COVID-19 outbreaks across Europe from social media. *Scientific Reports, 11*, 2147. https://doi.org/10.1038/s41598-021-81333-1

Luce, E. (2023, April 19). The new Washington Consensus. *Financial Times*. https://www.ft.com/content/42922712-cd33-4de0-8763-1cc271331a32

Maçães, B. (2020, June 15). *The attack of the civilization-state*. NOEMA. https://www.noemamag.com/the-attack-of-the-civilization-state

Magdy, S. (2023, February 11). Sudan military finishes review of Russian Red Sea base deal. *Associated Press*. https://apnews.com/article/politics-sudan-government-moscow-803738fba4d8f91455f0121067c118dd

Mahbubani, K. (2020). *Has China won? The Chinese challenge to American primacy*. PublicAffairs.

Mair, J., Clark, T., Fowler, N., & Snoddy, R. (Eds.). (2017). *Brexit, Trump & the media*. Abramis.

Maley, W. (2021). *The Afghanistan wars* (3rd ed.). Red Globe Press.

Malhotra, D. (2025, August 26). *Not just BRICS: Building a Russia-India-Saudi axis.* New Eastern Europe. https://neweasterneurope.eu/2025/08/26/not-just-brics-building-a-russia-india-saudi-axis/

Markowitz, J. (2023). Arctic shock: Utilizing climate change to test a theory of resource competition. *Journal of Conflict Resolution, 67*(10), 1845–1872. https://doi.org/10.1177/0022002723115357

Marsh, S., & Chambers, M. (2022, February 22). *Germany freezes Nord Stream 2 gas project as Ukraine crisis deepens.* Reuters. https://www.reuters.com/business/energy/germanys-scholz-halts-nord-stream-2-certification-2022-02-22

Martina, M., & Slodkowski, A. (2024, November 26). *Trump camp says China is 'attacking' U.S. with fentanyl. They aim to fight back.* Reuters. https://www.reuters.com/investigates/special-report/drugs-fentanyl-china

Maté, A. (2019, November 13). *Ukrainegate impeachment saga worsens US-Russia Cold War: Interview with Stephen F. Cohen.* Pushback—The Grayzone. https://youtu.be/bpASSqz1hGc?t=1217

McCarthy, J. (2024, April 12). Four years ago, we were clapping health workers in the street. Now we're reducing their benefits. *The Irish Times.* https://www.irishtimes.com/opinion/2024/04/12/four-years-ago-we-were-clapping-health-workers-in-the-street-now-were-reducing-their-benefits

McTague, T. (2022, January 24). The tears of a clown. *The Atlantic.* https://www.theatlantic.com/international/archive/2022/01/boris-johnson-party-pressure/621325/

Mearsheimer, J. J. (2018). *The great delusion: Liberal dreams and international realities.* Yale University Press.

Mearsheimer, J. J. (2019). Bound to fail: The rise and fall of the liberal international order. *International Security, 43*(4), 7–50. https://doi.org/10.1162/isec_a_00342

Mearsheimer, J. J. (2022). The causes and consequences of the Ukraine war. *Horizons: Journal of International Relations & Sustainable Development, 21*, 12–27.

Mednick, S. (2023, August 13). Niger's junta gains the upper hand over the regional bloc threatening military force, analysts say. *Associated Press.* https://apnews.com/article/niger-coup-west-africa-military-jihadis-57900b121d1fa1499354ed21aca994d1

Miller, K. (2024, October 12). This is why Trump imagines he will win. *The New York Times.* https://www.nytimes.com/2024/10/12/opinion/trump-second-term.html

Milne, R. (2023, June 5). Arctic chill: Western nations fear China and Russia will exploit regional tensions. *Financial Times.* https://www.ft.com/content/ef7d5f39-4a59-4774-888c-ade3c2354b63

Mimbs Nyce, C. (2021, February 18). The real scandal of Ted Cruz's vacation. *The Atlantic.* https://www.theatlantic.com/newsletters/archive/2021/02/the-atlantic-daily-the-real-scandal-of-ted-cruzs-vacation/618089

Mishra, M., Yan, P., & Shroeder, R. (2022). TikTok politics: Tit for tat on the India-China cyberspace frontier. *International Journal of Communication, 16*, 814–839.

Mitchell, G. (2021, January 7). Clap for heroes: Nurses say they do not want return of applause. *Nursing Times.* https://www.nursingtimes.net/news/coronavirus/clap-for-heroes-nurses-say-they-do-not-want-return-of-applause-07-01-2021

Morone, J. A. (2024). Coronavirus and culture war: Blunders, defiance, and glimmers of solidarity. *Political Science Quarterly, 139*(2), 257–266. https://doi.org/10.1093/psquar/qqad071

Mukherjee, S. (2025, March 10). Covid's deadliest effect took five years to appear. *The New York Times.* https://www.nytimes.com/2025/03/10/opinion/covid-public-health-privatization.html

Murphy, C. (2022, October 25). The wreckage of neoliberalism. *The Atlantic.* https://www.theatlantic.com/ideas/archive/2022/10/democrats-should-reject-neoliberalism/671850

Mychajlyszyn, N. (2008). From Soviet Ukraine to the Orange Revolution: European security relations and the Ukrainian identity. In O. Schmidtke & S. Yekelchyk (Eds.), *Europe's last frontier? Belarus, Moldova, and Ukraine between Russia and the European Union* (pp. 31–53). Palgrave Macmillan.

Naval History & Heritage Command. (2010). *U.S. Navy in the "War on Terrorism" 2001–2010*. US Department of the Navy. https://www.history.navy.mil/research/library/online-reading-room/title-list-alphabetically/u/us-navy-world-2001-2010.htm

Ndongo, S., & Pigeaud, F. (2020, January). The Franc Zone: French neocolonialism in Africa. *Jacobin*. https://jacobin.com/2020/01/franc-zone-french-neocolonialism-africa

News Wires. (2023, February 9). Russia's Lavrov pledges support on lifting UN sanctions, defends Wagner on Sudan visit. *France 24*. https://www.france24.com/en/africa/20230209-russia-s-lavrov-meets-sudan-s-military-leaders-in-final-stop-of-africa-tour

Nichols, T. (2022, October 3). Trump, Putin, and the assault of anarchy. *The Atlantic*. https://www.theatlantic.com/newsletters/archive/2022/10/trump-putin-and-the-assault-of-anarchy/671641

Nilsen, T. (2019, August 7). *Russia deploys missile system 70 km from Norway's Vardø radar*. The Barents Observer. https://thebarentsobserver.com/en/security/2019/08/russia-deploys-bastion-missile-system-70-km-norways-vardo-radar

Norris, P., & Inglehart, R. (2019). *Cultural backlash: Trump, Brexit, & authoritarian populism*. Cambridge University Press.

O'Connor, T. (2019, May 23). Russia will 'take measures' against U.S. radar near its border, thought to be part of missile defense. *Newsweek*. https://www.newsweek.com/russia-us-radar-norway-defense-1434756

O'Sullivan, M. (2024, December 13). WENA-The Middle East has a new name for the west. *Forbes*. https://www.forbes.com/sites/mikeosullivan/2024/12/13/wenathe-middle-east-has-a-new-name-for-the-west

Orhan, E. (2022). The effects of the Russia-Ukraine war on global trade. *Journal of International Trade, Logistics & Law, 8*(1), 141–146.

Orozco, L. T. (2023, April 19). Like a glove: Nord Stream pipeline sabotage and American foreign policy. *Yale Review of International Studies*. https://yris.yira.org/column/like-a-glove-nord-stream-pipeline-sabotage-and-american-foreign-policy

Paige, H. (2025, April 4). The scramble for the Arctic is just getting started: Security in a multipolar Arctic. *Jacobin*. https://jacobin.com/2025/04/arctic-militarization-dual-use-multipolar

Pajon, C. (2023). France's Indo-Pacific approach: Salvaging the rules-based order and staying relevant. In Y. Hosoya & H. Kundnani (Eds.), *The transformation of the liberal international order: Evolutions and limitations* (pp. 65–74). Springer Nature.

Pandya, A. (2024, May 28). *Why the U.S. needs to accept a multipolar world order with dignity*. USANAS Foundation. https://usanasfoundation.com/why-us-needs-to-accept-multipolar-world-order-with-dignity

Parker, C. F., & Stern, E. K. (2022). The Trump administration and the COVID-19 crisis: Exploring the warning-response problems and missed opportunities of a public health emergency. *Public Administration*. https://doi.org/10.1111/padm.12843

Parker, K., & Horowitz, J. (2022, March 9). Majority of workers who quit a job in 2021 cite low pay, no opportunities for advancement, feeling disrespected. *Pew Research Center*. https://www.pewresearch.org/fact-tank/2022/03/09/majority-of-workers-who-quit-a-job-in-2021-cite-low-pay-no-opportunities-for-advancement-feeling-disrespected/

Pérez, A. (2020, October 30). *Fortress Europe: An authoritarian-populist construct?* Real Instituto Elcano. https://www.realinstitutoelcano.org/en/analyses/fortress-europe-an-authoritarian-populist-construct

Perry, S. L., Whitehead, A. L., & Grubbs, J. B. (2020). Culture Wars and COVID-19 conduct: Christian nationalism, religiosity, and Americans' behavior during the coronavirus pandemic. *Journal for the Scientific Study of Religion, 59*(3), 405–416. https://doi.org/10.1111/jssr.12677

Phillips, J. K., Ford, M. A., & Bonnie, R. J. (Eds.). (2017). *Pain management and the opioid epidemic: Balancing societal and individual benefits and risks of prescription opioid use*. National Academies Press.

Piketty, T. (2014). *Capital in the twenty-first century* (A. Goldhammer, Trans.). Belknap Press of Harvard University Press.

Pilkington, E. (2014, February 7). US official apologises to EU counterparts for undiplomatic language. *The Guardian*. https://www.theguardian.com/world/2014/feb/06/us-ukraine-russia-eu-victoria-nuland

Polakow-Suransky, S. (2023, December 27). The year geopolitical competition returned to Africa. *Foreign Policy*. https://foreignpolicy.com/2023/12/27/africa-geopolitics-sudan-niger-nigeria-mauritania-brics-wagner-prigozhin-2023.

Posen, A. (2023, March 24). America's zero-sum economics doesn't add up. *Foreign Policy*. https://foreignpolicy.com/2023/03/24/economy-trade-united-states-china-industry-manufacturing-supply-chains-biden

Pu, D., He, Y., Zhang, W., & Zhang, Y. (2023). Engaging the consumer in disinvestment in public healthcare: Concerns, perspectives & attitudes of older adults. *Journal of Evaluation in Clinical Practice, 29*(2), 320–328. https://doi.org/10.1111/jep.13769

Pustake, M., et al. (2022). SARS, MERS & COVID-19: An overview & comparison of clinical, laboratory & radiological features. *Journal of Family Medicine & Primary Care, 11*(1), 10–17. https://doi.org/10.4103/jfmpc.jfmpc_839_21

Rankin, A. (2023, April 10). Macron sparks anger by saying Europe should not be 'vassal' in US-China clash. *The Guardian*. https://www.theguardian.com/world/2023/apr/10/emmanuel-macron-sparks-anger-europe-vassal-us-china-clash

Reich, R. (2013, May 26). *Lessons from the world of tax avoidance: How nations can negotiate with global capital*. RobertReich.org. https://robertreich.org/post/51397984260

Reperant, L., & Osterhaus, A. (2017). AIDS, avian flu, SARS, MERS, Ebola, Zika... What next? *Vaccine, 35*(35), 4470–4474. https://doi.org/10.1016/j.vaccine.2017.04.082

Reuters. (2020, May 19). *Partly false: Series of viral outbreaks between 1957 and 2019 all originated in China*. Reuters. https://www.reuters.com/article/world/partly-false-series-of-viral-outbreaks-between-1957-and-2019-all-originated-in-idUSKBN22V2Z8

Reuters. (2024, November 7). Macron likens Europe to a herbivore as he calls for it to 'take back control'. *The Guardian*. https://www.theguardian.com/world/video/2024/nov/07/macron-likens-europe-to-a-herbivore-as-he-calls-for-it-to-take-back-control-video

Reuters. (2025, November 19). US secures $1 trillion Saudi spending commitments spanning nuclear energy to F-35s. *Reuters*. https://www.reuters.com/world/middle-east/us-secures-1-trillion-saudi-spending-commitments-spanning-nuclear-energy-f-35s-2025-11-19/

Reuters in Berlin (2015, July 8). NSA tapped German Chancellery for decades, WikiLeaks claims. *The Guardian*. https://www.theguardian.com/us-news/2015/jul/08/nsa-tapped-german-chancellery-decades-wikileaks-claims-merkel

Richardson, V. (2018, November 28). *Obama takes credit for U.S. Oil-and-Gas Boom: 'That Was Me, People.'* AP News. https://apnews.com/article/business-5dfbc1aa17701ae219239caad0bfefb2

Rickett, O., & Amin, M. (2024, May 6). *Sudan war: Russia hedges bets by aiding both sides in conflict*. Middle East Eye. https://www.middleeasteye.net/news/russia-sudan-war-saf-rsf-hedges-bets-both-sides-support

Roa, C. (2025, March 7). *Welcome to imperial America*. The Institute for Peace & Diplomacy. https://peacediplomacy.org/2025/03/07/welcome-to-imperial-america

Rodney Coates. (2025, January 27). Why Trump's tariffs can't solve America's fentanyl crisis. *The Conversation*. https://theconversation.com/why-trumps-tariffs-cant-solve-americas-fentanyl-crisis-245978

Rosenthal, E. (2017). *An American sickness: How healthcare became big business and how you can take it back*. Penguin.

Rosin, H., & Goldberg, J. (2024, October 31). Is journalism ready for a second Trump administration? *The Atlantic*. https://www.theatlantic.com/podcasts/archive/2024/10/is-journalism-ready-for-a-second-trump-administration/680467

Rossoliński-Liebe, G. (2015, June). *The Fascist Kernel of Ukrainian Genocidal Nationalism* (The Carl Beck Papers in Russian and East European Studies Nr 2402).

Roth, A. (2012, July 11). Journey by sea takes awkward turn in Russia. *The New York Times*. https://web.archive.org/web/20150205233822/https://www.nytimes.com/2012/07/12/world/europe/team-returns-to-alaska-after-4-day-detention-in-russia.html

Rotteveel, A. (2022). To what extent do citizens support the disinvestment of healthcare interventions? An exploration of the support for four viewpoints on active disinvestment in the Netherlands. *Social Science & Medicine, 293*, 114662. https://doi.org/10.1016/j.socscimed.2021.114662

Roubini, N. (2023, August 28). How can the US and China prevent a war? *The Guardian*. https://www.theguardian.com/business/2023/aug/28/how-can-the-us-and-china-prevent-a-war

Sachs, J. D. (2023, May 23). *The war in Ukraine was provoked—And why that matters to achieve peace*. Common Dreams. https://www.commondreams.org/opinion/the-war-in-ukraine-was-provoked-and-why-that-matters-if-we-want-peace

Sanders, B. (2024, March 18). A revolution in American foreign policy: Replacing greed, militarism, and hypocrisy with solidarity, diplomacy, and human rights. *Foreign Affairs*. https://www.foreignaffairs.com/united-states/revolution-american-foreign-policy-bernie-sanders

Sarotte, M. (2021). *Not one inch: America, Russia, and the making of post-Cold War stalemate*. Yale University Press.

Savage, L. (2023, April 19). Ordinary Americans are being forced to subsidize the military-industrial complex. *Jacobin*. https://jacobin.com/2023/04/military-industrial-complex-spending-tax-dollar-social-services

Schake, K. (2021, May 27). Biden brings more class warfare to foreign policy. *The Atlantic*. https://www.theatlantic.com/ideas/archive/2021/05/biden-foreign-policy-america-first-middle-class/618999

Scheidel, W. (2017). *The great leveler: Violence and the history of inequality from the Stone Age to the twenty-first century*. Princeton University Press.

Schwartz, I. (2023, January 10). *John Mearsheimer on Ukraine conflict: There are no realistic options, the West is screwed*. Real Clear Politics. https://www.realclearpolitics.com/video/2023/01/10/john_mearsheimer_on_ukraine_conflict_there_are_no_realistic_options_the_west_is_screwed.html

Serenko, A. (2023). The great resignation: The great knowledge exodus or the onset of the Great Knowledge Revolution? *Journal of Knowledge Management, 27*(4), 1042–1055. https://doi.org/10.1108/JKM-12-2021-0920

Serwat, L., Nsaibia, H., & Gurcov, N. (2023, August 2). *Moving out of the shadows: Shifts in Wagner Group operations around the world*. Armed Conflict Location & Event Data Project (ACLED). https://acleddata.com/report/moving-out-shadows-shifts-wagner-group-operations-around-world

Sharma, R. (2022, August 28). A post-dollar world is coming. *Financial Times*. https://www.ft.com/content/989b2e50-e8b5-474c-86a3-190c6881b235

Sherman, J., (2023, March 27). The problem with India's app bans. *Atlantic Council*. https://www.atlanticcouncil.org/blogs/southasiasource/the-problem-with-indias-app-bans

Shidore, S. (2023, September 1). American power just took a big hit. *The New York Times*. https://www.nytimes.com/2023/09/01/opinion/brics-expansion-america.html

Sibal, K. (2023, April 21). India exercising strategic autonomy finds resonance in Europe. *News 18*. https://www.news18.com/opinion/opinion-india-exercising-strategic-autonomy-finds-resonance-in-europe-7602007.html

Snider, T. (2022). *Partnering with neo-Nazis in Ukraine: An inconvenient history*. Antiwar.com. https://original.antiwar.com/ted_snider/2022/03/30/partnering-with-neo-nazis-in-ukraine-an-inconvenient-history

Solchanyk, R. (2001). *Ukraine & Russia: The post-Soviet transition*. Rowman & Littlefield.

Sorman, G. (2023, July 17). Bitterness and resentment in the Global South. *City Journal*. https://www.city-journal.org/article/bitterness-and-resentment-in-the-global-south

Spiegel Staff (2013, October 27). Embassy espionage. The NSA's secret spy hub in Berlin. *Der Spiegel*. https://www.spiegel.de/international/germany/cover-story-how-nsa-spied-on-merkel-cell-phone-from-berlin-embassy-a-930205.html

Spitznagel, E. (2022, October 22). 'Dr. Doom' predicts NYC destroyed by nukes, storms in next 20 years. *New York Post*. https://nypost.com/2022/10/22/dr-doom-nouriel-roubini-predicts-scary-demise-for-us

Stacey, K. (2020, July 2). India leads global backlash against Chinese Tech with App Bans. *Financial Times*. https://www.ft.com/content/4b47a4d6-9632-11ea-9afc-5eaad1e5d9bf

Standish, R. (2018, October 3). The new cold front in Russia's information war. *Foreign Policy*. https://web.archive.org/web/20181004142533/https://foreignpolicy.com/2018/10/03/the-new-cold-front-in-russias-information-war-nato-norway

Starkman, D., et al. (2021, October 19). *FAQ about the Pandora Papers & ICIJ*. ICIJ. https://www.icij.org/investigations/pandora-papers/frequently-asked-questions-about-the-pandora-papers-and-icij

Staun, J. (2017). Russia's strategy in the Arctic: Cooperation, not confrontation. *Polar Record, 53*(270), 314–332. https://doi.org/10.1017/S0032247417000158

Stevenson, A., & Mozur, P. (2024, November, 27). China has a new playbook to counter Trump: 'Supply Chain Warfare'. *The New York Times*. https://www.nytimes.com/2024/11/27/business/china-retaliation-skydio.html

Stiglitz, J. E. (2003). *Globalization & its discontents*. Norton.

Stiglitz, J. E. (2019). *People, power, and profits: Progressive capitalism for an age of discontent*. Norton.

Stoltenberg, J. (2023a, July 10). A stronger NATO for a more dangerous world: What the alliance must do in Vilnius—And beyond. *Foreign Affairs*. https://www.foreignaffairs.com/europe/stronger-nato-more-dangerous-world-vilnius-jens-stoltenberg;

Stoltenberg, J (2023b, September 7). *Opening remarks by NATO Secretary General Jens Stoltenberg at the joint meeting of the European Parliament's Committee on Foreign Affairs (AFET) and the Subcommittee on Security and Defence (SEDE) followed by an exchange of views with Members of the European Parliament*. NATO. https://www.nato.int/cps/en/natohq/opinions_218172.htm

Stone, K., & Kuttner, R. (2020, April 8). The rise of neo-feudalism. *The American Prospect*. https://prospect.org/economy/rise-of-neo-feudalism

Subtelny, O. (2009). *Ukraine: A history* (4th ed.). University of Toronto Press

Sullivan, J. (2023, April 24). A BRICS currency could shake the dollar's dominance. *Foreign Policy*. https://foreignpolicy.com/2023/04/24/brics-currency-end-dollar-dominance-united-states-russia-china

Susskind, D. (2024). *Growth: A history & a reckoning*. Harvard University Press.

SwissAid. (2025, November 4). *United Arab Emirates: More than ever a hub for conflict gold*. SWISSAID. https://www.swissaid.ch/en/media/united-arab-emirates-more-than-ever-a-hub-for-conflict-gold

Szporluk, R. (1993). Belarus', Ukraine and the Russian question: A comment. *Post-Soviet Affairs, 9*(4), 366–374. https://doi.org/10.1080/1060586X.1993.10641375

Taub, B. (2024, September 16). The dark time. *The New Yorker*.

Terajima, A. (2025, September 26). *Who sabotaged Nord Stream? 3 years on, investigations offer more questions than answers*. Kyiv Independent. https://kyivindependent.com/who-sabotaged-nord-stream-3-years-on-investigations-offer-more-questions-than-answers

Thomas, K., Silver-Greenberg, J., & Drucker, J. (2023, July 18). They lost their legs. Doctors and health care giants profited. *The New York Times*. https://www.nytimes.com/2023/07/15/health/atherectomy-peripheral-artery-disease.html

Thurow, L. (2001). *The zero-sum society: Distribution & the possibilities for economic change*. Basic Books.

TJN [Tax Justice Network]. (2021, March 22). *CFA Franc as a vivid symbol of colonial continuities in Francophone Africa*. Tax Justice Network. https://taxjustice.net/2021/03/22/the-cfa-franc-as-a-vivid-symbol-of-colonial-continuities-in-francophone-africa

Tong, E. (2024). Repercussions of the Russia-Urkaine war. *International Review of Economics & Finance, 89*, 366–390.

Tooze, A. (2021). *Shutdown: How COVID shook the world's economy*. Penguin.

Trading Economics (n.d.). Wheat. *Trading Economics*. https://tradingeconomics.com/commodity/wheat

Trebesch, C. (2023, September 7). *Ukraine Support Tracker: Europe clearly overtakes US, with total commitments now twice as large*. Kiel Institute for the World Economy. https://www.ifw-kiel.de/publications/news/ukraine-support-tracker-europe-clearly-overtakes-us-with-total-commitments-now-twice-as-large

Trump, D. (2019, February 6). *State of the Union, 2019*. CNN. https://edition.cnn.com/2019/02/05/politics/donald-trump-state-of-the-union-2019-transcript/index.html

Trump, D. J. (2025, September 5). *Restoring the United States Department of War*. The White House. https://www.whitehouse.gov/presidential-actions/2025/09/restoring-the-united-states-department-of-war/

Tsygankov, A. P. (2024). Russia, Ukraine, and the West: From mistrust to conflict. *The Journal of Slavic Military Studies, 37*(3–4), 287–309. https://doi.org/10.1080/13518046.2024.2418231

Tudoroiu, T. (2018). *Brexit, President Trump, & the changing geopolitics of Eastern Europe*. Springer International.

Turchin, P. (2023). *End times: Elites, counter-elites, and the path of political disintegration*. Penguin Press.

USEIA [US Energy Information Administration]. (2025, June 30). *U.S. Ending Stocks of Crude Oil (in million barrels), Weekly Petroleum Status Report*. USEIA. https://www.eia.gov/dnav/pet/pet_stoc_typ_d_nus_SAS_mbbl_a.htm

US Government Printing Office. (1990). *Agreement between the United States of America and the Union of Soviet Socialist Republics on the Maritime Boundary* (Treaty Document 101-22).

Varoufakis, Y. (2011). *The Global Minotaur: America, Europe and the future of the global economy*. Zed.

Walt, S. M. (2018). *The hell of good intentions: America's foreign policy elite and the decline of US primacy*. Farrar.

Wang, H. (1991). *America against America*. Literature and Art Publishing House.

Wang, P., & Catalano, T. (2023). Chinese virus. *Journal of Language and Discrimination, 7*(1), 26–51. https://doi.org/10.1558/jld.23484

Weaver, M. (2020, May 22). Pressure on Dominic Cummings to quit over lockdown breach. *The Guardian*. https://www.theguardian.com/politics/2020/may/22/dominic-cummings-durham-trip-coronavirus-lockdown

Weisman, J. (2024, September 5). Trump Praises Tariffs, and William McKinley, to Power Brokers. *The New York Times*. https://www.nytimes.com/2024/09/05/us/politics/trump-tariffs-william-mckinley.html

Wertheim, S. (2023, June 16). The tale the west tells itself about Ukraine. NYT. https://www.nytimes.com/2023/06/16/opinion/nato-ukraine-russia-peace.html

White, S., Korosteleva, J., & McAllister, I. (2008). A wider Europe? The view from Russia, Belarus and Ukraine. *Journal of Common Market Studies, 46*(2), 219–241. https://doi.org/10.1111/j.1468-5965.2007.00775.x

White, S., McAllister, I., & Feklyunina, V. (2010). Belarus, Ukraine and Russia: East or West? *The British Journal of Politics and International Relations, 12*(3), 344–367. https://doi.org/10.1111/j.1467-856X.2010.00410.x

Whitham, B. (2022, February 1). It's no surprise liberal democracy is giving way to authoritarianism. *The Conversation*. https://theconversation.com/its-no-surprise-liberal-democracy-is-giving-way-to-authoritarianism-174509

WHO Data. (2025). *Number of COVID-19 deaths reported to WHO: United States of America, 28 days to 6 July 2025*. World Health Organization. https://data.who.int/dashboards/covid19/deaths?m49=840

Wicker, R. (2024, May 29). America's military is not prepared for war—Or peace. *The New York Times*. https://www.nytimes.com/2024/05/29/opinion/us-military-war.html

Wickramasinghe, C., Steele, E., & Gorczynski, R. M. (Eds.). (2022). *Understanding the origin and global spread of COVID-19*. World Scientific.

Wilkins, H. (2023, March 14). *Russia could face local resistance against promised naval base in Sudan*. VOA. https://www.voanews.com/a/russia-could-face-local-resistance-against-promised-naval-base-in-sudan-/7003780.html
Wilson, D. (2003, October 1). *Dreaming with BRICs: The path to 2050*. Goldman Sachs Archives. https://www.goldmansachs.com/intelligence/archive/brics-dream.html
Wolff, R. (2020). *The sickness is the system: When capitalism fails to save us from pandemics or itself*. Democracy at Work.
Wolff, R. (2023, May 8). *Economic update: The emerging new world economy*. Democracy at Work. https://www.youtube.com/watch?v=2s6F97zYJ1Y
Wong, E., et al. (2023, May 3). How U.S. efforts to guide Sudan to democracy ended in war. *The New York Times*. https://nyti.ms/415xqQi
Woo, P. C. Y., Lau, S. K. P., Huang, Y., & Yuen, K. Y. (2006). Infectious diseases emerging from Chinese wet-markets: Zoonotic origins of severe respiratory viral infections. *Current Opinion in Infectious Diseases, 19*(5), 401–407. https://doi.org/10.1097/01.qco.0000244043.08264
Workman, D. (2023–2024). *Report card for trade surpluses and deficits by country*. World's Top Exports. https://www.worldstopexports.com/report-card-for-trade-surpluses-and-deficits-by-country
Yan, S. (2023). China and European strategic autonomy. In F. Attinà & Y. Feng (Eds.), *China & world politics in transition: How China transforms the world political order* (pp. 181–194). Springer.
Zhao, T., Lu, H., & Yin, M. (2022). Warnings regarding the potential coronavirus disease 2019 (COVID-19) transmission risk: Vaccination is not enough. *Infection Control & Hospital Epidemiology, 43*(5), 679–680. https://doi.org/10.1017/ice.2021.63
Zheng, J., & Zompetti, J. P. (2023). 'I'm not a virus': Asian hate in Donald Trump's rhetoric. *Asian Journal of Communication, 33*(5), 470–503. https://doi.org/10.1080/01292986.2023.2246509
Zhu, J. (2022). The rise and fall of ruling oligarchs: Fighting 'political corruption' in China. *China Review, 22*(2), 49–79, https://www.jstor.org/stable/48671499
Zucman, G. (2015). *The hidden wealth of nations: The scourge of tax havens*. University of Chicago Press.

Epilogue: History Instructs 10

Abstract

The epilogue explores how the same zero-sum mercantilist policies waged by the Latin city-states against the ecumenical Eastern Roman Empire in the 12–15th centuries were those that the Protestant nation-states waged against the ecumenical Western Roman Empire in the 16–19th centuries, and are those that the Revisionist civilization-states are waging against the ecumenical American empire today. In the end, like the Eastern and Western Roman emperors before them, American presidents are being reduced (by mercantilist policies) to the status and power of and by the very civilization-states over which they fancy themselves to rule. Influenced, but nevertheless skeptical of the debates between the neoliberal followers of Francis Fukuyama vs. Samuel Huntington, the defining feature of the zero-sum conflicts between the Civilization states in the twenty-first century is how they manage their images—either as benignly powerful security guarantors or Robin Hood-like challengers of the global status quo. Thus, the predictably convergent cycles of history churn away in rotations of various models of zero-sum political economies—or what has been called an "Infinite Dictatorship," in which one regime after another reimposes the same policies to enrich themselves and impoverish others. This occurs all while presenting their flawed forms of political economies as "win–win" or at least a divergence from the traditional zero-sum logic of haves and have-nots alike imprisoned within the same sovereign social pyramids. Thus the ubiquity of zero-sum thinking, as well as tribalism, becomes tantalizingly inescapable. The question then is not zero-sum versus non-zero-sum, but who wins and/or loses what and in which way. Thus, new, cooperative models arise which promise divergent possibilities of infinite growth, even as believers and critics converge in their views of the planet's finitude.

A. M. Feldman and Y. Stamos, *Zero Sum Political Economy*, World-Systems Evolution and Global Futures, https://doi.org/10.1007/978-3-032-18326-2_10

Convergence: Infinite Tyranny?

> And from the days of John the Baptist until now the kingdom of heaven suffers violence, and the violent take it by force.
>
> Matthew 11:12 (NKJV)

The modern Hebrew translation from the ancient Greek renders the end of this quote: "We must struggle for the Kingdom of Heaven!" Whereas the Greek passively recognizes the violence inherent in divinity, the Hebrew actively embraces it. The idea that might makes right is always recognized as a lie—the Hebrew כֹּחַ and the Greek δύναμιν both refer to the false power of human self-righteousness in Deuteronomy 8:18. But whether the ideology is leftist or rightist, as one author argues, that's never stopped the powerful from retrospectively justifying their self-righteousness—the ostensibly infinite dictatorship (del Pino, 2022).

In *Nineteen Eighty-Four*, George Orwell explained the rationale of power through the voice of his character O'Brien (a party apparachik): "The Party seeks power entirely for its own sake … If you want a picture of the future, imagine a boot stamping on a human face – forever." A *Little Red Book* quotation by Mao Zedong said something similar: "power grows out of the barrel of a gun." The implication is clear in both: power, especially self-righteous power, by its very nature, is zero-sum—a conclusion (in)famously made by the Catholic jurist and Nazism supporter, Carl Schmitt. So, in a convergence between 1930s Berlin and 2020s Washington, the Catholic lawyer and venture capitalist JD Vance disparaged his critics just as he was being elected US vice president in November, 2024, saying: "The thing that I kept thinking about liberalism in 2019 and 2020 is that these guys have all read Carl Schmitt – there's no law, there's just power. And the goal here is to get back in power" (Wallace-Wells, 2024).

Zero-Sum Tribalism

Schmitt's power in his own day was unquestioned. He justified Nazism with jurisprudential concepts, legal analogies and historical precedents regarding statehood, sovereignty and the political economies they've promulgated. The most important of his ideas pertained to socio-political mythmakings of "sovereignty," "ally" and "enemy," which could be implemented by the likes of Joseph Goebbels to manipulate publics with mythology and propaganda. His legal ideas about sovereignty resonate for their arbitrariness ascribed to the lawmaker: "Sovereign is he who decides on the exception" (1922/2005, p. 5). Schmitt's zero-sum political ideas about "us" versus "them" distinctions resonate for their tribalism: "The political is the most intense and extreme antagonism. It cannot be derived from other domains. The friend and enemy concept belongs only to the political" (1932/2007, p. 29). It's no surprise that he disdained the heterogeneity and compromise inherent in democracy; authoritarian 21st-c. regimes and their ideologues from Shigong in Beijing to Dugin in Moscow have happily followed suit (Jones, 2022; Mitchell, 2020).

It's also little surprise that Schmitt's jurisprudential ideas returned to fashion in the heated zero-sum political fights over Washingtonian supreme court appointments after the death of Antonin Scalia in 2016. American legal philosophers like Elizabeth Anderson warned that the zero-sum tribalism and self-righteous fights for legal power would politically lead the supreme court's reasoning "down the path to utter lawlessness, and open the door to dictatorship." For Anderson, Schmitt "offers some insight into the court majority's mind-set:" Schmittian assumptions about politics as a zero-sum struggle between friends and enemies can lead to a refusal to accept the other side as legitimate and, ultimately, to a Schmittian expansion of executive power" (Szalai, 2024a, 2024b). Hence that after Trump was convicted of felony charges by a jury of his peers, millions of his "law-and-order" supporters donned t-shirts declaring "I'm voting for the felon" since clearly the rule of law was subservient to the will of the populace (Frum, 2024).

The *Project 2025* playbook, which cast humans in the liberal *homo economicus* model as innately selfish, chauvinistic and brutal, combined legal justifications like "America First," MAGA white Christian nationalist mythology and the arbitrary executive decrees of the mid-late 2020s to point to exactly this. Similar pessimistic nihilism embedded in liberalism and rebranded as "human nature" would resurface continuously as yet more justification for the Leviathan: "We are innately biased against outsiders," writes David Smith (2011, p. 71), "This bias is seized upon and manipulated by indoctrination and propaganda to motivate men and women to slaughter one another." The same mythical storytelling justifying divine-right sovereign imperial power and tribalism which would perpetuate 20th-c. genocides could be repeated in the 21st (Stanley, 2020). Yuval Harari (2014, pp. 27–28) explicitly acknowledges the arbitrary mythology of power: "Any large-scale human cooperation – whether a modern state, a medieval church, an ancient city or an archaic tribe – is rooted in common myths that exist only in people's collective imagination." Yet for Harari, Schmitt's zero-sum tribalism was not eternal; he warned against the seeming inevitability of ethnic cleansing, that "peace can only be achieved if it includes providing the Palestinians with dignified lives in their homeland" (Ruiz, 2024).

Inevitability and Eternity

In their books *Religion as Make-Believe*, by Neil van Leeuwen and *Not Born Yesterday* by Hugo Mercier, they both argue that belief and delusion are essentially two sides of the same zero-sum coin: that self-identity is a fundamentally socioeconomic expression of belonging. In other words, zero-sum tribalism is presented by Schmittians as inevitably coefficient with the very nature of belief. But belief can also cut against inevitability itself. As long as the belief in the inevitability of politicized zero-sum tribalism persists, we will be doomed to a chosen self-fulfilling prophecy. When we choose otherwise, we liberate ourselves from unnecessarily condemning ourselves to repeating the very history we seek to avoid—this is simultaneously the promise and the paradox of liberalism.

Yet the atavistic, reactionary urge to forfeit responsibility alongside liberty itself comes as a response to the transformation of political discourse from inevitability to eternity—from liberalism to illiberalism. In the prophetic words of Timothy Snyder (2017): "The danger we now face is of a passage from the politics of inevitability to the politics of eternity, from a naive and flawed sort of democratic republic to a confused and cynical sort of fascist oligarchy" (p. 124). If, as Oswald Spengler (in)famously argued, only the power of blood is able to overcome the power of gold, then blood will be used to maintain gold in the twenty-first century as in every previous century. In other words, when money buys power, the truth is meaningless. This is why when Timothy Snyder and his students bind together "fascism" and "oligarchy," they knowingly bind together every century's great struggle between the powerful and the powerless—foedus and feudum, labor and capital—for millennia (what Lincoln called "the eternal struggle"). It's for this reason that increasing observers discuss twenty-first-century refeudalization as a logical result of the bewildering fashion for deregulation and privatization in the 1980s–00s: "The cultural remnants of feudalism remain. The red carpet. The bugle. Presidents like to be praised" (Murphy, 2025; Nicas, 2024).

Yet the idea that if one person has more, someone else must have less is always as wrong as the idea that might makes right. A sophisticated understanding of human relationships—which, we should note, requires human intelligence—reveals that we interact in a positive-sum world when we work together and assist one another. As the neoliberal pundit David Brooks (2024a, 2024b) writes,

> It seems banal, but division of labor was part of a constellation of ideas that liberated our civilization from the savage grip of zero-sum thinking. For millenniums before that, economic growth had been basically stagnant. Many people simply assumed that the supply of wealth was finite. If I'm going to get more of it, it will be the result of conquering you and stealing what you have. In a zero-sum mind-set, the basic logic of life is dog-eat-dog, conquer or be conquered. Property is theft. Predators win.

This is why the mass, cyclical government-sanctioned legal debt forgiveness program advocated by today's jubilee movement is based on the ancient Judaic tradition (Ross, 2021). In other words, redistribution and other reforms are necessary to maintain democracy and prevent Snyder's dark passage from inevitability to eternity (Stiglitz, 2023).

Awe and Absurdity

What inevitability and eternity have in common is their absurd, uncritical acceptance of injustice, inequality and war. What liberalism (literally, the belief in liberty) was originally meant to do was prevent this by promoting the opposites: justice, equality and peace. Yet as Thomas Mann (1938, p. 57) wrote, "War is a cowardly escape from the problems of peace," the problems of peace create the conditions for war. The seemingly deterministic cycles go back to Plato. In peacetime, the rich get richer benefiting from the exploitation and poverty of the poor in a perpetual contest of seeming economic free will masking an increasingly deterministic, zero-sum game, until war breaks out to end the charade's status quo, drive the money-changers from the temple and purge the mixture of sacred and profane, costing incalculable blood and gold. Creating misery on both individual and structural levels which eventually lead to war, wealth doesn't make societies better off—quite the opposite, and there's plenty of science since Machiavelli to prove it, even in a newspaper owned by Jeff Bezos (Matthewes & Sandsmark, 2017). As pope Benedict XVI (Josef Ratzinger) said (2010): "humanity has succeeded in unleashing a cycle of death and terror which they can no longer break out of." In the endless tribunal of posterity, the judgment of the past by the present unleashes real awe—torrential feelings of pride and shame playing an endless game of musical chairs between the forces of individual freedom and the common good. As one pundit put it, "you want to be five years ahead of history, not 15 years" (Klein, 2021). It doesn't matter when you're born; you will always swim in the sublime sea of hazard of human history.

Yet even if each succeeding generation pays thrice for the sins of their fathers (in remonstration, redemption and repetition), the generational labels are often of limited use, especially when they fulfill little more than Neil Howe's historical "astrology" rather than simply explaining Kondratiev's wave, Schumpeter's business cycle, Khaldun-Laffer's curve or Turchin's cliodynamics (Cohen, 2021; Green, 2023; Howe, 2023; Menand, 2021; Pinsker, 2020; Turchin, 2016; Turchin & Nefedov, 2009; Schumpeter, 1942; Bernard, 2014). The Overton Window theory which teaches that what's unthinkable in one moment becomes unquestionable the next shows that whereas the zero-sum injustice of every epoch's status quo is obvious when it's over, it's often impossible to conceive when it predominates. The irony, of course, is that necessary transformations and reformations are only possible *because* they're inconceivable.

American fatalism manifests itself in the shrugging passivity of historical repetition and the popular pointlessness of memory. It's not that some American historians haven't successfully learned its lessons and have attempted to warn their fellow Americans about the dangers of imperial hubris (Bacevich, 2022; Johnson, 2004a, 2004b, 2007, 2010). It's that many more give up before they even try. So it's bitterly ironic that a Georgetown history professor like Michael Kazin (2023) would self-anathematize, writing that "History has few true lessons to teach." In this way, such "chattering class" pontificators and pundits become liberal handwringing representatives and victims of the very absurd victimhood they diagnose, or as Oprah Winfrey's self-help book co-author Arthur Brooks (2023) puts it:

loquacious logophiles might have byzantine lives and find themselves in manifold precarious situations that lower their jouissance... We are evolved to use every advantage to get ahead in life, and humans often see resources as existing in a zero-sum environment, a bias that some psychologists have called "win–win denial."

Regardless of Brooks' logical inconsistencies and hypocritical religious positions (2023), his personal and political angst seems to reflect his elite position as a Harvard Business School professor—since "getting ahead" implies someone else falling behind (Dickson, 2015; Leithart, 2019). It seems to be a kind of Freudian signal anxiety—according to the *Dictionary of Psychology* (Sam, 2013), "the kind of anxiety that arises in response to internal conflict or an emerging impulse and functions as a sign to the ego of impending threat, resulting in the preemptive use of a defense mechanism"—but on a sociological, national or even civilizational scale and not so different from the collective alienations, ennuis, malaises and anomies discussed by Marx, Weber, Freud, Durkheim, Mauss, Veblen, and so on, which led to the miseries, boredoms and atavistic desires for heroism, bloodletting and chaos discussed by Polanyi, Frankl, Hoffer, Orwell, Huxley, Luxemburg, Arendt, and so on.

Like the post-2008 formula that "profits be privatized while costs be socialized," the Anglo-American apathy toward historical repetition is best expressed in its contrivance and fetishism of "creative destruction"—as long as the former is internalized while the latter is externalized. If the East seems to revere history, remember it well and repeat it intentionally, then the West seems to revile history, forget it quickly and repeat it unintentionally. The liberal paradox of American individualism is that it disempowers the individual from addressing structural problems; or as Simone de Beauvoir figured out Americans already in (1947, p. 94):

What is most striking to me, and most discouraging, is that they are so apathetic while being neither blind nor unconscious [...] They witness the rise, more ominous every day, of racism and reactionary attitudes, the birth of a kind of fascism. But they themselves don't feel responsible for anything because they don't think they can do anything in this world [...] In America, the individual is nothing. He is made into an abstract object of worship; by persuading him of his individual value, one stifles the awakening of a collective spirit in him. But reduced to himself in this way, he is robbed of any concrete power.

Every period of expansion, when civic institutions come to rely exclusively on expansion, is indicated by some form of individualism. Every period of unraveling, when myths of eternal expansion are used to maintain and justify the status quo, is indicated by some form of producerism or workaholism. And every period of decadence, when the absurd is consumed by the earnest, is indicated by some form of survival-of-the-fittest social Darwinism. An awful period of civic crisis and destruction usually follows. But history needn't be determined and time needn't be cyclical.

Liberalism's decadence, corruption and failure are the very result of its triumph, purity and success, as true in the 1790s and 1910s as in the 2020s. In each period, the middle classes, mental health, peaceful power transfers and democratic institutions decline; the inequality, corruption, authoritarianism (and now, sea levels) rise. The ruling classes get so out of touch that they pretend that the problems are individual instead of acknowledging that both the problems and solutions are structural. When the first era of liberalism failed in the 1910s–40s, it resulted in the rise of authoritarianism and the World Wars. The era of neoliberalism is failing again in the early twenty-first century and will likely have a similar result. Why do we continuously insist on forgetting the past and repeating the most monstrous chapters of our history for the sake of eternal liberal expansion on a planet with finite resources?

The failures of liberalism in the early twentieth century and neoliberalism in the early twenty-first century have both been caused by the same underlying paradox: structural reliance on steady growth (via unrepeatable governing and business practices) running up against the cosmic impossibility of further growth (Mazzucato, 2020, pp. 198–199). When the necessity for eternal expansion collides with the limits of sustainability, it produces the answer to the eternal question: if God is so powerful, what happens when he creates a force so great he cannot resist it? The answer is that it leads to vast zero-sum conflict between the forces of expansion and the forces of resistance; credit and debt; progress and regress. The paradox of zero-sum thinking is that it's the same as all other paradoxes: it's true until it isn't and, simultaneously, it isn't true until it is (Easterlin, 2017).

Divergence: Infinite Growth?

His eyes are staring, his mouth is open, his wings are spread. This is how one pictures the Angel of History. His face is turned toward the past. Where we perceive a chain of events, he sees one single catastrophe which keeps piling wreckage upon wreckage and hurls it in front of his feet. The angel would like to stay, awaken the dead, and make whole what has been smashed. But a storm is blowing in from Paradise; it has got caught in his wings with such violence that the angel can no longer close them. This storm irresistibly propels him into the future to which his back is turned, while the pile of debris before him grows skyward. This storm is what we call progress (Benjamin, 1973, p. 259; cited in Anderson, 2006, pp. 161–162).

The concept of religious progress through the birth and death of civilizations has the merit of calling attention to the fact that periods of historic decay may well be times of profoundest religious insights; for historic catastrophes break the power of the idolatrous worship of cultures and civilizations (Niebuhr, 1949, p. 111; Miller McDonald, 2025).

Just as Jesus' crucifixion was symbolic of the entire destruction of Israel a generation hence, religious prophecies have always centered around the rise and fall of various idolatries (Crossan, 1991; Fredriksen, 1999; Horsley, 2003; Levine, 2006; Sanders, 1985; Wright, 1996). Like any deity, the idolatry at the center of liberalism has different names which thinkers fight for inclusion and exclusion—but the so-called "free market" is the head of the golden calf. The divergent tradeoff is both implied and denied either between progress and regress, credit and debt or abundance and scarcity (lately called degrowth).

Progress and Regress

In every instance, liberalism's very fetish for "progress" is predicated on simultaneous regress, as every caste structure produces the conditions which undermine and eventually ruin itself. It's ironic that self-styled technocratic neoliberal progressives like Ezra Klein and Derek Thompson (2025) challenge the "eureka theory" of progress, which emphasizes individual inventors and moments of discovery. While acknowledging the importance of inventions, they argue that implementation and widespread adoption are equally crucial for social advancement. Consequently, they explain, this disconnect between innovation and implementation has contributed to stagnating "progress" in the United States, affecting areas like technological advancement, income growth, and life expectancy. "Progress is our escape from the status quo of suffering, our ejection seat from history," notes Thompson (2022a, 2022b), as he also points to its central position in American ideology. "In the past few decades, however, progress has faltered – and faith in it has curdled." So for Klein and Thompson, the emphasis on individual ability comes at the expense of structural utility; every generation's solutions become the next generation's problems—to be antithetically used to subvert or disparage the very history it makes (Harris, 2024).

In the United States as in Russia, history is manipulated as a weapon to justify the creative destruction of progress (Miller McDonald, 2025). James Fallows draws parallels between republican Rome and contemporary America, warning of civil confrontation: a short-term victory for demagogic reactionary forces (like Caesar's), possibly followed by a grand compromise. Scholars like Jeff Lowenstein and Danny Postel (2022, pp. 124–125) portray current political conflicts in the US as a fundamental threat to democracy, led by an authoritarian movement with fascist tendencies which, though both a symptom and a disease, feeds off the very cycle of misery it perpetuates. Commentators like Adrienne LaFrance (2023) and Hugh Hewitt (2023) describe increasing American domestic terrorism due to economic inequality, eroding faith in democratic institutions, identity-based polarization and demographic displacements which together create a powder keg of social tension with growing tendencies for political violence and authoritarian demagoguery. Such authoritarian demagoguery may temporarily dissipate, but similar or more revolutionary figures and movements will take the scene if the United States remains a post-democracy captured by virtue-signaling corporations and administered on their behalf by hand-wringing Democrats or forever-war Republicans (Hamid, 2020; Spang, 2020a, 2020b; Wood, 2020). Other pundits like James Fallows (2021) and Peter Wehner (2022) note the growing divide between coastal metros and struggling interior communities, with progressives (like Roman optimates) defending a system that benefits them at the expense of the plebeian majority—disenfranchised and marginalized working-class voters. The same American republicanism, literally embodied by Lincoln, was ironically used by a demagogue to legitimize his pyrrhic victory.

The 17th-c. New England poet Anne Bradstreet wrote about the "four monarchies" (from Daniel 2) and clearly considered the mid-17th-c. Anglican monarchy as an extension of the Roman monarchy: "The Tarquins they from Rome by force expel, In banishment perpetual to dwell; The Government they change, a new one bring, And people swear ne'r to accept of King." Her Puritan words were veiled criticism of the Anglican monarchy, which later inspired American republicanism—famously distilled in Benjamin Franklin's ostensible description of the 1787 US constitution: "a republic, if you can keep it" (McHenry, 1911, p. 87). Or, as Thomas Jefferson opined a few years earlier, authoritarian tyranny is always justified by the Hobbesian threat confusing anarchy with chaos: "for what oppression may not a precedent be found in this world of the *bellum omnium in omnia*?" Thomas Jefferson (1832, p. 114) rejected using Roman precedents to justify expanding government powers in America. He warned that without proper checks, the legislature or the executive could seize all authority, potentially reducing themselves to single-person rule and creating a dictatorship under a different name. More than four centuries passed from the overthrow and death of Tarquin to the reign of Julius Caesar when Rome was a republic. From Bradstreet's words, published in 1642, more than four centuries will have passed by the mid-twenty-first century. In the 2020s, the irony is that republicanism is rising in the UK even as monarchism is rising in the United States (driven by the likes of Curtis Yarvin). And Daniel 2's "Four monarchies" as successive Roman empires remain both credited and indebted—to Washington, Brussels, Moscow, Beijing.

Credit and Debt

Like most of history's greatest scholars, David Graeber's brilliance lay in his combination of meticulous scholarship, rigorous documentation and argumentation—and overt dedication to justice. By turning on its head the banal liberal theory that money began as a more efficient and formal replacement of informal barter (it was never informal barter, but rather informal debt), Graeber showed that the entire economic history of money was always an artifice: that it is in fact a history of debt. For Graeber (2011) and his coauthor David Wengrow (2021), the value of a unit of money lay in a fundamentally converse understanding of trust—trust and scarcity are two opposite sides of the same monetary coin—pun intended. Thus, economies built on trust are local and truly about free-trading, whereas economies built on scarcity are larger-scale and truly about debt-peonage.

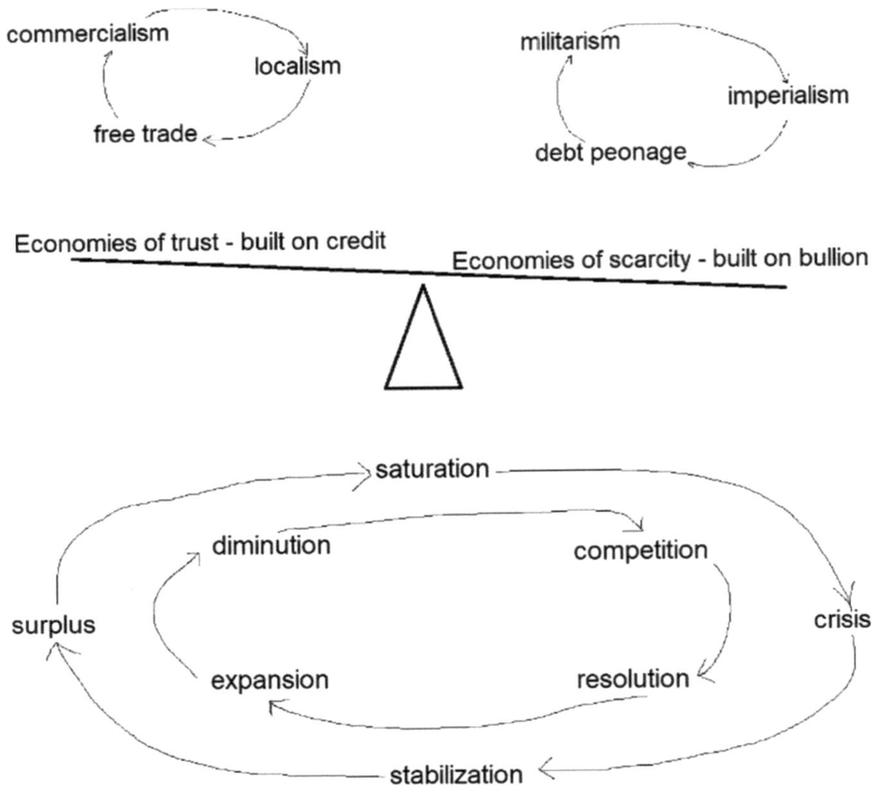

From this model can be easily extrapolated the basic problems with conventional historical models of political economy: its simplistically deterministic nature. One of the reasons Marx's ideas are discussed relatively seldomly in these pages is that while it's well known that his overtly linear understanding of economic history was as much a product of the liberal ideals of his generation as his imagination, the misguided followers of his doctrines made them into self-fulfilling prophecies from which escape seemed futile—for example, that rent-seeking speculation, farcical inequality, social darwinism and ideological cannibalism intrinsically indicate eras of decadence. Thus, thinkers from Robert Davies (1998) to Branko Milanovic (2021) could fit the history of Soviet political economy into a larger cycle of historical determinism back to the empires of antiquity. Such a cyclical deterministic model of imperial golden ages of various sovereignties would typically look like: expansion → surplus → diminution → saturation → competition → crisis → resolution → stabilization (Norberg, 2025; Slatyer, 2012).

Of course, what could be said about the USSR or the PRC could also be said of the USA, UK or EU: Anglophone, allied and European nations of the 2020s retain much the same deterministic political-economic institutions since they're structured to facilitate a zero-sum vertical system rather than a positive-sum horizontal system. The marked failures of the former are coefficient with the market failures of the latter. This is why a hand-wringing neoliberal economist like Brad DeLong would write:

There's someone in Bangladesh who would almost surely be a better economics professor than I am and is now behind a water buffalo. The market economy gives me and my preferences 200 times the voice and weight of his. If that isn't the biggest market failure of all, I don't know what your definition of market failure could possibly be (Lowrey, 2022).

The logic used by critics of the logic of Market Failure Theory (MFT) and Modern Monetary Theory (MMT) ironically falls apart on closer inspection: "governments in richer countries such as the United States also play a huge role. Whatever you think of restrictions on immigration, they *are* restrictions; they are heavy regulation of the labor market" (Henderson, 2022). One wonders if the author supports the very open borders, free trade policies and grotesque inequalities that eventually lead to demagoguery. It seems that critics of MFT and MMT are as compromised by inconsistency and hypocrisy—if not more—than the neokeynesian policies they criticize.

The real zero-sum issue is of course inequality itself—something which can be addressed by a potential Constitution for the entire earth (Ferrajoli, 2022). If Gresham's iron law of monetary cycles is that bad money drives out the good money, then the iron law of economic cycles is that economic inequality drives out equality. Whether a potential UBI (Universal Basic Income) is a necessary form of public safety-net welfare mandated by democracies or an institutionalized neo-potlatch charitable dependence is beside the point: if healthcare and housing are human rights, then the redistribution of wealth from rich to poor makes up for previous redistribution of wealth from poor to rich (like the funding for the NHS from tobacco corporations). Similarly, since tax and migration are opposite sides of the same coin (implied more in the work of Khaldun than Laffer); the former suggested that minimal tax rates are preferable due to capital flight and diminishing returns. But to suggest that his ideas support tax policies favored by Austrian school economists is absurd. If ibn Khaldun was a forerunner of the Austrian school of economics when it comes to tax policies, then Atilla the Hun was a forerunner of the borderless world when it comes to migration policies. As the journalist Sam Pizzigati (2018) asks, if we can implement an optimum tax rate, why not optimum inequality rates?

This also explains the increasing discussions of so-called circular economies. Popular among both back-to-the-land leftists and corporate conservatives, new models of circular economies propose to utilize "new" economic models and technologies to "return" to sustainability. The mental confluence of political economy and sustainability has simultaneously produced some of the best work on biodiversity economics and circular economics (Dasgupta, 2021). Yet like any other model, its success is jeopardized by whoever designs it. If fascist oligarchies are permitted to design and construct circular economies, they will benefit themselves at the zero-sum expense of democratic accountability; in other words, "doughnut economics" (Raworth, 2017).

Abundance and Degrowth

If in scientific inquiry Nietzsche and Darwin were to the nineteenth century what Foucault and Dawkins were to the 20th, then in political economy, Marx and Malthus were to the nineteenth century what Keynes and Hayek were to the twentieth century. The confluence between them all remains central to questions of abundance and scarcity.

Marx's ideas were to Nietzsche's what Malthus' were to Darwin: 19th-c. intellectual underpinnings of historical, philosophical and/or biological determinisms of scarcity. All assumed the structural constraints of finite land, bullion and other resources on earth, and all fell prey to the same trap of zero-sum logic, which doomed their imperial and/or empirical projects. With the 20th-c. downfalls of their respective liberal empires, Keynes, Hayek, Foucault and Dawkins replaced them, each envisaging various forms of achieving abundance through growth rather than mercantilism, but disagreed on how to do it. Just as Khrushchev conceived of the growth of Soviet economic power as a "battering ram with which we shall smash the capitalist system," they each ironically viewed growthism and abundance as a mercantile instrument to confront their ideological enemies (Alexander & Numbers, 2010; Lewontin et al., 1984; Skousen, 2007; Susskind, 2024, pp. 64–72, 188–192; Wapshott, 2011). So it's no surprise that the 21st-c. failure of Western imperial and empirical liberalism has produced a plethora of literature reexamining the legacies of these thinkers.

This is also true in Charles Mann's (2018a, 2018b) explanations of various versions of neomalthusian concerns about human overpopulation of Earth—as he describes it, the conflict between the Wizards (seeking technological eclipses) and Prophets (seeing logical apocalypses) (Hains, 2018; Linnér, 2003; Ridley, 2015; Gray, 2007). It is also as evident in the oligarchic domination and extraction of the world's finite resources (Blas & Farchy, 2021; Perry, 2023; Specktor, 2021) as it is prominent in the neomathusian-tinged conservationism of figures like David Attenborough (2018), Edward Wilson (2016), Jane Goodall (2015), Jared Diamond (2005), Bill McKibben (1998) and so on. One irony is that rather than astronomically growing, the trajectory of the world's 21st-c. population is subject to demographic debate about "leveling off," with oligarchs "kvetching" about a global population decreasing, rather than increasing (Cave et al., 2021; Chamie, 2022; Cilluffo & Ruiz, 2019; Goldstone & May, 2023; Kunzig, 2014; Roser & Ritchie, 2023; Rostow, 1998; Sanderson, 2013; Seidel, 2025; Reuters, 2014; UN Department of Economic & Social Affairs, 2024). "The implications of permanently slumped population growth are wide-ranging," Thompson writes (2022b), "Shrinking populations produce stagnant economies. Stagnant economies create wonky cultural knock-on effects, like a zero-sum mentality that ironically makes it harder to pursue pro-growth policies." In Elizabeth Warren's *Two Income Trap* (2016), later dates of reaching the traditional signs of adulthood (marriage, homeownership, parenthood, etc.) and increasing adolescent immiseration suggest greater political-economic inequality and instability in a given society, which in turn demonstrates massive demographic aging throughout the twenty-first century.

Global birthrates have declined to below replacement level (Anderson & Winthrop, 2025; Caldwell, 2020; Fraser, 2019; Milanovic, 2016; Piketty, 2022; Reeves, 2017; *The Economist*, 2023; Wilkinson & Pickett, 2009). This was just as true in the early twenty-first century as it was before the Black Death, 30 Years War, the French Revolution and Napoleonic Wars, WWI-WWII, etc. Since the 1970s, the 2020s' transformation from a half century of liberal hand wringing would be replaced by another half century of conservative hand wringing.

Another irony is that following the Meadows' legendary 1970s-era volume at the Club of Rome (*The Limits to Growth*), a number of newer books drawing on neomalthusian ideas and warning of the long-term dangers of population growth have appeared by various co-authors which have since become self-described "futurists," energy company CEOs and business school professors like Jørgen Randers and William Behrens III (Bardi, 2011; Jørgensen et al., 2015; Meadows et al., 1992, 2004; Randers, 2012). The greatest irony, of course, is that as one review of Daniel Susskind's *Growth: A History and a Reckoning* postulates, the main obstacles to U.S. economic growth are self-created rather than natural: artificial housing scarcity, excessive regulations hindering clean energy development, monopolistic practices, an ineffective and unjust tax system, etc. Thus, as based on Robert Gordon's *Rise & Fall of American Growth* (2017, esp. Figures 8-1, 16-2), artificial assumptions of "natural" malthusian caps give the lie to 21st-c. beliefs in 19th-c. levels of economic growth—growth (and efficiency) come at the expense of both equality *and* reality (Kahloon, 2024; Mitchell, 2021; Okun, 2015; Susskind, 2024, pp. 196–216).

The latest, 21st-c. front in the zero-sum conflict of Charles Mann's Wizards and Prophets is between those who adhere to the Degrowth and Abundance movements. Both movements consider themselves "progressive," but emphasize different solutions to the same problems of finitude. The former, led by Kohei Saito (2024) and Giorgios Kallis (2019), can be considered demand-side progressives who believe in the finite scarcity of resources and energy, the importance of prudently conserving them and thus the necessity of a "degrowth" ideology. The latter, led by Ezra Klein and Derek Thompson's *Abundance* (2025), can be considered supply-side progressives who believe resources can be made abundant with technological advancements in the energy sector and other inventive forms of production development. If the former dismiss the latter as advocating a kind of "neo-neoliberalism," the latter dismiss the former as advocating a kind of "ecosocialism" (Foster & Spéth, 2024; Gyauch-Lewis, 2024). Combined with the climate crisis of the twenty-first century, one commentator describes it as "the turn of climate skepticism toward the hardened lifeboat ethics of what is sometimes called eco-fascism" (Wallace-Wells, 2025). So it's ironic that the zero-sum nature of the history of political economy (and economic growth) is decontextualized at best or forgotten at worst, dooming liberalism's proponents to repeating the very past and fulfilling the very Malthusian prophecies they so fervently (and smugly) seek to avoid. In reality, liberalism and the zero-sum autarkies of mercantilism/feudalism (and later, fascism and communism) form the same recipe, except that one has the added ingredient of growth for the sake of man rather than God. As Simon Weil

(2002, p. 115) noted, "the real sin of idolatry is always committed on behalf of something similar to the State" since each requires human sacrifice at its altar.

At first glance, the Abundance and Degrowth ideologies seem to be two mutually inconsistent agendas that cannot coexist. Their mutual critiques are that the other side lacks imagination and refuses to accept ecological, ecumenical and/or economical reality. "The intransigence of such zero-sum disputes is a reminder of why win–win fantasies are so attractive in the first place," Jennifer Szalai (2024a, 2024b) writes, "Whatever the profound differences between degrowth's proponents and their critics, the scale of the climate crisis suggests one point of convergence: We need all the imaginative help we can get." Degrowthers like George Monbiot (2021) deny the possibility of compromise: "there is no such thing as green growth. Growth is wiping the green from the Earth." Abundantists like Holden Karnofsky expressly reject the idea of zero economic growth, arguing that growth facilitates positive-sum scenarios that benefit society as a whole, whereas stagnation could lead to purely zero-sum interactions. This view implies that economic expansion has been crucial for improving living standards, and its absence might result in more contentious resource allocation where gains for some necessarily mean losses for others (Klein & Karnofsky, 2021). Yet as Mariana Mazzucato (2020, p. 207) writes,

Too many green policies today are just minor adjustments to a trajectory that still favors the old waste-prone behaviors and the financial casino that worsens inequality. A healthy economy that works for the *whole* of society must tilt the playing field consistently to reward behaviors that help us achieve agreed and desirable goals. That means achieving coherence in a multiplicity of fields, from taxes to regulation, from business law to the social safety net.

This is the reason that Susskind (2024, pp. 2020–2221) advocates what he calls "weak degrowthism," which is "about demoting growth in the hierarchy of ends that a society might care about." He supports more direct democracies, economic equality and wealth taxes, which would "be a price worth paying for a fairer society." Yet his advocacy of loosening intellectual property rights to foster intellectual growth on a finite planet would ostensibly come at the zero-sum expense of corporate intellectual property hoarders like dominant media outlets and book publishers. Ultimately however, the competition between the Abundance and Degrowth agendas for hearts and minds presupposes their competition for power—the acute cause of the crisis (Haiven, 2014; Mulgan, 2020).

In the final analysis, it doesn't matter how much fact is parsed from interpretation if liberal democratic progressivism is only as powerful as its ideological understanding of power. The liberal approach to power has always been paradoxical: "Human power was implacable," as Edmund Fawcett (2018, p. 8) writes, "It could never be relied on to behave well. Whether political, economic or social, superior power of some people over others tended inevitably to arbitrariness and domination unless resisted and checked." Political economy ensures that liberal democracy is revealed as an oxymoron—the ouroboros, an absurd creature consuming its own tail whose cerebrospinal fluid is zero sum. If, as Malcolm X said, "power concedes nothing," then in the zero-sum calculation of liberal-democratic political economy, the political consumes the economic, growth consumes stability and liberalism consumes democracy.

It doesn't matter how often history shows the moral bankruptcy and futility of capitalist peace theory and antidemocratic realities stemming from the idolatry of liberal internationalism—as John Mearsheimer (2018), Paul Musgrave and Daniel Nexon (2013, pp. 131–148), Erik Gartzke (2007, pp. 166–191) and their ilk warn liberals like Thomas Friedman (1999)—war returns. In 1913, Rosa Luxemburg explained that accumulation begets militarization: "Militarism fulfils a quite definite function in the history of capital, accompanying as it does every historical phase of accumulation" (1951, pt. 3.32). Her mentee Hannah Arendt (1962a, 1962b, p. 151) added more:

The mob, begotten by the monstrous accumulation of capital, accompanied its begetter on those voyages of discovery where nothing was discovered but new possibilities for investment. The owners of superfluous wealth were the only men who could use the superfluous men who came from the four corners of the earth. Together they established the first paradise of parasites whose lifeblood was gold. Imperialism, the product of superfluous money and superfluous men, began its startling career by producing the most superfluous and unreal goods.

Just as the crises of the nineteenth and twentieth centuries consisted of failures of liberalism, the crisis of the twenty-first century is as afflicted by free will as it is by determinism—a problem as much of the ruling class as the ruled and as much of the present as the past and future. If grotesque economic inequality politically destabilizes societies (elites vs. lower-class wage-stagnation), then the political-economic and social expectations of the members of a given society are far more important to the general growth, wellbeing and stability of the society than their standard of living relative to their ancestors (Economist, 2020; Turchin, 2016, Fig. 13.6; Turchin & Nefedov, 2009). Economic resentment being an indicative factor of political instability, humans are not economically resentful of their better-off progeny just as we do not feel economically superior to our ancestors. Humans economically compare ourselves to others while we live—not abstract notions of past or future generations. "We are either asking people in the present to become poorer to protect other ends in the future, or we are asking people in the future to sacrifice some of those other ends so that people today can maintain their prosperity," Susskind (2024, p. 223) writes, "the fact that the growth dilemma now looms so large is itself a symptom of that same short-termism, an almost century-long failure to see that the pursuit of unfettered growth is creating immense problems for the future." For example, if Appalachia is to Trump what the Donbas is to Putin, then it's no surprise that the aggrieved and pain-tolerant denizens of such regions are caught in a 21st-c. geopolitical catch-22: given their simultaneous mineral wealths, material poverties and support for demagogues, their imagined future political enrichments are commensurate with their real present economic impoverishments.

The quotation usually misattributed to Bismarck—"By himself the individual can create nothing; he can only wait until he hears God's footsteps resounding through events and then spring forward to grasp the hem of his mantle – that is all"—suggests that because we are always caught in a paradoxical historical cycle as the pendulum of time swings back and forth, we are always bound within a catch-22 (Pflanze, 2020, p. 87). Together, we are bound by order, which ensures economic stability and economic consolidation, as a counter to chaos, in which the consolidation may be overthrown and wealth and power become up for grabs by the strongest. The conditions of this paradox, however, have always been zero-sum: as one opportunistic psychologist warns, either we are enslaved by order or we are haunted by chaos:

We are eternally caught between the most diamantine rock and the hardest of places: loss of group-centred belief renders life chaotic, miserable, intolerable; presence of group-centred belief makes conflict with other groups inevitable. In the West, we have been withdrawing from our tradition-, religion-, and even nation-centred cultures, partly to decrease the danger of group conflict. But we are increasingly falling prey to the desperation of meaninglessness, and that is no improvement at all (Peterson, 2018, p. xxxii).

The same awful powerlessness and deprivation of poverty also limits the harm that the impoverished can do to others. As Václav Havel (1987) explained, this makes solidarity and compassion uniquely available to the billions of victims of poverty and injustice, who can most clearly see how their status is dependent on those at the top of the pyramid, whose own wealth and power MUST be used to exploit, enslave or otherwise destroy others to stay afloat. Massive wealth cannot be maintained without engaging in the sadistic or sociopathic consumption of others' suffering. This is why potlatch initiatives have traditionally been so important—because they have always disguised the zero-sum nature of the social pyramid.

Determinisms are never singular—the unpredictable interactions between free will and determinism ensure that history is both cyclical and linear. The timelessness of Hegel's lord-bondsman dialectic was such that as impressed by Smithian growth as Marx was, the latter's "emphasis on economic structures as core components of social formations was an extreme case, but it reflects a much more general trend" (Arnason, 2003, p. 180). That the "Great-Man" theory of history is a delusion, perpetuated by the likes of Ayn Rand, Horatio Alger, Tina Turner and many before them is simply beside the point, since FDR's "mysterious cycles of history" ensured by predictably banal political economies would render individual control as limited as collective control unlimited. We can choose to either swim against the tides of time or go with the flow. Either way, the tides will rise and fall—not based on individual agency, but on collective action and reaction.

Like other prevailing thought patterns, zero-sum thinking often tends to function as a self-fulfilling prophecy (Davidai & Tepper, 2023). The pundit Ross Douthat's (2024) paradoxical prediction is perceptive: "the spirit of populism, its political psychology, needs a dose of the libertarian impulse, an element of American entrepreneurial can-do, to avoid becoming a purely defensive and zero-sum worldview." The presumption that only American entrepreneurialism can prevent zero-sum thinking is a self-fulfilling prophecy since it simultaneously presumes that other nations are incapable of non-zero-sum thinking, a naively liberal position which causes the very conflicts it seeks to prevent, and suspiciously similar to the older liberal zero-sum logic of Oliver Wendell Holmes Jr (1941, p. 36): "Between two groups of men that want to make inconsistent kinds of worlds I see no remedy except force… It seems to me that every society rests on the death of men." It's no surprise that Peter Theil and his ilk fret about an "antichrist" arising "like Eliezer Yudkowsky, Nick Bostrom and Greta Thunberg" to secure a single world government, reign in big tech and stem inequality. Such zero-sum thinking thus reinforces divisions and barbarizes the struggle between potential winners and losers; it pushes players to act in a way that harms themselves and precludes non-zero-sum outcomes even if other ways of playing would be in certain ways more beneficial to them (eg., drained vs clean swimming pools) (Blake, 2021). If zero-sum thinking is an example of a simultaneously both rational and irrational intellectual ouroboros inside a möbius strip, one that is simultaneously both real and unreal, then, it recalls Nietzsche's famous definition of nihilism: "*The highest values devalue themselves.*" There is no point; "why" has no answer' (*The Will to Power*, §2). If growth, freedom and rights are among the highest values, then they devalue themselves through zero-sum beliefs. If God is dead, then everything is possible.

Ultimately, if a zero-sum political economy is more politics than economics, the difference between free will and determinism is an illusion: zero-sum logic is everywhere and everywhen (Johnson et al., 2018; Rubin, 2003). Cooperative models might lead to better economic indicators even for the states, classes, corporations, or individuals on top. That would even be true for laissez-faire models in the original sense of the phrase, which would mean non-interventionism rather than interventionism to the benefit of corporations or interventionism in order to impose on others what *you* label as laissez-faire economics. But such modes of operation might decrease the difference between those at the top and those at the bottom. The history of political economy has always been a pyramid scheme—all the way back to pharaoh Khufu. The point of the Matthew Effect is that as long as humans compete for power in a world of finite resources, the competition will inevitably become deadly (Wolf, 2007). Hence, zero-sum thinking is just as apparent among the wealthy as among the poor—when the wealthy use zero-sum logic, it is the logic of rent-seeking; when the poor use zero-sum logic, either it is for the same end or it is for redistribution of finite wealth.

Cooperative models might lead to better economic indicators even for the states, classes, corporations, or individuals on top. But this is all about power, and power is relative. Even if one aims to hoard near-absolute power, one must see it as relative. And when wealth buys power, then truth becomes meaningless. Essentially, the neoliberal critique of Marxism is just as true in reverse, the larger the wealth disparity, the more power the few at the top have to influence political decision-making in ways that serve their own interests and increase their own wealth (at the expense—and often against the expressed democratic will—of the many at the bottom). If the arc of history is long and flexible, then it bends toward whomever happens to have the means to bend it.

This is both the predicament of our current geopolitical moment and the reason why extreme wealth inequality and democracy cannot coexist. Unchecked inequality does not find a natural equilibrium; it just spirals out of control and into the latest tanks, trenches and tupolevs. The larger the wealth disparity, the more power the few at the top have to influence political decision-making in ways that serve their own interests and increase their own wealth (at the expense—and often against the expressed democratic will—of the many at the bottom) (BBC, 2014; Gilens & Page, 2014). And the smaller the percentage of wealth that they need to spend to have people justifying and embellishing the disparity and their own position at the top: journalists, academics and lawyers work directly or indirectly for them while some folks reproduce such favorable discourses for free since they have fallen victim to the PR stunts of those who work for the super-rich and have idolized them or even aspire to be like them—deluding themselves that there is anything more than an infinitesimal possibility for this to happen the more the zero-sum game gets harsher and the deck gets stacked in favor of those already winning.

It is another irony that in order to attain or retain near-absolute power you have to see it as relative. It is not how much you pull yourself up by your bootstraps but how much you kick others out of the way or crush them under your heel. This is why the "end of history" was not followed by an era of peace and prosperity for all but by a frenzied struggle to destroy and subjugate anyone remotely defiant of or autonomous from neoliberal US hegemony (Sachs, 2024). This is why many Middle Eastern nations were devastated, why Yugoslavia was split up, why both Eurasia and Latin America were devastated by generations of corrupt cartels and oligarchies, why NATO expanded ever eastwards while refusing to include a Russia already ruined by Western-imposed "shock therapy" in a common security architecture, why Latin America has been plagued by countless coups—whether they be military, parliamentary, executive or judicial. And this is why elites refuse to make any real economic concessions to the plebs even after the 2008 crisis and instead increase their efforts to pit plebs against plebs in culture wars or literally national wars all the while extorting more wealth out of them—either directly through the overexploitation of their labor or indirectly through the overexploitation of the commons. This is why this book is written at the outset of Cold War II and potentially on the cusp of WWIII.

As Hannah Arendt (1962a, 1962b) observed, eras of chaos which break the stranglehold of concentrated wealth also tend to coincide with the deaths of tens of millions—all in the name of "progress." Adolf Eichmann justified his bureaucratic actions based on the Nazi ideals of progress: "I will gladly jump into my grave in the knowledge that five million enemies of the Reich have already died like animals." Afterwards, when peace and order are restored, prosperity leads to the gradual increase in inherited wealth and accumulation and economic inequality, which tends to cause the next cycle of chaos (Arendt, 1970). In other words, the rich get richer and the poor get poorer until a crisis point is reached and a period of chaos and destruction ensues, leading eventually to the reestablishment of order and stability—and the cycle repeats. It's little surprise that one of the most memorable lines in one of the most popular shows of the 2010s, *Game of Thrones*, came from the dragon queen Daenerys Targaryen—"I want to break the wheel"—who destroyed the world she sought to redeem.

This historiosophy of zero-sum thinking leading to seemingly (but not divinely-mandated) deterministic cycles of history may seem bleak at first glance—certainly given the common Whig-derived liberal western historiosophy that history moves in a linear fashion upward, onward and toward freedom, prosperity, or, in Martin Luther King Jr.'s famous formula, that the moral arc of the universe is long, but it bends toward justice. But given the discrediting of Whiggism in the 1850s and liberalism's repeated failures in the 1900s and 2010s, there is a much older and perhaps more useful (if not truer) conception of the "goal" of history (as Karl Jaspers put it)—the myth of Sisyphus. Today we think of Sisyphus as the worst metaphor of the human experience—Sisyphus was doomed by the gods to roll a heavy boulder up a hill everyday for eternity only for it to roll back down again and to have to repeat again the following day. It's a striking, if pessimistic, metaphor. It's also, as Albert Camus (1942) argued, worth reinterpreting optimistically: Sisyphus would come to appreciate the serenity of the eternal endeavor insofar that he always knew what tomorrow would bring because he had already learned from yesterday's instruction. For Sisyphus, the predictability of the past makes for a predictable future. Every schoolboy quotes the dictum that those who don't learn from the past are condemned to repeat it. But let's turn that on its head: the fact that history repeats because we never learn means that the future can be discernible if we squint, however faint it may at first appear—like a slowly approaching form bathed in light and shadow in the distance, or perhaps Snowpiercer bearing down on us in the cold tunnel of time.

You don't need a crystal ball to see that a 21st-c. Cold War II between Washington and Beijing will have overtones of the 20th-c. struggles between autarkic fascism and communism, or that proxy wars will be fought in various external theatres such as the Levant, Ukraine, Latin America, the Indo-Pacific Oceans or in space. You don't need to be able to read tea leaves to see that space will be to 21st-c. tech oligarchs what Mulligan's Valley was to the striking 20th-c. corporate overlords in Ayn Rand's *Atlas Shrugged*. You don't need to deal tarot cards to see that if the American Republic collapses into another zero-sum civil war for political-economic supremacy and/or survival, the resulting Augustan opera will resemble a Lucasian space empire which will last a few more generations until that too splinters into local dynasties competing for seemingly zero-sum wealth and power.

Yet none of these events are predetermined on a finite planet. Just as the over-arching lessons of the Revolutionary, Civil and World Wars were encapsulated in legal Rights (for all Citizens and Humans), the paradox of rights is that they're only as strong as those who either defend or attack them. When sovereignty comes before rights, then rule OF law becomes rule BY law—and those warning of a coming antichrist themselves become the chief architects of his arrival. A new global constitution and financial architecture which guarantee human rights for all by restraining the power of the few is the only way to prevent the very dystopian scenarios their self-appointed prophets seek to propagandize. Sisyphus would never ask himself Who is John Galt? Cassandra knew the answer long ago; he was murdered in his bathtub by his wife and Aegisthus had already replaced him!

References

Alexander, D., & Numbers, R. (Eds.). (2010). *Biology & ideology from Descartes to Dawkins*. University of Chicago Press.

Anderson, B. (2006). *Imagined communities: Reflections on the origin and spread of nationalism*. Verso.

Anderson, J., & Winthrop, R. (2025). *The disengaged teen: Helping kids learn better, feel better, and live better*. Crown.

Arendt, H. (1962a). *The origins of totalitarianism*. World Publishing. (Original work published 1951)

Arendt, H. (1962b). *Eichmann in Jerusalem: A report on the banality of evil*. Viking.

Arendt, H. (1970). *On violence*. Harcourt.

Arnason, J. (2003). *Civilizations in dispute: Historical questions & theoretical traditions*. Brill.

Attenborough, D. (2018, October 4). Population growth must come to an end. *EcoWatch*. https://www.ecowatch.com/david-attenborough-population-growth-2609996785.html

Bacevich, A. (2022). *On shedding an obsolete past*. Haymarket.

Bardi, U. (2011). *The limits to growth revisited*. Springer.

BBC. (2014, April 17). Study: US is an oligarchy, not a democracy. *BBC News*. https://www.bbc.com/news/blogs-echochambers-27074746

de Beauvoir, S. (1947). *America day by day*. Duckworth.

Benjamin, W. (1973). *Illuminations*. Fontana.

Benedict XVI. (2010, May 13). Apostolic journey to Portugal on the occasion of the tenth anniversary of the beatification of Jacinta and Francisco: Holy Mass on the Esplanade of the Shrine of Our Lady of Fátima. *Vatican*. https://www.vatican.va/content/benedict-xvi/en/homilies/2010/documents/hf_ben-xvi_hom_20100513_fatima.html

Bernard, L. (2014). Long-wave economic cycles: The contributions of Kondratieff, Kuznets, Schumpeter, Kalecki, Goodwin, Kaldor, and Minsky. *Review of Keynesian Economics, 2*(1), 87–107.

Blake, J. (2021, March 6). A drained swimming pool shows how racism harms White people, too. *CNN*. https://edition.cnn.com/2021/03/05/us/heather-mcghee-racism-white-people-blake/index.html

Blas, J., & Farchy, J. (2021). *The world for sale: Money, power and the traders who barter the earth's resources*. Oxford University Press.

Brooks, A. (2023, March 23). How smart people can stop being miserable. *The Atlantic*. https://www.theatlantic.com/family/archive/2023/03/intelligence-well-being-life-satisfaction-happiness/673476

Brooks, D. (2024a, January 4). What Biden needs to tell us. *The New York Times*. https://www.nytimes.com/2024/01/04/opinion/populism-trump-liberalism.html

Brooks, A. (2024b, January 5). From strength to strength. *Faithful Intellect*. https://faithfulintellect.com/from-strength-to-strength-by-arthur-c-brooks

Caldwell, C. (2020). *The age of entitlement: America since the sixties*. Simon & Schuster.

Camus, A. (1942). *The myth of Sisyphus and other essays*. Random House.

Cave, D., et al. (2021, May 22). Long slide looms for world population, with sweeping ramifications. *The New York Times*. https://www.nytimes.com/2021/05/22/world/global-population-shrinking.html

Chamie, J. (2022). Billionaires 'kvetching' about population collapse. In *Population levels, trends, and differentials* (pp. 99–100). Springer. https://doi.org/10.1007/978-3-031-22479-9_20

Cilluffo, A., & Ruiz, N. (2019, June 17). World's population is projected to nearly stop growing by the end of the century. *Pew Research Center.* https://www.pewresearch.org/short-reads/2019/06/17/worlds-population-is-projected-to-nearly-stop-growing-by-the-end-of-the-century.

Cohen, P. (2021, July 7). Generation labels mean nothing. It's time to retire them. *The Washington Post.* https://www.washingtonpost.com/opinions/2021/07/07/generation-labels-mean-nothing-retire-them

Crossan, J. D. (1991). *The historical Jesus: The life of a Mediterranean Jewish peasant.* Harper.

Dasgupta, P. (2021). *The economics of biodiversity.* Crown.

Davidai, S., & Tepper, S. (2023). The psychology of zero-sum beliefs. *National Review of Psychology, 2*, 472–482. https://doi.org/10.1038/s44159-023-00194-9

Davies, R. (1998). *Soviet economic development from Lenin to Khrushchev.* Cambridge University Press.

del Pino, L. (2022). *La dictadura infinita: La evolución autoritaria de un Occidente cobarde y cansado de sí mismo.* Esfera.

Diamond, J. (2005). *Collapse: How societies choose to fail or succeed.* Viking.

Dickson, E. (2015, December). Why Arthur Brooks is wrong about victimhood culture. *The Cut.* https://www.thecut.com/2015/12/arthur-brooks-is-wrong-about-victimhood-culture.html

Douthat, R. (2024, December 7). JD Vance, Elon Musk and the future of America. *The New York Times.* https://www.nytimes.com/2024/12/07/opinion/vance-musk-trump.html

Easterlin, R. A. (2017). Paradox lost? *Review of Behavioral Economics, 4*(4), 311–339. https://doi.org/10.1561/105.00000068

Economist. (2020, October 22). Can too many brainy people be a dangerous thing? https://www.economist.com/finance-and-economics/2020/10/22/can-too-many-brainy-people-be-a-dangerous-thing

Economist. (2023, June 1). Global fertility has collapsed, with profound economic consequences. https://www.economist.com/leaders/2023/06/01/global-fertility-has-collapsed-with-profound-economic-consequences

Fallows, J. (2021, August 13). Will the U.S. pass a point of no return? *The Atlantic.* https://www.theatlantic.com/notes/2021/08/will-us-pass-point-no-return/619739

Fawcett, E. (2018). *Liberalism: The life of an idea.* Princeton University Press.

Ferrajoli, L. (2022). *Per una Costituzione della Terra: L'umanità al bivio.* Feltrinelli.

Foster, J., & Spéth, A. (2024, June 1). Review of the month: Ecosocialism & degrowth. *Monthly Review, 76*(2). https://monthlyreview.org/2024/06/01/ecosocialism-and-degrowth

Frankl, V. E. (2006). *Man's search for meaning.* Beacon Press. (Original work published 1946)

Fraser, N. (2019). *The old is dying and the new cannot be born: From progressive neoliberalism to Trump and beyond.* Verso.

Fredriksen, P. (1999). *Jesus of Nazareth, King of the Jews: A Jewish life and the emergence of Christianity.* Vintage.

Freud, S. (1926). Inhibitions, symptoms and anxiety. In *The standard edition of the complete psychological works of Sigmund Freud*, Volume XX. (J. Strachey, et al., Trans.). Vintage, 1999 (Original work published 1925–1926).

Friedman, T. (1999). *The Lexus and the olive tree: Understanding globalization.* Farrar, Straus & Giroux.

Frum, D. (2024, May 30). Wrong case, right verdict. *The Atlantic.* https://www.theatlantic.com/politics/archive/2024/05/wrong-case-right-verdict-trump-guilty/678551/

Fukuyama, F. (1992). *The end of history and the last man.* Free Press.

Fukuyama, F. (2018). *Identity: The demand for dignity and the politics of resentment.* Farrar.

Gartzke, E. (2007). The capitalist peace. *American Journal of Political Science, 51*(1), 166–191. https://doi.org/10.1111/j.1540-5907.2007.00244.x

Gilens, M., & Page, B. (2014). Testing theories of American politics: Elites, interest groups, and average citizens. *Perspectives on Politics, 12*(3), 564–581. https://doi.org/10.1017/S1537592714001595

Goldstone, J., & May, J. (2023). How 21st century population issues and policies differ from those of the 20th century. *World, 4*(3), 467–476. https://doi.org/10.3390/world4030029

Goodall, J. (2015, October 15). Overpopulation, peace & the purpose of zoos. *ABC News: Religion & Ethics Report*. https://www.abc.net.au/listen/programs/religionandethicsreport/jane-goodall-zoos-world-peace-day-chimpanzees/7860972

Gordon, R. J. (2017). *The rise & fall of American growth*. Princeton University Press.

Graeber, D. (2011). *Debt: The first 5,000 years*. Melville House.

Graeber, D., & Wengrow, D. (2021). *The dawn of everything: A new history of humanity*. Farrar.

Gray, J. (2007). *Black mass: Apocalyptic religion and the death of utopia*. Farrar.

Green, D. (2023, July 21). 'The Fourth Turning Is Here' and 'End Times' review: Big wheel. *The Wall Street Journal*. https://www.wsj.com/arts-culture/books/the-fourth-turning-is-here-and-end-times-3439006b

Gyauch-Lewis, D. (2024, November 26). Abundance agenda: Neoliberalism's rebrand. *The American Prospect*. https://prospect.org/economy/2024-11-26-abundance-agenda-neoliberalisms-rebrand

Hains, T. (2018, August 15). Yes, Thanos was evil: Why advocates of population control are always wrong, from Malthus to Marvel. *Real Clear Politics*. https://www.realclearpolitics.com/video/2018/08/15/why_thanos_was_evil_advocates_of_population_control_are_wrong_from_malthus_to_marvel.html

Haiven, M. (2014). *Crises of imagination, crises of power*. Zed Books.

Hamid, S. (2020, June). The burden of being part of history. *The Atlantic*. https://www.theatlantic.com/ideas/archive/2020/06/burden-being-part-history/613327

Harari, Y. N. (2014). *Sapiens: A brief history of humankind*. Harper.

Harris, M. (2024, May 28). What's the matter with Abundance? *The Baffler*. https://thebaffler.com/latest/whats-the-matter-with-abundance-harris

Havel, V. (1987). *Living in truth*. Faber.

Havel, V. (1978). *The power of the powerless*. M.E. Sharpe.

Henderson, D. (2022, September 8). Brad DeLong's strange concept of market failure. *Econlib*. https://www.econlib.org/brad-delongs-strange-concept-of-market-failure

Hewitt, H. (2023, July 9). Despairing over today's divisions? Try reading some history. *The Washington Post*. https://www.washingtonpost.com/opinions/2023/07/09/current-divisions-historical-context

Hoffer, E. (1951). *The true believer: Thoughts on the nature of mass movements*. Harper & Row.

Holmes, O. W., Jr. (1941). Letter to Frederick Pollock, February 1, 1920. In M. Howe (Ed.), *Holmes-Pollock letters: The correspondence of Mr. Justice Holmes and Sir Frederick Pollock, 1874–1932* (Vol. 2). Harvard University Press.

Horsley, R. A. (2003). *Jesus and empire: The kingdom of God and the new world disorder*. Fortress Press.

Howe, N. (2023). *The fourth turning is here: What the seasons of history tell us about how and when this crisis will end*. Simon & Schuster.

Huxley, A. (1970). *Letters of Aldous Huxley*. Harper & Row.

Jefferson, T. (1832). Query XIII. In *Notes on the state of Virginia*. Lilly & Wait.

Johnson, C. (2004a). *Blowback: The costs and consequences of American empire* (2nd ed.). Metropolitan Books.

Johnson, C. (2004b). *The sorrows of empire: Militarism, secrecy, and the end of the republic*. Metropolitan Books.

Johnson, C. (2007). *Nemesis: The last days of the American republic*. Metropolitan Books.

Johnson, C. (2010). *Dismantling the empire: America's last best hope*. Metropolitan Books.

Johnson, S., Kim, S., Keil, F., & Goldstein, D. (2018). Psychological underpinnings of zero-sum thinking. *SSRN*. https://doi.org/10.2139/ssrn.3117627

Jones, D. (2022, August 23). Putin's geopolitical brain. *CIEO*. https://www.cieo.org.uk/research/putins-geopolitical-brain

Jørgensen, S., Fath, B. D., Nielsen, S. N., Pulselli, F. M., & Fiscus, D. A. (2015). *Flourishing within limits to growth: Following nature's way*. Routledge.

Judis, J. B. (2018). *The nationalism resurgence.* Columbia Global Reports.
Kahloon, I. (2024, June 3). High & higher. *The New Yorker.* https://www.newyorker.com/magazine/2024/06/03/growth-a-history-and-a-reckoning-daniel-susskind-book-review
Kallis, G. (2019). *Limits: Why Malthus was wrong and why environmentalists should care.* Stanford University Press.
Kazin, M. (2023, March 30). What would it take for one party to dominate America again? *The New York Times.* https://nyti.ms/3KjPXmM
Klein, E. (2021, October 8). David Shor is telling Democrats what they don't want to hear. *The New York Times.* https://nyti.ms/2WRI2qT
Klein, E. & Karnofsky, H. (2021, October 5). Transcript: Ezra Klein interviews Holden Karnofsky. *The New York Times.* https://www.nytimes.com/2021/10/05/podcasts/transcript-ezra-klein-interviews-holden-karnofsky.html
Klein, E., & Thompson, D. (2025). *Abundance.* Avid Reader Press.
Kunzig, R. (2014, September 19). A world with 11 billion people? New population projections shatter earlier estimates. *National Geographic.* https://www.nationalgeographic.com/science/article/140918-population-global-united-nations-2100-boom-africa
LaFrance, A. (2023, March 6). The new anarchy. *The Atlantic.* https://www.theatlantic.com/magazine/archive/2023/04/us-extremism-portland-george-floyd-protests-january-6/673088
Leithart, P. (2019, March 29). What Arthur Brooks gets wrong. *First Things.* https://firstthings.com/what-arthur-brooks-gets-wrong
Levine, A.-J. (2006). *The misunderstood Jew: The Church and the scandal of the Jewish Jesus.* Harper.
Lewontin, R., Rose, S., & Kamin, L. (1984). *Not in our genes: Biology, ideology & human nature.* Pantheon.
Linnér, B.-O. (2003). *The return of Malthus: Environmentalism & post-war population-resource crises.* White Horse.
Lowenstein, J., & Postel, D. (2022). We'll miss it when it's gone: The assault on -and the fight to save- democracy in the United States today". *Deusto Journal of Human Rights, 10,* 103–131.
Lowrey, A. (2022, September 3). The economist who knows the miracle is over. *The Atlantic.* https://www.theatlantic.com/ideas/archive/2022/09/brad-delong-economist-slouching-towards-utopia-book/671337
Luxemburg, R. (1951). *The accumulation of capital* (A. Schwarzschild, Trans.). Routledge & Kegan Paul. (Original work published 1913)
Mann, C. (2018a). *The wizard & the prophet: Two remarkable scientists & their dueling visions to shape tomorrow's world.* Knopf.
Mann, C. (2018b, March). Can planet Earth feed 10 billion people? *The Atlantic.* https://www.theatlantic.com/magazine/archive/2018/03/charles-mann-can-planet-earth-feed-10-billion-people/550928
Mann, T. (1938). *The coming victory of democracy.* Knopf.
Marx, K. (1992). *Early writings* (R. Livingstone & G. Benton, Trans.). Penguin Books.
Mathewes, C., & Sandsmark, E. (2017, July 28). Being rich wrecks your soul. We used to know that. *The Washington Post.* https://www.washingtonpost.com/outlook/being-rich-wrecks-your-soul-we-used-to-know-that/2017/07/28/7d3e2b90-5ab3-11e7-9fc6-c7ef4bc58d13_story.html
Mauss, M. (1954). *The gift: Forms and functions of exchange in archaic societies* (I. Cunnison, Trans.). Cohen & West.
Mazzucato, M. (2020). *Mission economy: A moonshot guide to changing capitalism.* Penguin.
McDonald, S. M. (2025). *Progress: How one idea built civilization and now threatens to destroy it.* St. Martin's Press.
McHenry, J. (1911). *The records of the Federal Convention of 1787* (Vol. III, M. Farrand, Ed.). Yale University Press.
McKibben, B. (1998). *Maybe one: A case for smaller families.* Holt.
Meadows, D. H., Meadows, D. L., & Randers, J. (1992). *Beyond the limits: Confronting global collapse, envisioning a sustainable future.* Chelsea Green.

Meadows, D. H., Randers, J., & Meadows, D. L. (2004). *Limits to growth: The 30-year update.* Chelsea Green.
Mearsheimer, J. J. (2018). *The great delusion: Liberal dreams and international realities.* Yale University Press.
Menand, L. (2021, October 11). It's time to stop talking about generations. *The New Yorker*. https://www.newyorker.com/magazine/2021/10/18/its-time-to-stop-talking-about-generations
Milanovic, B. (2016). *Global inequality: A new approach for the age of globalization.* Harvard University Press.
Milanovic, B. (2021). *Capitalism, alone: The future of the system that rules the world.* Harvard University Press.
Mitchell, D. (2021, May 7). Arthur Okun, class warfare, redistribution, and income growth. *Daily Economy*. https://www.aier.org/article/arthur-okun-class-warfare-redistribution-and-income-growth
Mitchell, R. M. (2020). Chinese receptions of Carl Schmitt since 1929. *Penn State Journal of Law & International Affairs, 8*(1), 181–206. https://insight.dickinsonlaw.psu.edu/jlia/vol8/iss1/8
Monbiot, G. (2021, September 29). 'Green growth' doesn't exist—Less of everything is the only way to avert catastrophe. *The Guardian*. https://www.theguardian.com/commentisfree/2021/sep/29/green-growth-economic-activity-environment
Mulgan, G. (2020). *The imaginary crisis (and how we might quicken social and public imagination).* Demos Helsinki. https://demoshelsinki.fi/new/wp-content/uploads/2020/04/the-imaginary-crisis-web.pdf
Murphy, C. (2025, June 3). Feudalism is our future. *The Atlantic*. https://www.theatlantic.com/magazine/archive/2025/07/government-privatization-feudalism/682888
Musgrave, P., & Nexon, D. (2013). American liberalism and the imperial temptation. In N. Parker (Ed.), *Empire and international order* (pp. 131–148). Ashgate.
Nicas, J. (2024, August 23). Pepe Mujica: Lessons from a bank-robbing guerrilla turned president. *The New York Times*. https://www.nytimes.com/2024/08/23/world/americas/pepe-mujica-uruguay-president.html
Niebuhr, R. (1949). *Faith & history.* Scribner.
Norberg, J. (2025). *Peak human: What we can learn from the rise and fall of golden ages.* Atlantic Books.
Okun, A. M. (2015). *Equality & efficiency: The big tradeoff*. Brookings Institution Press.
Orwell, G. (2021). *George Orwell: Visions of Dystopia.* Flame Tree Publishing.
Piketty, T. (2022). *A brief history of equality* (S. Rendall, Trans.). Harvard University Press.
Pinsker, J. (2020, February 21). Oh no, they've come up with another generation label. *The Atlantic*. https://www.theatlantic.com/family/archive/2020/02/generation-after-gen-z-named-alpha/606862
Pizzigati, S. (2018). *The case for a maximum wage.* Polity Press.
Perry, L. (2023, March 24). Why feminists should fear a declining birth rate. *UnHerd*. https://unherd.com/thepost/why-feminists-should-fear-a-declining-birth-rate/
Petersen, J. B. (2018). *12 rules for life: An antidote to chaos.* Random House.
Pflanze, O. (2020). *Bismarck and the development of Germany: The period of unification, 1815–1871.* Princeton University Press.
Polanyi, K. (2001). *The great transformation: The political and economic origins of our time.* Beacon Press. (Original work published 1944)
Randers, J. (2012). *2052: A global forecast for the next forty years.* Chelsea Green.
Raworth, K. (2017). *Doughnut economics: Seven ways to think like a 21st-century economist.* Chelsea Green.
Reeves, R. V. (2017). *Dream hoarders: How the American upper middle class is leaving everyone else in the dust, why that is a problem, and what to do about it.* Brookings Institution Press.

Reuters. (2014, September 22). World's population unlikely to level off anytime soon; May hit 12 billion by 2100. *The Washington Post*. https://www.washingtonpost.com/national/health-science/worlds-population-unlikely-to-level-off-anytime-soon-may-hit-12-billion-by-2100/2014/09/22/aa6689a0-3f68-11e4-9587-5dafd96295f0_story.html

Ridley, M. (2015, December 14). The long shadow of Malthus. *Standpoint Magazine*. https://standpointmag.co.uk/text-january-february-2016-matt-ridley-long-shadow-of-malthus/

Roser, M., & Ritchie, H. (2023, March 18). Two centuries of rapid global population growth will come to an end. *Our World in Data*. https://ourworldindata.org/world-population-growth-past-future

Ross, A. (2021, August 30). David Graeber was right: A debt free world is possible. *Novara Media*. https://novaramedia.com/2021/08/30/david-graeber-was-right-a-debt-free-world-is-possible

Rostow, W. (1998). *The great population spike and after: Reflections on the 21st century*. Oxford University Press.

Rubin, P. H. (2003). Folk economics. *Southern Economic Journal, 70*(1), 157–171. https://doi.org/10.2307/1061637

Ruiz, J. (2024, January 17). Yuval Noah Harari: 'Netanyahu built a coalition of messianic zealots and shameless opportunists'. *El País*. https://english.elpais.com/culture/2024-01-17/yuval-noah-harari-netanyahu-built-a-coalition-of-messianic-zealots-and-shameless-opportunists.html

Sachs, J. D. (2024, September 4). How the neocons chose hegemony over peace beginning in the early 1990s. *Racket News* [Substack]. https://www.jeffsachs.org/newspaper-articles/bfsmbpe4plx7cc6lgxhf37lx249r22

Saito, K. (2024). *Slow down: The degrowth manifesto* (B. Bergstrom, Trans.). Astra.

Sam, N. (2013, April 13). Signal anxiety. *Psychology Dictionary*. https://psychologydictionary.org/signal-anxiety

Sanders, E. P. (1985). *Jesus and Judaism*. Fortress Press.

Sanderson, W. C. (2013). *The end of world population growth in the 21st century: New challenges for human capital formation and sustainable development*. Routledge.

Schmitt, C. (2005). *Political theology* (G. Schwab, Trans.). University of Chicago Press. (Original work published 1922)

Schmitt, C. (2007). *The concept of the political* (G. Schwab, Trans.). University of Chicago Press. (Original work published 1932)

Schumpeter, J. A. (1942). *Capitalism, socialism, and democracy*. Harper & Brothers.

Seidel, J. (2025, January 18). 'Below the replacement rate': Alarming trend sweeping the globe. *News.com.au*. https://www.news.com.au/world/below-the-replacement-rate-alarming-trend-sweeping-the-globe/news-story/12fc2a64ce97866907575469ecca3eec

Skousen, M. (2007). *The big three in economics: Adam Smith, Karl Marx, & John Maynard Keynes*. Sharpe.

Slatyer, W. (2012). *Life/death rhythms of ancient empires—Climatic cycles influence rule of dynasties*. Trafford.

Smith, D. L. (2011). *Less than human: Why we demean, enslave, and exterminate others*. Martin's Press.

Snyder, T. (2017). *On tyranny: Twenty lessons from the twentieth century*. Bodley Head.

Spang, R. (2020a, April). The revolution is only getting started. *The Atlantic*. https://www.theatlantic.com/ideas/archive/2020/04/revolution-only-getting-started/609463/

Spang, R. (2020b, July). A revolution doesn't look like a revolution. *The Atlantic*. https://www.theatlantic.com/ideas/archive/2020/07/revolution-doesnt-look-like-revolution/613801

Specktor, B. (2021, July 19). Society is right on track for a global collapse, new study of infamous 1970s report finds. *LiveScience*. https://www.livescience.com/collapse-human-society-limits-to-growth.html

Stanley, J. (2020). *How fascism works: The politics of us and them*. Random House.

Stiglitz, J. E. (2023, September 1). Salvaging global democratic politics requires far-reaching economic reforms. *The Guardian*. https://www.theguardian.com/business/2023/sep/01/global-democratic-politics-economic-reforms

Susskind, D. (2024). *Growth: A history & a reckoning*. Harvard University Press.
Szalai, J. (2024a, June 8). Shrink the economy, save the world? *The New York Times*. https://www.nytimes.com/2024/06/08/books/review/shrink-the-economy-save-the-world.html
Szalai, J. (2024b, July 13). The Nazi jurist who haunts our broken politics. *The New York Times*. https://www.nytimes.com/2024/07/13/books/review/carl-schmitt-jd-vance.html
Thompson, D. (2022a, December 12). Why the age of American progress ended. *The Atlantic*. https://www.theatlantic.com/magazine/archive/2023/01/science-technology-vaccine-invention-history/672227
Thompson, D. (2022b, March 28). Why U.S. population growth is collapsing. *The Atlantic*. https://www.theatlantic.com/newsletters/archive/2022/03/american-population-growth-rate-slow/629392
Turchin, P. (2016). *Ages of discord: A structural-demographic analysis of American history*. Beresta Books.
Turchin, P., & Nefedov, S. A. (2009). *Secular cycles*. Princeton University Press.
UN Department of Economic & Social Affairs. (2024). *World population prospects 2024: Summary of results*. United Nations.
Veblen, T. (1994). *The theory of the leisure class* (R. Lekachman, Intro.). Penguin Books. (Original work published 1899)
Wallace-Wells, B. (2024, November 4). The convert: The sudden rise of J. D. Vance has transfixed conservative élites. Is he the future of Trumpism? *The New Yorker*. https://www.newyorker.com/magazine/2024/11/04/j-d-vance-profile
Wallace-Wells, D. (2025, January 11). You don't get disasters like the Palisades Fire without human failure. *The New York Times*. https://www.nytimes.com/2025/01/11/opinion/los-angeles-wildfire-build-fireproof.html
Wapshott, N. (2011). *Keynes/Hayek: The clash that defined modern economics*. Norton.
Warren, E., & Tyagi, A. W. (2016). *The two-income trap: Why middle-class parents are (still) going broke*. Basic Books.
Weber, M. (1922). *Economy and society*. University of California Press.
Weber, M. (1946a). *From Max Weber: Essays in sociology*. Oxford University Press.
Weber, M. (1946b). Science as a vocation. In H. H. Gerth & C. W. Mills (Eds.), *From Max Weber: Essays in sociology* (pp. 129–156). Oxford University Press.
Wilkinson, R., & Pickett, K. (2009). *The spirit level: Why more equal societies almost always do better*. Allen Lane.
Wilson, E. O. (2016). *Half-earth: Our planet's fight for life*. Norton.
Wehner, P. (2022, August 11). Now they're calling for violence. *The Atlantic*. https://www.theatlantic.com/ideas/archive/2022/08/trump-fbi-mar-a-lago-search-republican-reaction/671104
Weil, S. (2002). *The need for roots: Prelude to a declaration of duties toward mankind* (A. Wills, Trans.). Routledge.
Wolf, M. (2007, December 19). The dangers of living in a zero-sum world economy. *Financial Times*. https://www.ft.com/content/0447f562-ad85-11dc-9386-0000779fd2ac
Wood, G. (2020, December). Can history predict the future? *The Atlantic*. https://www.theatlantic.com/magazine/archive/2020/12/can-history-predict-future/616993
Wright, N. T. (1996). *Jesus and the victory of God*. Fortress Press.

Index

A

Abbasid (family), 40, 58
Abundantism, 44, 84, 248, 319, 320
Adams (family), 61
Addiction, 61, 182, 197, 204, 205, 265, 266
Afghanistan, 51, 175, 181, 197, 199, 263, 264, 266
Africa, 21, 35, 36, 50, 51, 112, 113, 127, 128, 149, 150, 161, 178, 226, 265, 285, 286, 288
Alger, Horatio, 115–118, 265, 322
America, 11, 18, 42, 50, 53, 55, 61, 62, 78, 79, 81, 83–88, 90, 93, 95, 96, 109, 113–116, 126, 130, 132, 150–152, 156, 158, 165, 175, 184, 185, 192, 194, 228, 234, 245, 250, 263, 265, 270, 271, 273–275, 278, 281–284, 289, 312, 314, 315
Anthropocene, 279, 280, 290
Antisemitism, 108, 128, 130
Arctic, 286
Area studies, 149, 226, 281, 314
Arendt, Hannah, 264, 312, 321, 324
Aristocracy, 41, 51, 80, 81, 84, 93, 115, 156–158, 188, 245
Aristotle, 8
Armenia, 272
Asia, 35, 36, 59, 113, 128, 150, 151, 176, 178, 226, 265, 273
Aspirationism, 93, 96, 106, 150, 241
Assad (family), 61, 284, 289
Athens, 81
Atlantic Ocean, 47, 91, 264, 270, 288
Australia, 36, 84, 89, 106, 129, 150, 193, 242, 275, 288
Austria, 61, 186
Autarky, 39, 147, 148, 155, 269, 274, 282
Authoritarianism, 29, 132, 177, 226, 270, 278, 312, 313

B

Balzac, Honoré de, 62
Beijing, 270, 278, 280, 309, 315, 325
Belarus, 275, 276
Bell (family), 92, 123
Berlin, 9, 112, 181, 197, 223, 264, 274, 283, 308
Bilderberg (family), 183
Birmingham, 88, 127
Bismarck, Otto von, 110, 116, 119, 321
Black Sea, 46, 47, 63, 120, 121, 275–277
Boeing (family), 62, 197, 199
Bonaparte (family), 59, 107
Bonaparte, Napoleon, 59, 93, 95, 107, 154
Bootstrapping, 115, 117, 130, 131
Borja (family), 63
Boss (family), 153, 155
Bourbon (family), 59, 95, 107, 113, 130, 279
Bourgeois, 88, 90, 91, 116, 129, 150, 274
Brazil, 42, 94, 95, 288
Brexit, 54, 237, 247, 265
Brussels, 164, 281, 315
Brzezinski (family), 179, 180, 280
Buddhism, 16, 25, 50, 52
Bulgaria, 34, 35, 109
Bush (family), 60, 175, 183, 184, 188, 190

C

California, 81, 199
Calvinism, 124
Cameralism, 153
Canada, 61, 84, 89, 117, 123, 243, 273, 275, 280

A. M. Feldman and Y. Stamos, *Zero Sum Political Economy*, World-Systems Evolution and Global Futures, https://doi.org/10.1007/978-3-032-18326-2

Capitalism, 11, 38, 54, 82, 105, 106, 109, 118, 123, 129, 132, 147, 155, 156, 158, 159, 165, 175, 176, 180, 189, 190, 192, 195–197, 200–203, 241, 243, 245, 249, 265, 269, 271, 273, 278, 290
Cargill-MacMillan (family), 60
Caribbean Sea, 95
Carnegie (family), 61, 116, 132
Cartels, 109, 148, 152, 153, 165, 186, 200, 223, 226, 324
Caste, 18, 25–27, 29, 34, 35, 40–42, 51, 53, 84, 191, 314
Centrism, 270
Charity, 8, 16, 25–28, 34, 39, 133, 247, 248, 267
Charles V, 48
Chauvinism, 90, 107, 111, 119, 120, 128, 161
Cheney (family), 60, 183, 184
China, 4, 17, 36, 41, 45, 53, 55, 59, 62, 79, 80, 82, 96, 127, 128, 151, 161, 177, 191, 192, 228, 229, 265–267, 270–273, 275, 277–289
Churchill, Winston, 160, 264
Clark, John, 109, 110, 146
Clinton, Bill, 60, 175, 183, 184
Clinton (family), 60, 175, 183, 184
Cold War I, 148, 154, 155, 183, 191, 194, 196, 199, 222, 223, 282, 286
Cold War II, 279, 284, 286, 289, 324, 325
Colonialism/settler colonialism, 11, 23, 84, 85, 112, 123, 200, 285
Columbus, Cristopher, 47, 63
Communism, 11, 114, 123, 147, 155, 160, 173–176, 178, 180, 188, 189, 191, 196, 266, 319, 325
Confindustria, 154
Confucianism, 16, 25, 50, 80
Conservatism, 10
Conspiracy theories, 108
Credit, 37, 43, 81, 108, 156, 175, 200, 229, 274, 313, 315
Crusades, 8, 44, 63

D

Da Gama, Vasco, 47, 63
Darwin, Charles, 125–128, 130, 133, 183, 318
Debasement, 43–46, 121, 158
Debt, 18, 19, 21, 37, 39, 42–44, 95, 154, 155, 157, 158, 161, 174, 182, 183, 198, 200, 201, 225, 227, 230–232, 239, 240, 244, 269, 282, 310, 313, 315
Decartelization, 152, 155
Decolonization, 176, 193
Denmark, 87, 115
Disney (family), 61
Durkheim, Emile, 132
Dynasties, 6, 16, 18, 20, 23, 34–36, 38–44, 47–53, 55, 57–63, 95, 97, 106, 109, 112, 114, 116, 119, 122, 132, 153, 155, 175, 180, 183, 184, 192, 201, 202, 223, 247, 250, 267, 279, 325

E

Economism, 10, 37, 79, 87, 88, 90, 94, 95, 99, 106, 108–111, 117, 118, 124, 146, 154, 155, 157–159, 162, 163, 182, 184, 189–192, 195, 196, 203, 204, 226, 227, 233, 235, 245, 247, 249, 264, 290, 317
Ecuador, 182
Ecumenism, 11, 62, 63, 82, 83, 88, 91, 95, 96, 113, 121, 122, 127, 147, 155, 223, 279, 320
Edison (family), 60
Egypt, 17, 18, 58, 164, 229, 275, 284
Eisenhower, Dwight, 10, 197, 273
Empiricism, 163, 318
England, 22, 44, 48, 54, 59, 83, 89, 92, 93, 111, 132, 133, 159, 230, 264
Environmentalism, 224, 238, 268, 290
Ethiopia, 112, 150, 284
Eugenics, 127–133, 152, 155, 161, 165, 183
Eurasia, 11, 16, 35, 39, 40, 45, 54, 58, 59, 62, 63, 96, 106, 107, 109, 114, 116–118, 147, 158, 176, 179, 193, 196, 199, 201, 224, 264, 283, 285, 324
Europe, 38, 44, 50, 54, 55, 63, 80, 82, 90, 92, 93, 110, 115, 121, 128, 131, 132, 150, 151, 155, 159, 160, 175, 177, 181, 192, 196, 226, 273, 276, 281

F

Fascism, 11, 114, 123, 126, 146, 159, 162, 174, 176, 178, 185, 310, 312, 319, 325
Feudalism, 11, 25, 29, 37, 41, 42, 48–57, 62, 80, 82, 92, 95, 98, 107, 116, 126, 130, 180, 223, 244, 249, 273, 278, 310, 319
France, 54, 63, 95, 109, 132, 149, 150, 156, 159, 176, 192, 239, 281, 285
Franco, Francisco, 155, 159
Freud, Sigmund, 10, 111, 117, 312

Friedman, Milton, 115, 163, 165, 166, 175, 185–187, 189–191, 197, 244
Fugger (family), 56, 123

G
Galton, Francis, 127, 128, 146
Game of Thrones, 325
Gaza, 263, 275, 284, 290
Genoa, 46, 55
Gentry, 248, 249
Georgism, 115
Germany, 109, 110, 121, 122, 132, 133, 147, 149, 151–153, 156, 157, 159, 161, 176, 177, 196, 225, 226, 239, 273, 274, 281, 282
Gompers, 119
Gompers, Samuel, 119
Gorbachev, Mikhail, 182, 284
Graeber, David, 17, 19, 24, 28, 44, 229, 240, 249, 315
Greece, 17, 48, 51, 61, 81, 132, 160, 176, 204, 225, 229, 239, 240, 275
Gresham's Law, 44, 317
Großunternehmen, 154
Growtherism, 11, 36–38, 46, 93, 108, 116, 124, 148, 157, 158, 160, 162, 163, 192, 200, 203, 224, 226, 227, 229, 230, 235, 273, 310, 319, 320

H
Habsburg (family), 42, 48, 56, 59, 61, 63, 95, 107, 108, 122, 185, 279
Haiti, 95, 263
Halford Mackinder, 114
Hanoverian (family), 95, 121
Hayek, Friedrich, 157, 159, 163, 165, 175, 185, 187, 189, 190, 318
Hegel, G.W.F., 90, 322
Herrenvolk democracy, 128, 129, 132
Hilton (family), 62
Hitler, Adolf, 63, 133, 149–151, 153, 154
Hohenzollern (family), 59, 121, 122
Holland, 176, 185
Hoover (family), 61, 124, 155, 156
Hudson River, 91
Hume, David, 78
Hungary, 34, 35, 177
Huxley, Aldous, 52, 312

I
Imperialism, 113, 114, 119, 123, 125, 126, 133, 148, 151, 159–161, 164, 176, 178, 194, 196, 197, 264, 321
India, 18, 21, 36, 45, 52, 106, 133, 147, 150, 191, 285–288
Indian Ocean, 325
Indonesia, 151, 193
Industrialism, 94
Inflation, 43, 123, 148, 155, 158, 161, 163, 165, 166, 174, 186, 200, 204, 222, 229, 249, 269, 278, 281
Insurance, 185, 186, 265
Iran, 193, 222, 280, 284, 289
Iraq, 51, 194, 198, 199, 263, 266
Ireland, 89, 106, 147, 225, 263
Iron law of oligarchy, 99, 129, 317
Israel, 18, 58, 164, 229, 275, 283, 284, 313
Istanbul/Constantinople, 8, 11, 38, 45–47, 49, 55, 120
Italy, 25, 50, 109, 112, 126, 147, 149, 150, 159, 176, 177, 225, 275

J
Japan, 34, 53, 95, 109, 127, 128, 147, 151, 152, 155, 156, 159, 161, 176, 188, 191, 192, 268, 273, 288
Jefferson, Thomas, 78, 83, 84, 315
Jerusalem, 89
Jim Crow, 131, 133
Jinping, Xi, 53, 264
John Kenneth Galbraith, 118

K
Kaczyński (family), 192
Kennedy (family), 61, 161, 243
Kennedy, John, 184
Keynes, John, 115, 122, 123, 130, 157–159, 189, 196, 204, 318
Khaldun, Ibn, 21, 51, 317
Kim (family), 60
Koch (family), 60, 183, 184, 241
Komnenos (family), 8, 40, 44, 50, 58
Korea, 53, 60, 113, 127, 128, 147, 159, 180, 191, 192, 197, 287, 289

L
Latin America, 54, 61, 109, 125, 161, 182, 193, 226, 243, 273, 288, 324, 325
Lenin, Vladimir, 40, 120, 264
Lerner, Abba, 158

Liberalism, 11, 79, 85, 93, 95–99, 105, 107–111, 113, 114, 116, 118, 123, 124, 146, 148, 155, 157–159, 165, 166, 173, 174, 182–184, 190, 195, 224, 288, 308–310, 312–314, 318, 319, 321, 325
Libya, 150, 229, 275, 286
Lincoln, Abraham, 39, 96–98, 310, 314
London, 78, 83, 87, 107, 108, 116, 118, 121, 126, 150, 197
Luxemburg, Rosa, 264, 312, 321

M
Mackinder, Harold, 114, 152, 179
Macron, Emmanuel, 277, 281, 289
Mafias, 57, 61, 62, 153, 202, 243
Mahan, Alfred, 114, 152
Malta, 263
Malthusianism, 129, 130
Mamluk (family), 40, 46, 51
Manifest destiny, 62, 113, 133
Marshall, Alfred, 110, 117, 118, 146, 153
Martin Luther King Jr., 131
Marx, Karl, 16, 39, 88, 89, 106, 117, 123, 164, 187, 195, 196, 312, 316, 318, 322
Matthew Effect, 88, 117, 323
Mauss, Marcel, 28, 117, 312
Mazzucato, Mariana, 80, 165, 175, 222, 227, 245, 313, 320
McKinley, William, 114
Medici (family), 90, 91, 116, 129, 150, 274
Mediterranean Sea, 164
Mencius, 27, 28
Mercantilism, 11, 43, 46, 48, 49, 54–57, 98, 107, 147, 154, 158, 275, 318, 319
Meritocracy, 134, 223, 231–234, 248, 268
Metternich, Klemens von, 264
Mexico, 125, 265, 287
Mississippi River, 86
Modernism, 54, 133
Morgan (family), 61, 86, 116
Morgenthau (family), 60
Morocco, 130
Moscow, 42, 147, 154, 160, 177, 178, 181, 182, 197, 276–278, 280, 309, 315
Mughal (family), 17, 40, 41, 51, 63
Mussolini, Benito, 126, 146, 150, 264
Myanmar, 52, 263

N
NATO, 34, 159, 160, 198, 199, 274, 276, 277, 280–282, 288, 324
Neoliberalism, 12, 132, 148, 159, 166, 174–176, 180, 182–184, 186, 188, 189, 191, 195, 196, 200, 201, 203–205, 221, 223, 224, 226, 231, 232, 235, 236, 238, 241–243, 245, 270, 274, 275, 278, 288, 313
Netanyahu, Benjamin, 284
New Delhi, 280, 287
New England, 85, 115, 314
New York, 85, 90, 91, 93, 107, 108, 115, 116, 121, 125, 152, 164, 188, 265, 275
New Zealand, 275
Nietzsche, Friedrich, 195, 318, 323
Nixon, Richard, 148, 163, 164, 174, 177, 190, 285
Noblesse oblige, 25, 28, 116
Nuclear warfare, 198, 263, 276, 289, 290

O
Obama, Barack, 60, 224, 247, 274, 277, 282
Oceania, 11, 113, 270, 273
Oligarchy, 97, 116, 153, 166, 191, 193, 224, 245, 310
Operation Barbarossa, 63
Orange (family), 185
Orban (family), 192
Orwell, George, 176, 177, 308, 312
Ottoman (family), 22, 38, 40, 41, 44, 47, 48, 51, 59, 63, 95, 108, 120–122, 279
Overton Window, 311

P
Pacific Ocean, 325
Pahlavi (family), 59, 122
Pakistan, 180, 287
Palaiologos (family), 47
Palestine, 106
Panama Canal, 125, 273
Papandreou (family), 61
Paris, 83, 87, 93, 123, 225
Pearson, Karl, 127, 128
Peasantry, 43, 53, 92, 131, 191
Philanthropy, 28, 29, 34, 223, 247, 248, 266
Philippines, 51, 61, 113, 114, 125, 151
Physiocracy, 79, 80, 82
Piketty, Thomas, 37, 38, 130, 190, 242, 264, 319
Plutocracy, 245
Poland, 40, 150, 280
Polanyi, Karl, 159, 184, 312
Potlatch, 25, 27–29, 33–35, 39, 42, 56, 58, 88, 97, 98, 112, 116, 117, 124, 132,

153, 155, 157, 182, 223, 248, 266, 322
Producerism, 119
Progress, 57, 78–80, 82, 91, 92, 94, 120, 127, 128, 130, 250, 272, 288, 313, 314, 324
Punditry, 108, 278, 288, 310, 311, 314, 322
Putin, Vladimir, 175, 191, 276, 277, 283–285, 288, 289

Q
Qajari (family), 59, 122
Qing (family), 17, 40, 53, 59, 82, 95, 108, 122, 127
Quandt (family), 155

R
Rand, Ayn, 188, 322, 325
Reagan, Ronald, 165, 175, 183, 184, 190, 192, 197, 202, 222, 237, 238, 263, 265, 275, 283
Redistribution, 81, 89, 90, 112, 115, 147, 157, 159, 161, 165, 193, 222, 227, 228, 235, 236, 310, 317, 323
Red Sea, 46, 286
Rent-seeking, 39–41, 50, 56, 82, 84, 86, 98, 110, 112, 113, 115–117, 149, 159, 242, 245, 316, 323
Reputation laundering, 28, 203, 266
Rhodes (family), 116, 224
Robber barons, 109, 116
Robinson, Joan, 118, 155, 193
Rockefeller (family), 61, 86, 116, 160, 180
Romania, 109, 178, 280
Romanov (family), 50, 59, 95, 96, 108, 119, 120, 122, 127, 279
Rome, 58, 62, 126, 146, 164, 314, 315, 319
Roosevelt (family), 60, 61, 150, 156, 184
Roosevelt, Franklin, 156, 157
Roosevelt, Theodore, 113, 114
Ruml, Beardsley, 157, 158
Rurikid (family), 58
Russia, 42, 47, 59, 62, 93, 96, 97, 128, 133, 149, 154, 191, 275–278, 280–283, 285–289

S
Sackler (family), 61, 266, 267
Sahel, 285, 286
Saigon/Ho Chi Minh city, 177, 264
Saudi (family), 51, 59, 60
Scandinavia, 34, 159, 161
Schmitt, Carl, 152, 179, 280, 308, 309
Serbia, 44, 109
Serfdom, 19, 51, 92, 95, 96, 98, 109, 118, 241, 243, 249
Silicon Valley, 243, 247
Singapore, 115, 226
Slavery, 18–21, 25, 42, 47, 51, 87, 90, 94–99, 105, 107–109, 112, 124, 129, 195, 243, 273, 288
Social Darwinism, 110, 126–128, 130–134, 148, 165, 183, 184, 231, 233, 234, 312, 316
South Africa, 22, 79, 89, 106, 113, 161, 288
Spain, 42, 48, 54, 63, 113, 155, 225
Spencer, Herbert, 106, 125–128, 146, 183, 184, 244
Stalin, Joseph, 63, 150, 176–179, 181, 264
Stiglitz, Joseph, 61, 165, 166, 221, 226, 245, 273, 279, 310
Sudan, 263, 286
Suez Canal, 160, 193
Susskind, Daniel, 90, 91, 93, 158, 163, 200, 225, 245, 247, 250, 279, 318–321
Sweden, 188
Switzerland, 126, 263
Syria, 51, 61, 164, 263, 284, 289
Syrian War, 263, 284, 289

T
Taiwan, 115, 128, 147, 159, 177, 263, 273, 275, 287
Talleyrand, Charles-Maurice, 264
Tellurocracy, 62, 279
Thalassocracy, 279
Thatcher, Margaret, 175, 192, 237, 238
Thessaloniki, 46
Tiffany (family), 189
Trastámara (family), 47, 63
Tribalism, 16, 20, 22–24, 42, 308, 309
Trotsky, Leon, 40, 106, 178
Trudeau (family), 61
Trump, Donald, 54, 247, 265, 267, 268, 270, 272, 273, 275, 278–280, 284–289, 309, 321
Trump (family), 60, 232, 237
Turchin, Peter, 62, 162, 224, 228, 233, 245, 264, 278, 311, 321
Turkey, 161, 229, 275, 280, 284

U
Ukraine, 51, 175, 201, 263, 274–278, 281–283, 285, 287, 288, 290, 325

V
Valois (family), 59, 63
Vanderbilt (family), 61, 86, 116
Veblen, Thorstein, 118, 312
Venice, 46, 54–56
Vietnam, 174, 177, 180, 182, 193, 197, 222, 264, 266
Volga River, 34, 35, 150

W
Wallace, Henry, 161
Wallenberg (family), 164
Walton (family), 60
Warburg (family), 124
Washington DC, 147, 153, 155, 160, 178, 192, 197, 199, 201, 246, 247, 270, 271, 278, 280, 288, 308, 315, 325
Washington, George, 78, 84, 85, 91, 179
Weber, Max, 312
Whiggism, 91, 98, 325
Wilson, Woodrow, 122, 123
World War I, 119, 123
World War II, 79, 185, 289

Y
Yeltsin, Boris, 175
Yemen, 263, 284

Z
Zaibatsu, 154, 155
Zedong, Mao, 53, 308

MIX
Papier aus verantwortungsvollen Quellen
Paper from responsible sources
FSC® C105338

If you have any concerns about our products,
you can contact us on
ProductSafety@springernature.com

In case Publisher is established outside the EU,
the EU authorized representative is:
Springer Nature Customer Service Center GmbH
Europaplatz 3, 69115 Heidelberg, Germany

Printed by Libri Plureos GmbH
in Hamburg, Germany